THE TRANSFORMATION OF ENFORCEMENT

This insightful book considers the phenomenon of the transformation of enforcement in European economic law while adopting a distinct global perspective. The editors identify and respond to the need for reflection on transformation processes in the area of enforcement by bringing together the leading international and European scholars in a variety of disciplines to share and compare experiences and learning in different areas of law.

Rooted in a wide and regulatory understanding of enforcement, this book showcases the transformation of enforcement with reference to both European economic law (especially transnational commercial law, competition law, intellectual property law, consumer law) and to the current context of significant global economic challenges. Comparative perspectives facilitate the formation of a holistic perspective on enforcement that reaches beyond distinct theoretical accounts, political agendas, regulatory systems, institutional patterns, particular remedies, industry sectors, and stakeholder perspectives. As the first comprehensive and comparative analysis of the enforcement of European economic law that reaches beyond closely confined areas of law, it constitutes a crucial contribution to the theoretical and policy questions of how to design a coherent European enforcement architecture in accordance with essential principles and objectives of the EU economic order.

This unique study will have broad appeal. By exploring enforcement transformations from a legal and a cross-disciplinary perspective, it will be essential reading for scholars, practitioners and policymakers from different disciplines.

The Transformation of Enforcement

European Economic Law in Global Perspective

Edited by
Hans-W Micklitz
and
Andrea Wechsler

•HART•
OXFORD • LONDON • NEW YORK • NEW DELHI • SYDNEY

HART PUBLISHING
Bloomsbury Publishing Plc
Kemp House, Chawley Park, Cumnor Hill, Oxford, OX2 9PH, UK

HART PUBLISHING, the Hart/Stag logo, BLOOMSBURY and the Diana logo are trademarks of Bloomsbury Publishing Plc
First published in Great Britain 2016

First published in hardback, 2016
Paperback edition, 2018

A catalogue record for this book is available from the British Library.

Library of Congress Cataloging-in-Publication Data

Names: Micklitz, Hans-W., editor. | Wechsler, Andrea, 1977– , editor.

Title: The transformation of enforcement : European economic law in global perspective/ edited by Hans-W Micklitz and Andrea Wechsler.

Description: Oxford ; Portland, Oregon : Hart Publishing Ltd, 2015. | "contains a selection of written contributions prepared for the European University Institute (EUI) June 2013 international conference on "The Transformation of Enforcement : European Economic Law in Global Perspective" organised as part of the larger project "European Regulatory Private Law : The Transformation of European Private Law from Autonomy to Functionalism in Competition and Regulation."—ECIP Introduction. | Includes bibliographical references and index. | Description based on print version record and CIP data provided by publisher; resource not viewed.

Identifiers: LCCN 2015045487 (print) | LCCN 2015044471 (ebook) | ISBN 9781849468923 (Epub) | ISBN 9781849468916 (hardback : alk. paper)

Subjects: LCSH: Trade regulation—European Union countries—Congresses. | Actions and defenses—European Union countries—Congresses. | Citizen suits (Civil procedure)—European Union countries—Congresses. | Law and globalization—European Union countries—Congresses.

Classification: LCC KJE6569.A8 (print) | LCC KJE6569.A8 T73 2015 (ebook) | DDC 343.2408/7—dc23

LC record available at http://lccn.loc.gov/2015045487

ISBN: PB: 978-1-50992-447-9
HB: 978-1-84946-891-6

Typeset by Compuscript Ltd, Shannon

To find out more about our authors and books visit www.hartpublishing.co.uk. Here you will find extracts, author information, details of forthcoming events and the option to sign up for our newsletters.

Contents

List of Contributors

Diego P Fernández Arroyo is Professor at the Sciences Po Law School in Paris, Co-director of the Global Governance Studies Program and Co-director of the Research Project Private International Law as Global Governance (PILAGG), Global Professor at the New York University (Paris), and Honorary Professor of the Buenos Aires and Cordoba Universities (Argentina).

Sandrine Clavel is Law Professor, University of Versailles (France), and Dean of the Law Faculty.

Naomi Creutzfeldt is ESRC Research Fellow, Centre for Socio-Legal Studies, University of Oxford, and Fellow of Wolfson College. She is also a civil and commercial mediator.

Katalin Cseres is Associate Professor of Law at Amsterdam Centre for European Law and Governance, Amsterdam Center or Law & Economics, University of Amsterdam.

Josef Drexl is Director of Max Planck Institute for Innovation and Competition.

Horst Eidenmüller is Freshfields Professor of Commercial Law and Professorial Fellow of St Hugh's College, University of Oxford. He has extensive experience as a mediator and arbitrator in national and international commercial conflicts.

Martin Fries is a Postdoctoral Researcher at the Center for International Law, University of Munich. He also practices as a lawyer, collaborative lawyer, and mediator.

Burkhard Hess is Executive Director of the Max Planck Institute Luxembourg for International, European and Regulatory Procedural Law, and Professor at the Universities of Heidelberg and Luxembourg.

Reto M Hilty is Director of Max Planck Institute for Innovation and Competition, and Professor at the Universities of Zurich and Munich.

Christopher Hodges is Professor of Justice Systems, Head of the Swiss Re/CMS Research Programme on Civil Justice Systems, and Fellow of Wolfson College, University of Oxford; Honorary Professor at China University of Political Science and Law, Beijing; and Solicitor, England and Wales (non-practising).

R Daniel Kelemen is Professor of Political Science and Jean Monnet Chair in European Union Politics at Rutgers University.

Hans-W Micklitz is Professor for Economic Law at the European University Institute, Jean Monnet Chair of Private Law and European Economic Law at the University of Bamberg, and Head of the Institute of European and Consumer Law in Bamberg.

Marcus Norrgård is Professor of Law at the University of Helsinki.

Andrea Renda is Senior Research Fellow at the Centre for European Policy Studies (Brussels), Director of International Economics at Istituto Affari Internazionali (Rome), and Senior Lecturer of Law and Economics, LUISS Guido Carli (Rome).

Boško Tripković is Research and Teaching Associate at the European University Institute.

Ianika N Tzankova is Full Professor at Tilburg Law School.

Robert Wai is Associate Professor at Osgoode Hall Law School, York University. He is called to the bars of British Columbia and New York.

Andrea Wechsler is Professor of Economic Law at Pforzheim University.

Christopher A Whytock is Professor of Law and Political Science at University of California, Irvine School of Law.

Marlene Wind is Professor and Director of CEP (Centre for European Politics) Department of Political Science University of Copenhagen, founding member of iCourts, Danish Centre of Excellence for International Courts, and Professor II at Pluricourts, Faculty of Public Law, Oslo University.

Part I

Introduction

1

Introduction: The Transformation of Enforcement—European Economic Law in Global Perspective

HANS-W MICKLITZ AND ANDREA WECHSLER

I. THE ORIGIN, PURPOSE AND CONTENTS OF THIS PUBLICATION

THIS BOOK ON *The Transformation of Enforcement—European Economic Law in Global Perspective* contains a selection of written contributions prepared for the European University Institute (EUI) June 2013 international conference on 'The Transformation of Enforcement—European Economic Law in Global Perspective'.[1] The conference was organised as part of the larger project 'European Regulatory Private Law: The Transformation of European Private Law from Autonomy to Functionalism in Competition and Regulation'.[2] The book investigates enforcement through the lens of the objective of the European Research Council (ERC) project—that is to analyse a normative model, which could shape a self-sufficient European private legal order in its interaction with national private law systems.

Within this larger project framework, this book answers one of the most pressing issues in current European economic law and its enforcement. In search for a new legal architecture for transnational economic transactions and their enforcement, numerous commentators have ventured into proposing new theories and bases for European economic law and transnational

[1] https://blogs.eui.eu/erc-erpl/event/transformation-of-european-law-enforcement/?instance_id (last visited 9 August 2015).

[2] See https://blogs.eui.eu/erc-erpl/ (last visit 10 August 2015) and on the design of the overall project H-W Micklitz and Y Svetiev (eds), *A Self-sufficient European Private Law—A Viable Concept?* EUI Working Paper 2012/31 (ERC-ERPL 01/2012); H-W Micklitz, Y Svetiev and G Comparato (eds), *European Regulatory Private Law—The Paradigm Tested*, EUI-ERC Law 2014/04.

private law.[3] Most of these research efforts have, however, focused upon either selected areas of law, such as competition law, consumer law and financial services, or selected issues in the realm of enforcement, such as, for instance, class actions.[4] Furthermore, most of the conceptual overarching research efforts have substantially neglected the realm of enforcement. Few researchers have devoted thoughts to the question of a coherent enforcement architecture for European economic law in an ever more transnational setting.[5] Thus, this is the first book which thoroughly examines and compares enforcement transformations in various areas of law. It brings together the leading international and European scholars in a variety of disciplines to share and compare the experiences and learnings in different areas of law. In doing so, the book draws upon an interdisciplinary approach that includes law, economics and political sciences. Ultimately, it adds to the existing body of literature in European economic law by offering a cross-disciplinary perspective that was formerly non-existent.

This publication is rooted in a wide and regulatory understanding of enforcement. It is argued that the system has turned into a regulated market for law enforcement. With the ultimate enforcement authority remaining vested in state institutions, the European enforcement regime can be characterised as a regulated market for rendering dispute resolution and justice. In this regulated market, the monopoly of enforcement by the state has been broken by the emergence of ever greater private enforcement powers in the shadow of the law. Justice is understood as a service and enforcement as a market. The guiding norm in the market for law enforcement service has become competition between the diverse enforcement mechanisms. Thereby, it is in particular traditional judicial avenues of law enforcement that are pressurised into redefining their role in this market for law enforcement. Building on this understanding of enforcement, it is argued that political agendas and functional approaches have led to the emergence of a distinct regulatory governance approach which aims at coping with

[3] *Les Grandes Théories du Droit Transnational* (2013) 1 *Revue internationale de droit économique* (special issue), with contributions from K Tuori; B Kingsbury, N Krisch, RB Stewart; H Muir Watt; Ch Joerges, F Roedel; F Cafaggi; R Zimmermann; G-P Calliess, M Renner; A Fischer-Lescano, G Teubner; P Schiff Berman, RIDE 2013, Numéro 1–2, 1–256.

[4] J Basedow, J Ph Terhechte and L Tichy (eds), *Private Enforcement of Competition Law* (Baden-Baden, Nomos, 2011); F Cafaggi and H-W Micklitz (eds), *New Frontiers of Consumer Protection—the Interplay between Private and Public Enforcement* (Cheltenham, Edward Elgar, 2009); Ch Hodges, *The Reform of Class and Representative Actions in European Legal Systems. A New Framework for Collective Redress in Europe* (Oxford, Hart Publishing, 2009); Special Issue on European Regulatory Private Law and Financial Services (2014) 10 *European Review of Contract Law* 473–595, with an editorial from H-W Micklitz and contributions from O Cherednychenko, Y Svetiev, A Ottow, H Marjosola and F della Negra.

[5] With regard to transnational regulation F Cafaggi (ed), *Enforcement of Transnational Regulation, Ensuring Compliance in a Global World* (Cheltenham, Edward Elgar, 2012); with regard to EU Law, M Cremona (ed), *Compliance and Enforcement of EU Law* (Oxford, Oxford University Press, 2012).

these dynamics of the enforcement market. That governance approach is constituted of three elements—that is, of national policies of deregulation and non-regulation, of re-regulation policies at the European level and of self-regulation at the transnational level. Several contributions in this book build upon these elements—in particular the section on globalising justice.

This approach to enforcement distinguishes itself from traditional notions of the legal services industry. It views the rendering of justice as the essential service to be provided by the law enforcement system. The notion of justice denotes thereby not only access to justice but also procedural and substantive justice. Whilst access to justice is considered a condition *sine qua non*, the emphasis is in particular on the outcome of legal proceedings in terms of procedural and substantive justice. This notion builds upon the European Union (EU) holistic approach to create a genuine area of justice in the EU[6] and even further a genuine concept of European justice termed access justice (*Zugangsgerechtigkeit*).[7] It builds on theories of justice such as Rawls' social contract-based concept of justice with its reference to reasonableness and fairness of outcomes in the light of often divergent conceptions for a good life and a just society[8] and recognises the importance of distributive justice[9] and retributive justice.[10] However, it goes beyond. Access justice adds a layer of moral rightness to the efficiency considerations associated with the regulated market approach, though not necessarily aiming at distribution, but at guaranteeing justice in the access to the different enforcement institutions. It allows for the consideration of a wide variety of enforcement goals from compensation and over deterrence to vindication. By looking at enforcement goals, this genuine notion of justice accounts for the ever more functional approach to a European market order. Enforcement serves the functional purpose of guarding the rule of law and the economic function of increasing social welfare in new welfare economic terms.

Support for this view of justice as a service meant to secure access justice (*Zugangsgerechtigkeit*) comes from growing expectations for transparent, efficient, effective and affordable dispute resolution. These expectations are not only expressed by players in the enforcement game; they are even reflected in the laws with intellectual property law, for instance, requiring

[6] W van Gerven, 'Of Rights, Remedies and Procedures' (2000) 37 *Common Market Law Review* 501–36.

[7] H-W Micklitz, 'Social Justice and Access Justice in Private Law' in H-W Micklitz (ed), *The Many Faces of Social Justice in Private Law* (Cheltenham, Edward Elgar, 2011) 3–60, also published in H-W Micklitz, 'Social Justice and Access Justice in Private Law' *EUI Working Paper 2011/02*

[8] J Rawls, *A Theory of Justice* (Harvard, Belknap Press, 1971); J Rawls, *Justice as Fairness: A Restatement* (Harvard, Belknap Press, 2001).

[9] R Nozick, *Anarchy, State and Utopia* (Jackson, Basic Books, 1974).

[10] Criminal justice theories ranging from retribution, deterrence, rehabilitation, incapacitation, reparation, denunciation.

enforcement to be 'effective, expeditious, deterrent'.[11] Evidence in support of this view of justice comes further from a dramatic increase in the number of attorneys and the size of the legal services industry in Europe.[12] Industry has, thus, come to gradually realise the potential in benefitting from the ever growing understanding of justice as a service. Nevertheless, the European legal services market with its strong reliance on public authorities and consumer organisations in, for instance, consumer law enforcement, is still far from the profit-driven market approach that can be observed in the US.[13] As a consequence, the level of litigation in Europe is still rather low, but a steady increase can be observed. The adoption of collective consumer redress mechanisms shows further that this notion of justice as a service is valid and triggers cross-border collaboration in the legal services sector. The implication of this notion of justice as a service is not only that there will be an enhanced role for the legal services sector; rather it also grants a more active role to judges and the enforcement institutions. As such, justice as a service stresses the continued importance of enforcement institutions and, in particular, of the need to adapt traditional judicial institutions to the expectations of the market.

In the light of this understanding and this theoretical model, the overall challenge of the book is to explain current enforcement developments. This endeavour is undertaken at a time in which enforcement issues are high on the agenda in many fields of European economic law. These issues can be clustered into developments in particular areas of law, in two major trends—fragmentation and collectivisation, and a new governance form.

First, novel institutions, novel enforcement mechanisms and novel remedies are constantly being created in each of many distinct areas of law, such as competition law, consumer law, intellectual property law, contracts law, regulatory private law and international commercial law. Thereby, the entire enforcement regime is undergoing a profound transformation that lacks precedent. In the realm of patent law, for instance, a new title and new institutions are being created in the framework of Article 118 TFEU (Treaty on the Functioning of the European Union) in the form of a Unitary Patent regime.[14] In consumer law, private enforcement services such as alternative

[11] 1869 UNTS 299; 33 ILM 1197 (1994).

[12] D Kelemen, *Eurolegalism: The Transformation of Law and Regulation in the European Union* (Harvard, Harvard University Press, 2011) 79–88.

[13] F Cafaggi, 'The Great Transformation. Administrative and Judicial Enforcement in Consumer Protection: A Remedial Perspective' (2009) 21 *Loyola Consumer Law Review* 496.

[14] Reg (EU) No 1257/2012 of the European Parliament and of the Council of 17 December 2012 implementing enhanced cooperation in the area of the creation of unitary patent protection. Council reg (EU) No 1260/2012 of 17 December 2012 implementing enhanced cooperation in the area of the creation of unitary patent protection with regard to the applicable translation arrangements. The text of the draft agreement on a Unified Patent Court is available here: http://register.consilium.europa.eu/pdf/en/12/st16/st16351-co03.en12.pdf (last visited 9 August 2015).

dispute resolution (ADR) and online dispute resolution (ODR) as well as self-regulatory enforcement mechanisms such as in the form of private arbitration are on the rise.[15] A strong drive towards collectivity characterises the introduction of general class actions for damages in several Member States as well as increased attention to the question of damages actions in antitrust law and the question of collective redress for consumers.[16] At the same time, cases such as C-415/11 *Mohamed Aziz* have shown that enforcement mechanisms have become a last resort to remedy social deficiencies of the national and European order.[17]

Second, an investigation into the transformation of enforcement in Europe reveals two major trends: first, the fragmentation of enforcement in Europe horizontally and vertically and, second, the collectivisation of enforcement in Europe. Both dimensions are considered to be interdependent. Policy-makers are countering the growing fragmentation of the services for law enforcement with ever stronger policy initiatives towards the collectivisation and coordination of claims on both the supply and demand side for justice. Collectivisation thus counterbalances horizontal and vertical fragmentation.[18]

Third, a closer analysis of the transformation of enforcement demonstrates the emergence of a new governance form for enforcement: traditionally compensatory and deterrent enforcement is being supplanted by regulatory enforcement that balances compensation, deterrence and vindication. Regulatory enforcement implies not only a novel regulatory function of enforcement[19] as opposed to traditional dogmatic enforcement rationales but indicates also the departure from traditional command-and-control regulation in the area of enforcement. Traditional regulation is replaced by novel cooperation mechanisms for dispute resolution between government and private actors and, thus, to some degree private regulatory litigation.

[15] KC Nobles, 'Emerging Issues and Trends in International Arbitration' (2012) 43 *California Western International Law Jounral* 77. See eg Dir 2008/52/EC of the European Parliament and of the Council of 21 May 2008 on certain aspects of mediation in civil and commercial matters, OJ L 136, 24.5.2008, 3–8.

[16] eg the Green Paper on Collective Redress for Consumers and its follow-up including collective ADR, the competition law 2005 Green Paper, the 2008 White Paper, the 2009 Proposal for a Council Directive on Rules Governing Actions for damages for infringements of Arts 101 and 102 of the Treaty, the Study on the Methods of Damages Calculation, Quantifying Antitrust Damages 2009, Proposal for a Directive on Antitrust Damages Actions 2013, EU Recommendation on common principles for injunctive and compensatory collective redress mechanisms 2013.

[17] HW Micklitz, 'Unfair Contract Terms—Public Interest Litigation before European Courts Case C-415/11 Mohamed Aziz' in V Colaert and E Terryn (eds), *Landmark Cases of EU Consumer Law—in Honour of Jules Stuyck* (Cambridge, Intersentia, 2013) 615–34.

[18] Note also the concept of diagonal fragmentation which will not be pursued in this article: Ch Joerges, 'The Idea of Three-Dimensional Conflicts of Law as Constitutional Form of Transnational Governance', *RECON Online Working Paper 2010/5*.

[19] Compare also O Lobel, 'New Governance as Regulatory Governance' in D Levi-Four (ed), *The Oxford Handbook of Governance* (Oxford, Oxford University Press, 2012).

It is argued that this development emanates from the interplay between deregulation and non-regulation at the national level, reregulation at the European level and self-regulation at the transnational level.

In the light of these developments, it is striking that neither the political agenda nor academic reflections have so far adopted a coherent analytical and conceptual approach to these and other enforcement transformations, not in order to build a coherent system but to come to a much deeper and clearer understanding of the changes in the enforcement structure. So far academic and political endeavours have rarely transgressed the close confines of distinct areas of economic law. The overarching question about the function and role of enforcement in a European and global legal order has entirely been neglected. Interconnections with developments in the rest of the world have likewise been disregarded. And finally, it is causes and consequences of these profound transformations that have so far only superficially been analysed by leading researchers in the field.

In response to these observations, this book contains a detailed and thorough overview, analysis and critique of the transformation of enforcement in the area of European economic law by leading European and international academics. As an original contribution it constitutes a multidisciplinary research effort on the transformation of enforcement in Europe and its global interdependences. It showcases the transformation of law enforcement with reference to both European economic law (especially transnational commercial law, competition law, intellectual property law, consumer law) and to the current context of significant global economic challenges. Comparative perspectives facilitate the formation of a holistic perspective on enforcement that reaches beyond distinct theoretical accounts, political agendas, regulatory systems, industry sectors and stakeholder perspectives. As the first comprehensive and comparative analysis of the enforcement of European economic law that reaches beyond closely confined areas of law, it constitutes a crucial contribution to the theoretical and policy questions of how to design a coherent European enforcement architecture in accordance with essential principles and objectives of the EU economic order.

II. STRUCTURE OF THE BOOK

The book is structured as follows. The introduction will be followed by six distinct parts and a conclusion. The rationale for the outline is the distinct logic, first, of building theoretical grounds, second, of looking at the demand and supply of justice through an institutional lens, third, of a distinct investigation of the Court of Justice of the European Union, and fourth, of investigating mechanisms for rendering justice. These analyses are then followed by a transnational lens that looks into transnational enforcement mechanisms. With this transnational perspective in mind, the outline then proceeds to an investigation of the governance of justice in such transnational settings and, in particular, the issue of public accountability of enforcement. The book closes with a conclusion.

Looking at the individual parts of the book in more detail, the second chapter focuses on the nature and concept of enforcement. It looks, in particular, into the role, nature and drivers of enforcement in post-national constellations. Thus, the second part is to address the theoretical question of how enforcement theories and cultures account for various modes of enforcements (for example public, private) and their interdependences as well as for enforcement transformations and subsequent policy adaptations. In this framework, Wai analyses enforcement in the shadows of transnational economic law whilst Whytock explores governance, rights and the market for dispute resolution services in relation to the enforcement of foreign judgments. And finally, Wind addresses the question of whether legal and political culture can explain the successes and failures of European law compliance.

The third part examines the supply and demand for justice. In essence, it analyses enforcement avenues and institutions with a particular focus on alternatives to traditional judicial enforcement avenues as well as the emergence of alternative and *sui generis* enforcement systems and their administration. Moreover, the part focuses on the demand for justice by a variety of stakeholders ranging from individuals to collectives and from public to private entities. It aims at exposing new avenues for justice to be rendered in a variety of areas of law. Selected examples are novel alternative dispute resolutions mechanisms as well as online dispute resolution mechanisms. The part will focus in particular on new and better modes of redress for consumers both in contract law and antitrust law. Ultimately, the third part seeks to examine the issues of fragmentation, privatisation, overspecialisation and the isolation of adjudication in Europe. In this framework, Eidenmüller and Fries analyse the design of an efficient consumer rights enforcement system in Europe. Hodges and Creutzfeldt discuss transformations in public and private enforcement, and Drexl focuses in his analysis on the interaction between private and public enforcement in European competition law.

The fourth part is devoted to an analysis of the role of the Court of Justice of the European Union (CJEU) in the enforcement of European Economic Law. It aims at delineating the role of the CJEU in comparison with further EU institutions as well as national courts and alternative dispute resolution mechanisms. In doing so, the fourth part draws specifically on specific areas of law, such as intellectual property law. Ultimately, it aims at delineating the proper role of the CJEU in the establishment of a European area of justice. In this framework, Kelemen explores the impact of the Court of Justice on the European Law Enforcement Architecture and Norrgard discusses alternatives to the CJEU in the field of intellectual property law.

The fifth part focuses on substantive law, procedural law and the law of remedies. It aims at discussing a wide range of provisions on conflict resolution ranging from settlements, procedural law to the law of damages. It thereby exposes the role and relevance of the choice of compensation schemes, such as rules for the calculation of damages, for each area of law as such. It thereby also discusses the interaction and interconnectedness of each of these mechanisms for the effectiveness and efficiency of law enforcement in each of the individual areas of law. In this framework, Hodges analyses the realities of US class actions whilst Hilty addresses the role of enforcement in delineating the scope of IP (Intellectual Property) rights. Tzankova, by contrast, reflects on the potential of case management for the resolution of mass disputes while Renda discusses private antitrust damages actions in the EU.

The sixth part addresses the wide variety of enforcement mechanisms in transnational settings. It exposes how interdependence, collaboration, co-existence, hybridisation, and competition exist between public and private national, European, transnational (for example international commercial arbitration), and international enforcement avenues and their transformations. The part looks in particular at enforcement networks and compliance mechanisms beyond compulsory enforcement mechanisms. Thus, Clavel discusses the relative merits of arbitration and state courts' litigation with a larger view on the challenges of transnational contractual enforcement. Cseres focuses on competition law enforcement beyond the nation-state and the question of whether this could be a model for transnational enforcement mechanisms.

The seventh part is devoted to discussing European economic law in its global interdependence with transnational enforcement mechanisms. The following questions will, inter alia, be addressed: what interdependence, collaboration, co-existence, hybridisation and competition exist between public and private national, European, transnational (for example international commercial arbitration), and international (for example WTO (World Trade Organization)) enforcement avenues and their transformations? Is a degree of national assertiveness required—and if so what degree—for sustained legitimacy of enforcement avenues as opposed to the acceptance of alternative sources of legitimacy for transnational enforcement? These questions are addressed by Hess in his contribution on the role of procedural law in the governance of enforcement in Europe. And Fernández Arroyo discusses the legitimacy and public accountability of global litigation with particular emphasis on the case of transnational arbitration.

Eventually, the conclusion by Wechsler and Tripković is, first of all, devoted to discussing the nature and characteristics of enforcement while addressing the overarching question of 'what is enforcement?'. It is further devoted to discussing transformations of enforcement in Europe (fragmentation, collectivisation) and ongoing challenges in designing a coherent, efficient and effective enforcement system for European economic law. It lies down the foundations for a theory of the transformation of enforcement through European integration.

The authors wish to express their gratitude to the following sponsors who have helped to make both the conference and this publication possible. On the one hand, this publication would not have been feasible without the support of the ERC grant for the 'European Regulatory Private Law' (ERPL) project.[20] On the other hand, the support by the Dr Theo and Friedl Schoeller Research Center for Business and Society was vital for the conference on which this publication is based.[21] Moreover, we thank the researchers of the ERC project and Boško Tripković for their support of the conference and this publication.

[20] European Research Council under the European Union's Seventh Framework Programme (FP/2007–2013)/ERC Grant Agreement n [269722].

[21] See www.schoeller-forschungszentrum.de/index.php?id=86&L=1 (last visited 9 August 2015).

Part II

Theorising Justice: Analytical and Multidisciplinary Perspectives on Enforcement

2

Enforcement in the Shadows of Transnational Economic Law

ROBERT WAI

AS THE EDITORS observe in introducing this book, enforcement in transnational economic law is experiencing change and experimentation in Europe and worldwide as part of the general process of regulation, de-regulation and re-regulation in economic governance. These changes are occurring both inside the nation state and across sovereign borders.[1] Transnational economic law reflects these broader changes in global society that have challenged the centrality of the nation state, changes that were identified some time ago as the move towards a postnational constellation.[2] Dynamism in transnational economic governance is leading to a reconfiguration not just of substantive norms and of procedures of law-making, but also procedures of surveillance, monitoring and enforcement.[3]

Other chapters in this volume track the expanded range of enforcement mechanisms in various subjects of transnational economic law, a space now characterised by vertical and horizontal fragmentation of enforcement authority, increased use of private law and private enforcement, new forms of cooperative and voluntary regulation, and hybrid forms of enforcement. In contrast, this chapter is primarily an exploration of alternatives for conceptualising the complexity of enforcement in transnational economic law. The conception of economic law as transnational requires consideration of the full array of norms and processes—state and non-state, international and national law, public and private law—that affect cross-border economic relations. Viewing transnational economic governance as a complex

[1] See, eg S Picciotto and D Campbell (eds), 'New Directions in Regulatory Theory' (2002) 29 *Journal of Law and Society* (special issue).

[2] J Habermas, *The Postnational Constellation* (trans Max Pensky, Cambridge, MIT Press, 2001) especially ch 4.

[3] See, eg W Mattli and N Woods (eds), *The Politics of Global Regulation* (Princeton, Princeton University Press, 2009); C Scott, F Cafaggi and L Senden (eds), 'The Challenge of Transnational Private Regulation: Conceptual and Constitutional Debates' (2011) 38 *Journal of Law and Society* 1 (special issue).

set of legal orders is already common, for example in efforts to describe international economic law as global legal pluralism[4] or as multilevel trade governance.[5] Any account of compliance or enforcement must more rigorously identify the enforcement characteristics of the various orders, and articulate the relationships among them.

This chapter begins by emphasising that the legal subject that this chapter defines as transnational economic law has always conceived of itself in relation to a plural range of state and non-state governance norms. If transnational economic law has always pragmatically accepted that its norms, plurally sourced, are effective, it has not, however, carefully articulated the reasons for their effectiveness. The result is an account of enforcement in which the centre of legitimate and effective enforcement authority remains the public law enforcement model of the sovereign state. This version of traditional 'legal centralism' positions both public international law and various forms of transnational private ordering as hierarchically inferior to the sovereign state's public authority.[6]

The plausibility of the legal centralist model of enforcement is challenged by the intensification of pluralism in transnational economic law, of which the two most salient aspects are the continuing increase of public international law treaties in economic law, recently in the form of preferential trade agreements and bilateral investment treaties, and the proliferation of new non-state norms, such as voluntary standards. This chapter suggests that both of these developments involve an ascendant and quite different model of enforcement in transnational economic law. If the enforcement model based on public law is a hierarchical model based on the monopoly of the sovereign state on legitimate legal enforcement, the enforcement model based on private ordering is a heterarchical or horizontal model based on conflict and cooperation among non-state actors. Recent discussions of enforcement in international law also emphasise horizontal enforcement, although important differences arise because the actors are states rather than private actors.

The turn to horizontal enforcement responds to normative and positive limits in transnational society on the hierarchical enforcement model based on the sovereign state. But the state law regime remains crucial in its own right and is also pervasively present in making horizontal enforcement more effective and legitimate. Horizontal ordering in a contemporary transnational context rarely 'just happens'. Rather, horizontal ordering is already

[4] eg FG Snyder, 'Governing Economic Globalisation: European Law and Global Legal Pluralism' (1999) 5 *European Law Journal* 143.

[5] C Joerges and E-U Petersmann (eds), *Constitutionalism, Multilevel Trade Governance and International Economic Law* (Oxford, Hart Publishing, 2011).

[6] M Galanter, 'Justice in Many Rooms: Courts, Private Ordering and Indigenous Law' (1981) 19 *Journal of Legal Pluralism* 1, 21.

embedded within a variety of other background entitlements and powers, including those constituted by crucial state legal processes. In conceiving of this role of state law, the chapter draws on models of enforcement in private law[7] that emphasise private ordering in the shadow of the law,[8] supplemented by the powerful insights of Hale and other critical scholars about the role of state law in constituting the 'coercive power' that actors bring to bear in horizontal enforcement.[9]

Reflection on horizontal enforcement helps to strengthen any account of how enforcement in transnational economic law could be effective in spite of the obvious limits of a standard public law model of enforcement. But in turn, reflection on how horizontal ordering occurs in the shadow of the law strengthens the account of the operation and promise of horizontal enforcement in transnational economic law. The conceptions of enforcement involved in the public law model, the private ordering model, the public international law model and the private law model reveal the diversity of enforcement in the field already, and also normalise the complex interaction of enforcement practices that we now see in transnational economic law. The different enforcement regimes are not simply alternatives, but are connected in the practice of transnational economic governance, casting and receiving variable shadows, always in relation to each other.

I. ENFORCEMENT, TRANSNATIONALISM AND PLURALISM IN TRANSNATIONAL ECONOMIC LAW

That enforcement in contemporary economic law would be plural and hybrid is hardly surprising given the basic history of the complex legal field that is identified as transnational economic law in this chapter. Precedent analyses of the legal aspects of cross-border economic transactions have

[7] This is part of a more general effort to distinguish different aspects of the relation between public law, private ordering and private law in global economic governance; see R Wai, 'Private v Private: Transnational Private Law and Contestation in Global Economic Governance' in H Muir Watt and D Fernandez Arroyo (eds), *Private International Law and Global Governance* (Oxford, Oxford University Press, 2014).

[8] The metaphor of the shadow of the law is well established in the domestic law context; eg Galanter (n 6) and R Mnookin and L Kornhauser, 'Bargaining in the Shadow of the Law: The Case of Divorce' (1979) 88 *Yale Law Journal* 950. I have explored its meaning in the transnational context in R Wai, 'Transnational Liftoff and Juridical Touchdown: The Regulatory Function of Private International Law in an Era of Globalization' (2002) 40 *Columbia Journal of Transnational Law* 209, 267, as have others, notably C Whytock, 'Litigation, Arbitration, and the Transnational Shadow of the Law' (2009) 18 *Duke Journal of Comparative & International Law* 449. In the broader governance context, see K Abbott and D Snidal, 'The Governance Triangle: Regulatory Standards Institutions and the Shadow of the State' in Mattli and Woods (n 3).

[9] R Hale, 'Coercion and Distribution in a Supposedly Noncoercive State' (1923) 38 *Political Science Quarterly* 470.

been variously known by such titles as international trade law, international economic law and the law of international business transactions. There are also many related specialised topics such as international commercial law, international finance and international investment.

The difficulty of even naming the legal field that deals with the law of cross-border economic activity partly relates to a common awareness of the complex and plural orders of laws relevant to the subject, whether those be domestic, foreign or international; public or private; substantive or procedural; state or non-state. These varied sources in turn generate norms that are diverse in content, scope and form, and that are not necessarily aligned and sometimes in conflict with each other.

How does transnational economic law deal with this kind of pluralism and complexity in relevant laws? Most standard courses and texts in subjects such as the law of international business transactions respond simply by being pragmatic. Depending on the particular sector being focused on (for example carriage of goods by sea), or sometimes the particular business problem to be resolved (for example a Japanese and a US business establishing a joint venture to manufacture goods in Japan),[10] lawyers and legal academics in these fields pragmatically bring to bear the range of instruments, whatever their sources, that are potentially relevant or useful to serving a client's interest. Pragmatic solutions to problems rather than formal categories define horizons.[11] National legislation, customary merchant practice, international treaties, private law rules about contract or property, and standard or customised contractual terms are all potential components of an eclectic mix of techniques available for use with respect to international transactions of various kinds. Overlaps or gaps in relevant state norms are simply challenges or opportunities that well-trained transactional lawyers deal with, for example, through the use of customised contractual arrangements,[12] or the turn to customary business practices.

Associated with a pragmatic pluralism in the field has been a ready acceptance of transnationalism.[13] Jessup's 1956 definition of transnational law included 'all law which regulates actions or events that transcend

[10] The sustained problem used throughout the exploration of the plural dimensions, including consideration of political and cultural dimensions, of legal and business practice of investment in Y Yanagida, DH Foote, ES Johnson Jr, JM Ramseyer and HT Scogin Jr (eds), *Law and Investment in Japan: Cases and Materials* 2nd edn (Cambridge, Harvard University Press, 2000).

[11] See, eg D Vagts (ed), *Transnational Business Problems* 2nd edn (New York, Foundation Press, 1998).

[12] See, eg D McBarnet, 'Transnational Transactions: Legal Work, Cross-Border Commerce and Global Regulation' in M Likosky (ed), *Transnational Legal Processes* (London, Butterworths, 2002).

[13] Vagts (n 11); R Goode, H Kronke and E McKendrick (eds), *Transnational Commercial Law: Text, Cases, and Materials* (Oxford, Oxford University Press, 2007).

national frontiers'.[14] Transnationalism in this understanding accepts that public international law may be important, but also recognises that many other kinds of law are crucial, including the de facto or intentional extraterritorial effects of domestic public law and private law, and the many varieties of non-state law and practice. This kind of frame fits well with the already pragmatically plural approach of the law of international business transactions. Indeed, many of the examples that Jessup cites to motivate a more general turn to transnational law are taken from cross-border economic transactions, such as 'an American oil company doing business in Venezuela; or the New York lawyer who retains French counsel to advise on the settlement of his client's estate in France'.[15]

The acceptance of multiple levels of governance, including both state and non-state sources and actors, is not new to the precedent fields of transnational economic law. A leading common law text on the law and practice of international trade could focus on national laws, but with reference as well to relevant international treaties, private law, private international law and contracts.[16] As strikingly, customary non-state business norms of the *lex mercatoria* have long been central to defining the laws of international trade.[17] Non-state norms are traced as effective standards, sometimes in the absence of state regulation, sometimes as sources for state legal orders (for example bills of exchange and bills of lading in international carriage of goods), and often as continuing sources of private norm-setting even after the emergence of relevant state law (for example the substantive norms of maritime law, maritime insurance, letters of credit or trade-delivery terms). In addition, transnational economic law has always seemed untroubled by the emergence of new dynamic mixes of sources, including hybrid forms of law; for example, a legal regime for franchises produced through the combined effect of a national public regulation on franchises, national private laws of contract and the customised terms of particular franchise agreements. Because of such pragmatic pluralism, an international business transactions lawyer is not much troubled by the creation of new hybrid regimes such as international investment treaties that combine international treaty provisions with dispute resolution through arbitration with private party access.

[14] P Jessup, *Transnational Law* (New Haven, Yale University Press, 1956) 2.

[15] ibid, 3–4.

[16] C Murray, D Holloway and D Timson-Hunt (eds), *Schmitthoff's Export Trade: the Law and Practice of International Trade* 11th edn (London, Sweet & Maxwell, 2007).

[17] Goode et al (n 13) 12–18. Schmitthoff (n 16), while not theorising systematically the sources of norms, repeatedly identifies the role of international mercantile custom; eg 'trade terms have been developed by international mercantile custom and have simplified the sale of goods abroad' (Schmitthoff (n 16) 9).

II. THE DEFAULT TO THE PUBLIC LAW ENFORCEMENT MODEL

If transnational economic law has always recognised the importance of plural legal norms in practice, how has it conceived of enforcement of those norms? The field's pragmatism seemed to bracket elaboration of a theory of enforcement that expressly reflected on why these plural norms were followed in practice, what the different forms of enforcement involved with each kind of law were, or how they connected to each other. Instead of a detailed theory of enforcement, those working on fields of transnational economic law simply believed that the messy mix of state and non-state norms related to international business transactions were observed by almost all business actors almost all of the time.[18]

Mostly, the pragmatic but under-theorised approach to enforcement in traditional economic law seemed to fall back on the standard public law model of enforcement through the modern sovereign state. Various international and non-state sources of norms were openly acknowledged, and there was a belief that these would be effective through significant party compliance. But the legal enforcement of even these norms remained linked ultimately to the sovereign state as the authority with the legitimate and effective institutions needed to enforce norms. This account of enforcement that involves at least one stage where state officials are permitted to potentially use force is very much the traditional account of enforcement in both international and domestic law that Hathaway and Shapiro have recently cast as the 'modern state conception' of enforcement.[19] The standard story on enforcement mirrored the general legal centralist response to the insights of legal pluralism, 'the pretentions of the official law to stand in a relationship of hierarchic control to other normative orderings in society'.[20]

In earlier periods of transnational economic law, including during the era of the General Agreement on Tariffs and Trade (GATT) prior to the institutions of the World Trade Organization (WTO), there was limited emphasis even on public international law frames. Instead, a text on the law of international trade would feature the frame of relevant national laws and regulation (for example tariff and border control laws; tax legislation; commercial, insurance and financial laws) that intentionally or effectively related to transnational economic activity.[21] Jessup's discussion

[18] To loosely paraphrase Henkin's well-known observation about international law, to be discussed below; L Henkin, *How Nations Behave: Law and Foreign Policy* 2nd edn (New York, Columbia University Press, 1979) 47.

[19] O Hathaway and S Shapiro, 'Outcasting: Enforcement in Domestic and International Law' (2011) 121 *Yale Law Journal* 252.

[20] Galanter (n 6) 21.

[21] Schmitthoff (n 16) added but barely integrated a new final chapter on the WTO in its 2007 edition. See also eg the state law centre to the approach to foreign investment in Yanagida et al (n 10).

of transnational law identified that in many of the areas where states had the power to deal with domestic problems with transnational elements such as antitrust matters, assertions of sovereign jurisdiction went well beyond any narrow territorial definition, and many of the formal bases for jurisdiction had become legal fictions.[22] In that sense, the extraterritorial effects of many kinds of national regulation could be seen to readily extend to matters of the international economy.

The traditional model then arrayed around the public law of the sovereign state the other plural norms relevant to transnational economic law. National laws would be supplemented by international treaties in particular areas, such as the GATT or the Convention on Contracts for the International Sale of Goods, as well as any relevant non-state instruments and norms, such as those related to maritime insurance. But especially at the level of enforcement, the traditional centrality of the sovereign state to both kinds of norms was emphasised, or, rather, assumed.

In international law, state consent determines the legality and legitimacy of international law and institutions, whether treaty based or customary. In its early decision inaugurating the WTO era, the Dispute Settlement Body emphasised that

> the *WTO Agreement* is a treaty—the international equivalent of a contract. It is self-evident that in an exercise of their sovereignty, and in pursuit of their own respective national interests, the Members of the WTO have made a bargain. In exchange for the benefits they expect to derive as Members of the WTO, they have agreed to exercise their sovereign according to the commitments they made in the *WTO Agreement*.[23]

And especially in relation to enforcement, the effectiveness of international treaties was linked to voluntary implementation of international law obligations in domestic regulation by national sovereign authorities. For example, the tariff binding commitments made by contracting parties to the GATT would have their legal expression in national tariff laws and administration. This emphasis continues in dynamic areas of economic law such as controls on cross-border bribery, which while the subject of an international treaty,[24] centres its measures on domestic public law enforcement under statutes like the Foreign Corrupt Practices Act in the United States.[25]

[22] Jessup (n 14) 70.

[23] *Japan—Taxes on Alcoholic Beverages*, WT/DS8/AB/R, WT/DS10/AB/R, WT/DS11/AB/R, 15.

[24] OECD Convention on Combating Bribery of Foreign Public Officials in International Business Transactions (1997).

[25] P Lattman, 'Ralph Lauren to pay fine over bribery in Argentina' *International Herald Tribune* (Paris, 24 April 2013) 18. The cash settlement as part of two non-prosecution agreements with the US Justice Department and the SEC concerning mundane but illegal payments to Argentine customs officials permitted the company to reduce inspections and paperwork on product imports.

In the other direction, private actors, norms and processes (such as bargaining or reputational pressure) might all be considered to be important to the actual practice of transnational economic law. However from a legal enforcement perspective, these private norms and processes were seen to be actually or potentially subject to the ultimate monopoly of state sovereigns on the legitimate use of power. Contractual and customary norms related to international transactions were understood to depend on state legislatures, administration and courts for their enforcement, and customary practices, such as those of banks with respect to instruments of transnational payments such as documentary credits, ultimately relied on the support or at least tolerance of such practices by states. This sense of enforcement mirrored a traditional understanding of a legitimated sovereign state hierarchically overseeing the realm of non-state norms. There may have been much awareness that the practice of compliance among private actors was much less orderly, but this was not a focus in theorising enforcement.

III. CONTEMPORARY CHALLENGES TO THE PUBLIC LAW ENFORCEMENT MODEL: INTERNATIONAL LAW AND TRANSNATIONAL PRIVATE ORDERING

This traditional but crude account of the centrality of the public law model of enforcement in transnational economic law has become increasingly implausible in the last two decades, particularly as the norms and processes being generated by international law and non-state orders have continued apace.

The number of international law instruments related to the transnational economy since the end of the Cold War is impressive, most notably the multilateral Uruguay Round Agreements, but especially in recent years the proliferation of preferential trade agreements and bilateral investment treaties. From an enforcement perspective, what is most challenging about these instruments is the institutional overlay on sovereign state authority, most notably in the pairing of expanded substantive obligations in the Uruguay Round Agreements with the establishment of the World Trade Organization as a full-fledged institution including strengthened dispute settlement functions. The inadequacy of a public law account to account for these new institutional features of transnational economic governance is further challenged by new forms of enforcement such as investor–state arbitration.

At least as important to enforcement has been the proliferation and great awareness of non-state ordering mechanisms in transnational economic regulation.[26] Contract-based cooperative regimes directed towards planning,

[26] T Buthe and W Mattli, *The New Global Rulers: The Privatization of Regulation in the World Economy* (Princeton, Princeton University Press, 2011).

creating commitments and enabling reliance have proliferated, most spectacularly and controversially, in some core areas of financial regulation before the 2008 crisis.[27] Beyond such cooperative private ordering, attention has also turned to the increasing use of non-state forms of contestation between non-state actors. Contemporary forms of corporate social responsibility—sourced in public law, international law, or non-state standards, including voluntary standards—have relied on pressure from non-state actors as part of the context for transnational economic activity. Through direct action, private ordering mechanisms such as publicity campaigns, consumer boycotts and shareholder pressure create enforcement pressure in economic law, including in the cross-border context.[28]

The turn to non-state forms of enforcement is itself clearly contested. The failures of self-regulation have been implicated in the 2008 financial crisis. Similarly, the critiques of branding campaigns are many, including problems of legitimacy and effectiveness, given the episodic nature of such pressure, and its dependency in turn on forms of unevenly distributed private power, such as the power of affluent consumers. Nonetheless, the sense that some of the most effective forms of enforcement in transnational economic law have moved into the realms of non-state ordering is hard to avoid.

There is one obvious and striking parallel in the way in which both international law and non-state private ordering challenge the assumptions about enforcement under the domestic public law model. Both emphasise models of horizontal enforcement among actors arrayed without an overarching authority such as a sovereign state with legitimate and effective control over mechanisms of enforcement.[29] To explore this parallel, this chapter will first look at the expanded analysis of this mode of enforcement in relation to private ordering including transnational private ordering, and then see how it has been adopted in influential contemporary analyses of international law.

IV. HORIZONTAL ENFORCEMENT THROUGH TRANSNATIONAL PRIVATE ORDERING

The major alternative to the domestic public law model for enforcement in transnational economic law is enforcement through private ordering.

[27] FJ De Graf and C Williams, 'The Intellectual Foundations of the Global Financial Crisis: Analysis and Proposals for Reform' (2009) 32 *University of New South Wales Law Journal* 390; A Riles, *Collateral Knowledge: Legal Reasoning in the Global Financial Markets* (Chicago, University of Chicago Press, 2011).

[28] eg C Sabel, D O'Rourke and A Fung, *Ratcheting Labor Standards: Regulation for Continuous Improvement in the Global Workplace* (World Bank, 2000).

[29] This parallel in horizontal enforcement is noted in relation to two possible paradigms for viewing the investment treaty area in A Roberts, 'Clash of Paradigms: Actors and Analogies Shaping the Investment Treaty System' (2013) 107 *American Journal of International Law* 48, 58.

Interest in non-state enforcement tracks a more general turn in economic law towards private ordering mechanisms, especially market mechanisms, rather than state processes.[30] The contemporary pairing of *lex mercatoria* with non-state dispute settlement, such as arbitration, has been an important source example for such dramatic conceptualisations of the field of economic law as 'global law without a state'[31] or as 'transnational private governance'.[32]

A. The Proliferation of Non-State Norms in Transnational Economic Governance

The interest in non-state enforcement through private ordering is connected to the proliferation of non-state norms related to the transnational economy. The traditional examples of non-state private ordering in transnational law include customary trade delivery terms in the international sale of goods, rules about maritime transport and bills of lading in relation to carriage of goods, standard terms with respect to marine insurance, and customary practices with respect to bills of exchange and documentary credits.[33] More recently, the number and variety of non-state private regulations observed in transnational economic relations have proliferated.[34] These include standard setting by important transnational non-governmental actors such as the International Organization for Standards (ISO).[35] The Equator Principles of risk management principles in relation to environmental and social risks are voluntarily followed by major financial institutions

[30] See, eg D Charny, 'Nonlegal Sanctions in Commercial Relationships' (1990) 104 *Harvard Law Review* 375, and, of course, S Macaulay, 'Non-Contractual Relations in Business: A Preliminary Study' (1963) 28 *American Sociological Review* 1955.

[31] G Teubner, '"Global Bukowina": Legal Pluralism in the World Society' in G Teubner (ed), *Global Law Without a State* (Aldershot, Dartmouth Publishing, 1997).

[32] eg A Stone Sweet, 'The New Lex Mercatoria and Transnational Governance' (2006) 13 *Journal of European Public Policy* 627.

[33] In turn many of these customary standards have became the basis for domestic state laws (eg in the UK, the Marine Insurance Act incorporating the Lloyd's Marine Policy and Institute Cargo Clauses; Carriage of Goods by Sea Act applying the Hague-Visby Rules; Bills of Exchange Act), or have been standardised by various non-state institutions such as the International Chamber of Commerce (INCOTERMS for trade terms; Uniform Customs and Practice for Documentary Credits (UCP 600) for documentary credits). For a teleological reading, see KP Berger, *The Creeping Codification of the Lex Mercatoria* (The Hague, Kluwer, 1999) and *The Creeping Codification of the New Lex Mercatoria* (Austin, Wolfers Kluwer, 2010).

[34] See C Cutler, *Private Power and Global Authority: Transnational Merchant Law in the Global Political Economy* (Cambridge, Cambridge University Press, 2003); Scott, Cafaggi and Senden (n 3).

[35] eg *Environmental Management—The ISO 14000 Family of International Standards* 2nd edn (International Standards Organization, 2010). Generally, on the rise of international standards in relation to global governance, and on private and multi-stakeholder processes, see eg Abbott and Snidal (n 8); Buthe and Mattli (n 26).

in providing international project finance.[36] Another recent variant are the Guiding Principles on Business and Human Rights, sponsored and adopted by the UN Human Rights Council, but developed by a consultation process including mainly non-governmental actors, and centred around voluntary standards.[37] Direct reference or incorporation of non-state standards in international treaties, such as the Agreement on Technical Barriers to Trade (TBT) among WTO member states, further augments the importance of non-state international standards.[38]

B. Non-State Horizontal Enforcement

The proliferation of law-like private governance norms and processes, paired with doubts about the effectiveness of public authorities, have led to alternative theoretical accounts that use non-state social interaction as a frame for understanding both norm generation and enforcement in the contemporary transnational economy.

Although non-state norm generation need not be paired with private enforcement, privately selected normative standards do seem to invite processes of non-state power including market pressure brought by potential or existing customers or counterparties, shareholders and providers of financing. For example, problematic aspects of derivatives seem well suited to be determined and controlled by market actors protecting their interests by avoiding substantively problematic products or discounting purchase price. Alternatively, parties could negotiate an appropriate balance of protections through supporting contractual arrangements. In that process, model contracts such as the Master Agreement of the International Swaps and Derivatives Association could be used.[39] The provision of contractual arrangements could include both substantive and procedural provisions, including in relation to dispute resolution and enforcement. A variety of non-state forms of dispute resolution, notably arbitration, could be used, further evidencing the significance of private process rather than standard state regulation through public law.

The most important accounts of such enforcement based on non-state private ordering in transnational economic relations have not surprisingly turned to economic theory, in particular new institutional economics.[40]

[36] The Equator Principles III, effective from 4 June 2013.

[37] Guiding Principles on Business and Human Rights.

[38] Agreeement on Technical Barriers to Trade, Art 2.4.

[39] Riles (n 27) ch 1.

[40] See, eg G-P Calliess and P Zumbansen, *Rough Consensus and Running Code: A Theory of Transnational Private Law* (Oxford, Hart Publishing, 2010) 113–18 for a general theory of transnational private law that recognises some of the basic insights of new institutional economics.

New institutional economics emphasises the functional need to address enforcement in any more complex economic relation involving uncertain information, lack of trust and the need for reliance over time.[41]

While state institutions can perform enforcement functions and reduce transaction costs, the new institutional economics also show how effective governance can develop from the self-interested choices of rational actors even without the state. For example, vertical integration is one, hierarchical, private solution to problems of transaction costs.[42] Various forms of more horizontal based market solutions are also available. For example the sale of potentially poor quality goods or financial products can be controlled by parties discounting price to reflect transaction costs to cover due diligence, cost of insurance or loss provision. Otherwise, parties can privately negotiate protection through supporting contractual arrangements, such as substantive terms guaranteeing quality or fitness for purpose. Still other private ordering alternatives would allow for procedural or institutional protections to secure quality, such as deposits or hostages, provision by parties of specific assets, procedures for inspection or third party verification, and dispute resolution of various forms.[43]

The relationship between state and non-state enforcement regimes in the new institutional economics is frequently under-elaborated; the main account of their relationship is as functional alternatives. For example Williamson in describing various forms of credible commitments made through private ordering, including asset specificity as a form of hostage, expressly contrasts this emphasis on private ordering against a model of centralism based on state enforcement.[44] The new institutional economics accepts that state-based institutions can be functional to these purposes, including being more effective or less costly than non-state based solutions. North, in particular, emphasises that third party enforcement through state institutions may be necessary to achieve economic development in modern economies involving extensive markets based on significant impersonal exchange among strangers.[45]

The new institutional economists also recognise that state and non-state forms can coexist in the same society. North observes how many forms such as exchange of hostages, ostracism of merchants, reputational damage, kinship ties and 'ideological commitments to integrity and honesty' are part of the 'complex institutional framework of formal rules, informal constraints,

[41] D North, *Institutions, Institutional Change and Economic Performance* (Cambridge, Cambridge University Press, 1990); O Williamson, *The Economic Institutions of Capitalism* (New York, Free Press, 1985).

[42] See, eg North, ibid ch 4; R Coase, 'The Nature of the Firm' (1937) 4 *Economica* 386.

[43] For a short summary, see North (n 41) ch 4. For a more elaborate survey, see Williamson (n 41).

[44] Wiliamson (n 41) 164–66.

[45] North (n 41) ch 7.

and enforcement that together make possible low-cost transacting'.[46] But while he and Williamson are aware that a number of these non-state institutions, such as contracts, in turn rely on state enforcement, they do not focus on the inter-relationship.

The emphasis on non-state forms of enforcement is also found in the related and influential work of Ostrom on common resource management regimes. Ostrom argues that collective action models such as the tragedy of the commons obscure the capacity of non-state based local communities to build enduring, self-governing institutions for governance of a commons.[47] Her empirical studies emphasise instead that norms on appropriation and provision of a commons can be made effective through local institutions rather than external authorities, in particular monitoring, conflict resolution and graduated sanctions attended to by local appropriators with interests in the commons or actors accountable to the appropriators.[48] 'Quasi-voluntary compliance', a term she takes from Levi, can arise from coercion by external actors, but also from 'contingent self-commitments and mutual monitoring'.[49] Ostrom does acknowledge that effective and sustainable local governance of commons frequently occurs in a larger organisation of multiple levels or layers of nested enterprises.[50] In her analysis of groundwater basin management in the Los Angeles metropolitan area, for example, she emphasises how a non-hierarchical form of 'polycentric public-enterprise game' included significant use of litigation and other state law venues and strategies. But her emphasis remains on the mixed character of these management regimes, in a system involving significant roles for private water companies and producer associations, and in which there is neither centralised ownership nor centralised regulation.[51]

For enforcement in the transnational economy, the functionality of non-state institutions is especially promising because they help private actors in international transactions deal with weak or absent public law institutions. The revival of trade in the middle ages, for example, has been traced to how the combination of the law merchant and institutional arrangements of the Champagne fairs provided a basis for expansion of cross-border trade even without established state law or state enforcement of contracts.[52]

[46] ibid, 58.

[47] E Ostrom, *Governing the Commons: The Evolution of Institutions for Collective Action* (Cambridge, Cambridge University Press, 1990).

[48] ibid, 88–102.

[49] ibid, 94–100, citing M Levi, *Of Rules and Revenue* (Berkeley, University of California Press, 1988) ch 3.

[50] eg E Ostrom, *The Future of the Commons: Beyond Market Failure and Government Regulation* (London, Institute of Economic Affairs, 2012) 81–82.

[51] Ostrom (n 47) 136.

[52] P Milgrom, D North and B Weingast, 'The Role of Institutions in the Revival of Trade: The Law Merchant, Private Judges and the Champagne Fairs' (1990) 2 *Economics and Politics* 1. On the role of the merchant guilds in enforcement, see A Greif, P Milgrom and B Weingast, 'Coordination, Commitment, and Enforcement: The Case of the Merchant Guild' (1994) 102

They view the Champagne fairs as non-state institutions that enhanced a reliable reputation system in support of merchant law norms, even in the absence of effective state institutions. Among the other attributes of the fairs were the provision of a private court system to hear complaints of merchants, the potential incarceration of those found to have cheated while at a fair, and the practice of refusal of entry to merchants to subsequent Champagne fairs who were not in good standing for failure to make good on prior judgments against them.[53]

Even after the rise of sovereign states with their enforcement capacities and authority, the various forms of non-state enforcement techniques often continue to exist.[54] The result is almost always that some combination of state and non-state techniques are deployed to provide the necessary security for transactions. This blend accords with the pragmatic pluralism of the international business transactions scholar. In this sense, non-state actors, so long as they are not blinded by parochial prejudice, could structure their relationships without borders.

C. Horizontal Enforcement and Non-Cooperative Private Ordering

The development of contractual and other cooperative institutional solutions may obscure that horizontal enforcement also anticipates non-cooperative forms of conflictual pressure. Even where negotiation fails, there is room for 'private' pressures to enforce norms that do not depend on state enforcement. In Ellickson's powerful conception based on his study of the disputing practice among Shasta County ranchers, there is 'order without law' through a mix of different mechanisms mostly understood not just to sit outside the range of state law, but also outside the zone of more 'consensual' private arrangements.[55]

On the issue of cost-sharing for boundary fences, for example, Ellickson found that neighbours believed in a non-state norm different from the background California state law. At the level of enforcement, strikingly, neighbours relied neither on complaints to public officials, nor appointments of third parties, nor even an ex ante arrangement such as a contract, but ex post pressure after a failure to pay, such as the 'pointed verbal request

Journal of Political Economy 745. There is critical commentary on these accounts of the merchant institutions; see eg E Kadens, 'The Myth of the Customary Law Merchant' (2012) 90 *Texas Law Review* 1153.

[53] Milgrom, North and Weingast (n 52) 20.

[54] North (n 41) 35.

[55] R Ellickson, *Order without Law: How Neighbours Settle Disputes* (Cambridge, Harvard University Press, 1991).

(implicitly backed by the threat of informal sanctions)', sometimes acted on as in 'borrowing' a piece of neighbour's equipment.[56]

In the context of cattle trespass disputes, Ellickson notes

> four types of countermeasures, listed in escalating order of seriousness: (1) self-help retaliation; (2) reports to county authorities; (3) claims for compensation informally submitted without the help of attorneys; and (4) attorney-assisted claims for compensation. The law starts to gain bite as one moves down the list.
>
> ... Not only are most trespass disputes in Shasta County resolved according to extralegal rules, but most enforcement actions are also extralegal.[57]

The most common countermeasures were the self-help measures, such as truthful negative gossip, but also 'tougher' forms such as herding offending animals to inconvenient locations or threats of harm to animals.[58] Ellickson, like the new institutional economists, puts little emphasis on the relationship among these measures other than as functional alternatives of varying degrees of severity.

Nonetheless, Ellickson's typology highlights that the spectrum of extra-legal ordering includes many that are directly conflictual and not mediated by cooperative ex ante institutions such as a merchant court. In this sense, they are similar to other kinds of direct action forms of contestation, used as well in the transnational context, such as the shaming campaigns associated with anti-branding activism, or the pressure deployed through consumer or shareholder boycotts.[59]

V. HORIZONTAL ENFORCEMENT IN PUBLIC INTERNATIONAL LAW

In both its conflictual and cooperative forms, the analysis of horizontal enforcement among private actors, in an interesting convergence, has also been deployed to ground recent theories of enforcement in international law.

Like the pragmatic international business transactions lawyer, some leading public international lawyers have premised their belief in the effectiveness of international law on Henkin's observation that it is 'probably the case that almost all nations observe almost all principles of international law and almost all of their obligations almost all of the time'.[60]

The causes of this empirical observation are much debated. Henkin links compliance with a variety of influences including the desire to act legally, but especially the importance to states and governments of reputation.

[56] ibid, 79–81.
[57] ibid, 57.
[58] ibid, 58.
[59] N Klein, *No Logo: Taking Aim at the Brand Bullies* (Toronto, Knopf Canada, 2000).
[60] Henkin (n 18) 47.

International law enhances these reputational concerns by making linkages between state behaviour across different episodes, different issue areas and different configurations of states. Other scholars connect the concern for compliance and reputation to a dynamic process of interaction and internalisation through which relevant state and non-state actors move towards compliance.[61]

But a major focus in recent international law scholarship on compliance is on horizontal pressures for compliance more like those found in private ordering rather than standard hierarchical public law enforcement. This view of international law primarily as a mechanism to resolve problems of cooperation among autonomous actors is influenced by economics, but also by international relations as the source discipline of much of the strategic analysis and game theory that has been in turn so influential in economics. This is a story then of complex interdisciplinary movement of ideas and concepts.[62]

In international law, this convergence in approach intensified after the end of the Cold War, with international relations scholars developing some modest hopes for an effective international regime premised on rational choice models still based on national self-interest.[63] The starting point for such work remained the classic realist structure of anarchy in which key units of power are arranged without any kind of supranational leviathan.[64] Whether modelled as tragedy of the commons, problems of public goods or prisoner's dilemmas, the focus was on resulting problems of cooperation generated because actors in an anarchic structure fail to achieve their interests because of lack of trust in other actors. Problems of strategy and game theory ensue.[65]

Such modelling provides a basis for claiming that international treaties and institutions allow states to advance their rational self-interest in achieving various kinds of cooperative goods. The fit to the international economic policy is obvious. The main theories of international trade, including theories of absolute advantage and comparative advantage, are premised on the

[61] H Koh, 'Transnational Legal Process' (1996) 75 *Nebraska Law Review* 181.

[62] J Trachtman, *The Economic Structure of International Law* (Cambridge, Harvard University Press, 2008) 76–80 helpfully discusses together parallel developments in literatures in international law, international regimes, social norms and industrial organisation.

[63] See, eg the significant expansion of interest in international law in the journal *International Organization*, such as the special issue of the journal published as J Goldstein, M Kahler, RO Keohane and A-M Slaughter (eds), *Legalization and World Politics* (Cambridge, MIT Press, 2001).

[64] The key work in the move to view international economic regimes as the outcome of rational choice and cooperation among sovereign actors is R Keohane, *After Hegemony: Cooperation and Discord in the World Political Economy* (Princeton, Princeton University Press, 1984).

[65] See, eg D Baird, R Gertner and R Picker, *Game Theory and the Law* (Cambridge, Harvard University Press, 1992).

mutual benefits that will accrue to states if they overcome a myopic focus on self-interest and instead realise the cooperative benefits of maximum aggregate production through liberal trade advanced by forgoing protectionist tariffs and other impediments to trade.[66]

Strategic analysis of problems of collective action could point to the imposition of an overarching authority, for example a supranational authority enforcing free trade norms. But the realist emphasis has instead been on functional alternatives to centralised enforcement through a supranational leviathan.[67] In particular, various forms of horizontal enforcement, such as tit-for-tat retaliation in an iterated relationship could provide adequate enforcement.[68] This is a relentlessly functional approach to international law that considers it as simply one alternative 'to reach efficient and stable strategic equilibria of cooperation: of achievement of joint games where there are temptations to defect'.[69] Similarly, for Trachtman, international organisations that function well reflect the choice of sovereign states as the best means among alternative institutional arrangements for achieving cooperative goals.[70]

An emphasis on horizontal enforcement makes sense of the enforcement apparatus currently available in international economic law. Even the WTO Dispute Settlement Understanding (DSU), among the most impressive procedures in contemporary international law, lacks any supranational enforcement capacity. Instead, a panel that finds a violation of a Uruguay Round treaty typically recommends that the Member found to be in violation come into compliance with its treaty obligations.[71] Although the DSU now provides for improved 'monitoring and surveillance' procedures, the most serious remedy in the event of refusal of a Member to comply is the possibility that the Dispute Settlement Body will authorise a complaining Member to withdraw concessions.[72] This is essentially authorisation of retaliation, the most traditional form of horizontal enforcement.

This emphasis on the horizontal nature of enforcement in even the most advanced of international law regimes for dispute settlement matches the more chastened approach to international law associated with the 'limits of

[66] eg M Trebilcock and R Howse, *The Regulation of International Trade* 3rd edn (London, Routledge, 2005) 2–4.

[67] Most mainstream analyses in international relations of international law deemphasise the importance of centralised Austinian style enforcement; see eg KW Abbott, RO Keohane, A Moravcsik, A-M Slaughter and D Snidal, 'The Concept of Legalization' in Goldstein et al (n 63) 34.

[68] J Setear, 'An Iterative Perspective on Treaties: A Synthesis of International Relations Theory and International Law' (1996) 37 *Harvard International Law Journal* 139.

[69] Trachtman (n 62) 23 and ch 3.

[70] ibid, 24 and ch 5.

[71] Dispute Settlement Understanding, Art 19.1.

[72] ibid, Art 22.

international law' school.[73] This approach builds from the realist tradition in international relations, with its scepticism towards allegedly naïve, utopian tendencies of international law.[74] International law, and specifically compliance and enforcement of international law, is treated as a matter primarily of national self-interest. Goldsmith and Posner characterise much of customary and conventional international law as situations of coincidence of interests or problems of coordination, in which enforcement is not a problem because the interests of states to act in a consistent fashion already align. Similarly, they see other examples of compliance as really situations of coercion, in which a non-compliant state faces such coercive power of another state that compliance becomes beneficial under a cost–benefit analysis. Goldsmith and Posner do see a role for customary international law in bilateral repeated prisoner's dilemmas.[75] They also accept that international treaties may provide informational focal points that 'align expectations about which behaviours count as cooperation'.[76] International law can also provide monitoring and dispute resolution mechanisms that provide information and transparency about whether compliance or cheating is occurring. International law processes might also deploy effective reputational pressure by linking behaviour across time and across different parties,[77] such that the costs of non-compliance are increased beyond the myopic calculation of a single episode.

More recently Hathaway and Shapiro's interest in 'outcasting'[78] as the normal form of enforcement in international law also shares the focus on horizontal methods of enforcement found among private actors, but in a more positive vein. Hathaway and Shapiro argue that modelling enforcement on the internal sanction powers of a modern domestic state with control over the use or threats of use of physical force is a very crude account of enforcement of law. Instead of threats of physical force, outcasting encourages compliance by denying law-breakers the benefits of social cooperation and membership. Hathaway and Shapiro also emphasise that international institutions often themselves do not impose sanctions, but authorise other actors to do so. They consider enforcement through 'external outcasting' as normal in international law, for example in the WTO.[79] The ultimate sanction for non-compliance is understood not to be direct punishment by

[73] J Goldsmith and E Posner, *The Limits of International Law* (Oxford, Oxford University Press, 2005). See also E Posner, *The Perils of Global Legalism* (Chicago, University of Chicago Press, 2009).

[74] EH Carr, *The Twenty Years' Crisis 1919–1939* 2nd edn (London, Macmillan, 1946); H Morgenthau, *Politics Among Nations: The Struggle for Power and Peace* (New York, Alfred A Knopf, 1948).

[75] Goldsmith and Posner (n 73) 41–42.

[76] ibid, 86.

[77] ibid, 101.

[78] Hathaway and Shapiro (n 19).

[79] ibid, 307.

the WTO or threats of physical force. Rather, the incentive to comply is provided by the loss of the protections and benefits provided by states and linked to compliance with the WTO.

From this base, a more constructivist approach to international law would emphasise that national interests are often either ill-defined or involve complex conflicts among various constituencies internal to any sovereign state. In that context, international law treaties and procedures can play more of a role in influencing the perception of state interests, rather than simply occasioning a strategic cost–benefit analysis based on simply calculable national interests.[80] Moreover, international law norms can play a role in creating benchmarks for private decision-making, as well as in shifting decision-making power among elites or other groups within states.[81]

This last distinction is not just a point about attribution of compliance pull. For it relates to an important distinction between horizontal enforcement of international law as compared to that of private ordering. International law and institutions are the product of public authorities deriving legitimacy from their domestic political process. This potentially creates a normative authority not found in equivalent institutions generated purely by the interaction among private actors. Among the consequences would be that international law and institutions may be able to play more of a role like that of states with respect to influencing and constituting the terrain of horizontal enforcement and thereby addressing important limits on the effectiveness and legitimacy of models of horizontal enforcement for transnational economic law.

VI. THE LIMITS OF TRANSNATIONAL PRIVATE ORDERING AS ENFORCEMENT

The rational choice analysis of new institutional economics and institutionalist international relations theory contributes much to explaining compliance and enforcement in transnational economic law. However, it is also important to recognise the limits of this perspective for a legal analysis.

Issues of legitimacy and in particular exclusion of certain kinds of issues, interests and actors are addressed only in a very limited way in most horizontal enforcement analyses. Third parties to contracts are the classic example, but broader externalities in environmental protection, competition policy or financial stability may not be adequately internalised in the actions of two parties engaged either in bilateral cooperation or conflict. The failed reliance on private regulation before the 2008 financial crisis highlighted that the

[80] R Howse and R Teitel, 'Beyond Compliance: Rethinking Why International Law Really Matters' (2010) 1 *Global Policy* 127.

[81] ibid, 130.

legitimacy of state law and public regulation through state institutions, in contrast to private ordering, is premised on the authority of a public government charged with plenary representation of the interests of all members of the society, and having a core task of aggregating and defending a shared public interest of the society.[82]

Even as between negotiating parties, private ordering solutions are very much the consequence of the starting distribution of private power of the parties negotiating. In that sense, private enforcement can simply reflect power relations of domination, often harshly and indiscriminately coercive, rather than reflecting any logic of respect for the preferences or efficiency, let alone fairness.[83] Similarly, private ordering is generally ill-suited to situations involving claims of distributive justice, where no cooperative solution exists but instead difficult choices about conflicting claims are needed.[84] Although difficult, these are the kinds of policy issues that comprise a significant part of what makes law more than simply apologetic for brute power.

At the international level, a related critique of transnational private regulation has been made from a developing country perspective, in which it is argued that powerful private actors may have as much or more influence over private norms and in private enforcement as legitimate but weak public authorities of developing country states.[85]

These kinds of policy concerns about private ordering have all been evident since the financial crisis in 2008, where a key contributor to crisis has been identified as naïve, motivated or ideological reliance on non-state actors for regulation and governance in financial services.[86] The premise that market actors would self-protect by avoiding risky assets, discounting price, or requiring contractual or other customised protection turned out to be based on inaccurate assumptions including (a) behavioural biases and mistakes; (b) structural incentives towards misinformation and excessive risk, including for various intermediaries such as originating lenders and rating agencies; and (c) inadequate attention to power and knowledge imbalances between parties. The market regulation approach also crucially failed to adequately internalise costs to third parties and to the public interest including the risks to stability of the entire financial system.[87]

[82] See generally, Cutler (n 34) ch 7.

[83] Galanter (n 6) 25.

[84] For one version of this critique of the focus in international economic law on cooperative benefits, see R Wai, 'The Commercial Activity Exception to Sovereign Immunity and the Boundaries of Contemporary International Legalism' in C Scott (ed), *Torture as Tort: Comparative Perspectives on the Development of Transnational Human Rights Litigation* (Oxford, Hart Publishing, 2001) 232–39.

[85] See, eg A Anghie, *Imperialism, Sovereignty, and the Making of International Law* (Cambridge, Cambridge University Press, 2005).

[86] Among many examples, see RA Posner, *A Failure of Capitalism: The Crisis of '08 and the Descent into Depression* (Cambridge, Harvard University Press, 2009).

[87] eg De Graf and Williams (n 27).

Private power can be deployed to counter or control private power.[88] Certain liberal traditions of the market understand the virtues of the market as including not just its capacity to generate private cooperative benefits through increased total production, but also the market as a social and regulatory order that deploys private power to control private power.[89] To work this way, however, market design must attend to how competition or contestation can be destroyed by agglomerations of private power. Unfortunately, some contemporary private governance is careless in attending to agglomerations and abuses of private power, and ideologically blinded to the importance of public institutions in providing the context and rules of the game that help to protect against such abuses. A liberal account of productive governance through deployment of private power against private power requires a better sense of the interaction between state institutional context and private ordering. From the perspective of enforcement, private ordering analyses have the tendency to underestimate or deemphasise the function of state institutions in constituting the terrain of powers and interests at play in private ordering so as to generate more representative or effective regulatory outcomes.

A focus on this relationship is characteristic of the regime of private law, to which I now turn as both a distinctive site for enforcement, but also as containing a useful, underlying conceptual model for enforcement.

VII. THE MODEL OF ENFORCEMENT IN TRANSNATIONAL PRIVATE LAW

A. Private Law as a Substantive Regime of Transnational Economic Governance

I have argued elsewhere that domestic private law regimes are important sites of transnational governance because many private actors depend on the institutions of private law to support their economic activity, such as for contract and property enforcement.[90] This reliance on private law foundations in domestic courts continues even in cutting-edge sectors such as derivatives markets.[91] Thereby national private law institutions become touchdown sites of the transnational economy and de facto institutional sites of transnational economic governance. From the perspective of this book, these sites of private law are especially interesting because while often thought of as facilitative institutions for cooperative transactions, they are

[88] See Wai (n 7).

[89] These liberal conceptions of countervailing private power are discussed in ibid, 43–45.

[90] Wai (n 8).

[91] J Braithwaite, 'Standard Form Contracts as Transnational Law: Evidence from Derivatives Markets' (2012) 75 *Modern Law Review* 779.

also potentially sites for enforcement by one private party of non-cooperative claims it makes against another private party.[92] Private law potentially disposes of significant governance stakes through defining property entitlements, demarking the boundaries of contract enforcement and providing tort compensation for injury.[93]

Transnational litigation of private law claims is a form of enforcement in transnational governance[94] that has been a high-profile transnational response to business misconduct since at least the litigation after the disaster at the Union Carbide plant in Bhopal in 1984.[95] Ongoing private law claims in the United States against British Petroleum and others arising from the Deepwater Horizon accident,[96] suits in English courts by Nigerian fisherman harmed by oil spills of Royal Dutch Shell,[97] negligence litigation against financial companies including rating agencies related to the sale of 'toxic financial products',[98] and litigation in Ecuadorian courts against Chevron as the successor corporation to Texaco in relation to ecological harms from its Lago Agrio operations,[99] all provide examples of the continuing relevance of transnational private litigation as a site for transnational economic governance.

Regardless of the effectiveness of transnational private litigation, what is of particular interest for this chapter is the nature of the enforcement model involved. In particular, transnational private litigation involves the provision of dispute resolution venues and enforcement mechanisms through state institutions that allow private power to contest private power. The state does not initiate, investigate or prosecute such claims. Rather litigation is premised on private ordering by parties including whether and how to bring a claim in the state venues. Regardless of whether it is a contract, property or tort relationship, the dispute is a form of contestation of the private behaviour of one party by another private party.[100] But equally crucial

[92] Wai (n 7).

[93] Wai (n 8).

[94] R Wai, 'Transnational Private Litigation and Transnational Governance' in P Mueller and M Lederer (eds), *Criticizing Global Governance* (London, Palgrave Macmillan, 2005).

[95] For a sense of the potential but also the many limits of such litigation, see eg U Baxi and A Dhanda (eds), *Valiant Victims and Lethal Litigation: The Bhopal Case* (Bombay, NM Tripathi, 1990) and J Cassels, *The Uncertain Promise of Law: Lessons from Bhopal* (Toronto, University of Toronto Press, 1993).

[96] See, eg Campbell Robertson and Clifford Krauss, 'BP May Be Fined Up to $18 Billion for Spill in Gulf' *New York Times* (New York, 5 September 2014) A1.

[97] See, eg Christopher Adams and William Wallis, 'Shell agrees to £55m deal with Nigerian fisherman over oil leaks' *Financial Times* (London, 7 January 2015) 4.

[98] See, eg Jamie Smyth and Sam Fleming, 'S&P loses appeal over rating of toxic financial products' *Financial Times* (London, 7/8 June 2014) 8.

[99] Provincial Court of Sucumbios, Lago Agrio, Ecuador, Judgment of Case No 2003-0002, 14 Feb 2011, largely upheld on appeal by the Ecuador Supreme Court 12 November 2013, although the damage award was reduced to $9.5 billion.

[100] Wai (n 7).

is that this form of private enforcement is an alternative to pure direct action or use of a non-state institution, for the state plays a crucial enabling role.

B. Private Law and Private Dispute Resolution Procedures in Transnational Business Relations

If private law sometimes provides a state process for the adjudication of substantive claims under private law by one private party against another, it may also support the use of dispute resolution procedures for conflict and disputes that seemingly have less state presence. As Collins notes in his account of 'regulating contracts', the core of the planning activities performed by contract lawyers include not just customised substantive terms, but also planning for foreseeable and unforeseeable contingencies, construction of 'non-legal sanctions or self-enforcing legal sanctions such as security interests', and customisation of dispute resolution and remedies.[101] In this way, contracts can expressly provide for customised layers of non-state procedures to assist with compliance, with state law moving increasingly towards being background support for what look primarily like non-state procedures for disputing and resolving disputes, including deposits, inspections, outside monitoring, complaint processes, mediation and arbitration.[102] The spectrum of contract-based governance functions can operate in transnational contracts as well, utilising private ingenuity combined with background state law supports. So, any law of contract that enables enforcement in domestic courts of, for example, a contractual provision for a deposit or bond to secure obligations in a cross-border context functions as transnational private law.

But even in promoting non-state forms of private dispute settlement, the state presence remains, so long as we have not moved into a closed autopoietic system in which it does not even occur to parties to resist system norms to use non-state norms and processes.[103] Although set up as an alternative to civil litigation in state courts, for example, the effectiveness of arbitration as an enforcement regime depends crucially on the support of state courts. In narrow form, international commercial arbitration is private dispute resolution other than state courts. But arbitration relies for its effectiveness on the background support of state law processes.[104] In particular, through legislation and decisions of courts themselves, state institutions have been conscientious to support the use of arbitration in the transnational context,

[101] H Collins, *Regulating Contracts* (Oxford, Oxford University Press, 1999) 151.

[102] R Wai, 'The Interlegality of Transnational Private Law' (2008) 71 *Law & Contemporary Problems* 107, 122.

[103] Teubner (n 31) above. My doubts are outlined in Wai (n 102) 112–20.

[104] Wai (n 8) 220–22; Whytock (n 8).

through, for example, decisions to decline jurisdiction if arbitration had been agreed to, and willingness to enforce arbitral awards as effectively as domestic civil court judgments.[105] I have characterised this reliance of arbitration on state processes as a leading example of the 'touchdown' of global economic relations in existing state processes, and therefore that international commercial arbitration occurs very much in the shadow of the law.[106]

VIII. INTERACTIONS OF TRANSNATIONAL ENFORCEMENT: TRANSNATIONAL PRIVATE ORDERING IN THE SHADOWS OF THE LAW

The examples of transnational litigation and arbitration both provide crucial insight as to the nature of enforcement overall in transnational economic law. In particular, the model of enforcement in private law is one that exemplifies the 'transnational shadow of the law'.[107] This metaphor should be pushed further to emphasise how wide and deep these shadows are, signalling the extent of the inter-relationship among different kinds of transnational economic law norms. Such inter-relationships also seem to characterise many of the forms of enforcement that we are now seeing more generally in transnational economic law. It is to this characterisation that this chapter therefore now turns by way of conclusion.

A. Back to Hale: The Deeper Shadow of the Law

Private law can be viewed as exemplary of a mixed system in which private ordering is enabled but regulated as a means of achieving both cooperation and contestation among private actors.[108] The non-state disputants drive this form of legalism in terms of assertion of claims, framing of arguments and marshalling of evidence.[109] But equally there is a clear presence of the state in this process in providing enabling institutions, such as courts, and substantive norms including mandatory, default and permissive provisions.

Building on this frame, contemporary legal scholarship has highlighted how other forms of disputing and private ordering, such as negotiation, occur in the shadow of the state law. Mnookin and Kornhauser's study of

[105] See generally, Y Dezalay and B Garth, *Dealing in Virtue: International Commercial Arbitration and the Construction of a Transnational Order* (Chicago, University of Chicago Press, 1996).

[106] Wai (n 8) 267.

[107] ibid and Whytock (n 8).

[108] Wai (n 7).

[109] R Kagan, *Adversarial Legalism: The American Way of Law* (Cambridge, Harvard University Press, 2001) 9.

divorce law in the United States highlighted how contemporary family law provisions permitted substantial degrees of private ordering.[110] The resulting private ordering in terms of negotiated settlements with respect to both monetary and child-related responsibilities reflect a mix of non-legal factors such as parental preferences and financial endowments, and 'bargaining endowments' created by legal rules.[111] This is neither pure private ordering nor state-mandated regulation: modern divorce law is a mixed system that looks very much like how private law is organised.

This view of how state law relates more generally to non-state normative systems has been generalised by Galanter to reflect a 'centrifugal' view of the role of state courts in distributing 'regulatory effects' in a society.[112] In this view, the difference between negotiation and regulation can almost disappear with a spectrum of intermediate instances that partake of both.[113]

Another way to deepen the conception of the shadow of the law is to recover the historical frame of legal realism that many decades ago powerfully traced the constitutive effects of law on the distribution of power in society. Robert Hale in particular provided a powerful framework for thinking about the relationship of legal and non-legal power, including specifically with respect to the market economy.[114] This insight has been developed powerfully in critical legal writing in recent decades,[115] and its forceful articulation offers insights to unexpected topics like enforcement in transnational economic law.

Duncan Kennedy observes that one crucial insight of Holmes, Hale and the realists was to see that the stakes of law are both less than the state enforcement power in 'criminalist' sanction mode, but also more than that mode because law is pervasively influential on social ordering: 'the whole point of the realist analysis is that the apparently nondirective background rules of contract, property and tort do powerfully *influence* the social order that emerges from bargaining, even though they neither compel nor forbid that ordering'.[116] The potential application of this frame to social change is wide, for example, Kennedy tracks the play of 'legal cards' by actors along other cards in the process of stability and change in low income housing markets in urban areas.[117]

[110] Mnookin and Kornhauser (n 8).

[111] ibid, 966.

[112] Galanter (n 6) 6. For the transnational connection of radiating effects, see Whytock (n 8) 455.

[113] Galanter (n 6) 9.

[114] Hale (n 9).

[115] D Kennedy, 'The Stakes of Law, or Hale and Foucault!' in *Sexy Dressing etc: Essays on the Power and Politics of Cultural Identity* (Cambridge, Harvard University Press, 1993).

[116] ibid, 119.

[117] D Kennedy, 'Legal Economics of US Low Income Housing Markets in Light of "Informality" Analysis' (2002–2003) 4 *Journal of Law and Society* 41, 47.

For Hale the economy can be understood as a competition among various private actors to influence each other through their relative coercive power. This is a kind of generalised competition of private power versus private power. But Hale highlights what many economists and also many contemporary lawyers fail to discern clearly, which is that state law is pervasive in constituting the private power of competing actors. Most obvious is that private property depends on the deployment of state law to define and enforce private property entitlements.[118]

Hale recognises that some private power originates from non-legal sources. To take a contemporary example, technology, like a particular kind of fencing in ranching country, can be a non-legal basis for appropriation and exclusion. But legal regimes can also provide such coercive power, such as through intellectual property laws and legal enforcement of restrictive contractual provisions. The relation of legal and non-legal techniques is strikingly revealed when they are functionally substitutable. Burk for example compares the state apparatus connected to a copyright or patent law regime and the potentially equivalent technological regime, such as digital rights management (DRM) systems in relation to file-sharing or genetic use restriction technologies (GURTs) that prevent or moderate the use and reproduction of a good beyond the terms on which it has been transferred to the user.[119] Technical and legal forms of regulation can therefore be compared in terms of effectiveness, but also in terms of competing policy values, such as issues of access, disclosure and innovation, or unconscionability.[120] Under one view, technology that imposes restrictions that would be treated as improper in the equivalent legal regime (whether patent law, contract law or other forms of state law) should not be legally permitted, as part of a more general understanding of the proper setting for technology as including 'legal constraints on code'.[121]

Like Hale, contemporary critical thinkers see that law's constitutive role often does sit quite closely behind seemingly non-legal sources of coercive power such as economic resources or engineering capacity. For example, the possibility of using most technologies can be prohibited or made difficult by state law that treats efforts to hack, decipher or render useless technological restrictions as a crime or a tort or a violation of a property right.[122] In a similar vein, libel law can make into potential torts private efforts to use communications to exercise reputational pressure.

Bringing Hale to functionalist approaches to private enforcement highlights that the connections between state law and private ordering are

[118] Hale (n 9) 471–74.

[119] D Burk, 'DNA Rules: Legal and Conceptual Implications of Biological "Lock-Out" Systems' (2004) 92 *California Law Review* 1553.

[120] ibid, 1565–75.

[121] ibid, 1568–69.

[122] ibid, 1561–71.

manifold and pervasive, constituting the terrain for both cooperative and conflictual private pressure.[123] The new institutionalists do not fully acknowledge the many and deep shadows cast by state law over private ordering solutions. In Ellickson's account of Shasta County, state laws do figure as one part of an escalation strategy in cattle trespass disputes moving from self-help retaliation to 'attorney-assisted claims for compensation'.[124] But even for a legal scholar like Ellickson, state law enforcement strategies mainly figure as alternative, and less preferred, strategies to horizontal enforcement, rather than configuring the terrain and form of horizontal strategies themselves.

B. Hale and Jessup: Enforcement and the Stakes of Transnational Law

The insights concerning private ordering in the shadow of the law should be extended to the deeper effects described by Hale, and simultaneously expanded to address the transnational context. Whytock has convincingly argued that the shadow of the law metaphor captures well the relationship between arbitration and state processes.[125] In the realm of enforcement, the simple point is that arbitration relies on compliance by private parties with arbitral awards, which in turn only happens with the active support in the background of the mandatory enforcement of the state private law regime. Can the metaphor be developed still more deeply to provide a model of the relationship between various forms of enforcement in transnational economic law? Hale's framework of legal and non-legal bases for coercion (or bargaining or dispute resolution) can be combined with Jessup's insights about the plural transnational law to tell us more about the transnational shadow of law.

A key starting observation, again, is that background regimes of law in transnational economic relations are crucial because the dedicated regimes in the foreground of transnational economic law offer nothing like the hierarchical public law enforcement of domestic law. There are no supranational equivalents of the criminalist or even of the private law kind. Transnational law then seems to depend on domestic state regimes performing these functions in the transnational realm, or on enforcement and compliance through private ordering.

Combining the insights of Hale and Jessup broadens awareness of the forms of law that can cast a shadow on compliance in the transnational context. A perspective on the transnational shadow of the law that reflects the

[123] Hale (n 9) 475–77, is sceptical of the distinction between threats and promises, arguing that both require the force of law behind them to be effective as pressure.

[124] Ellickson (n 55) 57.

[125] Whytock (n 8).

insights from Hale also highlights that most forms of law, for the domestic as much of the transnational, depend not on a simple crude application of coercive state enforcement, but rather on the varied effects on private ordering generated by a wide variety of state and non-state legal orders.

The kinds of effective law in the cross-border context are varied. Private ordering can obviously turn on the transnational effects of enforcement of standard public law. So, the practices of a multinational bank in foreign markets may be directly changed as a result of prosecutions and negotiated settlements with financial or securities regulators in Britain and the United States.[126] Public international law can cast a shadow over processes of interstate bargaining.[127] But if international law influences the reputational or other calculations of state governments, then this will be reflected in the domestic state law enforcement model as well: for example, a change to the vigour of public enforcement in domestic tax laws or securities regulation. If one accepts, against the sceptical 'limits' approach, that international law exercises broader compliance pull over actors because of its formal status as the product of consent by legitimated states rather than simply single states or private actors, then international law may very well be able to cast a structuring shadow over bargaining not just among states, but among different actors within and across states. Non-state actors face the enforcement effects of international law if a state implements international law obligations, but private ordering can also be influenced by the operation of public international law through other mechanisms, for example, as sources of normative benchmarks for private actors, even without any direct formal obligations.[128]

Such attention to the multiple legal backgrounds to private action makes normal an understanding of how private law produces transnational effects. The state apparatus is not a guarantee of enforcement, but structures the kind of private ordering—whether that be litigation, negotiation, claiming or retaliation—that otherwise occurs.

At its most inclusive, the shadows of enforcement potentially run in many directions. As Galanter has suggested, in some configurations the relation between non-state legal orders and the state law system might best be imagined as law in the shadow of private ordering.[129] There are examples of this reversal at the level of substantive norms, where national

[126] eg 'Deutsche Bank Pays Record Fine for Libor Manipulation' *Financial Times* (London, 23 April 2015) ($2.5 billion settlement with the UK Financial Conduct Authority and the US Department of Justice, the Commodity Futures Trading Commission and the New York Department of Financial Services).

[127] M Busch and E Reinhardt, 'Bargaining in the Shadow of the Law: Early Settlement in GATT/WTO Disputes' (2001) 24 *Fordham International Law Journal* 158; Howse and Teitel (n 80) 132–33.

[128] Howse and Teitel (n 80) 131.

[129] Galanter (n 6) 23.

courts and legislation in areas such as bills of exchange essentially codified well-established customary practices.[130] Another instance is the move from private standard-setting towards instruments such as the TBT Agreement of the WTO, and through that conduit to changes in national public regulation.[131]

Acknowledging and deploying the wider and deeper shadows of transnational law is especially important in the transnational context where such awareness will always be in competition with doubts about the effectiveness of enforcement of different regimes whether the de facto limits of national public law regulation, the existential critiques of public international law based on its lack of supranational enforcement, the procedural and practical hazard of private litigation, or the 'soft' character of many forms of non-state standards.

New understandings of contemporary enforcement in transnational economic law may also follow.

i. Inter-regime Interactions

For example, a single regime or a group of regimes could engage in 'self-conscious appraisal and design of the relation between competing normative orders' in the transnational space, including pursuing coexistence or coherence with other regulatory regimes.[132] Inspired by private international law, for example, one can set a model that emphasises coexistence and comity with respect to other normative orders.[133] Even where there is potential conflict, an awareness of the simultaneous existence of heterarchical orders can help shape a more tailored approach and context-specific approach to issues such as recognition and enforcement of foreign judgments. In this sense, transnational economic law may use techniques[134] from private international law such as the separation of questions of substance and process,[135] distinctions between questions of governing law and questions of jurisdiction, and *dépeçage* of applicable norms based on different aspects of what might seem a single transnational legal relation.[136]

130 Cutler (n 34) chs 4 and 5.

131 Howse and Teitel (n 80) 131–32.

132 Galanter (n 6) 28.

133 See, eg R Wai, 'Conflicts and Comity in Transnational Governance: Private International Law as Mechanism and Metaphor for Transnational Social Regulation through Plural Legal Regimes' in Joerges and Petersmann (n 5); K Knop, R Michaels and A Riles, 'From Multiculturalism to Technique: Feminism, Culture, and the Conflict of Laws Style' (2012) 64 *Stanford Law Review* 589.

134 Knop, Michaels and Riles (n 133).

135 Compare to the parallel move from substantive to procedural review in by the WTO Dispute Settlement Body with respect to national regulatory measures challenged as trade violations, see A Lang, *World Trade Law After Neoliberalism* (Oxford, Oxford University Press, 2011) 320–43.

136 Wai (n 102) 123–25.

A self-conscious awareness of multiple enforcement regimes also would assess enforcement in transnational economic law as involving potential issues of strategic regime shifting and forum shopping, for example between the trade and investment regimes.[137]

ii. Enforcement Hybrids

Viewing enforcement as involving a broader transnational shadow of the law helps explain enforcement hybrids that mix elements of different normative sources.

Such hybrids form part of new governance approaches to enforcement in domestic public regulation that are increasingly common in transnational economic law, for example with respect to labour standards[138] or human rights.[139] New governance techniques focus on deploying greater participation of non-state actors in effective regulation.[140] For example, graduated sanctions deemphasise mandatory public law enforcement, and instead see enforcement measures as including a wide spectrum of carrots and sticks.[141] The turn to new governance techniques is partly justified by weakness in public law enforcement powers, but also partly argued to result in regulation that is more efficient, effective and experimental. All of these arguments but especially the argument from regulatory gaps have generated significant interest in developing processes in the transnational realm that combine private pressure with public incentives and influences.[142] New governance looks to compliance through structured techniques such as transparency requirements and certification of monitors of private actors that influence private governance.[143] In doing so, the best of this work understands that what is involved is private governance in the shadow of the law[144] often involving varied forms of public law intervention, including 'default hybrids', such as the regulatory penalty defaults that shape the nature of private ordering that occurs in environmental regulation.[145]

[137] eg S Puig, 'International Regime Complexity and Economic Law Enforcement' (2014) 17 *Journal of International Economic Law* 491.

[138] Sabel, O'Rourke and Fung (n 28).

[139] JG Ruggie, 'Global Governance and "New Governance Theory": Lessons from Business and Human Rights' (2014) 20 *Global Governance* 5.

[140] G de Búrca and J Scott (eds), *Law and New Governance in the EU and the US* (Oxford, Hart Publishing, 2006).

[141] Most famously the pyramid of responsive regulation in I Ayres and J Braithwaite, *Responsive Regulation: Transcending the Regulation Debate* (Oxford, Oxford University Press, 1992).

[142] Ruggie (n 139) 5–6.

[143] See eg Sabel, O'Rourke and Fung (n 28).

[144] de Búrca and Scott (n 140) 9.

[145] See, eg B Karkkainen, 'Information-forcing Regulation and Environmental Governance' in de Búrca and Scott (n 140).

More generally, we see significant expansion in transnational economic law of hybrids of public and private enforcement. The international investment treaty regime is the most obvious example of 'private enforcement' of international economic law, in which the main enforcement venue has shifted to a form of non-state dispute resolution, but constituted by public international law treaties.[146] Such hybridity with respect to enforcement is also evident in the existing WTO system. As already noted, the remedies in dispute settlement at the WTO rely heavily on voluntary compliance, with the ultimate sanction being authorisation to a complaining member state to withdraw concessions, that is, a form of horizontal enforcement. Other parts of the WTO system suggest even greater complexity in enforcement. For example, with respect to dumping, the approach of the WTO is not to provide any direct international level processes of dispute settlement, but rather to permit Member States to deploy domestic trade remedy law to impose anti-dumping duties on imported dumped goods.[147] WTO-level oversight in this context is not directed towards direct control of dumping, but rather to regulate the domestic trade remedy law of states that provide for enforcement of anti-dumping duties under their domestic law.

In addition to significant substantive provisions (such as standards for duration of copyright and patent protection), the Agreement on Trade Related Aspects of Intellectual Property Rights (TRIPS) expressly attends to

> the provision of effective and appropriate means for the enforcement of trade-related intellectual property rights, taking into account differences in national legal systems.[148]

The detail with which Part III of the TRIPS Agreement attends to domestic enforcement, including civil remedies and criminal penalties, has been described as constituting 'a largely unprecedented degree of control by an international regime over domestic civil and administrative procedures'.[149] Such procedural provisions are in turn 'enforced' by the normal processes for state-to-state dispute resolution and enforcement under the Dispute Settlement Understanding.[150]

Reflexive awareness of the plural nature of enforcement and the creation of hybrid forms of enforcement demonstrate how the complex shadows of enforcement in transnational economic law may be creatively deployed going forward, both to facilitate more compliance and settlement, but also

[146] A Sykes, 'Public versus Private Enforcement of International Economic Law: Standing and Remedy' (2005) 34 *Journal of Legal Studies* 631.

[147] GATT 1994, Art VI and the Agreement on Art VI of the General Agreement on Tariffs and Trade 1994.

[148] TRIPS Agreement, Preamble.

[149] Trebilcock and Howse (n 66) 415.

[150] TRIPS Agreement, Art 64.

to bring in a wider range of policy objectives. Complexity and interaction among public law, international law, private law and private ordering of enforcement have been long present in the traditions of transnational economic law. More open and careful analysis of their distinctions and interactions is essential to understanding the possibilities of enforcement in any postnational constellation of economic law.

3

Enforcement of Foreign Judgments: Governance, Rights, and the Market for Dispute Resolution Services

CHRISTOPHER A WHYTOCK

ENFORCEMENT—ALONG WITH rulemaking and rule application—is a basic function of any system of governance.[1] The effectiveness of a governance system depends significantly on compliance with the rules it produces.[2] Compliance, in turn, depends in the first instance on ex ante background factors that influence a person's understanding of the legitimacy of a governance system and its rules and the expected costs and benefits of non-compliance.[3] Enforcement is the process of obtaining a person's compliance or punishing a person's non-compliance when ex ante background factors fail to elicit compliance.[4]

In a governance system with courts, one basic type of enforcement is the enforcement of court judgments. For example, if background factors do not lead a judgment debtor to comply with a money judgment in the first instance, enforcement measures may then be taken to compel payment to the

[1] See AM Kjaer, *Governance* (Cambridge, Polity Press, 2004) 10 (defining governance as 'the setting of rules, the application of rules, and the enforcement of rules').

[2] See K Raustiala, 'Compliance and Effectiveness in International Regulatory Cooperation' (2000) 32 *Case Western Reserve Journal of International Law* 387, 388 ('Compliance ... is typically an important aspect of the production of institutional effectiveness, but not the only aspect').

[3] See JG March and JP Olsen, 'The Institutional Dynamics of International Political Orders' (1998) 52 *International Organization* 943 (distinguishing the logic of appropriateness and the logic of consequences in decision-making); TR Tyler, *Why People Obey the Law* (Princeton, Princeton University Press, 1990) (analysing the role of legitimacy in compliance).

[4] Two clarifications are in order. First, enforcement is not necessarily a precondition for compliance. A well-designed governance system that attends to background factors will tend to elicit compliance without enforcement. Second, there can, of course, be a relationship between background factors and enforcement. eg, punishment at the enforcement stage may feed back into the background cost–benefit analysis, thus enhancing future compliance by other persons without enforcement.

judgment creditor. A standard enforcement measure is execution, whereby a court issues an order directing an enforcement agent (such as a sheriff or *huissier de justice*) to seize property of the judgment debtor, sell it, and deliver the proceeds to the judgment creditor in satisfaction of the judgment. The enforcement of court judgments is an important governance function because courts themselves perform important governance functions.[5] They offer dispute resolution services in the form of litigation, and in the process they authoritatively interpret rules and apply them to particular situations. From the perspective of political science, courts not only resolve discrete disputes, but also contribute to the authoritative allocation of resources within a society, thus answering a basic question of governance: Who gets what?[6]

When national courts decide cases involving parties of different nationalities or activities that occur or have effects in the territory of more than one nation, they engage in what I call *transnational judicial governance*.[7] In addition to determining the rights and obligations of transnational actors, they regulate extraterritorial activity and they allocate governance authority among nations, between national and international institutions, and between private and public actors. For example, in transnational regulatory litigation, national courts apply national regulatory norms to determine rights and obligations of transnational actors.[8] In transnational public law litigation, '[p]rivate individuals, government officials, and nations sue one another directly, and are sued directly, in a variety of judicial fora, most prominently, domestic courts',[9] based on rights derived from both national

[5] See M Shapiro, *Courts: A Comparative and Political Analysis* (Chicago, The University of Chicago Press, 1981); M Shapiro and AS Sweet, *On Law, Politics, And Judicialization* (Oxford, Oxford University Press, 2002); CN Tate and T Vallinder (eds), *The Global Expansion of Judicial Power* (New York, NYU Press, 1995); RA Dahl, 'Decision-Making in a Democracy: The Supreme Court as a National Policy-Maker' (1957) 6 *Journal of Public Law* 279; CA Whytock, 'Domestic Courts and Global Governance' (2009) 84 *Tulane Law Review* 67.

[6] The 'who gets what' question has long preoccupied scholars of domestic systems of governance. See, eg HD Lasswell, *Politics: Who Gets What, When, How* (New York, Whittseley House, 1936). *cf* RM Cover, 'Dispute Resolution: A Foreword' (1979) 88 *Yale Law Journal* 910, 911 (noting that courts both solve disputes and distribute resources); M Shapiro, 'From Public Law to Public Policy, or the "Public" in "Public Law"' (1972) 5 *Political Science & Politics* 410, 413 (discussing 'judicial allocation of values').

[7] For an in-depth analysis of transnational judicial governance, see Whytock (n 5) and CA Whytock, 'Transnational Judicial Governance' (2012) 2 *St John's Journal of International & Comparative Law* 55. *cf* TL Putnam, 'Courts Without Borders: Domestic Sources of US Extraterritoriality in the Regulatory Sphere' (2009) 63 *International Organization* 459 (exploring how domestic courts have come to regulate persons and conduct outside their states' borders by claiming jurisdiction over transactions with local and extraterritorial elements).

[8] See generally HL Buxbaum, 'Transnational Regulatory Litigation' (2006) 46 *Virginia Journal of International Law* 251, 253–54 (examining the rise in cases brought in US courts under the Alien Tort Claims Act, applying international law norms to secure remedies for violation of those norms that would not otherwise be available).

[9] HH Koh, 'Transnational Public Law Litigation' (1991) 100 *Yale Law Journal* 2347, 2348 (discussing how traditional domestic litigation and traditional international law litigation have merged to form a blended body of 'transnational' public law).

and international law. And in transnational private litigation, national courts resolve transnational disputes under different nations' private law rules (for example rules governing torts, contracts and property)—rules that reflect these nations' respective distributive and regulatory policies.[10]

The same multinational connections that enable transnational judicial governance can also create special enforcement challenges. If a court in one nation (N1) issues a money judgment but the judgment debtor has no assets in N1, enforcement may be impossible there. The judgment creditor may then seek enforcement in another nation (N2) where the judgment debtor does have assets. From N2's perspective, the N1 judgment is a foreign judgment. The problem is that sovereignty principles and related customary international law principles on jurisdiction generally prohibit nations from taking enforcement measures in the territory of other nations. Moreover, there is no general rule of international law requiring nations to enforce foreign judgments. Therefore, the ability to enforce the N1 judgment in N2 depends on the willingness of an N2 court to order enforcement against the judgment debtor's N2 assets, which in turn depends on N2's private international law (conflict of laws) rules.

The stakes are high both for nations, because the enforcement of foreign judgments is one factor that determines the quality of transnational judicial governance, and for individual litigants, because the enforcement of foreign judgments affects their legal rights. In this chapter, I analyse the rules of foreign judgment enforcement from both perspectives. I do so comparatively, with a focus on the private international law rules of the European Union (EU) and United States (US) applicable to foreign judgments in civil and commercial matters, in order to highlight how different approaches strike different balances between two sets of enforcement values: governance values and rights values. Part I provides an overview of governance values and rights values. Part II examines a spectrum of ideal-type and real-world approaches to foreign judgment enforcement—ranging from always enforce, to the US and EU approaches to their respective internal judgments (full faith and credit and the Brussels I Regulation), to national treatment of external judgments, to never enforce—and explains how they score on different governance values and rights values. Part III is more conjectural. It proposes lessons of this chapter's analysis for the design of private international law rules governing foreign judgments, and speculates about the causes and consequences of the evolution of the law of foreign judgments in the transatlantic area—including implications for the transnational market for dispute resolution services.

[10] See generally R Wai, 'Transnational Private Litigation and Transnational Governance' in M Lederer and PS Müller (eds), *Criticizing Global Governance* (New York, Palgrave Macmillan, 2005) 243 (analysing transnational private litigation).

I. ENFORCEMENT VALUES

Although enforcement is a basic governance function, it would be a mistake to understand enforcement in purely functional terms, because enforcement—like private international law generally—implicates important societal values. In the context of foreign judgment enforcement, enforcement values can be placed roughly into two categories: governance values and rights values.[11]

A. Governance Values

Governance values focus on policies facilitating, guiding or restraining collective activity.[12] These values have implications that extend beyond the parties to particular disputes.[13] Governance values include *efficiency*, which is concerned with avoiding the expenditure of societal resources to re-litigate issues that have already been litigated, and with reducing transaction costs in transnational business.[14] If N2 declines to enforce an N1 judgment, duplicative public resources of N2's legal system and private resources of the litigants will be expended if the claimant subsequently pursues the same claim in N2. These costs can be avoided—and efficiency thus increased—if N2 renders duplicative litigation unnecessary by enforcing the N1 judgment.

Closely related to efficiency is the principle of *repose*, which emphasises 'the need to put to rest quarrels and disputes that have arisen so that the energies of individuals and the resources of society can be devoted to more constructive tasks'.[15] One way of understanding repose is in terms of public and private opportunity costs. If N2 declines to enforce the N1 judgment

[11] For a preliminary sketch of these two types of values and their application to EU and US private international law, see CA Whytock, 'Faith and Scepticism in Private International Law: Trust, Governance, Politics, and Foreign Judgments' (2014) 7 *Erasmus Law Review* 113.

[12] See RO Keohane, *Power and Governance in a Partially Globalized World* (London, Routledge, 2002) 245–46 (defining governance as 'the processes and institutions, both formal and informal, that guide and restrain ... collective activit[y]').

[13] See Whytock (n 5) 31.

[14] See R Michaels, 'Recognition and Enforcement of Foreign Judgments' in *Max Planck Encyclopedia of Public International Law*, available at www.mpepil.com (noting that 'the general public has an interest in avoiding resources spent on re-litigation and in international decisional harmonies'); AT von Mehren and DT Trautman, 'Recognition of Foreign Adjudications: A Survey and a Suggested Approach' (1968) 81 *Harvard Law Review* 1601, 1603–04 (noting 'desire to avoid the duplication of effort and consequent waste involved in reconsidering a matter that has already been litigated'). See also J Lookofsky and K Hertz, *EU-PIL: European Union Private International Law in Contract and Tort* (New York, JurisNet, 2009) 135 (noting importance of foreign judgment enforcement to 'promote efficiency and economy in international business').

[15] AT Von Mehren, 'Recognition and Enforcement of Foreign Judgments—General Theory and the Role of Jurisdictional Requirements' (1981) 167 *Recueil des Cours* 20–22.

and the plaintiff files the same claim against the defendant in N2, then N2 will spend public resources for its courts to adjudicate the claim that it could otherwise spend on other judicial matters, and the parties will spend private resources on litigation that they could otherwise spend on more beneficial endeavours. N2's enforcement of the N1 judgment would bring the dispute to an end and avoid these public and private opportunity costs.

Another governance value is *certainty*, which helps 'establish the security of contracts, promote commercial dealings, and generally further the rule of law among states that are interdependent as well as independent'.[16] Among the uncertainties of transnational litigation is uncertainty about whether an N1 judgment will be enforced in other nations. This uncertainty can lead to financial and contractual uncertainty, because it is unclear whether a judgment that otherwise would establish the parties' financial and contractual responsibilities will ultimately be given effect. This uncertainty can be avoided, and the parties' planning for the future facilitated, if N2 enforces—and is expected to enforce—N1 judgments.

A somewhat different governance value is *comity*. Comity is the respect that one nation gives to another nation as a legally equal sovereign. Comity may 'foster ... stability and unity in an international order' by avoiding conflict among nations and by promoting reciprocity in the respect that nations give to each other.[17] N2 may owe no international legal obligation to N1 to enforce an N1 judgment, but by nevertheless enforcing it N2 furthers the value of comity, thus avoiding the offence to (and perhaps conflict with) N1 that could be caused by N2's refusal to respect the judgment, and encouraging N1 to reciprocate by enforcing N2 judgments.

B. Rights Values

Foreign judgment enforcement also implicates rights values. These values focus on justice for particular litigants in particular cases. One rights value is *correctness*, including both substantive and procedural correctness. As Arthur von Mehren puts it, the 'principle of correctness ... expresses the

[16] AF Lowenfeld, 'International Litigation and the Quest for Reasonableness: General Court on Private International Law' (1994) 245 *Recueil des Cours* 109. See also Von Mehren and Trautman (n 14) 1603–04 (noting 'interest in fostering stability and unity in an international order in which many aspects of life are not confined to any single jurisdiction ...'); Michaels (n 14) 2 (referring to 'transnational legal certainty' as a value underlying the enforcement of foreign judgments).

[17] Von Mehren and Trautman (n 14) 1603–04. See also Michaels (n 14) 2 ('Dutch authors, in particular Voet and Huber, developed [the principle of] comity, defined much later by the United States Supreme Court in [*Hilton v Guyot*] a decision denying recognition to a French judgment as "neither a matter of absolute obligation on the one hand nor of mere courtesy and good will ... it is the recognition which one nation allows within its territory to the legislative, executive or judicial acts of another ..."').

concern that legal justice, as understood by the society in both substantive and procedural terms, be done'.[18] Simply put, there is value in reaching an outcome that is just and legally correct—both substantively and procedurally. N2's enforcement of an incorrect N1 judgment would be at odds with the value of correctness. For this reason, the judgment debtor may want the N2 court to subject the N1 judgment to some degree of procedural or substantive scrutiny before it is enforced, or it may wish to have the N2 court review the judgment in its entirety (*révision au fond*) to ensure a correct outcome.

Closely related to the value of correctness are *property rights*. At least in the case of money judgments, the standard enforcement measure is execution, a process whereby the judgment debtor's property is seized and sold to satisfy the judgment. If the judgment is not legally correct, then the taking of the judgment debtor's property to satisfy the judgment would not be legally justified, leading to a violation of the judgment debtor's property rights. For this reason, the judgment debtor may want the N2 court to scrutinise the N1 judgment to serve not only the intrinsically important value of correctness, but also the value of protecting the judgment debtor's property rights.

Another rights value implicated by foreign judgment enforcement is *access to justice*. Access to justice requires not only court access, but also a remedy when a person is legally entitled to one.[19] A plaintiff may be able to obtain court access in N1 to pursue a claim against a defendant. But if the N1 court issues a judgment in the plaintiff's favour, the defendant refuses to satisfy the judgment and only has assets in N2, and N2 refuses to enforce the judgment, then the plaintiff may lack a remedy altogether and thus be denied meaningful access to justice. Moreover, in some cases a plaintiff—for either legal or practical reasons—may lack access to an N2 court where the prospective judgment debtor has assets. If N2 both fails to provide court access and refuses to enforce an N1 judgment, the result may be a transnational access-to-justice gap.[20] When N2 enforces an N1 judgment, N2 helps complete the plaintiff's access to justice rights by providing a legal remedy.[21]

Governance values and rights values are not mutually exclusive. Protecting rights in particular cases can advance broader governance values, and governance values like efficiency and certainty can benefit individual

[18] Von Mehren (n 15) 20–22.

[19] CA Whytock, 'Foreign State Immunity and the Right to Court Access' (2013) 93 *Boston University Law Review* 2033; CA Whytock and CB Robertson, 'Forum Non Conveniens and the Enforcement of Foreign Judgments' (2011) 111 *Columbia Law Review* 1444, 1472.

[20] Whytock and Robertson (n 19) 1472.

[21] See XE Kramer, 'Cross-Border Enforcement and the Brussels I-Bis Reg: Towards a New Balance Between Mutual Trust and National Control Over Fundamental Rights' (2013) 60 *Netherlands International Law Review* 343, 367 ('The abolition of exequatur has ... been justified by the desire to enhance access to justice and the right to an effective remedy, as guaranteed by Art 47 of the EU Charter and Arts 6 and 13 of the ECHR. ... From the perspective of the judgment creditor, the interests are evidently to enforce his rights as a result of a judgment in an efficient way'.).

litigants. On the other hand, no approach to foreign judgment enforcement can simultaneously maximise all of these values.[22] Value trade-offs are therefore inevitable, and different approaches to foreign judgment enforcement will entail different trade-offs.

II. A SPECTRUM OF APPROACHES TO FOREIGN JUDGMENT ENFORCEMENT

In the absence of a global treaty on foreign judgment enforcement, there are diverse private international law approaches to foreign judgments. One way to arrange these approaches is along a spectrum indicating the extent to which they tend to favour enforcement, from a categorical always-enforce approach, to the usually-enforce approach that the US and the EU take to their respective internal judgments, to the sometimes-enforce approach that nations tend to take to external judgments, to a categorical never-enforce approach. These approaches strike different trade-offs among various governance values and rights values.

A. Always Enforce

One approach to foreign judgments is *always enforce*. This approach scores high on governance values. By enforcing the N1 judgment, N2 makes duplicative litigation unnecessary, brings the parties' dispute to a close, and gives respect to N1's legal system, thus furthering the values of efficiency, repose, certainty and comity. The always-enforce approach has mixed scores on rights values. On the one hand, it promotes access to justice by ensuring that a plaintiff can obtain a remedy based on a foreign judgment. On the other hand, it does so without regard to correctness and property rights, and therefore scores low on those values.

B. Usually Enforce: Full Faith and Credit and Internal US Judgments

A more nuanced approach is to *usually enforce* foreign judgments. An example is the US full-faith-and-credit approach. The full-faith-and-

[22] See Von Mehren (n 15) 22 ('Embracing one [principle] to the complete exclusion of the other would be intolerable. Assigning an absolute value to correctness would create an enormous social and economic burden, unduly reward the disputatious, and undermine the security of transactions and relations that is essential if economic and social life are to go forward. On the other hand, giving full scope to the principle of repose would require that full and absolute finality be given to every determination made by an adjudicator of first instance. But … a system of justice that, in the name of repose, denied in every case a second chance would be perceived as fundamentally unjust. … [A] tension persists between the two principles and no solution can ever be entirely stable nor demonstrably correct'.).

credit clause—contained in Article IV, Section 1 of the US Constitution—provides that

> [f]ull faith and credit shall be given in each state to the public acts, records, and judicial proceedings of every other state.

A federal statute—28 USC § 1738—implements the full-faith-and-credit clause by requiring that all courts in the United States, including both state and federal courts, give full faith and credit to the judicial proceedings of US states.[23]

Full faith and credit is sometimes called an 'iron law' because it can require one state (S2) to enforce another state's (S1) judgment even if the judgment is based on a mistake of fact or law.[24] If the judgment debtor wishes to challenge the S1 judgment on the merits, it must do so in S1's courts—for example, by appealing to an S1 appellate court—but it cannot do so in S2.[25] There are narrow exceptions to the general rule. Full faith and credit does not require S2 to enforce an S1 judgment if the S1 judgment was obtained by fraud or if the S1 court did not have jurisdiction. However, if the S1 court heard the issue of fraud or jurisdiction and decided against the judgment debtor, the S2 court must give full faith and credit to that decision.[26]

The US Supreme Court has stated that there is no 'roving public policy exception' to full faith and credit.[27] According to the Court, '[t]he full faith and credit clause is one of the provisions incorporated into the Constitution by its framers for the purpose of transforming an aggregation of independent, sovereign States into a nation ... [W]e are aware of [no] considerations of local policy or law which could rightly be deemed to impair the force and effect which the full faith and credit clause ... require[s] to be given to [a money] judgment outside the state of its rendition'.[28] But 'the issue will not stay buried; like the mythical Phoenix, the notion that there is a "public policy" exception to the Iron Law of Full Faith and Credit keeps trying to rise from the ashes'.[29] As one expert opines, however, 'the Supreme Court

[23] See 28 USC 1738 ('The ... judicial proceedings of any court of any ... State, Territory or Possession ... shall have the same full faith and credit in every court within the United States and its Territories and Possessions as they have by law or usage in the courts of such State, Territory or Possession from which they are taken'.).

[24] WM Richman, WL Reynolds and CA Whytock, *Understanding Conflict of Laws* 4th edn (New Providence, LexisNexis, 2013) 388.

[25] ibid.

[26] ibid, 393–94.

[27] *Baker v General Motors* 522 US 222, 233–34 (1998). See, eg, Restatement (Second) of Conflict of Laws § 103 ('A judgment rendered in one State of the United States need not be recognized or enforced in a sister State if such recognition or enforcement is not required by the national policy of full faith and credit because it would involve an improper interference with important interests of the sister State'.); *Reading & Bates v Baker Energy Resources* 976 SW 2d 702 (Tex App 1998); *Blackwell v Haslam*, 2013 WL 3379364 (Tenn App 2013).

[28] *Baker v General Motors* (n 27) 233–34 (citations omitted).

[29] WL Reynolds and WM Richman, *The Full Faith and Credit Clause* (Westport, Praeger, 2005) 102.

has not endorsed [a public policy exception] and its precedents seem to negate it'.[30]

The US full-faith-and-credit approach is not far from the always-enforce ideal type, and thus scores high on governance values, as well as on the rights value of access to justice (albeit not as high as the always-enforce approach). By allowing for the possibility of non-enforcement in S2 on the ground of fraud or lack of S1 jurisdiction, the US full-faith-and-credit approach falls short of maximising the governance values of efficiency, repose and certainty. Because full faith and credit applies to the S1 court's decisions on its own jurisdiction and on claims of fraud, however, the value of comity nevertheless should ordinarily be protected. To a slightly greater extent than the always-enforce approach, the US full-faith-and-credit approach furthers the rights values of correctness and property rights by providing some protection against enforcement when the S1 judgment was a result of fraud or the S1 court lacked jurisdiction. Any trade-off against access to justice due to the fraud exception would seem to be an equitable one in cases where it is the judgment creditor who committed the fraud.

C. Usually Enforce: The Brussels I Regulation and Internal EU Judgments

The private international law rules governing the enforcement of a judgment of a court of one EU member (M1) in another EU member (M2) are contained in the recently recast Brussels I Regulation.[31] These rules lie farther from the always-enforce end of the spectrum than the rules of US full faith and credit, but, as explained below, they are getting closer. Under the Brussels I Regulation, there is a general rule requiring enforcement of an M1 judgment in M2, unless one of the grounds for refusing enforcement listed in Article 45(1) is found to exist:[32]

> On the application of any interested party, the recognition of a judgment shall be refused:
>
> (a) if such recognition is manifestly contrary to public policy (*ordre public*) in the Member State addressed;
> (b) where the judgment was given in default of appearance, if the defendant was not served with the document which instituted the proceedings or with an equivalent document in sufficient time and in such a way as to enable him to

[30] SC Symeonides, 'Choice of Law in the American Courts in 2013: Twenty-Seventh Annual Survey' (2014) 62 *American Journal of Comparative Law* 223, 319.

[31] Reg No 1215/2012 of 12 December 2012 on jurisdiction and the recognition and enforcement of judgments in civil and commercial matters (recast) [2012] OJ L351/1 (hereinafter Brussels I Reg).

[32] See Brussels I Reg, Art 46 ('On the application of the person against whom enforcement is sought, the enforcement of a judgment shall be refused where one of the grounds referred to in Article 45 is found to exist'.).

arrange for his defence, unless the defendant failed to commence proceedings to challenge the judgment when it was possible for him to do so;
(c) if the judgment is irreconcilable with a judgment given between the same parties in the Member State addressed;
(d) if the judgment is irreconcilable with an earlier judgment given in another Member State or in a third State involving the same cause of action and between the same parties, provided that the earlier judgment fulfils the conditions necessary for its recognition in the Member State addressed; or
(e) if the judgment conflicts with: (i) [the special jurisdictional provisions of] Sections 3, 4 or 5 of Chapter II where the policyholder, the insured, a beneficiary of the insurance contract, the injured party, the consumer or the employee was the defendant;[33] or (ii) [the exclusive jurisdiction provisions of] Section 6 of Chapter II.[34]

Overall, the Brussels I Regulation—like the US full-faith-and-credit approach—scores high on the governance values of efficiency, repose, certainty and comity. In one respect, the Brussels I Regulation may score even higher on these values because lack of personal jurisdiction is not a ground for refusing enforcement (except pursuant to Article 45(1)(e), where the judgment conflicts with the Brussels I Regulation's special jurisdictional provisions designed to protect weak parties—but even then, Article 45(2) provides that M2 shall be bound by the findings of fact on which M1 based its jurisdiction).[35] However, this difference should not be overstated because, as noted above, under the US law of full faith and credit, S2 must give full faith and credit to an S1 court's jurisdictional rulings. The most salient difference in terms of governance values is the Brussels I Regulation's public policy exception, which entails a trade-off against the values of efficiency, repose, certainty and comity. However, because the public policy ground is very narrow, this difference, too, should not be overstated.[36]

[33] These provisions are intended to protect parties assumed to be relatively weak. See M Bogdan, *Concise Introduction to EU Private International Law* 2nd edn (Groningen, Europa Law Publishing, 2012) 53 (noting that the equivalent special jurisdictional provisions in the Brussels I Reg are intended 'to protect the weaker party (the person claiming insurance benefits, the consumer, the employee) against being sued in other Member States than his own, while at the same time giving the same weaker party the option to sue in his own country even when the defendant is domiciled in another Member State').

[34] For example, 'in proceedings which have as their object rights *in rem* in immovable property ... the courts of the Member State in which the property is situated' has exclusive jurisdiction. Brussels I Reg, Art 24(1).

[35] See P Hay, 'The Development of the Public Policy Barrier to Judgment Recognition Within the European Community' (2007) 6 *The European Legal Forum* 289, 290 (noting that the Brussels I Reg's recognition command is in this respect *stronger* than US full faith and credit 'because it is combined with jurisdictional bases that must be observed by rendering courts').

[36] See P Stone, *EU Private International Law* 2nd edn (Cheltenham, Edward Elgar Publishing, 2010) 239 (noting that the ECJ has 'consistently emphasised' that the public policy exception 'should operate only in exceptional cases').

Similar to US full faith and credit, the same features that make the Brussels I Regulation score high on governance values make it score lower on the rights values of correctness and property rights, and relatively high on access to justice.[37] The absence of a fraud ground and a general jurisdictional ground for refusal of enforcement might suggest an even lower score on correctness and property rights (and a higher score on access to justice) than US full faith and credit. The public policy exception, however, may allow non-enforcement in a limited number of exceptional instances of fraud, particularly if the fraud is found to have precluded a fair trial,[38] and in addition to the limited special jurisdictional grounds for refusal noted above, there are protections for the right to adequate notice in Article 45(1)(b) applicable to default judgments. More broadly, the public policy exception can be understood as providing a 'safety net' that furthers the values of correctness and property rights by allowing M2 to refuse enforcement of an M1 judgment where M1 failed to provide procedural rights—including those fair trial rights assured by Article 6(1) of the European Convention on Human Rights[39]—which would go beyond the grounds for refusal expressly available under the US law of full faith and credit. These doctrinal nuances defy measurement. Comparative empirical analysis of actual court decisions in US full-faith-and-credit and EU Brussels I Regulation enforcement cases would ultimately be necessary to evaluate which approach scores higher on various governance values and rights values.

There is, however, a trend in the EU's internal approach to foreign judgments in a direction that reflects a further emphasis on the governance values of efficiency, repose, certainty and comity and the rights value of access

[37] Perhaps the EU emphasis on these governance values at the expense of the rights value of correctness was most clearly expressed in the ECJ's judgment in *Turner*, a jurisdiction case, in which it ruled that a court of one EU member (in this case the United Kingdom) is prohibited from issuing an antisuit injunction barring a party from pursuing proceedings in the same case in a court of another EU member (in this case Spain) 'even where that party is acting in bad faith with a view to frustrating the existing proceedings': Case 159/02 *Turner* [2004] ECR I-3565, para 31. One US commentator argues that the ECJ's approach in *Turner* 'elevates a quest for efficiency over a quest for equity'. R Brand, 'Hague Academy of International Law' (2011) 358 *Recueil des Cours* 9, 177. See also Case C-116/02 *Gasser* [2003] ECR I-14693, para 54 (requiring Austria to dismiss a case under the first-court-seized rule where suit was first filed in Italy, despite the parties' exclusive choice-of-court agreement selecting an Austrian court). Art 31 of the recast Brussels I Reg changes the rule announced in *Gasser* by prioritising courts with exclusive jurisdiction under a choice-of-court agreement.

[38] CMV Clarkson and J Hill, *The Conflict of Laws* 4th edn (Oxford, Oxford University Press, 2011) 197. For an analysis of EU Member Court decisions on the applicability of the Brussels I Reg's public policy exception in cases where fraud is alleged, see Burkhard Hess, Thomas Pfeiffer and Peter Schlosser, *Report on the Application of Reg Brussels I in the Member States* (Sep 2007, Study JLS/C4/2005/03), available at ec.europa.eu/civiljustice/news/docs/study_application_brussels_1_en.pdf.

[39] XE Kramer, 'Cross-border Enforcement in the EU: Mutual Trust versus Fair Trial? Towards Principles of European Civil Procedure' (2011) 2 *International Journal of Procedural Law* 202, 219 ('A safety net for the violation of fair trial principles is provided [by the Brussels I Reg] at the enforcement level through the ground of refusal relating to public policy'.).

to justice: EU law has made it progressively easier to enforce EU Member judgments in other EU Members. Most notably, one of the highlights of the recast Brussels I Regulation is the elimination of *exequatur*—that is, a declaration of enforceability by M2—as a prerequisite for enforcement of an M1 judgment in M2. In certain specialised areas of EU law, *exequatur* had already been abolished.[40] But implementing this change for judgments in civil and commercial matters more generally is an important step toward facilitating the enforcement of foreign judgments within the EU—albeit arguably at the expense of the values of correctness and property rights. As Peter Stone argues, '[t]he effect of the change—will usually be to reduce from an already low level the protection which a defendant can obtain from the courts of his own country'.[41] Similarly, Andrew Dickinson argues that *exequatur* provides significant protection against fraudulent enforcement proceedings.[42] Moreover, according to a recent study, the jurisprudence of the European Court of Human Rights 'clearly recognizes the value of exequatur or similar proceedings for the protection of human rights of the judgment debtor'.[43] But others note that exequatur rarely resulted in non-enforcement anyway, and argue that in any event the ability of a judgment debtor to apply for refusal of enforcement and appeal a decision to deny that application renders the elimination of exequatur inconsequential from a rights perspective.[44] For example, Peter Hay argues that 'abolition of the exequatur streamlines the recognition process, but ... does not change it much substantively'.[45] Similarly, Samuel Baumgartner argues that 'the abolition of the declaration of enforceability sounds like a bolder move than it really is'.[46]

[40] See European Commission, 'Impact assessment accompanying the proposal for a regulation of the European Parliament and of the Council on jurisdiction and the recognition and enforcement of judgments in civil and commercial matters (recast)' SEC(2010) 1547 final, 15 (hereinafter Impact Assessment) (noting abolition of *exequatur* in Reg 805/2004 of 21 April 2004 establishing a European enforcement order for uncontested claims [2004] OJ L143/15, Reg 1896/2006 of 12 December 2006 creating a European Order for Payment Procedure [2006] OJ L399/1, Reg 861/2007 of 11 July 2007 creating a European Small Claims Procedure [2007] OJ L199/1, and Reg 4/2009 of 18 December 2008 on jurisdiction, applicable law, recognition and enforcement of decisions and cooperation in matters relating to maintenance obligations [2009] OJ L7/1).

[41] Stone (n 36) 265.

[42] A Dickinson, 'Surveying the Proposed Brussels I bis Reg—Solid Foundations but Renovation Needed' (2010) 12 *Yearbook of Private International Law* 247, 267.

[43] T Schilling, 'The Enforcement of Foreign Judgments in the Jurisprudence of the European Court of Human Rights' (January 2012) 4, available at works.bepress.com/theodor_schilling/9.

[44] See B Hess, *Note on the Proposal for a Regulation of the European Parliament and of the Council on Jurisdiction and the Recognition and Enforcement of Judgments in Civil and Commercial Matters (Recast)* (Brussels, European Parliament, 2011), available at www.europarl.europa.eu/RegData/etudes/note/join/2011/453201/IPOL-JURI_NT(2011)453201_EN.pdf.

[45] P Hay, 'Notes on the European Union's Brussels-I "Recast" Regulation: An American Perspective, European Legal Forum' (2013) *The European Legal Forum* 1, 6.

[46] SP Baumgartner, 'Changes in the European Union's Regime of Recognizing and Enforcing Foreign Judgments and Transnational Litigation in the United States' (2012) 18 *Southwestern Journal of International Law* 567.

But whether or not this move significantly undermines the rights values of correctness and property rights, it indicates a stronger EU emphasis than before on the governance values of efficiency, repose, certainty and comity. In fact, these governance values are expressed in the Brussels I Regulation itself. As its preamble notes, it is essential to eliminate '[c]ertain differences between national rules governing jurisdiction and recognition of judgments [that] hamper the sound operation of the internal market' and to put in place rules 'to ensure rapid and simple recognition and enforcement of judgments',[47] in furtherance of 'the objective of free circulation of judgments in civil and commercial matters'.[48] Regarding *exequatur* specifically, the preamble explains that 'the aim of making cross-border litigation less time-consuming and costly justifies the abolition of the declaration of enforceability prior to enforcement in the Member State addressed'.[49]

D. Sometimes Enforce: The US Approach to External Judgments

US full-faith-and-credit applies only to judgments from within the US and the Brussels I Regulation applies only to judgments from within the EU. In that sense, they both deal with 'internal' judgments. Private international law regarding 'external' judgments is generally farther from the always-enforce end of the spectrum than private international law regarding internal judgments. Some nations only enforce an external N1 foreign judgment if a treaty with N1 requires them to do so, and some only enforce based on reciprocity—that is, if N1 would enforce an N2 judgment under the same circumstances.[50] In other nations, including the United States, private international law takes a more nuanced *sometimes enforce* approach to external foreign judgments by combining a general rule in favour of enforcement with a list of grounds for refusal.[51]

In the US, state law (not federal law) generally provides the rules governing the enforcement of external foreign judgments. For many years, the most common approach among US states was legislation based on the Uniform Foreign Money-Judgments Recognition Act, which was approved by the National Conference of Commissioners on Uniform State Laws (Uniform Law Commission) in 1962 (1962 Act). The 1962 Act has three mandatory and six discretionary grounds for refusal:

(a) A foreign judgment is not conclusive if
    (1) the judgment was rendered under a system which does not provide impartial tribunals or procedures compatible with the requirements of due process of law;

47 Preamble 4 of Brussels I Reg.
48 ibid, preamble 6.
49 Above n 47, recital 26.
50 Lookofsky and Hertz (n 14) 137–40.
51 R Brand, 'Hague Academy of International Law' (2011) 358 *Recueil des Cours* 9, 103.

(2) the foreign court did not have personal jurisdiction over the defendant; or
(3) the foreign court did not have jurisdiction over the subject matter.

(b) A foreign judgment need not be recognized if
(1) the defendant in the proceedings in the foreign court did not receive notice of the proceedings in sufficient time to enable him to defend;
(2) the judgment was obtained by fraud;
(3) the ... [claim for relief] on which the judgment is based is repugnant to the public policy of this state;
(4) the judgment conflicts with another final and conclusive judgment;
(5) the proceeding in the foreign court was contrary to an agreement between the parties under which the dispute in question was to be settled otherwise than by proceedings in that court; or
(6) in the case of jurisdiction based only on personal service, the foreign court was a seriously inconvenient forum for the trial of the action.[52]

By including a wide range of grounds for refusing enforcement, the 1962 Act scores lower on the governance values of efficiency, repose, certainty and comity and on the rights value of access to justice than either the US full-faith-and-credit or the EU Brussels I Regulation approaches to internal judgments. In terms of the values of correctness and property, the 1962 Act scores relatively high by requiring or allowing an N2 court in the US to refuse enforcement when it finds one of the enumerated procedural defects or fraud.

In 2005, however, the Uniform Law Commission adopted a new uniform act to replace the 1962 Act: the Uniform Foreign-Country Money Judgments Recognition Act of 2005 (2005 Act). The 2005 Act adds two discretionary grounds for refusal not contained in the 1962 Act, providing that a court need not recognise a foreign-country judgment if:

(7) the judgment was rendered in circumstances that raise substantial doubt about the integrity of the rendering court with respect to the judgment; or
(8) the specific proceeding in the foreign court leading to the judgment was not compatible with the requirements of due process of law.[53]

This change invites US judges to more closely scrutinise the specific foreign proceedings leading to a judgment. Traditionally, the failure of due

[52] See ss 3 and 4 of Uniform Foreign Money-Judgments Recognition Act of 1962 (1962). See ss 481 and 482 of the Restatement (Third) of Foreign Relations Law of the United States attempts to restate the common law of foreign judgment enforcement, and it is for the most part consistent with the 1962 Act.

[53] See s 4(c) of 2005 Act. Moreover, in 2005, the American Law Institute adopted a proposed federal statute on the recognition and enforcement of foreign judgments that included a mandatory version of the 2005 Act's judicial integrity exception. See American Law Institute, 'Recognition and Enforcement of Foreign Judgments: Analysis and Proposed Federal Statute' s 5(a)(ii) (2006) (barring recognition or enforcement if 'the judgment was rendered in circumstances that raise substantial and justifiable doubt about the integrity of the rendering court with respect to the judgment in question') (hereinafter ALI Proposed Statute).

process in a particular case has not been sufficient to refuse enforcement.[54] Nevertheless, a growing number of US States are enacting legislation based on the 2005 Act, and today there are already more 2005 Act States than 1962 Act States.[55] Thus, the 2005 Act and its new case-specific grounds for refusal are rapidly becoming the norm in US law.

The shift toward new case-specific grounds for non-enforcement is a shift towards a greater emphasis on the rights values of correctness and property. On the other hand, this trend cuts against the governance values of efficiency, repose, certainty and comity. Commentators in the US are not unaware of these costs. For example, the American Law Institute rejected a case-specific due process exception in its proposed federal statute on foreign judgments, explaining that '[s]uch a detailed inquiry into the foreign judgment is inconsistent with the pro-enforcement philosophy of [the 1962] Act'.[56] Similarly, the US Court of Appeals for the Seventh Circuit has expressed the concern that a case-specific approach would be 'inconsistent with providing a streamlined, expeditious method for collecting money judgments rendered by courts in other jurisdictions' and 'would in effect [allow] a further appeal on the merits ... thus converting every successful multinational suit for damages into two suits ...'.[57] Concerns from an access to justice perspective have also been raised.[58] But these concerns ultimately have not carried the day, as suggested by the increasingly widespread adoption of the 2005 Act by US States.

[54] See s 4 of 1962 Act (providing systemic but not case-specific due process exception). However, based on a review of US court decisions, one scholar has concluded that even when courts apply the systemic due process standard, they in fact tend to consider case-specific factors. See PB Stephan, 'Unjust Legal Systems and the Enforcement of Foreign Judgments' in PB Stephan (ed), *Foreign Court Judgments and the United States Legal System* (Leiden, Brill, 2014).

[55] The US Virgin Islands and 15 states have legislation based on the 1962 Act: Alaska, Connecticut, Florida, Georgia, Maine, Maryland, Massachusetts, Missouri, New Jersey, New York, North Dakota, Ohio, Pennsylvania, Texas and Virginia. However, two of these states—Massachusetts and Virginia—have introduced pending legislation based on the 2005 Act. See www.uniformlaws.org/LegislativeFactSheet.aspx?title=Foreign%20Money%20Judgments%20Recognition%20Act (last visited 4 March 2014). The District of Columbia and 18 states have adopted legislation based on the 2005 Act: Alabama, California, Colorado, Delaware, Hawaii, Idaho, Illinois, Indiana, Iowa, Michigan, Minnesota, Montana, Nevada, New Mexico, North Carolina, Oklahoma, Oregon, Washington. In addition, legislation based on the 2005 Act has been introduced in Massachusetts, Mississippi and Virginia. See www.uniformlaws.org/LegislativeFactSheet.aspx?title=Foreign-Country%20Money%20Judgments%20Recognition%20Act (last visited 4 March 2014).

[56] See s 5, comment c, of ALI Proposed Statute.

[57] *Society of Lloyd's v Ashenden*, 233 F 3d 473, 477 (7th Cir 2000).

[58] CA Whytock, 'Some Cautionary Notes on the "Chevronization" of Transnational Litigation' (2013) 1 *Stanford Journal of Complex Litigation* 467, 479; Whytock and Robertson (n 19).

E. Never Enforce

Finally, as a point of comparison, it is helpful to consider a categorical *never enforce* approach. By preventing enforcement of an N1 judgment in N2, this approach scores low on the governance values of efficiency, repose, certainty and comity. It has mixed scores on rights values, however. It is agnostic as to the value of correctness in the sense that it refuses enforcement without any inquiry into the judgment's actual substantive or procedural correctness. It scores high on the value of property rights because it categorically protects the judgment debtor's N2 property from being used to satisfy the N1 judgment (albeit in an unprincipled way that is not linked to correctness). And it scores low on the value of access to justice by preventing a successful plaintiff from obtaining a remedy in N2 based on the N1 judgment, even in situations where the judgment debtor's only assets are in N2.

III. BROADER IMPLICATIONS: DESIGN, CAUSES AND CONSEQUENCES

The analysis presented above has implications for the design of private international law rules on foreign judgment enforcement. It also raises questions about the factors that influence how these rules evolve and about the impact of various approaches to foreign judgment enforcement on the market for dispute resolution services.

A. Fundamental Design Principles

As demonstrated above, different approaches to foreign judgment enforcement reflect different trade-offs between different enforcement values. These trade-offs are inevitable because governance values and rights values cannot be simultaneously maximised. For example, as this chapter's analysis shows, scores on the values of efficiency, repose, certainty, comity and access to justice tend to be inversely correlated with scores on the values of correctness and property rights. This means that in any effort to design or reform private international law rules, a single-minded focus on a particular subset of these values is likely to result in rules that have unintended negative consequences for other values. This suggests two fundamental principles of design for rules governing foreign judgments:

— First, the implications of the rules for all governance and rights values should be thoroughly analysed before settling on a given approach.
— Second, the inevitable trade-offs among these values should be made explicitly and transparently by lawmakers.

B. Explaining the Evolution of Foreign Judgment Enforcement

Stepping back from design principles, what factors might explain—as a matter of positive theory—how the law of foreign judgments evolves from the never-enforce end of the spectrum toward the always-enforce end of the spectrum (or vice versa)?

— First, the evolution of private international law rules governing foreign judgments is likely to be strongly influenced by cross-national patterns of procedural and substantive legal convergence. Specifically, other things being equal, as cross-national procedural and substantive convergence increases, procedural and substantive grounds for refusal are likely to decrease. This is because procedural grounds for non-enforcement are less necessary if the nations involved have similar procedural rules, and substantive grounds for non-enforcement—such as public policy—are less important if those nations have similar substantive law and policy.

It would seem that there is more procedural and substantive convergence among US States than among EU members, and more convergence in each of these cases than among nations globally. Therefore, it is not surprising that the US internal full-faith-and-credit approach is closest to the always-enforce approach, with the EU's internal Brussels I Regulation approach slightly farther away from it, and the US approach to external foreign judgments still farther away. This may also help explain the rejection of the European Commission's proposal to eliminate the public policy exception in the recast Brussels I Regulation.[59]

— Second, the evolution of private international law rules governing foreign judgments is likely to be strongly influenced by levels of mutual trust among nations. Specifically, other things being equal, as mutual trust increases, grounds for refusal are likely to decrease.

In the EU, the concept of mutual trust has played an animating role in private international law since at least the early 1990s. In *Sonntag v Waidmann*,

[59] European Commission, 'Proposal for a Regulation of the European Parliament and of the Council on Jurisdiction and the recognition and enforcement of judgments in civil and commercial matters (recast)' COM(2010) 748 final, (hereinafter Brussels I Recast Proposal). The proposal did add, however, a limited right for a judgment debtor to 'apply for a refusal of recognition or enforcement of a judgment where such recognition or enforcement would not be permitted by the fundamental principles underlying the right to a fair trial' (Art 46) and it preserved the public policy ground for certain specified defamation and collective redress claims (Art 37). See Kramer (n 21) 365 (noting that the proposed removal of the public policy exception was 'extensively debated' and arguing that '[t]he protection of public policy is to be regarded as a matter of the rule of law and has always been regarded as a necessary safety valve in private international law').

a 1993 case before the European Court of Justice, Advocate General Darmon stated in his opinion that

> [t]he principle of the recognition of judgments is based on the Member States' mutual trust in their respective legal systems and judicial institutions. This trust allows the Member States to waive their internal rules on the recognition and enforcement of foreign judgments.[60]

The recast Brussels I Regulation explicitly links the abolition of exequatur to mutual trust:

> Mutual trust in the administration of justice in the Union justifies the principle that judgments given in a Member State should be recognised in all Member States without the need for any special procedure. ... As a result, a judgment given by the courts of a Member State should be treated as if it had been given in the Member State addressed.[61]

Conversely, where there is less mutual trust, more grounds for refusal are likely. In the US, both of the new case-specific exceptions added by the 2005 Act were justified in terms of a lack of 'mutual trust' even though the exact words are not used. As the Study Report for the 2005 Act pointed out regarding its new case-specific due process exception, '[t]here is less expectation that foreign courts will follow procedures comporting with U.S. notions of due process and jurisdiction or that they will apply substantively tolerable laws, and there may be suspicions of unfairness or fraud'.[62] The Reporter's Notes to a draft of the 2005 Act also noted support for the 2005 Act's case-specific judicial integrity exception based on the perception that 'bribery and other forms of judicial misconduct can be a real issue with regard to certain foreign country judgments'.[63] The federal statute

[60] Opinion of Advocate General Darmon in Case C-172/91 *Sonntag v Waidmann* [1993] ECR I-1963, paras 71–72.

[61] Recital 26 of Brussels I Recast. X Kramer, 'Procedure Matters: Construction and Deconstructivism in European Civil Procedure' (2012) 33 *Erasmus Law Lectures* 18 ('Based on this pillar [mutual trust], the European Commission wishes to abolish the permission of courts for the enforcement of judgments rendered in another EU Member State. The idea is that if there is full mutual trust, this permission (called *exequatur*) is no longer required').

[62] K Patchel, Study Report on Possible Amendment of the Uniform Foreign Money-Judgments Recognition Act, 25 June 2003, 26, available at www.uniformlaws.org/shared/docs/foreign%20country%20money%20judgments%20recognition/ufmjra_apr04_studyrpt.pdf.

[63] Discussion Draft of 2005 Act, October 2004, 7. The American Law Institute's commentary on the corruption ground for non-enforcement in its proposed federal statute on foreign judgments also expresses distrust, noting 'concerns about corruption in the judiciaries of certain countries'. The drafters acknowledge that '[t]he defense of possible corruption in the rendering court is one that has not traditionally been an explicit ground for nonrecognition or nonenforcement by courts in the United States'. But they explain that 'concerns about corruption in the judiciaries of certain countries and the effect of corruption in the particular case led to inclusion of this additional defense'.

on the recognition and enforcement of foreign judgments proposed by the American Law Institute in 2005 justified its mandatory judicial integrity exception in similar terms:

> The defense of possible corruption in the rendering court is one that has not traditionally been an explicit ground for nonrecognition or nonenforcement by courts in the United States. However, concerns about corruption in the judiciaries of certain countries and the effect of corruption in the particular case led to inclusion of this additional defense.[64]

It is noteworthy that the European Commission has also used lack of mutual trust as a reason for not extending the Brussels I regime to non-EU members, raising concerns that 'companies might not always get a fair trial and an adequate protection of their rights before the courts of a third State' and that '[s]uch problems can notably arise in countries where the judiciary cannot be considered to be independent or is riven by corruption'.[65] Similarly, in his opinion in *Owusu v NB Jackson*, Advocate General Léger explained that the EU established the simplified Brussels Convention mechanism for recognition and enforcement

> in a specific context characterised by mutual trust between the Member States of the Community regarding their legal systems and their judicial institutions. However, the same situation does not necessarily prevail in relations between Member States and non-Contracting States. That is why this mechanism of the Convention applies only to judgments given by courts of a Member State in the context of their recognition and enforcement in another Member State.[66]

These two conjectures imply that further substantive and procedural convergence between EU members on the one hand and US states on the other hand, accompanied by measures to build an area of transatlantic mutual trust in the administration of justice, could improve prospects for the ratification and implementation of the Hague Convention on Choice of Court Agreements and, perhaps eventually, on a more generally applicable framework for the transatlantic enforcement of foreign judgments.

C. Enforcement of Judgments and the Market for Dispute Resolution Services

Yet another consideration is the effect of different approaches to foreign judgment enforcement on the market for dispute resolution in civil and commercial matters. This market has two dimensions: an international

[64] ALI Proposed Statute (n 53) 60 (comment d on s 5).

[65] Impact Assessment (n 40) 20.

[66] Opinion of Advocate General Léger in Case C-281/02 *Owusu v NB Jackson and others* [2005] ECR I-1383, para 144.

dimension, which involves competition among nations, and a public–private dimension, which involves competition between national courts and arbitration. The law of foreign judgments affects both dimensions of competition.

— First, other things being equal, rules favouring enforcement of judgments among a group of nations is likely to increase competition among the courts of those nations.

Absent such rules, a plaintiff will have a strong incentive to sue in the courts of a nation (N1) where the defendant has assets, even if the courts of another nation (N2) are more efficient or otherwise more appropriate. This is because if the plaintiff sues in N2 and obtains a favourable judgment there, it may not be possible to enforce that judgment in N1. In contrast, with rules favouring the enforcement of N2 judgments in N1 (and vice versa), the plaintiff's choice of court will not depend so heavily on concerns about enforcement, and competition between N1 and N2 courts will instead be based primarily on their other respective advantages and disadvantages as providers of dispute resolution services.

Of course other considerations (especially jurisdictional rules) can also affect this competition. But holding those considerations constant, the implication is that competition among national courts would be greater among US states and among EU members where rules favour enforcement of internal judgments than between courts in the US and courts in the EU. A party may prefer an EU member's courts, but sue in the US because that is where the defendant's assets lie (or vice versa). This distorts the international dimension of competition for dispute resolution services in the transatlantic area. A further implication is that an EU–US judgment enforcement agreement or a multinational agreement with enforcement provisions (such as the Hague Convention on Choice of Court Agreements) could enhance the international dimension of competitiveness of the market for dispute resolution services in the transatlantic area.

— Second, other things being equal, rules favouring enforcement of judgments among a group of nations is likely to increase competition between the courts of those nations and arbitration.

Private international law rules governing the enforcement of foreign judgments has an important impact on this public–private dimension of the market for dispute resolution services. One of the major advantages of arbitration as a method of transnational dispute resolution is that most nations tend to enforce foreign arbitral awards, subject to narrow and exclusive grounds for refusal, in accordance with the Convention on the Recognition and Enforcement of Foreign Arbitral Awards (New York Convention) and similar regional arrangements. This gives parties an incentive to select arbitration even if they otherwise have strong reasons to prefer litigation in a national court (such as a desire for an appellate review process). The lack of an analogous treaty regime for the enforcement of foreign judgments distorts this dimension of the market for dispute resolution services.

If, for example, the Hague Convention on Choice of Court Agreements enters into effect for a significant number of nations, enforcement issues will no longer tip the scale in favour of arbitration to the extent they do now.[67] And even now, where litigation in an EU member's courts is at least as attractive to a claimant as arbitration, the Brussels I Regulation's rules on enforcement should significantly level the playing field when the respondent has assets in at least one EU member's territory, and the same would seem to be the case internally to the US full-faith-and-credit regime.

None of the foregoing is meant to suggest that unbridled competition for dispute resolution services is necessarily desirable. The point is simply that when designing an approach to foreign judgment enforcement, private international law-makers should be attentive to the implications of their rules for both the international and public–private dimensions of the market for dispute resolution services. Further interdisciplinary study of the implications of different approaches to foreign judgment enforcement for governance values and rights values, and of the causes and consequences of variation across different approaches, promises to provide important foundations for understanding and reforming private international law in the transatlantic area and beyond.

[67] Brand (n 37) 149–51.

4

Can Legal and Political Culture Explain the Successes and Failures of European Law Compliance?

MARLENE WIND

I. INTRODUCTION

TODAY FEW DISPUTE the Court of Justice of the European Union's (CJEU) historical role in promoting and shaping European integration over the past 50 years. In the literature, it is often argued that the CJEU constitutionalised the treaties without much resistance, and that national courts and private litigants willingly accepted and actively enforced this new legal order. In much legal scholarship, the success and impact of European law at the national level is, however, left untheorised and understudied. Interestingly, it is somehow just assumed that once a directive or a regulation is adopted and formal enforcement mechanisms are in place, the law works. Also the classical political science literature on legal integration is blind to the barriers of enforcement. Here the focus has mainly been on how actors have exploited the new European legal possibilities to go to court to defend their rights. However, as I will argue below both perspectives ignore how legal, political and administrative culture at the national level often creates barriers to the intended effective implementation of European law. Drawing on the more recent Europeanisation and implementation literature, this chapter argues that in order to make EU law enforcement work better, it is essential to understand how and to what degree so-called 'veto players' operate and how different legal and political cultures enhance or inhibit an efficient working of European law at the national level.

II. FROM 'LAW IN THE BOOKS' TO 'LAW IN ACTION'

If one glances through the most critically acclaimed well-recognised EU law textbooks from recent years, it is hard to find even one single chapter covering the practical on-the-ground implementation of EU law. It is rather puzzling however that the issue of how EU law is transposed and complied with after the law is issued is so understudied. The main issue is thus what happens when national civil servants at all levels of administration take over? Opening the black box to investigate this is essential, in particular because we see a clear variation in the transposition and implementation from one country to the next. The truth is that we know very little about this or about the de facto on-the-ground compliance with EU law. The main focus of the majority of the law books on Europe that we use teaching prospective EU bureaucrats, lawyers or law researchers, have thus been centred on the institutional design, the competence of the Court of Justice, instruments of compliance, legal principles, the preliminary ruling procedure, infringement procedures etc.[1] What is equally if not more important to understand is however what happens *after* a legislative bill has become law. When studying EU law implementation we should therefore move from 'law on paper' to real living law for those meant to be affected—namely national bureaucracies, courts, politicians, companies, Non-Governmental Organisations (NGOs), and citizens on the ground. While it is obviously also important to teach students the law in the books, it should be just as crucial for future bureaucrats and lawyers, as well as for NGOs and companies dealing with EU legislation on a day to day basis, to understand and be able to detect, not only the many obstacles, barriers and veto points encountered at the national level, but also the facilitators to a correct implementation of EU law in the individual member states. As Treib puts it:

> [P]utting a piece of legislation or a government programme into practice does not happen automatically, nor is it a purely technical or apolitical affair. Instead, long delays and attempts at shrinking seem to be a matter of everyday business in the field of implementation. In other words, if we are interested in the extent to which a particular polity is able to solve the problems with which it is confronted, we need to study not only the way it reaches decisions and the character of the resulting legal output, but also the way in which the law is executed in practice.[2]

As mentioned above, it is also important to try to understand and even explain the rather large variation among Member States in European legal implementation and compliance. Why do some Member States comply faster with some directives, or other pieces of law, while others do not comply at all? And is it possible to measure differences in implementation and compliance levels? These are all issues that researchers within political science have been looking at for some time now. It is, however, mainly within implementation and Europeanisation research that these studies are

[1] See: P Craig and G de Búrca, *EU Law: Texts, Cases and Materials* (Oxford, Oxford University Press, 2011); D Chalmers, G Davies and G Monti, *European Union Law, Cases and Materials* 2nd edn (Cambridge, Cambridge University Press, 2010).

[2] O Treib, 'Implementing and Complying with EU Governance Outputs' (2014) 9 *Living Reviews in European Governance* 1, 5.

conducted tracing the fate of specific directives across several Member States in order to detect differences in the transposition and implementation phase.

This research is primarily focused on obstacles to Europeanisation, implementation and compliance with EU law. Others—in particular American EU scholars—have their focus elsewhere and are much more interested in what they see as the opposite phenomenon: Europe becoming more and more alike and comparable to the US—also when it comes to implementation and compliance.[3] The argument is here that citizens and companies allegedly have discovered how to use national courts across the continent to claim their (EU) rights and thereby help enforce EU law. As this contribution will argue this narrative is, however, questionable as it is situated at a very abstract (almost moral) level holding limited empirical evidence when you dig a bit beneath the surface. As my data shows, whether based on wishful thinking or abstract theorising, little suggests that an increased number of national litigants, civil society mobilisation, preliminary rulings and competitive national courts are creating a European adversarial system which—on a broad scale—helps enhance the integration and harmonisation of European law. Rather the opposite. However, like many lawyers, who believe that structures and laws themselves can change behaviour, this perspective is mostly interested in comparing the EU and the US at a very abstract level.

The article will start off by sketching out the literature positing that the EU and not least its Member States have adopted an American style adversarial legal culture which promotes and enhances the enforcement of European law. It will then move on to take a brief look at the literature on 'Europeanisation' and implementation with a focus on the empirical study of barriers and variance in the transposition of EU law. The final and last section will then use the legal culture in the anti-adversarial Nordic Member States as an example of how we—at a general level—need to include a better understanding of how legal cultures, types of democracy, administrative typologies etc may obstruct or sometimes even enhance the enforcement of European law. The overall argument will be that only thorough case studies of what happens to specific directives and regulations, when met by veto players and other actors at the national level, can help us make sense of variation in compliance across Member States.

III. HAS THE EU REALLY BECOME AMERICANISED?

In particular, American literature on European legal integration has emphasised the degree to which a gradual process, with the Court of Justice as a

[3] RD Kelemen, 'The Americanisation of European Law? Adversarial Legalism *á La Européenne*' (2008) 7 *European Political Science* 32.

dominant player, smoothly transformed Europe from an intergovernmental organisation to a semi-federal construction.[4] What is often focused on in this narrative is how, in particular, the Court of Justice was successful in building a 'new legal order'—with its supremacy and direct effect clauses—turning national judges, ordinary citizens and business lobbies into effective enforcers of European law. According to this long heralded thesis, the development bears strong resemblances to the American political system where 'adversarial legalism'—coined by Kagan—is a significant feature and where most disputes are solved in the courtroom.[5] The perspective sees legal entrepreneurs as empowered by this system and argues that the integration process set in motion 'linked processes of deregulation and reregulation that are encouraging the spread of American legal style across all European Union (EU) member states'.[6] Though Kagan is more sceptical of whether this is actually the case,[7] there seems to be a somewhat broad consensus among the above mentioned authors that the old European styles of regulation are long overdue and that the American counterpart is more up to date, as Kelemen has phrased it:

> European integration has unleashed both economic and political pressures that encourage the spread of adversarial legalism as an approach to governance. The creation of a single European market has been based on a dual process of economic liberalization or deregulation at the national level coupled with reregulation at the European level. This process has undermined informal national styles of regulation based on closed, insider networks and trust among repeat players and has pressured regulators to rely on more formal, transparent and judicially enforceable approaches to regulation ... The EU's limited implementation and enforcement capacity makes it tempting for policy makers to effectively privatize government by enlisting private parties and national courts to enforce EU policies.[8]

The problem with these rather sweeping conclusions is of course that it paints a very general and—in my analysis—superficial picture of the

[4] JHH Weiler, 'The Transformation of Europe' (1991) 100 *Yale Law Journal* 2403; KJ Alter, *Establishing the Supremacy of European Law* (Oxford, Oxford University Press, 2001); A Stone Sweet, *The Judicial Construction of Europe* (Oxford, Oxford University Press, 2004); M Shapiro, 'The Globalization of Law' (1993) 1 *Indiana Journal of Global Legal Studies* 37; Kelemen (n 3).

[5] RA Kagan, 'Should Europe Worry About Adversarial Legalism?' (1997) 17 *Oxford Journal of Legal Studies* 165. Kagan defines adversarial legalism partly in the following manner: 'What, then might one mean by the "Americanization" of European law? I will define it as the adoption by Western European countries of laws, legal practices, and legal frameworks that had been adopted in the United States significantly earlier and that represent significant disparities from long-standing European traditions ... The US has also been distinctive in enabling entrepreneurial lawyers to aggregate many individual tort claims into a single class action, not infrequently demanding millions of dollars in damages'. RA Kagan, 'The "Non-Americanisation" of European Law' (2008) 7 *European Political Science* 21, 22ff.

[6] Kelemen (n 3) 33.

[7] Kagan, 'Should Europe Worry About Adversarial Legalism?' (n 5) and Kagan, 'The "Non-Americanisation" of European Law' (n 5).

[8] Kelemen (n 3) 33.

regulatory developments in Europe. Just like the rather widespread legal narrative of European law being in effect in Member States almost automatically after having been adopted politically, the social mobilisation thesis pays little attention to diversity of legal cultures and national barriers in the European legal landscape. For instance, when Kelemen describes the classical European ways of regulating as 'opaque' and as systems of regulation 'that relied on insider networks' arguing that 'the legal challenges, the growing diversity of players in liberalized markets simply rendered traditional systems of regulation unworkable',[9] concrete empirical evidence or even just examples would have been very helpful.

However, as I will demonstrate below, the thesis of the EU as a 'weak state' with limited enforcement capacity that almost automatically generates 'strong political incentives to rely on adversarial legalism as a mode of governance'[10] is simply too general a claim to make. While an Americanised development may have been a probable expectation if we follow a specific theoretical logic, the European reality today looks somewhat different exhibiting great variance among states and societies. Societal mobilisation in the form of litigation at the Member State level, which is central to the argument, does in other words not come about just because some broader European structures change or because it becomes possible for litigants at the national level to ask for preliminary references in their national courts. If there is no tradition to litigate against the State or if national courts refuse to forward cases to the European Court of Justice, little adversarial legalism will appear. Moreover, whether this or another scenario occurs is only detectable after in-depth case studies of civil-society relations and administrative and political democracy practices and traditions in individual Member States. National judges deciding about preliminary references or the enforcement of EU law may not always be eager to enforce European law or ask questions in Luxembourg but may be more attentive to national legal hierarchies and loyalties. Moreover, in some more corporatist countries, citizens simply do not use courts as a medium for dispute resolution.

The question is thus how we best study the enforcement of European Union law knowing that there are national differences that may obstruct or enhance implementation? Despite a heavy focus on Europeanisation among particularly European political scientists in recent years, the large majority of academics studying EU law enforcement are still inattentive to the *variation* between Member States in the implementation of European law. Hence we still know rather little about the day-to-day workings of the law at different governmental and regional levels and among different players like litigants and national courts. The consequence of this is not only ignorance

[9] ibid, 34.
[10] ibid, 35.

and suboptimal enforcement of EU law but often also a very uneven development of European rights protection across the Member States.

IV. THE 'COMPLIANCE SCALE' AND THE DIVERSE IMPACT OF EUROPEAN LAW

From available EU statistics, it is obvious that not all Member States comply equally well—or fast—with their European commitments. This is hardly breaking news. Studies have shown that some countries are falling behind in some areas while others are categorised as dutiful compliers.[11] In the literature on Europeanisation, this is often described as a question of how Member States 'respond' domestically to European law and of the 'actual policy impact' of European jurisprudence at the domestic level.[12]

But what is Europeanisation really about and how can the 'domestic impact' of Europe be studied more concretely? Can it help us to better understand compliance? According to Treib, implementation and compliance are two sides of the same coin:

> [M]ost compliance and implementation research is interested in both the process of how a given norm is being put into practice and in the outcome in terms of conformity. In this sense implementation and compliance are two sides of the same coin.[13]

If we follow Ladrech and start by looking at the broader and perhaps more fuzzy term of Europeanisation, we are however focusing more on norm diffusion than actual implementation: 'an incremental process reorienting the direction and shape of politics to the degree that EC political and economic dynamics become part of the organizational logic of national politics and policy-making'.[14] Börzel has described it as 'a process by which domestic policy areas become increasingly subject to European policy-making'.[15] Following Héritier et al, Europeanisation means:

> the process of influence deriving from European decisions and impacting member states' policies and political and administrative structures. It comprises the following elements: the European decisions, the processes triggered by these decisions as

[11] G Falkner, O Treib, M Hartlapp and S Leiber, *Complying with Europe: EU Harmonisation and Soft Law in the Member States* (Cambridge, Cambridge University Press, 2005).

[12] M Blauberger, 'With Luxembourg in Mind ... The Remaking of National Policies in the Face of ECJ Jurisprudence' (2012) 19 *Journal of European Public Policy* 109.

[13] Treib (n 2) 5.

[14] R Ladrech, 'Europeanization of Domestic Politics and Institutions: The Case of France' (1994) 32 *Journal of Common Market Studies* 69.

[15] T Börzel, 'Towards Convergence in Europe? Institutional Adaptation to Europeanization in Germany and Spain' (1999) 39 *Journal of Common Market Studies* 573, 574.

well as the impacts of these processes on national policies, decision processes and institutional structures.[16]

The primary focus of any Europeanisation research agenda is thus to study whether and to what degree new EU rules, norms, ways of doing things and ways of thinking impact and eventually create changes at the Member State level. Ultimately, it is to establish whether there is a *causal link* between the issuing of a European regulation and concrete legal change at the national and/or regional level. If no domestic change can be detected, the European measure has had no impact.[17] The causal link can be illustrated by this model:[18]

The mediating factors of Europeanisation

Cause →	Intermediate variables →	Effect
The amount of binding force in the EU regulation/ the political-judicial mechanism: • Treaties • Regulations • Directives • Judgments from CJEU • Recommendations • Norms and values	• Political, institutional capacity • Political, legal and institutional tradition • Veto-players and/ or mediating factors • Cultures of compliance	Effects on domestic level Specific rights and commitments for EU citizens, organizations and businesses Divergence or convergence

The most interesting dimension in this context is quite obviously the intermediate variables which are the elements that may obstruct, hinder but also occasionally enhance the actual domestic effect of a European measure. When looking at a concrete legal instrument, for instance European economic regulation in the competition area, one will thus look at the degree to which a Member State's political and institutional capacities create hindrances

[16] A Héritier, D Kerver, C Knill, D Lehmkuhl and M Teutsch, *Differential Europe. The European Union Impact on National Policymaking* (Lanham, Rowman & Littlefield, 2001). Radaelli, who is a well know expert on Europeanisation, describes the process in the following manner: 'Processes of (a) construction (b) diffusion and (c) institutionalisation of formal and informal rules, procedures, policy paradigms, styles, "ways of doing things" and shared beliefs and norms which are first defined and consolidated in the making of EU decisions and then incorporated in the logic of domestic discourse, identities, political structures and public policies'. C Radaelli, 'The Europeanization of Public Policy' in K Featherstone and C Radaelli (eds), *The Politics of Europeanization* (Oxford, Oxford University Press, 2003) 30.

[17] This does not necessarily mean that a Member State has omitted its obligation. That will depend on a concrete empirical analysis. It can also be explained by the fact that the measure is already in place or that there is a 'perfect fit' or match between the proposed European measure and existing national law.

[18] Adapted from M Kelstrup, DS Martinsen and M Wind, *Europa i forandring—en grundbog om EU's politiske og retlige system* (København, Hans Reitzel, 2012) 385.

to the full effect of the law. Looking at *political and institutional capacities* could be to analyse what type of state we are dealing with. Is it a centralised state which is highly regulated, a federal state, or a state with a high degree of local autonomy and self-rule? How is implementation of EU laws organised more specifically? Who is in charge of what and what checks are there on the degree to which a regulation in fact reaches its final destination? Research has found that the degree of centralisation and central oversight can influence whether a measure is implemented correctly and fully complied with. Another important aspect is whether there is a 'fit/misfit' between a European measure and the regulation already in place at the national level. The hypothesis is that the better the 'fit' is with existing regulation, the greater the likelihood that an EU measure will in fact be implemented and complied with. The fit/misfit hypothesis can be useful in concrete studies of implementation where it becomes critical not just to focus on the European law in question, but equally on the existing legal framework in place in a specific area in the Member State. This may thus give us a better understanding of how difficult it will be to get the full effect of any specific EU initiative or whether difficulties in the implementation is to be expected. Political, legal and institutional traditions tell us something about the political norms and ways of doing things which have been built over decades, or even centuries in a Member State, and which can either hinder or encourage a certain European regulatory measure, practice or mechanism. Is there, for instance, a longstanding tradition for aiding national companies financially or with special privileges? Are these compensated either directly or indirectly for social or other reasons? These are all matters that could influence the handling of a specific anti-trust or agricultural regulation. Or if the EU wants to introduce flexicurity to combat unemployment this might be welcomed by the Nordic welfare states, but considered highly 'unfitting' in other Member States due to long hailed traditions for privileging those who already have a job compared to those outside the workforce. Another example is the preliminary ruling procedure with which the present author has been occupied.[19] This mechanism may—as several studies have shown—be welcomed by judges and litigants in Germany and France,[20] but be very unwelcome in countries with no tradition for judicial review by courts at the national level and where parliamentary supremacy is regarded as the only legitimate way of conducting politics (more on this below).[21]

[19] M Wind, 'The Nordics, the EU and the Reluctance Towards Supranational Judicial Review' (2010) 48 *Journal of Common Market Studies* 1039.

[20] Alter (n 4).

[21] M Wind, 'When Parliament Comes First. The Danish Concept of Democracy Meets the European Union' (2009) 27 *Nordic Journal of Human Rights* 272; Wind (n 19); M Wind and JE Rytter, 'In Need of Juristocracy? The Silence of Denmark in the Development of European Legal Norms' (2011) 9 *International Journal of Constitutional Law* 470; M Wind, 'Who is Afraid of European Constitutionalism? The Nordic Distress with Judicial Review

Studies of national veto players could similarly entail a focus on lobby groups with strong interests (and influence) on the implementation of EU law. In environmental policy areas, for instance, this would be agricultural lobby groups (farmer's organisations), but it could also be environmental groupings which are influential when it comes to shaping the transposition of European law into national law.[22] Another highly relevant sector to look at would be civil servants and the administrative culture in the ministries of the Member States. Are those civil servants who give advice on and administer the implementation of European legal rules interpreting regulations or directives narrowly or expansively? Either way, administrative culture matters and impacts enforcement of European law. A god example is when we detect differences in opinion, tradition and practice between for instance the Ministry of Justice and the Ministry of Environment, or between the Ministry of Environment and those agencies on the ground responsible for the actual implementation of European environmental directives. Studies show that civil servants (and the administrative culture) may act as gatekeepers and veto players for the correct implementation of European law.[23] As we are to see below in the example I draw out from a study on the Danish and Swedish judges and ministerial civil servants, veto players can also be institutional actors who function as gate-keepers to the CJEU. By creating barriers to the full functioning of the preliminary reference mechanism, they in fact prevented litigants from having their case heard.[24] This research thus showed how civil servants played an active role in deciding which cases, coming out of the national courts, should reach the CJEU in the first place—resulting in very few preliminary references.[25] Civil servants may also be important veto players when it comes to deciding whether a court case, coming out of the CJEU, should have any legal effect at all in the national legal order, in particular, when it is a case based on a preliminary reference procedure between the Court and another Member State. Should this case have any bearing on us? Or should we regard it as too specific

and Constitutional Democracy', *iCourts Working Paper* no 13, forthcoming in C Franzius, F Mayer and J Neyer (eds), *Modelle des Parlamentarismus im 21. Jarhundert. Neue Ordnungen von Recht und Politik; Recht und Politik in der Europäschen Union* (Berlin, NOMOS Verlag, 2015).

[22] RA Cichowski, *The European Court and Civil Society, Litigation, Mobilization and Governance* (Cambridge, Cambridge University Press, 2007).

[23] A study has shown that it is far from enough just to look at formal implementation of EU law into the Member States as formal implementation is merely self-reported figures coming out of the ministries themselves. Most of these reports only focus on whether a directive has been transposed in time, but there is nothing about the actual implementation. See Kelstrup et al (n 18).

[24] M Wind, DS Martinsen and GP Rotger, 'The Uneven Legal Push for Europe' (2009) 10 *European Union Politics* 63; Wind (n 19).

[25] Wind (n 19). See also P Pagh, 'Præjudicielle forelæggelser og Juridisk specialudvalg' (2004) *Ugeskrift for retsvæsen* 305.

with no general or principal consequences for the overall interpretation of Union law? In other words, it will often be the civil servants (but also the national courts in subsequent cases) who ultimately decide whether a particular ruling is significantly similar to specific conditions in a particular Member State to eventually change national law and practice.[26] At the end of the day the civil servants are rarely framed for having undermined EU law as such. Rather it is a matter of interpretation and legal and political culture. Where does your loyalty lie? With the state you serve and the majority in parliament or with European law and the citizens or firms who's rights may have been infringed? In several studies, Martinsen has shown that in a Nordic context, where judicial review and courts play a minor role and where health care is tax-financed, CJEU case law has challenged national prerogatives by giving patients more rights and trans-European opportunities for treatment abroad. She demonstrated that civil servants for years deliberately ignored the European case law and, as patient organisations would never test their government's administration in court because there is no tradition for doing so, civil servants ended up as the main gate-keepers for citizens' trans-border health rights.

What also matters when it comes to the transposition of EU law into the Member State's legal order is thus the degree to which we are dealing with a very litigious society or not. In the Nordic countries for instance, there is no tradition for going to court to defend your rights, in particular not your European rights. Disputes and disagreements are solved outside the courtroom in a dense corporatist structure. Also, if the national courts have no tradition for challenging the lawmakers through the exercise of judicial review, there will be little mobilisation and almost no focus on (European) rights which can be enforced in the courtroom.[27]

Studying a Member States' compliance culture is also of salience when enforcement and effectiveness are at stake. Gerda Falkner has done a very cited study categorising countries into three different compliance regimes, or as she calls it 'Worlds of Compliance': 1) The world of law observance; 2) the world of domestic politics; 3) the world of neglect.[28] A fourth 'the world of dead letter' has later been added by Falkner.[29] This primarily concerns Central and Eastern European countries, Italy and Ireland and signifies that law is only law on paper but rarely implemented.[30]

[26] DS Martinsen and K Vrangbæk, 'The Europeanization of Health Care Governance: Implementing the Market Imperatives of Europe' (2008) 1 *Public Administration* 169.

[27] M Gøtze, *The Evolution of EU Administrative Law and the Contributions of Nordic Administrative Law* (Brussels, European Parliament, 2011); Wind (n 19).

[28] Falkner (n 11) 317–41.

[29] G Falkner and O Treib, 'Three Worlds of Compliance or Four? The EU-15 Compared to New Member States' 46(2) *Journal of Common Market Studies* 293–313.

[30] ibid.

Falkner simply lumped EU countries into the different categories after having carefully studied how EU social regulation was implemented in the different Member States. Where some countries were reported to have complied fully and on time with specific directives, others met directives with domestic political barriers, while some simply ignored the directives until an infringement case was launched against it. However, without going too much into details, Falkner's typology has been criticised for being too simplistic and for relying too much on official implementation statistics coming from the national ministries themselves.

When we want to understand how and to what degree EU law works and is adopted as intended at the Member State level, it is however not enough simply to look at the 'barriers' to the full working of European law. It is also important to acquire an understanding of the degree of change resulting from any European legal measure. This can be done by scaling the Europeanisation process. The model below, based on Radaelli, illustrates how this can be done.[31]

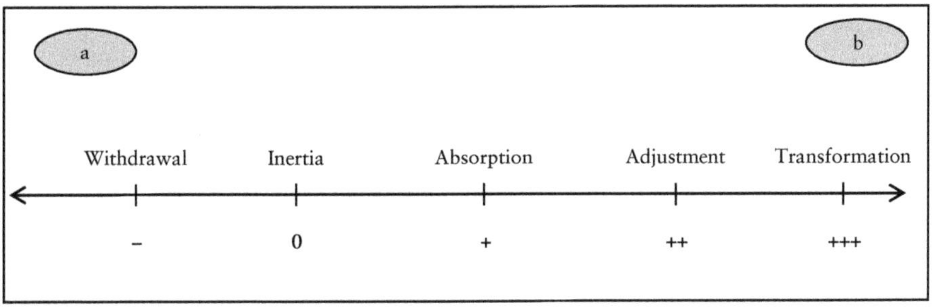

This scale is meant to illustrate the ways in which any given EU law measure can be received in the Member States once it is issued. It is important to note that we are dealing with a typology here which can be helpful when trying to make sense of the transposition process on a scale from non-implementation to complete transformation of national law in accordance with a new EU law. Withdrawal thus symbolises a complete national rejection of a new European measure through inaction, inertia, the conscious creation of 'red tape', barriers and obstruction. Absorption implies on this scale that the measure has resulted in only cosmetic changes. Adjustment is closer to the intended substantial effect of any particular European law or measure. And finally transformation symbolises a radical change of national practices and rules as a consequence of the adoption of a new European regulation.[32] But how can we use all this? It provides us with a guide or a pair of spectacles through which we will know what to look for when studying implementation

[31] Radaelli (n 16) 35.
[32] Radelli (n 16). See also Kelstrup et al (n 18) 377.

of EU law, or, if you perceive this as a compliance-scale, studying compliance in particular.

V. WHEN THE OTHERWISE OBEDIENT NORDICS OBSTRUCT

One of the questions that the sweeping literature on European constitutionalisation has omitted is the issue of how we make sense of the fact that Member States are different and have different legal and political traditions. Not only may administrative traditions diverge but the same goes for the behaviour and thinking of other actors like national courts or litigants. Different Member States often respond differently to the Court or the EU decision-making system as such. If we look at a previous study of the Nordic courts and judges, it becomes clear just how important it is to leave behind old textbooks and formal studies of EU law which often stay on the surface. However, it also suggests that there is little evidence that the European Union as such is becoming Americanised and adapting to adversarial legalism, at least not across the board. The fact that the EU launched a preliminary ruling system and introduced supremacy and direct effect thus tells us little about how the Member States have responded to these new mechanisms and eventually accommodated them over the years. Just to give one example out of many, the below analysis of the attitude and behaviour of the German lower courts towards the 'new' European legal order of preliminary references and supremacy is thus hard to recognise when looking to the Nordic experiences:

> Lower court judges, with the luxury of focusing only on the case at hand, are usually less concerned with the coherence of the national legal system. In addition, the preliminary ruling mechanism allows lower courts to appeal to an authority outside the national legal system, securing an authoritative counter-precedent to the interpretations of national supreme courts. As long as a lower court agrees with ECJ interpretations, ECJ decisions actually lend legal credibility to a lower court decision and thus bolster the influence of the lower court within the national legal system. As such, references to the ECJ have become a convenient means to circumvent higher courts.[33]

Despite these very sweeping conclusions about the entire European development based on a few country case studies, you find no support whatsoever for this 'court competition-thesis' in the Nordic countries. Here the 'feeling' of 'judicial empowerment' in lower courts is non-existent. A survey of Danish and Swedish judges conducted some years ago revealed that no

[33] Alter (n 4) 49. See also KJ Alter, 'Explaining National Court Acceptance of European Court Jurisprudence: A Critical Evaluation of Theories of Legal Integration' in A-M Slaughter, A Stone-Sweet and J Weiler (eds), *The European Courts and National Courts* (Oxford, Hart Publishing, 1998) 225–50.

lower judge wanted to challenge their superior colleagues in the Supreme Courts, and lower as well as higher court judges were sceptical of letting a 'foreign' supranational court overrule the national majority in parliament.[34] Alter's general theory of 'court competition' thus cannot account for the variance in preliminary reference patterns across Member States.[35] In Denmark and Sweden, where the majority of national judges (still) are recruited from the Ministry of Justice, concerns about the 'coherence of the national legal system' are still highly prevalent, and lower courts have only occasionally forwarded questions to the CJEU. The study of the Nordic judges mentioned in brief above[36] demonstrated that due to legal and political culture, and not least the lack of experience with judicial review at the national level, almost no preliminary references were sent by lower Danish and Swedish courts. Also, the Supreme Courts were highly reluctant and the Swedish Government even received an infringement case in 2004 for forwarding too few cases to the CJEU. Despite the fact that the Nordics are normally regarded as law abiding Member States (see Falkner's study above), there has been no desire, neither by the judges nor by the civil servants in the Ministry of Justice, to let the CJEU interfere in the national legal order through preliminary references. And if not asked for advice the CJEU will of course have scarce possibilities to influence national law. What is then the explanation for this rather peculiar behaviour? As indicated already, the Nordic countries are majoritarian democracies and thereby per definition highly sceptical of judicial review by courts in general. Having no tradition for setting aside majoritarian decisions at the national level (in Denmark it has only happened once in 165 years!), working closely together with the CJEU and letting litigants try their cases at a supranational court would, according to the judges and civil servants interviewed and included in our large scale survey,[37] imply introducing judicial review through the back door. This is something they—on a broad scale—thought was a very bad idea. Moreover, in Denmark the Ministry of Justice not only advises the courts about whether a preliminary question should be forwarded, they also help draft the questions in order to limit their scopes.[38] That the Nordic countries have a relatively low number of infringement cases is, as one civil servant explained, rather simple: 'we do not want to go to court, so if an infringement case is approaching, we normally strike a last minute compromise to avoid that procedure'.[39] Thus a tradition for 'no one over or above

[34] Wind (n 19); Wind (n 21).

[35] Wind et al (n 24).

[36] See Wind (n 21); M Wind and A Føllesdal, 'Introduction—Nordic Reluctance Towards Judicial Review under Siege' (2009) 27 *Nordic Journal of Human Rights* 131; Wind (n 19); Wind et al (n 24); Wind and Rytter (n 21).

[37] The survey can be studied in Wind (n 19).

[38] Pagh (n 25); Wind (n 19).

[39] Interview with anonymous high ranked civil servant from the Ministry of Justice.

the parliament' and no judicial review at the national level not only explains the reluctance towards supranational judicial review—in particular in sensitive areas—but also explains why CJEU case law sometimes is completely ignored in this part of Europe.

Legal cultures can also explain a general sceptical approach to supranational courts and bodies. Nordic courts and the Nordic legal education systems are fierce defenders of a dogmatic black letter law tradition (separating 'is' from 'ought'). They thus regard both the Luxembourg and the Strasbourg court as far too dynamic—not to say political. Summing up it is possible to list a number of specific features (or variables) that may explain why some Member States—even the law abiding ones—are very far indeed from any kind of Americanisation.

Variables that define countries with a low degree of litigation and less independent courts include:

- Very homogenous societies
- Few minorities
- Corporatist governmental structure
- Citizens have no tradition for challenging their governments in court
- No tradition for judicial review (majoritarian democracies)
- High trust in the state: Willingness to pay high taxes
- Very little emphasis on citizens rights—in particular European rights
- Very little emphasis on the division of powers between different branches of government

In more general terms one can say that legal, political but also administrative and institutional features of any given Member State thus become incredibly important to take into account when estimating their compliance with EU law. It will in other words be overly simplistic to assume, as much legal literature still does, that a law implements itself once enacted, and that law will work and become adopted similarly in all Member States. This is why a much better understanding of legal and political cultures in the Member States may help us to better understand the successes and failures of compliance with European law.

VI. CONCLUSION

What can this small essay tell us about the study of compliance? First and foremost it tells us that culture is back, and that European law cannot be studied in isolation from insights coming from political science. The literature on implementation is in other words valuable for understanding how, why and whether compliance with EU law works at all. As Treib argues: 'Policy implementation … refers to "what happens after a bill becomes law" … or, as one scholar put it, to the process of "translating policy into action"'.[40] It is the latter part which is often left out in legal textbook-presentations and in sweeping narrations about the almost 'automatic' Americanisation of European law.

Implementation studies also tell us that only detailed comparative case analyses of specific directives or regulations will give us the 'true story' of how European law really works on the ground. It is of course an exaggeration to say that the constitutionalisation thesis is writ wrong and that the European integration process has not changed Europe and the Member States in even quite radical ways. Legal contestation and social mobilisation have in many ways become an everyday practice with individuals and firms as insistent law enforcers. However, this is something that will have to be studied and analysed empirically. It cannot just be assumed. In order to fully comprehend, and perhaps also predict where the problems in the enforcement of European law may lie in the future, we will thus have to go back to a thorough comparative analysis of European legal traditions, types of democracy, and administrative practices. Only by understanding these broad, but very sticky phenomena, can we—perhaps—predict upcoming compliance problems at the national level but also more ambitiously improve European law-making itself.

[40] Treib (n 2) 5, footnote omitted.

Part III

The Supply and Demand Side of Justice: Stakeholders and Institutions

5

*Against False Settlement: Designing Efficient Consumer Rights Enforcement Systems in Europe**

HORST EIDENMÜLLER AND MARTIN FRIES

I. INTRODUCTION

CONSUMER SATISFACTION HAS now been at the core of EU legal policymaking for more than a decade. With ever more information duties for traders, withdrawal rights for consumers, the policing of standard contract terms in B2C (Business To Consumer) contracts, and mandatory substantive consumer protection rules regarding sales and service contracts, the European Commission (Commission) tries to support consumer confidence and boost the single market. According to this programme, barriers to Union-wide trade are to be eliminated step-by-step until contracting with parties from other Member States becomes as easy as contracting in domestic commerce.[1]

Whereas the EU has, for a long time, focused on strengthening substantive consumer rights, it appears that only quite recently did it come to the Commission's attention that, according to Holmes' famous 'acid test', for

* This article is a reprint with minor revisions of H Eidenmüller and M Engel, 'Against False Settlement: Designing Efficient Consumer Rights Enforcement Systems in Europe' (2014) 29 *Ohio State Journal on Dispute Resolution* 269. The authors thank the participants of the EUI Conference on 'The Transformation of Enforcement' in Florence (27–28 June 2013), the participants of the University of Frankfurt Conference on 'Alternatives to Formalization–Formalization of Alternatives?' in Frankfurt (20–21 July 2013) as well as the participants of the University of Amsterdam Conference on 'Private Law and the Basic Structure of Society' in Amsterdam (31 January 2014) for their feedback and discussions.

[1] See Commission, 'Communication from the Commission to the European Parliament, the Council, the European Economic and Social Committee and the Committee of Regions on Cross-Border Business to Consumer e-Commerce in the EU' COM (2009) 557 final, 16, 47. However, it is important to note that the law is not the only barrier to cross-border shopping. Transaction (shipping) costs, in particular, are not taken into account by Eurobarometer but most likely create a notable obstacle to cross-border trade. Their relative weight is significant, especially in cases with a low transaction value.

consumer rights to be effective, there must be effective sanctions if such rights are not respected.[2] And since most consumers are not jurists, the enforcement mechanism must be easily manageable for the layperson if the consumers themselves—as opposed to legal professionals—are supposed to use it. It is not the fuss that can be expected to meet the requirements of the forum; rather, the forum has to be fitted to the fuss.[3]

Very much in this spirit, the most recent consumer protection legislation in the EU focuses on designing efficient consumer rights enforcement mechanisms in Europe.[4] With its Directive on Consumer Alternative Dispute Resolution (ADR) and its Regulation on Consumer Online Dispute Resolution (ODR),[5] the EU aims to provide a feasible and easily accessible framework within which consumers can pursue their rights quickly and effectively.[6] Through a network of extra-judicial conciliation bodies and an EU online conflict allocation scheme, consumer disputes shall be resolved speedily and in a cost-efficient manner. However, the newly envisaged EU landscape for the resolution of small-stakes B2C disputes has the effect of sidelining state courts. Specifically, conflicts are shifted to private or semi-private service providers who supposedly follow the consumers' interests by putting efficiency above judicial scrutiny and the observance of due process standards.

This paper argues that this is a detrimental development. The 'settlement euphoria' that inspires the European push towards a non-judicial dispute resolution landscape is misguided on both justice and efficiency grounds. It is simply contradictory to set up a sophisticated system of mandatory consumer protection rights and to then leave the 'enforcement' of these rights to non-legal private providers, which are not trained or incentivised for this task and which operate outside the procedural safeguards of the

[2] OW Holmes, 'The Path of the Law' (1997) 110 *Harvard Law Review* 991, 995.

[3] FEA Sander and SB Goldberg, 'Fitting the Forum to the Fuss: A User-Friendly Guide to Selecting an ADR Procedure' (1994) 10 *Negotiation Journal* 49. See also C Duve, H Eidenmüller and A Hacke, *Mediation in der Wirtschaft* 2nd edn (Köln, Otto Schmidt, 2011) 351–53.

[4] See Commission, 'The EU Justice Scoreboard: A Tool to Promote Effective Justice and Growth' COM (2013) 160 final; E Dubois, C Schurrer and M Velicogna, 'The Functioning of Judicial Systems and the Situation of the Economy in the European Union Member States' (European Commission for the Efficiency of Justice, Strasbourg, 15 January 2013) 638, www.ec.europa.eu/justice/effective-justice/files/cepej_study_justice_scoreboard_en.pdf; B Hess, 'Study No JAI/A3/2002/02 On Making More Efficient the Enforcement of Judicial Decisions Within the European Union' (2004) www.ec.europa.eu/civiljustice/publications/docs/enforcement_judicial_decisions_180204_en.pdf.

[5] Dir 2013/11/EU of the European Parliament and of the Council of 21 May 2013 on Alternative Dispute Resolution for Consumer Disputes and Amending Reg (EC) No 2006/2004 and Dir 2009/22/EC [2013] OJ L165/63 (Dir on Consumer ADR); Commission Reg (EU) No 524/2013 of the European Parliament and of the Council of 21 May 2013 on Online Dispute Resolution for Consumer Disputes and Amending Reg (EC) No 2006/2004 and Dir 2009/22/EC [2013] OJ L165/1 (Reg on Consumer ODR).

[6] See Dir on Consumer ADR (n 5) 1; Reg on Consumer ODR (n 5) 2.

court system. To put it differently: mandatory consumer protection rights attempt to correct market failure. Hence, enforcing these rights should not be returned to the market. This move is also inefficient because 'false settlement' compromises proper behavioural incentives for businesses. Further, a new and heavily regulated private enforcement architecture alongside the state courts would undoubtedly significantly increase the total transaction costs of the dispute system. Finally, even if ADR decisions are non-binding on the consumer, access to the courts will be at least de facto considerably impaired. Instead, consumer rights should be enforced in streamlined court proceedings specifically designed to meet the requirements of B2C disputes arising from small-stakes[7] sales or service contracts in particular.[8]

This chapter starts with describing current developments in the field of consumer behaviour, consumer law, and the institutional handling of consumer conflicts (Part II). On this basis, the chapter discusses fundamental principles of dispute systems design for efficiently enforcing consumer rights (Part III) and attempts to develop a coherent model for an efficient consumer rights dispute system regarding small-stakes B2C transactions (Part IV). This in turn leads to a critique of the recent EU legislation on consumer ADR and ODR (Part V). The final section concludes and summarises the main results of the paper (Part VI).

II. THE CASE FOR CONSUMER RIGHTS DISPUTE SYSTEMS DESIGN

Dispute systems design has a long tradition, especially in the United States of America. It deals with adapting the design of a certain conflict resolution procedure to the needs of its users.[9] It tries to do this by establishing rules, principles or institutions that, taken together, allow a *systematic* management of a specific type of conflict. By shifting its regulatory focus from the substantive rights of consumers to the procedural framework for handling

[7] We will assume that small-stakes disputes are cases in which the amount in dispute is lower than €1000.

[8] This is also one of the core recommendations drawn from the so-called Oxford Study. See CJS Hodges and S Vogenauer, 'European Civil Justice Systems: Findings of a Major Comparative Study on Litigation Funding and Costs' (The Foundation for Law, Justice and Society, 2010) 9, www.fljs.org/sites/www.fljs.org/files/publications/Hodges.pdf.

[9] See WL Ury, JM Brett and SB Goldberg, *Getting Disputes Resolved: Designing Systems to Cut the Costs of Conflict* 2nd edn (San Francisco, Jossey-Bass Publishers, 1993). See also Duve, Eidenmüller and Hacke (n 3) 325; A Kupfer Schneider, 'Building a Pedagogy of Problem-Solving: Learning to Choose Among ADR Processes' (2000) 5 *Harvard Negotiation Law Review* 113; LB Bingham, 'The Next Step: Research on How Dispute System Design Affects Function' (2002) 18 *Negotiation Journal* 375; FEA Sander and L Rozdeiczer, 'Matching Cases and Dispute Resolution Procedures: Detailed Analysis Leading to a Mediation-Centered Approach' (2006) 11 *Harvard Negotiation Law Review* 1; H Eidenmüller and A Hacke, 'Institutionalisierung der Mediation im betrieblichen Konfliktmanagement' (2003) *Personalführung* 20.

B2C conflicts, the EU enters the domain of consumer rights dispute systems design.

A. Recent Developments in Consumer Behaviour and Consumer Law

The current European legislation for enforcing consumer rights and resolving B2C disputes follows a somewhat long-term and steady increase in cross-border e-commerce[10] and, consequently, in cross-border consumer disputes. With the rise of the Internet, many consumers have learned to shop online in a sophisticated manner and to exploit differences in price.[11] They have also gained access to products and services that were previously unavailable to them. Today, for numerous consumers, national borders play only a secondary role in the selection of a contract partner. With growth rates clearly in the double-digit area per year, e-commerce, since the turn of the millennium, is among the fastest growing sectors of the European economy, and there are no signs that this trend might reverse in the foreseeable future—quite the contrary.[12]

Coinciding with this development, the EU has taken significant steps to boost consumer confidence even further by setting up a comprehensive and mandatory system of consumer rights in B2C transactions. These include far-reaching information duties for businesses, the policing of standard contract terms, rules on product and service quality, remedies for breach of contract and withdrawal rights. Many of these rights are ineffective, inefficient and redistribute between consumer segments.[13] This has not stopped the EU from pushing full force in the direction of ever more consumer protection—literally at all costs. The current *acquis communautaire*, the Common Frame of Reference (CFR),[14] and the Draft Common European

[10] Since the turn of the millennium, cross-border online shopping within the EU has notably increased. One in 10 EU consumers (10%) purchased online from a seller/provider in another EU country in 2011/2012 compared with 6% in 2006. European Commission, 'Consumers' Attitudes Towards Cross-Border Trade and Consumer Protection' (TNS Political and Social, Directorate-General for Health and Consumers, Flash Eurobarometer 332, 2012) 6, www.ec.europa.eu/public_opinion/flash/fl_332_en.pdf (Flash Eurobarometer 332).

[11] 56% of EU citizens with Internet access have in the 12 months before the survey purchased goods or services online. ibid, 11.

[12] Of all cross-border purchases, the ratio of online business was 18% in 2002, rising to 27% in 2006, and reaching 46% in 2011 (ibid, 14). See The European Opinion Research Group EEIG and EOS Gallup Europe, 'Public Opinion in Europe: Views on Business-to-Consumer Cross-Border Trade' (Health and Consumer Protection Directorate-General and Enterprise Directorate-General, Standard Eurobarometer 57.2, Flash Eurobarometer 128, Report B, 2002) 7, www.ec.europa.eu/public_opinion/archives/ebs/ebs_175_fl128_en.pdf.

[13] See H Eidenmüller, F Faust, HC Grigoleit, N Jansen, G Wagner and R Zimmermann, 'Towards a Revision of the Consumer Acquis' (2011) 48 *Common Market Law Review* 1077; H Eidenmüller, 'Why Withdrawal Rights?' (2011) 7 *European Review of Contract Law* 1, 5.

[14] For the academic Draft Common Frame of Reference (DCFR) see C von Bar, E Clive and H Schulte-Nölke, 'Principles, Definitions, and Model Rules of European Private Law' (Study

Sales Law (DCESL) proposed in 2011,[15] reflect the EU's legal policy in this respect over the past two decades. On the level of private international law, Article 6(2) of the Rome I Regulation has also been designed to ease cross-border trade as it assures the consumer that he will usually be guaranteed, at a minimum, the consumer protection level of his home state. Hence, the consumer can conduct transactions in any Member State without having to be concerned with the respective substantive law.

B. The Current State of Judicial Consumer Rights Enforcement

However, the concept of boosting cross-border trade and the single European market by mandatory rights of consumers and by (minimum) harmonisation of the European Member States' laws in this respect, comes with an important caveat: as second year law students learn all over the world, the value of a right depends heavily on the mode of its enforcement and, in particular, the costs associated with this enforcement. This turns the attention to the question concerning the extent to which consumer rights in small-stakes cases are nowadays effectively enforced in the EU.

Rights enforcement is first and foremost the task of the public courts. Most European Member States allow small-stakes claims to be brought to local courts whose jurisdiction depends on a claim value lower than a certain amount, for example, €5000 in Germany.[16] Furthermore, many Member States do not require parties to be represented by an attorney before such courts.[17] In 2006 and 2007, the EU itself established a European order for

Group on a European Civil Code and the Research Group on EC Private Law, European law publishers, 2009) www.ec.europa.eu/justice/policies/civil/docs/dcfr_outline_edition_en.pdf. See also H Eidenmüller, F Faust, HC Grigoleit, N Jansen, G Wagner and R Zimmermann, 'The Common Frame of Reference for European Private Law—Policy Choices and Codification Problems' (2008) 28 *Oxford Journal of Legal Studies* 659.

[15] Commission, 'Proposal for a Regulation of the European Parliament and of the Council on a Common European Sales Law' COM (2011) 635 final. See also H Eidenmüller, N Jansen, E-M Kieninger, G Wagner, R Zimmermann, 'The Proposal for a Regulation on a Common European Sales Law: Deficits of the Most Recent Textual Layer of European Contract Law' (2012) 16 *Edinburgh Law Review* 301; Eidenmüller et al (n 13) 1077.

[16] s 23 No 1 Gerichtsverfassungsgesetz (GVG). In England and Wales, small claims courts handle cases up to a value of £10,000 (≈ €11,700), whereas Danish small claims courts' jurisdiction is restricted to a maximum amount in dispute of DKK 50,000 (≈ €6700). Lower maximum thresholds can be found in Northern Ireland and Scotland (£3000 ≈ €3500), Ireland (€2000), and Spain (€900). In the United States, maximum amounts in dispute also vary: For example, California small claims courts handle cases up to $5000 amount in dispute, while Illinois applies a maximum amount of $10,000.

[17] eg, Germany (s 78 Zivilprozessordnung (ZPO)), France (art 827 Code de procédure civile (CPC)), and the United Kingdom (customary right to self-representation) do not require parties to be represented by an attorney. In some small claims courts in the US, such as in California (California Code of Civil Procedure (Cal CCP) s 116.530), it is even forbidden to be represented by a lawyer in a small claims procedure.

payment procedure and a small claims procedure for claims with a value of up to €2000, which applies to all Member States except Denmark.[18] The goal is to make 'access to justice' a reality even for low-value claims. At the same time, reforms that have made the right to file a claim dependent on a previous unsuccessful settlement attempt or mediation have been repealed in many Member States—sometimes because such reforms were deemed unconstitutional for limiting parties' access to the courts.[19]

Even though Member States have made considerable advances to ease access to their respective small claims courts, the caseload of these courts is steadily decreasing. In Germany, for example, the caseload of the local small claims courts (*Amtsgerichte*) has declined continuously by more than two per cent per year over the last 10 years—despite significant GDP (Gross Domestic Product) growth rates.[20] This trend is a general one, that is it is visible also with respect to high-stakes B2B (Business To Business) disputes. However, it has become a specific *problem* only for consumers. The situation in other Member States is not different.[21] An explanation for this phenomenon could be that there are fewer and fewer small-stakes contracts or at least fewer and fewer conflicts arising out of these contracts. Both conjectures, however, are highly implausible. It seems much more

[18] The European order for payment procedure was established by Reg (EC) No 1896/2006 of the European Parliament and of the Council [2006] OJ L399/1. XE Kramer provided a first evaluation: XE Kramer, 'Enhancing Enforcement in the European Union: The European Order for Payment Procedure and Its Implementation in the Member States, Particularly in Germany, the Netherlands, and England' in CH van Rhee and A Ucelac (eds), *Enforcement and Enforceability—Tradition and Reform* (Antwerp, Intersentia Publishers, 2010) 17. The European small claims procedure was established by Reg (EC) No 861/2007 of the European Parliament and of the council [2007] OJ L199/1. See J Stuyck, E Terryn, V Colaert, T Van Dyck, N Peretz, N Hoekx and P Tereszkiewicz, 'An Analysis and Evaluation of Alternative Means of Consumer Redress Other than Redress Through Ordinary Judicial Proceedings' (European Commission, Health and Consumer Protection Directorate-General, 2007) ec.europa.eu/consumers/archive/redress/reports_studies/comparative_report_en.pdf; G Haibach, 'The Commission Proposal for a Regulation Establishing a European Small Claims Procedure: An Analysis' (2005) 13 *European Review of Private Law* 593.

[19] In Italy, the Corte Costituzionale (judgment dated 24 October 2012, file no 272/2012) struck down the statutory mediation requirement in late 2012; however, its re-introduction was enacted in June 2013; for a critical analysis, see G De Palo and LR Keller, 'The Italian Mediation Explosion: Lessons in Realpolitik' (2012) 28 *Negotiation Journal* 181. In Germany, most states (*Länder*) have cut back the statutory requirement (s 15a EGZPO) for smallest-stakes claims (amount in dispute lower than €750) to be conciliated or mediated before they can be brought to court.

[20] Statistisches Bundesamt, 'Fachserie 10, Reihe 2.1, Rechtspflege: Zivilgerichte' (Destatis, Wiesbaden, 2012) 12, www.destatis.de/DE/Publikationen/Thematisch/Rechtspflege/GerichtePersonal/Zivilgerichte2100210127004.pdf?__blob=publicationFile.

[21] In the United Kingdom, the number of small claims hearings decreased by almost one third within a decade, according to the Ministry of Justice. Ministry of Justice, 'Judicial and Court Statistics 2011' (National Statistics, 2011) 17, www.gov.uk/government/uploads/system/uploads/attachment_data/file/217494/judicial-court-stats-2011.pdf. A study on statistics of US small claims courts in 28 states showed an average 14% decrease in caseload between 2008 and 2010. See National Center for State Courts, 'Small Claims Fall Sharply in Last Two Years' (Court Statistics Project, 2013) www.courtstatistics.org/Civil/2012W5CIVIL.aspx.

likely that the transaction costs associated with going to court are prohibitively high for many consumers, and increasingly so: consumers have to spend a three-digit amount in court fees for most claims no matter how low the amount in dispute happens to be.[22] Consumers are mostly wary of bringing a suit without a lawyer, which generates expensive legal costs, and a significant amount of time is also invested in preparation, that is, opportunity costs are incurred that will often far exceed the amount in dispute.[23] Hence, using existing state court proceedings to solve these disputes seems to become increasingly inefficient.

The situation is even more problematic for distance transactions in general, and cross-border cases in particular. Here, the geographical distance between at least one party and the competent court, language differences and a lack of knowledge as to the applicable substantive law pose major obstacles that trigger even higher transactions costs for resolving disputes through the court system. No one, for example, will seriously consider suing a trader located in another Member State 1000 miles away for a defective Blu-ray player bought over the Internet for €100. It cannot be denied that this negatively impacts on trade and economic growth if no other efficient consumer rights enforcement and dispute resolution mechanisms are available.

C. Recent Legislation on Consumer Dispute Resolution

Against this background of increasing numbers of distance contracts and systemic deficiencies in the European Member States' small claims procedures, regulators all over the world are attempting to modernise consumer dispute resolution processes.

i. EU Legislation

As already mentioned, the EU has recently passed a Directive on Consumer ADR and a Regulation on Consumer ODR in order to weave the newly emerging conflict resolution schemes into a comprehensive system of alternative dispute resolution for B2C transactions.

The Directive aims to set up a network of locally available ADR entities to provide fast and low-cost dispute resolution for consumer conflicts arising out of sales and service contracts.[24] Traders need not participate, but, as

[22] Under German law (ss 3, 34, appendix 1 no 1210 GKG), eg, since 2013 even claims amounting to €1 or less result in court fees of more than €100.

[23] Only about one third of EU customers agree that it is easy to resolve disputes with sellers/providers through the courts. See Flash Eurobarometer 332 (n 10) 118.

[24] Directive on Consumer ADR (n 5) 70.

soon as they do, they must provide information on competent ADR entities on their homepage.[25] The EU wants every consumer to know about this low-threshold mechanism.[26] At the same time, the Directive is not targeted at taking cases away from the public small claims courts, but at settling cases that now remain unresolved.[27]

Parallel to the ADR Directive, the Regulation on Consumer ODR enables the EU to set up a Union-wide online platform for consumers, whereby consumers can easily obtain information on a competent ADR entity to handle their case and can immediately file an online complaint.[28] Both regulations, together, aim to build a comprehensive out-of-court consumer dispute resolution framework[29] to bridge the gap between direct negotiations between traders and consumers on the one hand, and the public courts on the other.

ii. United States Regulation

While the attempt to establish a cyber court in the state of Michigan was eventually abandoned in 2012, it is relevant to note that it would have only provided a framework for medium and large-stakes disputes.[30] And yet it might have served as a role model for a low-cost procedure for small claims, too. In any event, it seems unlikely that the technological build-up in US civil procedure will, in the medium term, exceed the scope of Federal Rule of Civil Procedure 43(a), which permits testimony by videoconferencing under certain circumstances.[31]

[25] ibid, 75–76.

[26] Ibid, 67–68.

[27] ibid, 68. Whether consumers can be forced into a consumer ADR procedure in standard terms is another issue. On this issue, see ibid at 70, 75 and see below section V, B, 3.

[28] This platform is quite similar to the one proposed by RC Bordone, already 15 years ago, which in turn referred to the famous (offline) multi-door courthouse idea, brought up by FEA Sander; RC Bordone, 'Electronic Online Dispute Resolution: A Systems Approach-Potential, Problems and a Proposal' (1998) 3 *Harvard Negotiation Law Review* 175, 199; FEA Sander, 'Varieties of Dispute Processing' (1976) 70 *Federal Rules Decision* 79, 131. The similar attempt by UNCITRAL to establish an ODR procedure has not yet been completed. See RA Brand, 'Party Autonomy and Access to Justice in the UNCITRAL Online Dispute Resolution Project' (2012) 10 *Loyola University Chicago International Law Review* 11. See also Working Group III, '2010 to Present: Online Dispute Resolution' (UNCITRAL, Working Group Documents) www.uncitral.org/uncitral/commission/working_groups/3Online_Dispute_Resolution.html.

[29] See Regulation on Consumer ODR (n 5) 4; Directive on Consumer ADR (n 5) 70 ('ensuring that consumers can … submit complaints … to entities offering … alternative dispute resolution procedures').

[30] See LM Ponte, 'The Michigan Cyber Court: A Bold Experiment in the Development of the First Public Virtual Courthouse' (2002) 4 *North Carolina Journal of Law & Technology* 51.

[31] This, however, already saves significant costs. For example, in Travis County, Texas, the so-called I-Jury Online Impaneling makes online answering of jury summons possible. This saves more than $100,000 per year in jury costs as unnecessary physical appearances are avoided. It also reduces the number of summons and the number of scheduled impaneling sessions, saving more than $25,000 per year in rent. See National Center for State Courts,

However, in the wake of the latest financial crisis, there has been increased public awareness of particular consumer needs such as protection against fraudulent financial investment advice. In 2010, Section 1011 of the Dodd-Frank Act laid the foundation for the formation of the Consumer Financial Protection Bureau (CFPB) in mid-2011, a federal agency responsible for consumer protection in the field of financial products and services. Amongst other services, the CFPB enables consumers to submit an online complaint on any bank-related issue such as money transfers, loans, mortgages, credit cards or credit reports.[32] The difference between the CFPB complaint and the EU ODR complaint is, however, that the EU service will not be restricted to financial issues and will not handle the complaint itself, but rather simply forward it to a competent ADR entity. A similar service does not exist in the US so far.

iii. Experience from Australia

Apart from the US and the EU, the country with the most significant experience regarding modern public small claims procedures is Australia. The Supreme Court of Victoria and the civil courts in Brisbane have experimented with facilitating court procedures through digital technology. However, the service currently provided is still restricted to comprehensive electronic document management support.[33] Other countries have mimicked this approach and have started electronic case filing at least for the written proceedings.[34]

For the time being, the efforts of public providers of innovative consumer dispute resolution have thus far been unsystematic. Legislators worldwide strive to make their judiciaries capable of competing with private dispute resolution providers. In order to avoid compromising fundamental due process values of civil procedure—while maintaining systemic coherence—there is a considerable need to define crucial principles of consumer rights dispute systems design for legislators to follow if they create new schemes of procedural consumer protection.

'Technology in the Courts', www.ncsc.org/Topics/Technology/Technology-in-the-Courts/Resource-Guide.aspx.

[32] See Consumer Financial Protection Bureau, 'Submit a Complaint', www.consumerfinance.gov/complaint/.

[33] See, eg, Queensland Courts, 'Electronic Trials (eTrials)' (2012) www.courts.qld.gov.au/information-for-lawyers/electronic-trials-etrials; Supreme Court of Victoria, 'E-Filing', www.supremecourt.vic.gov.au/home/forms+fees+and+services/efiling+and+case+management/.

[34] See, eg, Bayerisches Staatsministerium der Justiz und für Verbraucherschutz, 'Stand der Informationtechnik in der Bayerischen Justiz' (2013) www.justiz.de/BLK/laenderberichte/bayern.pdf (the AUGEMA programme facilitating the summons procedure in the central Bavarian court for decisions on summons in Coburg).

III. PRINCIPLES OF CONSUMER RIGHTS DISPUTE SYSTEMS DESIGN

To outline principles of consumer rights dispute systems design is a prescriptive rather than a descriptive task. This task does not focus on what new developments in the field of consumer dispute resolution *currently* look like, but on how dispute systems *should* be designed and which maxims they should follow. The term 'principles' in this regard means objectives and quality criteria that shape the design of a dispute resolution system and, consequently, its functioning.

A. Justice Criteria

The first fundamental set of principles that consumer rights dispute systems must reflect relates to questions of justice. Here, 'justice' comprises enforcement of substantive consumer rights, respect for established due process values, and access to judicial proceedings.

i. Consumer Rights Enforcement

It is not a matter of course that the enforcement of substantive consumer rights is or should be one of the guiding principles of consumer dispute resolution procedures.[35] Consumer satisfaction ranks high in current legal policy-making.[36] But while the meaning of this concept and its measurement are open to doubt, consumer satisfaction surely cannot be equated with the enforcement of consumer rights pure and simple.[37]

Especially in today's ADR world, parties' interests are widely held in higher esteem than their legal positions.[38] This is because interests are perceived to

[35] CJS Hodges, 'Collectivism: Evaluating the Effectiveness of Public and Private Models for Regulating Consumer Protection' in W van Boom and M Loos (eds), *Collective Enforcement of Consumer Law* (Groningen, Europa Law Publishing, 2007) 205, 207 (contends that 'the primary focus now is on improving the ability of consumers to realise their rights'). For a different focus, see L Mulcahy, 'The Collective Interest in Private Dispute Resolution' (2013) 33 *Oxford Journal of Legal Studies* 59 (who emphasises the value of precedence and of the collective interest in private adjudication).

[36] See, eg, IPSOS INRA, 'Consumer Satisfaction Survey' (European Commission, Health & Consumer Protection Directorat-General, 2007) www.ec.europa.eu/consumers/cons_int/serv_gen/cons_satisf/consumer_service_finrep_en.pdf; European Commission, 'Making Markets Work For Consumers: Questions and Answers on the 2011 Consumer Markets Scoreboard' (EU MEMO/11/718, 2011) 6, www.europa.eu/rapid/press-release_MEMO-11-718_en.pdf.

[37] According to Art 47 of the Charter of Fundamental Rights of the European Union, everyone whose rights and freedoms guaranteed by the law of the Union are violated has the right to an effective remedy before a tribunal. Consumer satisfaction does not necessitate such a right. Charter of Fundamental Rights of the European Union (2000/C 364/01) [2000] OJ L364/20.

[38] The importance of the parties' interests for value creation in conflict resolution has been stressed primarily by Fisher, Ury and Patton. See R Fisher, WL Ury and B Patton, *Getting to Yes* 2nd edn (London, Penguin Books, 1991). See also C Provis, 'Interests vs Positions: A Critique

be related to the future, which seems to matter more than succeeding in court, that is, successfully enforcing a right with respect to an issue relating to or having happened in the past. ADR proponents point out that parties to a conflict want to save time and transaction costs, eliminate litigation risk and maintain the relationship with their respective counterparts.[39] The latter aspect often plays an important role when parties decide to attempt mediation instead of bringing suit. However, the nature of the respective dispute has a considerable impact on the importance of this pro-ADR argument. The preservation of relationships is hardly relevant for consumers and thus, does not push in the direction of alternative dispute resolution in B2C conflicts. As long as they transact on a sufficiently competitive product or services market, consumers can immediately turn to other traders and will have no interest at all in maintaining a sound relationship with their counterparts.

This is especially true for distance contracts. Whereas in contracts among locals or within a small industry, parties might not want to burn bridges, a consumer can shop from an almost unlimited number of traders around the world. Thus, she can easily walk away at no cost; it is first and foremost the trader who is interested in a harmonious business–consumer relationship. This is all the more true as the vast majority of consumer disputes arise from alleged malperformance by the trader.[40] In this case, consumer confidence will have already been lost in most cases, and the customer will rarely ever contract with the business again. Hence, as long as the further interests of the consumer—a speedy and low-cost process at little risk—are met, consumer protection will mean enforcing consumer rights rather than reaching a consensus between business and consumer or realising some other diffuse idea of consumer satisfaction.

This argument is supported by research on the social costs and benefits of litigation. Beyond the individual interests of consumers, the social function of enforcing their rights is that only then will those rights be fully honoured by businesses. In other words, in case of suboptimal consumer rights enforcement, these rights will be diluted and hence will be the proper incentive for

of the Distinction' (1996) 12 *Negotiation Journal* 305 (critical on the differentiation between interests and positions).

[39] See P Cortés, 'The Potential of Online Dispute Resolution as a Consumer Redress Mechanism' (2007), www.ssrn.com/abstract_id=998865; see F Abedi and SSA Yusoff, 'Consumer Dispute Resolution: The Way Forward' (2011) 2 *Journal of Global Management* 204.

[40] Eurostat, 'Consumers in Europe' (Statistical Books, European Commission, 2009) 54, www.ec.europa.eu/eurostat/documents/3217494/5713579/KS-DY-09-001-EN.PDF/35c63f24-25fe-42a8-8ba3-8f4ff19ae3e9?version=1.0. In 2011, one out of five consumers experienced a delay in delivery, and one out of 20 consumers a complete failure of delivery from a distance contract with a contractor in the consumer's own country. See Flash Eurobarometer 332 (n 10) 92.

traders to respect them.[41] If a trader anticipates that, should she breach a contract, some alternative dispute resolution scheme will be in place leading to a compromise solution that does not fully compensate the consumer for the harm suffered, breach will occur even if it is inefficient. Hence, consumer dispute resolution systems should aim at full enforcement of substantive consumer rights.[42] Further, the enforcement of rights should be made public to establish precedential value.[43] A financial institution, for example, that violates fiduciary duties towards consumers in selling products to them that earn the institution a commission,[44] should be held accountable in all relevant cases. The institution's liability should not be limited to compensating an individual consumer who eventually dared to pursue her rights.[45] An individual enforcement level of significantly less than 100% can be tolerated only if it is compensated by complementary enforcement mechanisms, including, for example, unfair competition suits by competitors or forceful collective redress by consumer organisations.

Consequently, even though it is certainly true that consumers are primarily interested in getting good value for money and not in enforcing the law at all costs, a dispute system for B2C conflicts should, in principle, be rights-based.[46] Consumer rights, if honoured, delineate cases in which consumers do indeed get good value for money. By contrast, alternative dispute resolution procedures for B2C conflicts that are primarily aimed at satisfying the interests of the parties will usually produce compromise solutions that result in a suboptimal enforcement level, benefitting businesses yet harming consumers. Sure enough, the majority of cases brought to small

[41] S Shavell, 'The Social Versus the Private Incentive to Bring Suit in a Costly Legal System' (1982) 11 *Journal of Legal Studies* 333; S Shavell, 'The Fundamental Divergence Between the Private and the Social Motive to Use the Legal System' (1997) 26 *Journal of Legal Studies* 575; H Eidenmüller, *Vertrags- und Verfahrensrecht der Wirtschaftsmediation* (Köln, Otto Schmidt, 2000) 7.

[42] A necessary caveat to the statement in the text is that full enforcement of substantive consumer rights is warranted on efficiency grounds only if those rights are efficient in the first place—which is certainly not the case with respect to the existing European consumer rights acquis in its totality. See above s II.A.

[43] OM Fiss, 'Against Settlement' (1984) 93 *Yale Law Journal* 1073; DR Hensler, 'Our Courts, Ourselves: How the Alternative Dispute Resolution Movement Is Re-Shaping Our Legal System' (2003) 108 *Penn State Law Review* 165.

[44] For consistent case law by the German Federal Court of Justice (BGH) on this issue see Judgment dated 12 February 2004, file no III ZR 359/02, BGHZ 158, 110; Judgment dated 19 December 2006, file no XI ZR 56/05, BGHZ 170, 226; Decree dated 19 July 2011, file no XI ZR 191/10 (2011) 64 *Neue Juristische Wochenschrift* 3227.

[45] On the case of Crédit Suisse, see M Engel, 'Failure at the Lower Levels' (2011), www.ssrn.com/abstract_id=1927238.

[46] Hence, we strongly disagree with CJS Hodges, I Benöhr and N Creutzfeldt-Banda, who wish to 'go beyond the legal standards' and base decisions on codes of business practice, fairness, or equity. However, they also say that their 'position is somewhat confused'. See CJS Hodges, I Benöhr and N Creutzfeld-Banda (eds), *Consumer ADR in Europe* (Oxford, Hart Publishing, 2012) 412.

claims courts today also settle or otherwise do not proceed to judgment.[47] However, these settlements are usually reached following a clear judicial instruction regarding the merits and risks of the respective cases, thus in the darkest possible shadow of the law.[48] Hence, the outcome of small claims courts' proceedings is rights-based regardless of whether a judgment is delivered or not.

A further consequence of this assessment relates to the qualifications of persons that are competent to administer rights-based processes. Clearly, only trained jurists can be entrusted with this job. If the goal of the process is rights enforcement, only legal professionals are in a position to do justice to this goal.

ii. Due Process Values

Apart from the enforcement of substantive consumer rights, several due process values have emerged from the laws of civil procedure of many Member States that are reflected in primary and secondary EU law and thus belong to the 'procedural acquis' of the EU.[49]

Among these values are the neutrality of any involved third party or dispute resolution provider, adequate competence of such party regarding the respective resolution standard—which might be substantive consumer law—and her accountability. Accountability, here, is understood as referring to the responsibility of the dispute resolution entity for the results achieved and, as the case may be, the reversibility of decisions. If a decision hinges on the interpretation of European law, accountability involves referring a case to the European Court of Justice (ECJ). This indirectly ensures decision quality and uniform application of consumer law throughout the whole of the European Union.

In addition, accessibility of the relevant procedure is of increasing importance. Dispute resolution mechanisms must be easy to initiate, simple to conduct, available at no or low cost for consumers, etc. If such mechanisms involve large amounts of paperwork, a lengthy procedure drawn out over several months and a disproportionately high cost to the consumer (eg, €50

[47] See, eg, Ministry of Justice, 'Judicial and Court statistics 2011' (National Statistics, UK, 2012) www.justice.gov.uk/downloads/statistics/courts-and-sentencing/jcs-2011/judicial-court-stats-2011.pdf; Statistisches Bundesamt (n 20) 18.

[48] The term 'shadow of the law' was introduced by RH Mnookin and L Kornhauser. See RH Mnookin and L Kornhauser, 'Bargaining in the Shadow of the Law: The Case of Divorce' (1979) 88 *Yale Law Journal* 950.

[49] See T Andersson, 'Harmonization and Mutual Recognition' in MT Andenæs, B Hess and P Oberhammer (eds), *Enforcement Agency Practice in Europe* (London, British Institute of International and Comparative Law, 2005) 245–46; B Hess, 'Improving the Interfaces Between Arbitration and European Procedural Law' (2010) 6(1) *Les Cahiers de l'Arbitrage (Paris Journal of International Arbitration)* 17.

for the enforcement of a €100 claim), chances are high that the consumer will not pursue his claim.

The above-mentioned principles and values might be regarded as rules of law only applying to the judiciary in its traditional sense. However, since handling consumer conflicts along consumer rights will be widely perceived as a public task, it is paramount that legislators obey these due process values regardless of how the concrete dispute system eventually takes shape.

iii. Access to Justice

Apart from the enforcement of consumer rights and due process values, a third fundamental principle of justice in dispute systems design is unconditional access to justice.[50] Especially for typically weak parties, it is essential to have the right to be heard in court[51] and not to be deprived of the possibility to bring suit by the law or by a contractual provision agreed to without proper reflection.[52]

Access to justice is particularly important where businesses are generally allowed to unilaterally propose terms and conditions to the contract in the fine print. Since court proceedings entail unwanted publicity and may lead to disadvantageous precedents from the businesses' perspective, traders might try to exclude legal recourse in their standard business conditions and restrict complaints to alternative dispute resolution. Even though a consumer signs a contract indicating that she has read and accepts the general terms and conditions, it is commonly recognised that this is no meaningful form of consent; nobody truly studies these clauses in advance of signing. Hence, consumers also typically do not wish to waive their right of access to justice because they happen to have signed a contract purporting a waiver of that right. However, if they later find themselves in an alternative dispute

[50] This principle is also rooted in Art 6(1) of the European Convention on Human Rights. See GP Calliess, 'Online Dispute Resolution: Consumer Redress in a Global Market Place' (2006) 7 *German Law Journal* 647–48; P Cortés, 'Developing Online Dispute Resolution for Consumers in the EU: A Proposal for the Regulation of Accredited Providers' (2011) 19 *International Journal of Law and Information Technology* 1, 4–6.

[51] Hence, we understand justice as being provided by the state by conceptual necessity. By contrast, J Malbon believes that justice can also be supplied by out-of-state courts. J Malbon, 'Consumer Complaints' in J Malbon and L Nottage (eds), *Consumer Law and Policy in Australia and New Zealand* (Sydney, The Federation Press, 2013) 339, 358.

[52] See European Union Agency for Fundamental Rights, 'Access to Justice in Europe: An Overview of Challenges and Opportunities' (2011) www.fra.europa.eu/sites/default/files/fra_uploads/1520-report-access-to-justice_EN.pdf. For the respective discussion in the United States, see RM Alderman, 'The Future of Consumer Law in the United States—Hello Arbitration, Bye-Bye Courts, So-Long Consumer Protection' (2007), www.ssrn.com/abstract_id=1015517.

resolution procedure, they are prevented from exactly such access, at least for as long as the procedure lasts or as long as they cannot terminate it.[53]

B. Efficiency Criteria

Apart from questions of justice, efficiency plays an important role in modern dispute systems design.[54] Efficiency means maximising social welfare on a cost–benefit basis.[55] On the benefits side, fully enforcing consumer rights is, as already discussed, not only a justice issue but also mandated on efficiency grounds. Further, conflict resolution procedures differ in how well they protect a party's reputation, which secures future business. This, however, does not imply that processes and results should be kept confidential. First, as already discussed, protecting one's reputation usually is important only for traders because, other than businesses which are regularly rated in review sites, consumers rarely 'carry around' a negative reputation as a contracting party.[56] Second, securing future business is not an end in itself. On efficiency grounds, market participants who generate business only by engaging in dubious or even fraudulent practices should rather be forced to leave the market.

On the costs side, the law generally should reduce transaction costs and thereby facilitate trade.[57] Conflict resolution costs comprise the direct system costs associated with the procedure and its administration and supervision, regardless of whether these are borne by both parties, one of the

[53] Hesitant, but generally open to dispute resolution clauses in standard terms, LK Hofmeister, *Online Dispute Resolution bei Verbraucherverträgen* (Baden-Baden, Nomos, 2012) 326.

[54] L Susskind and J Cruikshank, *Breaking the Impasse: Consensual Approaches to Resolving Public Disputes* (New York, Basic Books, 1987) 21–26. See CA Costantino and C Sickles Merchant, *Designing Conflict Management Systems: A Guide to Creating Productive and Healthy Organizations* (San Francisco, Jossey-Bass Publishers, 1995) 171–72, 194–96; S Smith and J Martinez, 'An Analytic Framework for Dispute Systems Design' (2009) 14 *Harvard Negotiation Law Review* 123; O Rabinovich-Einy and E Katsh, 'Technology and the Future of Dispute Systems Design' (2012) 17 *Harvard Negotiation Law Review* 151.

[55] See Oxford Dictionaries, 'Efficient', www.oxforddictionaries.com/definition/english/efficient (referring to maximum productivity). See also A Sen, 'The Concept of Efficiency' in M Parkin and AR Nobay (eds), *Contemporary Issues in Economics* (Manchester, Manchester University Press, 1975) 196; H Eidenmüller, *Effizienz als Rechtsprinzip* 3rd edn (Tübingen, Mohr Siebeck, 2005) 41.

[56] Even where generating negative customer reputation is feasible, market organisers step back. An interesting example of this phenomenon is the feedback rating on eBay. Since 2008, sellers can only give positive feedback to buyers, whereas buyers can still rate a business negatively. An exception to this asymmetric policy is credit-reporting schemes, which allow banks to determine whether a potential customer has a low creditworthiness.

[57] This recommendation is rooted in the Coase Theorem. See R Coase, 'The Problem of Social Cost' (1960) 3 *Journal of Law & Economics* 1; Eidenmüller (n 55) 63; Calliess (n 50) 658.

parties or a third party, such as the general tax payer (for example, in case of legal aid awarded to one of the parties). Moreover, there are usually substantial opportunity costs, most notably the time that parties must invest in the process. Procedural efficiency is increased where dispute resolution is not only free of unnecessary cost drivers and redundant complexity, but also fast and reliable.[58] Together with the tenet of a rights-based solution, this provides the background for a coherent model for a consumer rights dispute system in B2C transactions.

IV. A MODEL FOR A CONSUMER RIGHTS DISPUTE SYSTEM IN B2C TRANSACTIONS

Against this background, a sound normative model for a consumer dispute system would be comprised of a low-entry initiation mode, a simple but rights-based resolution procedure, the observance of due process standards and the quick enforceability of results.

A. Initiation

Initiation of the dispute resolution procedure must be comprehensible to the 'average consumer' with modest means and without the assistance of a lawyer. Currently, the best way to realise this is an online standard complaint form that an aggrieved individual can complete on her own by entering her basic data and the reasons for the complaint. The complaint form must not be complex; it is to collect only the most fundamental facts and allegations of the case. It should further involve the capability to upload documents to support the alleged claim.

The value of this kind of complaint form essentially depends on its actual accessibility to the consumers. This fundamentally means that the average consumer should know about the chance to initiate dispute resolution in this way. This in turn presupposes sufficient information, not only from state agencies or consumer organisations, but also from the involved trader himself.

[58] On the importance of technology in saving procedural costs, see DA Larson, '"Brother, Can You Spare a Dime?" Technology Can Reduce Dispute Resolution Costs When Times Are Tough and Improve Outcomes' (2011) 11 *Nevada Law Journal* 523. It is, however, not a necessity that the procedure be free for consumers; contrary to the opinion of Z Tang, this can even cause perverse incentives for the consumer. Z Tang, 'An Effective Dispute Resolution System for Electronic Consumer Contracts' (2007) 23 *Computer Law & Security Review* 42, 48.

B. Resolution Procedure

The core model procedure of consumer dispute resolution would begin with an asynchronous online exchange between both parties aimed at resolving the issue through plain communication. The trader should be given the possibility to respond to the consumer's argument and to upload relevant documents on his part within 10 business days. Still, the complexity of the process should be limited. A well-structured online tool that contrasts the opinions of both parties and accentuates shared views as well as disagreements can help keep the conflict matter manageable.[59]

It is debatable whether the model procedure should allow for the taking of evidence. To include such procedural steps means to considerably increase the complexity of the system at the risk of the consumer no longer finding her way through the process. Also, evidentiary issues rarely arise in practice, as most cases can and will be resolved by acknowledgement, waiver or another form of settlement. On the other hand, excluding questions of proof from the model procedure might provoke abusive consumer complaints with customers opportunistically alleging business malperformance in order to compensate for their own mistakes. A compromise in this regard would be a procedure that does not include evidentiary issues but that allows the case to be referred to a different, more elaborate process if the conflict is escalated to a level on which issues of proof become decisive.

C. Enforcement and Publication

Eventually, the outcome of the dispute resolution should be binding at least on the business and also easily enforceable. Even for small claims, consumers must be able to mandate a marshal to collect the debt with the full force of the public enforcement machinery, if necessary. Only then does the process give both parties a strong incentive to comply with the procedural outcome.

Apart from that, if the outcome of the dispute resolution scheme is not a settlement but the decision of a third party, it should be published so that other traders and consumers can adjust their behaviour to the new precedent. The publication of results is also important because it helps dispute resolution providers arrive at consistent decisions that do not contradict each other. Finally, it also serves to vindicate crucial public policies and principles beyond the private interests of the parties, such as antitrust laws, which are easily violated in non-public settlements.[60]

[59] A good, although not perfect tool is the recently modernized Juripax technology. See https://web.archive.org/web/20150502180929/http://www.juripax.com/EN/software.php.

[60] Hensler (n 43) 196 (calling this 'achiev[ing] social change').

This brief sketch of a model consumer conflict resolution procedure raises the question of where this dispute system should ideally be set up, that is, who should administer it. Which entity is best equipped to establish a rights-based, low-cost dispute resolution procedure that observes due process standards and can lead to an easily enforceable and public award? The answer to this question is simple: It is the state. The model described is a modern court proceeding for small claims in B2C disputes. It is the public courts who are in a unique position to enforce consumer rights. Failure in the modernisation of civil procedure in many Member States should not lead the legislature to remove public courts' involvement in small claims procedures and to allocate original tasks of the judiciary to private service providers.[61] This even holds true in the international realm with its idiosyncratic procedural problems: Just because cross-border rights enforcement poses a legislative challenge, there is no reason whatsoever to lower the sights and set the goal of proper rights enforcement aside.

V. A CRITIQUE OF THE RECENT EU LEGISLATION ON CONSUMER ADR AND ODR

Against this background, the recent EU legislation on consumer ADR and ODR raises major concerns as to the enforcement of mandatory consumer rights, the compliance with fundamental values of due process, and the efficiency (welfare) effects associated with it.

A. Visions for Viable Consumer Dispute Resolution

The EU model for a Union-wide consumer dispute resolution system is composed of local dispute resolution entities established by the Member States in accordance with the Directive on Consumer ADR and an online clearinghouse set up by the EU itself following the Regulation on Consumer ODR. The underlying vision of this model is to build a new civil justice system not based on courts, but rather, on private or semi-private settlement and decision bodies operated by chambers of commerce, trade associations, consumer organisations, or entirely private service providers.[62] The EU aims

[61] This problem is not sufficiently reflected in the otherwise prudent proposal by P Cortés. See P Cortés, 'Developing Online Dispute Resolution for Consumers in the EU: A Proposal for the Regulation of Accredited Providers' (2011) 19 *International Journal of Law and Information Technology* 1.

[62] See Directive on Consumer ADR (n 5) 64 ('system of redress'); ibid, 68 ('ADR procedures should not be designed to replace court procedures'). See also Regulation on Consumer ODR (n 5) 3. Currently, about half of the existing ADR entities notified to the European Commission are based in Germany. However, German ADR entities are less focused on consumers,

to achieve full regional and sector coverage of those services throughout all Member States so that consumers can consistently choose a cheap and accessible alternative to the formalised small claims procedure in public courts.[63] The EU envisions a collaborative relationship between consumers, traders and regulators, which might in the future even impose an obligation to use the alternative system before bringing suit.[64]

The EU vision is not the one and only alternative. It is also conceivable, and indeed quite realistic, for there to be massive improvements in the existing small claims court systems in the Member States. Such improvements would, inter alia, result in more efficient court proceedings and the use of modern technology for case filings as well as for the conduct of hearings. Legislators might also consider the use of new public enforcement mechanisms, such as collective redress, punitive damages, consumer advocates,[65] public shaming and similar measures, to make up for individual enforcement deficits. Indeed, the EU now, at least very cautiously, recommends that Member States introduce collective redress schemes.[66] Finally, court modernisation could be pushed and supported by innovation in private dispute resolution services. Such services could and should coexist beneficially with the public courts.[67]

B. Adherence to Fundamental Principles of Procedural Quality

Whereas the latter vision fully respects and adheres to fundamental principles of procedural quality, the recent EU regulation does so only to a very limited extent.

and thus, play a less important role than the highly frequented ADR bodies in other countries, eg, the Financial Ombudsman in the United Kingdom handling alone about one-fifth of about 0.5 million cases per year in the EU; Alleweldt (n 41) 13.

[63] Directive on Consumer ADR (n 5) 66, 71.

[64] CJS Hodges, 'Consumer ADR in Europe' (2012) 11 *Zeitschrift für Konfliktmanagement* 195, 196.

[65] See L Nottage, 'The New Australian Consumer Law: What About Consumer ADR?' (2009) 9 *Queensland University of Technology Law and Justice Jounal* 176, 192; Malbon and Nottage (n 51) 350.

[66] See Directive on Consumer ADR (n 5) 66. See also Commission, 'Recommendation of XXX on Common Principles for Injunctive and Compensatory Collective Redress Mechanisms in the Member States Concerning Violations of Rights Granted Under Union Law' COM (2013) 3539/3.

[67] Typically, private adjudication schemes will follow economic considerations rather than public court procedures. See WM Landes and RA Posner, 'Adjudication as a Private Good' (1979) 8 *Journal of Legal Studies* 235. This, however, does not necessarily weaken the case for the courts; it only emphasises the function of private providers to serve as a potential (technological) role model.

i. Justice

Given that consumer justice demands rights-based proceedings, mandatory consumer rights should be enforced by judges or other legal professionals who possess a keen understanding of the law and operate on the basis of fundamental due process principles. In stark contrast, the EU regulation requires natural persons in charge of consumer ADR to only have a general understanding of the law.[68] This is an extremely vague standard. It is also clearly not a qualification that supports the full enforcement of consumer rights.[69] Rather, it aims at raising consumer satisfaction—whatever that means and however it is measured—under the guise of consumer protection.[70]

It is also questionable how Member States will effectively monitor the performance and neutrality of dispute resolution providers if they decide or settle disputes according to criteria that have not been transparently established beforehand.[71] Any result may be justified or rationalised as increasing consumer satisfaction. The existing ombudsman entities employ numerous employees whose qualification to handle complicated legal issues is doubtful. Whereas the head ombudsman is often a renowned jurist,[72] there is no transparent mechanism to ensure appropriate staffing.[73] Further, enforcing private providers' decisions in contested cases will certainly not be easier and often will be more difficult than enforcing a small claims court judgment.[74]

[68] See Directive on Consumer ADR (n 5) 72.

[69] However, CJS Hodges argues that the 'advantage of ADR mechanisms is that they are essentially outside national court systems'. Hodges (n 35) 205, 226. This is a distinct disadvantage if the mechanism in question is a rights-based dispute resolution procedure that is administered by non-legal providers.

[70] Against the background of the UNCITRAL ODR Project, R Brand argues that access to courts is not access to justice and that only an easily accessible ODR scheme could offer 'the hope of real justice'. Brand (n 28) 11. Similarly, J Hörnle sees 'greater access to justice' through out-of-court ODR. J Hörnle, *Cross-Border Internet Dispute Resolution* (Cambridge, Cambridge University Press, 2009) 89. This understanding of justice seems questionable as it reloads the concrete and traditional idea of justice with the abstract and vague standard of consumer satisfaction.

[71] Close monitoring of the qualification of neutrality is especially important where the respective dispute resolution mechanism was not chosen by both parties. See F Steffek et al, 'Guide for Regulating Dispute Resolution (GRDR): Principles and Comments' in F Steffek and H Unberath (eds), *Regulating Dispute Resolution: ADR and Access to Justice at the Crossroads* (Oxford, Hart Publishing, 2013) 13, 26.

[72] For example, the Danish Consumer Ombudsman was previously Head of the Property Law Division in the Danish Ministry of Justice; the German Insurance Ombudsman previously served as President of the German Federal Supreme Court.

[73] It is quite telling that the 'Competency Model' set out by the UK Legal Ombudsman splendidly rolls out numerous factors of the staff's competencies on 11 closely typed pages—without mentioning legal skills at all. See Legal Ombudsman, 'Competency Model' (2010), www.legalombudsman.org.uk/downloads/documents/job_docs/OLC_Competency_Model.pdf.

[74] It is, however, not impossible that decisions by private dispute resolution providers come with higher voluntary compliance. See Hodges (n 64) 197.

Finally, the new EU system appears to violate core procedural values such as the right to be heard in court, the possibility to appeal, and the public accountability of decision makers.[75] Whereas the ECJ currently ensures consistent consumer law application throughout the whole EU, referring cases to ADR entities creates significant fragmentation as to the interpretation and application of consumer rights. The consumer dispute system designed by the EU promises effective consumer protection but will yield hardly more than effective consumer sedation.

ii. Efficiency

In terms of procedural efficiency, the EU scheme indeed facilitates complaint filing by making use of modern communication technology. It also aims at offering a fast-track procedure that is simple to initiate and easy to comprehend, even for the average consumer. Moreover, traders who participate in the alternative dispute resolution scheme have to provide information to competent ADR entities so that factual obstacles to the procedure are reduced.

At the same time, the regulatory burden for setting up the EU mechanism is huge. Public authorities in all Member States will have to supervise private ADR providers, their expertise, independence, impartiality and effectiveness. The EU itself must not only build an online platform for conflict allocation; it must also create an online case management tool for a comprehensive electronic handling of cases. Hence, a new court-like system will emerge next to the small claims courts in every Member State. This will result in an inefficient duplication of resources. It would be much more prudent and efficient to modernise the existing judicial infrastructure in the Member States and provide a court-run, electronic small claims procedure based on the model sketched above.

This rival vision of improving the existing court system builds on the independence and expertise of judges instead of setting up a completely new infrastructure that would be difficult to monitor. It also facilitates competition between state and private proceedings and uses this competition as a discovery process:[76] if private dispute resolution providers come up with innovative (technical) solutions, these elements may later be adopted in the state proceedings. Such competition is, unfortunately, stifled by regulating consumer ADR and ODR in the way the EU currently does.

[75] The example of the Irish Financial Services Ombudsman shows that accountability of the ADR entities and reversibility of decisions does significantly lower the desirability of a scheme: In 2010, only about one out of three complaints was eventually decided by the Ombudsman. See Financial Services Ombudsman, 'Financial Services Ombudsman Annual Report 2010' (2011) 17, www.financialombudsman.ie/documents/FSO_AR_2010_EN_WEB.pdf.

[76] The value of competition as a 'discovery process' was first highlighted by FA von Hayek. FA von Hayek, *Freiburger Studien* (Tübingen, Mohr Siebeck, 1969) 249.

iii. Access to Justice

A further, but no less pressing, aspect is compliance with the fundamental right of access to justice. Article 1 of the Directive on Consumer ADR emphasises that the use of alternative dispute resolution be voluntary for the consumer and should not prevent her from exercising her right of access to the judicial system. Similarly, Article 10(1) states that Member States

> shall ensure that an agreement between a consumer and a trader to submit complaints to an ADR entity is not binding on the consumer if it was concluded before the dispute has materialized and if it has the effect of depriving the consumer of his right to bring an action before the courts for the settlement of the dispute.[77]

Prima facie, this suggests that consumers cannot be pulled into an ADR procedure in the general terms and conditions of a trader. However, on a closer look, the issue is not that simple. Recital 45 of the ADR Directive makes it quite clear that the wording in Article 10(1) only relates to ADR procedures that *permanently* take the case out of the state court system such as arbitration:

> In cases where a dispute could not be resolved through a given ADR procedure whose outcome is not binding, the parties should subsequently not be prevented from initiating judicial proceedings in relation to that dispute.[78]

In other words, a mediation or conciliation clause in a trader's general terms and conditions would not fall foul of the Directive on Consumer ADR.

Sure enough, the Directive 93/13/EEC on unfair terms in consumer contracts includes provisions against unfair small print in consumer contracts. Article 3(3), Annex (1)(q) suggests that a clause may be regarded as unfair if it excludes or hinders the consumer's right to take legal action. Nevertheless, arbitration clauses are not necessarily invalid because legal action is broadly understood in Annex (1)(q) to mean any procedure that is 'covered by legal provisions', and arbitration surely will, in most cases, be covered by such provisions. It is a question of the applicable national consumer protection law whether such a clause is invalid or not.[79] Most Member States' laws guard the consumer against unexpected arbitration clauses and deem them void.[80] Against this background, the new Directive on Consumer ADR does not provide additional protection.

[77] Directive on Consumer ADR (n 5) 75.

[78] ibid, 68.

[79] Case C-168/05 *Elisa María Mostaza Claro v Centro Móvil Milenium SL* [2006] ECR I 10421 (concerning a mobile phone contract with an arbitration clause); G Wagner, 'Keine Präklusion des Einwandes der Nichtigkeit einer Schiedsvereinbarung wegen Missbräuchlichkeit in Verbraucherverträgen' (2007) 5 *German Arbitration Journal* 49. On mandatory binding arbitration in consumer disputes, see EG Thornburg, 'Going Private: Technology, Due Process, and Internet Dispute Resolution' (2000) 34 *UC Davis Law Review* 151.

[80] See BGH (2005) 58 *Neue Juristische Wochenschrift* 1125. (In Germany, for example, s 1031(5) of the Code of Civil Procedure provides that consumer arbitration clauses must be

Temporary action waivers such as waivers associated with a mediation or other ADR procedures not binding on the consumer are a different matter, however. In most Member States, these waivers are unobjectionable even if included in the general terms and conditions of a trader. Moreover, they do not violate Annex (1)(q) of Directive 93/13/EEC as consumers maintain the right to bring suit once alternative dispute resolution has failed.[81]

However, the said waivers are hardly less problematic: They urge consumers to try alternative dispute resolution,[82] and even though consumers may initiate adversarial proceedings thereafter, they will not pursue such proceedings in most cases. As every mediation practitioner will confirm, it takes a lot of stamina and determination to fight a 50/50 settlement proposal achieved as the outcome of a consensual and often laborious procedure—stamina and determination that the average consumer typically does not have.[83] And even if the consumer completely loses out in an ADR procedure, she will likely be prevented from going to court. After all, if one 'expert' already told her that she has no case, why would she go through all the hassle and costs again, only to be told a second time?

At the same time, this dispute system is highly attractive for businesses. By pushing cases into ADR schemes, they can minimise the risk of negative publicity associated with public proceedings that highlight illegal commercial practices. The most active and stubborn consumers will be paid off—in secrecy, and possibly only partially. No effective sanctions will be administered in the great mass of the cases. At the same time, advocating ADR schemes as effective consumer dispute resolution tools appears to be an accommodating policy position. It significantly reduces the political pressure to introduce public collective redress schemes in the European Union that would effectively address the issue of mass damages in consumer contracts—apparently the nightmarish litigation risk of businesses.[84]

stipulated separately in order to be valid). The English Regulation from 1999 implementing Dir 93/13/EEC states that binding arbitration clauses shall be void except if negotiated individually. See Codice dei Consumatori, Art 36(2) (It), www.andec.it/public/80%2004-Codice_del%20 Consumo%20_En.pdf?idPP=1365&idPulsante=861 (Italy goes one step further by declaring the respective standard business conditions void even if it was negotiated individually).

[81] Case C-317/08 *Rosalba Alassini v Telecom Italia SpA* [2010] ECR II-3989 (concerning contracts for the provision of telephone services, including a clause making reference to the court proceedings conditional upon an attempt to settle the dispute out of court). See, eg, G Wagner, *Prozessverträge* (Tübingen, Mohr Siebeck, 1998) 445; Eidenmüller (n 41) 14.

[82] Steffek et al (n 71) 13, 29 (postulating the principle of 'initiation control' which is hardly compatible with the urge towards an out-of-court procedure).

[83] See H Roth, 'Bedeutungsverluste der Zivilgerichtsbarkeit durch Verbrauchermediation' (2013) 68 *Juristenzeitung* 637, 643.

[84] *Am Express Co v Italian Colors Rest* [2013] 133 S Ct 2304 (confirming the validity of arbitration clauses in consumer contracts in the United States). See also PL Murray, 'Die Flucht aus der Ziviljustiz' (2006) 11 *Zeitschrift für Zivilprozess International* 295, 300.

This is all the more problematic if ADR entities predominantly deliver judgments or opinions in favour of traders—as they frequently do.[85] It is no wonder given that these entities are primarily financed by businesses. Even with these financial arrangements, ADR entities publicly stress their independence and neutrality, and there certainly is no strong empirical support thus far for the assumption that financing schemes might lead them to systematically discriminate against consumers. However, the bad taste prevails, especially where businesses own[86] a process of consumer rights enforcement.[87] Also, public courts are an institution, which is perfectly designed according to the principles of autonomous and unbiased decision-making. This calls for the judiciary to maintain full sovereignty over the interpretation and application of consumer protection law. To shift jurisdictional responsibilities to private or semi-private providers might improve access to some private form of justice in many Member States; but at the same time it will worsen access to independent public justice in countries with an efficient judiciary.[88] Public justice, however, serves an important role even where the amounts in dispute are low because with these kinds of disputes, the total societal damage is usually much larger. Just think of an unfair clause in a mobile phone contract that harms millions of customers, but where each individual customer only suffers a loss in the order of €1–€10.[89] To lure consumers into a settlement here is to seriously compromise consumer rights. In other words: If the EU aims at effectively protecting consumers, it should better guard against false settlement.[90]

C. The Call for the European Union

If the EU refrained from establishing an alternative small claims civil system, what could instead be done to foster innovative and efficient dispute

[85] See Ombudsmann für Versicherungen, 'Jahresbericht 2012', 89 (reporting that only 36% of consumer complaints against businesses, apart from life insurance complaints, brought to the German Insurance Ombudsman were completely or partly successful. In almost two out of three cases, the consumer completely failed and one out of four complaints was considered improper action and thus dismissed). See also P of Matravers, 'Alternative Dispute Resolution: An English Viewpoint' (2008) 74 *Arbitration* 406, 408 (saying of compulsory mediation in the UK: 'You can take a horse to water, but you cannot make it drink. To which those in favour of compulsory mediation reply, "yes, but if you take a horse to water it usually does drink"'.).

[86] See CA Costantino, 'Second Generation Organizational Conflict Management Systems Design: A Practitioner's Perspective on Emerging Issues' (2009) 14 *Harvard Negotiation Law Review* 81, 85 (on ownership of dispute systems to be designed).

[87] See AB Kinon, 'Power Before Interests in Dispute System Design' (2012) 17 *Harvard Negotiation Law Review* 273 (urging for increased awareness of power in dispute systems design in a slightly different context).

[88] Roth (n 83) 641. See generally Hodges (n 64) 197.

[89] Mulcahy (n 35) 66.

[90] This conclusion hints at the well-known article entitled 'Against Settlement' by O Fiss; see Fiss (n 43).

resolution procedures for consumer conflicts? What does the better role model for the EU itself look like?

In fact, the EU has only a limited capacity to influence the civil procedure laws of its Member States. The principle of conferral laid down in Article 5(2) Treaty on European Union (TEU) requires a specific legal basis for any action taken by the EU. A harmonisation measure regarding civil procedure laws cannot be based on Article 114 Treaty on the Functioning of the European Union (TFEU) on the establishment and the functioning of the internal market because the special competence of Article 81 TFEU rules out the application of Article 114 TFEU.[91] Article 352 TFEU does not allow for the harmonisation of civil procedure laws in the Member States either.[92] Hence, it is first and foremost Article 81 TFEU, which can serve as a legal basis for harmonising Member States' civil procedure rules. With respect to other ADR instruments, the EU has thus with good reason solely relied on Article 81 TFEU, for example, in the case of the European Mediation Directive.[93] However, this legislative competence of the EU is limited to cross-border cases. This constraint also holds for the conceivable introduction of a European class action. Against this background it is quite telling that the Commission did not even mention a legal basis in the TFEU when it recently recommended the consideration of common principles for injunctive and compensatory collective redress mechanisms in the Member States.[94]

Instead of considering measures not provided for in the TFEU, the EU would better act as a role model for the use of electronic infrastructure and similar improvements in small claims courts. A first step in this regard might be to streamline the procedure at the ECJ and the General Court, the two courts of the Court of Justice of the European Union. These courts eat up huge amounts of money from the Member States by using up to 13 judges per case and employing costly offline procedures that involve the presence of persons from many Member States as well as work for

[91] The ECJ has repeatedly decided that measures that come within the limits of a specific legislative competence cannot be based on Art 114 TFEU. See Case C-155/91 *European Commission v Council* [1993] ECR I-939; Case C-491/01 *The Queen v Secretary of State for Health ex parte BAT* [2002] ECR I-11543; Case C-411/06 *European Commission v Parliament & Council* [2009] ECR I-7585. See also S Leible and A Staudinger, 'Article 65 of the EC Treaty in the EC System of Competencies' (2001) 1 *The European Legal Forum* 225, 234 (referring to the principle of subsidiarity, Art 5(3) TFEU).

[92] Case C-436/03 *European Parliament v Council* [2006] ECR I-3733 (clearly stating that TFEU Art 352 does not allow for such harmonisation. Apart from that, the unanimity requirement of Art 352 TFEU often makes the Commission refrain from even attempting to make use of this legislative competence).

[93] See, eg, Council Dir 2008/52/EC of 21 May 2008 on certain aspects of mediation in civil and commercial matters [2008] OJ L136/3 (solely relying on Art 81 TFEU).

[94] Commission (n 66).

legions of interpreters. Furthermore, the EU could technologically update its own e-justice portal, including its small claims procedure.[95] By modernising the procedures already directly governed by EU law, the EU could set a good example and thereby even free up resources, which the Member States could use to improve the operation of their own small claims courts. The EU also could support and supplement the Member States in their attempts to trim their procedural laws. Such measures can easily be based on Article 169(2)(b) TFEU.[96] Member States who today refrain from modernising their small claims procedures because of lacking resources or legislative lethargy would then be encouraged to follow the lead by the EU and thereby help consumers to effectively pursue their rights.

VI. SUMMARY

With the Directive on Consumer ADR and the Regulation on Consumer ODR, the EU aims to create a new consumer conflict resolution scheme that satisfies the needs of businesses and consumers more effectively than the small claims courts in the Member States currently do. However, from the perspective of dispute systems design, this policy move is highly problematic. The benefit of easy accessibility of the new system comes with severe flaws:

i) The new system is not geared towards the *effective enforcement of consumer rights*. However, less than full enforcement compromises the EU's policy of protecting consumers in B2C transactions by mandatory substantive provisions. It also leads to inefficient behavioural incentives for traders.
ii) The new system also compromises *due process values*. The right to be heard, the right to appeal a judgment, the right to publicly criticise, the right to discuss the ADR procedure and its outcome, and the accountability of the neutral third party—all these are not necessarily guaranteed.
iii) The new system establishes a comprehensive, quasi-judicial landscape of ADR providers next to the courts. The private providers

[95] Interestingly, the Union's own small claims procedure, established in 2009, is rather an embarrassing role model for the handling of low-value disputes. See F Vicari, S Linkevicius, K Vaksmaa and P Stańczak, 'ECC-Net European Small Claims Procedure Report' (ECC-Net, 2012) 23, www.ec.europa.eu/consumers/ecc/docs/small_claims_210992012_en.pdf (establishing that only 12% of the Member States can confirm that more than five (!) cases have been initiated since 2009; the remaining Member States report up to five cases or that there are no data available).

[96] I Benöhr, 'Alternative Dispute Resolution for Consumers in the EU' in Hodges, Benöhr and Creutzfeld-Banda (n 46) 7.

must be heavily regulated to secure minimum service standards. The transaction costs associated with this are significant. This duplication of resources—public courts and heavily regulated private ADR providers—is *inefficient*.

iv) Finally, the new system will de facto prevent consumers from fighting an ADR decision or opinion even if it is non-binding on them. Hence, it is also highly problematic because it reduces *access to justice*.

The best institution to realise the goals of a rights-based and efficient consumer dispute resolution system is not a private or semi-private provider but the state. It is simply contradictory to craft a comprehensive set of substantive and mandatory consumer protection rights and then leave the enforcement of these rights to private or semi-private bodies whose independence and impartiality is questionable and who are staffed not necessarily with trained jurists but with 'professionals' who may only have some superficial understanding of the law. Mandatory consumer protection rights attempt to correct market failure. Enforcement of such rights should be entrusted to public courts, not returned to the market. The EU would do much better in modernising its own courts and proceedings and should work towards a Union-wide consensus for the modernisation of small claims courts procedures in all Member States.

6

Transformations in Public and Private Enforcement

CHRISTOPHER HODGES* AND NAOMI CREUTZFELDT**

THIS CHAPTER MAPS a series of major innovative developments that are occurring across Member States in the 'enforcement' of what has traditionally been considered to be public regulatory law and in the delivery of redress for breach of private consumer liability law. It notes the adoption of various techniques that deliver what is now called 'redress', irrespective of whether the actors, adjudicative forum or categorisation of the law involved might traditionally have been categorised as 'public' and 'private' 'enforcement'. Thus, it highlights a transformation in the traditional categorisation of substantive law into the binary distinction between public and private law, and its replacement by a functional approach in which the former categorisation is largely irrelevant, since various hybrids or combinations of public and private techniques come to the fore in order to deliver the desired outcome—that of redress.

I. THE TRADITIONAL BINARY CATEGORISATION

Traditionally, techniques to enforce law have been categorised into the two separate and distinct fields of 'public enforcement of public law by public authorities' and 'private enforcement of private law by private parties'. A classic example of public enforcement by public authorities is when the police or public prosecutor institute criminal proceedings in a criminal court. A public regulatory body can also, in some jurisdictions, commence criminal or administrative proceedings (in a criminal or administrative court). An example of private enforcement by private parties is when a private

* Research funding from the Swiss Reinsurance Company Limited, European Justice Forum, and law firm CMS.

** This work was supported by the Economic and Social Research Council (grant number ES/K00820X/1).

party whose substantive private law right has been infringed institutes a civil action in a civil court to vindicate it, often claiming compensatory damages or an injunction. In a number of situations, especially in collective actions, a representative or intermediary is required (representative association, third-party funder and lawyer).

These two traditional categories—public and private—involve three main aspects. First, the type of *substantive law* involved is categorised into public or private law. The public law category includes administrative and criminal law. Second, there is the categorisation of the *forum*, and hence of the procedure: a criminal/administrative tribunal or a court that adjudicates private rights. Third, there is the categorisation of the *actors* who instigate the proceedings: state officials (public prosecutors, regulatory agencies, the police) or private parties (and their representative intermediaries, lawyers).

However, examples discussed below show that mixed variations of all these three variables now exist. Thus, the public–private categorisation, in all three of the above aspects, has started to crumble. The examples below illustrate that in everyday enforcement of the law there is not necessarily a clear cut divide between public and private aspects in the substantive law, forum or actors involved, but rather a mixed approach. The real issue is *purposive*: what mechanism works best in delivering the ultimate desired outcome, whether it be behavioural compliance with regulatory requirements or providing redress for loss or damage?

Some examples of this hybrid or mixed new approach can be summarised as follows. First, in some jurisdictions, officials can now institute civil proceedings for civil sanctions in a civil court, instead of criminal proceedings in a criminal court for criminal sanctions. Second, private parties in many states can piggy-back a private claim onto the end of criminal proceedings, in which criminal courts can award compensation to victims of crime. The compensation might be based on public law provisions such as a 'compensation order', or on the private law of civil damages. Third, the process of adjudication by a court can be short-circuited in various ways. Criminal or administrative enforcement can be resolved by plea-bargains, involving undertakings as to future conduct or payment of fines and/or compensation. Civil proceedings can be avoided or ended through negotiation between the parties, perhaps involving the assistance of third parties such as through mediation or other 'alternative dispute resolution' (ADR) techniques. Similarly, fourth, the 'tribunal' that processes the complaint may be a state entity (court, administrative court/tribunal or some other tribunal), or a newer type of ADR entity, such as a public/statutory ombudsman or a private entity (arbitrator, private ombudsman, ADR entity, some other third party).

Not all of these new structures or new techniques currently exist in every Member State, but a survey across all Member States reveals a remarkable range of options. A considerable amount of innovation and experimentation is occurring. This chapter aims to map some of the main developments. It is not intended here to give a full picture of all such developments or a full picture of the status in every Member State. Rather, various particular examples have been selected in order to illustrate striking innovations.

II. REDRESS IN CRIMINAL PROCEEDINGS

The purpose of criminal sentencing in the UK was restated in 2003 in a striking fashion: the traditional value of 'punishment' remained, but added to it were the additional purposes of the reduction of crime (including its reduction by deterrence), the *reform and rehabilitation* of offenders, the *protection* of the public, and the making of *reparation* by offenders to persons affected by their offences.[1] A shift has occurred here from concepts of authoritarian enforcement and punishment towards softer techniques of responsive justice[2] and reparation by offenders.

This shift can be exemplified by the reformation and diversity of approaches now adopted towards payment of money to victims of crime. First, European jurisdictions have a long history of compensation for victims of violent crime, paid by the state, now subject to EU harmonisation.[3] Second, driven by a need to respond effectively to drug and mafia traffickers, legislation has emerged aimed at removing the proceeds of crime from offenders, removing what appear to be excessive assets on the basis that they are illicit 'lifestyle' proceeds of extensive and criminal activity.[4] Third, a policy has emerged of making those who commit crime compensate their victims. This approach is linked with the spread of restorative justice approaches to behaviour control, as alternatives to more authoritarian sentencing. In the UK, public authorities

[1] Criminal Justice Act 2003, s 142.

[2] See D Sullivan and L Tifft (eds), *Handbook of Restorative Justice* (Abingdon, Routledge, 2006); D Miers and J Willemsens (eds), *Mapping Restorative Justice: Developments in 25 European Countries* (Leuven, European Forum for Victim-Offender Mediation and Restorative Justice, 2004); I Aertsen, R Mackay, C Pelikan, M Wright and J Willemsens, *Rebuilding Community Connections—Mediation and Restorative Justice* (Strasbourg, Council of Europe, 2004). In the United Kingdom, restorative justice was first extensively used in relation to juvenile crime: see Home Office, *Restorative Justice: the Government's Strategy* (London, Home Office, 2003).

[3] Dir 2004/80/EC of 29 April 2004 relating to compensation to crime victims [2004] OJ L261/15, Arts 1 and 2. See also Council Framework Decision of 15 March 2001 on the standing of victims in criminal proceedings (2001/220/JHA), and Proposal for a Directive establishing minimum standards on the rights, support and protection of victims of crime COM(2011) 275 final, 18 May 2011. See also Council of Europe Recommendation No R(85) 11 on the position of the victim in the framework of criminal law and procedure; Recommendation No R(87) 21 on assistance to victims and the prevention of victimization; Recommendation No R(2000) 19 on the role of the public prosecution in the criminal justice system; and the European Convention on the compensation of victims of violent crimes (1983). In the UK see the Victims of Violent Intentional Crime (Arrangements for Compensation) (European Communities) Regs 2005/3396.

[4] See Dir 2014/42/EU of 3 April 2014 on the freezing and confiscation of instrumentalities and proceeds of crime in the European Union [2014] OJ L127/39. In the UK, confiscation orders, recovery orders and forfeiture orders under the Proceeds of Crime Act 2002, ss 6–13, 240–43, 266, 298. See also the Crime and Courts Act 2013, s 48.

may seek a compensation order as part of criminal enforcement, and from 2013 criminal courts are *required* to consider making a compensation order to victims.[5] Fourth, since the financial crisis, this has coincided with a desire to reduce public expenditure on compensation to victims of crime. An example is the UK extension of the 'victims' surcharge', in effect a statutory fine payable in addition to any penalty imposed by the court.[6]

In many Member States, those who have suffered damage may 'piggyback' a civil compensation claim onto a criminal prosecution through the *partie civile* mechanism. In essence, the private parties are saved the bother and expense of investigating and prosecuting a case, and their claims for damages will be adjudicated by the court (or a special civil master appointed and overseen by the criminal judge) in a second phase of the proceedings. Voet has described the use of this technique in various large cases in Belgium, where it was used to resolve mass damages claims since a private class action mechanism was not available.[7] Belgium found that the technique produced results but is considering introducing various improvements. Although the *partie civile* mechanism exists in many jurisdictions, Voet has identified that it is only where the criminal courts are *required* to resolve a civil claim by a private party (rather than having discretion not to do so) that the technique is used in large or mass cases. Adoption of such a wider approach may have advantages and is worth reviewing.

Thus, various mechanisms exist under which compensation may be claimed and paid to victims of crime in which it is unnecessary for the criminal and civil aspects and procedures to operate independently of each other. Various fused hybrid mechanisms exist, clearly in order to save costs and time. Such techniques are uncontroversial, and are quietly being extended.

III. REGULATORS' ENFORCEMENT POLICIES AND POWERS

In parallel with developments in criminal law, but to an even greater extent, enforcement policy and practice in regulatory law has also been transformed away from 'command and control' authoritarianism and 'deterrence'. Extensive academic research has found that many enforcers, in a range of different circumstances, have moved away from basing regulatory design on a theory of 'command and control' model and from basing enforcement policy on theories of deterrence or 'rational economic actors'. Instead,

[5] The Legal Aid, Sentencing and Punishment of Offenders Act 2012, s 63. See previously the Criminal Justice Act 2003, s 142(e).

[6] Anti-Social Behaviour, Crime and Policing Act 2014, s 179, amending the Criminal Justice Act 2003, s 161A.

[7] S Voet, 'Public Enforcement & A(O)DR as Mechanisms for Resolving Mass Problems: A Belgian Perspective' in C Hodges and A Stadler (eds), *Resolving Mass Disputes: ADR and Settlement of Mass Claims* (Cheltenham, Edward Elgar, 2013).

they adopt enforcement policies based on restorative justice and responsive regulation, and on behavioural psychology,[8] largely on the basis that such approaches have been found to be more effective in delivering *compliance*.[9] Such a shift opens the door to refocusing 'regulatory enforcement' away from the mirage that deterrence will affect behaviour in most situations and towards supporting arrangements that support compliance, education, constant learning and improvement. Such a shift therefore entails far less reliance on imposition of public penalties (as enforcement) and instead use of a range of 'smarter' tools that support particular *behaviour*.

Policies issued by the Organisation for Economic Co-operation and Development (OECD) have also stressed not only Better Regulation objectives of efficiency but also the advisability of adopting effective, evidence-based approaches to enforcement that promote compliance rather than merely sanction infringement.[10] OECD policy was highly influenced by policies developed in the UK and by responsive regulation theories and practices. The OECD has recently strongly recommended a responsive regulation approach to all member states.[11]

UK policy on regulatory enforcement was (re)stated by Macrory in 2006 to comprise six Penalty Principles:[12]

1. Aim to change the behaviour of the offender;
2. Aim to eliminate any financial gain or benefit from non-compliance;
3. Be responsive and consider what is appropriate for the particular offender and regulatory issue, which can include punishment and the public stigma that should be associated with a criminal conviction;
4. Be proportionate to the nature of the offence and the harm caused;
5. Aim to restore the harm caused by regulatory non-compliance, where appropriate; and
6. Aim to deter future non-compliance.

[8] Two accessible texts from a great volume of research are TR Tyler, *Why People Obey the Law* (Dartmouth CA, Yale University Press, 2006) and D Kahneman, *Thinking, Fast and Slow* (London, Allen Lane, 2011).

[9] The classic texts are I Ayres and J Braithwaite, *Responsive Regulation: Transcending the Deregulation Debate* (Oxford, Oxford University Press, 1992); J Braithwaite, *Restorative Justice and Responsive Regulation* (Oxford, Oxford University Press, 2002). For some examples see CJS Hodges, 'Encouraging Enterprise and Rebalancing Risk: Implications of Economic Policy for Regulation, Enforcement and Compensation' [2007] *European Business Law Review* 1231.

[10] Recommendation of the Council on Regulatory and Policy Governance (Paris, OECD, 2012); OECD Best Practice Principles for Regulatory Policy: Regulatory Enforcement and Inspections (OECD, 2014); Dispute Resolution and Redress. Review of the 2007 Council Recommendation (Paris, OECD, 22–23 April 2013).

[11] OECD Best Practice Principles for Regulatory Policy: Regulatory Enforcement and Inspections (OECD, 2014).

[12] R Macrory, *Regulatory Justice: Making Sanctions Effective* (London, HM Treasury, 2006); reprinted in R Macrory, *Regulation, Enforcement and Governance in Environmental Law* (Oxford, Hart Publishing, 2010).

Since then, all major UK regulatory authorities have been required to issue enforcement policies that conform to and take account of the Macrory Principles.[13] The introduction to the Code stressed:

> the need for regulators to adopt a positive and proactive approach towards ensuring compliance by:
>
> — helping and encouraging regulated entities to understand and meet regulatory requirements more easily; and
>
> — responding proportionately to regulatory breaches.[14]

Enforcers of regulatory law now have the ability to use not just criminal powers but also the alternative of *civil sanctions*, inspired by Macrory, including imposing discretionary requirements that the offender must take steps specified by the regulator, within a stated period, designed to secure (a) that the offence does not continue to recur (a 'compliance requirement') and (b) that the position is restored, so far as possible, to what it would have been if no offence had been committed (a 'restoration requirement').[15] If a person refused to comply with a discretionary requirement or undertaking, the enforcer could decide to bring a prosecution for the original offence.[16] A recodification of enforcement powers has extended policy and powers on securing redress and changes in behaviour.[17]

IV. REDRESS BY REGULATORS

The expansion of regulatory enforcers' policy from '(deterrent) enforcement' to supporting compliance inherently involved a focus on delivering good outcomes for the ultimate beneficiaries of regulation. Thus, considerations of reparation and redress arose, for example to benefit consumers who had been mis-sold insurance or financial products, or overcharged by energy companies, or to ensure that damage to the environment was not just sanctioned but repaired. Hence, enforcers' roles widened to include delivery of *restorative outcomes* as well as affecting economic operators' behaviour. Some regulators resisted such an expansion in their roles, which they regarded as

[13] Under the Regulatory Enforcement and Sanctions Act 2008, Legislative and Regulatory Reform Act 2006, s 22 (2) and (3), and Regulators' Compliance Code (2007), now Regulators' Code (Department for Business Innovation & Skills, 2013). For a review of the enforcement policies of various agencies see C Hodges, *Law and Corporate Behaviour: Integrating Theories of Regulation and Enforcement* (Oxford, Hart Publishing, 2015).

[14] Regulators' Code (n 13) para 1.3.

[15] Regulatory Enforcement and Sanctions Act 2008, s 42. See *Regulatory Enforcement and Sanctions Act 2008: Guidance to the Act* (London, Department for Business Enterprise and Regulatory Reform, July 2008) at www.berr.gov.uk/file47135.pdf.

[16] *Regulatory Enforcement and Sanctions Act 2008: Guidance to the Act*, ibid para 50. The coercive background is, therefore, strongly similar to the powers of Nordic Consumer Ombudsmen explained below.

[17] Consumer Rights Act 2015.

involving taking on aspects that were more appropriate if remaining in the traditional sphere of private law enforcement, that is through civil damages claims. But other regulators found that they could not only deliver mass redress effectively and efficiently, but do so more swiftly and at lower overall cost than if public and private aspects remained to be pursued through separate avenues. Further, *all* the behavioural, sanctioning, compliance and restorative aspects of a case could be resolved *together* at the same time through initiative taken by a regulatory authority that has sufficiently wide powers.[18] The leading exponents of this revolutionary innovative shift have been in Denmark and the UK.[19]

The Danish national consumer law enforcement officer (called, slightly confusingly, the Consumer Ombudsman) has a toolbox of enforcement powers, which include the normal prosecution powers but also, since 2005, the power to commence proceedings for mass redress. The redress power has confused some commentators, since it is contained in the Class Action Law: whilst any party affected may start a class action on an opt-in basis, only the Consumer Ombudsman may do so on an opt-out basis. As a result, almost no private class actions have been commenced in Denmark (a large bank case failed after several years' litigation). But instead, the Consumer Ombudsman uses the threat of his collective redress power regularly in enforcement discussions with traders. Since it is a powerful weapon amongst a powerful armoury, he has not yet had to commence redress proceedings, since traders agree settlements, which include *all* aspects, such as agreement to cease infringement, undertaking not to repeat, agreement to make changes in systems and practice, repayment of customers, and maybe public sanctions. This is an extremely efficient and effective system, and offers advantages for traders, consumers and the state.

The same approach has been adopted by virtually all public regulators in the UK. The history is complex and has taken several years to develop. The (former) Financial Services Authority has always possessed a wide range of investigation and sanctioning powers. As part of these, it has since 2000 had powers to seek or make a Restitution Order[20] and an order for a scheme that multiple firms review past business, which would determine the nature and extent of the failure, establish the liability of authorised persons to make compensation payments, and determine the amounts payable by way of compensation payments.[21] The mass redress power has proved to be effective in various cases, and avoided a need for those who had suffered loss to

[18] Such powers should be, and are, subject to effective transparency, and review of their exercise by courts, legislators and others: such matters are beyond the scope of this chapter.

[19] The authors have seen highly effective examples adopted by the Lithuanian Telecommunications Authority, and a less successful attempt by the Irish Financial Services Ombudsman.

[20] Financial Services and Markets Act 2000 (FSMA), s 383.

[21] ibid, s 404.

instigate private litigation. Arrangements agreed between the regulator and banks usually also included undertakings that specified behavioural changes would be implemented by the banks for their future conduct, so that the mischief would not be repeated. But use of these powers received little publicity until a series of major scandals in the trading activities of financial institutions came to light from the mid-2000s.

In 2010 the consumer redress scheme power was revised, and has now been widely and effectively used. The (new) Financial Conduct Authority (FCA) may make a consumer redress scheme[22] where it considers a widespread problem exists and a court would award redress to consumers.[23] The regulator can make rules requiring a relevant firm to establish and operate a consumer redress scheme, which may include requirements for the firm to investigate whether it has failed to comply with the law, to determine whether the failure has caused or may cause loss to consumers, to determine what the redress should be, and to make the redress to the consumers.[24] Where a consumer makes a complaint to the Ombudsman in relation to an act or omission of a firm that is covered by a consumer redress scheme, the Ombudsman is required to determine the complaint by reference to what, in the Ombudsman's opinion, the determination under the consumer redress scheme should be or should have been, and may make an appropriate payment award.[25] In effect, therefore, the Ombudsman applies the solution mandated by the regulator, and decides if the business has done what the regulator required.

Since 2010, compensation has been paid in a sequence of financial cases, either as a result of agreements between the financial services regulator and financial institutions, or as a result of the use of the formal powers. Like the Danish experience, the FCA finds that virtually all cases are resolved by agreement with banks: these wrap up agreements to desist in ongoing illegal activity such as mis-selling, to undertake not to repeat such activity, to clarify what internal changes are made to ensure and monitor such ongoing

[22] Financial Services Act 2010, ss 14 and 26(3), significantly extending s 404 of the FSMA. The new rules were brought into force from 12 October 2010 by The Financial Services Act 2010 (Commencement No 1 and Transitional Provision) Order 2010/2480. The FSA decided not to apply for civil sanction powers under the Regulatory Enforcement and Sanctions Act 2008 since it concluded that having them would not make a material difference to the effectiveness of its enforcement action.

[23] FSMA, s 404, as amended by Financial Services Act 2010, s 14: the power for the Authority to make rules requiring each relevant firm (or each relevant firm of a specified description) to establish and operate a consumer redress scheme arises where it appears to the Authority that there has been a widespread failure to comply with applicable requirements and as a result, consumers have suffered loss or damage in respect of which, if they brought legal proceedings, a remedy or relief would be available.

[24] FSMA, s 404(4)–(7). A firm may apply to the Tribunal for a review of any rules made by the Authority: s 404D.

[25] FSMA, s 404B. The award is subject to the Ombudsman's upper limit, but he may recommend that the firm pay a larger amount: s 404B(5) and (6).

behaviour, to submit to an agreed sanction such as a fine, and to pay redress to victims.

Outside the financial sector, a number of other regulatory agencies, operating in different sectors, have also been given extended powers to seek civil sanctions, which can include issuing restoration notices and accepting undertakings to compensate.[26] Similar mass redress powers to those of the FCA have been given to regulators in the energy sector so as to improve both payment of redress to consumers, and the regulator's leverage in bringing redress about.[27] Some regulators have brought about payment of redress without having formal redress powers but simply by leveraging their influence, and that of the ability to 'name and shame' traders who value their reputations in competitive markets.

For example, on 9 March 2012 the energy regulator, Ofgem, accepted an energy company's offer to invest £4.5 million to help vulnerable customers and consequently reduced a penalty for breach of marketing rules to £1.[28] In November 2012, Ofgem secured a commitment from E.ON to pay back around £1.4 million (an average rebate of £14.83, including eight per cent interest) to approximately 94,000 consumers who were incorrectly charged exit fees or overcharged following price rises that were incorrectly implemented too early.[29] In addition, E.ON agreed to make an additional payment of around £300,000 as a goodwill gesture to a consumer fund which they run in partnership with Age UK.[30]

The competition authority has also been given a somewhat complex redress power, although that technique has been somewhat overlooked because the focus has tended to be on the related introduction of an opt-out class action.[31]

In summary, it has been seen that both criminal and regulatory enforcement have diversified their policy objectives, enforcement policies and techniques. Public officials have assumed responsibility for delivering good *outcomes*, and this involves delivering redress. Where redress powers are

[26] Empowering Orders may be made under the Regulatory Enforcement and Sanctions Act 2008. Examples are The Environmental Civil Sanctions (England) Order 2010/1157 and The Environmental Civil Sanctions (Miscellaneous Amendments) (England) Order 2010/1159.

[27] Energy Act 2013. See the *Consultation on a Proposed New Power for Ofgem to Compel Regulated Energy Businesses to Provide Redress to Consumers* (Department of Energy and Climate Change, April 2012), 12D/060, available at: www.decc.gov.uk/assets/decc/11/consultation/4975-consultation-on-a-proposed-new-power-for-ofgem-to-.pdf.

[28] Details of Ofgem's decision are available at: www.ofgem.gov.uk/Media/PressRel/Documents1/EDF%20press%20notice%20March%209%202012.pdf.

[29] *Ofgem secures £1.7 million for consumers following E.ON error* (Ofgem press release, 27 November 2012), available at: www.ofgem.gov.uk/Media/PressRel/Documents1/20121127_EON_Press_Release.pdf.

[30] The Engage Fund, run in partnership with Age UK Group, helps fund services to maximise incomes of older people by providing benefits advice and financial help through benefits health checks carried out either face to face or by telephone in local Age UK offices enabling some to be lifted out of fuel poverty.

[31] Consumer Rights Act 2015.

well designed, they not only deliver redress swiftly and cheaply, avoiding any need for private enforcement, but also are more efficient in resolving the regulatory, behavioural aspects with those ongoing enterprises whose businesses are not inherently criminal.

The regulatory techniques are both powerful and effective. They deliver full compensation (without deduction of transactional cost) to consumers, often providing small individual amounts, very quickly, with minimal transactional cost to the public budget. The regulator can oversee that payments are made properly by traders, and take enforcement action where this is not done. The regulator is also in a position to engage in ongoing monitoring of traders' behaviour, to ensure that it has changed. The dual involvement of both a regulatory enforcer and an ombudsman is also highly significant, as discussed below.

V. ADR: MEDIATION, ARBITRATION AND ODR

Alternative dispute resolution (ADR), as its name implies, evolved as a means of avoiding courts and civil procedure in resolving civil disputes by adopting alternative means. ADR can also involve a number of *techniques* that can be deployed before or alongside a civil process, or in a discrete context, such as mediation, early neutral evaluation, mini-trial. Such techniques do not typically exist within particular permanent *structures*, such as exist for courts and arbitration 'courts'. EU support for ADR has been growing for some time.[32] Mediation has been adopted by the EU generically for cross-border claims, and includes requirements on confidentiality of processes and enforceability of agreements.[33] In common law judicial procedures it is enthusiastically supported but in some civil law jurisdictions it remains controversial.[34] Various national rules of civil procedure have been amended in the last decade to integrate the use of mediation with court-based claims. The influential pioneer was England and Wales in the fundamental reform of the Civil Procedure Rules introduced in 1999.[35]

[32] Commission Recommendation 98/257/EC on the principles applicable to the bodies responsible for out-of-court settlement of consumer disputes [1998] OJ L155/31; Commission Recommendation 2001/310/EC on the principles for out-of-court bodies involved in the consensual resolution of consumer disputes [2001] OJ L109, 56–61; European Code of Conduct for Mediators, 2004, see http://europa.eu.int/comm.justice_home/ejn/adr_ec_code_conduct_en.pdf.

[33] Dir 2008/52/EC of the European Parliament and of the Council of 21 May 2008 on certain aspects of mediation in civil and commercial matters [2008] OJ L136/3.

[34] See H Eidenmüller in this volume; G Wagner, 'Private Law Enforcement though ADR: Wonder Drug or Snake Oil?' (2014) 51 *Common Market Law Review* 165.

[35] Pursuant to Lord Woolf, *Access to Justice: Interim Report to the Lord Chancellor on the Civil Justice System in England and Wales* (London, HMSO, 1995) and Lord Woolf, *Access to Justice: Final Report* (London, HMSO, 1996). See D Dwyer (ed), *The Civil Procedure Rules Ten Years On* (Oxford, Oxford University Press, 2009).

A key feature of the English reform was to combine court procedure with mediation, and make settlement a formal goal of civil process. All these developments are well known and not discussed further here, save for a few observations.

Mediation involves the encouragement of negotiation with the aim of resolving disputes quickly and by agreement of the parties. This may result in settlements that are not necessarily wholly consistent with a strict, formal application of 'the law'. But maybe the parties do not wish to pay for a comprehensive investigation and adjudication into the rights and wrongs of the parties, and simply wish for a swift or cost-proportionate solution that is tolerably consonant with a law-abiding society. Justice comes at a price. Are judges always right? At what price? The key drivers in the innovation towards mediation are user-friendliness, less formality in procedure, and more humanity and accessibility.

Businesses or individuals whose rights have been infringed do not necessarily seek 'vindication of the law' through payment of full compensation in every case; they might want to be listened to seriously, to have their concerns heard, to receive an explanation of what happened and why, to have an 'opponent' apologise or undertake to behave differently in future, or to accept less by way of money than a strict application of the law would mandate. It may not be clear where right lies in a case, or it may be too complicated and expensive to deliver a forensically correct answer. Accordingly, claims have long been settled on the basis of negotiation and settlement. These factors underpin the rise in negotiation, plea-bargaining and mediation.

Arbitration is a form of ADR. It involves a distinct pathway and a tribunal that is separate from the system of state or international courts. It has long been widely accepted, especially for commercial disputes. More recently, online commerce has adopted an arbitration model under the title of ODR (online dispute resolution).[36] It is widely believed that the explosion of online trading across the world could not have occurred without support for the essential element of trust that an ODR system is believed to provide.[37] In fact, many such systems do not incorporate a dispute resolution or decision-making mechanism, but are based on feedback of customer complaints and the threat that publication of adverse comments would attract disciplinary action by the trading platform provider.

[36] See J Hörnle, *Cross-Border Dispute Resolution* (Cambridge, Cambridge University Press, 2009); P Cortés, *Online Dispute Resolution for Consumers in the European Union* (London, Routledge, 2011).

[37] L Del Luca, C Rule and Z Loebl, 'Facilitating Expansion of Cross-Border E-Commerce—Developing a Global Online Dispute Resolution System (Lessons Derived from Existing ODR Systems—Work of the United Nations Commission on International Trade Law)' (2012) 1 *Penn State Journal of Law & International Affairs* 59.

VI. CONSUMER ADR

Consumer ADR is easily confused with ADR and mediation but although consumer dispute resolution (CDR) uses classical ADR *techniques*, such as mediation or some form of adjudicative decision-making, it occupies its own permanent *structures* in Europe. For cross-border claims, a network of national European Consumer Centres (ECC-Net)[38] and related system for financial claims (FIN-Net)[39] were created, to advise, signpost and facilitate negotiation and resolution of consumer disputes. Issues over the misapplication of Internal Market law by public authorities are facilitated through the SOLVIT[40] network, created in 2002 as a free-of-charge online problem solving network in which EU Member States work together to solve problems without legal proceedings. ADR has been encouraged or mandated in sectoral legislation for a significant number of types of disputes, including E-commerce,[41] markets in financial instruments (MiFID),[42] postal services,[43] general services,[44] payment services,[45] consumer credit,[46] telecoms,[47] energy,[48] bus and coach passenger rights[49] and mortgages.[50]

[38] Council Resolution of 25 May 2000 on a Community-wide network of national bodies for the extra-judicial settlement of consumer disputes [2000] OJ C155/1. See www.eejnet.org/filing_complaint.

[39] See ec.europa.eu/internal_market/finservices-retail/finnet/index_en.htm.

[40] See ec.europa.eu/solvit/site/index_en.htm.

[41] Dir 2000/31/EC of 8 June 2000 on certain legal aspects of information society services, in particular electronic commerce, in the Internal Market [2000] OJ L178.

[42] Dir 2004/39/EC of 21 April 2004 on markets in financial instruments [2004] OJ L145.

[43] Dir 2008/6/EC of 20 February 2008 amending Dir 97/67/EC with regard to the full accomplishment of the internal market of Community postal services [2008] OJ L52.

[44] Dir 2006/123/EC of 12 December 2006 on services in the internal market [2006] OJ L376.

[45] Dir 2007/64/EC of 13 November 2007 on payment services in the internal market [2007] OJ L319.

[46] Dir 2008/48/EC of 23 April 2008 on credit agreements for consumers [2008] OJ L133.

[47] Dir 2009/136/EC of 25 November 2009 amending Dir 2002/22/EC on universal service and users' rights relating to electronic communications networks and services, Dir 2002/58/EC concerning the processing of personal data and the protection of privacy in the electronic communications sector and Reg (EC) No 2006/2004 on cooperation between national authorities responsible for the enforcement of consumer protection laws [2009] OJ L337, and Dir 2009/140/EC of 25 November 2009 amending Dirs 2002/21/EC on a common regulatory framework for electronic communications networks and services, 2002/19/EC on access to, and interconnection of, electronic communications networks and associated facilities, and 2002/20/EC on the authorisation of electronic communications networks and services [2009] OJ L337.

[48] Dir 2009/72/EC of 13 July 2009 concerning common rules for the internal market in electricity [2009] OJ L211, and Dir 2009/73/EC of 13 July 2009 concerning common rules for the internal market in natural gas [2009] OJ L211.

[49] Reg (EU) No 181/2011 of 16 February 2011 concerning the rights of passengers in bus and coach transport [2011] OJ L55.

[50] Dir 2014/17/EU of 4 February 2014 on credit agreements for consumers relating to residential immovable property [2014] OJ L60.

CDR currently exists in a wide range of different arrangements,[51] which are not yet subject to harmonisation.[52] The main types are:

— Arbitration, sometimes with mediation as a first stage;[53]
— Official quasi-arbitration but non-binding adjudication;
— Regulated arbitration;
— Complaint functions within public regulatory authorities;[54]
— Private sector ombudsmen, sometimes regulated; decisions are sometimes accepted as de facto binding by trader members, sometimes not;
— Statutory ombudsmen, binding on the firm if the consumer accepts the otherwise non-binding award.

In 2013 the EU has specifically espoused CDR in its search for 'simple, fast and low-cost' ways of resolving consumer disputes,[55] given dissatisfaction with general court procedures, and adopted forms such as small claims procedures[56] or collective actions.[57] Research has indicated various

[51] A 2009 study identified 750 national CDR schemes across the EU: Civic Consulting, *Study on the Use of Alternative Dispute Resolution in the European Union*, 16 October 2009, available at: ec.europa.eu/consumers/redress_cons/adr_study.pdf.

[52] For a review of national systems see C Hodges, I Benöhr and N Creutzfeldt-Banda, *Consumer ADR in Europe* (Oxford, Hart Publishing, 2012); J Stuyck, E Terryn, V Colaert, T Van Dyck, N Peretz, N Hoekx and P Tereszkiewicz, *An Analysis and Evaluation of Alternative Means of Consumer Redress Other than Redress through Ordinary Judicial Proceedings: Final Report* (Catholic University of Leuven, 17 January 2007), available at: ec.europa.eu/consumers/redress/reports_studies/index_en.htm.

[53] Arbitration of consumer disputes, especially under pre-contract standard clauses, runs into a series of obstacles, under ECHR Art 6, CFHR Art 47, Dir 93/13/EEC of 5 April 1993 on unfair terms in consumer contracts [1993] OJ L95, and national arbitration law, such as the UK Arbitration Act 1996, ss 89–91, the Swedish Arbitration Act, s 6.

[54] Two recent examples in which these functions have been outsourced are the creation of the Energy Ombudsman in Germany in place of the *Bundesnetzargentur* in 2013 and the outsourcing of the Passenger and Complaints Team by the UK Civil Aviation Authority in 2015.

[55] Dir 2013/11/EU of 21 May 2013 on alternative dispute resolution for consumer disputes and amending Reg (EC) No 2006/2004 and Dir 2009/22/EC (Dir on consumer ADR) [2013] OJ L165/63, recital 4.

[56] Commission Reg (EC) 861/2007 of the European Parliament and of the Council of 11 July 2007 establishing a European Small Claims Procedure [2007] OJ L 199/1. See G Haibach, 'The Commission Proposal for a Regulation Establishing a European Small Claims Procedures: An Analysis' [2005] *European Review of Private Law* 293–601; E Hondius, 'Towards a European Small Claims Procedure' in L Thévenoz and N Reich (eds), *Liber amicorum Bernd Stauder, Consumer Law* (Geneva, Schulthess, 2006) 131; J Baldwin, 'Is There a Limit to the Expansion of Small Claims?' in MDA Freeman (ed), *Current Legal Problems* Vol 56 (Oxford, Oxford University Press, 2004) 313; CJ Whelan (ed), *Small Claims Courts—A Comparative Study* (Oxford, Clarendon Press, 1990) 253.

[57] See R Mulheron, *The Class Action in Common Law Legal Systems: A Comparative Perspective* (Oxford, Hart Publishing, 2004); C Hodges, *The Reform of Class and Representative Actions in European Legal Systems: A New Framework for Collective Redress in Europe* (Oxford, Hart Publishing, 2008); D Hensler and C Hodges, 'The Globalisation of Class Actions' (2009) 622 *Annals of the American Academy of Political and Social Science* (special issue) 7–345.

problems with small claims procedures,[58] and that they would generally only be used by European consumers if the amount involved exceeds around €200.[59] A 2011 Commission survey found that the majority (53 per cent) of people would only go to court for financial loss somewhere between €101 and €2,500.[60] The Commission made proposals to amend the European Small Claims Procedure (ESCP) in 2013[61] after finding that its use is still 'rather limited compared to the number of potential cases'.[62] The aims for the ESCP stated in the supporting policy documents make almost no reference to consumer claims, and appear largely directed at small business claims. Possible harmonisation of collective actions has been discussed for many years, with no formal proposal yet being made for harmonising legislation, given the recognised difficulty of identifying the right mix of safeguards against the potential for abuse, and the need to balance safeguards against abuse with enabling access.[63] A rough model was published in 2013[64] but empirical evidence is that national collective actions are generally little used since other more attractive options exist.[65]

By contrast, CDR schemes have been shown to be low-cost and quick. The vast majority are free or of minimal cost to consumers (below €50) and are settled within a short period of time (an average of 90 days).[66] From July 2015, the EU has mandated the creation of a pan-EU network of CDR

[58] C Crifò, 'Europeanisation, Harmonisation and Unspoken Premises: The Case of Service Rules in the Regulation on a European Small Claims Procedure (Reg No 861/2007)' (2011) 30 *Civil Justice Quarterly* 283 ('an ungainly juggernaut'; 'the legal landscape appears, far from simplified, further complicated'); XE Kramer, 'Small Claim, Simple Recovery?' (2011) 1 *ERA Forum* 119. See also XE Kramer and EA Ontanu, 'The Functioning of the European Small Claims Procedure in the Netherlands: Normative and Empirical Reflections' (2013) 3 *Nederlands Internationaal Privaatrecht* 319–28 ('the number of cases handled in the ESCP is limited ... Apparently consumers still find it difficult to find their way to this procedure ... the duration of the procedure is on average three to five months').

[59] J Stuyck et al (n 52) 41.

[60] *Special Eurobarometer 342, Consumer empowerment* (European Commission, 2011), para 5.5.3, available at: ec.europa.eu/consumers/consumer_empowerment/docs/report_eurobarometer_342_en.pdf.

[61] Proposal for a Reg of the European Parliament and of the Council amending Reg (EC) No 861/2007 of the European Parliament and the Council of 11 July 2007 establishing a European Small Claims Procedure and Reg (EC) No 1896/2006 of the European Parliament and of the Council of 12 December 2006 creating a European order for payment procedure COM (2013) 794 final.

[62] Report from the Commission to the European Parliament, the Council and the European Economic and Social Committee of 19 November 2013 on the application of Reg (EC) No 861/2007 of the European Parliament and of the Council establishing a European Small Claims Procedure COM(2013) 795.

[63] European Parliament Resolution of 2 February 2012 'Towards a Coherent European Approach to Collective Redress', 2011/2089(INI); European Commission, MEMO/08/741, 4.

[64] Commission Recommendation of 11 June 2013 on common principles for collective redress mechanisms in the Member States for injunctions against and claims on damages caused by violations of EU rights COM(2013) 3539/3.

[65] See C Hodges, 'Collective Redress: A Breakthrough or a *Damp Sqibb*?' (2014) 34 *Journal of Consumer Policy* 67–89.

[66] Civic Consulting (n 51) 33.

entities capable of handling every type of consumer–trader dispute.[67] CDR entities will be regulated by competent authorities against conformity with minimum criteria.[68] Those traders who belong to CDR entities are required to publish information identifying them, and notify them to consumers who raise disputes.[69] Cross-border disputes may be channelled through an EU ODR platform to the appropriate CDR entity in the relevant Member State.[70]

The sheer scale of the number of consumer claims that are already handled by some CDR systems is impressive, and indicates their potential in resolving barriers to access to justice based on cost–benefit (dis)proportionality and lack of user-friendliness and accessibility of other traditional mechanisms. The UK Financial Ombudsman Service currently receives over two million inquiries a year, of which it resolves over 400,000 disputes. Many of the disputes involve similar issues, so the system provides mass and collective redress.[71] Around 11,000 claims are processed annually by the 50 sectoral dispute Boards in the Netherlands. In Finland, Sweden, Norway and Denmark, virtually no consumer claims have gone to court for many years, since they go through the CDR system. In those states also, medical negligence or product liability litigation is processed through the no fault compensation schemes, and not the courts.[72]

The CDR system is still in early phases of development, with various issues to resolve. However, since the CDR approach will expand as a result of the 2013 EU legislation, this is looking like a major revolution in the architecture of European legal systems. It also raises the issue of what the residual function may be for the courts.

Susskind, who has prophesied that information technology will replace lawyers,[73] and others, have called in 2015 for the adoption of an online dispute resolution function by courts, known as HM Online Court (HMOC), to replace the normal court service for all small claims.[74] That proposal overlooks a number of impediments: Small claim numbers have already fallen far below the number of claims that are resolved by ombudsmen or other ADR systems, and it will not be justifiable for the courts' budget to

[67] Dir 2013/11 (n 55).

[68] ibid, Arts 5–11. The criteria are: Expertise, independence, impartiality, transparency, effectiveness, fairness, liberty and legality.

[69] ibid, Arts 13–15.

[70] Reg (EC) No 524/2013 of 21 May 2013 on online dispute resolution for consumer disputes (Reg on consumer ODR) [2013] OJ L165/1.

[71] See Annual Reports of the Financial Ombudsman Service at www.financial-ombudsman.org.uk.

[72] C Hodges, 'Nordic Compensation Schemes for Drug Injuries' (2006) 29 *Journal of Consumer Policy* 143.

[73] R Susskind, *The End of Lawyers? Rethinking the Nature of Legal Services* (Oxford, Oxford University Press, 2008).

[74] Online Dispute Resolution Advisory Group, *Online Dispute Resolution for Low Value Civil Claims* (London, Civil Justice Council, 2015).

stretch to establishing such a system for the small numbers when the cost can be privatised through the ADR system.

An important function of ombudsmen systems is the ability to provide functions that are wider than mere dispute resolution. Ombudsmen systems provide extensive consumer advice functions and, together with regulators, form part of an integrated mechanism for affecting trading behaviour.[75] Indeed, the combination of regulatory authorities and an ombudsman system can be particularly effective. Consumers can access ombudsmen easily, and have their issues considered quickly. Many contacts merely seek advice or triage on whether an issue is or is not a right to compensation. Effective ombudsmen systems capture, collate and publish comprehensive data on what issues are emerging in market trading, and which traders give rise to which problems. The aggregated information gives a clear picture of issues in the marketplace, and can be recorded and fed back to traders, markets, consumers and regulators, all of whom can then react. Circulating this data to traders, consumers, markets and regulators has been shown to have salutary effects on trading behaviour, and to improve standards. Regulators, in particular, can intervene swiftly to stop infringing behaviour. They can also ensure that traders pay mass compensation without delay, failing which claims may be made to the ombudsmen. Making claims, individually or collectively, in slow court systems, with added bureaucracy and cost, no longer looks an attractive option for consumer–trader disputes. The 2013 legislation therefore mandates close relations between CDR entities and regulators.[76]

In short, a major shift is taking place for consumer–trader disputes. In place of consumers being required to institute private litigation if a trader fails to respond to a complaint, they may raise complaints with a new corpus of independent entities that replace public courts. These CDR entities, whether they operate on mediation-arbitration or ombudsman models, are required to apply the same substantive law as courts, but their expertise and operational ability is simply quicker and cheaper than many courts, and they often include arrangements that underpin compliance with awards by traders (that is the enforcement of judgment stage).[77]

VII. ANALYSING THE TRANSFORMATIONS

This chapter has identified a considerable degree of innovative new approaches to enforcement of law and resolution of disputes. It has been

[75] C Hodges, 'Consumer Ombudsmen: Better Regulation and Dispute Resolution' (2015) *ERA Forum* 593.

[76] Dir on Consumer ADR (n 55) Art 17.

[77] Details vary between schemes. In the Netherlands, trade associations guarantee payment of a monetary award by a member firm. See Hodges, Benöhr and Creutzfeldt-Banda (n 52).

found that a range of new techniques are being developed to deliver the *objectives* of behavioural compliance and of redress. Those objectives constitute restatements of what used to be called regulation and compensation, respectively delivered through criminal, administrative and/or regulatory structures and private law.

This chapter noted at the start three aspects of the traditional public–private divide that have changed: *substantive law, forum* and *actors*. Particularly striking examples can now illustrate changes in each of these aspects. First, the principles of the private law of damages still underpin payment of compensation or redress when a compensation order or consumer redress scheme is invoked in criminal or regulatory processes, but the details of damages law are in practice often of little importance. The principle of full redress is simply applied. Second, one of the most dramatic transformations is the shift in forum for delivering consumer redress, from courts to CDR entities, ombudsmen or even regulators. Third, various changes have occurred in the actors involved: the intermediaries in private litigation are lawyers, but those in new redress mechanisms are regulators and CDR entities.

The outcome is a shift away from the traditional binary private and public enforcement model to a three pillar model, in which ADR, and especially ombudsmen, provide a key central pillar, functioning as both part of the dispute resolution system (like litigation through private enforcement) and as part of the regulatory system (like public enforcers, who also assume some redress responsibilities).

Where does this leave courts—do they disappear? Of course not. Ombudsmen are capable of deciding points of law, as private arbitrators have long decided points of law. But there is a significant argument that law should be made by parliaments, regulators and courts. The court provides the opportunity for an open, fully transparent and rational exposure and debate of the facts, law and issues. It is precisely because that process takes resources and time that make the process expensive and (comparatively) slow—but those features are also its strengths.

Change will not occur at the same time in every Member State. Some systems such as Germany have strong court systems, in which litigation is supported by insurance. They have been resistant to the idea of mediation, and the spread of ADR and ombudsmen has been slow. But the economic force of the need to provide better value court processes at lower cost if access to justice is to be maintained, coupled with consumer pressure for justice that grows with the slow realisation that many consumer claims already fall below the court's net because of cost and the slow responsiveness of the system, and pressure from regulators to increase control over markets through data that can only be provided by ombudsmen systems, will force change. In Central and Eastern European States, there is a Communist hangover of dislike of both courts and public bodies, so ombudsmen provide a new neutral option.

The scale and significance of all these shifts of course raises important issues. For example: Is justice still upheld? Is the law applied, and fairly? What controls are necessary on the new entities involved? There is no space remaining to address these issues here. But it is important to realise how fundamental are the changes that are occurring, and how irreversible.

The development of these new structures and techniques has occurred consistently for reasons of trying to find quicker, cheaper and more effective *outcomes*. What is important is to identify and adopt a technique, and structure, or combination of the above, that delivers the desired outcomes in the particular circumstances—whether amicable resolution or formal declaration of rights, whether payment of redress or a real change in future behaviour—and to do so effectively and economically efficiently. The categorisations are unimportant. What are important are outcomes, costs and speed. The crucial policy principles are purposive and economic.

For example, the imposition of traditional deterrent sanctions in criminal, regulatory or private law might no longer be thought sufficiently to affect future behaviour and its effectiveness has been questioned in many criminal and commercial contexts. New approaches seek to support *compliance* by different means. A further clear example is that private enforcement of rights is often unsatisfactory for consumers: affecting traders' behaviour requires the power that public regulators can wield, and consumer redress can be delivered effectively through a well-designed combination of regulators and ombudsmen.

The debate over class actions is another example. A fundamental question that that debate has thrown up is whether the claim that court litigation-based procedures can really be considered to deliver redress adequately or at acceptable cost. The traditional claim is that class actions deliver 'judicial economy', but, when exposed to the light of empirical reality, the evidence tends to indicate that class actions have to include either economic features that provide major incentives so as to induce commercial intermediaries (lawyers and/or funders) to invest in them, or such major safeguards against conflicts of interest and abuse by intermediaries that the mechanism offers minimal incentives to anyone, and significant barriers, such that it is ineffective as a means of delivering redress. In the former situation, also, the redress delivered to those who deserve compensation can be significantly reduced by the costs skimmed off by intermediaries.

The debate on class actions and on private enforcement of competition law also highlights the claim that private enforcement affects corporate behaviour; that 'regulation by litigation' works. Closer scrutiny of this claim also reveals significant cracks in its validity. Any ex post facto 'enforcement' faces a challenge in its assertion that it will produce significant future ex ante effects on the behaviour of a particular corporate defendant or of other firms. The claim is based on the theoretical assumptions, first, that every commercial firm makes every decision solely on the basis of rational assessments of the costs and benefits of a proposed course of action, valuing every decision with complete 20:20 foresight and calculation and, second, that every firm can be considered to be a single entity with its own *animus* and can completely control the activities of every employee. This is not the place to examine these assumptions,[78] but it can be noted that they have come under withering attack from various quarters, notably cognitive and behavioural psychology. The result is that the primacy of litigation as a means of corporate behaviour-control—regulation—has collapsed. This realisation has coincided with a number of statements from the EU as to the primacy of public enforcement over private enforcement, such as in competition law.[79] It also coincides with the financial crisis, in which responses aimed at affecting the behaviour of bankers and financial markets firmly strengthen public regulatory mechanisms and largely ignore private enforcement as mechanisms for affecting behaviour.

VIII. CONCLUSIONS

The extent to which European legal systems are undergoing innovation in techniques, mechanisms, procedures and architectural structures is impressively large. The developments are driven by pragmatic considerations of finding techniques that work well, in terms of effectiveness and efficiency. Some existing techniques and structures have been found to be wanting, and new approaches have been identified that offer improvements in some respects. In this process, we will lose some cherished features but gain some advantages. Some new options might be faster and cheaper but threaten some pre-existing values. Nothing is ever perfect. Innovation is disruptive. But it is clear that innovation in European legal systems is underway, is producing multiple fundamental changes, and is far from over.

[78] CJS Hodges, *Law and Corporate Behaviour: Integrating Theories of Regulation, Enforcement, Compliance and Ethics* (Oxford, Hart Publishing, 2015).

[79] Proposal for a Dir of the European Parliament and of the Council on certain rules governing actions for damages under national law for infringements of the competition law provisions of the Member States and of the European Union COM(2013) 404.

7

The Interaction Between Private and Public Enforcement in European Competition Law

JOSEF DREXL

I. INTRODUCTION

ON 26 NOVEMBER 2014, the Directive on actions for damages for infringements of national and EU competition law was finally adopted by the EU legislature.[1] This final text of the Directive differs in several regards from the previous Commission Proposal of 11 June 2013.[2] The new Damages Directive marks a highly important step towards promoting private enforcement of competition law after many years of discussion.

Of course, an analysis of the Directive would now be extremely timely.[3] Yet competition law enforcement is not limited to private enforcement, nor is private enforcement limited to damage claims. This is why this chapter takes a more holistic approach to assess the current situation of enforcement of competition law in the European Union.

The following analysis will demonstrate that modern competition law enforcement is characterised by many tensions that often require new legal mechanisms for calibrating conflicting concerns and sometimes also difficult decisions where such conflicts cannot be overcome.

[1] Dir 2014/104/EU of the European Parliament and of the Council of 26 November 2014 on certain rules governing actions for damages under national law for infringements of the competition law provisions of the Member States and of the European Union [2014] OJ L349/1.

[2] Commission Proposal of 11 June 2013 for a Dir of the European Parliament and the Council on certain rules governing actions for damages under national law for infringements of the competition law provisions of the Member States and of the European Union COM(2013) 404 final.

[3] For a first analysis see C Kersting, 'Die neue Richtlinie zur privaten Rechtsdurchsetzung im Kartellrecht' (2014) *Wirtschaft und Wettbewerb* 564; H Schweitzer, 'Die neue Richtlinie für wettbewerbsrechtliche Schadensersatzklagen' (2014) *Neue Zeitschrift für Kartellrecht* 335. See also E Clark and R Sander, 'Navigating the Quantum Minefield in Cartel Damages Cases' (2015) 6 *Journal of European Competition Law & Practice* 153.

The most obvious tension is that between public enforcement and private enforcement.[4] As will be explained in the next section, the Commission's initiative to harmonise the law on damage claims, from a historical perspective, was triggered by a hard-felt need to strengthen enforcement of EU competition law in general (part II, below). In this sense, private enforcement spreads a second layer of remedies over public enforcement.

Several national laws of the Member States even add criminal sanctions, especially in cases of cartels. This two-pronged and sometimes even three-pronged system of sanctions, however, causes frictions. The currently most discussed friction relates to leniency programmes. Enforcement of private damage claims could severely undermine the willingness of cartel members to apply for leniency. At the same time, the success of private law suits for damages often depends on the plaintiffs having access to the leniency applications submitted to the competition agency (part III, below).

Another tension stems from the interaction between substantive competition law on the one hand and the regulation of remedies and procedures of competition law enforcement on the other hand (part IV, below). Effective enforcement depends on legal certainty as to whether there is an infringement of competition law or not. In the field of enforcement against cartels, this is mostly a problem of evidence. In other fields of competition law, such as in the field of abuse of dominance, even the substantive law question of whether a certain conduct is to be considered an abuse can be highly complex. The complexity of unilateral conduct cases has even increased in recent years for several reasons. This complexity has led to new enforcement mechanisms that allow for quick resolution at the price of avoiding final decisions that contribute to legal certainty. In areas where public enforcement fails to produce legal certainty, private parties are less likely to bring private claims to the courts.

Another conflict regards the entitlement to damage claims (part V, below). The question is whether these claims should only be granted to the direct purchaser or also to indirect purchasers, including final consumers. In this regard, achieving both effective enforcement and compensation of the victims is a most difficult task whose fulfilment raises an array of difficult legal questions.

Finally, in the context of private enforcement in particular, modern competition law demonstrates a tension between the underlying economic theory and normative values and considerations (part VI, below).

[4] There are also voices that question the appropriateness of private enforcement of competition law. See W Moeschel, 'Should Private Enforcement of Competition Law Be Strengthened?' (2013) 6(2) *Global Competition Litigation Review* 1.

II. RECENT HISTORY OF THE DEVELOPMENT OF COMPETITION LAW ENFORCEMENT IN THE EU

Within the last 10 to 15 years, enforcement of competition law in the EU has undergone a fundamental change. This is mostly due to two developments, the decentralisation of EU competition law enforcement through Regulation 1/2003,[5] on the one hand, and the strengthening of private enforcement, on the other hand.

The decision to decentralise public enforcement of EU competition law was mostly driven by the backlog of applications for an individual exemption according to Article 101(3) TFEU (Treaty on the Functioning of the European Union) (ex-Article 81(3) EC) under the former Implementation Regulation 17/62.[6] There was the risk that this backlog would increase even more with the introduction of the more economic approach to the system of block exemptions. Ever since the adoption of the Block Exemption Regulation on Vertical Agreements in 1999[7] the Commission has favoured and promoted a system that relies on market-share thresholds as a proxy for market power and a criterion for the exemption. This, however, created additional work for the Commission. While prior to this system change undertakings with large market shares were also able to benefit from a block exemption on the condition that they only included clauses in their agreements that were explicitly exempted, as of the introduction of the market-share approach such undertakings would have had to apply for an individual exemption. Of course, the upcoming enlargement of the EU by 10 Member States on 1 May 2004 gave a clear signal that the problem would become even more acute. This explains why, in addition to transferring the power of enforcing Articles 101 and 102 TFEU to national competition agencies,[8] Regulation 1/2003 made Article 101(3) TFEU directly applicable[9] and thereby liberated the Commission from its duty of ex ante control of agreements that were not block-exempted. As a consequence, since the entry into force of Regulation 1/2003 on 1 May 2004, undertakings have to 'self-assess' the conformity of their agreements with Article 101(1) and (3) TFEU.

Obviously, these changes gave rise to concerns that they would weaken the respect of competition law and the effectiveness of its enforcement. The transfer of power to both national authorities and national courts[10] did not contribute much to responding to this problem. Competition authorities

[5] Council Reg (EC) No 1/2003 on the implementation of the rules on competition laid down in Arts 81 and 82 of the Treaty [2003] OJ L1/1.

[6] EEC Council Reg No 17: First Reg implementing Arts 85 and 86 of the Treaty [1959–1962] OJ (English special edition) series I, 87.

[7] Commission Reg (EC) No 2790/1999 of 22 December 1999 on the application of Art 81(3) of the Treaty to categories of vertical agreements and concerted practices [1999] OJ L336/21.

[8] Art 5 Reg 1/2003 (n 5).

[9] See Art 1(2) Reg 1/2003 (n 5).

[10] See Art 6 Reg 1/2003 (n 5).

usually do not start investigations as long as there are no complaints about allegedly restrictive agreements; and contracting parties are hardly likely to bring cases to the courts as long as they share the common interest in applying their potentially restrictive agreement.

These problems were already foreseeable prior to the adoption of Regulation 1/2003. Therefore, they may have influenced the former European Court of Justice (ECJ, now CJEU) in its *Courage* decision in 2001, in which the Court strengthened private enforcement by recognising claims of 'any individual' for damages caused to this person by a contract or any other conduct that restricts competition.[11] It is worth noting that the contract at stake in *Courage* was one that fell within the scope of application of the Block Exemption Regulation on Vertical Agreements. By allowing the purchaser of beer who had entered into a 20 year lease contract for a pub with a brewery and, thereby, had agreed to purchase a minimum quantity of beer from the brewery (so-called beer tie), to collect damages, the ECJ developed a rule that made it more likely that cases on restrictive agreements would be brought to the courts. In addition to Article 101(2) TFEU, which only provides for nullity of the restrictive agreement, the Court managed to justify damage claims by the principle of full effectiveness of EU law.[12] Thereby, the Court not only extended the entitlement to damage claims to all victims of restrictive agreements, it also transferred two other principles that guarantee minimum protection of victims under national damage claims, namely, the principles of equivalence and effectiveness, to the field of EU competition law.[13] According to the principle of equivalence, the rules and procedures that apply to damage claims for the violation of EU competition law 'shall not be less favourable' than those applicable to infringements of national competition law. According to the principle of effectiveness, national laws must not 'render practically impossible or excessively difficult' the exercise of rights conferred by EU competition law.[14]

In the subsequent *Manfredi* case,[15] another referral case regarding damage claims of Italian consumers who had become victims of an insurance cartel, and the most recent *Kone* case,[16] the ECJ applied these two principles

[11] Case C-453/99 *Courage v Crehan* [2001] ECR I-6297, para 26. This was most recently confirmed in Case C-557/12 *Kone v ÖBB-Infrastruktur* EU:C:2014:1317, paras 21–23.

[12] *Courage v Crehan* (n 11) paras 25 et seq.

[13] ibid, para 29 (with a reference to Case C-261/95 *Palmisani v INPS* [1997] ECR I-4025, para 27).

[14] Both formulas are also used in Art 4 of the new Damages Dir (n 1).

[15] Joined Cases C-295/04 and C-298/04 *Manfredi et al v Lloyd Adriatico et al* [2006] ECR I-6619.

[16] Case C-557/12 *Kone v ÖBB-Infrastruktur* EU:C:2014:1317 (confirming liability of cartel members for excessive umbrella pricing of non-cartel members). For a critical view on this judgment see A Fritzsche, 'Jedermann kann–Anmerkungen zum Kone-Urteil des EuGH (Rs C-557/12) zum Schadensersatz bei kartellbedingt eintretenden Preisschirmeffekten' (2014) *Neue Zeitschrift für Kartellrecht* 428.

and thereby clarified several sub-issues and concepts of the law on damage claims, such as causation and the limitation period for bringing such claims.

This case law of the ECJ produced an immediate impact in the Member States. Germany, for instance, changed its law on damage claims in 2005 by broadening the entitlement to damage claims and introducing a provision that binds the courts in so-called follow-on actions to previous final decisions of courts and competition agencies within the EU regarding the anti-competitive nature of the specific conduct. Such changes led to a sudden increase of damage claims brought to the courts[17] and convinced the Commission to launch its initiative for drafting an EU legal instrument on damage claims.[18] Also other EU Member States experienced an increase in damage claims brought to the courts in more recent years.[19]

III. COORDINATING PRIVATE DAMAGE CLAIMS WITH LENIENCY PROGRAMMES AND SETTLEMENTS

As can be learned from the analysis of the *Courage* and *Manfredi* cases above, the ECJ's decision to strengthen private enforcement first developed in the framework of vertical agreements and then went on to horizontal cartels. Without any doubt, damage claims have by now proven to be most important in price cartel cases. In contrast to the United States, where victims of price cartels can use pre-trial discovery, in the EU, the level of private enforcement traditionally remained low due to procedural limitations to collecting evidence on the existence of a cartel in particular. Therefore, also in terms of strengthening private enforcement, it was of utmost importance to promote the detection of existing cartels through leniency programmes. By granting immunity from the imposition of fines to the cartel member who successfully applies for leniency, competition authorities have managed to increase the detection rate considerably. Decisions of competition authorities against cartels can then be relied upon by the victims for bringing their damage claims to the courts against the cartel members. Competition law can help to strengthen the positive effect of leniency on enforcement by providing a binding effect to the agency decisions in the proceedings that

[17] See generally BJ Rodger (ed), *Competition Law, Comparative Private Enforcement and Collective Redress across the EU* (The Hague, Kluwer Law International, 2014). On follow-on actions in the UK see also M Furse, 'Follow-on Actions in the UK: Litigating Section 47A of the Competition Act 1998' (2013) 9 *European Competition Journal* 79.

[18] See Green Paper–Damages actions for breach of the EC antitrust rules, 19 December 2005, COM(2005) 672 final; White Paper on Damages actions for breach of the EC antitrust rules, 2 April 2008, COM(2008) 165 final.

[19] See, eg, M Kuipers, S Tuinenga, S Wisking, K Dietzel, S Campbell and A Fritsche, 'Actions for Damages in the Netherlands, the United Kingdom, and Germany' (2015) 6 *Journal of European Competition Law & Practice* 129.

have private damage claims as their object.[20] In contrast to the Commission Proposal, the new Damages Directive does not fully adopt this approach. Whereas Article 9(1) of the Directive accepts this binding effect in principle, Article 9(2), which was not included in the Commission Proposal, clarifies that Member States are not obliged to provide more than prima facie evidence of a violation based on final decisions of courts or agencies of other EU Member States.[21] Follow-on actions in cartel cases show that damage claims are not an alternative to public enforcement. Rather, they strengthen enforcement in general by adding private law remedies to administrative sanctions and fines.

Although detection of cartels through public enforcement is quintessential for the success of private damage claims, the recognition of damage claims runs the risk of undermining the effectiveness of public enforcement. Members of cartels are less likely to apply for leniency if they risk having to compensate the victims according to the national rules on damage claims.

In the US, this problem is addressed by 'detrebling' the damages to be paid by the leniency applicant who cooperates in compensating the victims of the cartel, while the other members of the cartel have to pay treble damages.[22]

In the EU, Member States do not usually provide for double or treble damages to be paid in competition cases. Article 3(1) of the Damages Directive only provides for 'full' compensation and, in Article 3(3), it even prevents Member States from overcompensation 'whether by means of punitive, multiple or other types of damages.' In the EU, the problem is more of a procedural nature. The question that needs to be addressed is whether and to what extent potential victims of a cartel can claim access to the files of competition authorities in order to collect information on the liability of the leniency applicant.[23]

The CJEU addressed this question for the first time in the *Pfleiderer* case.[24] This case arose from proceedings before the German competition authority, the *Bundeskartellamt*. In line with the authority's leniency

[20] See, eg, s 33(4) of the German *Gesetz gegen Wettbewerbsbeschränkungen* (Act against Restraints of Competition).

[21] In contrast, s 33(4) of the German Act against Restraints of Competition provides for a binding effect also of decisions of national competition agencies and national courts of other EU Member States that confirm that an infringement of Art 101 or 102 TFEU has occurred.

[22] See, in particular, SD Hammond and BA Barnett, 'Frequently Asked Questions Regarding the Antitrust Division's Leniency Program and Model Leniency Letters', 19 November 2008, Question 20, available at www.justice.gov/atr/public/criminal/239583.htm (accessed 18 March 2015).

[23] Nevertheless, there are also voices in Europe that favour immunity of leniency applicants from civil liability. See AK Singh, 'Disclosure of Leniency Evidence: Examining the Directive on Damages Action in the Aftermath of Recent ECJ Rulings' (2014) 7(4) *Global Competition Litigation Review* 200, 211–12.

[24] Case C-360/09 *Pfleiderer v Bundeskartellamt* [2011] ECR I-5161.

notice,[25] Pfleiderer AG, a large manufacturer of wood panel imitations and a victim of the European decor paper cartel, was denied access to information the *Bundeskartellamt* had received from other authorities of the European Competition Network (ECN). Through the denial, and based on the principle of confidentiality, the authority aimed to protect the interests of the leniency applicant. While the CJEU made clear that only national procedural rules decide on the issue of access, the Court, by relying on the principle of effectiveness, also stated that those rules must not render the implementation of EU law impossible or excessively difficult.[26] Based on the consideration that leniency programmes are 'useful tools' for detecting and stopping infringements of competition law,[27] the Court concluded that the effectiveness of competition law enforcement would be seriously compromised if documents relating to the leniency procedure were too easily provided to a person wishing to bring a damage claim to the courts despite the fact that the leniency applicant had already benefited from the grant of an exemption from the fine.[28] Since the CJEU also took note of the role of damage claims for guaranteeing full effectiveness of EU competition law as developed in *Courage* and *Manfredi*,[29] it finally advocated a 'weighing exercise' to be engaged in by the national courts on a case-by-case basis.[30] Accordingly, the Court concluded that the victims of a cartel are not per se precluded from seeking information on the leniency application, but that it is for the courts of the Member States, on the basis of their national laws, to determine the conditions of such access by weighing the interests protected by EU law.[31]

The CJEU's weighing approach confirms the conflict that exists between public and private enforcement. Yet it provides relatively little guidance to national authorities and courts as to the results of such a weighing. In the *Pfleiderer* case, the referring Bonn Local Court (*Amtsgericht* Bonn) finally rejected the application for access to the files, based on the need to promote effective detection of cartels and the personal interest of the leniency applicant in confidential treatment of the leniency information.[32] Thereby, the Court also took account of the interests of the victim by stating that, in the concrete case, the ability of the victim to bring a damage claim to the court

[25] Point 22 of *Bekanntmachung 9/2006 über den Erlass und die Reduktion von Geldbußen in Kartellsachen–Bonusregelung*, 7 March 2006, available at www.bundeskartellamt.de/SharedDocs/Publikation/DE/Bekanntmachungen/Bekanntmachung%20-%20Bonusregelung.pdf?__blob=publicationFile&v=7 (accessed 18 March 2015).

[26] *Pfleiderer v Bundeskartellamt* (n 24) para 24.

[27] ibid, para 25.

[28] ibid, para 26.

[29] ibid, paras 28–30.

[30] ibid, para 31.

[31] ibid, para 32.

[32] *Amtsgericht* Bonn, 18 January 2012, Case 51 Gs 53/09, available at www.openjur.de/u/453131.html (accessed 18 March 2015).

was not seriously curtailed thanks to the information that was nevertheless provided by the *Bundeskartellamt*.[33]

In a subsequent decision of 6 June 2013, on the referral of the Vienna Higher Regional Court (*Oberlandesgericht Wien)*, the CJEU had the opportunity to further clarify the *Pfleiderer* holding.[34] The Austrian court was seized by an association of undertakings against the Federal Cartel Authority (*Bundeskartellbehörde*) to get access to the files of proceedings relating to a European cartel in the chemical industry with the objective of preparing actions for damages against the cartel members including the leniency applicant. According to the Austrian Law on Cartels (*Kartellgesetz*), however, persons who are not parties to the proceedings in competition cases before the Authority are only entitled to access to the documents of these proceedings on the condition that all parties to the proceedings give their consent. Thereby, the Austrian law does not leave any discretion to the Authority or the court to decide otherwise even if legitimate interests of the third party would advocate such access. By relying on the *Pfleiderer* decision, the Vienna Higher Regional Court doubted whether it was still allowed to deny access to the files in the underlying case of proceedings involving an infringement of EU competition law without weighing the interests of the parties concerned in the individual case. The CJEU indeed confirmed that a rule such as the Austrian one which, in a very rigid form, excluded any weighing of the interests of the parties would seriously compromise the effectiveness of the enforcement of Article 101 TFEU and of the rights of the persons seeking access to the files.[35] Such a rule would, if the parties have no other way of collecting evidence, render nugatory the right to compensation which is recognised as a matter of EU law.[36] Yet the CJEU also took account of the conflicting confidentiality interests of the leniency applicant and the public interest in guaranteeing effective detection of infringements.[37] Therefore, the CJEU recalled its holding in *Pfleiderer* according to which national courts need to balance the interests of the parties on a case-by-case basis when they decide on whether third parties should be granted access to the documents of competition law proceedings.[38] Finally, the CJEU clearly stated that access can only be denied if there is a 'risk that a given document

[33] ibid, para 42.

[34] Case C-536/11 *Bundeswettbewerbsbehörde v Donau Chemie* EU:C:2013:366. See also R Hempel, 'An der schönen blauen Donau—Akteneinsicht in Kronzeugenanträge im Fluss' (2014) *Zeitschrift für Wettbewerbsrecht* 203; N Hirst, 'Donau Chemie: National Rules Impeding Access to Antitrust Files Liable to Breach EU Law' (2013) *Journal of European Competition Law & Practice* 484; F Neumayr, H Kühnert and V Schaumburger, 'The Gordian Knot of Access to Files: Legislation will have to resolve it' (2014) 7(4) *Global Competition Litigation Review* 185, 189.

[35] ibid, para 31.

[36] ibid, para 32.

[37] ibid, para 33.

[38] ibid, para 34.

may actually undermine the public interest relating to the effectiveness of the national leniency programme'.[39]

It is quite questionable whether the final text of the Damages Directive is in line with the principles stated by the CJEU in its jurisprudence.[40] Indeed, Article 6(6) of the Directive by and large follows the Commission Proposal by generally excluding access of private claimants to the leniency statements and settlement submissions. The European legislature takes this decision not only in order to maintain incentives for cartel members to cooperate with the agency, but also to protect cooperating undertakings against being exposed to liability under worse conditions than other cartel members that are unwilling to cooperate.[41] Yet the Directive's approach is not without any balancing of interests. Rather, the European legislature's decision rests on the assumption that the right of the injured parties to compensation will not be unduly curtailed if the exclusion of access is strictly limited to the said documents.[42] This explains why Article 6(7) of the Damages Directive gives private claimants a right to request access of the national court to the leniency statements and settlement submissions

> for the sole purpose of ensuring that their contents fulfil the definitions [for leniency statements and settlement submissions] in points (16) and (18) of Article 2.[43]

This excludes access of the private claimant or other third parties to the documents, but empowers the court to control whether a refusal to grant access to documents is indeed covered by the exception made by Article 6(6) of the Directive. Furthermore, in the case that only parts of a relevant document are covered by the exception, Article 6(8) provides that other parts are disclosed in accordance with the rules of Article 6.[44]

The *Pfleiderer* case, as it was finally decided by the referring German court, seems to confirm that damage actions will not necessarily fail if

[39] ibid, para 48.

[40] See also Clark and Sander (n 3) 161 (also highlighting the conflict of the Directive with the CJEU's judgments) and in more detail Singh (n 23) 206–09.

[41] See Recital 26 of the Dir in this regard.

[42] Accordingly, Recital 26 concludes:

> In order to ensure that that exception [from disclosure] does not unduly interfere with the injured parties' right to compensation, it should be limited to these voluntary and self-incriminating leniency statements and settlement submissions.

[43] On the contents of a settlement submission see Commission Notice on the conduct of settlement procedures in view of the adoption of Decisions pursuant to Art 7 and Art 23 of Council Reg (EC) No 1/2003 in cartel cases [2008] OJ C167/1, para 20.

[44] The EU legislature further explains its view in Recital 27 as follows:

> The rules in this Directive on the disclosure of documents other than leniency statements and settlement submissions ensure that injured parties retain sufficient alternative means by which to obtain access to the relevant evidence that they need in order to prepare their actions for damages. National courts should themselves be able, upon request of a claimant, to access documents in respect of which the exemption is invoked in order to verify whether the contents thereof fall outside the definitions of leniency corporate statements and settlement submissions laid down in this Directive. Any content falling outside those definitions should be disclosable under the relevant conditions.

victims are denied access to the leniency statements. Yet, against the principles stipulated by the CJEU, Article 6(6) goes too far by preventing the national court from weighing the interests on a case-by-case basis.[45] In the more recent *EnBW* judgment, the CJEU accepted that the Commission applies a presumption according to which the interests in excluding access to the leniency documents prevail. But the Court also clarified that it should also be possible to show that there is an overriding public interest in the disclosure of such documents.[46]

On the other hand, it is not true that cooperation with the agencies necessarily increases the risk of being exposed to private damage claims.[47] Cartel members also benefit as far as the binding effect of an agency decision is concerned. According to Article 9 of the Damages Directive, leniency applicants and cartel members that offer settlements may indeed be better off than cartel members that are unwilling to cooperate since the binding effect of final decisions is limited to the

> nature of the infringement and its material, personal, temporal and territorial scope as determined by the competition authority or review court in exercise of its jurisdictions.[48]

Since leniency programmes result in immunity for the applicants, private applicants will have to prove the involvement of the leniency applicant in the cartel and its particular role. A binding effect of an agency decision on the existence of the cartel has to be denied for damage actions against the cartel member that was granted immunity even as a matter of the rule of law, since this member did not take part in the proceedings that led to the decision against the other members and had no right to appeal against such a decision.[49] In contrast, settlement submissions result in final decisions[50]

[45] The Explanatory Memorandum to the Commission's Proposal (at 14) describes the exemption as 'absolute protection'. In this context, the Commission refrains from citing the *Pfleiderer* decision of the CJEU. In the sense of a conflict with the case law of the CJEU see also Schweitzer (n 3) 342–43. For a most recent empirical study on the factors that influence the decision of firms to apply for leniency see CT Hoang, K Hüschelrath, U Laitenberger and F Smuda, 'Determinants of Self-reporting Under the European Corporate Leniency Program' (2014) 40 *International Review of Law and Economics* 15.

[46] C-365/12 P *Commission v EnBW Energie Baden-Württemberg* EU:C:2014:112, para 100. On this case see also Neumayr, Kühnert and Schaumburger (n 34) 186–87.

[47] Doubts were also expressed by the High Court of Justice of England and Wales of 6 June 2012, *National Grid Electricity Transmission Plc v ABB & Others* [2012] EWHC 1717 (Ch), para 37 (Roth J).

[48] Recital 31 of the Damages Dir (n 1).

[49] See also J Bornkamm, in E Langen and H-J Bunte (eds), *Kartellrecht, Kommentar, Band 1: Deutsches Kartellrecht* 10th edn (Cologne, Luchterhand, 2010) § 33 GWB para 171; V Emmerich, in U Immenga and E-J Mestmäcker (eds), *Wettbewerbsrecht, Band 2: GWB* 4th edn (Munich, CH Beck, 2007) § 33 para 79 (both authors arguing in this sense with regard to the binding effect under German competition law, which does not contain any explicit personal limitation of this effect).

[50] See Commission Notice on Cartel Settlements (n 43) paras 28–33.

and the imposition of—however reduced—fines against undertakings that enter into such settlements. Nevertheless, a settlement decision sets the fine only according to the statements of the undertaking, and as these statements are accepted by the agency, without including a decision on the involvement of this undertaking in the cartel. Therefore, also with regard to undertakings entering into settlements, private plaintiffs should not be able rely on a binding effect of the decisions.

The absence of any decision on which private claimants can rely in the form of follow-on actions pursuant to Article 9(1) of the Damage Directive shows why it is so important that private claimants get access to the documents held by the agencies as the most important source of information that can help them to prove their damage claims against leniency applicants and undertakings that settle their cases.

The fact that private enforcement can be undermined by the mere lack of final decisions on which private claimants can rely also characterises cases on abuse of market dominance (Article 102 TFEU), which nowadays are often terminated by commitment decisions under Article 9 Regulation 1/2003.[51] Such decisions only make commitments binding on the undertakings that enter into such commitments. They do not confirm that there was indeed a violation of competition law.[52] Hence, commitment decisions do not constitute a sufficient basis for follow-on damage claims pursuant to Article 9(1) of the Damages Directive.[53]

[51] On private enforcement in the context of Art 102 TFEU see generally F Louis, 'Promoting Private Antitrust Enforcement: Remember Article 102' in P Lowe and M Marquis (eds), *European Competition Law Annual 2011: Integrating Public and Private Enforcement of Competition Law—Implications for Courts and Agencies* (Oxford, Hart Publishing, 2014) 85; M-O Mackenrodt, 'Private Incentive, Optimal Deterrence and Damage Claims for Abuses of Dominant Positions' in M-O Mackenrodt, B Conde Gallego and S Enchelmaier (eds), *Abuse of Dominant Position: New Interpretation, New Enforcement Mechanisms?* (Berlin, Springer, 2008) 165; HKS Schmidt, 'Private Enforcement—Is Article 82 EC special?' in M-O Mackenrodt, B Conde Gallego and S Enchelmaier (eds), *Abuse of Dominant Position: New Interpretation, New Enforcement Mechanisms?* (Berlin, Springer, 2008) 137.

[52] In the same sense D Ashton and D Henry, *Competition Damages Actions in the EU—Law and Practice* (Cheltenham, Edward Elgar, 2013) para 4.087. See also Recital 22 Reg 1/2003 (n 5) (stating that commitment decisions do not restrict the power of national authorities and courts to apply Arts 101 and 102 TFEU since such application would not give rise to conflicting decisions).

[53] This conclusion seems to be shared by the Commission. See Commission, 'Commitment decisions (Article 9 of Council Regulation 1/2003 providing for a modernised framework for antitrust scrutiny of company behaviour)–Frequently asked questions and answers', MEMO/04/217, 17 September 2004, available at europa.eu/rapid/press-release_MEMO-04-217_en.htm (accessed 18 March 2015) ('Article 9 decisions are silent on whether there was or still is a breach of the EU competition rules. Thus a customer or a competitor possibly seeking private enforcement in national courts still needs to prove the illegality of the former behaviour to obtain compensation for damages'.)

IV. TENSION BETWEEN SUBSTANTIVE LAW AND PRIVATE ENFORCEMENT

Price-cartel cases are simple cases with regard to the substantive standard applied to the infringement of competition law, but difficult cases when it comes to proving damage claims. Victims of cartels often face considerable problems in producing evidence on the existence of the infringement. In addition, damage claims are also difficult with regard to proving causation and calculating the amount of damages.

Private enforcement, however, is not limited to price cartels. In more complex cases of non-hard-core restrictive agreements and unilateral restraints in particular, the more economic approach advocated by the Commission has considerably increased the complexity of the assessment of individual cases. For such cases, victims take additional risks when they bring cases to the courts.

In such cases, legal certainty is crucial. After the entry into force of Regulation 1/2003, the Commission largely relies on guidelines as a means to instruct national courts on how EU competition law should be enforced in individual cases. Those guidelines, however, are characterised by several drawbacks: first, they have no binding effect on national courts. These courts may develop their own ideas on how to apply the law and, in particular, may prefer to refer cases to the CJEU for preliminary judgments. Second, the guidelines are not formulated as traditional legal rules, but as guidance on how to analyse cases from a perspective of economics. Thereby, the guidelines often tell the enforcers which considerations need to be taken into account without providing clear and foreseeable insights on which results enforcers will reach in individual cases when they follow that guidance.[54] Third, in the framework of Article 101(3) TFEU, the Commission has lost its own role of providing more legal certainty in the course of its case law ever since the undertakings have been told under Regulation 1/2003 that they have to self-assess the conformity of their agreements with competition law.

Similar problems arise in the framework of the enforcement of Article 102 TFEU. As already pointed out, the Commission nowadays prefers to terminate public enforcement actions in the form of commitment decisions under Article 9 of Regulation 1/2003. Those decisions are often poorly reasoned and, more importantly, can hardly be appealed by the alleged infringer of competition law to the European courts.[55] In particular, many of the economically most important cases have been terminated by commitment

[54] For similar concerns see Louis (n 51) 88–89.

[55] See Case C-441/07 P *Commission v Alrosa* [2010] ECR I-5949, paras 42 (stating that the Commission's assessment must be 'manifestly incorrect') and 48 (arguing that undertakings are aware that the 'concessions they make may go beyond what the Commission could itself impose on them in a decision adopted under Article 7 of [Reg 1/2003] after a thorough examination').

decisions. These decisions do not provide much, if any, help to the victims of the alleged infringement for arguing a private damage claim.

In addition, economic and technological change increases the problem of uncertainty. Particularly in cases in which intellectual property rights are at stake, or which in a broader sense present issues of innovation, competition law enforcers can hardly ever give clear answers to the question of whether there was indeed an infringement. In these cases, enforcers usually have to perform a balancing exercise already at the level of substantive law by assessing and weighing different kinds of effects on both static price competition and competition for innovation.

An example of this is provided by the *Boehringer* case, in which the Commission started an investigation in 2007. The case concerned allegations that Boehringer, a German pharmaceutical company, had applied for and obtained blocking patents with the aim of disturbing research and development efforts of its Spanish competitor, Almirall, in order to protect its own market-dominant position in the market of medicine for the treatment of chronic obstructive pulmonary disease (COPD). The Commission closed the case without any decision in 2011, after Boehringer agreed to remove its blocking patents. The Commission announced the termination as a big win for consumers suffering from COPD.[56] Yet whether Almirall could seriously consider bringing a damage claim against Boehringer for the loss it had incurred in past years is highly doubtful. The assessment of blocking patents under Article 102 TFEU may belong to the most disputed competition law issues for which no case law exists.[57] In the Pharmaceutical Sector Inquiry Report the Commission had already considered the potential anti-competitive effect of blocking patents.[58] But such a sector inquiry itself only serves as a fact-finding mission and is not meant to replace later investigations and decisions against individual undertakings.[59]

Legal uncertainty, the application of alternative new mechanisms for terminating investigations, including commitment decisions in particular, and the threat of potential damage claims create a kind of vicious circle.

[56] Commission, 'Antitrust: Commission welcomes improved market entry for lung disease treatments', Press release IP/11/842, 6 July 2011, available at europa.eu/rapid/press-release_IP-11-842_en.htm (accessed 18 March 2015).

[57] See the critical views of L Kjølbye, 'Article 82 EC as Remedy to Patent System Imperfections: Fighting Fire with Fire? (2009) 32 *World Competition* 163; J Straus, 'Patent Application Obstacle for Innovation and Abuse of Dominant Market Position under Article 102 TFEU?' (2010) 1 *Journal of European Competition Law & Practice* 189. More in favour of applying competition law see J Drexl, 'AstraZeneca and the Sector Inquiry: When do Patent Filings Violate Competition Law?' in J Drexl and N Lee (eds), *Pharmaceutical Innovation, Competition and Patent Law—A Trilateral Perspective* (Cheltenham, Edward Elgar, 2013) 290.

[58] Commission, 'Pharmaceutical Sector Inquiry Final Report, Part I' (8 July 2009), paras 1092 and 1118, available at ec.europa.eu/competition/sectors/pharmaceuticals/inquiry/staff_working_paper_part1.pdf (accessed 18 March 2015).

[59] This is also confirmed by the Commission. ibid, paras 1088 and 1096.

The fact that the victims of alleged infringements of competition law may sue for damages increases the incentive of undertakings to give in more easily to the accusations of the competition authority and to settle without a binding decision on which the victims could rely. Such concessions are made in a situation of uncertainty in which neither the authority nor the undertakings can know for sure how the courts would later decide. Hence, while victims are in need of more legal certainty as an incentive to bring their damage claims to the courts, the availability of such actions in principle produces the opposite effect, namely, that undertakings are more willing to do anything to avoid a clarification of the legal situation. Competition authorities like commitment decisions as a highly effective means of public enforcement. But, as can be seen, these decisions are not capable of producing sufficient legal certainty. They undermine the right of victims to compensation and create an imbalance of power between the authority and the alleged infringer to the disadvantage of the latter. These problems may lead to over-enforcement of competition law, namely, in cases in which undertakings accept the action of the authority although courts would otherwise decide against the authority.[60] Finally, the tension between public and private enforcement that arises from uncertainty regarding the substantive standards of competition law generally questions the respect of the rule of law in competition law enforcement.

Yet these problems do not exclude private enforcement completely. As can be seen from the practice of courts, private enforcement may still play a most important role in cases in which the victims of allegedly anti-competitive conduct rely on competition law as a defence in order to counter an action of the alleged infringer against the victim. Such a scenario was also presented in the *Courage* case.[61] There, the brewery sued the pub operator based on the lease and beer delivery contract for payment of past supplies, which triggered the defendant to counterclaim for damages based on an infringement of Article 101 TFEU. In the *Huawei* case, which was most recently decided by the CJEU, the defendant relied on a duty to license at fair, reasonable and non-discriminatory (FRAND) terms under competition law as a defence against an action for infringement of a standard-essential patent.[62] In its referral, the District Court (*Landgericht*) of Düsseldorf did not only ask whether there was an infringement of Article 102 TFEU. Rather, the referral was for the most part triggered by the so-called *Orange Book* decision of the

[60] This is even implicitly confirmed by the CJEU in Case C-441/07 P *Commission v Alrosa* [2010] ECR I-5949, para 48.

[61] See n 11, above.

[62] Case C-170/13 *Huawei Technologies v ZTE* EU:C:2015:477. See also the referral decision of the Düsseldorf District Court (*Landgericht*) Düsseldorf of 21 March 2012, Case 4b O 104/12, available at openjur.de/u/617729.html (accessed 18 March 2015).

German Federal Supreme Court (*Bundesgerichtshof*),[63] in which the Court made it quite difficult for the petitioner of a standard-essential patent to rely on competition law against a claim for injunctive relief of the patent owner. Hence, *Huawei* provided the CJEU with the opportunity to further develop the principles on effective private enforcement after *Courage* and *Manfredi* for yet another set of cases. This example shows that in practical cases that are characterised by highly complex legal issues private enforcement is not at all limited to stand-alone actions for damages, but also includes reliance on competition law as a defence. Unfortunately, the European legislature in the Damages Directive has not taken account of this much broader picture and all topics of private enforcement.

V. TENSIONS REGARDING THE ENTITLEMENT TO DAMAGE CLAIMS

Damage claims for infringements of competition law present a large array of complex legal issues. The perhaps most difficult issue relates to the persons who are entitled to assert damage claims.

In cartel cases in particular, there are two groups of persons who could in principle claim a right to compensation under the *Courage* case law, namely, direct and indirect purchasers. Any competition law has to fix rules that decide under which conditions one or the other group of persons is entitled to claim damages. There are two factors that influence these rules: first, the question of who is entitled to damage claims is very much influenced by general concepts of national private law, such as causation and the rules on calculating damages. In the European context, this means that, without harmonisation of these rules, the situation for damage claims as a tool of private enforcement would vary considerably among the Member States. Therefore, it is no surprise that the new Damages Directive addresses the issue. Second, the decision on who is entitled to claim damages is also influenced by the policy considerations that play a crucial role in the framework of competition law. The basis for these considerations was indeed prepared by the ECJ in the *Courage* decision.

The *Courage* decision itself is characterised by a considerable tension that arises from the simultaneous need to create incentives for effective private enforcement and the need to compensate the person that has actually suffered economic loss. On the one hand, the Court relies on the principle of full effectiveness and, therefore, establishes the rule that 'any person' that has suffered a loss due to an infringement of EU competition law can claim

[63] Federal Supreme Court (*Bundesgerichtshof*) of 6 May 2009, Case KZR 39/06, *Orange Book* (2010) 41 *International Review of Intellectual Property and Competition Law* 369 (English translation).

compensation. This has to lead to the conclusion that Member States must not exclude indirect purchasers, including final consumers, from compensation if overcharges were passed from direct purchasers to them in the supply chain.[64] On the other hand, the ECJ also highlighted a second principle, according to which Member States may apply rules that guarantee that damage claims do not lead to an unjust enrichment of the victim.[65] The problem is simply that granting the right to damages either to indirect or to direct purchasers can lead to under-deterrence, while entitlement of both direct and indirect purchasers would over-deter by obliging the cartel members to compensate two groups of persons for the same economic loss.

Concentration of the damage claim on the level of direct purchasers by excluding the so-called passing-on defence may increase the likelihood that damage claims are brought to the courts since the damages on the subsequent levels of the supply chain are spread among numerous victims and thereby reduce the interest of individual victims to go to court. On the other hand, the direct purchaser may also prefer to refrain from legal action if such action would disturb established business relations with the supplier. Also, exclusion of the passing-on defence may curtail consumer protection. In the frequent case of the passing-on of the overcharge in the supply chain, the passing-on defence would lead to an unjustified enrichment of direct purchasers, while the consumers are excluded from compensation. Hence, balancing the interest in effective enforcement and the interest in compensating the person who has ultimately suffered from the cartel requires procedural reforms in view of collective redress of highly dispersed indirect purchasers, including consumers.[66]

This, however, does not exhaust all problems. While it seems possible to identify the entitlement of the person who has in the end suffered the economic loss from a theoretical point of view, this result also needs to be guaranteed in separate court proceedings of the direct and indirect purchasers (consumers) against the cartel members. This highlights the relevance of the rules on the burden of proof. These rules have to guarantee that the cartel members do not get away with the competition law infringement without

[64] This was also the interpretation of the Commission in its 2008 White Paper (n 18) ch 2.1, 4. In this regard, EU law differs considerably from the situation in the US, where the Supreme Court has excluded both the so-called passing-on defence of cartel members and damage actions of indirect purchasers. See *Hanover Shoe, Inc v United Shoe Machinery Corp* 392 US 481 (1968); *Illinois Brick Co v Illinois* 431 US 720 (1977). However, under state competition law, the rule is often a different one. Also, in 2007, the US Antitrust Modernization Commission recommended changing this rule so as to allow actions of indirect purchasers. See Antitrust Modernization Commission, Report and Recommendations, 2007, 267, available at govinfo.library.unt.edu/amc/report_recommendation/toc.htm (accessed 18 March 2015).

[65] *Courage v Crehan* (n 11) para 30.

[66] Collective consumer actions were already considered in the Commission's 2005 Green Paper (n 18) ch 2.5, 8–9. In the 2008 White Paper (n 18) ch 2.1, 4, the Commission confirmed a clear need for mechanisms of collective redress for consumers.

having to compensate anybody or, conversely, that cartel members have to compensate multiple purchasers at different levels in the supply chain. The first situation would arise if a cartel member successfully relied on the passing-on defence and also won in proceedings with indirect purchasers due to problems the latter had in proving that the damage was passed on to them. The second situation would arise if the passing-on defence was not available or failed, and at the same time the indirect purchasers succeeded with their damage claims as well.

These issues were first discussed in the national arena after the ECJ's *Courage* decision. Again, Germany is a good example. In 2005, the German legislature clarified that the mere fact that the relevant goods or services were resold to indirect customers in the supply chain does not exclude damage claims of the direct purchasers.[67] In the later so-called *ORWI* judgment of 2011, the German Federal Supreme Court (*Bundesgerichtshof*) discussed the question of how to deal with damage claims of indirect purchasers and the passing-on defence in more detail.[68] The underlying case related to the indirect industrial purchasers of paper that were affected by a European-wide cartel of paper producers. Against the backdrop of the *Courage* decision, the Federal Supreme Court confirmed that German national law does not and must not exclude actions of indirect purchasers since such exclusion would seriously compromise the full effectiveness of EU competition law.[69] Nevertheless, the Court in the end left the question open of whether EU law makes the entitlement of indirect purchasers mandatory by explaining that such damage claims of indirect purchasers are already mandated by the objectives of competition law since the law would otherwise deny compensation to those persons who most frequently suffer economic loss in cartel cases.[70] Moreover, the Court also acknowledged that the recognition of damage claims of indirect purchasers has to go hand in hand with the passing-on defence against claims of direct purchasers, which, in turn, could undermine effective enforcement.[71] Yet the Court rejected these concerns and

[67] s 33(3), 2nd sentence, Act against Restraints of Competition reads:

If a good or service is purchased at an excessive price, a damage shall not be excluded on account of the resale of the good or service.

In Germany, this rule is generally understood as one that clarifies that the general principles for the calculation of damages do apply.

[68] Federal Supreme Court (*Bundesgerichtshof*) of 28 June 2011, Case KZR 75/10—ORWI (2012) 43 *International Review of Intellectual Property and Competition Law* 487 (English translation). See also FW Bulst, 'Das ORWI-Urteil des Bundesgerichtshofs im Lichte des Unionsrechts' (2012) *Zeitschrift für Wettbewerbsrecht* 70; M Harmann-Rüppel and P Ludewig, 'Entscheidung für die Passing-On-Defence im deutschen Recht' (2012) *Zeitschrift für Wettbewerbsrecht* 90; C Kersting, 'Zur Anspruchsberechtigung indirekter Abnehmer im Kartellrecht nach dem ORWI-Urteil des BGH', (2012) *Juristen-Zeitung* 777.

[69] Federal Supreme Court (*Bundesgerichtshof*) of 28 June 2011, Case KZR 75/10—ORWI (n 68) paras 15–17.

[70] ibid, paras 24–26.

[71] ibid, para 28.

the proposal to concentrate damage claims on the level of direct purchasers by highlighting the role of damage claims to compensate only those who have incurred actual loss.[72] Most interestingly, the Federal Supreme Court rejected the view that the principle of full effectiveness of EU competition law makes damage claims of direct purchasers mandatory by highlighting that, according to the *Pfleiderer* decision of the CJEU, the rights of individuals need to be weighed against the public interest in effective enforcement.[73] Yet, regarding the burden of proof, the Court also clarified that it is for the indirect purchaser to prove that there is a causal link between the cartel and the passing-on of the surcharge to the indirect purchaser[74] and, thereby, because of the economic complexities of pricing in downstream markets, rejected any presumption of a passing-on of the surcharge.[75] On the other hand, the Court also held that the fact that the direct purchaser fixes his or her own price does not interrupt the causal link as such, since such decisions are influenced by this party's own costs.[76] According to these considerations the Court confirmed that there was a passing-on of the surcharge to the indirect purchaser.[77] Since the claim was brought by an indirect industrial purchaser, the question had to be answered of whether the defendant could rely on the passing-on defence with respect to the indirect purchaser as well.[78] According to the Court, the damage claim comes into existence with the purchasing contract. The fact that the damage was later passed on to the next level of the supply chain is only considered by the Court according to the doctrine of *Vorteilsausgleichung*.[79] Under this doctrine the defendant can rely on later benefits accruing to the victim provided that there is an adequate causal link between the injury and the benefit and that taking account of the benefit neither contradicts the underlying policy objectives of the damage claims nor unjustifiably exonerates the defendant.[80] According to the Court, also in the light of the principle of full effectiveness of EU law, it is the defendant who bears the burden to prove that these requirements for a *Vorteilsausgleichung* are fulfilled.[81] The Court sees these principles in line with the amendment of 2005, where the legislature basically left it to the courts to apply the doctrine of *Vorteilsausgleichung*.[82] Finally, the

[72] ibid, para 29.
[73] ibid, paras 37–38.
[74] ibid, para 44.
[75] ibid, para 45.
[76] ibid, para 48.
[77] ibid, para 49.
[78] ibid, paras 55–77.
[79] On this see H Köhler, 'Kartellverbot und Schadensersatz' (2004) *Gewerblicher Rechtsschutz und Urheberrecht* 99, 102.
[80] Federal Supreme Court (*Bundesgerichtshof*) of 28 June 2011, Case KZR 75/10—ORWI (n 68) para 58.
[81] ibid, para 64.
[82] Ibid, paras 66–67 (on s 33(3), 2nd sentence, Act against Restraints of Competition).

Federal Supreme Court also addressed the risk that the defendant might lose two subsequent proceedings against purchasers on different levels in the supply chain. In this regard, the Court hints at the possibility of the defendant to extend the law suit of the plaintiff to subsequent purchasers who might sue at a later stage.[83] Of course, in this regard the problem arises that the subsequent purchasers are extremely numerous and that quite often they cannot be identified easily by the defendant. In this regard, the Federal Court of Justice is to be criticised for too easily wiping an obvious problem off the table by pointing out that, in such instances, the economic loss is so fragmented that damage claims of those purchasers can hardly be successfully argued.[84] This argument is only convincing against the backdrop of the current German system that does not offer any means of collective redress of consumers. If such a system were introduced at a later stage, the procedural approach to coordinating damage claims of purchasers of different levels of the supply chain would have to be reconsidered.

Indeed, the new Damages Directive also puts a particular emphasis on actions of indirect purchasers and the availability of the follow-on defence. The obvious risk of overcompensation is addressed in Article 12(1) of the Directive. This provision requires the Member States both to guarantee that anyone who suffers harm, including direct and indirect purchasers, can claim compensation and to ensure that total compensation does not exceed the harm caused by the infringement. This result can only be reached if a passing-on of the overcharge to indirect infringers is taken into account for the damage claims of potential victims on the different levels of the supply chain. Accordingly, Article 13 therefore allows the defendant to rely on the passing-on defence, but still puts the burden on the defendant to prove that the overcharge was passed on to the next level of the supply chain.

Damage claims of indirect purchasers are dealt with by a different provision.[85] According to Article 14(1) of the Directive, the burden of proof for whether the overcharge was passed to the claimant—and for the amount of compensation—rests on the claimant. While this seems to be in line with the standard of proof required by the German Federal Supreme Court in *ORWI*, Article 13(2)(1) provides for an important presumption in favour of indirect purchasers in the form of a prima facie case of passing-on. According to these rules, a passing-on is deemed to be established if the claimant presents proof for the following cumulative requirements, namely,

[83] ibid, para 73.

[84] ibid, para 74.

[85] See also M Strand, 'Indirect Purchasers, Passing-on and the New Directive on Competition Law Damages' (2014) 10 *European Competition Journal* 361. On the pros and cons of damage claims of indirect purchasers see generally A Fuchs, 'Anspruchsberechtigte, Schadensabwälzung und Schadensbemessung bei Kartellverstößen' in O Remien (ed), *Schadensersatz im europäischen Privat und Wirtschaftsrecht* (Tübingen, Mohr Siebeck, 2012) 55, 62–67.

that (1) the defendant has committed an infringement of competition law, that (2) the infringement resulted in an overcharge for the direct purchaser and that (3) the claimant had purchased goods or services that were the subject of the infringement, or purchased goods or services derived from or contained such goods or services. If this very low standard of proof is fulfilled, it is for the alleged infringer to prove that the overcharge was not passed on to the claimant (Article 14(2)(2) of the Directive). As Recital 41 explains, Article 14 is meant to react to the obvious problems that indirect purchasers have to face when they have to prove their claims. By mentioning consumers in Recital 41, the Commission acknowledges the consumer-protection orientation of the rebuttable presumption of the passing on of the overcharge under Article 14(2).

From these rules on burden of proof it arises that there is a clear risk that a defendant may lose his or her case in proceedings with both direct and indirect purchasers. Therefore, in Article 15, the Damages Directive takes account of the need to coordinate actions of purchasers from different levels in the supply chain in order to avoid multiple liability of the competition law infringer. However, Article 15 proves to be rather modest. Article 15(1) only stipulates an obligation of national courts seized of an action for damages to 'take due account' of actions brought by claimants from another level in the supply chain and relating to the same infringement, of judgments resulting from such actions and of relevant information in the public domain resulting from public enforcement cases. Neither this provision nor the recitals explain how Member States can implement such an obligation without deviating from the fundamental principle of mere *inter partes* effects of private law judgments. Indeed, Article 15 provides that national courts are only obliged to coordinate their proceedings under the condition that they 'are able, by means available under Union and national law', to do so. According to Article 15(2) of the Directive, this includes the respect of the rule on the coordination of parallel proceedings in different Member States as contained in the Brussels I Regulation 1215/2012 on jurisdiction and enforcement.[86]

Unfortunately, neither the procedural approach of the German Federal Supreme Court nor that of the Commission Proposal will be able to fully guarantee that infringers of competition law will not either avoid paying at all or have to compensate multiple claimants from different levels in the supply chain. A solution would have been possible by harmonising substantive law. Just as indicated by the ECJ in *Courage*, damage claims could

[86] According to the Explanatory Memorandum to the Commission Proposal, at 4.4,17–18, parallel proceedings initiated by claimants from different levels in the supply chain are considered related ones in the sense of Art 30 of the Brussels I Regulation so that Courts could stay proceedings in order to prevent irreconcilable judgments or could even consolidate the actions.

be granted to both direct purchasers—without recognising the passing-on defence—and indirect purchasers. This would lead to a situation in which the defendant has to satisfy the claims of the purchaser that brings the first action. Once the defendant has satisfied the claimant from one level in the supply chain, this would also fulfil the obligation to compensate claimants from other levels in the supply chain. For this case, the law should provide for rules on bilateral compensation between the claimants from different levels in the supply chain. This solution was also the preferred choice in a decision of the Berlin Higher Regional Court (*Kammergericht*) of 2009.[87] This approach maximises incentives to bring damage claims to the court for all parties and would make it more likely that cartel members indeed have to compensate for the infringement without imposing on them a risk of multiple liability. Yet this approach did not find the support of the German Federal Supreme Court in the *ORWI* case.

To many, it may come as a surprise that the Damages Directive does not contain anything on collective redress of consumers, although this was an important element of the earlier policy considerations of the Commission, especially in the White Paper of 2008.[88] Yet, on the very day when it published its Proposal for the Damages Directive, the Commission also adopted a Recommendation on collective redress mechanisms that facilitate the enforcement of all rights that citizens have under EU law.[89] This Recommendation mirrors a widening of the perspective in two regards: first, the Recommendation goes beyond the enforcement of competition law by covering all rights of EU citizens, including general consumer rights

[87] Berlin Higher Regional Court (*Kammergericht Berlin*) of 1 October 2009, Case 2 U 10/03, *Berliner Transportbeton*, paras 103–26, available at www.gerichtsentscheidungen.berlin-brandenburg.de/jportal/portal/t/279b/bs/10/page/sammlung.psml?pid=Dokumentanzeige&showdoccase=1&js_peid=Trefferliste&documentnumber=1&numberofresults=1&fromdoctodoc=yes&doc.id=KORE230912009&doc.part=L&doc.price=0.0#focuspoint, accessed 18 March 2015, following R Bechtold, *GWB* 6th edn (Munich, CH Beck, 2008) s 33 para 24. A similar proposal however for statutory reform in this sense was submitted by J Drexl, 'Zur Schadensersatzberechtigung unmittelbarer und mittelbarer Abnehmer im europäisierten Kartelldeliktsrecht' in A Heldrich et al (eds), *Festschrift für Claus-Wilhelm Canaris zum 70. Geburtstag* Vol I (Munich, CH Beck, 2007) 1339, 1356–59.

[88] White Paper (n 18) ch 2.1, 4. See also P Buccirossi and M Carpagnano, 'Is it Time for the European Union to Legislate in the Field of Collective Redress in Antitrust (and How)?' (2013) 4 *Journal of European Competition Law & Practice* 3 (claiming the introduction of such redress not only for consumers but also SMEs).

[89] Recommendation of the Commission on common principles for injunctive and compensatory collective redress mechanisms in the Member States concerning violations of rights granted under Union Law, C(2013) 3539/3, available at eur-lex.europa.eu/legal-content/EN/TXT/?qid=1398263020823&uri=OJ:JOL_2013_201_R_NS0013 (accessed 18 March 2015). On its role for competition law enforcement see D-PL Tzakas, 'Collective Redress in the Field of EU Competition Law: The Need for an EU Remedy and the Impact of the Recent Commission Recommendation' (2014) 41(3) *Legal Issues of Economic Integration* 225.

in particular.[90] Accordingly, the Recommendation was prepared by several cooperating Directorates General (DG), including DG Competition. Second, the Recommendation is not limited to collective redress of consumers alone, but applies to the rights of all EU citizens. As to the first aspect, while it is understandable that the Commission prefers a comprehensive approach to collective redress in different fields, the broader perspective runs the risk of missing the necessary coordination between emerging national systems of collective redress in the Member States and the peculiar needs in the field of competition law enforcement.[91] As to the second aspect, the broader perspective deserves to be supported since collective redress in competition matters in particular is needed not only to serve the interests of consumers but also of small businesses.[92]

In the earlier debate on private enforcement of EU competition law, the most important issue was whether group actions should be based on an opt-out or an opt-in principle. The Recommendation follows the latter approach.[93] The issue of collective redress was probably the most relevant one that contributed to considerably postponing the Commission's Proposal for the Damages Directive. This was mostly due to concerns that the EU could run the risk of importing the highly problematic model of class actions in antitrust cases from the United States. These concerns also explain why the issue of collective redress was dissected from the legislation on damage claims for competition law infringements and why the Commission only chose to adopt a non-binding recommendation.

VI. TENSION BETWEEN ECONOMIC THEORY AND NORMATIVE CONSIDERATIONS

The last tension that is to be addressed closely relates to that between substantive law and the effectiveness of private enforcement (see part IV, above). With regard to the substantive law standards, it was pointed out that the criteria for assessing competition law infringements, under the influence of the 'more economic approach', nowadays tend to be more influenced by arguments of economic theory than in the past. In this regard, it has to be

[90] Recital 7 of the Recommendation mentions

> consumer protection, competition, environment protection, protection of personal data, financial services legislation and investor protection.

For a critical assessment of this horizontal approach see M Dawson and E Muir, 'One for All and All for One? The Collective Enforcement of EU Law' (2014) 41(3) *Legal Issues of Economic Integration* 215.

[91] On the current systems of collective redress in the Member States in competition law matters see Ashton and Henry (n 52) paras 6.072–6.156.

[92] According to Recital 6 of the Recommendation collective redress mechanisms should not only be available to natural but also to legal persons.

[93] Paras 21 to 24 of the Recommendation (n 89).

added that the strengthening of private enforcement is also driven by economic considerations. Under such considerations, damage claims are characterised by changing objectives. While damage claims, from a perspective of traditional private law, are designed to compensate private parties for harm that was caused to them by others, private enforcement in economic terms receives a both preventive and public-law connotation as a means to create additional incentives to deter undertakings from infringing competition law in the first place.[94] This coincides with the traditional role attributed to the recognition of individual rights according to the principle of full effectiveness of European law. Rights of the individual follow a utilitarian rationale. The individual is vested with rights in the public interest, namely, to enhance the respect of EU law. From this perspective, the most important reason for recognising private damage claims is not to compensate victims for the harm that was done to them, but to strengthen enforcement and the respect of EU competition law as such.

As can be seen from the analysis, the debate on damage claims and private enforcement is largely characterised by the conflict between normative and economic considerations. In the light of economic considerations, there are also good arguments for introducing double or even treble damages in order to increase the deterrent effect of private enforcement. But such multiple damage awards would collide with the normative consideration that the victim should only be compensated for the harm incurred and should not benefit from unjustified enrichment.

Such conflicts between economic and normative considerations also show up in additional regards. The Commission, under the impression of the economic approach, nowadays states that competition law should enhance efficiency and consumer welfare. Consumer interests and consumer harm have made it to the centre of the assessment of competition cases.[95] At the same time competition economists would argue that competition law is only designed to protect consumers and not competitors.[96] Yet the same

[94] On this public-law dimension of private enforcement see M-A Frison-Roche, 'Efficient and/or Effective Enforcement' in J Drexl, L Idot and J Monéger (eds), *Economic Theory and Competition Law* (Cheltenham, Edward Elgar, 2009) 211. Because of the public law connotation of private enforcement, it would be wrong to assume a fundamental conflict between the objectives of public and private enforcement. See also Singh (n 23) 209–11 (rejecting such a fundamental conflict).

[95] This tendency is most clearly expressed in the Communication from the Commission—Guidance on the Commission's enforcement priorities in applying Art 82 of the EC Treaty to abusive exclusionary conduct by dominant undertakings [2009] OJ C45/7.

[96] US American enforcers have complained in the past that Europeans protect competitors, while US enforcers protect competition. See, for instance, the immediate reaction of the US DoJ on the 2007 judgment of the European Court of First Instance in Case T-201-04 *Microsoft v Commission* [2007] ECR II-3601: US Department of Justice, 'Assistant Attorney General for Antitrust, Thomas O. Barnett, Issues Statement on European Microsoft Decision', Press Release of 17 September 2007, available at www.justice.gov/atr/public/press_releases/2007/226070.pdf, accessed 18 March 2015. This view is however quite rightly opposed by scholars such as EM Fox, 'We Protect Competition, You Protect Competitors' (2003) 26 *World Competition* 149.

economists would argue that consumer welfare and protection of competitors can also be enhanced by granting damage claims to competitors.[97] This does not appear contradictory in an analytical framework based on economic theory, since, in this framework, even private rights only serve the public objective of enhancing economic efficiency. Also granting a right to competitors—for instance in cases of exclusionary abuses under Article 102 TFEU—to be compensated for the harm that they suffer makes economic sense.[98] The higher the number of self-interested advocates that bring private claims to the courts, the more likely it will be that 'efficient' competition law will be respected. But from a normative perspective, it certainly makes no sense to argue that a competition law that grants damage claims to competitors does not protect these competitors.

Of course, especially with regard to damage claims arising from cartels, the new Damages Directive can also be seen as an instrument that promotes consumer welfare in particular. However, it is not blind to more normative considerations. By responding to the CJEU's principle to accord private remedies to all individuals that suffer harm from an infringement of competition law, the Damages Directive clarifies that its rules also apply *mutatis mutandis* to upstream restraints of competition that harm suppliers.

VII. CONCLUSION

In its historical context, the *Courage* decision of 2001, which established the foundations of the European law on damage claims for infringement of EU competition law, can be understood as a strategy of the former ECJ to strengthen enforcement in view of the upcoming decentralisation of the enforcement of Articles 101 and 102 TFEU and the implementation of the market-share approach of the new type of Block Exemption Regulations. Nowadays, the development of private enforcement is very much driven by cases relating to price cartels. While initially private damage claims were considered an alternative to public enforcement, especially in cases where competition authorities are no longer informed on potentially anti-competitive agreements, private enforcement in price-cartel cases mostly takes place in the form of 'follow-on actions' in which the victims of the cartel rely on previous public enforcement actions of the competition authorities. Recent cases on price cartels show that there is a tension between private and public enforcement; the interest of the victims of price cartels in also getting compensation from leniency applicants undermines the public interest in

[97] Damage claims of competitors are potentially most relevant for private enforcement of Art 102 cases. See Mackenrodt (n 51) 182–83.

[98] Yet damage claims of competitors may lead to over-deterrence. See Mackenrodt (n 51) 184–86 (still not rejecting the appropriateness of damage claims of competitors).

enhancing the detection of cartels by protecting leniency applicants against access of victims to the documents delivered by the leniency applicant. In order to solve the problem, the CJEU requires national courts to engage in a weighing of the interests on a case-by-case basis. This requirement is not sufficiently mirrored by the new Damages Directive, which provides for a general delimitation of different kinds of documents to which access will be granted or not.

With the particular focus of current practice on price cartels and damage claims, there is a risk that the role of private enforcement in other areas of competition law enforcement where already the assessment of competition law infringement raises highly complex issues of law and economics is not sufficiently taken into account. The trend towards less formal mechanisms of public enforcement in this field, including the increasing use of commitment decisions and settlements, acts against the interest of victims in legal certainty and, thereby, undermines their possibilities of bringing stand-alone damage claims against alleged infringers. Yet in this field of more complex competition cases, private enforcement plays a major role as a defence in proceedings initiated by alleged infringers. This dimension of private enforcement has largely been overlooked so far and is not sufficiently addressed by the new Damages Directive, for instance, when the victims argue a duty to license under EU competition law as a defence against an intellectual property (IP) infringement claim.

The debate on who should be entitled to sue for damages in case of price cartels and whether a passing-on defence should be recognised or not raises complex legal issues influenced by traditional private law concepts in the Member States and complex policy issues regarding effective enforcement of EU competition law. The debate on this question can be understood as an example of the conflict that arises between the public interest in deterring from infringement in a most effective way and normative considerations relating to the function of damage claims to compensate the purchaser who has ultimately had to pay the price of the cartel. This conflict between economic and normative considerations can be identified as an overall theme that characterises policy decisions that have to be made in the context of regulating private enforcement in general. This conflict therefore also influences the question of whether private enforcement should also build on the introduction of collective redress of the victims of cartels from the lowest level in the supply chain.

Part IV

Shaping Justice: The Court of Justice of the European Union

8

The Impact of the Court of Justice on the European Law Enforcement Architecture

R DANIEL KELEMEN

I. INTRODUCTION

THE ENFORCEMENT ARCHITECTURE for European economic law has been transformed profoundly over the past three decades. While the styles of economic regulation that had prevailed at the national level in post-War west European states differed in many ways, they shared important common features—particularly when compared to the more judicialised, litigious style of regulatory enforcement that prevailed in the United States.[1] Across a wide variety of fields of economic regulation, European approaches relied on relatively closed networks of bureaucrats and regulated interests to develop and implement policies in close concertation. Public authorities generally resolved conflicts with regulated interests informally, through negotiation and compromise, seldom turning to the courts to bring enforcement litigation. Regulators enjoyed considerable discretion in pursuing their regulatory objectives, as courts rarely intervened to challenge their regulatory decision-making. Enforcement litigation brought by private actors was an even greater rarity. Concepts like 'regulation through litigation' or the 'private attorney general' were seen as distinctly American phenomena, anathema to European modes of regulation. However, since the relaunch of the Single Market project in the mid-1980s, the European Union (EU) has both undermined traditional national styles of regulation in EU Member States and encouraged the rise of a distinctive legal and regulatory style which I have termed Eurolegalism.[2] Eurolegalism is a regulatory style

[1] RA Kagan, *Adversarial Legalism: The American Way of Law* (Cambridge MA, Harvard University Press, 2001).

[2] RD Kelemen, *Eurolegalism: The Transformation of Law and Regulation in the European Union* (Cambridge MA, Harvard University Press, 2011). As I explain in the book, Eurolegalism is a distinctive European variant of the American legal style that Robert Kagan (n 1) has labelled 'adversarial legalism'.

distinguished by an emphasis on strict, judicialised enforcement of detailed legal norms through a combination of public enforcement and the broad empowerment of private actors to assert their legal rights. As I put it earlier:

> Across policy areas ranging from employment discrimination to consumer protection to antitrust to securities regulation to the free movement rights of workers, students, and even medical patients, we can observe more coercive legal enforcement, more rights claims, and a growing judicial role in shaping policy.[3]

In short, with the rise of Eurolegalism, the enforcement of economic law in Europe has become more judicialised, more coercive and has come to rely more heavily on private actors.

The Court of Justice of the European Union (CJEU)[4] has played a central role in this transformation, but it has by no means been the only driver of the trend. As I explain below, the rise of Eurolegalism and the transformation of enforcement is a product of the combined impact of economic liberalisation and political fragmentation associated with the process of European integration. Functional pressures associated with the project of creating a single market along with political incentives generated by the structure of EU institutions have led policy-makers to rely on a more adversarial, litigious approach to enforcement. Judges did not create Eurolegalism—neither supranational judges of the CJEU nor the national judges who enforce EU law. But judges have been more than merely passive participants in the transformation of regulatory style. The CJEU has seized on the opportunities that EU policy makers handed to it, accelerating the rise of Eurolegalism through its case law and frequently pushing it beyond what most lawmakers intended.

This chapter explores how the rise of Eurolegalism has transformed the enforcement architecture of European economic law, with a particular emphasis on the role the CJEU has played in the process. The analysis sheds light on questions such as: Why has the volume and strictness of centralised enforcement of economic law by the Commission increased? Why has the EU so actively promoted decentralised enforcement of European economic law by private parties before national courts? And what role has the CJEU played in promoting a more coercive, judicialised and litigious approach to enforcement? The remainder of the chapter is divided into four sections. Section II summarises my arguments concerning the rise of Eurolegalism and the resulting transformation of patterns of enforcement. Section III highlights the impact of the CJEU on these trends. Section IV considers the emerging judicial architecture of enforcement in the EU, highlighting challenges currently facing the CJEU. Section V concludes.

[3] Kelemen (n 2) 5.

[4] Following the new nomenclature, I refer to the CJEU when referring to the EU's supranational judiciary as a whole (including the Court of Justice and the General Court). When referring to the Court of Justice specifically, I use the acronym ECJ.

II. THE RISE OF EUROLEGALISM AND THE TRANSFORMATION OF ENFORCEMENT

European integration has encouraged the spread of Eurolegalism through two closely intertwined causal mechanisms: economic liberalisation and political fragmentation. First, economic liberalisation associated with the process of establishing a single market has undermined traditional national approaches to regulation including their less coercive, less judicialised approaches to enforcement. Deregulation at the national level has been coupled with reregulation at the EU level, but the greater number and diversity of market players in pan-European liberalised markets has led EU policy-makers to rely on more formal, transparent approaches to regulation backed by enforcement litigation brought by both public and private actors. Consider, for example, an area such as securities regulation.[5] National governments across Europe had relied on approaches to securities regulation that emphasised informal, flexible self-regulation by stock exchanges themselves and by the repeat players (such as listing firms and financial intermediaries) who operated on these exchanges. This approach was tenable in relatively closed markets, where the number of listing firms and financial intermediaries was limited, and where market actors and regulators formed a cosy network of repeat players. However, these informal, self-regulatory systems, which limited market entry and tended to favour insiders, stood in the way of the EU's efforts to create a single market for financial services. Moreover, the approach to regulation that prevailed in these national systems clearly could not be replicated in a liberalised, dynamic pan-European market for financial services, where there would be more (and more diverse) market players, less trust and where new entrants to national markets would demand transparent, even-handed enforcement of clear legal rules. Thus, the drive to create a single financial market involved both deregulation and reregulation: deregulation that dismantled national regulatory regimes and reregulation that established an EU-based securities regulatory regime, which emphasised transparent legal rules and judicial enforcement by both public and private actors. This example highlights why the creation of 'freer' markets can require more rules and why deregulation of market entry is often followed by juridical reregulation that emphasises strict enforcement.[6]

Second, beyond the impact of these economic shifts, the political fragmentation rooted in the EU's very institutional architecture has also played a role in encouraging the rise of Eurolegalism. The EU's institutional structure is characterised both by horizontal fragmentation at the EU level

[5] Kelemen (n 2) ch 4.

[6] S Vogel, 'Why Freer Markets Need More Rules' in M Landy, M Levin and M Shapiro (eds), *Creating Competitive Markets: The Politics of Regulatory Reform* (Washington DC, Brookings Institution Press, 2007).

where policy-making power is divided between the Council, the European Parliament and the European Commission and by vertical fragmentation that divides policy-making authority between institutions at the EU level and the Member State administrations who implement most EU law. Also, the EU has an extremely weak administrative apparatus.[7] The EU sets many of the rules that govern economic and social life in a diverse polity with over 500 million people spread across 28 member states, yet its bureaucracy—with just over 43,000 employees[8]—is a tiny fraction of the size of its Member States' bureaucracies.[9] The EU's administrative bureaucracy in the Commission and other bodies simply lacks the capacity to effectively oversee the implementation and enforcement of the EU's enormous corpus of rules. Finally, despite its administrative weakness, the EU does possess a relatively strong and independent judicial system, led by the Court of Justice in Luxembourg and including the vast network of national courts who actively participate in the EU judicial order. This fragmented institutional structure generates a variety of principal-agent problems, because the political principals crafting laws at the EU level (the European Parliament (EP), the Council and the Commission) are concerned about controlling the discretion of the agents (Member State administrations) who will be implementing these policies. This distrust encourages lawmakers to enact laws that spell out in detail the actions that national administrations must take and to invite courts to play an active role in enforcing these laws. Lawmakers do this both by creating bases for the European Commission to bring enforcement litigation before the European Court of Justice (ECJ) and by harnessing national courts and private litigants to play a key role in enforcement, as a way to make up for the weaknesses of the EU's central administrative apparatus and to ensure that EU policies are implemented and enforced across the Union.

The European Parliament, the Commission and even Member State governments in the Council support this judicialised approach to enforcement, which ties the hands of Member State governments and exposes them to the potential of both public and private enforcement litigation.[10] But—as

[7] RD Kelemen, 'The Politics of Eurocracy: Building a New European State?' in N Jabko and C Parsons (eds), *The State of the European Union, Volume 7: With US or Against US? European Trends in American Perspective* (Oxford, Oxford University Press, 2005).

[8] I include in this figure the 33,000 staff of the European Commission, the roughly 5000 staff of the EU's various decentralised regulatory agencies, the roughly 2500 staff of the European Central Bank, the roughly 2000 staff of the European Investment Bank and the roughly 800 staff of Europol. If one were to include employment in all EU institutions (including staff of the Council, Parliament, Court of Justice, External Action Service and other entities), the total number of EU personnel approaches 60,000.

[9] RD Kelemen, 'Building the New European State? Federalism, Core State Powers and European Integration' in P Genschel and M Jachtenfuchs (eds), *Beyond the Regulatory Polity: The European Integration of Core State Powers* (Oxford, Oxford University Press, 2014).

[10] Kelemen (n 2) 26.

I discuss in greater detail in the next section—the ECJ too has played an active role, offering expansive interpretations of the substantive and procedural rights created by EU treaties and secondary legislation, pressing national courts to facilitate private enforcement and making rulings that strictly enforce EU economic laws against recalcitrant member states.

As a result of these dynamics, EU economic regulation is full of detailed, judicially enforceable provisions, many of which are framed as rights that economic actors may enforce before national courts. Policy makers have framed policies in the language of individual rights even where rights-based approaches were clearly not the norm at the national level in EU Member States.[11] This can be seen across the spectrum of economic policy, in fields ranging from competition policy, to securities regulation, to consumer protection, to environmental policy, to employment discrimination regulation, to Eurozone governance. Concerning employment discrimination, the Race Directive and Framework Equal Treatment Directive create a number of provisions that can be enforced by workers who suffer discrimination on the basis of race, age, disability, religion and sexual orientation.[12] In consumer protection law, consumers have enforceable rights with regard to product liability, advertising, unfair commercial practices,[13] and sector-specific rights in areas ranging from air passenger rights[14] to patient's rights.[15] In the field of securities regulation, shareholders enjoy a range of rights that they can enforce against listing companies and financial intermediaries.[16] In the field of competition policy, the 'modernisation' reforms were designed to encourage private parties to take enforcement action against firms who violate EU competition rules.[17]

[11] ibid, 45; G de Búrca, 'The Language of Rights and European Integration' in G More and J Shaw (eds), *New Legal Dynamics of European Union* (Oxford, Clarendon Press, 1995).

[12] D Mabbett, 'The Development of Rights-Based Social Policy in the European Union' (2005) 43 *Journal of Common Market Studies* 97. These anti-discrimination rules of course build on long-established EU protections against employment discrimination on the basis of sex.

[13] S Weatherill, *EU Consumer Law and Policy* (Cheltenham, Elgar European Law, 2005); S Weatherill and U Bernitz, *The Regulation of Unfair Commercial Practices under EC Directive 2005/29* (Oxford, Hart Publishing, 2007).

[14] Kelemen (n 2) 1–4; S Garben, 'Sky-High Controversy and High-Flying Claims? The Sturgeon Case Law in Light of Judicial Activism, Euroscepticism and Eurolegalism' (2013) 50 *Common Market Law Review* 15.

[15] A Kaczorowska, 'A Review of the Creation by the European Court of Justice of the Right to Effective and Speedy Medical Treatment and Its Outcomes' (2006) 12 *European Law Journal* 345; S Greer and S Rauscher, 'Destabilization Rights and Restabilization Politics: Policy and Political Reactions to European Union Healthcare Services Law (2011) 18 *Journal of European Public Policy* 220.

[16] Kelemen (n 2) ch 4.

[17] A Wigger and A Nölke, 'Enhanced Roles of Private Actors in the EU Business Regulation and the Erosion of the Rhenish Model of Capitalism: The Case of Antitrust Enforcement' (2007) 45 *Journal of Common Market Studies* 487; N Reich, 'The "Courage" Doctrine: Encouraging or Discouraging Compensation for Antitrust Injuries?' (2005) 42 *Common Market Law Review* 35; C Hodges, 'Competition Enforcement, Regulation and Civil Justice: What Is the Case?' (2006) 43 *Common Market Law Review* 1381.

The rise of Eurolegalism has not only transformed enforcement by establishing substantive rights, it has also led to the establishment of a host of procedural rights and remedies and to a broad effort to enhance access to justice for private parties before national courts. For a system of regulatory governance based on adversarial legalism to operate, it is not enough to simply establish rights; private parties must be ensured access to justice. For every right, there must be a remedy (*ubi jus, ibi remedium*), and impediments to access to justice and differences in national procedural rules and remedies could prevent citizens and firms from enforcing their rights. Traditionally, many of the procedural rules and institutions found in national systems of civil justice and in administrative law in European countries deterred private parties from enforcing their rights. Rules concerning litigation finance—from the loser pays rule to the absence of contingency fee arrangements, rules concerning collective actions, and limits on damages all worked to discourage enforcement litigation. If the EU was to ensure that legal persons could realise the economic rights it had created, it had to guarantee them effective and equivalent access to justice and remedies across the Union.[18]

Under the banner of creating a 'Genuine European Area of Justice',[19] the EU is leading a broad effort to increase access to justice and to encourage the harmonisation of procedural law in ways that will facilitate private enforcement.[20] As a result, national systems of civil justice and administrative law are being transformed gradually in ways that facilitate access to justice and private enforcement. EU legal integration is encouraging changes that may reduce the cost to plaintiffs of bringing litigation (that is, through changes to the rules governing collective actions and conditional fee arrangements) and increase the potential rewards (for example through changes to rules on damage awards) that successful plaintiffs may realise.[21]

With these changes in Europe's legal landscape, not only has enforcement by public authorities become more judicialised and coercive, private actors too have been given greater opportunities and incentives to bring enforcement actions. The impact of this transformation of enforcement can be seen by tracing in detail changes in affected policy areas—such as competition policy, securities regulation, employment discrimination, environmental

[18] C Harlow, 'A Common European Law of Remedies?' in C Kilpatrick, T Novitz and P Skidmore (eds), *The Future of Remedies in Europe* (Oxford, Hart Publishing, 2000).

[19] Presidency Conclusions, Tampere European Council, 15–16 October 1999, Section B.

[20] HE Hartnell, 'EUstitia: Institutionalizing Justice in the European Union' (2002) 23 *Northwestern Journal of International Law and Business* 65; C Hodges, 'Europeanization of Civil Justice: Trends and Issues' (2007) 26 *Civil Justice Quarterly* 96; C Hodges, 'European Union Legislation' (2009) 622 *Annals of the American Academy of Political and Social Science* 78; C Hodges, 'From Class Actions to Collective Redress: A Revolution in Approach to Compensation' (2009) 1 *Civil Justice Quarterly* 41; Kelemen (n 2) ch 3.

[21] Kelemen (n 2) ch 3.

policy and many more.[22] It can also be seen by surveying aggregate measures reflecting broad changes in the 'European legal field'.[23] As I have detailed elsewhere, since the mid-1980s, EU Member States have seen a dramatic increase in the number of attorneys and the size of their legal services industries.[24] Likewise, the volume of judgments rendered by the ECJ and the General Court has more than tripled since the latter court was established,[25] which reflects increases in various enforcement actions including infringement proceedings and enforcement actions before national courts referred to the ECJ under the preliminary ruling procedure.

While it is clear that Eurolegalism is spreading across the EU, it is important to emphasise that the pace of its spread and the precise forms it takes vary considerably across policy areas and countries. We have observed the spread of Eurolegalism across a wide range of policy areas—including areas mentioned above such as securities regulation, competition policy, workplace discrimination policy, health care policy, and consumer protection policy and other sensitive areas such as industrial policy[26] and Eurozone fiscal governance.[27] Nevertheless, there are clearly some areas where Eurolegalism has spread more slowly or not at all. Generally, we can expect Eurolegalism to take root more quickly in areas of law, such as securities or competition policy, dominated by corporations or other well-resourced actors, than in areas such as anti-discrimination law where potential litigants face resource constraints and other obstacles to access to justice. In some fields, Eurolegalism may fail to take root at all, as Francesca Bignami demonstrates in her study of the data privacy field.[28] Yet, Reich and Micklitz's study of litigation surrounding the Unfair Contract Terms Directive (UCTD) reminds us that while the dynamics of Eurolegalism may fail to take root in a policy area initially, they may later come to life in a rapid surge of judicial activity.[29] Future studies of European governance and the spread of Eurolegalism need to systematically explore and explain variations in the timing and scale of the phenomenon across policy areas and Member States.

[22] Kelemen (n 2).

[23] A Vauchez, 'The Force of a Weak Field: Law and Lawyers in the Governance of the European Union' (2008) 2 *International Political Sociology* 128; A Vauchez and B de Witte (eds), *Lawyering Europe: European Law as a Transnational Social Field* (Oxford, Hart Publishing, 2013).

[24] Kelemen (n 2) 79–88.

[25] ibid, 90.

[26] B Rehder, '"Adversarial Legalism" in the German System of Industrial Relations?' (2009) 3 *Regulation and Governance* 217.

[27] RD Kelemen and T Teo, 'Law, Focal Points and Fiscal Discipline in the United States and the European Union' (2014) 108 *American Political Science Review* 355. In the realm of Eurozone fiscal governance, the 2012 Fiscal Compact Treaty promotes a form of Eurolegalism by calling on national courts to play a central role in enforcing structural balanced budget rules.

[28] F Bignami, 'Cooperative Legalism and the Non-Americanization of European Regulatory Styles: The Case of Data Privacy' (2011) 59 *American Journal of Comparative Law* 411.

[29] H-W Micklitz and N Reich, 'The Court and Sleeping Beauty: The Revival of the Unfair Contract Terms Directive (UCTD)' (2014) 51 *Common Market Law Review* 771.

III. THE ARCHITECTURE OF ENFORCEMENT

A central governance dilemma facing the EU is that its policy-making ambitions far exceed its administrative enforcement capacity. Member governments transfer more authority to the EU in treaties and agree to the adoption of more and more secondary legislation, but they have steadfastly refused to allow the European Commission to expand to the scale necessary to effectively oversee this growing body of EU law. Of course, the EU relies primarily on national administrations to implement and enforce its policies, but as they may not always act as reliable agents of the Union, Brussels needs mechanisms through which to ensure that EU law is effectively implemented and enforced.

Given the political impediments to expanding the Commission bureaucracy, the EU has sought to strengthen its enforcement architecture in two other ways. First, the EU has expanded its regulatory capacity in a decentralised fashion, establishing more than 30 specialised European agencies spread out to locations across Europe, such as the European Medicines Agency in London, the European Securities and Markets Authority in Paris, the European Food Safety Authority in Parma and the European Asylum Support Office in Valletta.[30] These EU agencies are not enforcement bodies per se, but they do bolster the EU's administrative capacity both directly—insofar as they perform regulatory functions such as information gathering or rulemaking—and indirectly insofar as they serve as hubs of networks of national regulatory authorities and work to harmonise the activities of these national authorities.[31]

It seems likely that the role of EU agencies in the Union's enforcement architecture will increase in the years to come. Since the early years of the Community, the role of EU agencies in the process of regulatory implementation and enforcement has been constrained by the ECJ's *Meroni* doctrine.[32] In *Meroni*, the Court held that Community law does not allow the delegation of discretionary regulatory powers to bodies not established in the EU's Treaties. EU agencies are established through secondary legislation—not by the Treaties—and the ECJ has long interpreted the *Meroni* doctrine to severely limit the decision-making powers that could be granted to agencies.[33] However, in a 2014 ruling, the ECJ effectively reinterpreted

[30] RD Kelemen, 'The Political Foundations of Judicial Independence in the European Union' (2012) 19 *Journal of European Public Policy* 43; RD Kelemen and AD Tarrant, 'The Political Foundations of the Eurocracy' (2011) 34 *West European Politics* 922.

[31] RD Kelemen and G Majone, 'Managing Europeanization: The European Agencies' in J Peterson and M Shackleton (eds), *The Institutions of the European Union* (Oxford, Oxford University Press, 2012) 238.

[32] Case C-9/56 *Meroni v High Authority* [1957–58] ECR 133.

[33] Communication from the Commission of 25 July 2001 'European governance—A white paper' COM (2001) 428 final [2001] OJ C287/1, 24.

the *Meroni* doctrine, opening the way for EU agencies to exercise greater regulatory powers. The ruling concerned the EU's Short Selling Regulation,[34] which had granted a new EU agency—the European Securities and Markets Authority—the power to ban short selling during market emergencies. The United Kingdom brought a legal action before the ECJ seeking to strike down this provision of the Short Selling Regulation, claiming it had delegated a large degree of discretionary rule-making power to an EU agency in violation of the *Meroni* doctrine. In its January 2014 ruling,[35] the ECJ rejected the UK's claims and upheld the Regulation. Although the ECJ did not explicitly overrule *Meroni*, it offered a very expansive interpretation of the scope of decision-making authority that could be granted to an EU agency without the delegation constituting 'excessive' discretionary power. In other words, the ruling is likely to open up the way for the delegation of greater regulatory powers to EU agencies.

Second, and more importantly, in order to promote the enforcement of EU law the EU is seeking to construct a European judiciary. In section II above, I outlined the combination of forces that have led the EU to promote a highly judicialised mode of governance—Eurolegalism. Governing through Eurolegalism requires judges. Of course, it requires much else besides—including the development of an entire 'legal field'[36] of academics, lawyers and litigants surrounding EU law. But as a mode of governance that relies heavily on judicialisation and decentralised enforcement, Eurolegalism cannot function without an adequate supply of judges. Thus the emergence and development of Eurolegalism requires both a contingent of judges at the EU level large enough to handle the volume of cases seeking adjudication, and it requires national judges to act as reliable guardians of EU law in the cases involving EU law that are brought before them. In other words, the EU has had to find ways to both expand courts at the EU level and gradually convert more and more national courts, so that they would see themselves—and act—not simply as elements of a national judiciary but as geographically dispersed courts in a European Union judicial order.

The judicial architecture of enforcement in the EU has expanded dramatically in recent decades and its transformation continues. The ECJ was originally composed of seven justices, and in its early years the ECJ struggled to cultivate ties with a handful of national courts that might send it references for preliminary rulings. This was hardly the recipe for a judicial architecture on which a highly legalistic, judicialised enforcement regime might be built. However, over the ensuing decades the 'EU judiciary'—comprising both the

[34] Reg (EU) No 236/2012 of 14 March 2012 on short selling and certain aspects of credit default swaps [2012] OJ L86/1.

[35] Case 270/12 *United Kingdom v Parliament and Council*, judgment of 22 January 2014, not yet reported.

[36] Vauchez (n 23); Vauchez and de Witte (n 23).

supranational courts and the national courts that cooperate with it—has grown along several dimensions.

First, the ECJ which is composed of one judge per Member State[37] has grown with each enlargement, expanding the number of justices to 28. This growth in itself might not have helped the ECJ to handle more cases, but the ECJ took advantage of its growth and established a system of hearing cases in smaller chambers (of three, five or 13 judges).[38] Thus, the ECJ effectively transformed itself from one court to several. Today, the ECJ hears nearly all of its cases in chambers of three or five judges, with only particularly significant cases going before the Grand Chamber of 15 judges or before the Full Court. Beyond growing the ECJ internally, new courts were also created. In the Single European Act, the Member States agreed to expand the EU judiciary by creating a lower chamber, the Court of First Instance (now the General Court). They adhered to the one judge per Member State approach, thus doubling the number of EU-level judges with the creation of this new court. Also, in 2004 a seven judge Civil Service Tribunal was established to hear EU staff cases, removing them from the dockets of the ECJ and Court of First Instance. Thus, today the EU's supranational judiciary effectively has 63 judges arrayed across three courts, which divide themselves into a total of 22 smaller chambers. It is this growth in the Luxembourg based courts—along with procedural reforms—which has now allowed the CJEU to hear over a thousand cases a year with shorter waiting times than in the past.

Debates about further expansion of the EU-level judiciary are ongoing. In 2011, the Court of Justice requested that the Council add 12 additional judges to the General Court in order to deal with its mounting backlog of cases and the lengthy delays in rendering judgments.[39] Though the Member States agreed in principle to the need to expand judicial capacity, they could not agree on how to allocate the proposed 12 additional judges between the 27 (later 28) Member States. Finally, last October Member States agreed to a plan to phase in the addition of 28 additional judges to the General Court (one additional judge per Member State). However, the EU has yet to move ahead with the addition of any judges. The Council's proposal to phase in 28 additional judges remains stalled in the European Parliament,

[37] Whenever the number of Member States was even, States would appoint an additional judge by collective agreement such that the total number of judges on the Court would be odd. This was necessary because the Court makes decisions by majority vote. However, with the accession of Croatia and the enlargement of the EU to 28 Member States, a 29th judge was not appointed.

[38] Hearing cases in chambers was permitted under Art 165 of the Treaty of Rome.

[39] Council of the European Union, Interinstitutional File 2011/0901 (COD), Brussels 7 April 2011.

and the General Court itself is resisting the measure, so it remains to be seen whether, and if so how and when, the CJEU will be expanded.[40]

While the expansion of EU-level courts has occurred in one location—at the CJEU on the Kirchberg Plateau in Luxembourg—it seems likely that we may soon see specialised EU-level courts begin to spread across Europe. In 2013, 25 EU Member States agreed to establish a system of patent courts—which would collectively be known as the Unified Patent Court (UPC).[41] This new patent court system would operate within the framework of EU law, but would not be housed within the structure of the CJEU. The UPC would have its appellate court in Luxembourg, but have main trial courts in Paris, London and Munich, with a series of local division courts spread out across the European Union. Though the system was due to be launched in 2015, only six Member governments have ratified the agreement thus far and Spain has a pending legal action before the ECJ seeking to annul the two regulations that form the basis for the new unitary patent system and the UPC.[42] As a result the launch of the UPC is likely to be delayed. Nevertheless, given the broad political support for the scheme, it remains unlikely it will be abandoned altogether.

While gradually expanding the EU-level judicial architecture, the EU has also steadily expanded its judicial architecture at the national level. The effectiveness of European law has always depended on the ECJ's relationship with national courts who send it cases (via the preliminary ruling procedure), recognise the supremacy of European law and apply European law and ECJ rulings domestically. Convincing the courts of the original six Member States to recognise the supremacy of European law and to send cases to the ECJ was a vital step in the process of European legal integration.[43] Since that crucial founding period, the ECJ, and more generally the EU, have worked to bring the national judiciaries of new Member States into the interlocking system of national and EU level courts.[44] Thus, the network of national courts that cooperate (and sometimes conflict) with the ECJ in the interpretation and application of EU law has expanded with the enlargement of the EU from six to 28 Member States.

But the EU has done more than just invite national courts to participate in the process of EU law. The EU has slowly and steadily worked to achieve a more profound transformation—the conversion of national courts into

[40] V Pop, 'Companies Restless at Slow Pace of EU Justice' *Wall Street Journal* (New York, 26 March 2015).

[41] Agreement on a Unified Patent Court [2013] OJ C176/1.

[42] CJEU, 'Advocate General's Opinion in Case C-146/13 *Spain v Parliament and Council* and Case C-147/13 *Spain v Council*', Press Release No 152/14, Luxemburg, 18 November 2014.

[43] K Alter, *Establishing the Supremacy of European Law* (Oxford, Oxford University Press, 2001).

[44] D Piana, *Judicial Accountabilities in New Europe* (Farnham, Ashgate, 2010).

European courts that see themselves, and behave, as integral elements in a European judicial order. Today thousands of judges across the 28 States of the European Union are trained in European law, participate in EU-related judicial networks and engage with the EU courts in Luxembourg. EU policy-makers have significantly ramped up judicial training and exchange programmes working through central institutions such as the Academy of European Law, the European Judicial Training Network, through various horizontal networks of jurists and through national judicial training institutes. The European Commission recently conducted surveys of judicial training on EU law at European legal training institutes and at national legal training institutes,[45] and is determined to see far more judges trained in European law as part of its broader goal that 50 per cent of all legal practitioners in the EU will receive training on EU law by 2020.[46]

While the EU is pressing ahead with its effort to gradually convert national courts into reliably 'European' courts, the process is neither smooth nor uniformly successful. Courts in Nordic Member States continue to be very reluctant to use the preliminary ruling procedure,[47] and some new Member States have shown similar reluctance.[48] There are continuing tensions between the ECJ and national courts, with courts such as the German and Czech constitutional courts challenging the ECJ over supremacy and other critical doctrines.[49] Recent challenges to the independence of the judiciary in Hungary, Bulgaria and Romania have raised new questions about the EU's ability to rely on national courts to enforce European law and, more generally, about the EU's ability to function as a community under the rule of law.

This observation brings us back to the questions posed by the editors of this volume concerning whether the EU has in place or can develop a European enforcement architecture in accordance with essential principles and objectives of the EU economic order. With an ever growing body of European economic law and a growing, increasingly diverse and sometimes unreliable network of thousands of national courts, the ECJ faces a

[45] See: European Commission, 'Building Trust in EU-Wide Justice: A New Dimension to European Judicial Training', COM(2011) 551 final; Directorate General for Internal Policies, *Judicial Training in the European Union Member States* (Brussels, European Parliament, 2011); European Commission, *Report on European Judicial Training 2011* (Luxemburg, Publications Office of the European Union, 2012).

[46] 'European Commission sets goal of training 700,000 legal professionals in EU law by 2020' (Commission Press Release IP/11/1021 of 13 September 2011).

[47] M Wind, 'The Nordics, the EU and the Reluctance Towards Supranational Judicial Review' (2010) 48 *Journal of Common Market Studies* 1039.

[48] M Bobek, 'Learning to Talk: Preliminary Rulings, the Courts of the New Member States and the Court of Justice' (2008) 45 *Common Market Law Review* 1611.

[49] A Dyevre, 'The German Federal Constitutional Court and European Judicial Politics' (2011) 34 *West European Politics* 346; A Dyevre, 'Judicial Non-Compliance in a Non-Hierarchical Legal Order: Isolated Accident or Omen of Judicial Armageddon?', Max Planck Institute for International and Comparative Law, Working paper, January 2012; E Jones and RD Kelemen, 'The Euro Goes to Court' (2014) 56 *Survival: Global Politics and Strategy* 15.

monumental task in seeking to maintain the coherence of Community legal order and ensure respect for the rule of law.[50] To be sure, EU law-makers and the ECJ have taken important steps to encourage national courts and national legal systems to strengthen access to justice such that private parties can enforce EU economic law (and other law) before national courts. However, the impact of these initiatives varies greatly across Member States and policy areas, and where corrupt or inefficient national judicial systems impede access to justice, the decentralised enforcement of EU economic law may remain more of an aspiration than a reality.

IV. THE ROLE OF THE COURT OF JUSTICE

The discussion of the rise of Eurolegalism above demonstrates that repeatedly and across many policy areas, EU lawmakers in the Parliament, Commission and Council have promoted a judicialised mode of economic governance that relies on both public and private enforcement litigation. This trend is the product of deeply rooted functional pressures and political incentives—not simply the creation of activist judges. Yet, it is also clear that the ECJ itself has played a central role in the rise of Eurolegalism and in the construction of the EU's enforcement architecture more generally. The ECJ has an institutional self-interest in promoting deeper European integration and in asserting for itself a central role in EU governance. The fragmented political structure of the EU makes it difficult for EU political actors to secure the agreement (by qualified majority or sometimes unanimity) necessary to rein in the ECJ when it expands the bounds of EU law beyond what they may have envisaged. With this 'joint decision trap' shielding it, the ECJ can make expansive interpretations of EU law and enforce the law strictly against non-compliant states with little fear of political reprisal.[51]

The ECJ has played an active role in promoting an expansive interpretation of the scope of substantive and procedural rights in EU law and in promoting the decentralised enforcement of EU law by private actors before national courts. Considering these actions, many critics of the ECJ accuse the Court of being activist and self-aggrandising.[52] Perhaps it is.

[50] K Lenaerts, 'The Rule of Law and the Coherence of the Judicial System of the European Union' (2007) 44 *Common Market Law Review* 1625; H Rasmussen, 'Present and Future European Judicial Problems after Enlargement and the Post-2005 Ideological Revolt' (2007) 44 *Common Market Law Review* 1661.

[51] F Scharpf, 'The Joint-Decision Trap Revisited' (2006) 44 *Journal of Common Market Studies* 845; Kelemen (n 30).

[52] See for instance: H Rasmussen, *On Law and Policy in the European Court of Justice* (Dordrecht, Martinus Nijhoff, 1986); F Scharpf, 'Legitimacy in the Multilevel European Polity' (2009) 1 *European Political Science Review* 173; M Everson, 'Is the European Court of Justice a legal or political institution now?' *The Guardian* (London, 10 August 2010); R Herzog and L Gerken, 'Stoppt den Europäischen Gerichtshof', *Frankfurter Allgemeine Zeitung* (Frankfurt, 8 September 2008) 8.

But we must also recognise that political actors have *invited* the ECJ—backed by national courts—to play this role. At most, critics of 'judicial overreach' can only fault the ECJ for the enthusiasm with which it has accepted this invitation.

To appreciate the role the ECJ has played in the rise of Eurolegalism, we must look back to the role the ECJ played in shaping the foundations of today's EU legal order. Landmark ECJ doctrines such as direct effect (*Van Gend*)[53] and supremacy (*Costa*)[54] were necessary in order to establish a legal order in which EU law could be enforced in the face of contradictory national law and in which private parties could play a role in enforcing their EU rights. The ECJ has repeatedly offered expansive interpretations of the scope of EU substantive and procedural rights[55] that created more bases for private rights claims. The ECJ and General Court have played a decisive role in shaping EU administrative law, holding that national courts are obliged to alter national rules of administrative procedure when doing so is necessary to ensure the full and effective protection of EU rights.[56] Likewise, the ECJ has played a crucial role by insisting that national legal systems and national courts ensure effective judicial remedies when enforcing EU directives.[57] For instance, the Court has required Member State legal systems to lift statutory damage caps and to ensure that damage awards provide for full compensation for damages suffered (*Marshall II*).[58] In the field of competition policy, the ECJ established in *Courage*[59] that individuals who suffer damages as a result of private actors' violations of EU competition law could hold them liable for the damages suffered.

We should also recognise the role the ECJ has played in shaping the very judicial architecture that underpins Eurolegalism. First, the ECJ used the

[53] Case C-26/62 *Van Gend en Loos v Nederlandse Administratie der Belastingen* [1963] ECR 1.

[54] Case C-6/64 *Costa v ENEL* [1964] ECR 583.

[55] R Cichowski, *The European Court, Civil Society, and European Integration* (Cambridge, Cambridge University Press, 2007); A Stone Sweet, *The Judicial Construction of Europe* (Oxford, Oxford University Press, 2004); G de Búrca and B de Witte, *Social Rights in Europe* (Oxford, Oxford University Press, 2005); JA Caporaso and S Tarrow, 'Polanyi in Brussels: Supranational Institutions and the Transnational Embedding of Markets' (2009) 63 *International Organization* 593; Alter (n 43); M Shapiro, 'Rights in the European Union: Convergent with the USA?' in Jabko and Parsons (n 7).

[56] Kelemen (n 2) 54; A Ward, 'The Limits of the Uniform Application of Community Law and Effective Judicial Review: A Look Post-Amsterdam' in Kilpatrick, Novitz and Skidmore (n 18); W van Gerven, 'Bridging the Gap Between Community and National Laws: Towards a Principle of Homogeneity in the Field of Legal Remedies?' (1995) 32 *Common Market Law Review* 679.

[57] P Craig and G de Búrca, *EU Law: Text, Cases, and Materials* 4th edn (Oxford, Oxford University Press, 2008) 309–20; A Ward, *Judicial Review and the Rights of Private Parties in EU Law* 2nd edn (Oxford, Oxford University Press, 2007) 39–41.

[58] Case C-271/91 *Marshall v Southampton and SW Area Health Authority* [1993] ECR I-2367.

[59] Case C-453/99 *Courage v Crehan* [2001] ECR I-6297.

discretion it enjoyed under the Treaty of Rome with respect to its own internal organisation in order to develop the Chamber system, which eventually allowed it to dramatically increase its capacity to hear cases. Second, with regard to increasing the size of the CJEU, the Court of Justice has periodically been proactive in communicating to the Council of Ministers the importance of increasing the size of the Court or of instituting other procedural reforms in its statute such that it could perform its judicial function effectively. Most recently, the ECJ has requested that the Council of Ministers help it address the growing backlog of cases before the General Court by adding 12 new judges.[60] Third and finally, the ECJ has from the outset played an active role in seeking to transform national courts into European courts. It has mostly done this in an inviting manner, cultivating ties with national judges who would participate in the preliminary ruling system early on,[61] and eventually institutionalising extensive training programmes on EU law for visiting judges. ECJ judges have also been active through their scholarship and outreach activities in promoting acceptance among national judiciaries of the Court and its doctrines.[62] But the ECJ has mixed its warm embrace of national judges with the occasional cold shower, as for instance when it asserted the principle that member states could be held liable for damages suffered by individuals as a result of infringements of EU law attributable to national courts of last instance.[63]

V. CONCLUSION

Legalistic and adversarial approaches to enforcement, particularly ones that rely on private parties to bring enforcement litigation, were traditionally seen as elements of an American regulatory style, what Kagan has called adversarial legalism,[64] or what Farhang has identified as integral to America's 'Litigation State'.[65] This American-style approach was quite out of step with the approaches that prevailed in Western Europe, which were more informal and relied more on concertation between regulators

[60] Council of the European Union (n 39). Also see V Skouris, 'The Court of Justice of the European Union: A Judiciary in a Constant State of Transformation' in P Cardonnel, A Rosas and N Wahl (eds), *Constitutionalizing the EU Judicial System* (Oxford, Hart Publishing, 2012).

[61] AM Burley and W Mattli, 'Europe Before the Court' (1993) 47 *International Organization* 41; Alter (n 43).

[62] For a review of the recent EU legal history literature that explores these activities in the early Court, see M Pollack, 'The New EU Legal History: What's New, What's Missing' (2013) 28 *American University International Law Review* 1257.

[63] Case C-224/01 *Gerhard Köbler v Republik Österreich* [2003] ECR I-10239; Case C-173/03 *Traghetti del Mediterraneo SpA, in liquidation v Repubblica Italiana* [2006] ECR I-1209.

[64] Kagan (n 1).

[65] S Farhang, *The Litigation State: Public Regulation and Private Lawsuits in the United States* (Princeton, Princeton University Press, 2010).

and stakeholders than on courts and private enforcement actions. With the rise of Eurolegalism across a wide range of policy areas, enforcement of economic law is being transformed. Public authorities, from the European Commission to the national authorities that act to implement and enforce EU law, have come to take a more coercive approach and to rely more on litigation than they did in the past. Private actors too have been encouraged to play a greater role in enforcement, though the degree to which they have mobilised to play this role and the degree to which national legal systems afford them access to justice continues to vary considerably across Member States and policy areas. Ironically, while the EU appears to be embracing its own form of Eurolegalism with the support of the CJEU, there are indications that the US is seeking to limit its reliance on adversarial legalism and the 'litigation state', with the US Supreme Court leading the drive to restrict private enforcement.[66]

[66] S Burbank and S Farhang, 'Litigation Reform: An Institutional Approach' (2014) 162 *University of Pennsylvania Law Review* 1543.

9

Alternatives to the Court of Justice of the European Union in the Field of Intellectual Property Law

MARCUS NORRGÅRD

I. INTRODUCTION

INTELLECTUAL PROPERTY LAW has during the last 25 years made a remarkable transition from a field of law based almost solely on national and international law to a cornerstone of modern EU private law. From the first tentative steps of the Directive on Semiconductor Topographies in 1986[1] and the Trademark Directive in 1988[2] the EU has ventured deep into many questions of intellectual property (IP) law, including such controversial issues as enforcement and patents on biotechnological inventions. All attempts have not been successful. The EU patent package was discussed for over 40 years before a compromise solution was reached, and it still remains uncertain whether a sufficient number of countries will ratify the agreement. Quite a few projects have, however, succeeded in harmonising EU intellectual property law.

IP legislation has over the years increasingly moved from the national parliaments to the EU level. Now trademark and design law are to a large part harmonised.[3] Patent law is still mainly in the national domain. Copyright is somewhere in between: there are quite a few copyright directives, but no all-encompassing piece of EU legislation.

[1] Council Dir 87/54/EEC of 16 December 1986 on the legal protection of topographies of semiconductor products [1987] OJ L24/36.

[2] First Council Dir 89/104/EEC of 21 December 1988 to approximate the laws of the Member States relating to trade marks [1989] OJ L40/1.

[3] Graeme Dinwoodie, 'The Europeanisation of Trade Mark Law' in A Ohly and J Pila (eds), *The Europeanization of Intellectual Property Law: Towards a European Legal Methodology* (Oxford, Oxford University Press, 2013) 76: 'extensive and deep Europeanization of trade mark law'.

After quite intensive substantive regulation of intellectual property, the European Union moved to questions of enforcement, first by entering into the TRIPS Agreement (1994)[4] (together with the Member States) and later by adopting the Enforcement Directive (2004/48/EC).[5] It is widely recognised that substantive rules require efficient enforcement in order to be of relevance. Thus it was more than natural that the EU would want to venture into the regulation of enforcement as well.

The Court of Justice of the European Union (CJEU) has had a fundamental harmonising role in the interpretation of directives, regulations and also—to a certain degree—international agreements.[6] Without one court vested with the power to interpret the legislative acts of the EU, harmonisation could have been disharmony—like the case has been with the European Patent Convention (EPC) where national Supreme courts have reached different conclusions in, for example, such a fundamental question as scope of protection.

It is quite clear that the CJEU has played an important part in harmonising IP law, and continues to do so. Sometimes the CJEU has played the part of the 'judicial activist' and sometimes not.[7] There is however one issue I would like to address in this paper, albeit rather speculatively, but none the less. Invoking the CJEU through the means of a preliminary reference procedure delays the overall time of the proceedings quite considerably. The more EU legislation is introduced in the field of intellectual property law, the greater the role of the CJEU and the greater the risk of delay.

I would like to take this opportunity to look at alternative—hopefully faster—ways of dealing with the question of IP law harmonisation in Europe. In all the alternatives some other court takes the place of the CJEU leaving the CJEU with matters of more fundamental magnitude.

[4] Agreement on Trade-Related Aspects of Intellectual Property Rights ('TRIPS'), Annex 1C of the Marrakesh Agreement Establishing the World Trade Organization, signed in Marrakesh, Morocco on 15 April 1994, available at: www.wto.org/english/tratop_e/trips_e/t_agm0_e.htm, 1.9.2014.

[5] Dir 2004/48/EC of 29 April 2004 on the enforcement of intellectual property rights [2004] OJ L195/16.

[6] The CJEU has, for example, in a few cases discussed the interpretation of the TRIPS Agreement. See, eg, Case C-431/05 *Merck Genéricos—Produtos Farmacêuticos Lda v Merck & Co Inc and Merck Sharp & Dohme* [2007] ECR I-7001. See also Case C-53/96 *Hermès International v FHT Marketing Choice* [1998] ECR I-3603.

[7] The judgment in Case C-5/08 *Infopaq International A/S v Danske Dagblades Forening* [2009] ECR I-6569 can be mentioned as a copyright case where the CJEU showed judicial activism. The CJEU harmonised the concept of 'originality' although the legal basis for such harmonisation is debatable. See, for example, Niklas Bruun, 'Mätäkuun juttu—EYT:n tekijänoikeustulkinta', available at: www.iprinfo.com/julkaisut/iprinfo-lehti/lehtiarkisto/2009/IPRinfo_4-2009/fi_FI/Matakuun_juttu__EYTn_tekijanoikeustulkinta/.

II. THE ROLE OF THE CJEU IN IP LITIGATION

The CJEU has a significant, threefold role in intellectual property law. First, the CJEU gives preliminary rulings in matters referred to it by national courts.[8] Second, the CJEU acts as an appeals court in questions regarding the registration of community trademarks and designs.[9] Third, in rare cases actions for annulment of EU legislation may be of relevance in intellectual property.[10]

Community trademark and design applications are decided by the Office for the Harmonization in the Internal Market (Trademarks and Designs) (OHIM) in Alicante, Spain. Such applications can be refused either by OHIM by its own motion or on the basis of an opposition by a third party.[11] In the first instance appeals against a refusal go to the boards of appeal of the OHIM.[12] Appeals against decisions of a board of appeal go to the General Court and from there to the CJEU.[13]

Intellectual property appeals form a considerable part of the General Court's decision-making activities.[14] During 2008–2012, an average of 31 per cent of the decided cases at the General Court were intellectual property law cases.[15] In absolute numbers the figure has varied between 168 (2009) and 240 (2011) decided IP cases. The duration of the proceedings in IP cases at the General Court have been around 20 months.[16] The CJEU has

[8] Art 267 of the Treaty on the Functioning of the European Union ('TFEU') OJ C326/47.

[9] According to Arts 263(1) and 256(1) TFEU the General Court has jurisdiction to review the legality of acts of bodies, offices or agencies of the Union intended to produce legal effects vis-à-vis third parties. In accordance with Art 115(1) of Council Reg (EC) No 207/2009 of 26 February 2009 on the Community trade mark [2009] OJ L78/1 ('CTMR'), OHIM is a body of the Community. See also Art 65 CTMR.

[10] In 1998, the Netherlands brought an action for annulment of the Dir 98/44/EC of 6 July 1998 on the legal protection of biotechnological inventions [1998] OJ L213/13 ('Biotech Directive'). See Case C-377/98 *Netherlands v Parliament and Council* [2001] ECR I-7079. The latest example is Spain's challenge of Reg No 1257/2012 of the European Parliament and of the Council of 17 December 2012 implementing enhanced cooperation in the area of the creation of unitary patent protection [2012] OJ L361/1 and Reg No 1260/2012 of 17 December 2012 implementing enhanced cooperation in the area of the creation of unitary patent protection with regard to the applicable translation arrangements [2012] OJ L361/89 (Cases C-146/13 and C-147/13 *Spain v Parliament and Council*, nyr).

[11] OHIM examines absolute grounds for refusal by its motion, relative grounds of refusal, however, only after opposition from a third party. See Arts 7–8 CTMR and Art 45 CTMR.

[12] Arts 61–62 CTMR.

[13] Art 65 CTMR and Art 263 TFEU.

[14] Court of Justice of the European Union, *Annual Report 2012* (Luxembourg, Publications Office of the European Union, 2013) 143: 'With 210 cases brought to a close and 238 new cases, intellectual property proceedings represented, in terms of numbers of cases, a significant source of the Court's activity …'.

[15] Decided cases in 2008: 605, of which 171 were IP cases (28.26%). Decided cases in 2009: 555, of which 168 were IP cases (30.27%). Decided cases in 2010: 527, of which 180 were IP cases (34.16%). Decided cases in 2011: 714, of which 240 were IP cases (33.61%). Decided cases in 2012: 688, of which 210 were IP cases (30.52%).

[16] 2008: 20.4 months. 2009: 20.1 months. 2010: 20.6 months. 2011: 20.3 months. 2012: 20.3 months.

during the same period (2008–2012) decided an average of 34 IP cases per year. The number includes both appeals and preliminary references.

Preliminary references have played a pivotal role in EU legal integration.[17] This applies also to intellectual property law, although the amount of preliminary references per year does not come anywhere close to the number of appeals in trademark and design cases. In 2008 the CJEU gave six preliminary rulings in IP cases, in 2009 in 14 cases, in 2010 in 10 cases, in 2011 in 20 cases and in 2012 in 20 cases.

In both cases—appeals and preliminary references—the average proceedings last around 20 months in the CJEU. The average duration of the proceedings in 2008–2012 has varied from 11.5 months in *Schenker*[18] to 41 months in *The Wellcome Foundation.*[19] There is however a major difference between appeals and preliminary references. In appeals the whole case is disposed of with the decision of the General Court (GC)/CJEU. In preliminary rulings, the case is still to be adjudicated by the national courts. The case has also been dealt with in one or two national instances before reaching the CJEU. Combined with the proceedings at the CJEU the proceedings as a whole risk taking too long.[20] It has been noted that 'the preliminary reference procedure has grown rapidly and today is in danger of becoming a victim of its own success'.[21] A delay of this magnitude not only is an issue of delay, but it soon also becomes an issue of access to justice and harmonisation if national courts do not, as has been suggested, ask for preliminary rulings because of the long time it takes to get them.[22]

Among others, Broberg and Fenger have considered how to reform the preliminary reference system. They start off by observing that the high number of preliminary references has led to a situation where it takes inconveniently long to receive an answer from the Court of Justice.[23] Although the CJEU has taken steps to make the proceedings quicker, the authors consider

[17] T de la Mare and C Donnelly, 'Preliminary Rulings and EU Legal Integration: Evolution and Stasis' in P Craig and G de Búrca (eds), *The Evolution of EU Law* (Oxford, Oxford University Press, 2011) 363.

[18] Case C-93/08 *Schenker SIA v Valsts ieņēmumu dienests* [2009] ECR I-903.

[19] Case C-276/05 *The Wellcome Foundation Ltd v Paranova Pharmazeutika Handels GmbH* [2008] ECR I-10479.

[20] See also M Broberg and N Fenger, *Preliminary References to the European Court of Justice* (Oxford, Oxford University Press, 2010) 6: 'An important consequence of the large number of references is that the average time taken to deal with each reference is now substantial'. de la Mare and Donnelly (n 17) 375: 'The financial and temporal costs of a preliminary reference represent a significant barrier to CJEU access'.

[21] Broberg and Fenger, ibid 5. cf de la Mare and Donnelly (n 17) 364: 'the procedure has been over-extended—under pressure both from national courts and the CJEU—in ways which, if left unchecked, may ultimately undermine its usefulness in future EU evolution'.

[22] Broberg and Fenger (n 20) 6: 'Presumably, the considerable time it takes to obtain a preliminary ruling deters a number of national courts from using this procedure even though otherwise the nature of the main proceedings justifies doing so'.

[23] ibid, 25.

a few alternative ways of making the system faster in the future. The authors note that the future challenge is to 'achieve a balance where the Court is not asked to treat more cases than it can handle while still ensuring that Community law is being developed primarily by the Court of Justice itself'.[24] If no measures are taken it is not unlikely that both the unity and the impact of the Court's decisions will diminish as their number increases and as they deal more frequently with questions of secondary importance or of interest only in the context of the case concerned.[25]

The authors consider five different types of ways of making the proceedings more efficient.[26] First, they look at whether it would be possible to transfer preliminary ruling cases to the General Court. According to Treaty on the Functioning of the European Union (TFEU) Article 256(3)

> The General Court shall have jurisdiction to hear and determine questions referred for a preliminary ruling under Article 267, in specific areas laid down by the Statute.

This possibility has, however, not been used as of yet.[27] Broberg and Fenger think it might be possible to transfer, for example, trademark cases. They also note that it might create synergy effects to transfer cases. If trademark cases would be sent to the GC, there seems to be no good reasons why copyright, design and patent cases would not follow.

Second, they consider so-called green light procedures, where the national court would suggest a solution in its referral and the Court of Justice would limit itself to giving a 'green light' to the proposal, with or without modifications. Third, they consider whether the Court of Justice might apply a similar system to the US Supreme Court's *certiorari* system. This kind of docket control would mean that the Court of Justice would itself choose which cases to adjudicate. In essence it could choose the important ones and disregard the cases of lesser importance. The authors note some drawbacks with this kind of system, and suggest also some remedies. Fourth, they suggest limiting the right to refer to courts of last instance. Also this proposal has its pros and cons, as the authors note. Finally, the authors consider creating regional courts to do part of the work of the Court of Justice, although they find it to be a 'radical way of relieving the preliminary reference pressure on the Court of Justice'.[28]

One alternative not expressly considered by the authors is to speed up CJEU proceedings by not asking for an opinion of the Advocate

[24] ibid.
[25] ibid, 25 et seq.
[26] ibid, 26 et seq.
[27] See also A Dashwood, M Dougan, B Rodger, E Spaventa and D Wyatt, *Wyatt and Dashwood's European Union Law* 6th edn (Oxford, Hart Publishing, 2011) 210.
[28] ibid, 32.

General (AG). In *Svensson* the Court did however just that.[29] Proceedings lasted in all about 16 months, which is shorter than normal. The problem with *Svensson* is that it concerns a question that has been at the centre of the European copyright discussion since the late 1990s, namely linking. Solutions had to some degree been found, but generally speaking the situation was not clear. In *Svensson*, however, the court seemingly easily reached a less than self-evident solution. Without the AG's opinion it has been rather difficult to know what the court actually did decide, and—more troubling—what the decision means outside the very specific factual situation presented in *Svensson*. Proper adjudication without the AG's opinion would, I think, require that the Court adapts its reasoning: the grounds for the decision must be more deliberative in order for the reader to understand why a certain interpretation has been reached.

The CJEU has also tried to speed up proceedings by not giving a judgment at all, but rather contents itself with giving a reasoned order. According to Rule 99 of the Rules of Procedure of the Court of Justice,[30] the CJEU can decide a preliminary ruling matter by reasoned order in three situations: the question is identical to a question on which the Court has already ruled, the reply may be clearly deduced from existing case law or the answer 'admits of no reasonable doubt'. For example, in C-535/13 *Honda v Patmanidi* the CJEU disposed of a trademark issue relating to parallel imports in just nine months.[31] The main downside of a reasoned order are the briefly stated grounds.

These different alternatives are important in their own right. They focus, however, on the preliminary reference system only. What if harmonised interpretations were achieved without the CJEU? I will look at a few different alternative ways of already reaching harmonised decisions before the case reaches the CJEU.

III. BUILDING BLOCKS OF AN IDEAL COURT SYSTEM IN IP LAW

When analysing whether a court structure is ideal, the fundamental right to access to justice and fair trial should be taken into account. According to Article 6 of the European Human Rights Convention everyone is entitled to a fair and public hearing within a reasonable time by an independent and impartial tribunal established by law. Article 13 provides that everyone whose rights and freedoms are violated shall have an effective remedy before a national authority. Article 47 of the EU Charter on fundamental

[29] Case C-466/12 *Svensson et al* v *Retriever Sverige AB*, judgment of 13 February 2014, nyr.

[30] Rules of Procedure of the Court of Justice [2012] OJ L265/1, as amended by the Amendment of the Rules of Procedure of the Court of Justice [2013] OJ L 173/65.

[31] Case C-535/13 *Honda v Patmanidi*, judgment of 17 July 2014, nyr.

rights provides in a similar manner that everyone whose rights and freedoms guaranteed by the law of the Union are violated has the right to an effective remedy before a tribunal and that everyone is entitled to a fair and public hearing within a reasonable time by an independent and impartial tribunal previously established by law. The European Human Rights Court in Strasbourg has repeatedly found that proceedings that last too long breach the right to a fair trial.[32]

On a more general level, any procedural system should be fast, cost-effective and lead to correct decisions.[33] It is clear that no existing court can achieve all the requirements at the same time. The different requirements should be viewed more as principles that are fulfilled more or less, instead of rules that apply either or. For instance, the questions of time, costs and correctness are seldom so clear-cut that it is possible to pinpoint at what stage delay, increased costs and not perfectly correct decisions become a problem. It should however be noted that an inefficient court system—one which is slower, costlier and more error-prone—can through efficiency-enhancing measures be made better as regards all these principles. I would argue—quite uncontroversially, I think—that the preliminary reference system is not optimally efficient in the light of costs, timeliness and correctness of decisions. As was briefly touched upon above, several measures have been taken in order to make the preliminary reference proceedings more efficient. It should however be remembered that efficiency has not traditionally been the main concern in preliminary reference matters. In the trademark case C-206/01 *Arsenal Football Club v Matthew Reed*, the High Court of Justice of England and Wales did not follow the judgment of the CJEU. Although the Court of Appeal later overturned the decision by the High Court, the 'delicacy of the relationship between the Court of Justice and the national courts, and the care the Court needs to take when rendering preliminary rulings' has been noted.[34] In spite of this, it could be argued that private law, especially intellectual property law, has reached a stage of harmonisation and maturity where more emphasis should be put on the efficiency of the court proceedings than on balancing the powers of the European Union

[32] ECHR judgment of 19 April 2007 in the case of *Vilho Eskelinen and Others v Finland* (2007) 45 EHRR 43. ECHR judgment of 7 June 2001 in the case of *Kress v France* ECHR 2001-VI, 41. ECHR judgment of 28 October 1999 in the case of *Zielinski and Pradal and Gonzalez and Others v France* ECHR 1999-VII, 95.

[33] To this effect, see also The ALI/UNIDROIT Principles of Transnational Civil Procedure, especially Principle 7 ('The court should resolve the dispute within a reasonable time'), and comment P-7B ('Prompt rendition of justice is a matter of access to justice and may also be considered an essential human right, but it should also be balanced against a party's right of a reasonable opportunity to organize and present its case'), available at www.unidroit.org/english/principles/civilprocedure/ali-unidroitprinciples-e.pdf.

[34] Dashwood et al (n 27) 217 et seq. Case C-206/01 *Arsenal Football Club v Matthew Reed* [2002] ECR I-10273.

in relation to the Member States. On the other hand, smartly designed measures may increase not only efficiency, but also trust in the CJEU.

In the EU there should be one court with the power to give binding decisions on the interpretation of primary and secondary legislation. If the CJEU were replaced by some other court, the need for a highest court to give binding, harmonising decisions, would still remain. It goes without saying that a system without such a harmonising court could be problematic. It would lead to a situation as that in patent law. Although the European Patent Convention to a large part harmonises patent law on a *legislative* level, the lack of a highest adjudicator in Europe in patent law has led to a situation where the English, the Germans, the French, the Dutch and other countries all have their own ways of interpreting the EPC.[35] There is a dialogue between the courts, especially between the German and the English courts, and the interpretations are not necessarily as far away from each other as they were when the EPC entered into force.[36] It remains, however, a fact that EPC Member States are free to have their own interpretations and to a large part they use this freedom.

IV. ALTERNATIVE MODELS FOR THE ROLE OF THE CJEU

A. Introduction

Three different models of dispute resolution are presented and discussed as alternatives to the CJEU in the field of intellectual property law. The Unified Patent Court (UPC) is the first model. It tries to evade the jurisdiction of the CJEU and build a system of national courts sitting in multinational compositions through an international agreement. The second model is the model introduced by TFEU Article 257 with a specialised court attached to the General Court. This represents a more EU-centric court alternative than the UPC. The last alternative represents an interesting mix of national courts and EU courts. It was presented in the 1989 Community Patent Convention and it was never accepted. As an idea it is however worth noting.

It should be noted that the enforcement of both Community trademarks (CTMs) and Community design rights (CDRs) take place exclusively in national courts (save for the preliminary references) although the national courts are called 'community trademark courts' or 'community design courts'. In practice the regular IP courts act as community courts in the

[35] See, for instance, J Pagenberg and WR Cornish (eds), *Interpretation of Patents in Europe. Application of Article 69 EPC* (Cologne, Carl Heymanns Verlag, 2006).

[36] This type of dialogue has taken place especially between the English and German courts. See, for instance, A Keukenschrijver, 'DE—The German Practice' in Pagenberg and Cornish (n 35) 78.

CTM and CDR cases. From an EU law perspective this in essence means that the national courts have the same role in CTM and CDR cases as in other types of private law cases involving EU law, namely the national courts have a duty to enforce EU law. Therefore the court structure in CTM and CDR cases does not provide us with an alternative to the current system.

B. The Unified Patent Court

The first model for intellectual property litigation is the Unified Patent Court (UPC), which is not yet set in place. Many of the necessary steps in order to make the UPC a reality have been taken. The Agreement on a Unified Patent Court has been agreed upon, although not yet ratified by a sufficient number of Member States, and the EU regulations on unitary effect have been adopted. The rules of procedure are being drafted and discussed.[37] At this point in time everything indicates that the UPC will become reality.

The UPC agreement establishes the UPC for the settlement of disputes relating to European patents and European patents with unitary effect. In effect, the UPC would be a national court common to the contracting states (UPC Agreement, Article 1). It would thus not be a community court as such. It would have the same obligations as any national court to take into account EU law and to refer cases for a preliminary ruling to the CJEU (UPC Agreement, Articles 1(2) and 21).[38]

The reason for the UPC being a *national* court instead of a supranational community court is an interesting one. Between 1975 and 2009 different community patent regimes were devised and suggested.[39] The latest, the

[37] The 17th draft of 31 October 2014.

[38] See also UPC Agreement, preamble ('CONSIDERING that, as any national court, the Unified Patent Court must respect and apply Union law and, in collaboration with the Court of Justice of the European Union as guardian of Union law, ensure its correct application and uniform interpretation ...') and Statute of the Unified Patent Court, Art 38. This would, for instance, mean that it would be possible for UPC as for any national court to state as P Craig, 'The Jurisdiction of the Community Courts Reconsidered' (2001) 36 *Texas International Law Journal* 555, 557: 'It is clear that properly understood we have three types of Community Court, not just two: we have the ECJ, the CFI *and* national courts'.

[39] Community patent regimes have, without success, been suggested in 1975, 1989, 2000 and 2009. There have generally been many components making up the community patent regime. One component has been the patent itself (how to acquire it, infringement, validity, assignment etc), and another very important and rather complex component has been the litigation system. Furthermore, the language regime has been at the centre of discussions. For a discussion on the 1975 and 1989 Community Patent Conventions, see, for example, A Benyamini, *Patent Infringement in the European Community* (New York, VCH Weinheim, 1993) 10–19. For the 2000 proposal, see Proposal for a Council Reg on the Community patent, COM(2000) 412 final. For the 2009 proposal, see Revised Proposal for a Council Reg on the Community patent (Council Doc 8588/09 of 7 April 2009). In the 2009 proposal, the court structure was of particular interest, see Draft Agreement on the European and Community Patents Court and Draft Statute—Revised Presidency text (Doc 7928/09 of 23 March 2009).

2009 proposal, was disqualified by the CJEU on the ground that it would not have been compatible with the EU treaties.[40] The Draft Agreement on the European and Community Patents Court devised an international court with its own legal capacity, which would have had exclusive jurisdiction in infringement and validity cases. The CJEU viewed such a court as being 'outside the institutional and judicial framework of the European Union' and that it would deprive the national courts their right to interpret and apply EU law and the CJEU its powers to reply by preliminary ruling to the national courts' questions.[41] This would have—according to the CJEU—altered 'the essential character of the powers which the Treaties confer on the institutions of the European Union and on the Member States and which are indispensable to the preservation of the very nature of European Union law'.[42] Creating a court outside the court structure recognised by the EU treaties was therefore not possible.

The now signed, but not yet ratified, Agreement on a Unified Patent Court builds, however, on the idea that the UPC would be a *national court* common to the contracting states. Thus the UPC would be a court with the same powers and obligations in relation to EU law as any national court, including a right and obligation to make preliminary references. The UPC is thus something similar to the Cour de Justice Benelux, which is a joint court of Belgium, the Netherlands and Luxembourg established in 1965 with jurisdiction in certain specified legal areas (such as trademark law). The CJEU has in Case C-337/95 *Parfums Christian Dior SA ja Parfums Christian Dior BV v Evora BV* clearly stated that a court common to several Member States is acceptable in the light of EU law.[43] Therefore it seems natural that a similar court structure was proposed for the UPC.

The UPC would comprise a Court of First Instance and a Court of Appeals. The Court of First Instance would not geographically be in one place, but instead it would have a central division and local and regional divisions (UPC Agreement, Article 7(1)). Any Member State has the right to request a local division, which in essence means that all contracting Member States may, if they so wish, have at least one local division (UPC Agreement, Article 7(3)). It is possible to have a further local division for every 100 cases per calendar year that have been commenced in that Contracting Member State (UPC Agreement, Article 7(4)). The central division would be divided between Paris, London and Munich.

The division of competence between the central division and the local and regional divisions is provided for in detail in the UPC Agreement. For this

[40] Opinion 1/09 [2011] ECR I-1137.

[41] ibid, para 89.

[42] ibid.

[43] Case C-337/95 *Parfums Christian Dior SA ja Parfums Christian Dior BV v Evora BV* [1997] ECR I-6013.

study, it is not necessary to look at it in detail, but the starting point is that infringement cases would go to the local or regional divisions depending on the defendant's domicile or place of infringement, whereas the central division would handle invalidity cases. There are however so many exceptions to these starting points (UPC Agreement, Article 33) that the UPC cannot be characterised as a bifurcated system (which is characterised by infringement and invalidity being adjudicated in different courts).

The Court of Appeal, which would have its seat in Luxembourg, would sit in a multinational composition of five judges (UPC Agreement, Article 9).

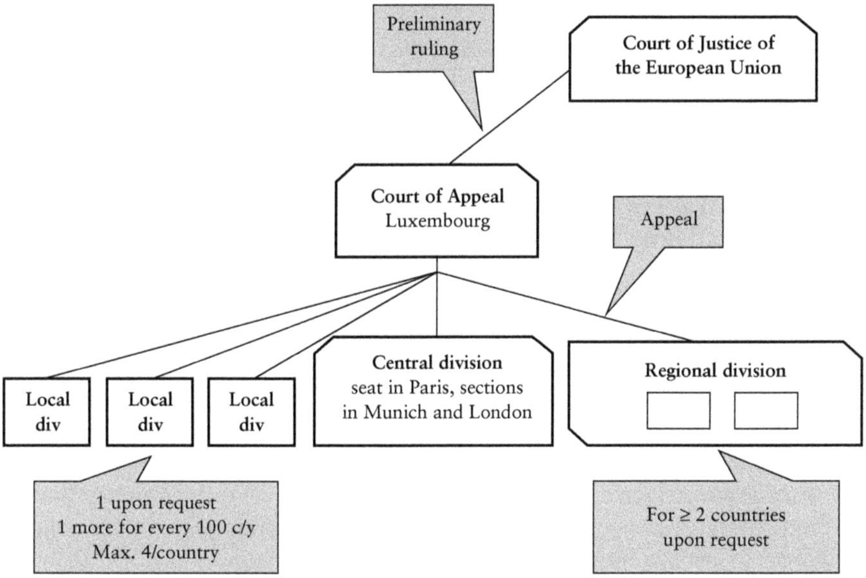

Quite a lot of thought and effort was put into trying to *avoid* the CJEU's jurisdiction.[44] The UPC is interesting for our purposes because it exemplifies a situation where national states surrender some of their sovereignty through an international agreement to a court that some or even most of the time sits in session with non-nationals in majority and outside the borders of the country in question. In principle there does not seem to be any legal objections to copy the UPC-model to other IP rights as well.

[44] This is clear, for example, in the light of the fact that the provisions on infringing acts were moved from the Reg No 1257/2012 of 17 December 2012 implementing enhanced cooperation in the area of the creation of unitary patent protection [2012] OJ L361/1, to the Agreement on the UPC. See, for example, H Ullrich, *Harmonizing Patent Law: The Untamable Union Patent* (Max Planck Institute for Intellectual Property & Competition Law Research Paper No 12-03) 45, fn 148, available at ssrn.com/abstract=2027920 ('This shows that every possible attempt is made to escape EU law').

In practice a UPC-like court structure also in other types of intellectual property law would mean that the new court would adjudicate infringement and validity already in the first instance instead of the normal national courts. Appeals would go to a centralised Court of Appeal sitting in a multinational composition. Although the Court of Appeal would have an obligation to make preliminary references to the CJEU, it might be easier for the CJEU to adopt a 'green light', docket control or some other controlling mechanism since the Court of Appeal would have the responsibility to oversee harmonisation of IP law. The CJEU could focus on general EU law and fundamental rights and the UPC-like court could focus on intellectual property law.

In principle this type of solution seems to be acceptable in the light of EU law much in the same way as the UPC is. It would be up to the Member States to jointly agree to set up a common court with a UPC-like structure. The EU Commission, Parliament or Council would not be needed for this. However, politically and economically setting up a UPC-like court structure might not be feasible in the foreseeable future, at least as long as IP litigation on the national level works fairly well.

C. Specialised First Instance Court Attached to the General Court

The second model is the Article 257 TFEU model: A specialised first instance court attached to the General Court. Article 257 TFEU provides that the European Parliament and the Council, acting in accordance with the ordinary legislative procedure, may establish specialised courts attached to the General Court to hear and determine at first instance certain classes of action or proceeding brought in specific areas. Appeals are heard by the General Court.

The same provision requires that specialized courts are created only for certain classes of action or proceedings brought in specific areas. It would seem clear that intellectual property disputes fall within this category taking especially into account the fact that the Commission originally suggested that the Community Patent Court would be created on the basis of the predecessor of Article 257 TFEU.[45] Intellectual property law is anyhow a well-defined area of law, although there are obvious connections with contract law, competition law and the law of remedies.

It has been suggested that a specialised IP court could be created in order to take care of trademark and design appeals cases (500–700 cases a year

[45] Proposal for a Council Decision establishing the Community Patent Court and concerning appeals before the Court of First Instance, COM/2003/0828 final.

as shown above) that now are decided by the General Court.[46] Such a court would have many benefits: it would be a specialised IP court, which most likely would attract judges specialised in IP, which would further increase the legitimacy and status of the judgments.

A specialised court attached to the General Court would not, however, touch upon how to deal with preliminary references. The problem is, if possible, more pressing in those cases. Preliminary reference cases in IP cases frequently involve complex questions, which would require a solid understanding of IP law. The judges at the CJEU are as a rule not, however, specialists in IP—nor should they be. They should have a broad understanding of EU law. The problem is, however, that many of the IP law questions that reach the CJEU touch only in part on general EU law principles. Usually they revolve around specific, but quite diverse, questions of IP law doctrine, such as likelihood of confusion (trademark law), originality (copyright law), intermediary liability (copyright law) or admissibility of linking (copyright law). At times, the IP community has struggled in either understanding the CJEU's reasoning or accepting the judgments. Therefore I will here toy with the idea of creating a novel forum also in other types of IP cases, primarily infringement and invalidity cases. These are today taken care of by national courts together with the CJEU through the preliminary ruling system. The preliminary rulings are the Achilles heel of the system: handling a case before a national court in two or three instances combined with a preliminary ruling leads to significant delays. Providing for a more efficient solution would be called for.

Creating a specialised court could be one solution. Article 257 TFEU provides that the Parliament and the Council 'may establish specialised courts attached to the General Court to hear and determine at first instance certain classes of action or proceeding brought in specific areas'. The problem is that the court needs to be 'attached to the General Court' and a 'first instance' court. What is meant by 'attached' leaves many questions open. This could either be interpreted as physical attachment (as with the European Union Civil Service Tribunal, which is located in Luxembourg) or merely as a legal attachment meaning that the specialised court would have its seat 'attached' to the General Court, but it could have divisions in different Member States similarly to the UPC.

That the provision requires that the specialised court should hear cases 'at first instance' seems to preclude the national courts from hearing cases. The provision is clearly not designed for a preliminary ruling system where national courts and the specialised EU court would collaborate.

[46] H Brady, *Twelve Things Everyone Should Know About the European Court of Justice* (London, Centre for European Reform, 2014) 43, available at: www.cer.org.uk/sites/default/files/publications/attachments/pdf/2014/hugo_brady_12_things_ecj_22.07.14-9313.pdf.

Collaboration need not be in the form of a preliminary ruling system, but can also be, for example, in the form of first instance national courts and an EU appeals court.

Furthermore, if the provision is to be interpreted as a physical attachment, it seems clear that it would have such great drawbacks that it would never be a realistic option for an EU IP court. One single IP court for the whole of the EU would be overburdened with cases, on the one hand, and on the other, litigants with limited economic resources would most likely be scared off. In essence such a court would on the one hand risk being too slow and too expensive an alternative. In short it would most likely be much worse than the current system. The only positive side of such a system would be that it would most certainly harmonise case law in Europe.

If, however, the attachment criterion could be interpreted as meaning a mere legal attachment, first instance divisions could be created in every EU Member State in much the same way as with the UPC. The provision does not however allow for appeal within the specialised court, which means that appeals from the divisions would go to the General Court, which would risk being overburdened by appeals. It is however clear that the specialised court would hear cases already in the first instance with a possibility of appeal (on points of law or facts, depending on the statute) to the General Court. It has been noted, quite correctly I think, that the provision does not allow for specialised courts only in the appeals phase.[47]

D. CPC-Style National Courts in the First Instance with a Common Appeals Court

The last model is the 1989 Community Patent Court (CPC) model. The general outline of the 1989 CPC alternative comprises national courts in the first and second instances (albeit called community patent courts) and a common appeal court. A system of division of labour between the national appeal courts and the common appeal court is devised. For the sake of argument, it is not necessary to present the 1989 CPC alternative in all its intricacies. It is enough to understand that it consists of national courts and a common appeal court. The rationale is clearly that the national community patent courts would deal with the bulk of litigation and only in questions appealed that require a harmonised solution would the question go to the common appeal court. There is nothing in the TFEU or other EU legislation that would allow for a CPC-style solution.

[47] M Brosinger, O Fischer, A Früh, T Jaeger and M Postl, *Der Reformvertrag von Lissabon—IP und Wettbewerbsaspekte* (Stand, September 2008) 58, available at: papers.ssrn.com/sol3/papers.cfm?abstract_id=1340861.

V. DISCUSSION AND TENTATIVE CONCLUSIONS

The question is whether any of the above presented models could replace the CJEU in intellectual property law cases. As a starting point it is clear—in the light of the TFEU and the general principles of EU law—that the CJEU should under any circumstance retain its power to interpret the treaties and fundamental rights. It is less certain that the CJEU actually should be the one interpreting directives and regulations in substantive private law questions.[48] The CJEU has been criticised for not providing the highest expertise available in IP matters.[49] Bearing in mind that especially larger member states have specialised judges dealing with IP matters, this critique is not only unsurprising, but to some degree also warranted. Adding to this the time it takes to process a case at the CJEU, it is clear that the current situation is far from ideal. It is neither fast nor cost-effective and if also the correctness of its decisions is put into question, the system is not ideal. There is also the risk that the present model means that the CJEU has less time to devote to the 'big' questions of EU law, such as general EU law and fundamental rights.

It would, however, be no small feat to replace the CJEU with one of the alternatives presented above. As especially the European discussions on patent law have taught us, intellectual property law can be high on the national and European political agenda. Language regimes, balance of power between individual Member States etc have put projects in jeopardy. Nevertheless, and regardless of political will now (or even in the foreseeable future), it is important to look at alternatives to the current system.

The alternatives presented above represent different approaches to how the balance between the EU and the Member States should be solved. At one end of the spectrum lies the EU-centric court system of TFEU Article 257. It requires that already the *first* instance is attached to the General Court. A first instance centralised EU court neither seems necessary nor appropriate.

[48] See, for example, R Kraßer, 'Effects of an Inclusion of Regulations Concerning the Content and Limits of the Patent Holder's Rights to Prohibit in an EU Regulation for the Creation of Unitary European Patent Protection', 7, available at: www.eplawpatentblog.com/2011/October/Opinion%20Prof%20Krasser%20EN.pdf: 'However, the court would be overstretched by the expected quantity of questions submitted. As the "constitutional court" of the EU, it should not be obliged to address individual issues in a specialised field'.

[49] A Ohly, 'Towards a Unified Patent Court in Europe' in Ohly and Pila (n 3) 215: 'Within the patent community there are strong concerns as to the role of the CJEU. These concerns stem partly from the fact that there is not much enthusiasm about the case law of the CJEU in trade mark and copyright law, but also from the quality of the few patent law cases which the Court has decided so far. The judges of the CJEU are generalists; many have constitutional or administrative law background. Hence, they lack detailed knowledge of and experience in intellectual property law …'. See also Robin Jacob, 'Opinion', 2 November 2011, available at: www.eplawpatentblog.com/2011/November/Robin%2020Jacob%2020Opinion%2020re%2020Arts.pdf: 'And it is far from certain that the rulings of the non-specialist CJEU would be clear' and 'I know of no one in favour of involvement of the CJEU in patent litigation. On the contrary all, users, lawyers and judges are unanimously against it.'

Although I do not have any figures, the number of first instance IP cases must be quite high. One court—even if it were modelled in line with the UPC with local or regional divisions in the first instance—would require quite substantial resources in order to work properly. The primary reason for invoking this kind of highly centralised solution is to maximise harmonised interpretations in case law. On the other hand it is the higher instances that secure harmonisation and there is no need, as far as I can see, for a centralised solution in the *first* instance. It is furthermore quite an intrusion on national procedural autonomy to take away first instance jurisdiction from the Member States.

At the other end of the spectrum are the current CTM/CDR courts of the Member States, which in essence relies totally on the Member States. They appoint courts that act as CTM/CDR courts. Essentially it does not differ from the normal national court system as no Member State seems to have introduced new, separate courts for CTM/CDR cases. Since the preliminary reference system is applied in CTM/CDR cases, it does not solve any problems because it represents the present model.

Close to this system is the UPC which is a national court sitting in multinational composition with local and/or regional divisions in different member states. Harmonisation is achieved since the Court of Appeal is centralised. If a similar system was created for other types of intellectual property, at least the Court of Appeal would most likely be required to ask for a preliminary ruling from the CJEU or—in the alternative—appeals to the CJEU/General Court would have to be provided for. Also this model is rather far-reaching in that it is unclear why, in general IP matters, there would *in the first instance* be a need for a complex structure of national courts sitting in multinational compositions. This model could, possibly, solve the problems of delay and harmonisation. The question of cost and languages could become controversial since already in the first instance it might happen that a case is to be heard in a different Member State than what the current system provides for, thus possibly requiring more travel than before, thus increasing the costs of the system.

This leads us to the last model, which is modelled after the 1989 CPC: a court structure based on a first instance court with a strong local presence, much like Community Trademark Courts and Community Design Courts. Appeals from a first instance court would however not go to the national Courts of Appeal but to a centralised Court of Appeal, which would guarantee harmonised interpretations of EU law and be highly specialised and knowledgeable in IP matters. The CJEU's role would be limited to questions of a higher magnitude. The Court of Justice would (in IP cases) have its primary role in deciding fundamental EU law questions, such as those relating to the Treaties establishing the European Union and the Charter on Fundamental Rights. The centralised Court of Appeal, not the CJEU, would be the instance responsible for ensuring harmonised interpretations of EU IP law.

The interplay between the Court of Appeal and the CJEU would have to be solved in some novel way, for instance by requiring the Court of Appeal to ask for preliminary rulings in fundamental EU law questions only. If, and this is a big if, maximum harmonisation is the aim, then I would suggest that this kind of system with national first instance courts, and a centralised appeals court, would be best suited to solve the puzzle of effectiveness (both as to time and costs) and harmonisation. Creating a common court of appeal seems possible in the light of CJEU's opinion 1/09, in which the structure of the UPC was accepted.

These alternatives and also the proposed reforms of the CJEU procedure show that it is ultimately a question of balancing the interest of harmonisation with other principles, such as national procedural autonomy. It is generally assumed that the CJEU is necessary in order to harmonise interpretations in IP law. If however any of the reforms presented above by Broberg and Fenger of the CJEU would become reality, many of them would lead to lesser harmonisation. A green light procedure, a *certiorari* system and creating regional courts to do part of the work of the Court of Justice would be equal to admitting that harmonisation cannot be attained at any price and instead leave some wiggle room for the national courts. Perhaps, in the end, the real question is how much harmonisation we really need and want. Now, it is essentially the national courts that decide whether and when to ask for a preliminary reference. The slow processing time in the CJEU probably is reflected in the national courts' willingness to ask for preliminary rulings, which in itself in a way disharmonises law.

In the alternative court systems presented above the first or second instance or both would be centralised, thus providing even more harmonisation than the CJEU provides today because all cases appealed would go to a court responsible for harmonising case law in IP matters. Although from a purely theoretical, substantive law point of view, this kind of maximum harmonisation would be of interest, it is questionable whether that really is optimal from the point of view national procedural autonomy and other concerns. On the other hand, no harmonisation is not ideal either, as the European Patent Convention shows.

The present preliminary reference system emphasises harmonised interpretation since Article 267 TFEU mandates the highest court to make a preliminary reference unless the question is *acte clair*. Dealing with delay in the present or future system of preliminary references might not be possible unless we openly adopt some kind of a doctrine of margin of appreciation giving the national courts rather more than less leeway in the interpretation of directives and regulations. If we want to hold on to maximum harmonisation, the only way to solve the problem of delays seems to be to substantially increase resources at the CJEU or transfer preliminary references to the General Court and increase resources there (TFEU Article 256(3)) or adopt some of the alternative court structures proposed above.

Part V

Rendering Justice: Procedures, Compensation, Sanctions

10

*US Class Actions: Promise and Reality**

CHRISTOPHER HODGES

THE TRADITIONAL COLLECTIVE action narrative argues that aggregating individual claims *should* produce 'judicial economy', or at least procedural economy, by sharing overall cost across multiple claims, thereby lowering the cost of individual cases, and thus increasing access to justice. It is also argued that aggregation gives the claimant side a lot of power, especially where the defendant cannot recover costs (as often in the USA, and under the old position in England under legal aid). In analysing the extent to which those points apply in aggregate mechanisms for civil claims, it is important to differentiate between different models, since the effect of the different funding mechanisms and rules on cost shifting produce entirely different situations. Indeed, strong European political statements have criticised the American class action model.

In analysing the US class action model and the emerging European collective action model, wider questions have been raised. First, the empirical evidence shows that *any* class action will have problems, notably selectivity in the types of case that are pursued (with some cases not being taken at all by intermediaries), high cost and poor repayment of claimants. Delay is a problem in the EU but not the USA. Second, these features are largely produced in the USA because the system loads the mechanisms so as to assist claimants. To European eyes, that policy produces major conflicts of interest for the intermediaries, and potential for abuse. On the other hand, where the EU models introduce safeguards against abuse, the mechanism becomes unattractive to intermediaries and funders.

This chapter will examine the empirical evidence on US class actions. It will first set out the ideal: The intended benefits of aggregating similar individual claims. These are facilitating procedural economy, increasing access to justice and providing deterrence against law-breaking. There follows a

* Research funding is received from international law firm CMS, the European Justice Forum and the Swiss Reinsurance Company Limited.

summary of the most significant empirical research into a number of aspects of how class actions operate in practice, from which it will be noted that reality falls somewhat short of the ideal. The main subjects addressed are: Selectivity of types of case, and the reasons for that; particular evidence on major case types, notably securities cases; transactional costs; reduction in damages paid to claimants, especially in consumer cases; the difficulty of identifying the extent to which cases and settlements have merit; forum shopping; and how the financial incentives generate conflicts of interest and abuse. It is then noted that various important shifts have occurred in US class action practice, moving cases firstly away from individual court proceedings towards multi-district management, which has produced effects on settlement, and secondly in consumer cases away from litigation entirely towards contractual arbitration. The chapter ends by drawing general conclusions, both on the US class action system and general implications for Europe and elsewhere.

I. THE OBJECTIVES OF AGGREGATION OF CLAIMS

There are two primary objectives of aggregating individual civil claims into a single coordinated procedure: to achieve procedural economy, and thereby to increase access to justice.[1] Both these goals are simple to grasp. It should be more efficient to process a single procedure than many similar claims. The concept is sometimes referred to as one of facilitating judicial economy in achieving efficient case management. There may also be economies of scale in relation to the transactional costs of claimants and defendants.[2] That incremental cost reduction might also facilitate an incremental increase in the number of cases that are economic for claimants to bring, thereby achieving the second goal of increasing access to justice. That second goal is particularly relevant in facilitating individual claims that are small in value, so that they become viable and relevant rights are vindicated and not flaunted. This goal recognises the fact of cost-effectiveness, in that some claims are individually too small to be worth processing given the cost of using the court system.

These objectives are somewhat changed by what occurs in practice. In the USA, it is well established that the requirement for court certification of a class action provides a major hurdle, but if a class is certified then the chances of settlement are very high.[3] The settlement of cases, as opposed

[1] CJS Hodges, 'Collective Actions' in P Cane and HM Kritzer (eds), *The Oxford Handbook of Empirical Legal Studies* (Oxford, Oxford University Press, 2010).

[2] RG Bone, 'Class Action' in CW Sanchirico (ed), *Procedural Law and Economics* (Cheltenham, Edward Elgar, 2012).

[3] B Garth, IH Nagel and SJ Plager, 'The Institution of the Private Attorney General: Perspectives from an Empirical Study of Class Action Litigation' (1987–1988) 61 *Southern California Law Review* 353.

to judicial determination, provides economies for the court and the parties. So the reality is that judicial economy is irrelevant, and the true objective is *procedural* or *process* economy. Indeed, despite the impression that mass litigation is extensive in the USA, such claims appear to constitute a small part of the judicial administrative workload, time being spent on certification and settlement hearings.[4]

A third objective applies under the American model, namely deterrence, on the theory that imposing internalisation of the cost of undesirable external costs created by a business, or the imposition of additional punitive damages, will deter future breaches of the law. The deterrence objective appears in some European writing and policy statements (on competition law and sometimes financial services) but less frequently in some areas than its ubiquitous appearance in US literature. The extent to which evidence supports the theory that private enforcement, or public enforcement, in fact deters corporate behaviour has been questioned and this extensive topic is not discussed further here.[5] However, it is important to highlight an important structural difference that American reliance on deterrence leads to in contrast with European structures, which now follows.

II. THE US MODEL

The encouragement of private enforcement is a particular feature of the USA's legal system.[6] Class actions are a deeply political weapon and activity within the system of American democracy and separation of powers.[7] The political ideology is to empower individual citizens to exercise their personal freedom to exert their rights. That model is held to maximise adherence to the law by maximising the number of enforcement agents within the

[4] Damage class actions constituted at most only 2.7% of all civil cases filed in all federal courts from 1972 to 1977: R Bernstein, 'Judicial Economy and Class Actions' (1978) 7(2) *The Journal of Legal Studies* 349. In California between 2000 and 2006, class actions were less than one-half of one per cent of all civil litigation: H Heiman, *Findings of the Study of California Class Action Litigation, 2000–2006* (San Francisco, Judicial Council of California, Administrative Office of the Courts, 2009).

[5] C Hodges, *Law and Corporate Behaviour: Integrating Theories of Regulation, Enforcement, Compliance and Ethics* (Oxford, Hart Publishing, 2015).

[6] C Hodges, 'Objectives, Mechanisms and Policy Choices in Collective Enforcement and Redress' in J Steele and W van Boom (eds), *Mass Justice* (Cheltenham, Edward Elgar, 2011).

[7] BG Garth, 'Power and Legal Artifice: The Federal Class Action' (1992) 26 *Law & Society Review* 237 ('The class action is a politically empowering legal artifice'); RA Kagan, *Adversarial Legalism: The American Way of Law* (Cambridge MA, Harvard University Press, 2001); W Haltom and M McCann, *Distorting the Law: Politics, Media, and The Litigation Crisis* (Chicago, University of Chicago Press, 2004); WV McIntosh and CL Cates, *Multi-Party Litigation: The Strategic Context* (Vancouver, UBC Press, 2009).

population, and is said to avoid disadvantages of enforcement by public agencies, such as capture[8] and limited resources.[9]

The above account contains one major assumption, namely that individual citizens can assert right by themselves. That assumption appears to be illusory. The reality is that the enforcement of law is overwhelmingly only achieved where intermediaries are involved.[10] Thus, public enforcement requires officials, and private enforcement typically requires lawyers, and funders. The class action encourages private lawyers to be intermediaries, and to perform the dual roles of litigation funder and professional representative, by providing a series of economic incentives. This model can be contrasted with the emerging European model where ombudsmen or other Alternative Dispute Resolution (ADR) entities and public regulatory agencies function as intermediaries, increasingly funded by business. In the US litigation system, lawyers acting as 'private attorneys general'[11] investigate and challenge potential wrongdoing and negotiate the imposition of deterrent penalties under the authority of the court system.[12]

In accordance with this model, the system includes an absence of barriers to investigation, and incentives to litigate and to succeed in settlements. First, access to evidence is through wide powers of discovery, deposition of witnesses of fact and interrogatories. Second, there are liberal rules on pleading allegations (notice pleading) and on liability. Third, the financial incentives are: no requirement on plaintiffs to fund a case; funding by lawyers, which may be on a contingency (no win no fee) arrangement and on a percentage of the recovery; funding in class actions typically being awarded by the court based on a percentage of the damages; no risk to a plaintiff of having to pay costs in the event of failure (that is no cost shifting); requirements on defendants to pay costs under many statutes;[13] levels of damages that are intended to provide deterrence and to cover plaintiffs' healthcare costs; the potential for punitive or triple damages; and the ability to exert significant bargaining power through assembling mass claims. Fourth, there

[8] S Farhang, 'Public Regulation and Private Lawsuits in the American Separation of Powers System' (2008) 52 *American Journal of Political Science* 821.

[9] See eg EA Bardach and RA Kagan, *Going by the Book: The Problem of Regulatory Unreasonableness* (Philadelphia PA, Temple University Press, 1982); J-J Laffont and J Tirole, 'The Politics of Government Decision-Making: A Theory of Regulatory Capture' (1991) 106(4) *Quarterly Journal of Economics* 1089.

[10] Much of the European debate can be viewed as revolving around whether intermediaries should be private lawyers, consumer associations, public regulators, private ADR entities, or quasi-public ombudsmen.

[11] SN Subrin and MYK Woo, *Litigating in America* (New York, Aspen Publishers, 2006).

[12] S Shavell, *Economic Analysis of Accident Law* (Cambridge MA, Harvard University Press, 1987) 277; S Issacharoff, 'Regulating after the Fact' (2007) 56 *DePaul Law Review* 375, 377; D Rosenberg, 'The Causal Connection in Mass Exposure Cases: A "Public Law" Vision of the Tort System' (1984) 97 *Harvard Law Review* 849, 853.

[13] See S Farhang, *The Litigation State: Public Regulation and Private Lawsuits in the US* (Princeton NJ, Princeton University Press, 2010).

may be elements of public sanctioning: Decisions on liability and penalties being made by juries, and the possibility of punitive damages.

The US class action model is the opt-out procedure: a single representative plaintiff brings a case that is deemed to be sufficiently similar to a class of others such that determination of the exemplar can and will determine and bind all the rest—unless an individual in the class opts out, and prefers not to bring his case or to proceed with an individual case. On the opposite model, every individual has to opt-in to a collective case. The three primary justifications for an opt-out model are: achieving maximal deterrent effect, maximising procedural efficiency and encouraging comprehensive settlement. Mulheron's comparison of initial opt-out rates in the United States, Australia and Canada (not take up rates) found higher mean participation rates with opt-out procedures (0–40 per cent) than opt-in (0.03–100 per cent).[14]

Each US State has its own rule on class actions. At federal level the rule is Rule 23 of the Federal Rules of Civil Procedure. These rules all differ in some respects: such details are unnecessary for the purposes of the current analysis. The Federal Rule provides the following main types of class actions:

- Injunctive and declaratory relief (Rule 23(b)(2) and Rule 23(b)(1)(A)). Civil rights cases and other cases seeking institutional change, discrimination, pollution.
- Monetary compensation (Rule 23(b)(3) and Rule 23(b)(1)(B)). This covers:
  - Mass torts. Products, transport crashes, building collapses, oil spills.
  - Securities and shareholders.
  - Other financial injury, often aiming at restitution of illegal gains, for example employment, antitrust, and consumer cases (involving a wide range of legal theories).

Although the class action mechanism has a long history in USA,[15] usage unexpectedly took off in the mid-1960s. This massive increase had three main origins: first, a crisis occurred in civil and social rights for which no clear political or social solution was available;[16] second, Rule 23 of the Federal Rules of Civil Procedure was liberalised in 1966 almost by accident; and third, those two elements combined with Congress' move to introduce a one-way fee shift in civil rights cases so as to encourage their resolution through the courts.[17] Lawyers seized on the opportunities of expanding

[14] R Mulheron, *Reform of Collective Redress in England and Wales: A Perspective of Need* (London, Civil Justice Council, 2007).

[15] SC Yeazell, *From Mediaeval Group Litigation to the Modern Class Action* (New Haven, Yale University Press, 1987).

[16] SC Yeazell, '*Brown*, the Civil Rights Movement, and the Silent Litigation Revolution' (2004) 57 *Vanderbilt Law Review* 1975.

[17] Farhang (n 13).

private enforcement, and Congress enacted ever more one-way fee shifts in preference to public enforcement of regulatory rules.[18]

It should be remembered that individual cases can be aggregated through various other techniques, including consolidated trials, protection and reorganisation under bankruptcy, and informal aggregation.[19] An important further procedure used by federal judges for collecting similar class actions together for coordinated pre-trial processing is under the multi-districting rule (MDL).[20] The MDL procedure has been found to have some advantages for plaintiffs (through increasing cost sharing, information sharing and division of labour among multiple plaintiffs) and for defendants (notably over deposition of witnesses).[21] It can be favoured where claims do not satisfy the class action certification procedure, such as where individual product liability claims have multiple individual issues.

III. REALITIES FROM EMPIRICAL EVIDENCE

Empirical research into the real world of collective litigation builds up to a picture of reality that is strikingly different from the idealistic picture set out above. In the 1960s, class actions developed as a means of providing an 'avenue open to a minority to petition for redress of grievances',[22] using litigation as 'a form of political expression'.[23] Since then, the focus has shifted from social policy reform cases to issues of market regulation of business activity, addressing issues of consumer protection, safety, market competition, investor protection, prisoners' rights, environmental protection and genocide. Civil rights cases tend to seek injunctive relief (Rule 23(b)(2)), whereas the commercial cases, especially securities cases, seek damages on an opt-out basis (Rule 23(b)(3)).[24] Fitzpatrick found that the vast majority of federal class action settlements in 2006 and 2007 provided cash relief

[18] ibid.

[19] See DR Hensler, 'Revisiting the Monster: New Myths and Realities of Class Actions and Other Large Scale Litigation' (2001) 11 *Duke Journal of Comparative & International Law* 179.

[20] 28 USC § 1407 (1997).

[21] SM Olson, 'Federal Multidistrict Litigation: Its Impact on Litigants' (1983) 13(3) *Justice System Journal* 341. See also Judicial Conference of the United States, Advisory Committee on Civil Rules, *Report of the Advisory Committee on Civil Rules and the Working Group on Mass Torts to the Chief Justice of the United States and to the Judicial Conference of the United States* (1999). See also MS Williams and TE George, 'Who Will Manage Complex Civil Litigation?: The Decision to Transfer and Consolidate Multidistrict Litigation' (2013) 10(3) *Journal of Empirical Legal Studies* 424; DF D'Onfro, 'Multidistrict Litigation: A Surprising Bonus for *Pro Se* Plaintiffs and a Possible Boon for Consumers' (2010), available at ssrn.com/abstract=1563.

[22] *NAACP v Button* 371 US 415 (1963), 431.

[23] ibid, 429.

[24] TE Willging, LL Hooper and RJ Niemic, *Empirical Study of Class Actions in Four Federal District Courts: Final Report to the Advisory Committee on Civil Rules* (Washington DC, Federal Judicial Centre, 1996).

(82 per cent), but a substantial number provided injunctive or declaratory relief (23 per cent) or in-kind relief (six per cent).[25] Every single securities settlement provided cash to the class and almost none of them provided in-kind, injunctive or declaratory relief. Consumer cases had the greatest percentage of settlements providing for in-kind relief (30 per cent). Civil rights cases had the greatest percentage of settlements providing for injunctive or declaratory relief (75 per cent), though almost half of civil rights cases also provided some cash relief (49 per cent).

Tens of thousands of individual claims are settled outside the courts through high-volume personal injury law practices that aggressively advertise and mass produce the resolution of claims with defendant insurers, typically with little client interaction, cursory investigation of facts, without initiating lawsuits, much less taking claims to trial ('settlement mills').[26] Such repeat players agree claims at settlement sums based not on trial-centred precedents but on formulaic going rates based on previous settlements tied to the gravity of the claimant's injury (akin to a no fault tariff), on the basis that this cooperation was economically profitable in avoiding litigation.[27]

In contrast to the regulatory power directed at market participants, the US Government is generally immune from suit under the doctrine of sovereign immunity. The Federal Tort Claims Act (FTCA) provides a limited waiver for circumstances where the United States is acting in a manner akin to a private person (for example providing medical care at a Veterans' Hospital) and where the private person would be liable under applicable state law. But the FTCA specifically exempts claims based on performance or non-performance of a discretionary function.

Issues of concern that arise in relation to the US private enforcement system and its reliance on class actions are selectivity in the types of cases pursued, transactional costs, reductions in levels of damages paid to plaintiffs, potential imbalance in the incentives for plaintiff lawyers to force defendants to settle irrespective of merits, conflicts of interest by plaintiff lawyers, and the potential for abuse, such as a tendency to target large companies, which are regarded as 'deep pockets'.[28] Despite the huge literature asserting the doctrinal value of the US theory and practice of class actions, it is striking that there is relatively limited reliable empirical research.[29]

[25] BT Fitzpatrick, 'An Empirical Study of Class Action Settlements and their Fee Awards' (2010) 7(4) *Journal of Empirical Legal Studies* 811.

[26] NF Engstrom, 'Run-of-the-Mill Justice' (2009) 22 *Georgetown Journal of Legal Ethics* 148.

[27] ibid.

[28] JC Alexander, 'Do the Merits Matter? A Study of Settlements in Securities Class Actions' (1991) 43 *Stanford Law Review* 497 (finding that every company in the cohort of companies making an initial public offering (IPO) with a market loss over $20 million was sued but smaller IPOs were not sued).

[29] See N Pace, 'Class Actions in the United States of America: An Overview of the Process and the Empirical Literature' (2007), available at: globalclassactions.stanford.edu/sites/default/files/documents/USA__National_Report.pdf.

It should be stressed that the issues listed above are intentional features of the US policy on private enforcement of law. However, European politicians have rejected the US model as abusive.[30] Farhang has noted that many US scholars suggest that, compared to administrative regulation, private enforcement regimes (1) produce inconsistency and uncertainty (since policy emanates from a multitude of litigants and judges); (2) mobilise less policy expertise; (3) are needlessly adversarial, subverting cooperation and voluntary compliance; (4) are extremely costly; and (5) are painfully slow and cumbersome.[31]

A. Type Selectivity

Studies have shown that certain types of class actions occur far more frequently than others. This is unsurprising given the driver of the significant financial incentives for intermediaries. One consequence of the American policy of private enforcement has been called a systemic failure of the ability for ordinary citizens to solve their legal problems, despite the seemingly high volume of litigation in the country. The incidence of reported problems for individuals in a number of first world states is relatively consistent, with the exception of Japan, which reports lower rates.[32] However, Hadfield found a striking difference in the rate at which people do nothing in response to legal difficulties between the United States (29 per cent or higher),[33] the United Kingdom (3–5 per cent), The Netherlands (10 per cent) and Slovakia (18 per cent), which she attributed to the availability of substantially more resources in the latter three states than in the United States that are devoted to the provision of problem solving and legal services for ordinary citizens.[34]

It would be logical to assume that expert lawyers would prefer to concentrate on cases that would maximise their income. Kritzer has illuminated

[30] Green Paper on Consumer Collective Redress, COM(2008) 794 final, para 48 (US-style class actions produce 'abuse' caused by a 'toxic cocktail' of causes); European Parliament resolution of 2 February 2012 on 'Towards a Coherent European Approach to Collective Redress' 2011/2089(INI), para 2 (noted 'efforts made by the US Supreme Court to limit frivolous litigation and abuse of the US class action system'); Communication from the Commission 'Towards a European Horizontal Framework for Collective Redress', COM(2013) 401 final.

[31] Farhang (n 8). See E Bardan and R Kagan (n 9); F Cross, 'Rethinking Environmental Citizen Suits' (1989) 8 *Temple Environmental Law & Technology Journal* 55; RA Kagan (n 7); RB Stewart and CR Sunstein, 'Public Programs and Private Rights' (1981–1982) 95 *Harvard Law Review* 1193.

[32] GK Hadfield, 'Higher Demand, Lower Supply? A Comparative Assessment of the Legal Resources Landscape for Ordinary Americans' (2009) 37 *Fordham Urban Law Journal* 129.

[33] *Supporting Justice: A Report on the Pro Bono Work of America's Lawyers* (Chicago, American Bar Association, 2005).

[34] ibid.

the fact that local law firms respond to the cases that are brought to them.[35] However, the most lucrative types of class action case are clearly concentrated in a small number of law firms, who aim to commence actions quickly in response to external stimuli and thus pre-empt competitors. Large class actions are clearly concentrated amongst a small number of expert law firms that bring cases quickly in response to external triggers.[36]

Several studies have found that securities cases are consistently[37] by far the largest category of class actions, comprising roughly 40 per cent of all federal class actions, whilst consumer, employment, employee benefits, antitrust and other cases each constitute perhaps plus or minus 10 per cent of cases, with civil rights some way behind.[38] Some class actions are brought under state law, such as insurance cases that are based on state statutes.[39]

i. Securities Cases

The policy of encouraging private enforcement of securities legislation is well established.[40] Enforcement actions taken by the Securities and Exchange Commission (SEC) imposing regulatory penalties as an alternative to damages seem to be used in different scenarios to class actions, and occurred rarely before 2006.[41]

Securities class actions have been strongly criticised. In 1991 Alexander asserted that recovery depended on the occurrence of the triggering event of a large loss, and did not require proof that a securities violation had actually occurred.[42] The result was that securities class actions operated as insurance

[35] HM Kritzer, *The Justice Broker* (New York, Oxford University Press, 1990) (finding little relationship between the type of fee arrangement and the amount of time that lawyers invest in their cases); HM Kritzer, 'Lawyer Fees and Lawyer Behaviour in Litigation: What Does the Empirical Literature Really Say?' (2002) 80 *Texas Law Review* 1943.

[36] Willging, Hooper and Niemic (n 24); AV Thakor, JS Nielsen and DA Gulley, *The Economic Reality of Securities Class Action Litigation* (Navigant Consulting and the US Chamber Institute for Legal Reform, 2005).

[37] See securities.stanford.edu. See also Cornerstone Research, *Securities Class Action Filings. 2008: A Year in Review* (2009); and annual surveys by NERA, such as R Comolli and S Starykh, *Recent Trends in Securities Class Action Litigation: 2014 Full-Year Review Settlement Amounts Plummet in 2014, but Post-Halliburton II Filings Rebound* (NERA, 2015).

[38] DR Hensler, B Dombey-Moore, B Giddens, J Gross, EK Moller and NM Pace, *Class Action Dilemmas: Pursuing Public Goals for Private Gain* (RAND Institute for Civil Justice, 2000); T Eisenberg and GP Miller, 'Attorney Fees in Class Action Settlements: An Empirical Study' (2004) 1(1) *Journal of Empirical Legal Studies* 27; BT Fitzpatrick, 'An Empirical Study of Class Action Settlements and their Fee Awards' (2010) 7(4) *Journal of Empirical Legal Studies* 811.

[39] NM Pace, SJ Carroll, I Vogelsang and L Zakaras, *Insurance Class Actions in the United States* (RAND Institute for Civil Justice, 2007).

[40] Approval of private enforcement of securities violations was given by the Supreme Court in *Herman & MacLean v Huddleston*, 459 US 375, 380 (1983).

[41] J Larsen, E Buckberg and B Lev, *SEC Settlements: A New era Post-SOX* (NERA, 2008).

[42] JC Alexander, 'Do the Merits Matter? A Study of Settlements in Securities Class Actions' (1991) 43(3) *Stanford Law Review* 497.

against market losses but only benefitted a small number of institutional investors against market losses from a speculative investment, and benefitted small investors little, whilst destroying shareholder value. In 2004 Choi expressed concern over three problems: frivolous suits; lack of incentives for plaintiff attorneys to focus on smaller companies; and the agency problem between plaintiffs' attorneys and the plaintiff class.[43] Frivolous suits appeared to be encouraged by the fact that Directors' and Officers' insurance policies would not pay if directors or officers were found guilty of violating the securities laws, so cases often settle irrespective of merits in order to maintain insurance cover.

Coffee asserted in 2006 that securities class actions impose enormous penalties but achieve little compensation and limited deterrence, because of basic circularity (pocket-shifting): damages imposed on a corporation fall on diversified shareholders, and enable larger and swifter investors at the expense of employees or smaller long-term investors.[44] Such actions may effectively deter firms from issuing shares or making forward predictions. Coffee noted that securities settlements only recover a very small share of investor losses: the annual ratio of settlements to losses published by NERA never exceeded 7.2 per cent in cases recorded from 1991 to 2004, and had recently been under three per cent, whereas attorney costs constituted 32 per cent of settlements.[45] He noted that senior management were highly likely to be named as defendants, but not outside directors or auditors (four per cent) or underwriters. However, such insiders rarely contributed financially to the settlement.[46] Where the defendant was a solvent corporation, its insurer would cover everything up to the policy limits, and the corporation would pick up the balance. The amount and structure of directors and officers (D&O) insurance has been found to be a significant factor, and payment to the plaintiffs' class is agreed for every claim that survives the motions stage,[47] thereby failing to provide authoritative guidance about merit at settlement.[48]

Based on the 2005 filing rate, Miller et al found that over a five year period the average public corporation faced a 10 per cent probability that

[43] SJ Choi, 'The Evidence on Securities Class Actions' (2004) 57 *Vanderbilt Law Review* 1465.

[44] JC Coffee, Jr, 'Reforming the Securities Class Action: An Essay on Deterrence and its Implementation' (2006) 106 *Columbia Law Review* 1534.

[45] ibid.

[46] Dunbar NERA study 1995 found that insurers paid 68.2% and corporations 31.4%, so at most 0.4% was paid by individual directors. BS Black, BR Cheffins and M Klausner, 'Outside Director Liability' (2006) 58 *Stanford Law Review* 1055.

[47] EM Fich and A Shivdasani, 'Financial Fraud, Director Reputation, and Shareholder Wealth' (2007) 86 *Journal of Financial Economics* 306.

[48] T Baker and SJ Griffith, 'How the Merits Matter: Directors' and Officers' Insurance and Securities Settlements' (2009) 157 *University of Pennsylvania Law Review* 755.

it would face at least one shareholder class action.[49] However, they found that the probability of dismissal rose from 19.4 per cent in 1993–1995 to 40.3 per cent in 2003–2005, attributed to the introduction of reforms under the Private Securities Litigation Reform Act of 1995 (PSLRA), including a presumption that the largest stockholder would be representative plaintiff and be incentivised to control the class attorneys, avoiding a 'race to the courthouse' by competing lawyers.[50] In response to charges that plaintiff class action attorneys had begun filing securities fraud cases in state courts to evade the 1995 Act, Congress passed the Securities Litigation Uniform Standards Act of 1998[51] to provide for removal of state class actions to the federal courts except in certain specified circumstances. In 2014, Krishnan et al found that 12 per cent of all merger and acquisition offers in 1999 and 2000 were challenged in the courts across the USA.[52]

Securities cases are generally commenced in response to bad stock price performance, and triggering events, notably false/misleading statements/failure to disclose, stock price manipulation and illegal business practices.[53] Some cases occur below $2 million that are settled quickly for perhaps half that figure on a nuisance basis (strike suits).[54]

Erickson's 2011 analysis of over 700 different types of corporate lawsuits (including shareholder derivative suits, securities class actions, Securities and Exchange Commission (SEC) enforcement actions and criminal prosecutions) revealed that they do not target different types of corporate wrongs, but often target the same alleged misconduct, the same defendants and the same corporate coffers.[55] Her data demonstrated that certain types

[49] RI Miller, T Foster and E Buckberg, *Recent Trends in Shareholder Class Action Litigation: Beyond Mega-Settlements, is Stabilization Ahead?* (NERA, 2006).

[50] For the somewhat limited effects see JD Cox and RS Thomas, with D Kiku, 'Does the Plaintiff Really Matter? An Empirical Analysis of Lead Plaintiffs in Securities Class Actions' (2006) 106 *Columbia Law Review* 1587; JD Cox, RS Thomas and L Bai, 'There Are Plaintiffs and ... There Are Plaintiffs: An Empirical Analysis of Securities Class Action Settlements' (2008) 61(2) *Vanderbilt Law Review* 355; MA Perino, 'Institutional Activism Through Litigation: An Empirical Analysis of Public Pension Fund Participation in Securities Class Actions' (2012) 9(2) *Journal of Empirical Legal Studies* 368; LA Baker, MA Perino and C Silver, 'Setting Attorneys' Fees in Securities Class Actions: An Empirical Assessment' (2013) 66(6) *Vanderbilt Law Review* 1677; LA Baker, MA Perino and C Silver, 'Is the Price Right? An Empirical Study of Fee-Setting in Securities Class Actions' (2015) *Columbia Law Review* (forthcoming).

[51] Pub L 105-353, 112 Stat 3227 (1998); codified in scattered sections of 15 USC, including s 78bb(f)(1).

[52] CNV Krishnan, RW Masulis, RS Thomas and RB Thompson, 'Jurisdictional Effects in M&A Litigation' (2014) 11(1) *Journal of Empirical Legal Studies* 132.

[53] R Bauer and R Braun, 'Long-Term Performance of Distressed Firms: The Role of Class Action Lawsuits' (2010) Netspar Discussion paper 10/2010-007, available at http://arno.uvt.nl/show.cgi?fid=100123; P Povel, R Singh and A Winton, 'Booms, Busts and Fraud' (2007) 20(4) *Review of Financial Studies* 1219.

[54] Cox, Thomas and Bai (n 50) found 20% of cases were of this type.

[55] JM Erickson, 'Overlitigating Corporate Fraud: An Empirical Examination' (2011) 96 *Iowa Law Review* 49.

of lawsuits consistently outperform others, creating a litigation hierarchy within corporate law. She concluded that those findings 'raise critical questions about traditional theories of deterrence, suggesting that more may not always be better when it comes to combating corporate fraud'.[56]

ii. Tort claims

From the 1960s to the mid-1990s mass tort cases, notably against manufacturers of pharmaceuticals,[57] aircraft, motor vehicles and tobacco, were a considerable focus of class actions. A major structural consideration in the purpose of injury compensation has been to provide cover through the tort system to compensate for the limited population overage and high cost of healthcare.[58] A review of 312 product liability and 297 non-product liability litigation events against automotive manufacturers found that the frequency of law suits was generally proportionate to the market share of companies.[59]

However, a sequence of decisions in the mid-1990s made certification more difficult, partly because of concern that certification put defendants under intense pressure to settle (discussed in Section IV below), and partly Supreme Court decisions such as *Castano v American Tobacco Company*[60] and *In re: Rhone-Poulenc Rorer, Inc*,[61] holding to a strict interpretation of the Rule 23 requirements, notably that the proposed class contained claims in which common issues did not predominate over individual issues.

After these decisions, commentators predicted that products liability plaintiffs would file fewer class actions in federal court, perhaps moving such filings to state courts whenever possible.[62] In fact, the number of personal injury lawsuits remained fairly steady, and cases were shifted to the MDL procedure, leading to an increase in non-class settlements.[63]

[56] ibid.

[57] See eg M Green, *Bendectin and Birth Defects: The Challenges of Mass Toxic Substances Litigation* (Philadelphia, University of Pennsylvania Press, 1996).

[58] US Census 2005. See also SD Sugarman, *Doing Away with Personal Injury Law: New Compensation Mechanisms for Consumers and Business* (New York, Quorum Books, 1992); R Avraham and M Schanzenbach, 'The Impact of Tort Reform on Private Health Insurance Coverage' (2007) *Northwestern University School of Law Public Law and Legal Theory Series* No 07–16.

[59] S Govindaraj, P Lee and D Tinkelman, 'Using the Event Study Methodology to Measure the Social Costs of Litigation—a Re-Examination Using Cases from the Automotive Industry' (2007) 3(2) *Review of Law & Economics* 342.

[60] 84 F 3d 734 (5th Cir 1996).

[61] 51 F 3d 1293 (7th Cir 1995).

[62] See, eg, LS Mullenix, 'Abandoning the Federal Class Action Ship: Is There Smoother Sailing for Class Actions in Gulf Water?' (2000) 74 *Tulane Law Review* 1709 (arguing that 'many class counsel have abandoned the federal courts in favor of what are perceived to be more receptive state court forums').

[63] TE Willging and EG Lee III, 'From Class Actions to Multidistrict Consolidations: Aggregate Mass-Tort Litigation After *Ortiz*' (2010) 58(4) *Kansas Law Review* 775.

Further, claims arising out of the 9/11 disaster were diverted from being made through the courts to a specially-established compensation fund,[64] as with the 2010 BP Gulf oil spill.[65]

iii. Antitrust Cases

Private enforcement was mandated by the Sherman Act, which provided a right of action for any person 'injured in his business or property' by virtue of an antitrust violation to sue for 'threefold the damages by him sustained, and the costs of suit, including a reasonable attorney's fee'.[66] The US Antitrust Division believes 'individual accountability through imposition of jail sentences is the single greatest deterrent' to cartel activity.[67] A senior US public enforcer has said that a private enforcement system may in fact hinder, rather than help, the public authorities in their enforcement of competition laws.[68]

DuVal's study of antitrust class actions between 1966 and 1973 found that the contribution of the class action had enabled types of plaintiffs to sue who would otherwise have been unable to do so because of the size of their claims.[69] On the other hand, Ginsburg and Brennan argued that judicial resolution of antitrust cases in the 1960s created a 'plaintiff's picnic', with the courts construing the antitrust laws to protect firms from their competitors without regard to whether the defendant had caused any injury to the competitive process.[70] An explosion of cases after the war peaked in 1975–1979, at which point private litigation exceeded public enforcement by a ratio of 20–1, and stabilised in the 2000s in the 9–1 range.[71] The private 'follow on' actions that used to be filed routinely have dwindled in number since the Supreme Court's decision in *Twombly*.[72]

[64] GK Hadfield, 'Framing Choice between Cash and the Courthouse; Experiences with the 9/11 Victim Compensation Fund' (2008) 42(3) *Law & Society Review* 645.

[65] LS Mullenix, 'Prometheus Unbound: The BP Gulf Coast Claims Facility as a Means for Resolving Mass Tort Litigation—A Fund Too Far' (2011) 71(3) *Louisiana Law Review* 819.

[66] 15 US Code s15(a).

[67] SD Hammond, 'Ten Strategies for Winning the Fight Against Hardcore Cartels', Paper presented at Paris Working Party No 3 Prosecutors Program, 18 October 2005.

[68] JT Rosch, 'Does the EU Need a System of Private Competition Remedies to Supplement Public Law Enforcement?', speech at 2011 LIDC Congress, Christ Church, Oxford, 23 September 2011.

[69] BS DuVal, Jr, 'The Class Action as an Antitrust Enforcement Device: The Chicago Experience (I)' (1976) 1(3) *American Bar Foundation Research Journal* 1021; BS DuVal, Jr, 'The Class Action as an Antitrust Enforcement Device: The Chicago Experience (II)' (1976) 1(4) *American Bar Foundation Research Journal* 1273.

[70] DH Ginsburg and L Brannon, 'Determinants of Private Antitrust Enforcement in the United States' (2005) 29 *Competition Policy International* 37.

[71] DA Crane, *The Institutional Structure of Antitrust Enforcement* (Oxford, Oxford University Press, 2011). See also *Sourcebook of Criminal Justice Statistics Online*, available at: www.albany.edu/sourcebook/pdf/t5412007.pdf.

[72] *Bell Atlantic Corp v Twombly* 550 US 544 (2007).

Class members in DuVal's cohort obtained relief in less than one-third of terminated class actions, and one-third were dismissed without any settlement.[73] Most class settlements fell far short of the aggregate damages sustained by the class. Antitrust class actions were burdensome because they were large, involving more parties and attorneys, greater discovery and greater potential recovery.

The 'Georgetown Study' of 1985,[74] which examined some 1900 cases filed in five US District Courts in 1973–1983, found that the system included both bad cases and meritorious cases that would not have been brought by the government, whilst around 80 per cent of cases settled after two years, and of those that proceeded to trial the plaintiffs won less than 30 per cent. A quarter of private cases were follow-ons to public enforcement.

The threat of costly civil class action litigation initiated under federal and/or state laws has the potential to force settlement on extortionate terms, because if it is initiated under federal law, defendants face the prospect of joint and several liability without a right to contribution. Crane's review of the antitrust evidence concluded that cases were easy to bring, costly to defend, unlikely to be involuntarily dismissed by the courts, and hence likely to coerce the defendant to pay a substantial settlement to be rid of the case.[75] He argued that much private antitrust litigation was motivated by businesses seeking a strategic advantage in the marketplace rather than by publicly minded private Attorneys General. Elzinga and Wood also concluded that many private antitrust lawsuits were strategically motivated.[76] Snyder and Kauper found evidence that the private antitrust remedy was often used to subvert, rather than promote, competition.[77]

iv. Employment Disputes

Employment claims (yearly average 29.3 per cent) were the largest types in Heiman's study of 3711 class actions filed between 2000 and 2005 in California.[78] A study of the class actions certified between 1979 and 1984 in the Northern District of California found that the clear majority were employment discrimination cases.[79] These were heavily dependent on

[73] DuVal (n 69).

[74] *Georgetown Study of Private Antitrust Litigation: Papers from the Georgetown Conference on Private Antitrust Litigation* (Airlie House, Virginia, 8–9 November 1985). See also LJ White (ed), *Private Antitrust Litigation: New Evidence, New Learning* (Cambridge MA, MIT Press, 1988) 3.

[75] Crane (n 71) 58.

[76] KG Elzinga and WC Wood, 'The Costs of the Legal System in Private Antitrust Enforcement' in White (n 74) 134.

[77] EA Snyder and TE Kauper, 'Misuses of the Antitrust Laws: The Competitor Plaintiff' (1991) 90 *Michigan Law Review* 551.

[78] Heiman (n 4).

[79] Garth (n 7).

obtaining initial information and analysis from the public authority, the Equal Employment Opportunity Commission (EEOC).[80] Several cases ended with a remedy that depended on governmental action to oversee it.

v. Consumer Actions

Amounts claimed by and paid to individual consumers in class actions are typically small. Hensler et al found that estimated losses in their 1995–1996 consumer suits ranged from an average of $3.83 to an average of $4550; in five of the six cases the average was probably less than $1000.[81]

Further, sums actually paid to consumers are often far less than the sums envisaged in the settlement. The reason is that although a class can be created by an opt-out certification procedure and then processed without the involvement of class members other than the lead plaintiff, after a settlement has been negotiated class members normally, in classes where claimants are numerous and dispersed such as consumer claims at least, need to opt-in so as to collect their individual entitlements. Studies have found that there appear to be substantial variations in take up rates: Hensler found rates varying from 30 per cent to 100 per cent,[82] with the result that far less was paid out to plaintiffs than had been agreed in settlements. Pace confirmed the finding in the RAND insurance study, and noted reasons why individuals might not claim.[83]

Analysis of 15 small-stakes consumer class actions settlements against some of the largest banks in MDL claims consolidated in 2009 found that between one per cent and 70 per cent of class members received some compensation, ranging from $13 to $90, representing between six per cent and 69 per cent of average class member damages, and being largely dependent on the underlying strength of the class' claims.[84] Class members who had to complete forms negotiated very high payments as percentages of claimed losses (over 90 per cent) whereas those in automatic settlements had lower rates (37 per cent to 75 per cent).[85] Even providing personal notices to people to return claim forms produces limited comprehension and response rates.[86]

[80] Garth, Nagel and Plager (n 3).

[81] Hensler (n 38).

[82] ibid.

[83] Pace (n 39). See also NM Pace and WB Rubenstein, 'How Transparent are Class Action Outcomes? Empirical Research on the Availability of Class Action Claims Data' (2008) RAND Institute for Civil Justice Working Paper; Willging, Hooper and Niemic (n 24).

[84] BT Fitzpatrick and RC Gilbert, 'An Empirical Look at Compensation in Consumer Class Actions' (2015) 11 (4) *New York University Journal of Law & Business* special issue.

[85] ibid.

[86] TC Bartsh, FM Boddy, BF King and PN Thompson, *A Class-Action Suit That Worked: The Consumer Refund in the Antibiotic Antitrust Litigation* (Lexington MA, Lexington Books, 1978).

Various studies observed that opt-in rates rise as the sums available increase, but rates may be noticeably low below say $1000: The 'it just ain't worth it' syndrome applies to opting into settlements as much as to initiating litigation and opting in to class actions. It has also been found that the number and percentage of opt-outs may depend on the type of the claim: more opt-out in mass tort to bring individual actions.[87] Accordingly, questions remain to be answered whether the opt-out class mechanism is effective and economical, and in what circumstances.

The consequences of a low opt-in rate are that, first, attorneys' fee recovery ratio is higher than it appeared when the settlement was agreed and fees were approved by the court, second, the sum paid by the defendant leaves an undistributed amount (perhaps dealt with by a *cy pres* payment), and third, either deserving plaintiffs go uncompensated, or a question arises over whether the enterprise was worth the cost, assuming it had legal merit.

B. Damages and Costs

Both damages awarded and plaintiffs' lawyers' transactional costs are substantial in class actions. This is consistent with the twin goals of the US legal system: first, to create sufficiently attractive incentives to encourage intermediaries to assume risk (and to insulate representative plaintiffs from any risk) and, second, to impose large penalties that will have a deterrent effect on corporate behaviour, thereby acting as regulation. As Hensler et al pointed out, determination of whether the fees of attorneys or other service-providing intermediaries are reasonable is a political judgment, influenced by local social factors.[88] It also depends on the extent to which the goals of deterrence, regulation and the delivery of adequate redress are achieved.

[87] Eisenberg and Miller (n 38).

[88] Hensler (n 38) (class attorneys received substantial fees in all successful suits, ranging from about half a million dollars to $75 million, representing the equivalent of average hourly fees ranging from $320 to almost $2,000); Eisenberg and Miller (n 38) (mean fee award of 21.9% in court-approved class actions in 1993–2002; injunctions or coupons had no material effect on the fee); T Eisenberg and G P Miller, 'Attorneys' Fees and Expenses in Class Action Settlements: 1993–2008' (2010) 7(1) *Journal of Empirical Legal Studies* 248 (extending the data set to 2008 found that the overwhelmingly important determinant of the fee was the size of the class recovery, with a strikingly linear relationship between fee awards and recoveries; in larger cases, fees being 21% to 27% of recoveries); T Eisenberg, GP Miller and MA Perino, 'A New Look at Judicial Impact: Attorneys' Fees in Securities Class Actions after *Goldberger v Integrated Resources, Inc*' (2009) 29 *Washington University Journal of Law and Policy* 5; Pace (n 39) (class attorneys' fees in 48 insurance class actions ranged from $50,000 to $50 million, and in 27 calculable cases represented from 12% to 41% of the common fund; in 36 calculable cases, class attorney fees had a median of 47% of the sums actually distributed); S Govindaraj, P Lee and D Tinkelman, 'Using the Event Study Methodology to Measure the Social Costs of Litigation—a Re-Examination Using Cases from the Automotive Industry' (2007) 3(2) *Review of Law & Economics* 342 (in a series of large antitrust cases, class attorney fees were usually 30% or one-third for recoveries under £100 million; for recoveries over that sum and

Eisenberg and Miller's 2004 study found that the average class action recovery in the cases studied was $138.6 million and aggregate class action recoveries averaged $5.13 billion per year.[89] The average recovery of the top 20 per cent of their cases was $613 million, and the average for the top 10 per cent of cases was $1.08 billion. The gross recovery across Eisenberg and Miller's 370 cases (in 2002 $) had a mean of $100 million and median of $11.6 million. In the four federal districts studied in the Class Action Reports set of cases the mean recovery was $35.4 million, and median $7.6 million.[90] The mean recovery did not noticeably increase over the decade studied, and the median level of individual recoveries ranged from $315 to $528 and the maximum awards ranged from $1505 to $5331 per class member.[91] The total sums agreed in all federal class action settlements in 2006 and 2007 were, respectively, $22 billion and $11 billion, of which between 76 and 73 per cent respectively was in securities cases.[92]

Fees awarded by judges, almost always as a result of agreed settlements, are usually based on a percentage of the total settlement amount, tapering as the size of the common fund increases in size.[93] Some judges have auctioned appointment as class counsel, so as to adopt a market mechanism to identify lowest prices.[94] It is rare for private bodies to object to fees,[95] but it appears that few if any class members object to fees or settlements.

Over the past 50 years, direct tort costs in the US grew more than 100-fold from less than $2 billion in 1950 to $254.7 billion in 2008, exceeding Gross Domestic Product (GDP) growth by an average of over two percentage points.[96] The authors estimated that in 2008 personal tort costs were $94.2 per person and business tort costs were $160.5. Total tort costs peaked in 2009 at equal to 1.79 per cent of the GDP of the United States. A United States federal government analysis in 2002 concluded that excessive tort litigation costs in 2000 were an $87 billion drag on the

below $500 million, fees were between 20% and 33.3%; and recoveries over $500 million the range was between 5.2% and 33.3%; fees for the largest recovery of £3.383 million were $219.90 million); Fitzpatrick (n 38) (in all federal class action settlements in 2006-2007, most fee awards were strongly related to settlement size, and between 25% and 35% of the settlement sum).

89 Eisenberg and Miller (n 38).

90 Willging, Hooper and Niemic (n 24).

91 ibid.

92 Fitzpatrick (n 38).

93 Hensler (n 38).

94 LL Hooper and M Leary, *Auctioning the Role of Class Counsel in Class Action Cases: A Descriptive Study* (Washington DC, Federal Judicial Centre, 2001). Of all the cases, 12 were securities and two antitrust; eight had terminated and all of them settled. The number of bids ranged from two to 21, average seven, median eight.

95 TF Burke, Lawyers, Lawsuits, and Legal Rights. The Battle over Litigation in American Society (Berkeley, University of California Press, 2002).

96 *2009 Update on US Tort Costs Trends* (Towers Perrin, 2009).

national economy.[97] In 2006 nearly one in six jury awards were $1 million or more, and over seven per cent of businesses experienced a liability loss of $5 million or more during the previous five years.[98] In 2005 the annual tort cost for small United States businesses was $98 billion. This equated to $20 per £1,000 of revenue. Small businesses bore 69 per cent of US business tort liability but took only 19 per cent of revenues. They paid $20 billion of their tort costs out of pocket, as opposed to through insurance.[99] In 2006 and 2007, a series of reports raised concerns over the risk of litigation to corporate markets.[100] Nevertheless, Palmer and Sanders found that stock market reaction to 'blockbuster' jury damages awards (amounting to $100 million or more) was trivial in 11 of a set of 17 cases identified in 2004, and reaction only occurred where the ratio of total award to market capitalisation was in excess of nine per cent.[101] They concluded that awards that seem large are unimportant to (deep pocket) companies that have much larger market capitalisation, despite the fact that they face almost constant litigation.

In 2006, 40 per cent of the largest companies spent $5 million or more on litigation, excluding settlements and awards.[102] A 2009 poll of top American business lawyers found that 97 per cent consider that the American civil justice system is 'too expensive'.[103] A survey of 500 US Chief Executives by the Conference Board found that lawsuits caused 36 per cent of their companies to discontinue products, 15 per cent to lay off workers and eight per cent to close plants.[104] A Gallup survey of US small businesses found that 26 per cent of owners said that fear of liability kept them from releasing new products, services or operations to the market.[105] Over 200 insurance

[97] *An Economic Analysis of the US Tort Liability System* (US Council of Economic Advisers, 2002).

[98] *US Tort Costs and Cross-Border Perspectives; 2005 Update* (Towers Perrin-Tillinghast, 2006).

[99] *Tort Liability Costs For Small Business* (US Chamber Institute for Legal Reform, 2007). Small businesses are defined here as those with less than £10 million annual revenues and at least one employee in addition to the owner. The tort cost increased 13% from 2002 to 2005.

[100] Committee on Capital Markets Regulation, 'Interim Report' (2006), available at: www.capmkts.org/pdfs/11.30Committee_Interim_ReportREV2.pdf; Commission on the Regulation of US Capital Markets in the 21st Century, 'Report and Recommendations' (2007), available at: www.capitalmarketscommission.com; MR Bloomberg and CE Schumer, 'Sustaining New York's and the US's Global Financial Services Leadership' (2007), available at: www.schumer.senate.gov/SchumerWebsite/pressroom/special_reports/2007/NY_REPORT%20)FINAL.pdf.

[101] M Palmer and TB Sanders, 'Surprise! Most Blockbuster Jury Awards Are Ignored by the Stock Market' (2010) 6(2) *Review of Law & Economics* 145.

[102] *Fourth Annual Litigation Trends Survey Findings* (New York, Fulbright & Jaworski, 2007).

[103] *Civil Litigation Survey of Chief Legal Officers and General Counsel belonging to the Association of Corporate Counsel* (Denver, Institute for the Advancement of the American Legal System, 2010).

[104] US Senate Commerce Committee Report on Product Liability Reform Act of 1997.

[105] *National Small Business Poll* (National Federation of Independent Businesses, 2002).

companies failed in the United States in the decade prior to 2006.[106] High litigation risks and stringent regulations were the principal factors in a 2007 Report that New York is in danger of losing its status as world financial centre.[107]

In contrast to the United States' tort costs, European tort costs as a percentage of GDP in 2003 were said to be 0.6 per cent in Poland and Denmark, 0.7 per cent in France and UK, 1.1 per cent in Germany and 1.7 per cent in Italy.[108] However, one should be careful to make the right comparisons. If the US litigation system is intended to include a significant element of public enforcement, then it is illogical to compare the total costs of litigation or tort in USA (that is damages and transactional costs) with the costs of litigation in other jurisdictions. It would be more relevant to compare, first, the total costs of public and private enforcement of different jurisdictions and, second, the ratio of public to private enforcement costs.

Analysis of 127 resolved class action suits filed in, or removed to, federal court in 2009, resolved by 1 September 2013, and referred to in two leading reporter journals found that 41 (31 per cent) had been dismissed on the merits by court (dismissal on the pleadings or grant of summary judgment for the defendant, 45 (35 per cent) had been dismissed voluntarily or settled individually with the lead plaintiff, without any relief for other class members, and 40 (33 per cent) had been settled as a class.[109] Thus, in nearly two-thirds of resolved cases in this set, class members received nothing.

C. Merits

However, the criteria for class certification do not, perhaps surprisingly, include a review of the merits of a case.[110] There is limited data on whether cases or settlements have good or poor merits. Although courts approve settlements and fee proposals by plaintiff attorneys, it is extremely rare for courts to question the merits of settlements, or reject them.

[106] AM Best, 'Rising Number of P/C Company Impairments Continues Trend' March 10, 2003, quoted in D Deal, R Hartwig, JM Hudgins, H Moskowitz, CP Vollweiler, C West, R Woollams, *Tort Excess 2005: The Necessity for Reform from a Policy, Legal and Risk Management Perspective* (US Chamber of Commerce, 2005).

[107] Bloomberg and Schumer (n 100). Significantly, the authors were political opponents.

[108] *US Tort Costs and Cross-Border Perspectives; 2005 Update* (Towers Perrin-Tillinghast, 2006). The data in this analysis was obtained from the insurance industry, but the basis for these European figures is not transparent.

[109] *Do Class Actions Benefit Class Members? An Empirical Analysis of Class Actions* (Mayer Brown LLP, 2013), available at www.mayerbrown.com/files/uploads/Documents/PDFs/2013/December/DoClassActionsBenefitClassMembers.pdf. The publications from which the data set was assembled were *The BNA Class Action Litigation Reporter* and *Mealey's Litigation Class Action Reporter*.

[110] CR Sunstein, R Hastie, JW Payne, DA Schkade and WK Viscusi, *Punitive Damages: How Juries Decide* (Chicago, University of Chicago Press, 2002).

Hensler at al's conclusion was that benefits and costs are very difficult to assess.[111] They found that class counsel were sometimes simply interested in finding a settlement price that the defendants would agree to, rather than in finding out what class members had lost, what defendants had gained, how likely it was that defendants would actually be held liable if the suit were to go to trial, and negotiating a fair settlement based on the answers to these questions.

Lawyers shape their clients' expectations and goals to what is realistically attainable within the legal system, often to only recovering money.[112] Meili has found that in consumer class actions, rather than *de*flating the unrealistic expectations of clients in individual cases, lawyers deliberately *in*flate the expectations of their clients, encouraging them to look beyond individual monetary compensation and focus on relief of the entire class.[113] He found that if their clients refuse to be so encouraged, the lawyers do not adopt them as named plaintiffs, and that named plaintiffs who give a deposition are given an incentive award ranging between $500 and a few thousand dollars.

D. Forum Shopping

Hensler et al found evidence of patterns of 'shopping' for judges who would be more favourable to class actions in their 1995 and 1996 cases, with nearly 60 per cent of reported class action decisions in state courts, especially in consumer, citizens' rights and tort cases.[114] The 2007 RAND study of insurance class actions also found clustering, with two jurisdictions in particular (Miami-Dade County, Florida, and Cook County, Illinois) accounting for about 17 per cent of their state cases.[115] Beisner and Miller noted evidence of a disproportionately high volume of class action filings in three counties, where the annual filings increased substantially between 1998 and 2000.[116] A study of 2816 commercial contracts (mainly credit and security agreements) found that jury trial was only waived in 20 per cent of them generally, but in 80 per cent of those that designated Illinois as the forum.[117]

[111] Hensler (n 38).

[112] T Relis, 'It's Not About the Money! A Theory on Misconceptions of Plaintiffs' Litigation Aims' (2007) 68 *University of Pittsburgh Law Review* 341.

[113] S Meili, 'Perceptions of Consumer Class Actions: The Views of Plaintiffs' Lawyers and their Clients', unpublished, February 2010.

[114] Hensler (n 38).

[115] Pace (n 39).

[116] JH Beisner and J Davidson Miller, *They're Making a Federal Case Out of It … In State Court* (Civil Justice Report, 2001).

[117] T Eisenberg and GP Miller, 'Do Juries Add Value? Evidence from an Empirical Study of Jury Trial Waiver Clauses in Large Corporation Contracts' (2007) 4(3) *Journal of Empirical Legal Studies* 539.

At federal level, Fitzpatrick found that the class action settlements approved in 2006 and 2007 in four Circuits constituted a much larger share than the share of all civil litigation that those Circuits resolved.[118] He suggested that there were many securities cases in the financial districts of Boston and New York, and large corporate presence also in Chicago and San Francisco. Eisenberg and Miller found the same heavy concentration of federal class actions in their study of opinions delivered between 1993 and 2008.[119] They found that of the 95 federal district courts, more than half of all class actions in their data set occurred in five courts, which they noted also tended to be ones with large populations. The Southern District of New York accounted for 28 per cent of the securities cases. The Eastern District of Pennsylvania led in antitrust and consumer cases. The Northern and Eastern Districts of California were leaders in employment cases.

A general shift of cases to federal courts occurred under the Class Action Fairness Act (CAFA) of 2005. However, a 2005 study found that both state and federal courts certified classes in fewer than one in four cases filed as class actions.[120] Although state courts approved settlements awarding more money to the class than did federal courts, that difference was a product of the size of the class: Individual class members on average were awarded more from settlements in federal courts than in state courts.

A further 2007 study of 88 districts estimated that an average of 5300 class actions per year were filed in federal courts from July 2001 through June 2006 (including original filings and removals from state courts), excluding class actions brought by *pro se* litigants, those involving prison conditions or habeas corpus claims, or where the United States government was a plaintiff.[121] They found a 46 per cent increase in class action activity in the study districts as a whole in the six month period January through June 2006, compared to the first six months of the study period in 2001. Much of that increase was in cases involving federal law, especially labour class actions.

E. Financial Incentives, Conflicts of Interest and Abuse

A system designed to deliver widespread *general* deterrence through an ex post facto mechanism involving mass non-specialist enforcers should

[118] BT Fitzpatrick, 'An Empirical Study of Class Action Settlements and their Fee Awards' (2010) 7(4) *Journal of Empirical Legal Studies* 811.

[119] Eisenberg and Miller (n 88).

[120] TE Willging and SR Wheatman, *An Empirical Examination of Attorneys' Choice of Forum in Class Action Litigation* (Washington DC, Federal Judicial Center, 2005).

[121] TE Willging and EG Lee III, *The Impact of the Class Action Fairness Act of 2005: Third Interim Report to the Judicial Conference Advisory Committee on Civil Rules* (Washington DC, Federal Judicial Centre, 2007).

logically aim at facilitating the achievement of results that have high impact on the market at large.

The 'private attorney general' concept is thoroughly embedded in the United States legal system but has not escaped strong criticism from some commentators.[122] In 1987 Garth, Nagel and Plager's analysis of all federal class actions in the Northern District of California certified between 1979 and 1984 found that there had been a 'dramatic shift' from the initial model of the Lone Ranger or bounty hunter engaged in private law enforcement to a preoccupation with economic logic over incentives to sue.[123] The private attorney general model does not support advocacy before administrative agencies, only courts.[124] Garth, Nagel and Plager found that a significant number of class action private attorneys tended to 'piggyback' their cases on governmental investigations, even to the extent of copying the government's complaint. For example, antitrust and securities cases depended largely on the investigative activities of governmental agencies. They commented:

> A lawyer dependent on fees from a successful lawsuit naturally looks for the easy victories; creativity and innovation in the generation of the lawsuit are unlikely. Indeed, it looks as if the mercenary lawyers limit themselves largely to 'no research' lawsuits because of the efficiency of such a strategy. ... The mercenary lawyer takes fewer risks in defining the scope of the class. Accordingly, the attorney's goal is to reduce the reach of the suit and the breadth of the defendants' exposure so as to both maximise class certification and the probability of an expeditious and favourable settlement.[125]

In the result, Garth et al concluded that the 'legal mercenary' model of private attorneys 'cannot fully realize the ideals implicit in the model of a private, institutional antidote to, or substitute for, governmental machinery'.[126] By contrast, they found that the 'social advocate' model, involving publicly paid lawyers, delivered the best enforcement of public law goals. A federally funded legal services programme was established in 1965 as part of the 'War on Poverty', and ran in parallel with a notable stream of civil liberties and environmental cases.[127] Garth et al found that 50 per cent of the certified

[122] See JC Coffee, Jr, 'Rescuing the Private Attorney General: Why the Model of the Lawyer as Bounty Hunter is not Working' (1983) 42 *Maryland Law Review* 215; JC Coffee, Jr, 'Understanding the Plaintiff's Attorney: The Implications of Economic Theory for Private Enforcement of Law Through Class and Derivative Actions' (1986) 86 *Columbia Law Review* 669; Garth, Nagel and Plager (n 3); LM Grosberg, 'Class Actions and Client-Centered Decisionmaking' (1989) 40 *Syracuse Law Review* 709 (arguing that it is a delusion to suggest that the 'client' is the decision-maker in class actions, and that class action lawyers act like public officials).

[123] Garth, Nagel and Plager (n 3).

[124] *Webb v Board of Education of Dyer County*, 471 US 234 (1985).

[125] Garth, Nagel and Plager (n 3).

[126] ibid, 395.

[127] Such as *Associated Industries v Ickes* 134 F2d 694, 704 (2d Cir 1943); *NAACP v Button* 371 US 415 (1963); *Newman v Piggie Park* 390 US 400, 402 (1968); *Alyeska Pipeline Service Co v Wilderness Society* 421 US 240 (1975)

class actions in their 1979–1984 cohort was the product of law firms created directly by broad funding agencies[128] trying to generate legal power for the unrepresented and underrepresented in society. But there the private foundations had retreated and federal funding had shrunk for the Legal Services Corporation, whose cases had fallen from 3584 in 1976 to 736 in 1986.[129] Garth concluded that the 'private attorney general' model works well when there is either subsidised social advocacy or a genuine governmental commitment to promote strong efforts by mercenary law enforcers. They suggested that efforts to reform the model and to create an antidote or substitute for governmental machinery—an effective enforcement institution independent of the vagaries of government—would fail unless they confront this basic proposition.

Garth et al did identify some examples of private enforcement independent of government, but they concluded that there were very few such cases and the limiting conditions were 'severe indeed'.[130] The most important characteristic of such cases was that there were one or more aggrieved plaintiffs who sought legal representation and who were armed at the outset with the facts necessary to prove a violation of the law affecting a large but easily identifiable group of persons. These facts were simple and largely undisputed in the crucial respects; the lawyers could proceed much as they would in a relatively simple private lawsuit, without investing in significant research.

IV. SHIFTS: MDL AND ARBITRATION

Two important shifts have occurred in US practice in recent years in addition to the points noted above, such as the Congressionally mandated shift from state to federal courts for class actions. The points noted here are the increase in the use of the MDL procedure and the shift in consumer and employment mass from litigation to arbitration.

Various studies have demonstrated that class actions that have survived a class certification hearing are then transferred for centralised case management under the MDL procedure, even if thought they may share only one common issue.[131] The transfer is decided by the Multidistrict Litigation Panel of federal judges.

[128] Notably ACLU, NAACP, the Sierra Club.

[129] *In Camera* 10 Class Action Rep 93 (1987).

[130] The cohort contained six out of 46 such cases, dealing with length of pre-trial detention, a pension plan, a company acquisition, insurance provisions restricting access on basis of race, and medication for mental patients.

[131] MH Redish and JM Karaba, 'One Size Doesn't Fit All: Multidistrict Litigation, Due Process, and the Dangers of Procedural Collectivism' (2015) 95 *Boston University Law Review* 95 (commenting that MDL amounts to a strange cross between The Wild West and political smoke-filled rooms of the twentieth century, which is hardly a combination that augurs well for either due process or the rule of law).

It has been noted above that courts expressed concern that class certification led inexorably to settlement on commercial grounds and irrespective of merits, and the total financial impact of the litigation could be so large as to run the risk of 'betting the company' and its survival on the decision of a single jury. In 1995, the Seventh Circuit decertified a class of haemophiliacs who had received blood contaminated with HIV, because the risk of bankruptcy put defendants 'under intense pressure to settle'.[132] In 1996, the Fifth Circuit overturned a decision certifying a nationwide class action by cigarette smokers, on the basis that the 'risk of facing an all-or-nothing verdict presents too high a risk, even when the probability of an adverse judgment is low'.[133] In 1996, the Sixth Circuit overturned the certification of a class of individuals who claimed injuries as a result of penile implants manufactured by the defendants.[134] In 1997 and 1999, the US Supreme Court reversed massive class settlements involving asbestos-related injuries. In *Amchem Products, Inc v Windsor*[135] it held that a proposed class of present and future asbestos claimants could not be certified as an opt-out class under Federal Rule of Civil Procedure 23(b)(3), since the claims were too disparate and 'sprawling' to be joined in a single representative class action.[136] In 1999, in *Ortiz v Fibreboard Corp*,[137] the Supreme Court again rejected an asbestos class settlement, on the basis that the settlement failed to satisfy the Rule 23(b)(1)(B) requirements for certification of asbestos claims against a single corporate defendant that the defendant had limited funds to pay the aggregated claims.[138]

In 1998, Federal Rule of Civil Procedure 23(f) enabled defendants to obtain appellate interlocutory review of federal district court decisions certifying class actions, which led to fewer cases being certified.[139] As noted above, PSLRA of 1995 and the 2005 CAFA had the effect of shifting most major class actions to federal court. The combined effect of these developments and the 1997 introduction of the MDL procedure resulted in a major increase in cases being transferred to the MDL procedure. Since then, many courts require that plaintiffs prove substantial portions of their cases on the merits at class certification, and several of the class certification requirements (class definition, numerosity, commonality, adequacy

[132] *In re Rhone-Poulenc Rorer Inc* 51 F 3d 1293 (7th Cir 1995).

[133] *Castano v Am Tobacco Co* 84 F3d 734, 746 (5th Cir 1996) (citing *Rhone–Poulenc* 51 F3d at 1298).

[134] *In re Am Med Sys, Inc* 75 F3d 1069 (6th Cir 1996).

[135] *Amchem Products, Inc v Windsor* 521 US 591, 622–25 (1997).

[136] ibid, 624–28.

[137] *Ortiz v Fibreboard Corp* 527 US 815, 864–65 (1999).

[138] ibid, 851.

[139] RH Klonoff, 'The Decline of Class Actions' (2012) 90 *Washington University Law Review* 1.

of representation, Rule 23(b)(2) and Rule 23(b)(3)), became considerably more difficult to establish.[140]

Once cases were transferred under the MDL procedure, they were rarely returned to originating courts. In 2010, 2012 and 2013, the Judicial Panel on Multidistrict Litigation remanded respectively only 3.425 per cent, 3.1 per cent, and 2.9 per cent of cases to their original districts.[141] A strong rationale for retaining cases was the hope of forcing a global settlement. For plaintiff attorneys, doctrinal uncertainties over weak claims could be avoided by packaging plaintiffs together in a global settlement. For defendants, as many cases as possible could be resolved in one stroke. Thus, the shift of products liability cases to the MDL resulted in non-class settlements.[142] Over time, however, the Panel has become more selective in the cases that it does and does not refer.[143]

The Supreme Court imposed a significant restriction in securities cases in 2014. At class certification for actions alleging violation of section 10(b) of the Securities Exchange Act, a presumption applies that plaintiffs relied on the misstatement. In *Halliburton v Erica P John Fund* ('Halliburton II'), the Supreme Court held that 'defendants must be afforded an opportunity before class certification to defeat the presumption through evidence that an alleged misrepresentation did not actually affect the market price of the stock'.[144] This was expected to reduce the number of certifications, albeit add to the already high cost of certification hearings.[145]

The second main shift has occurred in cases based on contract claims, such as consumer trading and employment. Businesses have inserted arbitration clauses that oust court jurisdiction in relation to disputes. In 2011, the Supreme Court upheld the validity of such arbitration clauses, notwithstanding the inability of consumers or employees to negotiate such standard terms in *Conception*[146] and affirmed the waiver of rights in 2013 in *American Express*.[147] As a result, a general move away from litigation towards arbitration is anticipated, and has accompanied a major growth in interest in ADR and online dispute resolution (ODR) systems.

The combined effects of the shifts noted above are viewed as presaging major transformations in the US legal system.[148] Fitzpatrick considers that

[140] ibid.

[141] EC Burch, 'Remanding Multidistrict Litigation' (2014) 73 *Louisiana Law Review* 399.

[142] Willging and Lee III (n 63).

[143] EG Lee, CR Borden, MS Williams and KM Scott, 'Multidistrict Centralization: An Empirical Examination' (2015) 12(2) *Journal of Empirical Legal Studies* 211–35.

[144] *Halliburton Co v Erica P John Fund, Inc* 134 S Ct 2398, 2412 (2014).

[145] Comolli (n 37).

[146] *AT&T Mobility v Conception* 131 S Ct 1740 (2011).

[147] *American Express Co v Italian Colors Restaurant* 133 S Ct 2304 (2013).

[148] MH Redish, 'Rethinking the Theory of the Class Action: The Risks and Rewards of Capitalistic Socialism in the Litigation Process' (2014) 65 *Emory Law Journal* 451 (the class action relationship between client and attorney should no longer be viewed as principal-

the logical conclusion of the Supreme Court's *Concepcion* and *American Express* decisions will be that businesses will eventually be able to eliminate virtually all class actions that are brought against them, including those brought by shareholders.[149] Accepting 'the evolving dysfunction of the American class action' Mullenix has called for the restriction of the class procedure to injunctive remedies and encouraging more public regulatory enforcement.[150]

V. CONCLUSIONS

There is a significant level of class action activity in the United States, although the number of class actions is small compared to the general volume of litigation. Class actions differ in size and can include a lot of claimants. They cover a range of subject matter, the largest group being securities cases. There has been a shift away from social issues to cases that are driven by outcomes that are about money. Welfare cases are frequently initiated by public organisations so as to raise topical welfare and political issues. Individuals often initiate employment discrimination cases, in which a sense of grievance or public fairness is often a necessary motivator. The process can transform employment discrimination victims into activists, but they do not always personally benefit from the outcome in the way initially envisaged.

Money cases are mainly directed at large corporations with 'deep pockets'. Cases that parallel, or are based on, breach of public regulatory law, such as antitrust and consumer fraud statutes, tend to be brought subsequent to findings of infringement by public agencies (piggy-back). Securities cases are brought against large firms when share prices fall.

The class action mechanism enables enormous amounts of money to be claimed, even though individual consumer claims typically involve low sums. The success rates of class actions may be lower than expected, at least for some types of claims. Even though total notional settlement amounts may appear large, sums actually reaching individual claimants may be modest. These issues raise questions over the efficiency and effectiveness of the class action procedure that are unresolved.

The certification stage acts as a watershed for the outcome of a class action. A significant percentage of cases never reach certification stage, either because they are dropped or because a settlement is negotiated. Almost

agent but as guardian-ward, and the system is plagued by externalities and perverse economic incentives); GM Vairo, 'Is the Class Action Really Dead? Is that Good or Bad for Class Members?' (2014) 64 *Emory Law Journal* 477 (utility as a prosecution tool has been compromised but certification for settlement purposes remains).

149 BT Fitzpatrick, 'The End of Class Actions?' (2015) 75(1) *Arizona Law Review* 161.

150 LS Mullenix, 'Ending Class Actions as We Know Them: Rethinking the American Class Action' (2014) 64 *Emory Law Journal* 399.

all class actions that are certified are settled and not tried. Settlements are usually negotiated on the basis of what the defendant will pay, and the agreed total sum is divided amongst the class. As a consequence, settlements can be based on incomplete evidence and incomplete understanding of the merits of a case. There are suggestions that this system of negotiated settlements, intermediaries' conflicts of interest, high transaction costs (especially discovery and large fees) produces some cases in which merits are poor ('blackmail settlements') and some cases in which a court might have awarded a higher total sum. Courts almost invariably approve proposed settlements. Significant issues remain over whether settlements are fair to possible future class members.

Under the US model, financial incentives are necessary to motivate private intermediaries to undertake law enforcement activities. Unquestionably, the US situation involves large economic forces. The justification for this model should rest on evidence that the size of the incentives is reasonable and not excessive, that the level of enforcement activity is justified on the basis of meritorious cases and settlements, that the costs imposed on defendants are justified and proportionate, that the system produces an adequate number of fair outcomes, and that illegal behaviour is adequately deterred, or that an adequate level of ongoing compliance with law is created. Reliable data on several of these requirements is scarce and difficult to verify, other than in relation to levels of transactional costs, damages and attorney compensation. The US model is clearly one that involves large sums of money changing hands. But do the outcomes justify the costs? The most important issue is whether claims that are brought, and particularly settled, have sufficient merit, and on that there is little reliable evidence but much assertion. A further issue concerns what anti-abuse mechanisms should be deployed, and how effective they are. Again, there is very little reliable understanding of how (and how well) different controls work.

The outcomes of class actions are difficult to assess. A great deal turns on the extent to which the system is effective in regulating corporate behaviour through deterrence based on large financial penalties. On that issue, there is little reliable empirical evidence, other than some that finds adverse financial impacts on firms and sometimes of employees.

As might be expected for a system in which there are high economic incentives to settle, since PSLRA 59 per cent of the cases resolve (whether through settlement or dismissal) within three years from first filing.[151] This contrasts with the slowing effect of various safeguards thought necessary in European collective action models.

There are the following lessons from this rich and valuable experience for other jurisdictions that are contemplating the design of effective methods of collective redress. The starting point is to define the goals, such as

[151] Comolli (n 37).

delivering redress, regulating behaviour or raising social and political issues. Certain types of procedure may be more or less appropriate for achieving individual goals. The empirical evidence that a particular procedure is capable of achieving a particular goal should be clear. For example, is it clear that private enforcement deters? Reliable sources of funding are needed in order to bring mass litigation. If public funding is not available, then certain types of case will not be brought, and there may be an access to justice gap. If reliance is placed on private funding, significant financial incentives may be required, and this will raise issues of conflicts of interest and increase the potential for abuse. Safeguards may be needed to control the system.[152] However, it is difficult to calibrate safeguards, and they may struggle to control large financial interests. A catch 22 situation arises that powerful financial incentives may be needed to incentivise private enforcement, which inherently creates abuse, but if significant balancing safeguards are imposed then litigation will be significantly dampened.[153] The dominance of private enforcement and class actions in the US system has chilled development of alternative means of achieving acceptable behaviour (through various forms of regulatory mechanisms) and delivering redress (through alternative dispute resolution, ombudsmen, compensation schemes or other means). Such alternative mechanisms are emerging strongly in Europe.[154] It is necessary to decide which mechanisms are most effective, efficient and desirable, and this evaluation should be based on empirical evidence. The history of collective actions in Europe indicates a low level of demand by judges for collective rules.[155] A way forward may be to prioritise pathways so that cases are funnelled through effective mechanisms in preference to others, in which case the collective action may end up as a last resort.[156]

[152] R Money-Kyrle and C Hodges, 'Safeguards in Collective Actions' (2012) 19(4) *Maastricht Journal of International and Comparative Law* 477.

[153] C Hodges, 'Collective Redress: A Breakthrough or a Damp Sqibb?' (2014) 34 *Journal of Consumer Policy* 67.

[154] C Hodges and A Stadler (eds), *Resolving Mass Disputes: ADR and Settlement of Mass Claims* (Cheltenham, Edward Elgar, 2013); C Hodges, 'Mass Collective Redress: Consumer ADR and Regulatory Techniques' (2015) *European Review of Private Law* (forthcoming).

[155] Hodges (n 153).

[156] Since the above was written, an expert account of the rise and fall of different types of class actions can be found in JC Coffee Jr, *Entrepreneurial Litigation: Its Rise, Fall, and Future* (Boston, Harvard University Press, 2015).

11

The Role of Enforcement in Delineating the Scope of Intellectual Property Rights[*]

RETO M HILTY

I. PARTICULARITIES OF THE ENFORCEMENT OF INTELLECTUAL PROPERTY RIGHTS

FOR AN 'ORDINARY' lawyer it may be difficult to understand why the enforcement of intellectual property (IP) rights is a special issue. In fact, it's hard to imagine that during a very cold winter like in early 2012 tens of thousands of people would demonstrate in the streets for weeks against an international treaty aiming at a strengthening of enforcement tools in other fields of law than IP, for instance related to tort law, criminal law or labour law—on the contrary: either people would not feel concerned at all or they would understand that such laws were enacted to protect their own interests and that therefore stricter enforcement tools made sense.

Why is that so different in the case of IP law? Why for instance did an incredible number of people oppose the Anti-Counterfeiting Trade Agreement (ACTA) in such a striking way that even a vast majority of European parliamentarians—rarely impressed by demonstrators, but used to deciding upon the advices of professional lobby groups—largely changed their views and voted against this treaty in July 2012?[1]

* The author wishes to thank Ansgar Glatt for his valuable support in searching for documents.

[1] See www.europarl.europa.eu/news/en/news-room/content/20120703IPR48247/html/European-Parliament-rejects-ACTA: 478 MEPs voted against ACTA, 39 in favour, and 165 abstained; they obviously were impressed by a petition addressed to the European Parliament, signed by 2.5 million people; see https://beck-online.beck.de/?VPATH=bibdata%2Freddok%2Fbecklink%2F1018995.htm&LINKNOTE=off. A side-effect was that the rather specific issue of copyright enforcement surprisingly quickly was brought from academic discussion to broader public awareness; see eg E Kirschbaum and I Ivanova, 'Protests Erupt Across Europe Against Web Piracy Treaty' *Reuters* (11 February 2012), available at: www.reuters.com/article/2012/02/11/us-europe-protest-acta- idUSTRE81A0I120120211; D Lee, 'Acta protests: Thousands take to streets across Europe' *BBC News Technology* (11 February 2012), available at: www.bbc.co.uk/news/technology-16999497.

There are a number of reasons why enforcement of IP law seems to be particularly challenging. However, one should rather not overestimate those exceptional circumstances during the winter of 2012. On the one hand it is certainly true that the protestors against ACTA[2]—rightly—felt what copyright lawyers have been discussing for more than one decade now, namely the 'digital dilemma': The internet provides for an unprecedented freedom and for access to almost all content in our world—but legal regulation (and copyright law in particular) increasingly impedes the possibilities to make use of this freedom.

On the other hand, did these people on the street really understand what exactly they were opposing? If they had known the text of the proposed agreement and if they had been aware of the current legal situation, they would have detected that nothing much was intended to change—at least not in Europe or in the US.[3] Rather we may assume—and the pictures of protestors that went around the world confirmed this—that the demonstrations were mainly based on good feelings: an important part of the motivation to protest might have been a sensation of helplessness towards certain political establishments, nourished by the secret negotiations on ACTA by a selected group of countries under the lead of the US administration, ultimately leading to a fear of censorship on the internet.[4]

For the moment, ACTA seems to be off the agenda; the demonstrators have gone home to their children and back to work. Politicians have also gone back to business as usual. Brussels continues to declare that only strong IP rights and rigorous enforcement will foster the European economy;[5] Washington unwaveringly opposes any kind of IP limitations.[6]

[2] It should be noted, however, that platforms like the former European alliance 'Stop Acta'—organised by the copyright-critical Pirate Party in lots of European countries—invoked these people to take to the streets.

[3] T Hoeren, 'ACTA ad acta? Überlegungen zum urheberrechtlichen "Shitstorm"' (2012) *MultiMedia und Recht* 137; see for the full text of the downvoted ACTA: trade.ec.europa.eu/doclib/docs/2011/may/tradoc_147937.pdf.

[4] This is in line with the fact that a lot of demonstrators wore the 'Guy Fawkes' mask, a historical symbol for political resistance. This mask became popular through the movie 'V for Vendetta' by Lana and Andy Wachowski and was not only used by the No-ACTA protests but also by the hacker group 'Anonymous' and the Occupy movement.

[5] Most recently eg Communication from the Commission to the European Parliament, the Council and the European Economic and Social Committee 'Towards a renewed consensus on the enforcement of Intellectual Property Rights: An EU Action Plan' COM/2014/0392 final, eur-lex.europa.eu/legal-content/EN/TXT/HTML/?uri=CELEX:52014DC0392&from=EN; see also below nn 24 and 61.

[6] If the USA after rancorous opposition finally agreed to the Marrakesh Treaty to Facilitate Access to Published Works for Persons Who Are Blind, Visually Impaired or Otherwise Print Disabled, signed on 27 June 2013, see www.wipo.int/treaties/en/ip/marrakesh/, this was indeed a remarkable *succès d'estime* for the numerous associations for blind people who had been fighting a hard struggle for years; this singular easing of the US negotiators, however, hardly marks a turnaround.

The Western industry continues to blame India for rejecting pharmacy patents or for granting compulsory licensing, and Apple, Samsung and many others unabatedly battle out their IT-patent wars. But nobody is going back to the street to demonstrate against the IP system.

Nevertheless, this 'normality'—and the silence on the street—might be deceptive. Enforcement of IP law remains a hot issue which deserves much more attention than the current debate—notably in Europe, related to the evaluation of the Enforcement Directive of 2004[7]—seems to grasp.[8] In fact, we should be concerned that the current perspective on IP enforcement is largely one-sided: we only—or at least primarily—focus on the right holders, a perspective which indeed is caused by the law itself.[9]

Admittedly, it is not easy to explain why an individual right recognised by legislation (like copyright) or even granted by a state authority—for example a patent, design right or trademark—should not be enforceable like any other right: namely, to its full extent.[10] Surely it does not make much sense to establish individual rights which cannot be enforced unconditionally, insofar as a right and its enforcement actually belong together like the two sides of a coin. Therefore, if we detect elements of faultiness within the IP system, it's rather confusing to call for 'remedy' on the side of enforcement. Nevertheless, there are at least two reasons why it would not be appropriate to enforce IP rights 'blindly'.

II. THE ONE-SIDED PERSPECTIVE OF IP LAW

First, it would be simplistic to perceive the holder of an individual right—related to an invention, a work or something similar—as a 'property owner' and to conclude therefrom that third parties should be excluded from any use of such subject matters of protection. The very notion of 'property'—notably in its understanding in a civil law context—is misleading, at least as long as 'intellectual property' is put on the same level as tangible property.[11]

[7] Dir 2004/48 of 29 April 2004 on the enforcement of intellectual property rights 157 OJ L45-86.

[8] See ec.europa.eu/internal_market/consultations/docs/2012/intellectual-property-rights/summary-of-responses_en.pdf.

[9] See below in s III.

[10] RM Hilty, 'Legal Remedies Against Abuse, Misuse and Other Forms of Inappropriate Conduct of IP Right Holders' in RM Hilty and K-C Liu (eds), *Compulsory Licensing* (Heidelberg, Springer, 2015) 377.

[11] See WM Landes and RA Posner, 'The Economic Structure of Intellectual Property Law' (2003) *Harvard University Press* 11–36; J Hughes, 'The Philosophy of Intellectual Property' (1988) 77 *Georgetown Law Journal* 287ff; LC Becker, 'Deserving to Own Intellectual Property' (1993) 68 *Chicago-Kent Law Review* 609ff; for a very detailed list of works about the general theories on intellectual property see PS Menell, 'Intellectual Property: General Theories' in B Bouckaert and G de Geest (eds), *Encyclopedia of Law & Economics: Volume II* (Cheltenham, Edward Elgar, 2000) 165–88.

This is of course an old story; as early as the nineteenth century the Pandects intensely discussed that and came to the conclusion that the (German) term '*geistiges Eigentum*' is inappropriate and should be avoided;[12] instead, the expression '*Immaterialgüterrecht*' was created and translated into certain other languages (for example Dutch, Swedish etc), but never to an extent that in leading languages—like English, French or Spanish—the term 'intellectual property' ever disappeared.[13]

In the meantime, the English language prevails all over the world and the term 'property' has become so common in all other languages that it seems hopeless to fight it on the linguistic level. This does not, however, mean that one would be able to understand the meaning of different variations of 'property' by reducing this term to the ownership of tangible subject matters.[14] Whereas it is unquestionable that the property owner of a car should be in the position of fending off third parties from driving it, it is not so clear why a patent or a copyright-protected work should not be made useful for any non-owners.[15] Basically what is called 'non-rivalry'—that the use of an invention, for example, by one actor does not 'naturally' exclude its simultaneous use by another one—makes a difference. Beyond that, the special relevance of those subject matters of 'property' for third parties needs to be considered.[16] In other words, the notion that IP rights solely have the function to prohibit non-authorised parties from using the subject matters of protection falls short because it ignores the fact that not all uses are of the same nature. In addition it disregards the fact that the use of a particular piece of (tangible) property by another party than its owner usually is not required as long as an identical or similar piece can be purchased and used. An invention, in contrast, possibly may not be substituted to solve a technical problem based on another solution (or a patented chemical substance may not be replaced by another one to cure certain diseases). Likewise,

[12] J Kohler, 'Die Idee des geistigen Eigenthums' (1894) 82 *Archiv für civilistische Praxis* 161; even today, scholars—*cf* M Rehbinder, *Urheberrecht* 16th edn (München, Beck, 2010) 46—and the infamous 'Pirate Party', enemy of today's copyright system (*cf* wiki.piratenpartei.de/Geistiges_Eigentum), appeal to avoid this well-known term. *Contra* A Ohly, 'Geistiges Eigentum?' (2003) *JuristenZeitung* 547.

[13] *cf* for the history of immaterial property rights: Rehbinder, ibid 7–22.

[14] Even beyond that language barrier the term remains subject to discussion; just recently, in 2012, the Supreme Court of the United Kingdom dealt with the expression 'intellectual property', *Phillips v Mulcaire* [2012] UKSC 28, [2013] 1 AC 1 [20].

[15] This may also not be concluded from the Preamble of TRIPS, which recognises 'that intellectual property rights are private rights'. Art 8 Para 1 rightly emphasises that Members may 'adopt measures necessary to protect public health and nutrition, and to promote the public interest in sectors of vital importance to their socio-economic and technological development', which makes clear that IP rights are not unconfined entitlements.

[16] In copyright law in particular a number of different interests are involved; see RM Hilty, 'Urheberrecht in der Informationsgesellschaft: "Wer will was von wem woraus?"—Ein Auftakt zum "zweiten Korb"' (2003) 47 *Zeitschrift für Urheber- und Medienrecht* 986–91.

works may have such relevance that the full prohibition of their use would be inappropriate.

To a certain degree, this is also reflected in the IP law. Certain use activities by third parties are explicitly or implicitly allowed, either by legislation or by jurisprudence.[17] In copyright law an entire EU Directive explains the conditions under which uses of a work are allowed;[18] in the field of patent law the international legislation in an early stage dealt with certain constellations—most prominently the 'improvement innovation'—in which a third party shall be allowed to use the subject matter of protection.[19] In contrast, no law permits non-owners of a car to use foreign cars, or homeless people to live in houses owned by someone else. Notably, uses of pre-existing works or innovation for the purpose of generating something new should be privileged if we do not want to pervert the function of IP rights—namely, to foster new developments and thereby the advancement of society—into the opposite.

In copyright law, this discussion has gained momentum under the term 'creative use', which may be understood in contrast to mere 'consumptive use'.[20] In patent law, this aspect is known as well; one example of the current debates on this challenge therefore revolves around 'experimental use'.[21] Most remarkably, however, the prevailing understanding of such privileged uses is related to the position of the right holder. Indeed, it is more or less common ground that there are exceptions and limitations to his right; but it is not recognised that the privileged user himself might dispose of his own right, namely, a 'right to use' the subject matter of protection of the right holder.[22]

[17] The legal instruments and their range diverge (of course) in every country. A significant distinction can be discovered between civil law and common law countries. This is best visible in copyright law; for a review on national copyright law systems all over the world see RM Hilty and S Nérisson (eds), *Balancing Copyright—A Survey of National Approaches* (Heidelberg, Springer, 2012).

[18] Dir 2001/29/EC of 22 May 2001 on the harmonisation of certain aspects of copyright and related rights in the information society, 167 OJ L10–19.

[19] Notably Art 5A of the Paris Convention; see today also Art 31 TRIPS; for more details see Hilty (n 10) 385.

[20] By granting a licence (creativecommons.org) the creator permits the use of his work under specific requirements with the benefit that his work is easily accessible and can be amended. RP Merges, 'A New Dynamism in the Public Domain' (2004) 71 *University of Chicago Law Review* 197–200; N Elkin-Koren, 'What Contracts Cannot Do: The Limits of Private Ordering in Facilitating a Creative Commons' (2005) 74 *Fordham Law Review* 375–422.

[21] 'An experiment with a patented article for the sole purpose of gratifying a philosophical taste, or curiosity, or for mere amusement, is not an infringement of the rights of a patentee', *Poppenhusen v Falke* 19 F Cas 1048 (CCSDNY 1861) (No 11, 279); EA Rowe, 'The Experimental Use Exception to Patent Infringement: Do Universities Deserve Special Treatment?' (2006) 57 *Hastings Law Journal* 921ff.

[22] See for more details about the law of users' rights: LR Patterson and SW Lindberg, *The Nature of Copyright: A Law of Users' Rights* (Athens, The University of Georgia Press, 1991) 191ff; for more details regarding the term 'user rights' in copyright law in different countries see RM Hilty and S Nérisson, 'Overview' in Hilty and Nérisson (n 17) 16ff. The Canadian Supreme Court used that phrase explicitly in *CCH Canadian Ltd v Law Society of Upper Canada* [2004] 1 SCR 339 No 48.

In other words, a 'neutral' perception is missing.[23] We accept that the party, the 'owner' of an invention, a work etc holds—enforceable (although to some extent limited)—exclusivity to use this 'property'. But we do not accept that other parties could also claim—and enforce—an independent right to use the subject matter of protection under certain conditions.[24]

At first view, however, one might believe that the opposite is true. In copyright law in particular, statutory limitations look like a 'right' to use (for example private copying, which is allowed in most Continental European copyright legislations). However, this is not the doctrinal understanding of such limitations, and if for instance technical protection measures (TPMs) are established with the effect that private copying factually is excluded, an enforcement of that statutory privilege is not feasible.[25] On the other hand, one might interpret the position of the licensee of a compulsory licence—primarily discussed in patent law—as a 'user right'. Those provisions, however, simply allow a third party to sue against the right holder on a case-by-case basis, proving that the statutory requirements for the grant of a licence are met, and yet incurring substantial transaction costs—and facing an entirely ambiguous outcome. In other words, there is neither a 'per se' enforceability related to such uses of third parties as it exists for the right holder nor a legally protected position *erga omnes*.

In view of that it becomes obvious that unreflected enforcement of IP rights to their full extent is not appropriate. If IP rights shall not fail to fulfil their functions—in particular to foster innovation and creation—their enforcement needs to be limited in order to meet a certain equilibrium between exclusivity and availability.

III. THE LACKING DIFFERENTIATIONS WITHIN THE IP LAWS

The second reason why the belief that IP rights should be enforced to their full extent is simplistic derives from the fact that even within one field of

[23] In respect of this relationship between right holder and user, the controversial question arises whether copyright law provides for an 'access-right'—'the right to control the manner in which members of the public apprehend the work', JC Ginsburg, 'From Having Copies to Experiencing Works: The Development of an Access Right in US Copyright Law' in G Hansen (ed), *US Intellectual Property Law and Policy* (Cheltenham, Edward Elgar, 2006) 47; see also TP Heide, 'Copyright in the EU and US: What "Access-Right"?' (2001) 48 *Journal of the Copyright Society of the USA* 363ff; the next question would be whether the right is granted in favour of the right holder or the user. Both options are controversial, but at least TPMs give the right holder de facto a right of access control; *cf* M Favale, 'The Right of Access in Digital Copyright: Right of the Owner or Right of the User?' (2012) 15 *The Journal of World Intellectual Property* 2, 11.

[24] This goes along with the fact that Art 17 (2) Charter of Fundamental Rights of the European Union, with its sole sentence on the topic, 'Intellectual property shall be protected', reflects in no way the users' interests. Recital 32 of Dir 2004/48/EC (n 7) explicitly refers to this provision; see also A Peukert, 'Intellectual Property as an End in Itself?' (2011) 33 *European Intellectual Property Review* 69.

[25] 'The digital code, in short, prevails on the legal code', Favale (n 23) 11.

law—like copyright, patent or trademark law—constellations vary widely. It is more or less common understanding today that the traditional 'one size fits all' approach is untenable.[26] The IP regimes, however, by no means make allowance for unequal constellations. Although different categories of works are exposed to completely different risks of unauthorised uses and other challenges for the right holders, and despite the fact that the conditions to commercialise them may be highly divergent, copyright legislation hardly knows any differentiations.[27] The same is true for the patent system, although it is hard to imagine that fast moving technologies—like in the IT industries—need identical legal protection as those in slowly evolving innovation fields. Beyond that, pharmaceutical industries, for instance, are obviously in need of much longer terms of protection to cover tremendous development and approval costs for drugs, whereas little steps of improvement in the field of mechanics—if at all innovative—quite often happen coincidentally and without substantial costs. Patent litigations, however, in no way take account of such differences.[28]

These undifferentiated legal approaches are more detrimental than it might seem at first instance—at least if one accepts that IP rights are not an aim in themselves, but that they need to meet certain utility concerns. Their very function may be understood as legal tools to safeguard market opportunities in terms of avoiding market failures.[29] Legal certainty with a view to possibilities of amortisation is supposed to incentivise potential investors.[30]

[26] See generally MW Carroll, 'One Size Does Not Fit All: A Framework for Tailoring Intellectual Property Rights' (2009) 70 *Ohio State Law Journal* 1361–434; C Schmidt, 'Comment: Some Economic Considerations Regarding Optimal Intellectual Property Protection' in A Kur and V Mizaras (eds), *The Structure of Intellectual Property Law. Can One Size Fit All?* (Cheltenham, Edward Elgar, 2011) 55; LC Thurow, 'Needed: A New System of Intellectual Property Rights' (1997) *Harvard Business Review* 95; presenting the benefits as well: G Dinwoodie, 'Remarks: "One Size Fits All" Consolidation and Difference in Intellectual Property Law' in Kur and Mizaras (eds), ibid 4ff, 14.

[27] Likewise, the current legal framework—especially in the EU (*cf* Art 5 Dir 2001/29/EC)—hardly allows for differentiations regarding limitations of the copyright. See A Metzger, 'Urheberrechtsschranken in der Wissensgesellschaft: "Fair use" oder enge Einzeltatbestände?' in M Leistner (ed), *Europäische Perspektiven des Geistigen Eigentums* (Tübingen, Mohr Siebeck, 2010) 121; see generally J Poeppel, *Die Neuordnung der urheberrechtlichen Schranken im digitalen Umfeld* (Göttingen, V&R Unipress, 2005) 124ff.

[28] Thurow (n 26) 103; DL Burk and MA Lemley, 'Is Patent Law Technology-Specific?' (2002) 17 *Berkeley Technology Law Journal* 1157ff.

[29] This utilitarian understanding of immaterial property rights was already reflected in the famous 'Copyright-Clause' of the Constitution of the United States of 1787 (Art I Sec 8 cl 8): 'The Congress shall have power … to promote the progress of science and useful arts …', see Menell (n 11) 130; see also Hilty (n 16) 986.

[30] Carroll (n 26) 1363; K Arrow, 'The Economic Welfare and the Allocation of Resources for Invention' in R Nelson (ed), *The Rate and Direction of Inventive Activity: Economic and Social Factors* (Princeton, Princeton University Press, 1962) 619ff; Thurow (n 26) 102ff; M Barrett, *Intellectual Property* 3rd edn (New York, Wolters Kluwer Law & Business, 2012) 2; Schmidt (n 26) 49.

Thus, IP rights are not necessarily directed at creators and inventors only, but also and even particularly at downstream industries taking commercial risks.

Having said that, we must be aware that legal tools to safeguard market opportunities should not go further than required. They solely should prevent frustrations of the investors facing insufficient prospects for profits in view of the behaviour of other market participants (for example imitators).[31] Beyond that, competitive forces have to prevail as far as possible; at the end of the day competition is the best driver for the emergence of the new. Any restriction to competition—including overly protected innovation or creation—enhances the likelihood that competitors rest on their laurels instead of meeting the challenge of dynamic markets.

In other words, IP rights only can fulfil their functions if the appropriate degree of legal protection is met.[32] However, while it is broadly recognised that under-exclusivity (in terms of insufficient protection) risks omitting possible investments in innovations, it is by far less commonly understood that over-exclusivity (in terms of overly limited competition) might have the same effect. In fact, as long as exclusivity hinders third parties from using the subject matter of protection, the right holder has good grounds to keep back investments in new ideas and products. 'Evergreening patents' in the field of pharmaceutical inventions provide a good example of such attempts: As long as basically identical, only slightly modified substances may be patented again shortly before the expiry of the underlying patent, there are no incentives to invest in substantially new drugs.[33]

Ideally, this delicate balance should be found within the IP system. Individual rights should from the outset be granted to the required degree of exclusivity only. This, however, is precisely not the case—and even worse: The mentioned 'one size fits all' pattern hardly allows for a differentiation of unequal constellations in accordance with the concrete circumstances.[34]

[31] Hilty (n 16) 995ff; RM Hilty, 'Vergütungssystem und Schrankenregelungen. Neue Herausforderungen an den Gesetzgeber' (2005) *Gewerblicher Rechtsschutz und Urheberrecht* 826; Patterson and Lindberg (n 22) 192.

[32] A Ohly, 'Free Access, Including Freedom to Imitate, as a Legal Principle—a Forgotten Concept?' in Kur and Mizaras (n 26) 101; M Senftleben, 'Overprotection and Protection Overlaps in Intellectual Property Law—The Need for Horizontal Fair Use Defences' in Kur and Mizaras (n 26) 137.

[33] The effect of this 'evergreening' practice is a de facto extended period of patent protection—even if the 'new' patent may often not be an invention in terms of Art 27 Para 1 TRIPS. *cf* R Chalmers, 'Evergreen or Deciduous? Australian Trends in Relation to the "Evergreening" of Patents' (2007) 30 *Melbourne University Law Review* 31ff; JJ Darrow, 'Debunking the "Evergreening" Patents Myth' (2010) 6 *Harvard Law Record* 131; J Mueller and D Chisum, 'Enabling Patent Law's inherent Anticipation Doctrine' (2008) 45 *Houston Law Review* 1106; AS Kesselheim, 'Intellectual Property Policy in the Pharmaceutical Sciences: The Effect of Inappropriate Patents and the Market Exclusivity Extensions on the Health Care System' (2007) 9 (3) *AAPS Journal* E308–E309.

[34] *cf* n 26.

Competition issues in particular may by no means be considered within the IP system. Only in very extreme cases—which hardly occur in practice—can anti-competitive effects of IP rights be corrected based on antitrust law.[35] In most situations, however, the requirements to apply antitrust law are not met, although even those IP rights that lie below the threshold of antitrust law may impact the forces of competition negatively.[36] In view of these shortcomings within the IP regime enforcement measures turn out to be an effective instrument to fine-tune the entire legal framework. In other words—although it may sound strange—the IP system as such would hardly lead to the adequate degree of exclusivity if all recognised or granted individual rights could be enforced to their full extent. Rather, enforcement proves to be the crucial layer to balance the system and to avoid unwanted dysfunctional effects of IP rights.

IV. THE LACKING DISCUSSION ON LIMITS TO ENFORCEABILITY

Having said this, it is remarkable, however, that possibilities to limit the enforceability of IP rights are rarely discussed in legal doctrine. Only very recently, in view of rather untypical developments, has this concern been addressed.[37] In fact, we increasingly become aware of litigation practices in which IP rights are no longer enforced with a view to the right holder's original interests in enforcement—mostly to ban imitators or copyists.[38] On the contrary the tool 'enforcement' is often used—or rather abused—for other purposes, be it to defend outdated business models, to squeeze undesirable competitors out of the market or other activities that do not correspond to the initial function of such IP rights.

[35] See leading cases C-241/91 P and 242/91 P *RTE (Magill)* [1995] ECR I-743; Case T-201/04 *Microsoft* [2007] ECR II-3601; Case C-418/01 *IMS Health* [2004] ECR I-5039.

[36] Especially the requirement of a 'dominant position within the internal market or in a substantial part of it' (Art 102 TFEU) is the toughest obstacle to overcome in the EU, because an IP right in most cases monopolises just the right itself, but not a market. In more detail: Hilty (n 10) 386; W Hübschle in KW Lange (ed), *Handbuch zum deutschen und europäischen Kartellrecht* 2nd edn (Frankfurt aM, Verlag Recht und Wirtschaft GmbH, 2006) 383 No 860; L Kempel, *Die Anwendung von Art 102 AEUV auf geistiges Eigentum und Sacheigentum* (Frankfurt aM, Lang, 2011) 44.

[37] *cf* A Ohly, 'Three Principles of European IP Enforcement Law: Effectiveness, Proportionality, Dissuasiveness' in J Drexl, RM Hilty, L Boy, C Godt and B Remiche (eds), *Technology and Competition. Contributions in Honour of Hanns Ullrich* (Brussels, Larcier, 2009) 257–75; W von Meibom and R Nack, 'Patents without Injunctions?—Trolls, Hold-ups, Ambushes, and Other Patent Warfare' in W Prinz zu Waldeck und Pyrmont, MJ Adelman, R Brauneis, J Drexl and R Nack (eds), *Patents and Technological Progress in a Globalized World* (Berlin, Springer, 2009) 495; Hilty (n 10) 387ff; *Contra*: 'Laws on intellectual property rights must be enforceable or they should not be laws', Thurow (n 26) 102.

[38] Hilty (n 16) 995.

Copyright law, for instance, has turned out to be an ideal gun to exact certain behaviours from consumers. One prominent example was delivered by the music industries during the first decade of our century; they ignored the request of a growing clientele for online music platforms and insisted on their selling of CDs instead. To support that business model, independent suppliers who were willing and able to satisfy the growing consumer preferences were criminalised, but not licensed—and also consumers of unauthorised online platforms increasingly were penalised.[39] With this strategy, the music industries absurdly raised the spiral between enforcement attempts and new forms of breaching copyright law; at the same time they lost their chance for a timely establishment of up-to-date business models.[40]

The IT markets attract public attention with deterrent examples of dysfunctional uses notably of software patents. Such patents seem to be an essential asset for survival of smartphone producers today—not to protect innovation, but in order to serve as a weapon in that heavily contested market.[41] In fact, it has become a common practice of big players within that market to sue each other more or less randomly, mutually alleging infringements of uncountable patents.[42] Courts quite often nullify such patents—but in certain cases they don't even have to decide the case. Instead, plaintiffs try to extort doubtful settlements with certain rivals—the winner is most likely the one who may throw the larger number of patents into the ring.

Other specific forms of dysfunctional patent litigation derive from the often debated 'patent trolls'.[43] Although this term is somehow lurid, the effect that such entities typically are not practising in the related technological field, but acquire patents in order to sue market participants instead—who usually are not truly infringing the questionable patents—may have dubious outcomes. Such legal actions may produce exorbitant costs to the account of (strategically chosen) defendants who ultimately will have to give up their prosecution of the litigation after a time because they can no longer afford it. One ulterior motive for such law suits may be to weaken

[39] With this approach a further problem has arisen: Criminalisation of (mostly) young people—so-called digital natives—who do not have a sense of wrongdoing whilst infringing an IP right; M Haedicke, *Patente und Piraten. Geistiges Eigentum in der Krise* (München, Beck, 2011) 13ff; Hilty (n 16) 984.

[40] MA Carrier, 'Copyright and Innovation: The Untold Story' (2012) *Wisconsin Law Review* 950–59.

[41] Von Meibom and Nack (n 37) 511; see also MA Lemley and C Shapiro, 'Patent Holdup and Royalty Stacking' (2007) 85 *Texas Law Review* 1994ff, 2025ff; DJ Goodman and RA Myers, '3G Cellular Standards and Patents' (2005) *'IEEE 2005 International Conference on Wireless Networks, Communications and Mobile Computing (2)'* 415–20 available at eeweb.poly.edu/dgoodman/wirelesscom2005.pdf.

[42] Infamous law suits—for example between Samsung and Apple or Motorola and Apple—frequently make it into the news.

[43] See J Stempel, 'New York Bears Down on Patent Trolls, Settles with Delaware Firm' *Reuters* (13 January 2014), available at www.reuters.com/article/2014/01/14/us-patent-trolls-settlement-idUSBREA0D05S20140114.

specific market participants—in certain cases so heavily that they ultimately become victims of unfriendly takeovers.[44]

Such strategies of right holders evolve over time and new expressions may be created in order to describe specific forms of behaviour. A currently fancy, but in truth exhumed term, is 'sham litigation' (also 'sham exception') which may be related to trademark law for instance—a field that by no means escapes from dysfunctional developments.[45] It basically describes competitors abusing the judicial system to prevent or delay the market entry of competing products. All those practices are characterised by the fact that IP rights are not utilised in line with their initial function, namely to foster new creations, innovation or a more effective or transparent marketing of products.[46] If IP rights under such constellations are enforced to their full extent, it is comprehensible that the IP system risks failing the purposes for which exclusive rights were established.

This increasing awareness of dysfunctional uses of IP rights, however, stands in contrast to the legal discussion. Notably on the level of international and European legislation, the question on how to limit inappropriate enforcement activities has hardly seriously been addressed; instead, all efforts have been invested in the establishment of global standards for an efficient enforcement of IP rights.[47] The most important tool in that respect has been the Agreement on Trade-Related Aspects of Intellectual Property Rights (TRIPS), being one treaty of the World Trade Organization (WTO) agreed on in 1994. The primary concern of this treaty—and the whole WTO—was globalisation; it was clear that with an ongoing opening of new markets, sensitive subject matters of IP protection would increasingly be available in developing countries—and that technology, but also cultural goods etc could easily be taken over or copied without adequate

[44] Lemley and Shapiro (n 41) 2008ff; differentiated with a view to non-practising entity (NPE) plaintiffs: M Risch, 'Patent Troll Myths' (2012) 42 *Seton Hall Law Review* 459; von Meibom and Nack (n 37) 497–503; A Ohly, '"Patenttrolle" oder: Der patentrechtliche Unterlassungsanspruch unter Verhältnismäßigkeitsvorbehalt? Aktuelle Entwicklungen im US-Patentrecht und ihre Bedeutung für das deutsche und europäische Patentsystem' (2008) *Gewerblicher Rechtsschutz und Urheberrecht Internationaler Teil* 790ff.

[45] *California Motor Transport v Trucking Unlimited* 404 US 511, 513 (1972); more detailed and with reference to the underlying Noerr-Pennington Doctrine: TA Balmer, 'Sham Litigation and the Antitrust Laws' (1980) 29 *Buffalo Law Review* 40; S Vezzoso, 'Towards an EU Doctrine of Anticompetitive IP-Related Litigation' (2012) 3 *Journal of European Competition Law & Practice* 530ff; also, the European Commission stated that lawsuits can under specific circumstances have an abusive character. Case T-111/96 *ITT Promedia NV v Commission* [1998] ECR II-2937 No 55. *cf* on inappropriate conduct in the field of trademarks: Hilty (n 10) 382; *cf* Case C-529/07 *Chocoladefabriken Lindt & Sprüngli v Franz Hauswirth* [2009] ECR I-4893.

[46] That is why the US Supreme Court in the first part of its definition of 'sham litigation' stated that 'the lawsuit must be objectively baseless in the sense that no reasonable litigant could realistically expect success on the merits', *Professional Real Estate Investors v Columbia Pictures Industries* 508 US 60 (1993).

[47] *cf* Peukert's study on different EU Regs and Dirs: Peukert (n 24) 67–71.

IP protection in those countries.[48] A related concern, however, was that underdeveloped countries might be willing to adopt proper provisions in their IP codes—but due to insufficient judicial systems such IP rights could not be enforced. Therefore, more than 20 provisions of TRIPS deal with issues of enforcement (including provisional measures, border measures and criminal procedures).

In the EU, first attempts to harmonise IP enforcement failed; 10 years after the enactment of TRIPS however—literally on the eve of the Eastern Expansion of the EU (and the growing fear of similar IP threats in the new EU Member States as in developing countries)—the Commission finally succeeded in implementing Directive 2004/48/EC on the enforcement of IP rights.[49] Similar to TRIPS, extended provisions of this Directive focus on the interests of the right holders.[50] On the other hand, both TRIPS and Directive 2004/48/EC remain extremely vague as to the interests of other parties involved.

Particularly missing are concrete legal remedies to oppose unjustified enforcement activities of right holders. This lack may be due to the aforementioned—disputable—premise that enforceable 'user rights' as such do not exist.[51] The consequence of this premise is that legal remedies to counter dysfunctional behaviours of right holders hardly exist. As a result, an appropriate adjusting on the level of enforcement—which is, as we have seen, the ultimate occasion to fine-tune unwanted effects of IP rights—risks failing. Notably, in view of the swelling discussion on unwanted effects of IP rights this common one-sided perception of the IP system is astonishing. It is especially alarming that the current evaluation of the Directive 2004/48/EC seems not to focus on a more balanced approach.[52]

V. POSSIBLE LEGAL REMEDIES

On the other hand, although concrete legal remedies are missing, it is not true that the concern of imbalanced enforcement as such has not been reflected in international and European legislation at all. In particular, Article 8 Paragraph 2 TRIPS explicitly recognises that Member States have

[48] P-T Stoll in J Busche, P-T Stoll and A Wiebe (eds), *TRIPs. Internationales und europäisches Recht des geistigen Eigentums. Kommentar* 2nd edn (Köln, Heymanns, 2013) Einleitung 1 No 29ff; the TRIPS Agreement also goes a problematic 'super-size-fits-all' way which relates to a similar problem as mentioned above: PK Yu, 'The Objectives and Principles of the TRIPS Agreement' (2009) 46 *Houston Law Review* 981.

[49] See n 7.

[50] *cf* Peukert (n 24).

[51] *cf* n 23.

[52] See the public consultation on the efficiency of proceedings and accessibility of measures by the European Commission from July 2013. Available at ec.europa.eu/internal_market/consultations/docs/2012/intellectual-property-rights/summary-of-responses_en.pdf.

the possibility to take appropriate measures 'to prevent the abuse of intellectual property rights by right holders'. Article 40 Paragraph 2 TRIPS relates to

> licensing practices or conditions that may in particular cases constitute an abuse of intellectual property rights having an adverse effect on competition in the relevant market.

Article 41 TRIPS not only requests Member States to ensure that enforcement procedures 'permit effective action against any act of infringement of intellectual property rights', but also that such procedures

> shall be applied in such a manner as to avoid the creation of barriers to legitimate trade and to provide for safeguards against their abuse.

In return, Article 48 TRIPS allows Member States (but does not oblige them) to

> order a party at whose request measures were taken and who has abused enforcement procedures to provide to a party wrongfully enjoined or restrained adequate compensation for the injury suffered because of such abuse.

Likewise, Article 50 Paragraph 3 TRIPS (and similarly Article 53 TRIPS) allows Member States

> to order the applicant to provide a security or equivalent assurance sufficient to protect the defendant and to prevent abuse.[53]

The determination of the legal instruments that might provide for the balance required by TRIPS, however, is left to the Member States, which certainly is the right approach in view of widely different legal traditions.[54] This is, however, also true with regard to the legal instruments ensuring sufficiently deterrent enforcement. Nevertheless, the EU has undertaken considerable efforts to harmonise the effects of legal enforcement tools; but the scope of the Directive 2004/48/EC[55] in essence is limited to that aforementioned one side of the coin.[56] Whether or not and to what extent EU Member States could confine the enforcement tools in their national laws

[53] For more details see Hilty (n 10) 384ff.

[54] Especially the principles of 'equity' allow a completely different approach. Ohly (n 37) 262; K Zweigert and H Kötz, *An Introduction to Comparative Law, chapter 14 III* 3rd edn (Oxford, Oxford University Press, 1998).

[55] Above n 7.

[56] This one-sided perspective may be traced back to Recital 32 of the Enforcement Dir 2004/48/EC that

> ensure[s] full respect for intellectual property, in accordance with Article 17 (2) of that Charter [of Fundamental Rights of the European Union].

Peukert (n 24) 69. This Art 17 (2) 'just' states: 'Intellectual property shall be protected'—which by no means is a certain base and which causes linguistic diversities in the Member States. See J Griffiths and L McDonagh, 'Fundamental Rights and European IP law—the case of Art 17 (2)

in order to acquire a functionally appropriate scope of exclusivity is not addressed concretely. Recital 17 solely requests a case-by-case approach;[57] further, Article 3 Paragraph 2 obliges the Member States to provide for measures, procedures and remedies that shall

> be effective, proportionate and dissuasive and shall be applied in such a manner as to avoid the creation of barriers to legitimate trade and to provide for safeguards against their abuse.[58]

But on the more concrete level related to injunctions and damages, Directive 2004/48/EC does not aim for any harmonisation of that upper limit of enforcement tools. Rather, flexibility is optional insofar as Article 11 only states that Member States

> shall ensure that, where a judicial decision is taken finding an infringement of an intellectual property right, the judicial authorities *may* issue against the infringer an injunction ...

This flexibility is reflected in the (very narrowly defined) requirements of Article 12, according to which

> the competent judicial authorities may order pecuniary compensation to be paid to the injured party instead of applying the measures provided ... if that person acted unintentionally and without negligence, if execution of the measures in question would cause him disproportionate harm and if pecuniary compensation to the injured party appears reasonably satisfactory.

To some extent this option may be understood as an application of the approach to reduce 'property' in terms of exclusivity to mere monetary compensation (so-called 'liability approach').[59]

of the EU Charter' in C Geiger (ed), *Constructing European Intellectual Property. Achievements and New Perspectives* (Cheltenham, Edward Elgar, 2013) 80.

[57] Recital 17 Dir 2004/48/EC:

> The measures ... in this Directive should be determined in each case in such a manner as to take due account of the specific characteristics of that case ...

Similar Recital 24:

> Depending on the particular case, and if justified by the circumstances, the measures, procedures and remedies ... should include prohibitory measures aimed at preventing further infringements of intellectual property rights.

Ohly (n 37) 265. For further arguments in favour of this flexibility: Hilty (n 10) 381.

[58] See Ohly (n 37) 257ff.

[59] See to this effect and its connection to abusive behaviour: J Phillips, 'eBay's Effect on Copyright Injunctions: When Property Rules Give Way to Liability Rules' (2009) 24 *Berkeley Technology Law Journal* 411ff; see generally G Calabresi and AD Melamed, 'Property Rules, Liability Rules, and Inalienability: One View of the Cathedral' (1972) 85 *Harvard Law Review* 1089–128; RP Merges, 'Contracting into Liability Rules: Intellectual Property Rights and Collective Rights Organizations' (1996) 84 *California Law Review* 1293–393; MA Lemley, 'Contracting Around Liability Rules' (2012) 100 *California Law Review* 463–86; see also Hilty (n 10) 392.

This (optional) setting related to injunctions in the EU Directive stands in contrast to its Article 13, which states that

> Member States shall ensure that the competent judicial authorities, on application of the injured party, *order* the infringer … to pay the right holder damages … (emphasis added)

In other words, the judicial authorities may have discretion whether or not they grant injunction, provided the national law allows for that discretion, whereas damages (as the case may be) shall be ordered in any case.[60] Thereby, one core issue—namely the limitation of enforcement and its possible replacement by pecuniary compensation—is by no means harmonised. The EU law on the contrary only requests the national laws to safeguard a minimal—but high-level (see Recital 10)—enforcement.[61] In contrast, an upper limit in terms of a 'ceiling' to enforcement activities based on national law is not stipulated.[62]

In the light of that, it is likely that the—from the outset very narrowly—provided flexibility by Article 11 respectively 12 of Directive 2004/48/EC to deny injunctive relief in certain cases will be used in diverse manners in different legal traditions. Whereas in the common law two equal layers—law and equity—allow for farther-reaching discretion of the judge, civil law approaches hardly concede similar autonomy to courts.[63] Although the principle of proportionality applied in civil law also implies a weighing of the interests involved to a certain degree, this would in practice hardly go beyond the estimation of damages, for instance.[64] Discretion to deny injunction and to grant damages instead would hardly be accepted. Thus, the law as such—in the face of the lacking criterion of equity—explicitly would have to allow for such discretion.

In consequence, if the European legislation earnestly aimed for such discretion of courts all over Europe, it would be unavoidable to alter Article 11

[60] Hilty (n 10) 389ff; A von Mühlendahl, 'Enforcement of Intellectual Property Rights—Is Injunctive Relief Mandatory?' (2007) 38 *International Review of Intellectual Property and Competition Law* 377.

[61] 'The objective of this Directive is to … ensure a high, equivalent and homogeneous level of protection in the internal market' (Recital 10 Dir 2004/48/EC).

[62] One special constellation of deficient ceilings derives from injunctions against innocent third parties for example in the case of website blocking, see M Husovec, 'Injunctions against Innocent Third Parties: The Case of Website Blocking' (2013) 4 *Journal of Intellectual Property, Information Technology and Electronic Commerce Law* 123.

[63] *cf* n 54.

[64] One of the rare cases is *OLG Jena* (Court of Appeal) (2008) *MultiMedia und Recht* 413. The Court denied injunctive relief because of dysfunctional conduct of the right holder based on s 242 German Civil Code, aiming to balance the involved interests. In the same litigation, however, the Federal Court of Justice of Germany found another way to solve the case: *BGH* (2010) *MultiMedia und Recht* 479; see W Bullinger and K Garbers-von-Boehm, 'Google-Bildersuche: Schlichte Einwilligung des Urhebers als Lösung?' (2010) *Gewerblicher Rechtsschutz und Urheberrecht—Praxis im Immaterialgüter- und Wettbewerbsrecht* 257.

into a mandatory provision. Beyond that, the unnecessarily narrow scope of Article 12 of Directive 2004/48/EC should be broadened. A benchmark might be the so-called 'four factor' test that has been developed in the US American jurisdiction (most prominently in the *eBay v MercExchange* case).[65] In an amended Directive, however, the criterion for a shifting from the property rule to a liability rule on a case-by-case basis should be detailed in view of the aim of unitary effects of national laws within the internal market.

Even if the denial of injunctive relief under certain circumstances was mandatory under European law, this might hardly suffice. Actual equity of arms would require additional amendments. Article 13 Paragraph 1 a) and b) of Directive 2004/48/EC, for instance, allows for different modes of calculating damages, including

> *at least* the amount of royalties or fees which would have been due if the infringer had requested authorisation to use the intellectual property right in question. (emphasis added)

Therewith, the capacity to harm an alleged infringer may be increased.[66] It is obvious that the threat potential of the right holder thus becomes even more important than in case of the compensation of proven damages only. However, even without enhanced amounts of damages, the plaintiff does by no means take a risk by suing alleged infringers beyond the actual scope of the related IP right.[67] Without any consequences—apart from possibly

[65] *eBay v MercExchange* 547 US 388 (2006). The 'four factor test' is a tool to determine whether a denial of injunctive relief is possible with the aim of reaching a better balanced patent system. *cf* to the fundamental case: E Elrefaie, 'Injunctive Relief Post *eBay* and the Various Applications of the Four-Factor Test in Differing Technological Industries' (2010) 2 *Hastings Science & Technology Law Journal* 219–42; Phillips (n 58) 416–34; B Petersen, 'Injunctive Relief in the Post-eBay World' (2008) 23 *Berkeley Technology Law Journal* 193–218; M Trimble, 'Injunctive Relief, Equity, and Misuse of Rights in US Patent Law' (2012) *Gewerblicher Rechtsschutz und Urheberrecht Internationaler Teil* 518–20; L O'Melinn, 'The Effects of eBay: Discretion, Statutory Damages, and Private Attorneys-General' (2008) 2 *Akron Intellectual Property Journal* 119–31; see also Hilty (n 10) 388.

[66] With regard also to intentional infringement and the flexible sanction, see Ohly (n 37) 273; T Dreier, 'Ausgleich, Abschreckung und andere Rechtsfolgen von Urheberrechtsverletzungen—Erste Gedanken zur EU-Richtlinie über die Maßnahmen und Verfahren zum Schutz der Rechte an geistigem Eigentum' (2004) *Gewerblicher Rechtsschutz und Urheberrecht Internationaler Teil* 709; Y Benhamou, 'Compensation of Damages for Infringements of Intellectual Property Rights in France, Under Directive 2004/48/EC and Its Transposition Law—New Notions?' (2009) 40 *International Review of Intellectual Property and Competition Law* 148ff.

[67] In Art 17 Sec 1 of the first draft of this Dir that is now Art 13 Sec 1 of Dir 2004/48/EC, the EU Commission even wanted

> to double the amount of the royalties or fees which would have been due if the infringer had requested authorization …

See Proposal for a Dir of the European Parliament and of the Council on measures and procedures to ensure the enforcement of intellectual property rights COM (2003) 46 final, 2003/2004 (COD).

losing the case—he may so to speak challenge the extension of the scope of protection. Under certain conditions, provisional and precautionary measures (Article 9 Directive 2004/48/EC) might suffice to stop a competitor—possibly not actually infringing the right at issue—in view of the defendant's risk of facing unforeseeable costs.

What is required, therefore, is correcting measures in the sense that an obviously arbitrary law suit without reasonable likelihood of an actual infringement of an IP right and without legitimate interests of the right holder in prohibiting certain business activities of a third party would entail similarly incisive consequences for the right holder as an unwarranted law suit to the detriment of an alleged infringer. Again, the establishment of appropriate legal tools could be left to the Member States. However, certain requirements for the application of such tools should be defined by European legislation in order to assure sufficient harmonisation of ceilings to enforcement in the national laws.

12

From Transnational Principles to European Rules of Civil Procedure: Reflections on the Potential of Case Management for the Resolution of Mass Disputes[*]

IANIKA N TZANKOVA

I. INTRODUCTION

DUE TO GLOBALISATION and industrialisation mass disputes increasingly occur in developed and developing economies.[1] Mass disputes are disputes involving a large number of claimants that seek remedies from another party, usually a corporation, for alleged infringements of their rights. The number of claimants poses a specific set of issues on the individuals or institutions dealing with mass disputes, varying from challenges related to the logistics of the resolution to more fundamental issues and due process concerns. Tackling such issues in order to avoid protracted litigation requires at least some degree of aggregation and concentration of the treatment of individual cases, and this creates a tendency for the 'confection' of the resolution process. That tendency could be viewed as problematic in relation to fundamental principles that guarantee

[*] This paper is based on a Feasibility Study of Case Management of Mass Disputes commenced at the request of The Hague Institute for Global Justice (THIGJ) by the author. Prof Dr Deborah R Hensler served as project advisor to the study. The author and the project advisor would like to thank THIGJ for the support it provided for the study. A related paper discussing solely the judicial case management of mass disputes was published in the Uniform Law Review (Ianika N Tzankova, 'Case Management: The Stepchild of Mass Claim Dispute Resolution' (2014) 19 *Uniform Law Review* 329).

[1] DR Hensler, 'How Economic Globalization is Helping to Construct a Private Transnational Legal Order' in S Muller, S Zouridis, M Frishman and L Kistemaker (eds), *The Law of the Future and the Future of Law* (Oslo, TOAEP, 2011).

individualised treatment and custom made outcomes, and thus needs to be adequately addressed.[2]

The EU Recommendation, which was presented on 11 June 2013 as part of a legislative package proposal, is a European initiative that has tried to capture the European culture in common principles of collective redress.[3] The Recommendation is a non-binding legal instrument drafted to promote the effective mitigation of a large number of individual claims, while limiting the likelihood of 'US-style' class actions by defining common principles to be applied across the Member States.

The Recommendation has an ambiguous character. It is unclear which method the Commission used to extract the alleged common principles from the great variety of collective redress regimes within the Member States.[4] Moreover, it seems to be a mix of a 'wish list' or demands of the business lobby, and (indeed) common European civil procedure features, rather than a snapshot of the status quo of the European thinking on collective redress. Defining common principles is a tough task, and the EU Recommendation should be viewed as a brave attempt to accomplish what at first sight seems a mission impossible, but probably also not much more than a brave attempt.

This paper will describe an alternative, bottom-up approach to the topic of collective redress by reporting on the results of a feasibility study on the case management of mass disputes.[5] Generally speaking, a distinction can be made between in-court, out-of-court (ADR (Alternative Dispute Resolution), special masters, tribunals, special commissions), or court-annexed (through court-appointed special masters or court related compensation schemes) mass claim dispute resolution. The courts in jurisdictions that have experience with the handling of mass disputes have developed various

[2] Various types of mass disputes are handled in different ways across jurisdictions. For example in Germany KapMuG deals only with financial cases, the Netherlands introduced sector driven compensation schemes for asbestos claims, in Belgium the criminal law takes care also of civil actions for damages etc.

[3] European Commission, 'Towards a European Horizontal Framework for Collective Redress', COM (2013) 401 final; Commission Recommendation of 11 June 2013 on common principles for injunctive and compensatory collective redress mechanisms in the Member States concerning violations of rights granted under Union Law [2013] OJ L201/60; European Commission, 'Proposal for a Directive on certain rules governing actions for damages under national law for infringements of the competition law provisions of the Member States and of the European Union', COM (2013) 404 final. See also C Hodges, 'Collective Redress: A Breakthrough or a Damp Squib?' (2014) 37 *Journal of Consumer Policy* 67.

[4] The European Law Institute (ELI) statement on collective redress demonstrates that some of the suggested 'common principles' are much less common within Europe than the EU Recommendation suggests. See for example the comments on opt-in and opt-out in the *Statement of the European Law Institute on Collective Redress and Competition Damages Claims* (Vienna, European Law Institute, 2014).

[5] The study was commissioned at the request of The Hague Institute for Global Justice. The idea for the project on judicial management of mass cases arose out of the 5th Annual Conference on the Globalization of Class Actions and Mass Litigation that took place in December 2011 in The Hague.

case management tools and techniques to handle that type of case. Some of those techniques include the use of consolidation mechanisms, or the use of ADR and special masters to help parties develop fair and efficient 'claim resolution facilities': facilities that distribute (settlement) funds to injured parties and provide them with remedies. Moreover, parties causing mass damages sometimes choose at their own initiative or under political pressure to use special masters and claim resolution facilities to distribute funds and run compensation schemes (for example the BP oil spill fund in the US). Also, at UN level and under UN reparation programmes it is more common to use claim resolution facilities to deal with, for example, property damages claims. The design and implementation of such claim resolution facilities pose yet another set of specific problems: how should the funds be divided, what are the relevant criteria and subcategories, how to deal with fraud claims, how to ensure due process, what kind of networks are needed and how to tackle logistical challenges to run the facilities in developing countries are just a few examples.

Although there are many parallels between the issues that individuals and institutions across jurisdictions face when dealing with mass disputes and there have been efforts to collect and disseminate the existing practical wisdom and experience, such efforts have so far been scattered or isolated, and often limited to a specific jurisdiction[6] or types of issues.[7] Moreover, individuals or institutions having to deal with a mass dispute are seldom aware of the existing expertise or are simply lacking the time, resources or skills to find and adjust the existing expertise to their own environment or to the needs of the specific case.

The goals of the feasibility study were to develop a better understanding of the cultural, jurisprudential and practical obstacles to a more efficient management of mass claim dispute resolution and—where appropriate—to develop tools for overcoming such obstacles. In other words the study aimed to explore the need for the collection of the existing practical wisdom and expertise for dealing with mass disputes, and the feasibility of presenting and disseminating these in a more uniform, neutral and user-friendly way.

[6] See Federal Judicial Center, 'Manual for Complex Litigation', 2004, available at: public.resource.org/scribd/8763868.pdf; A Hirsch and DM Sheehey, *Awarding Attorneys' Fees and Managing Fee Litigation* 2nd edn (Washington DC, Federal Judicial Center, 2005); BJ Rothstein and TE Willging, *Managing Class Action Litigation: A Pocket Guide for Judges* 3rd edn (Washington DC, Federal Judicial Center, 2010); Federal Judicial Center, 'Judges' Class Action Notice and Claims Process Checklist and Plain Language Guide 2010', available at: www.fjc.gov/public/pdf.nsf/lookup/notcheck.pdf/$file/notcheck.pdf; 'Procesreglement verzoekschriftprocedures handels- en insolventiezaken gerechtshoven', available at: www.rechtspraak.nl/Procedures/Landelijke-regelingen/Sector-civiel-recht/Documents/Procesreglement%20verzoekschrift procedures%20handel-%20en%20insolventiezaken%20Gerechtshoven.pdf.

[7] For example human rights, see HM Holtzmann and E Kristjansdottir (eds), *International Mass Claims Processes: Legal and Practical Perspectives* (Oxford, Oxford University Press, 2007).

Although the study was triggered by the case management issues that mass disputes pose for the judiciary, it followed a more functional approach and aimed to target a broader group of 'adjudicators', as not only judges, but also arbitrators, regulators and ombudsmen are expected to become more involved in the resolution of mass disputes in the future.

Generally speaking, at least three issues play a key role in the handling of mass disputes, and influence how adjudicators respond to mass disputes: lack of adequate administrative support and insufficient IT systems,[8] lack of adequate legislative implementation of aggregate devices for the handling of mass disputes, and lack of or insufficient case management. The feasibility study focused on the last two issues.

When legislatures enact new legislation to cope with mass disputes, the explanatory notes will often set out in general terms how the device should be used in practice, but the assumption is that the actors involved will have to 'shape' the new legislation. The courts are expected to establish and develop practical guidelines and practices. It is impossible to anticipate and regulate at the outset all practical implications of new legislation. However, when a legislature introduces novel procedural concepts such as aggregate devices for the handling of mass disputes, which implicitly or explicitly require a fundamental change of culture or approach, additional measures facilitating the transition are key for the success of the implementation.[9] The challenge is therefore to facilitate and structure such implementation processes, preferably in a cost-effective way. The implementation problem with respect to mass disputes is that the number of mass disputes within a jurisdiction is too low to justify the costs related to the development and implementation of management skills oriented training programmes or other kinds of supplemental devices.

The lack of or insufficient case management by the adjudicators handling a specific mass dispute is an important issue. It is evident that if adjudicators approach a mass dispute like an 'ordinary' bilateral dispute, they will face significant challenges. Also, if adjudicators do not make use of case management techniques,[10] do not discuss with the parties arrangements about communications and filing of documents or do not apply techniques to promote settlement, the mass dispute will probably make a good case for

[8] The limitation is dictated by the fact that the improvement of national court systems is an issue that can only be addressed by national legal systems.

[9] Even though the UK Rules of Civil Procedure introduced by Lord Woolf reflected the imposed change in litigation culture by the formulation of principles and overriding objectives, without customised judicial training, those would have become a dead letter. See JM Barendrecht and A Klijn, *Balanceren en vernieuwen: Een kaart van sociaal-wetenschappelijke kennis voor de Fundamentele Herbezinning Burgerlijk procesrecht* (Den Haag, Raad voor de Rechtspraak, 2004).

[10] For example: Schedule an early case management conference to identify relevant preliminary issues, discuss the sequence of relevant topics to address, determine a realistic but firm timetable, discuss the selection of test cases.

a contemporary version of Dickens' *Bleak House*.[11] When adjudicators are not exercising case management in the mass disputes, the question is whether this originates from a lack of familiarity with, and understanding of case management and aggregate litigation techniques, from statutory restraints, or from less tangible factors—like strong personal views and biases about the proper role of judges and the meaning of party autonomy—that are incompatible with the basic concept of case management.[12]

In addition, there are also problems related to claim resolution facilities. The extent of public control or monitoring of the design, implementation and functioning of claim resolution facilities varies. Furthermore, a distinction should be made between the design and implementation of claim resolution facilities dealing with personal injuries, and the design and implementation of claim resolution facilities dealing with other types of (financial) cases.[13]

The big numbers that are inherent to mass disputes also pose challenges on the calculation of damages that often takes place on a case-by-case basis. Calculation of damages in mass disputes may require the use of sampling or other statistical methods. In addition, there are also transparency issues. There are some examples of claim resolution facilities established at the instruction of a court, legislature, government or regulator, that have reported take-up rates (that is, the fraction of claimants who came forward relative to the total number of eligible claimants), the average amount of individual compensation, and the total costs of the distribution process (including compensation and transaction costs). However, there are no generally accepted guidelines or practices to secure proper functioning of claim resolution facilities.

When the claim resolution facilities are not the result of a governmental or legislative action, but of a judicial or (self or semi) regulatory intervention, there seems to be less attention for the results of the 'distribution stage'. Whether the design, functioning and outcome of the respective compensation scheme will be monitored, evaluated and reported, depends on the discretion and skills of a specific court or judge. This has at least two obvious disadvantages: there is no learning curve, and no possibility to evaluate not only whether the distribution process was successful at all, but also—if applicable—whether the preceding adjudicative process justified the time and effort.

[11] See en.wikipedia.org/wiki/Bleak_House.

[12] With respect to the implications of the concept of party autonomy for the funding of mass disputes see IN Tzankova, 'Funding of Mass Disputes: Lessons from the Netherlands' (2012) 8 *Journal of Law, Economics and Policy* 549.

[13] CJM van Doorn and IN Tzankova, 'De afwikkeling van massaschade via Claim Afwikkelingsfaciliteiten: een grensoverschrijdende verkenning' in LA van Heusden, JJ Westland, TC Gerverdinck, CAH Bikkers, CJM van Doorn and IN Tzankova (eds), *Massaal Procederen* (Den Haag, Boom Juridische Uitgevers, 2014).

The set of problems identified above becomes even more apparent in transnational mass disputes. On the one hand, the existing legal and institutional infrastructure can be improved only by a coordinated national or supranational institutional effort, which involves complicated political processes. On the other hand, the national judges confronted with the handling of mass disputes have varying legal and cultural backgrounds and case management skills.

Thus, three main groups of research questions, to be answered in an expert meeting complemented with a desk research and interview surveys, were formulated as follows:

- Is there a need for the collection of the existing expertise with regard to the case management of mass disputes, and what is the level of demand for the development of a toolkit and educational resources on the topic of case management of mass disputes?
- What are the cultural, jurisprudential and practical obstacles to a more efficient management of mass claim disputes?
- What tools would be appropriate to overcome such obstacles and implement case management practices in various jurisdictions? What are the main features of such tools, and who are the persons and organisations that need to be involved in the development process, including potential funding strategies?

The chapter proceeds as follows. Section II discusses the concepts of case management and claim resolution facilities, as the two main techniques for dealing with mass disputes in focus of the feasibility study. Section III further elaborates on the main research questions, the activities that were undertaken to clarify them, the research method and the results. Section IV concludes.

II. MASS DISPUTES AND THEIR RESOLUTION

Various legal systems have developed different mechanisms or techniques to deal with mass disputes in some aggregated or concentrated form.[14] The study focused on two techniques: case management and claim resolution facilities. The limitation of the study to those two will be explained in Section III.A. Below follows a brief discussion of the concepts and theoretical framework of case management and claim resolution facilities.

[14] DR Hensler, C Hodges and M Tulibacka (eds), 'The Globalization of Class Actions' (2009) 622 *Annals of the American Academy of Political and Social Science* (whole issue).

A. Case Management

i. Defining Case Management

The term case management refers to a subset of law practice management and covers a range of approaches and technologies used to leverage knowledge and methodologies for managing the life cycle of a case or matter more effectively.[15] Case management thus refers to the sophisticated information management and workflow practices that are tailored to meet the legal field's specific needs and requirements.[16]

One may wonder how case management relates to procedural law. Some have observed that 'Case management should be seen to incorporate not only procedural values, but also organizational values',[17] and that as such 'it stands between procedural law, which protects legal rights, and best practice'.[18] In other words: case management needs to be embedded within a legal framework and facilitated by the judicial organisation, but it in itself does not require an extensive body of rules.

In common law jurisdictions the term 'judicial case management' refers to the judge taking an active role in shepherding litigation to a conclusion, rather than leaving it to the lawyers to determine the chronology of key events.[19] There are various stages in civil litigation that occur before a trial is held or a decision is rendered. When a complaint is filed and a case is assigned to a judge, the 'managerial' judge sets forth a schedule for the submission or completion of the relevant pleadings, court appearances, briefing and deciding potentially dispositive motions, and other matters. In complex multi-party litigation, the judge will appoint committees of lawyers to represent plaintiffs and defendants, and often issue orders specifying how such committees are to be financed. The judge may appoint a 'special master' to facilitate communication among the lawyers, decide discovery disputes and encourage settlement. In the US virtually all class action and non-class mass litigation is managed in this fashion, usually with the full support of parties and lawyers.

Many civil law jurisdictions have some form of aggregate device to deal with mass disputes,[20] and most judges are familiar with the general concepts

[15] See www.encyclo.co.uk/define/Legal%20management.

[16] See generally M Spencer Dixon and D Foster, 'Capturing More Time … And Keeping Your Clients Happy While Doing It' (2007) *Law Practice Today*, available at: happs.americanbar.org/lpm/lpt/articles/bot03071.shtml. See also en.wikipedia.org/wiki/Legal_case_management.

[17] GY Ng, 'Case Management: Procedural Law v Best Practices' in CH van Rhee (ed), *Judicial Case Management and Efficiency in Civil Litigation* (Antwerp, Intersentia, 2008) 132.

[18] ibid, 113.

[19] J Resnik, 'Managerial Judges' (1982) 96 *Harvard Law Review* 374.

[20] Hensler, Hodges and Tulibacka (n 14) 7–29; PG Karlsgodt (ed), *World Class Actions: A Guide to Group and Representative Actions around the Globe* (Oxford, Oxford University Press, 2012).

that underlie judicial case management. Moreover, many scholars regard judicial control of civil litigation as a hallmark of continental 'inquisitorial' judging.[21] Contrary to common law systems, in civil law systems the judge is the one who examines the witnesses and drafts the report of the hearing. But apart from the field of evidence gathering, one may wonder whether the differences between the role of the judiciary in the adversarial and inquisitorial systems still exist to the extent traditionally prescribed by the respective procedural theories.[22] Nowadays the personal skills, style, preferences and background of the respective individuals seem to have much bigger influence on the actual case management of cases, than the question whether the adjudicator operates within an inquisitorial or adversarial system.

If one would try to come up with a description of judicial case management that would try to capture the core elements of that activity in a more uniform way, the Principles of Transnational Civil Procedure seem to be a good point of reference. Judicial case management as interpreted by these Principles[23]—and perhaps similarly understood in many other jurisdictions[24]—refers to an approach to the proceedings before a court, which holds that:

— the specific nature of the case should determine to a large extent the rules, directions and orders that govern the proceedings.
— rules, directions and orders of proceedings before a court should to a large extent be determined at a lower level. Ideally, judges, parties and attorneys are to determine to a large extent the proceedings before the court.
— it is the court that should primarily be responsible for the proceedings. Therefore the court should have the necessary procedural discretionary powers.
— the court's discretion should be discretion in the weak sense. The court is to use its powers to achieve the disposition of the dispute fairly, efficiently, and with reasonable speed.[25]

[21] JH Langbein, 'The German Advantage in Civil Procedure' (1985) 52 *The University of Chicago Law Review* 823; JC Reitz, 'Why We Probably Cannot Adopt the German Advantage in Civil Procedure' (1990) 75 *Iowa Law Review* 987; RJ Allen, S Kock, K Riecherberg and DT Rosen, 'German Advantage in Civil Procedure: A Plea for More Details and Fewer Generalities in Comparative Scholarship' (1988) 82 *Northwestern University Law Review* 705. For a discussion of the history of case management in Europe from the end of the 19th century see CH van Rhee (ed), *Judicial Case Management and Efficiency in Civil Litigation* (Antwerp, Intersentia, 2008).

[22] WDH Asser, HA Groen, JBM Vranken and IN Tzankova, *Een nieuwe balans* (Den Haag, BJu, 2003); WDH Asser, HA Groen, JBM Vranken and IN Tzankova, *Uitgebalanceerd* (Den Haag, BJu, 2006).

[23] R Turner, 'The Proactive Judge and the Provision of a Single Transnational Case Management System and its Associated Procedures' in M Andenas, N Andrews and R Nazzini (eds), *The Future of Transnational Civil Litigation: English Responses to the ALI/UNIDROIT Draft Principles and Rules of Transnational Civil Procedure* (London, BIICL, 2004).

[24] See also ibid, 73: 'the efforts of ALI/UNIDROIT… mirror…much of our own new rules'.

[25] RR Verkerk, 'What is Judicial Case Management? A Transnational and European Perspective' in CH van Rhee (ed), *Judicial Case Management and Efficiency in Civil Litigation* (Antwerp, Intersentia, 2008) 27–50, provided this summary of the Principles.

This suggests that the key words for a successful case management of any dispute are flexibility and creativity. The working definition of case management in this study emerges from the Principles of Transnational Civil Procedure. That definition captures the most distinct features of case management, as it is understood throughout various jurisdictions.

ii. Managing the Mass

Case management provides judges with the opportunity to handle mass disputes in a more efficient way. However, research on the utility and operation of case management in relation to mass disputes is generally lacking.[26] Case studies suggest that some civil law judges seem to experience more difficulty efficiently managing mass disputes compared to common law judges.[27] This is also a conclusion that follows from a study that was conducted by the University of Brussels (BEUC study).[28] The aim of the BEUC study was to track and evaluate the role of the judiciary in six European Member States when handling mass disputes. The study covered one common law jurisdiction,[29] and five non-common law jurisdictions.[30] One of the main conclusions was that the resolution of mass disputes in the five non-common law jurisdictions was problematic, even though they had introduced some kind of a collective action or another aggregate device to deal with mass disputes.

The conclusion with regard to the UK was different: the interviewed judges often used case management techniques to deal with mass disputes and to facilitate an out-of-court resolution by the parties, instead of using the Group Litigation Order (a statutory aggregate device available under the UK Civil Procedure Rules, and similar to the German KapMuG group proceedings).[31]

[26] In the European context there has been some empirical research about case assignment. See PM Langbroek and M Fabri, *The Right Judge for Each Case: A Study of Case Assignment and Impartiality in Six European Judiciaries* (Antwerp, Intersentia, 2007). The countries covered in the study are England and Wales, Germany, Italy, the Netherlands and Denmark.

[27] The Buncefield case study—N Creutzfeldt-Banda and C Hodges, 'Parallel Public and Private Responses: the Buncefield Explosion' in DR Hensler, C Hodges and IN Tzankova (eds), *Class Actions in Context: How Economics, Politics and Culture Shape Collective Litigation*, (Cheltenham, Edward Elgar, forthcoming), and Deutsche Telekom case study—A Halfmeier, 'Litigation Without End? The Deutsche Telekom Case and the German Approach to Private Enforcement of Securities Litigation' in Hensler, Hodges and Tzankova, ibid.

[28] Elodie Falla, 'Powers of the Judge in Collective Redress Proceedings', Research Paper submitted to BEUC (The European Consumer Organisation), February 2012, available at www.beuc.org/publications/2012-00227-01-e.pdf.

[29] The UK.

[30] Italy, Sweden, Spain, Portugal and Germany.

[31] The observation of two UK practitioners attending the conference Increasing Access to Justice through EU Class Actions, held at the EP in Brussels on 12 and 13 November 2012, was that 'cases get really messed up as soon as judges start using the GLO'.

The downside attributed to judicial case management has to do with the fear that the emphasis on efficiency might negatively influence the quality of the judicial work and its end product.[32] That criticism neglects the fact that in relation to mass disputes case management is a necessity rather than an option, as became apparent in the *Deutsche Telekom* case.[33]

iii. Case Management and Legal Culture

The question that emerges is: when adjudicators are not exercising case management in the mass disputes they are assigned to deal with, does this originate from a lack of familiarity with, and understanding of case management and aggregate litigation techniques, statutory restraints, or from less tangible factors like legal culture and strong personal views and biases about the proper role of judges and the meaning of party autonomy that are incompatible with the basic concept of case management? And if that is the case, could that be addressed?

An empirical study of case assignments and impartiality in six European judiciaries[34] seems to confirm that case management practices indeed reflect legal cultural traditions and preferences. The study shows that legal culture and tradition are decisive for the attitude of the case manager. For example, the more formalistic approach in Germany and Italy apparently originates from the cultural perception that this increases accountability and offers better safeguards for impartiality.[35]

But formality conflicts with flexibility and leaves little room for creativity. So if flexibility and creativity are instrumental for successful case management, could one conclude that there is no or little room for improvement of the case management of mass disputes in more legalistic or formalistic legal systems? In our view, such a premise would be too straightforward and simplistic.

In Germany, a jurisdiction with a more formal legal culture and case assignment tradition, a far-reaching specialisation within the courts is considered normal.[36] Although specialisation may reduce organisational flexibility, it may create room for specialised judicial educational case management programmes or training for the handling of mass disputes. Even within jurisdictions with a more formalistic legal culture there is room for

[32] Resnik (n 19); R Verkijk, 'Beyond Winning: Judicial Case Management and the Role of Lawyers in the Principles of Transnational Civil Procedure' in CH van Rhee (ed), *Judicial Case Management and Efficiency in Civil Litigation* (Antwerp, Intersentia, 2008) 132.

[33] See n 27.

[34] The study was general of nature and not focusing on mass disputes: Langbroek and Fabri (n 26).

[35] ibid, 24.

[36] ibid.

the improvement of case management practices, although that might require specific and further reaching implementation strategies.

To put it differently: an informal toolkit or a manual for the handling of mass disputes could be sufficient in jurisdictions with a more flexible legal culture, because notions of accountability and impartiality are considered there to be self-evident and internalised by the judicial services, so there is more flexibility for a judge to adjust the toolkit to a specific setting or context; whereas judicial case management training programmes that integrate the toolkit might be more appropriate in a formalistic legal environment, because a formalised training format would be viewed as less problematic from the standpoint of accountability.

It is hence important to properly manage the expectations. Sometimes an informal implementation approach will suffice, while sometimes a more formally embedded training programme would be appropriate if not necessary. The existing research suggests that generally speaking effective judicial case management is likely to flourish in an environment where: the rules of civil procedure do not prescribe a uniform procedural framework but differentiate between different types of cases; these rules leave the judge the necessary discretion to manage individual cases and the caseload as a whole; this discretion can only be exercised to promote certain well-defined goals, in particular efficiency, appropriate speed and moderate costs; the parties and their lawyers have a duty and the necessary incentives to co-operate;[37] and courts are provided with adequate resources.[38]

B. Claim Resolution Facilities

i. Defining Claim Resolution Facilities

'Claim Resolution Facility' (CRF) is a generic term used to describe a wide range of entities that process and resolve claims made against a potential funding source.[39] Their basis could be a national or international statutory instrument, a court order,[40] a settlement agreement, and they can even be

[37] Lawyers and parties will be more willing to cooperate when they are from the same network: Verkijk (n 32) 72–73 discusses some empirical data. Moreover, cooperating is more efficient, increases party autonomy and it boosts the independence of the lawyer (ibid 73–75).

[38] Van Rhee (n 21). The book discusses judicial case management in France, Scotland, Belgium and the Netherlands.

[39] FE McGovern, 'The What and Why of Claims Resolution Facilities' (2005) 57 *Stanford Law Review* 1361–62.

[40] DR Hensler, 'Alternative Courts? Litigation-Induced Claims Resolution Facilities' (2005) 57 *Stanford Law Review* 1429, discusses the 'privately designed, financed, and administered organizations for giving away money, established as a result of the settlement of mass litigation in trial or bankruptcy courts'.

established at the initiative of a party held responsible for an event that had caused mass damages. The CRF can be established proactively, prior to any litigation, after litigation, or it can even be integrated in the litigation by the decision-maker managing the case.[41]

McGovern[42] has identified nine different elements that appear in any CRF. Those relate to (1) the function of the facility,[43] (2) the paradigm or metaphor that best incorporates the characteristics of the facility,[44] (3) the source of authority or funding,[45] (4) the size and similarity of claims, (5) the organisation of the CRF,[46] (6) the eligibility criteria,[47] (7) the damage methodology,[48] (8) compensation[49] and (9) implementation.[50] Those elements will be explained in a bit more detail below.

There are generally two potential roles played by CRFs: determining both the total amount of damages and the allocation to each applicable individual, or performing only the allocation function. CRFs can also be set up to deal with non-monetary remedies. One of the first issues in establishing the legitimacy of CRFs is to determine the paradigm that best incorporates its characteristics. The tort paradigm is that the party that caused damage must internalise those costs by compensating the injured party for the precise amount of damages sustained. The welfare paradigm is that of a social safety net to ensure that no fundamental needs are unmet. The war reparations paradigm has a host of connotations, including retribution and compensation.

CRFs can be the product of a statute, administrative regulation, international mandate, class action, bankruptcy, group settlement or unilateral offer. Funding can come from a government, multiple defendants or a single defendant. Both the source of authority and the source of funding will affect the applicable paradigm as well as the choice of organisation, methodology and payment mechanisms. Typically, the more governmental the authority, the more legitimate the facility. The more ad hoc the source, the more burden on the facility to legitimise itself by its own design.

The tolerance for fine-tuned inequities in damage determination if there is a corresponding efficiency in claim processing will be much greater when

[41] McGovern (n 39) 1362.
[42] ibid, 1362–75.
[43] ibid, 1363–65.
[44] ibid, 1365–66.
[45] ibid, 1366–67.
[46] McGovern (n 39) 1368–70, where he also discusses various examples of CRFs designed on the basis of the inquisitorial model of decision-making.
[47] ibid, 1370–71.
[48] ibid, 1372–73.
[49] ibid, 1373–74.
[50] ibid, 1374–75.

the individual claimants share similar characteristics. The mere existence of potential funding will generate applications that present a difficult trade-off between errors and transaction costs. There are, however, certain standard options available to establish eligibility. There are at least 10 methods for assessing damages, varying from giving the same amount of payment to everyone to having a fully litigated trial before a jury of peers. The same facility may have several of these methodologies available depending upon the degree of certainty required before making a payment. The norm of compensation is money: cash, note, stock or other financial instrument. But there are instances where payment has been in-kind: medical operations, healthcare facilities, property repair etc.

One the most important variables in CRFs relates to the method of implementation and operation. Some facilities are subject to judicial hearings before, during and after operations. Other facilities are subject to court approval of their processes, but not their application. Once operational, some facilities are completely transparent, others are transparent only to each individual beneficiary, and still others are inscrutable to the lay observer.

ii. A Critical Assessment of CRFs

The extent of public control or monitoring of the design, implementation and functioning of CRFs varies. There are examples of claim resolution facilities established at the instruction of a court, legislature, government or regulator. However, there are neither general guidelines nor practices to secure proper monitoring of the functioning of CRFs. In 1990 the RAND Institute published a study about the—then new—phenomenon of CRFs.[51] The RAND study identified key questions to answer in order to know whether the increased role of CRFs was justified. The study was reprinted in 2004,[52] and it again proposed an agenda for research on CRFs.

The research agenda included the development of data related to the pattern of case outcomes, transaction costs and procedural justice. It also emphasised the need for information on how effective these facilities are in including those who are eligible for compensation under the plan and in foreclosing future litigation. Finally, it argued that judges, who must often approve the establishment and design of CRFs, should know more about claimants' responses to the facilities.[53]

[51] DR Hensler, 'Assessing Claims Resolution Facilities: What We Need to Know' (1990) 53 *Law and Contemporary Problems* 175; MA Peterson, 'Giving Away Money: Comparative Comments on Claims Resolution Facilities, Law and Contemporary Problems' (1990) 53 *Law and Contemporary Problems* 113.

[52] Hensler, ibid.

[53] ibid, 177–81.

Other key decisions with respect to CRFs include: the claims estimation strategies; the order of payments; the claimant outreach procedures; the establishment of a new, stand-alone organisation rather than the employment of an existing private or public agency to deliver compensation; the recruitment and staffing strategies; and the roles assigned to attorneys, both those representing claimants and those acting on behalf of the facilities.[54] Today, the RAND research agenda is still relevant. Although there have been some comparative studies on the functioning of CRFs,[55] there has not been much improvement of our knowledge about the functioning and optimal design of such facilities.

III. THE FEASIBILITY STUDY AND ITS RESULTS

A. Why Focus on Case Management and CRFs

i. Case Management as a Constant Factor

As was mentioned in section II, the focus of this study is on two specific techniques: case management and CRFs. This focus was originally triggered by the differences between jurisdictions that have adopted the adversarial and inquisitorial judicial styles; moreover, further research and policy developments revealed that there are more fundamental reasons for this choice.

The discussions about the resolution of mass disputes have been dominated by the controversy surrounding class and collective actions and other forms of aggregate dispute resolution, often resulting in inaction on the part of national or international legislatures to introduce adequate collective redress mechanisms.[56] At the same time, mass disputes continue to occur and to present significant challenges. The actual experiences with mass disputes have raised doubts whether collective redress is the only way to ensure the proper handling of mass disputes.[57]

On one hand, there are jurisdictions where judicial case management is well embedded in the legal system that seem to be capable of handling mass disputes despite the unavailability of class or collective action devices.[58] On the other hand, there are jurisdictions where class or collective actions formally exist, but where those devices have not been used much.[59] At the same time jurisdictions having a similar legal framework, seem to produce

[54] ibid, 184.

[55] Holtzmann and Kristjansdottir (n 7).

[56] The discussions on collective redress at EU level are probably illustrative of the status quo. See the documents in n 3.

[57] Creutzfeldt-Banda and Hodges (n 27).

[58] The US mass torts practice that does not allow the use of class actions is an example. Another example one could find in the UK: See ibid.

[59] Portugal is such an example.

different outcomes in terms of the speed and efficiency of the resolution and distribution process, apparently also as a result of differing case management styles and approaches.[60] Such observations raised the question whether a more pragmatic approach of the handling of mass disputes would result in more tangible effects on the resolution of mass disputes. Especially because all mechanisms used to deal with mass disputes, whether they are out-of-court, in-court or court-annexed at some point need proper case management.

ii. Increased Emphasis on ADR

Another reason to focus on case management and CRFs is the increased emphasis on the use of ADR within the EU (the Directive 2013/11/EU, ('the ADR Directive') and Regulation (EU) 524/2013 ('the ODR (Online Dispute Resolution) Regulation')). The underlying concept behind the ADR Directive is that there should be EU-wide access for consumers in every Member State to ADR entities which, in combination, comprehensively cover all business sectors in every territory, and which comply with a number of quality criteria.[61] Each Member State and the Commission will then list such qualified ADR entities. Inclusion in the list will be a guarantee that the ADR entity has the requisite characteristics to ensure an independent, impartial, transparent, effective, fast and fair resolution of the dispute in question. However, the ADR Directive does not address the collective resolution of consumer disputes, so the designated ADR entities need case management tools.

The impact of ADR is increasing also outside the field of consumer law. The introduction of the Dutch Act on Collective Settlements—that was enacted in 2005,[62] and which implicates the use of case management tools and CRFs—has been considered successful also outside the Netherlands. The UK, Germany and Belgium are considering the introduction of similar settlement schemes,[63] which is another indication that the significance of case management and CRFs within the EU will further increase.

iii. Claim Resolution Facilities (CRFs) and Corporate Social Responsibility (CSR)

On 16 June 2011, the UN Human Rights Council endorsed the 'Guiding Principles on Business and Human Rights: Implementing the United Nations

[60] Halfmeier (n 27), and Creutzfeldt-Banda and Hodges (n 27).

[61] Those entities would typically be Ombudsmen, Tribunals, Commissions, the doctrine speaks of 'CDR': Consumer dispute resolution. See C Hodges, I Benöhr and N Creutzfeldt-Banda, *Consumer ADR in Europe* (Oxford, Hart Publishing, 2013).

[62] Staatsblad 2005, no 380.

[63] In the UK this is considered in the context of antitrust enforcement, in Germany in financial matters, and in Belgium in the fields of consumer protection.

"Protect, Respect and Remedy" Framework'.[64] This framework of principles for governments and businesses (the 'Principles' or the 'Ruggie framework') rests on three pillars. The first is the State duty to protect against human rights abuse by third parties, including business enterprises, through appropriate policies, regulation and adjudication. The second is the corporate responsibility to respect human rights, which means that business enterprises should act with due diligence to avoid infringing on the rights of others. The third is the need for greater access for victims to effective remedy, both judicial and non-judicial. Each pillar is an essential component in an inter-related and dynamic system: the State duty to protect because it lies at the very core of the international human rights regime; the corporate responsibility to respect because it is the basic expectation society has of businesses in relation to human rights; and access to remedy because even the most concerted efforts cannot prevent all abuse.

Principle 22 stipulates that where business enterprises identify that they have caused or contributed to adverse impacts, they should provide for or cooperate in their remediation. The Principles use the term 'grievance mechanisms', meaning any routinised process through which grievances concerning business-related human rights abuse can be raised and remedy can be sought,[65] but the parallel with CRFs as discussed in section II.B above is evident. State-based grievance mechanisms may be administered by a branch or agency of the State, or by an independent body on a statutory or constitutional basis. They may be judicial or non-judicial. In some mechanisms, those affected are directly involved in seeking remedy; in others, an intermediary seeks remedy on their behalf.[66]

Principle 25 stipulates that States must take appropriate steps to ensure, through judicial, administrative, legislative or other appropriate means, that when business-related human rights abuse occurs within their territory and/or jurisdiction those affected have access to effective remedy. The remedies provided by the grievance mechanisms may take a range of forms the aim of which will be to counteract or make good any human rights harms that have occurred. Remedy may include apologies, restitution, rehabilitation, financial or non-financial compensation and punitive sanctions, as well as the prevention of harm through, for example, injunctions or guarantees of non-repetition.

Moreover, Principle 26 stipulates that States should ensure the effectiveness of domestic judicial mechanisms when addressing business-related human rights abuses, including considering ways to reduce barriers that

[64] The full text of the principles is to be found at www.business-humanrights.org/SpecialRepPortal/Home/Protect-Respect-Remedy-Framework/GuidingPrinciples.

[65] Commentary Principle 25.

[66] See the Comments on Principle 25. Principle 31 sets out the core criteria that such grievance mechanisms should meet.

could lead to a denial of access to remedy. One of the barriers discussed in the commentary to the principle are inadequate options for aggregating claims or enabling representative proceedings (such as class actions and other collective action procedures). Appropriate implementation of case management as discussed in this study could remedy such obstacles without the necessity of introducing formal aggregation devices such as class actions.

According to Principles 27–28, States should provide and facilitate non-judicial grievance mechanisms. One category of non-State based grievance mechanisms encompasses those administered by a business enterprise alone or with stakeholders, by an industry association or a multi-stakeholder group. They are non-judicial, but may use adjudicative, dialogue-based or other culturally appropriate and rights-compatible processes.[67]

The Ruggie framework places similar duties not only on the States but also on businesses by stipulating in Principles 29–30 that business enterprises should establish or participate in effective grievance mechanisms for individuals and communities who may be adversely impacted, and that businesses, multi-stakeholder and other collaborative initiatives that are based on respect for human rights-related standards should ensure that effective grievance mechanisms are available. The latter is to be achieved through codes of conduct, performance standards, global framework agreements between trade unions and transnational corporations, and similar undertakings. Again, this is exactly what CRFs could offer and achieve.

Principle 31 describes the effectiveness criteria which non-judicial grievance mechanisms should meet, and there is a clear link with the research agenda for the functioning of CRFs. The non-judicial grievance mechanisms should be sufficiently legitimate, accessible, predictable, equitable, transparent, rights-compatible and a source of continuous learning. The comments to that principle emphasise that poorly designed or implemented grievance mechanisms can risk compounding a sense of grievance amongst affected stakeholders, by heightening their sense of disempowerment. Linking the CRFs' research agenda to the Ruggie principles will help to identify which grievance systems and mechanisms work and how to design them. The most recent evaluations of the implementation of the Ruggie principles by businesses suggest that there is a need for such guidance.[68]

Finally, enhancing CSR through the development, proper implementation and monitoring of the functioning of grievance mechanisms or CRFs

[67] Commentary Principle 28.

[68] On 15 April 2013 a workshop took place in Berlin on the topic: Business and Human Rights Workshop—Putting the Ruggie Framework and the Guiding Principles into Practice. See the presentations on remediation and operational grievance mechanisms and human rights in the supply chain. For a report of the workshop see csreurope.org/ruggie-framework-and-guiding-principles-workshop-report-released.

can contribute to the development of the rule of law in developing and transitional countries by setting standards for a proper course of action.[69]

iv. Implications

The implication is that the study should follow a more functional approach that would build on two pillars: the collection of expertise for the handling of mass disputes irrespective of the institutional or jurisdictional setting and context, and the most optimal way to disseminate the collected expertise. The consequences of such an approach are:

- Ideally, the application or use of the end products would not be limited to a certain type of adjudicators.
- The focus would be on practical issues concerning the management of mass disputes, including the distribution stage.
- The project should have a global reach.
- The legal embedding of the case management techniques/best practices and CRFs in a specific institutional setting or jurisdiction falls outside the scope of the study, although certain minimum preconditions in terms of legal framework that influence effective case management should be recognised.

B. Activities and Results

This section elaborates on the three groups of main research questions, the research method and activities, and the results. The feasibility study started in August 2012 with the preparation of the expert meeting, which took place on 29 and 30 November 2012. The final report was delivered in October 2013. The study was centred on the two day expert meeting. Additional informal surveys and interviews were conducted between March and September 2013.

i. Activities: Consultation Document and Expert Meeting

The three main groups of research questions[70] were elaborated on in a consultation document and were further developed in a questionnaire. The questionnaire consisted of 23 sub-questions divided over three sections corresponding with the main research questions. The consultation document

[69] See the case studies discussed in E Kristjansdottir, A Nollkaemper and C Ryngaert (eds), *International Law in Domestic Courts: Rule of Law Reform in Post-Conflict States* (Anwerp, Intersentia, 2012).

[70] See Introduction (s I, p 250 above).

explained the background of the project, the phenomenon of mass disputes and the case management issues surrounding it, including an illustrative overview of state-of-the-art initiatives and tools with respect to the collection and dissemination of practical wisdom.

The consultation document was drafted on the basis of the literature available in English and Dutch, complemented with an informal survey and interviews with experts and stakeholders. The latter type of information gathering was essential given the often informal nature of the case management initiatives; information about them was not easily found in the public domain.

Furthermore the consultation document described the assumptions that needed to be tested in the subsequent expert meeting, together with a few potential end products of this project, such as a self-assessment test for case management, establishing the best practices and guidelines for the case management of mass disputes, and developing a case management training programme. The experts were requested to study the consultation document and the questionnaire in preparation of the meeting, but were not required to provide written answers to the questionnaire.[71]

ii. Assumptions to be Tested

One assumption that needed to be tested was that as a result of the globalisation and industrialisation mass disputes would occur more and more often in the future.[72] Some recent illustrative examples in various substantive fields of law are the PIP silicon breast implant claims,[73] off-label use of drugs such as Vioxx,[74] defective medical devices such as certain heart valves,[75] disputes arising from the global financial crisis such as Fortis[76]/Madoff[77]/Icesave[78], the Greek and Argentinean debts resulting in arbitrations,[79]

[71] Both the questionnaire and the consultation document are on file with the author.

[72] Hensler (n 1).

[73] See www.cosmeticsurgerylaw.co.uk/pip-implants-compensation-breast-implant-claim.html. Actions are also pending in France, the Netherlands, Australia and Germany.

[74] See www.msnbc.msn.com/id/6192603/ns/health-arthritis/t/report-vioxx-linked-thousands-deaths/#.UJEgDGewe_I. Litigation started in the US, Canada and Australia but not in Europe and the UK.

[75] See www.thompsons.law.co.uk/product-liability/shiley-heart-valves.htm.

[76] See www.ipe.com/news/misled-investors-file-class-action-against-fortis_38649.php#.UJEgVmewe_I.

[77] See jurist.org/paperchase/2011/11/madoff-victims-file-class-action-suit-against-jp-morgan.php.

[78] See www.businessweek.com/news/2011-12-07/landsbanki-islands-makes-3-6-billion-payment-on-icesave-claims.html.

[79] See criticallegalthinking.com/2012/02/27/the-abaclat-legacy-investment-arbitration-as-an-obstacle-to-greek-recovery/#fn-5590-7.

the Libor scandal[80], the Trafigura environmental case,[81] the Roman Catholic church abuses[82] and the Air Cargo cartel cases[83] etc.

Although class actions and group actions represent a relatively small percentage of the total number of cases within a jurisdiction,[84] numbers appear to be an inadequate indicator for the impact of such cases on the functioning of justice systems. Anecdotal evidence suggests that even one inadequately managed mass dispute can have a dramatic impact on the day-to-day operations of court systems and justice systems more in general.[85] The transactional[86] and emotional costs of such a negative impact are evident. Another assumption of the study is that the fact that mass disputes are not one-time events justifies measures aiming at the improvement of the case management skills of adjudicators.

The resolution of mass disputes is a complicated matter and there are many relevant legal issues to consider, that may vary per jurisdiction such as the standing to act,[87] funding, the requirements for the certification or admissibility of class and group actions,[88] the *res judicata* effect of judgments, recognition and enforcement issues etc. However, the feasibility study was limited to the case management of mass disputes, because it was believed to be a relatively universal and neutral topic. Irrespective of the legal infrastructure or the (un)availability of specific statutory devices to aggregate claims, at the end of the line there is an individual in charge of the resolution of a mass dispute who will face management challenges caused by the numbers inherent to mass disputes. The assumption was that there are certain universal issues related to the management of mass disputes that will always occur and there are certain case management techniques to deal with those issues. Still, one of the assumptions that needed to be tested in the expert meeting was whether the case management of mass disputes indeed could be treated isolated from the legal infrastructure within which the case manager operates and independently from the answer to the question, whether a legal system provides for a class action, group action or some other (regulatory or criminal) device for the resolution of mass disputes.

[80] See www.dailymail.co.uk/news/article-2168473/Libor-scandal-ruin-banking-giants-US-lawyers-prepare-sue-financial-firms-hundreds-BILLIONS.html.

[81] See www.thelawyer.com/trafigura-fee-day/1007136.article.

[82] See www.guardian.co.uk/law/2012/jul/12/catholic-church-loses-apeal-liability.

[83] See clen.law.unimelb.edu.au/go/news-and-events/discussion-group; www.ubmaviation news.com/News/Today-s-News/Talking-Point/Cargo-cartel-victims-sue-Air-France-KLM-and-Martinair-for-500m.

[84] US figures available from the Federal Judicial Center.

[85] In the Netherlands (*Dexia*), Germany (*Deutsche Telekom*), Belgium (*Lernout & Hauspie*) and Austria (disputes related to financial products).

[86] The *Dexia* case study in the Netherlands is an illustrative example of the potential waste of judicial and Legal Aid resources that mass disputes pose on society. For a discussion of the funding issue see Tzankova (n 12) 578–85, 589–90.

[87] For example individuals v organisations as class or group representative.

[88] Numerosity, commonality, adequacy of representation, predominance etc.

In sum, the assumptions that needed to be tested in the expert meeting were that:

- there was a need for collecting the existing expertise with regard to the case management of mass disputes;
- even if there were cultural, jurisprudential and practical obstacles to a more efficient management of mass claims, those could be overcome, at least to some extent if the case managers:
    - met certain competences, to be assessed through a self-assessment tool; and/or
    - received a customised training depending on the kind of mass disputes they would have to deal with.

iii. Overview State of the Art Initiatives

Most initiatives or tools related to the management of (mass) disputes and complex litigation are to be found in common law jurisdictions. The types of tools that will be discussed in more detail further below are guidelines, best practices, checklists and protocols, ad hoc task forces/designated judges and training programmes (a–c). Some of the related studies will be listed in sub-section d.

a. Manuals, Guidelines, Best Practices, Checklists and Protocols

Most materials with respect to the case management of mass disputes will not be found in statutory instruments, but in so-called secondary sources that, with just a few exceptions, are not binding and are merely developed as an extra aid or facility for the users (judges/lawyers). Some authors have warned that such secondary sources are lacking a constitutional basis, but have the potential of gaining or being attributed a 'natural authority'.[89] To avoid any potential confusion and to address such criticisms, the authors of manuals, protocols and guidelines state explicitly that those are not binding and are designed only as an aid for practitioners. The judge managing a mass dispute is free to use and modify or add to the toolbox depending on the needs of a particular case.[90]

The existing materials vary in content and scope but all have been drafted by professionals involved in the resolution of mass disputes, rather than by the legislature; sometimes they are drafted exclusively by judges,[91]

[89] AJ Simons, 'The Manual for Complex Litigation: More Rules or Mere Recommendations?' (1988) 62 *St John's Law Review* 493.

[90] See for an example the quote from Federal Judicial Center, 'Manual for Complex Litigation' (n 6) 28–29.

[91] The Manual for Complex Litigation and the Guidelines of the Amsterdam Court of Appeal, to be discussed further below, were drafted by members of the judiciary.

sometimes by judges and lawyers, and sometimes by judges, lawyers and scholars.[92] The overview of instruments below is illustrative rather than exhaustive, for a variety of reasons. Apart from a language barrier that prevents the identification and study of potential relevant materials in languages other than English, French and German, not all existing judicial case management initiatives are publicly available. For example, in the resolution of the *Dexia* matter[93] the Amsterdam District Court published an evaluation of the case management techniques and approaches it had developed and an overview of the challenges it had faced.[94] However, there is no publicly available information (yet) with respect to subsequent measures that were taken as a result of later Supreme Court rulings, which had significant logistical implications for the resolution of pending individual cases.[95]

The US Manual for Complex Litigation was established by the Federal Judicial Center and is probably one of the oldest and most distinctive examples of initiatives aiming to facilitate the case management of mass disputes and complex litigation.[96] The Manual is divided into a general section and sector-specific sections (for example antitrust, securities, employment, intellectual property). The general section defines general principles with respect to the role of the courts and the role of the lawyers. Some of the topics that are covered are: other judges/related litigation; sanctions; early supervision; preliminary matters (scheduling initial conference, interim measures, case management plan); discovery; techniques to promote settlement; the use of sampling; special masters and alternatives to promote settlements; ethical

[92] The Judicial Protocols of the American Bar Association that will be discussed in more detail further below at s III A ii are examples.

[93] *Dexia* was probably the first massive consumer mass claim dispute in the Netherlands. About 10% of Dutch households had a securities lease product that relied on big profits yet to be made on the stock markets. Between 1992–2003 Dexia sold over 700,000 lease-contracts to about 400,000 consumers. The product was invented in the mid 1990s. The idea was to make stock markets available for consumers in general and to not discriminate low incomes in particular. The 'bull market' in the 1990s made the product look like a risk-free investment. For a variety of tax-related reasons the product became very popular but by the end of 2001 the stock market crashed. The average loss per household with such a lease product amounted according to estimations of Consumentenbond to €3,000, but some households suffered losses of up to €50,000 and in exceptional cases even more. The case started rolling after the popular consumer TV show Radar broadcasted a TV-special about the product in early 2002. After the show an unusually high number (15,000–20,000) of disgruntled consumers contacted the TV show's service line. As a brand new owner of the acquired Dutch market leader, Dexia had to deal with the TV show and the subsequent complaints. After the TV show the consumers were redirected to a lawyer and a special purpose vehicle (SPV) was set up to represent the interests of the consumers who bought such a product. However, there was a large number of consumers (about 4,600) who were involved in individual proceedings. For various Dexia figures see also WAJP van den Reek and CLJM de Waal, 'De rechterlijke macht en financiële massaschade—De ervaringen van het team effectenlease van de rechtbank Amsterdam' (2009) *Trema* 275, 277.

[94] ibid.

[95] It required the hearing of witnesses in hundreds of cases.

[96] Federal Judicial Center, 'Manual for Complex Litigation' (n 6) 2004.

considerations; financial incentives issues; and costs and fees in mass disputes. Guidelines with respect to these issues have been published under the umbrella of the FJC as well.[97]

Another publication of the FJC is the pocket guide for judges managing class action litigation. It includes case management practices, suggestions for judicial review and administration of class settlements, especially regarding the disclosure of claims rates and actual payments to class members. Furthermore it contains an extensive coverage of the notice and claims processes.[98] The pocket guide refers to the Judges' Notice Checklist and Plain Language Guide that provides guidance with respect to the notice to class members.[99]

A task force of the Canadian Bar Association (CBA) has established judicial protocols consisting of best practices for judicial conduct in overlapping or multi-jurisdictional class actions. The protocols cover matters such as notice to class members, court-to-court communications and management of multi-jurisdictional class actions. The task force members were from the judiciary, as well as the plaintiff and defence class action bar.[100] The Canadian protocol is intended to mirror and support two similar judicial protocols related to multi-jurisdictional class actions established by the American Bar Association: the latter has adopted in 2011 as best practices the Protocol on Court-to-Court Communications in Canada-US Cross-Border Class Actions and a Notice Protocol: Coordinating Notice(s) to the Class(es) in Multijurisdictional Class Proceedings.[101] The protocols aim to facilitate coordination between the courts where possible while respecting judicial freedom and discretion.

Unlike the guidelines and protocols discussed, all of which state explicitly to be voluntary in nature, the guidelines established by the Amsterdam Court of Appeal in relation to the Dutch Act on Collective settlements (WCAM) have a less voluntary status.[102] These guidelines have to be followed by the Court and the parties. The Amsterdam Court of Appeal has exclusive jurisdiction to approve collective settlements and felt the need to establish guidelines for governing a case management conference after the filing of the petition, but prior to the fairness hearing. The WCAM did not provide for such a case management conference. During the case management conference the

[97] Hirsch and Sheehey (n 6).

[98] Rothstein and Willging (n 6).

[99] Federal Judicial Center, 'Judges' Class Action Notice and Claims Process Checklist and Plain Language Guide 2010' (n 6).

[100] See also www.cba.org/CBA/ClassActionsTaskForce/Main/.

[101] Available at: www.cba.org/cba/resolutions/pdf/11-03-A-bckd.pdf, and www.cba.org/CBA/resolutions/pdf/11-03-A-Annex03.pdf.

[102] The WCAM makes it possible that a settlement reached out of court and approved by the Court is binding on all group members who did not opt-out timely. See also Tzankova (n 12) 558–69.

Court and the petitioning parties discuss logistical matters and time lines related to the notices, the filing of an amended petition, additional exhibits or translations of materials required by the Court, the need for an interim ruling on specific issues such as jurisdiction, time line for objection etc. The evaluation of the WCAM has revealed that a case management conference is highly valued by the professionals involved and is essential for the proper instruction of the case. As a result, the Dutch legislature has amended the WCAM and codified the existing practice of a case management conference after the filing of a case.[103] The details however can still be found in the guidelines established by the Court of Appeal.

b. Judicial Training Programmes

Case management programmes designed specifically for the handling of class actions and complex litigation seem to exist in the United States. Although generally speaking various judicial training programmes exist within the EU, both at EU level and within the Member States, there seem to be no judicial training programmes focusing on the case management of mass disputes or complex litigation.

The situation with regard to arbitration institutes (such as the International Chamber of Commerce (ICC)) is similar to the European one although the ICC does provide guidelines on specific topics such as the managing of electronic document production, issues for arbitrators to consider when using experts, and issues to be considered when using IT in international arbitration.[104] So there is awareness about the importance of certain aspects of case management. Moreover, class arbitration is a relatively new and underdeveloped topic, which also explains the lack of training and other related initiatives.

c. Ad Hoc Judicial Task Forces: Designated Judges

As was already mentioned with regard to the *Dexia* case,[105] by 2007 the Amsterdam District Court was confronted with over 4,500 individual cases. The Court formed a special Judicial Task Force which at some point in the litigation consisted of a staff of nine full time judges and 35 clerks. The management problems originated from the fact that these individual consumers were represented by a large number of lawyers. Communications with the Court and arrangement of timetables were not easy to make. The judges assumed they could not aggregate claims because the factual circumstances

[103] Staatsblad 2013, 255.

[104] See www.iccwbo.org/about-icc/policy-commissions/arbitration/commission-rules,-reports-and-guidelines/.

[105] See n 94.

of the cases varied too much. At the same time, dealing with the claims on a case-by-case basis was not a realistic option, either because that would have taken years or because it would have had a negative impact on all other cases before that Court.

The Courts implemented a variety of case management measures. The first one was the draft of model judgments by three District Court judges to be used by judges throughout the country confronted with the resolution of similar cases. The models and templates were updated on a regular basis and integrated comments made by judges dealing with the cases. The models were meant as an aid and had no binding character. By the end of 2004, an informal working group was formed within the Amsterdam District Court consisting of about 10 members of the judiciary who became exclusively involved on both operational and judicial policy level in the resolution of the *Dexia* claims.

By the end of 2006, the number of individual cases had taken such proportions that the use of model judgments was not sufficient anymore, and a decision was taken to form an official Dexia Judicial Task Force (DJTF). The DJTF selected four test cases it considered representative for the various subgroups of claims and issued rulings in those cases making use of a formula for the calculation of damages, so parties in other cases would be able to figure out what the outcome in their case would be. That involved a margin of appreciation that would facilitate negotiations and out-of-court settlements. The approach attempted to streamline the resolution process, create uniformity and facilitate the out-of-court resolution of the case.

d. Claim Resolution Facilities

Knowhow with respect to the design and operation of claim resolution facilities resulting from court intervention is scarce,[106] and relates most of all to the design of the notice to be sent out to known and unknown group members.[107] As was observed in a study of the RAND Institute: 'a veil of secrecy can fall over class action litigation the moment the judge signs off on the agreement and ultimately, little information is available about how many class members actually received compensation and to what degree'.[108]

[106] FE McGovern, 'Distribution of Funds in Class Actions-Claims Administration' (2009) 35 *Journal of Corporation Law* 123, is one of the few publications addressing the issues of claim distribution and offering alternatives to cope with these issues.

[107] See www.kinsellamedia.com/Knowledge_Sharing.aspx, and www.rustconsulting.com/pdfs/ClaimFilingServices.pdf. See also TB Hilsee, SR Wheatman and GM Intrepido, 'Do You Really Want Me To Know My Rights? The Ethics Behind Due Process in Class Action Notice Is More Than Just Plain Language: A Desire to Actually Inform' (2005) 18 *Georgetown Journal of Legal Ethics* 1359.

[108] NM Pace and WB Rubenstein, 'How Transparent Are Case Outcomes: Empirical Research on the Availability of Class Action Claims Data', RAND Working Paper Series WR-599-ICJ, 2008.

e. Conclusion

The overview of existing mechanisms to facilitate and promote an effective management of mass disputes shows that the initiatives are stakeholder rather than legislature driven. Despite the differences between jurisdictions and contexts there are repeating themes such as notices and communication with the group, early case management conferences etc. The existing knowhow however is dispersed and—not surprisingly—tailored along the lines of the statutory provisions of the respective jurisdictions. The existing knowhow is not available in a functional format that would make it more easily accessible and applicable also in other jurisdictions or settings.

iv. Expert Meeting

The expert meeting aimed to bring together a small group of not more than 15 experts with diverse backgrounds: experts working in developed and developing countries around the globe,[109] operating within varying institutional settings: in-court/out-of-court/court-appointed, UN/international/national context, scholars/practitioners, high court/lower court judges. Given the relatively small number of experts, the preference was to invite experts who would combine multiple legal backgrounds and relevant expertise.[110]

Last minute cancellations were received from the experts from Canada, China and Argentina. This resulted in no experts attending from South America. In geographical terms Asia and Africa were underrepresented. In addition, securing the attendance of lower judges turned out to be a challenge for a variety of reasons. Some experts were not able to attend because of a heavy workload. Others experienced a language barrier.[111] Nevertheless, the background and expertise of the experts that came together was sufficiently diverse to cover the issues that needed to be addressed.

After the expert meeting additional desk research was conducted with regard to case management and CRFs. These results confirmed the results of the expert meeting and helped to further sharpen and develop the ideas about the follow-up of the project. Moreover, additional interviews with

[109] Including countries in Asia, North and South America, Africa, Europe and Australia.

[110] Let me offer a few examples. One expert's expertise related to civil procedure and arbitration and the functioning of multiple Asian legal cultures and jurisdictions (Singapore and Indonesia). Another expert had worked on judicial training programmes and civil justice reforms in several Asian jurisdictions (ao Laos and Cambodia), in addition to her experience as a Canadian practitioner dealing with mass disputes, and her academic experience with court-related resolution of mass disputes within the Australian legal system. Another expert combined South African judicial expertise in addition to his distinguished UN work, and a fourth expert had been working as a US court-appointed special master but also had relevant UN mass claim disputes experience.

[111] The expert meeting was conducted in English.

leaders of various institutions were conducted in order to identify potential partners and funding strategies to be able to properly address the next steps.

The outcome of the discussions during the expert meeting can be summarised as follows. There was agreement among the experts that it is best not to construct the project around the notion of 'universal' aspects or principles of management of mass disputes. In the first place, because the term 'universal' itself may have negative connotations in certain parts of the world and its use could, thus, affect the appeal of the project. More importantly, it is doubtful whether there are any truly universal aspects of management of mass disputes. It would be better to speak of 'uniformity' of some of the issues.

It was decided that it was better to think in terms of similarities in the way that mass disputes manifest themselves, and are or could be handled in smaller or larger groups of comparable countries or jurisdictions. For this reason, it was determined that it would be useful to start mapping the needs in terms of management of mass disputes in a variety of settings, which, it was expected, could show considerable differences. For example, the reliance on courts and the judiciary for the resolution of mass disputes in developing countries was considered problematic. The mapping of the 'state of the art' in terms of available knowledge of and experience with management of mass disputes should be deepened accordingly and may have to move beyond strictly adjudication-focused solutions towards out-of-court designed CRFs. Most importantly, to secure the success of the project, one should not forget the importance of the ownership of the project. It was considered of great importance to 'design' or organise this mapping project properly, involving relevant stakeholders.

There was agreement among the experts that, on the basis of the results of these mapping exercises, a toolkit on the management of mass disputes should be created. This toolkit should offer users a menu of options to deal with mass disputes and possible solutions to specific problems, rather than a strict set of rules. The options and solutions could be illustrated by means of case studies and should be viewed as a source of inspiration that enables users to develop a creative approach that is both effective and fitting in their context and domestic legal infrastructure. Therefore the collection of options should be called a 'toolkit' rather than 'best practices'.

The discussions made clear that some form of education on management of mass disputes would be necessary to allow beneficiaries to make good use of the toolkit, but that education alone would probably not be enough to bring about the necessary change in mentality or attitude to deal with mass disputes effectively and efficiently. Language barriers and insufficient IT infrastructure were pointed out as obvious barriers for a proper implementation in developing countries, and should be taken into account as well. The general feeling was that a training programme should be ideally developed after the mapping exercises as described above.

With respect to the substantive format of the toolkit, the experts endorsed the following approach and division of mass disputes: mass personal injury-property claims (catastrophes, product defect claims, environmental claims); financial claims (consumer claims, antitrust, securities, IP); rights (human rights, economic social rights, cultural rights, rights to property). In addition, when mapping the state-of-the-art with regard to the subsections, in-court and out-of-court processes, best practices, practical wisdom, case studies and solutions should be included in the toolkit.

In sum: the outcome of the expert meeting was that although the experts viewed such a comprehensive project as challenging and ambitious, there was a general agreement that there is a need for such a toolkit and that it would be good if the initiative could be taken forward keeping the various limitations and restrictions that were identified in mind. Furthermore, the experts agreed that it would be a good way to design the toolkit keeping in mind the different substantive fields of law and the fact that resolution could take place in and out of court, and in developed and developing countries. Last but not least, the toolkit should make sufficiently clear in its explanatory notes that it is merely that, a collection of good practices, options and solutions that can be selected and used at the discretion of the respective adjudicator that has to deal with mass disputes. That should be taken into account when designing the toolkit and drafting the explanatory notes to it.[112]

IV. FINAL REFLECTION

The harmonisation of civil procedure is an ambivalent topic for the European legislator because of the tension between the principle of procedural autonomy and the EC principle of effectiveness.[113] Defining common principles are then often offered as a next best approach. In the context of the resolution of mass disputes it turns out that even the identification and definition of common principles is a daunting task. Here a third option was discussed that eventually could lead to the definition of such common principles. That third option resembles a more pragmatic and functional approach to the issue. It argues that a first step could be the systemic and orderly collection of case management practices that proved useful in a defined category of cases, a toolkit that adjudicators could select or choose from when confronted with the resolution of a mass dispute. A toolkit that is unpretentious in its initial ambition, but has the potential to become a natural authority depending on the added value it manages to generate for its users.

[112] The Manual for Complex Litigation offers a good example in that respect

[113] See for a discussion of that tension IN Tzankova and MA Gramatikov, 'A Critical Note on two EU Principles: A Proceduralist View on the Draft CFR' in H-W Micklitz, L Niglia and S Waterhill (eds), *The Foundations of European Private Law* (Oxford, Hart Publishing, 2011).

13

Private Antitrust Damages Actions in the EU: Chronicle of an Attempted Golpe

ANDREA RENDA

I. INTRODUCTION

VERY OFTEN THE analysis of the impact of legal rules neglects or downplays the enforcement phase, and the behavioural aspects of compliance patterns. This is regrettable, since even apparently similar rules can produce widely diverging impacts, depending on how they are enforced and complied with. This is a key problem in European Union policy-making, since at the moment in which proposed legislation is evaluated, very little if anything is known about the mode of enforcement, and—relatedly—the ultimate effectiveness and efficiency of the proposed rules. As a result, even impact assessments never thought of enforcement for a long time.[1] The issue of enforcement arose in the EU debate particularly with respect to competition rules, most notably regarding the interplay between public and private enforcement. As a matter of fact, private enforcement of EC antitrust rules has been possible in the European Union since the 1957 Treaty of Rome, as Articles 101 and 102 TFEU (Treaty on the Functioning of the European Union) (ex 85 and 86) are directly applicable in Member States.[2] And indeed, since 1973 the European Commission has repeatedly expressed the view that private actions can provide a useful complement to its role as public enforcer.[3]

[1] Recently, A Renda, L Schrefler, G Luchetta, R Zavatta, *Assessing the Costs and Benefits of Regulation: Study for the European Commission* (Brussels, Centre for European Policy Studies, 2013), available at: ec.europa.eu/smart-regulation/impact/commission_guidelines/docs/131210_cba_study_sg_final.pdf, focused the attention on the lack of knowledge and tools in this field.

[2] Art 81(3) is directly applicable and enforceable only since 2004, after the modernisation of EC competition rules.

[3] WPJ Wils, 'Should Private Enforcement be Encouraged in Europe?' (2003) 26 *World Competition* 473, 478.

The role of private enforcement in complementing public enforcement by the European Commission and national competition authorities (NCAs) has been further stressed after the modernisation of EC competition law, and in particular after the Court of Justice of the European Union (CJEU) decisions in *Courage v Crehan*[4] and *Manfredi*.[5] The CJEU recognised that the full effectiveness of the Treaty would be put at risk if it were not open to any individual to claim damages for loss caused to him by conduct liable to restrict or distort competition. At the same time, the European Court of Justice (ECJ) held that there is an obligation to provide for effective means to exercise the right to compensation of damages suffered as a result of an antitrust infringement.

Against this background, private enforcement of antitrust laws has been found to be in a state of 'total underdevelopment' in a study completed in 2004 for the European Commission.[6] A few years later, Renda et al found that the situation had only marginally changed.[7] In Europe, public enforcement is by far the most common remedy for antitrust infringement, and statistics show that at most 10 per cent of antitrust litigation is initiated by a private claim before a national court.[8] On the contrary, in the United States the ratio of public to private enforcement is completely reversed: at least 90 per cent of legal actions for antitrust damages are initiated by private parties.[9]

Among the reasons that have caused such underdevelopment, most notable are Europe's exclusive focus on compensation rather than deterrence, which leads to the lack of punitive damages for competition infringements in the EU and in Member States; the absence of opt-out collective litigation and contingency fees in the European Union as opposed to the US; and the rather more complex and less plaintiff-friendly rules on access to evidence applied in Europe. Finally, legal uncertainty still exists as to whether and under what conditions private enforcement would be allowed before national courts: rules on the passing-on defence, existing civil procedure

[4] See eg Case C-453/99 *Courage Ltd v Bernard Crehan* [2001] ECR I-6297.

[5] Joined Cases C-295/04 and C-298/04 *Manfredi et al v Lloyd Adriatico Assicurazioni Spa e Assitalia Spa* [2006] ECR I-6619.

[6] D Waelbroeck, D Slater and G Even-Shoshan, *Study on the Conditions of Claims for Damages in Case of Infringement of EC Competition Rules: Comparative Report* (Brussels, Ashurst, 2004), available at ec.europa.eu/competition/antitrust/actionsdamages/comparative_report_clean_en.pdf.

[7] Waelbroeck, Slater and Even-Shoshan, ibid 27. See also the update provided by A Renda, J Peysner, AJ Riley, BJ Rodger, RJ Van Den Bergh, S Keske, R Pardolesi, E Leonardo Camilli and P Caprile, *Making Private Antitrust Damages Actions More Effective in the EU: Study for the European Commission* (Brussels, Centre for European Policy Studies, 2007), available at: ec.europa.eu/competition/antitrust/actionsdamages/files_white_paper/impact_study.pdf.

[8] See Renda et al (n 7).

[9] In 2004, 95.7% of all antitrust cases filed were private cases. See *Sourcebook of Criminal Justice Statistics Online*, Table 5.41.2004, available at: www.albany.edu/sourcebook/pdf/t5412004.pdf.

rules, the impact of previous decisions by the Commission or NCA on national courts and many other issues still wait for further clarification/ harmonisation at EU level.[10]

In 2013, the Commission finally tabled a proposal for a Directive on private antitrust damages actions, and the proposal completed the ordinary legislative procedure in November 2014. This chapter analyses the potential impact of the new Directive, with particular reference to the regulatory options that were available to the EU legislator. Section II below summarises the main findings of the economics literature in this field and shows the potential impact of private antitrust enforcement, whereas section III illustrates the evolution of the EU initiative on private antitrust enforcement up to the adoption of the recent Directive. Section IV concludes by comparing the potential welfare impact of an effective private antitrust enforcement system with the one expected from the current Directive.

II. THE IMPACT OF PRIVATE ANTITRUST ENFORCEMENT: INSIGHTS FROM LAW AND ECONOMICS

Why should the EU encourage more private antitrust damages actions in Europe? The overarching goals of enhanced private enforcement in the EU can be illustrated as follows:

— *Corrective justice*. An effective private enforcement secures that gains from anti-competitive conduct are transferred back to victims of anti-competitive conduct, and they are put in the same condition in which they would have been absent anti-competitive conduct—the so-called *Differenzmethode* or 'differential method'.[11]

— *Enhanced deterrence*. Currently antitrust law is not always entirely deterrent, since the probability of being sued and convicted is often low, and also since the resulting sanction is capped at 10 per cent of turnover. If one considers that the estimated detection rate of cartels is

[10] In some countries, the direct application of Art 101(3) could hinder the referral of antitrust cases to courts, since the uncertainty about the outcome is increased, see K Schmidt, 'Procedural Issues in the Private Enforcement of EC Competition Rules: Consideration Related to German Civil Procedure' in C-D Ehlermann and I Atanasiou (eds), *Effective Private Enforcement of EC Antitrust Law* (Oxford, Hart Publishing, 2003) 253.

[11] Many commentators argued that efficient incentives and optimal deterrence could be achieved by increasing the expected sanction imposed by public authorities. See eg RJ van den Bergh, W van Boom and M van der Woude, *The EC Green Paper on Damages Actions in Antitrust Cases: An Academic Comment* (Rotterdam, Erasmus University Rotterdam, 2006) 15, available at: ec.europa.eu/competition/antitrust/actionsdamages/files_green_paper_comments/ erasmus_university.pdf. Once the anti-competitive agreement is detected and sanctioned by the competition authority, it would be preferable to leave private parties to decide whether to sue or not for obtaining compensation and the annulment of the contractual agreement with their supplier. See also, on a more general note, AM Polinsky, 'Private Versus Public Enforcement of Fines' (1980) 9 *Journal of Legal Studies* 105.

approximately 13 per cent,[12] and that the average overcharge in cartels is estimated at approximately 25 per cent, it is clear that absent additional remedies it will often be more convenient to infringe and then, in isolated cases, pay a sanction than to exercise self-restraint in the first place. Private enforcement adds to the expected probability of being detected (whenever private parties have more information than public authorities), as well as to the expected sanction.

— *Ensuring that EU companies and citizens are put in similar conditions to exercise their right to damages and to conduct business on an equal footing throughout the territory of the EU.* Currently, Member States take very different approaches, with very different outcomes as regards the conditions for the exercise of the right to seek compensation of losses sustained as a result of antitrust infringements.[13]

— *Bringing competition law closer to the citizen.* Raising the awareness of citizens as regards the benefits of effective competition policy as well as their right to claim damage compensation in case of antitrust injury can contribute to the development of a solid culture of competition in Europe.[14]

— *Contributing to competitiveness, growth and jobs.* Since more competitive markets reduce allocative inefficiency by leading to greater output, lower prices and better quality, achieving the abovementioned goals would also contribute to European growth and employment, thus increasing EU competitiveness in light of the Lisbon goals.

However, as will be highlighted in the remainder of this chapter, setting up an effective antitrust damages action system is difficult and costly. A distinctive feature of enhanced antitrust private enforcement is that the benefits are most often very difficult to quantify. In jurisdictions where private damages actions are widespread, most of the cases settle before trial at undisclosed terms, whereas some of the upfront costs of private enforcement are easier to observe.[15] Also, the real deterrent effect of private antitrust damages actions is very difficult to measure, as it highly depends on undertakings' subjective expectations on the probability of detection, the probability of conviction and the expected exposure to damage awards.

An important risk of enhanced private enforcement lies in the potential for increased frivolous suits, as well as in a greater likelihood of Type I errors in adjudication, as courts are not always optimally placed to appreciate the

[12] Renda et al (n 7).

[13] Waelbroeck, Slater and Even-Shoshan (n 6).

[14] See eg, Case C-453/99 *Courage Ltd v Bernard Crehan* [2001] ECR I-6297.

[15] See eg IR Segal and MD Whinston, 'Public v Private Enforcement of Antitrust Law: A Survey', Stanford Law and Economics Olin Working Paper No 335/2006, available at: ssrn.com/abstract=952067.

features of a case, and may be captured by claimants into unmeritorious suits.[16]

Another risk of an ill-conceived system of damages actions is that of potential negative consequences of growth and employment, especially since increasing damage awards may face the limit of firms' ability to pay.[17] Langus and Motta show that stock markets react to news of a dawn raid, an infringement Decision and the Court of Justice judgment upholding the Commission's Decision, by reducing the firm's market value on average by respectively two per cent, 3.3 per cent and 1.3 per cent. Therefore, the successful prosecution of a firm for illegal behaviour might decrease its market value by more than six per cent.[18]

This, of course, does not mean that antitrust enforcement negatively affects market forces: to the contrary, if markets develop expectations that the convicted firm's profits will decrease overtime, this means that antitrust action is effective. At the same time, however, it is very important to ensure that private antitrust enforcement does not lead to a high amount of false convictions (Type I errors), as the mistakenly convicted firm would face important shortcomings in the market where it operates.

[16] Examples of strategic use of antitrust law are frequent in the economic literature, and are reported, inter alia by: WJ Baumol and JA Ordover, 'Use of Antitrust to Subvert Competition' (1985) 28 *Journal of Law and Economic* 247; W Breit and KG Elzinga, 'Private Antitrust Enforcement: The New Learning' (1985) 28 *Journal of Law and Economics* 405; WF Shughart II, *Antitrust Policy and Interest Group Politics* (New York, Quorum Books, 1990); JF Brodley, 'Antitrust Standing in Private Merger Cases: Reconciling Private Incentives and Public Enforcement Goals' (1995) 94 *Michigan Law Review* 1; S Shavell, 'The Fundamental Divergence between the Private and the Social Motive to Use the Legal System' (1997) 26 *Journal of Legal Studies* 575; RP McAfee and N Vakkur, 'The Strategic Abuse of Antitrust Laws' (2004) 1 *Journal of Strategic Management Education* 1; RP McAfee, HM Mialon and SH Mialon, 'Private v Public Antitrust Enforcement: A Strategic Analysis' (2008) 92 *Journal of Public Economics* 1863. Also the opposite is possible—that judges issue a mistaken judgment in favour of the defendant, leading to a Type II error. To clarify what we mean by Type I and II errors: Type I errors are defined as false condemnations, ie cases in which a court condemns a conduct that was not anti-competitive, or mandates compensation of harm for which there was no causation; a Type II error is defined as a false acquittal, ie a case in which a court fails to condemn a conduct, which was anti-competitive. One of the first papers to import this terminology was AA Fisher and RH Lande, 'Efficiency Considerations in Merger Enforcement' (1983) 71 *California Law Review* 1582.

[17] This was observed, among others, by R Kraakman, 'Corporate Liability Strategies and the Costs of Legal Controls' (1984) 93 *Yale Law Journal* 857, C Craycraft, JL Craycraft and JC Gallo, 'Antitrust Sanctions and a Firm's Ability to Pay' (1997) 12 *Review of Industrial Organisation* 171, and WPJ Wils, 'Is Criminalization of EU Competition Law the Answer?' (2005) 28 *World Competition* 117.

[18] G Langus and M Motta, 'The Effect of EU Antitrust Investigations and Fines on a Firm's Valuation', CEPR Discussion Paper No 6176/2007, available at http://www.cepr.org/pubs/dps/DP6176.asp. See M Motta, 'On Cartel Deterrence and Fines in the EU', written for and presented at the Meeting of the Economic Advisory Group on Competition Policy at the European Commission, Brussels, 14 September 2007. An earlier paper that used event studies analysis to infer the impact of antitrust enforcement on the stock market valuation of a firm is JM Bizjak and JL Coles, 'The Effect of Private Antitrust Litigation on the Stock-Market Valuation of the Firm (1995) 85 *American Economic Review* 436.

A. The 'Optimal Deterrence' Approach to Antitrust Enforcement

The law and economics literature has extensively explored the relative merits and the potential complementarity between public and private enforcement since the seminal contribution of Gary Becker and George Stigler, who argued that 'private attorneys general' motivated by their self-interest can enjoy an implicit advantage over public officials—rewarded by a fixed salary—and can thus remedy government failure leading to inaction in a number of antitrust cases.[19] This seminal contribution also led to the application of the theory of optimal sanctions to the problem of antitrust enforcement. Becker and Stigler also anticipated the problem of over-enforcement and 'race to damage', but observed that these problems did not affect the general idea that private enforcement could prove as efficient as public enforcement.

This conclusion was challenged by Landes and Posner,[20] but also Schwartz[21] and Posner,[22] mostly highlighting the risk that very high damage awards—required by the need to set optimal sanctions—would encourage an excessive number of plaintiffs to start competing for the damage award, thus leading to excessive litigation, over-deterrence and a consequent waste of resources. These observations shed more light on the inherent limits of private enforcement through optimal sanctions, and paved the way to a debate on the potential over-deterring effect of private damages actions. The resulting conclusion, however, did not imply that private enforcement ought to be abandoned, but highlighted the problem of striking the delicate balance between public and private enforcement.

In this respect, A Mitchell Polinsky observed that the risk of over-deterrence as illustrated by Landes and Posner is not so significant, since potential plaintiffs would only act in cases where the reward available was greater than the costs of enforcement.[23] Again, as noted by Roach and Trebilcock, this did not imply that private enforcement had to be abandoned: it meant that private enforcement is particularly efficient when the rewards available are greater than their enforcement costs. In all other cases, public enforcement could remedy the failure in the 'market for damage awards'.[24]

[19] GS Becker and GJ Stigler, 'Law Enforcement, Malfeasance and Compensation of Enforcers' (1974) 3 *Journal of Legal Studies* 1. See also K Roach and MJ Trebilcock, 'Private Enforcement of Competition Laws' (1997) 34 *Osgoode Hall Law Journal* 462.

[20] WM Landes and RA Posner, 'The Independent Judiciary in an Interest-Group Perspective', NBER Working Paper No w0110/1975, available at: ssrn.com/abstract=260301.

[21] W Schwartz, *Private Enforcement of the Antitrust Laws: An Economic Critique* (Washington, AEI Studies, 1981).

[22] See RA Posner, *Economic Analysis of Law* 2nd edn (Boston, Little Brown & Co, 4th edn 1992).

[23] AM Polinsky, 'Private Versus Public Enforcement of Fines' (1980) 9 *Journal of Legal Studies* 105.

[24] Roach and Trebilcock (n 19).

This early debate can help us shape our analysis. First, private enforcement must be looked at under the lens of rational individual behaviour—that is plaintiffs will decide to sue for damages only after a cost–benefit assessment of the merit of such action. Second, the imperfect information and limited resources available to public authorities are the main grounds for envisaging a role for private Attorney Generals in enforcing antitrust rules. Third, there is a limit to the magnitude of the damage award, that is the risk that litigation costs would significantly increase and the risk of over-deterrence, which could jeopardise the sustainability of the enforcement system, resulting in a misallocation of resources and a net loss to society.

Later contributions in the literature have further clarified some of the potential advantages of private enforcement. These include informational advantages, proximity to the violation and also increased legal certainty over the contours of antitrust law.[25] At the same time, the growing emphasis on potential inefficiencies of public enforcement has tilted the balance towards private enforcement. Arguments that move in this direction include the risk of capture of public authorities by private interest groups; inefficiencies linked to the behaviour and incentives of 'Weberian' bureaucrats often criticised in the 'new public management' and 'reinventing government' streams of literature; lengthy administrative procedures, the confirmation bias that affects public enforcers; the 'hindsight bias' or path-dependency of public enforcers; the desire to progress in career, etc.[26] In this respect, supplemental private enforcement can improve the accountability of public enforcers, by ensuring an alternative means of scrutiny in cases where public authorities arbitrarily decide not to proceed with an investigation.

Moreover, more effective private enforcement has an impact on deterrence by significantly affecting both the so-called 'availability bias' and challenging the 'overconfidence bias' as described by Wils.[27] In this respect,

[25] GL Priest and B Klein, 'The Selection of Disputes for Litigation' (1984) 13 *Journal of Legal Studies* 1–55.

[26] See for example: JC Coffee, 'Understanding the Plaintiff's Attorney: The Implications of Economic Theory for Private Enforcement of Law through Class and Derivative Actions' (1986) 86 *Columbia Law Review* 669; JC Coffee, 'The Regulation of Entrepreneurial Litigation: Balancing Fairness and Efficiency in the Large Class Action' (1987) 54 *The University of Chicago Law Review* 877; WPJ Wils, 'The Combination of the Investigative and Prosecutorial Function and the Adjudicative Function in EC Antitrust Enforcement: A Legal and Economic Analysis' (2004) 27 *World Competition* 201; and T Eger and P Weise, 'Limits to the Private Enforcement of Antitrust Law', German Working Papers in Law and Economics 2007/3, available at: www.bepress.com/gwp/default/vol2007/iss2/art3.

[27] WPJ Wils, 'Optimal Antitrust Fines: Theory and Practice' (2006) 29 *World Competition* 183, 196. Overconfidence bias leads prospective infringers to overestimate the gain and underestimate the probability of detection and punishment; whereas the availability bias leads individuals to 'rely disproportionately on those incidents which can easily be brought to mind, because they are recent, happened close to them, or were well publicized' (ibid). See also T Ulen and RB Korobkin, 'Law and Behavioral Science: Removing the Rationality Assumption from Law and Economics' (2000) 88 *California Law Review* 1051, and JI Krueger and DC Funder, 'Toward a Balanced Social Psychology: Causes, Consequences and Cures for the Problem-Seeing Approach to Social Behavior and Cognition' (2004) 27 *Behavioral and Brain Sciences* 1.

achieving effective—thus, well-conceived—private enforcement may be construed as a case of 'de-biasing through law'.[28] Finally, private enforcement can to a certain extent solve moral hazard problems, by leading potential offenders to take increased account of the consequences of anti-competitive actions when considering whether to undertake them.[29]

Private enforcement is superior to public enforcement in achieving corrective justice. Although sanctions imposed by public authorities could in principle be reallocated to society as a whole, direct damage awards can serve the goal of *restitutio in integrum*, that is putting victims of antitrust injury in the same condition in which they would have been, had the antitrust violation not occurred. In this respect, private enforcement can be seen as a reflection of antitrust injury as a tort law matter.

On the other hand, many authors also highlighted the potential risks connected with a replacement of public with private enforcement. According to Prichard, factors such as economies of scale in some types of investigation, superior investigative tools, the absence of appropriability, and the simplicity and flexibility of the fine represent efficiency advantages of public enforcement.[30] Furthermore, some authors see private enforcement as potentially undermining the effectiveness of public enforcement policies. The overlap between private goals and public policy objectives can in some cases lead to inconsistency of policy-making, and this problem is likely to be observed at EU level under the decentralised approach adopted by Regulation 1/2003.[31]

A possible way to maximise the effectiveness of antitrust while minimising the use of resources is by achieving the so-called 'optimal deterrence' in public enforcement. This requires that the expected sanction faced by undertakings wishing to adopt an anti-competitive conduct is just sufficient to deter that conduct without deterring also purely legal actions. If this is possible, then all illegal actions will be deterred, and there would not be any need for private enforcement. William Landes showed that to achieve optimal deterrence the damages from an antitrust violation should be equal to the violation's 'net harm to others', divided by the probability of detection.[32]

[28] See C Jolls and CR Sunstein, 'De-biasing Through Law', University of Chicago Law and Economics Olin Working Paper No 225/2005, available at: ssrn.com/abstract_id=590929.

[29] See, eg, Segal and Whinston (n 15).

[30] JRS Prichard, 'Private Enforcement and Class Actions' in JRS Prichard, WT Stanbury and TA Wilson (eds), *Canadian Competition Policy: Essays in Law and Economics* (Toronto, Butterworths, 1979) 237.

[31] Reg 1/2003 of 16 December 2002 on the implementation of the rules on competition laid down in Arts 81 and 82 of the Treaty [2003] OJ L 1/1. See JL Mashaw, 'Private Enforcement of Public Regulatory Provisions: The "Citizen Suit"' (1975) 4 *Class Action Reports* 29, 33.

[32] WM Landes, 'An Economic Analysis of the Courts' (1971) 14 *Journal of Law and Economics* 61; WM Landes, 'Optimal Sanctions for Antitrust Violations' (1983) 50 *University of Chicago Law Review* 652, 666–68. The theory of optimal deterrence has become widespread also amongst EU scholars—see eg, N Garoupa, 'A Note on Private Enforcement and Type I Error' (1997) 17 *International Review of Law and Economics* 423; C Harding and J Joshua, *Regulating Cartels in Europe: A Study of Legal Control of Corporate Delinquency* (Oxford, Oxford University Press, 2004); Wils (n 17); EL Camilli, 'Optimal Fines in Cartel Cases and the Actual EC Policy' (2006) 29 *World Competition* 575.

A decisional model based on benefit–cost analysis has been developed by many scholars, especially as regards the decision whether to form a (or join an existing) cartel. This can be described both in plain words, and by means of a simple formula. The underlying idea is that a firm will decide whether to create or join a cartel agreement only when the benefit is perceived as superior to the expected cost. As shown in the formula below, firms will expect to bear costs ($E(C)$), which include prospective fines and damage awards discounted at present value, and will compare such costs with the private benefit from participating in the cartel. The latter figure will be determined by the affected sales (AS) times the size of the mark-up on the competitive price (M). In summary, the firm will choose to create (or join) the cartel only if $E(C) < M \cdot AS$.[33] In the simplest model,[34] the expected cost will equal the expected fine or damage award times the probability that the cartel is discovered and convicted. A further refinement of this analysis implies that other prospective costs are taken into account, most notably prospective legal expenses and reputational ('stigmatisation') effects. In addition, the likelihood of settlement and the expected reduction of the sanction following a settlement transaction should be taken into account.

In the simple version of the model, the optimal fine would have to make the potential wrongdoer indifferent between joining a cartel and not joining. In other words, the expected cost should equal the expected benefit. This requires that the sanction F be equal to the expected benefit divided by the probability of conviction.

$$F = (markup * affected\ sales)/(probability\ of\ detection * probability\ of\ conviction)$$

More generally, when the probability of detection/conviction is low, the optimal sanction has to be remarkably higher than actual harm in order to satisfy the above optimality condition.[35] This has led some commentators to argue that:

— *Fines should be set at a very high level* in order to efficiently deter anti-competitive actions: Optimal sanctions estimated empirically in the literature were often several times higher than the actual overcharge. For example, Werden and Simon estimated that the optimal fine for the average cartel convicted by the Department of Justice from 1975 to 1980 was 111 times higher than the fine actually paid by the cartelists

[33] JM Connor, 'global Cartels Redux: The Amino Acid Lysine Antitrust Litigation 1996', 2007, available at: papers.ssrn.com/sol3/papers.cfm?abstract_id=1408070.

[34] As in RA Posner, *Antitrust Law* 2nd edn (Chicago, The University of Chicago Press, 2001).

[35] The simple formula shown here assumes that would-be cartelists are risk-neutral. The economic literature is split on this issue: on the one hand, Landes, 'Optimal Sanctions for Antitrust Violations' (n 32) and Posner (n 34) assume that the criminals are risk-neutral. As elaborated in AM Polinsky and S Shavell, 'The Economic Theory of Public Enforcement of Law' (2000) 38 *Journal of Economic Literature* 45, a more comprehensive approach to optimal deterrence requires attention to the risk attitudes of perpetrators.

in their sample;[36] whereas Gallo et al found that actual US fines were only 0.043 per cent of the optimal fine in their sample of 250 cartels for the period 1955–1993, and rose to approximately one per cent after 1985;[37] Wils finds that the optimal fine would reach 150 per cent of affected sales, and within the range of 5.0 to 7.5 times the overcharge;[38] Schinkel concludes that in the EU optimal fines would need at least an 83 per cent probability of detection, which is way greater than what empirical observation suggests.[39] Motta estimates that the minimum level of fine (relative to market turnover) necessary to deter cartel formation (if the competitive mark-up is 50 per cent and the demand elasticity is 0.6) is around 68 per cent per year of the relevant market turnover of the firm.[40] And Combe, under rather conservative assumptions, calculates the optimal sanction as being 6.6 times higher than the loss of consumer surplus, or—for a five year cartel—300 per cent of turnover![41]

— If the probability of detection cannot be raised beyond certain thresholds, then *optimal fines are inconsistent with ceilings* currently imposed on fines on both sides of the Atlantic; this includes: The 1987 US Sentencing Guidelines for criminal price fixing, which impose an upper limit of 80 per cent of the guilty firm's US affected sales;[42] the updated EC fining guidelines, which do not overcome 30 per cent of affected sales even in cases of 'gravity' and maintain, in any case, the cap of 10 per cent of the convicted firm's global turnover; and the Japanese

[36] GJ Werden and MJ Simon, 'Why Price Fixers Should Go to Prison' (1987) 32 *Antitrust Bulletin* 917, make several simplifying assumptions: the average M is at least 0.10, p is 0.10, the average duration of collusion is 74 months, and that the average interest rate is 10%.

[37] JC Gallo, KG Dau-Schmidt, JL Craycraft and CJ Parker, 'Criminal Penalties Under the Sherman Act: A Study in Law and Economics' (1994) 16 *Research in Law and Economics* 25, use a variant of the optimal sanction model, where a term ($AS \cdot 0.5M \cdot \varepsilon$) that represents the deadweight loss due to price fixing. They assume a monopoly pricing equilibrium, linear demand, a 10% mean overcharge, unitary elasticity ($\varepsilon = 1$), and a 15% detection probability. These assumptions imply that the deadweight loss is 5% of the income transfer, that Becker's net harm from price fixing is 0.105 of AS, and that F* is 0.70 of AS.

[38] Wils (n 17) applies model [6] in the context of cartels prosecuted in the European Union (EU). He assumes a 20% cartel overcharge, duration of five years, and a 33% probability of detection.

[39] MP Schinkel and J Rüggeberg, 'Consolidating Antitrust Damages in Europe: A Proposal for Standing in line with Efficient Private Enforcement', 2006, available at: ssrn.com/paper=903282 assumes a 25% overcharge, five year duration, fines of single damages, and a 30% annual depreciation rate; he also assumes that full amnesty and all cooperation discounts are granted by the EC.

[40] Motta (n 18).

[41] E Combe, 'Quelle Sanctions contre les cartels? Une Perspective Economique' (2006) *Revue Internationale De Droit Économique* 9.

[42] However, evidence suggests that half or less of all historical cartels exhibit long run price effects below 25%. See RH Lande and JM Connor, 'How High Do Cartels Raise Prices? Implications for Reform of the Antitrust Sentencing Guidelines' (2005) 80 *Tulane Law Review* 513.

cartel policy, where the Japanese Fair Trade Commission (JFTC) never overcame six per cent of Japanese affected commerce.

— *The setting of an optimal fine is hardly feasible*, also because too high fines will face the limit of the defendant's ability to pay. In particular, Werden and Simon observe that the optimal fine would lead several firms to bankruptcy.[43] Wils also claims that '[i]f such high fines were really imposed, many of the companies concerned would be forced into bankruptcy'.[44] Also, Craycraft et al found that in the US only 42 per cent of the firms would have been able to pay the optimal fine without falling into bankruptcy, and only 26 per cent by means of the highest measure of the operating funds.[45]

In other words, the theory of optimal fines depicts a world in which the impossibility to achieve a reasonably high probability of detection leads to the setting of too high fines, which would prove too burdensome for infringers that are actually convicted. In this respect, *private enforcement effectively acts as a complement to public enforcement in a second-best context*, where the optimal solution is impossible to achieve. Private enforcement contributes to more effective deterrence by: (i) Increasing the probability of detection p; and (ii) adding (or replacing) damage awards to the prospective fines imposed by public enforcers—depending on whether a private suit is stand-alone or follow-on.[46]

B. Assessing Incentives from the Victim's Viewpoint

In order to assess whether different policy initiative on private antitrust damages actions will stimulate (meritorious) lawsuits, it is important to find out whether the legal system puts potential claimants in a situation in which incentives to sue are sufficient to embark in litigation process. The plaintiff's incentive to sue has been framed in the literature as the result of a cost–benefit comparison, or as an investment decision.[47] Accordingly, such a decision is the result of a rational initiative undertaken by individuals or companies seeking a positive payoff.[48] Assume that the prospective costs

43 Werden and Simon (n 36).

44 Wils (n 27) 19.

45 Craycraft, Craycraft and Gallo (n 17) 175–76. The authors find that 95–100% of all firms fined for price fixing 1955–93 were able to pay their fines.

46 See Office of Fair Trading, 'Private Actions in Competition Law: Effective Redress for Consumers and Business Recommendations from the Office of Fair Trading', November 2007, OFT916resp, 13, s 3.4.

47 See B Cornell, 'The Incentive to Sue: An Option-Pricing Approach' (1990) 19 *Journal of Legal Studies* 173.

48 Several authors have contributed to the development of this literature, starting with Landes, 'An Economic Analysis of the Courts' (n 32). The model was then refined by J Gould, 'The Economics of Legal Conflicts' (1973) 2 *Journal of Legal Studies* 279, RA Posner,

for a plaintiff are the opportunity cost of time spent in litigation (OC_t) or settlement (OC_s), costs of access to courts (AC) and—depending on the fee allocation rule chosen—legal costs for litigation (LC_t) and settlement (LC_s). Expected rewards are the damages claimed (D), times the probability of winning at trial (w), and the expected settlement amount (S), times the probability to settle the claim before trial ($1 - p$).[49] The plaintiff will then sue whenever

$$p[wD - (OC_t + LC_t + AC)] + (1 - p)[S - (OC_s + LC_s)] > 0$$

where the opportunity cost of litigation is lower under settlement than under full litigation, due to shorter time ($OC_s < OC_t$); the same is for legal expenses ($LC_s < LC_t$); and for the total amount compensated, which tends to be a fraction of the total damage award when the case is settled before trial ($S < D$).[50] In other words, the plaintiff's net expected reward from filing suit has two main components: The reward from settlement and the reward from trial. The relative weight of these two components, of course, depends on the (perceived) likelihood of settlement and trial.

Based on the formula above, we can consider the impact that different procedural rules or damage multiples can exert on the plaintiff's incentive to sue. For example:

- Multiple damages increase the incentive to sue, as it increases D.
- A reversal of the burden of proof in favour of the plaintiff increases the incentives to sue, alongside with w.
- A one-way fee-shifting rule increases incentives to sue, as it removes LC_t and AC from the equation.
- All the rules that increase the probability of victory for the plaintiff (w) or increase the prospective cost of the defendant, in turn, have the effect of increasing the probability that the case will settle ($1-p$), and also the settlement amount (S).
- All means of funding private litigation increase the probability that the plaintiff will sue, of course, as they would reduce or eliminate LC_t and AC.

The plaintiff's decision to sue depends *in primis* on her subjective perception of p, w and S. With imperfect information, two cases may arise. First, the

'An Economic Approach to Legal Procedure and Judicial Administration' (1973) 2 *Journal of Legal Studies* 399, and S Shavell, 'The Social Versus the Private Incentive to Bring Suit in a Costly Legal System' (1982) 11 *Journal of Legal Studies* 333.

[49] The expected reward can also be different from the damage award. For example, it could be a settlement that takes place at some time prior to the trial, or include an increase in the plaintiff's business reputation.

[50] We assume that both the opportunity cost of litigation and the legal fees paid for litigating the case are greater than in the case of settlement. Consideration of time is also important, as the legal fees are to be paid upfront, whereas damages are awarded after the case has been adjudicated or settled.

plaintiff might overestimate the probability of winning at trial (w). For example, if the plaintiff incorrectly interprets the defendant's conduct, she may expect the judge to award damages; however, especially in cases where a rule of reason applies, the judge may find redeeming efficiencies and decide in favour of the defendant. Second, the plaintiff might mistakenly estimate the probability of settling the case ($1-p$). This can occur, for example, whenever the plaintiff expects the defendant to agree on the likelihood of plaintiff victory; whereas in reality, the defendant expects a different outcome—that is, the parties are both optimistic on the trial outcome. Accordingly, the defendant's expected reaction is important for the plaintiff's decision. If the defendant signals her nature of 'tough negotiator', the plaintiff may overestimate p, and may refrain from suing in order to avoid a costly and lengthy litigation.

Against this background, there are many ways in which claims can be facilitated. These include:

i) Making legal actions cheaper for the plaintiffs;
ii) increasing the prospective reward for plaintiffs, for example by multiplying damages;
iii) making evidence more easily available for plaintiffs at the pre-trial stage;
iv) allowing claims to be brought on a representative or collective basis;
v) facilitating follow-on actions by establishing previous public decisions as prima facie evidence in favour of the plaintiff.

As will be explained in section II below, the European Commission has initially considered almost all these options, and ended up discarding most of them in its final proposed Directive.

C. The Need to Avoid Frivolous and Unmeritorious Suits

One key concern shown by the European Commission during its decade-long debate on private antitrust enforcement has been the need to avoid generating a 'litigation culture', but rather creating a 'compensation culture'. The litigation culture, often attributed to the US legal system, is chiefly due to the existence of legal rules that are so plaintiff-friendly, that even plaintiffs that are not victims might consider suing for damages in order to secure advantages. Suits with negative expected value have been almost ignored in the early literature on suit, settlement and litigation incentives. Rosenberg and Shavell, Bebchuk, Katz and Bone shed more light on this issue, mostly relying on game theoretical models.[51]

[51] See D Rosenberg and S Shavell, 'A Model in Which Suits Are Brought for Their Nuisance Value' (1985) 5 *International Review of Law and Economics* 3; LA Bebchuk, 'Litigation and Settlement under Imperfect Information' (1984) 15 *RAND Journal of Economics* 404;

First, as regards fee allocation rules, a loser-pays rule such as the one applied—with variants—in EU countries seems to strike a more satisfactory balance than the 'each party bears her own cost' rule, as the two-way shifting mechanism discourages unmeritorious claims. Coupling the loser-pays rule with contingency fees would not create problems in this respect: as a matter of fact, the plaintiff will pay legal expenses (to her lawyer) if she wins, and will pay legal costs (to the defendant's lawyer) also if she loses.[52] Conditional fees, in this respect, may act as a slight disincentive since, if the plaintiff loses, she will have to pay the fees of both parties' lawyers. In this respect, coupled with the loser-pays, contingency fees may perform better than conditional fee agreements—in neither case would the plaintiff have an incentive to file unmeritorious suits, but in the latter case the plaintiff may be discouraged from initiating a damage action.[53] Therefore, the practical application of the loser-pays rule may create the opposite problem, that is of discouraging meritorious suits.[54]

Second, under full-fledged one-way fee-shifting and contingency fees, plaintiffs are greatly encouraged to file suit, as they would be fully indemnified from legal expenses. This situation will certainly lead to significant incentives to file both meritorious and unmeritorious suits. Such a finding is of course mitigated by the lawyers' decision: even under one-way fee-shifting, purely frivolous suits with low probability of success will be accepted by a lawyer only if they exhibit a significant potential for a positive settlement; otherwise, the lawyer will anticipate that the suit has a very low expected value for her, and will not accept the case. In this respect, contingency fees do not necessarily increase nuisance suits if compared with hourly fees: when the lawyer is more informed than the plaintiff about the relative merit of the case, she may suggest that the case is litigated and will charge fixed hourly fees even if she realises that the case has a negative expected value for the client.

Third, multiple damages can create incentives to file unmeritorious suits, especially if coupled with 'aggressive' fee allocation and legal cost rules. Especially in non-cartel cases, the threat of frivolous suits becomes significant and socially harmful, if plaintiffs face a significant windfall from punitive damages.[55] Besides cases in which multiple damages serve a clear

and LA Bebchuk, 'Negative Expected Value Suits' (1998) NBER Working Paper No W6474. See also A Katz, 'The Effect of Frivolous Lawsuits on the Settlement of Litigation' (1990) 10 *International Review of Law and Economics* 3; and RG Bone, 'Modelling Frivolous Suits' (1997) 145 *University of Pennsylvania Law Review* 519.

[52] LW Feuerstein, 'Two-Way Fee Shifting on Summary Judgment or Dismissal: An Equitable Deterrent to Unmeritorious Lawsuits' (1995) 23 *Pepperdine Law Review* 125, 128.

[53] Depends on whether the total legal costs change under the two arrangements.

[54] HM Kritzer, 'The English Rule' (1992) 78 *ABA Journal* 54.

[55] See, inter alia C Sharkey, 'Punitive Damages as Societal Damages' (2003) 113 *The Yale Law Journal* 347.

compensatory purpose—for example in absence of pre-judgment interest—all cases in which the expected value for the plaintiff is greater than the actual harm suffered can lead to frivolous suits. This also applies to negative expected value suits, where the plaintiff or her lawyer manage to settle successfully for a positive amount prior to trial.

Fourth, the impact of contingency fees on frivolous suits is ambiguous, and mostly depends on the risk attitude of the plaintiff, the plaintiff's lawyer, the information held by both subjects, and of course the merit of the case and the corresponding probability of victory at trial. As a general note, contingency fees may encourage frivolous suits when: (i) The plaintiff's lawyer is less informed than the plaintiff; (ii) the lawyer is optimistic about the probability of settling the case before trial; (iii) the plaintiff is shielded from the obligation to pay the defendant's legal costs.

Finally, the risk of frivolous suit can be effectively reduced if fee-shifting rules are corrected by ad hoc arrangements. These include procedural rules that force the losing plaintiff to pay the defendant's legal costs if the judge finds that the case was frivolous; and offer-of-judgment rules (like the US Federal Rule 68 and Part 36 of the English Civil Procedure rules), under which the defendant can make a settlement offer to the plaintiff; if the offer is rejected and the plaintiff loses at trial, then the defendant must be indemnified for legal expenses.[56]

Another possibility is adjusting pleading standards to avoid suits based only on anecdotal or barely circumstantial evidence. An example from US practice is the *Twombly* decision,[57] which was dismissed at the pleading stage by the District Court since evidence brought by the plaintiff was found consistent with pro-competitive, profit-seeking behaviour of the defendant Bell Atlantic. This decision was later reversed by the Second Circuit, as it had allegedly established a narrower pleading standard than the one provided by the Federal Rules of Civil Procedure. The Supreme Court decided in favour of heightened standards for allegations of conscious parallelism, and thus overturned the pleading standard in force since *Conley v Gibson*:[58] This will make dismissal prior to discovery more likely in the future.[59] As a result, pleading standards indeed can significantly affect the incentive to file suit and the likelihood of frivolous suits.

[56] See AW Katz, 'Indemnity of Legal Fees' in B Bouckaert and G de Geest (eds), *Encyclopedia of Law and Economics, Volume V: The Economics of Crime and Litigation* (Cheltenham, Edward Elgar, 2000).

[57] *Bell Atlantic Corp v Twombly* 550 US 544 (2007).

[58] *Conley v Gibson* 355 US 41 (1957).

[59] KN Hylton, 'Property Rules and Liability Rules, Once Again' (2006) 2 *Review of Law and Economics* 137.

D. An Analysis of the Potential Welfare Impact of Enhanced Private Enforcement in the EU

The complex picture outlined above reveals the mixed impact that enhanced private enforcement can exert on overall welfare. As demonstrated by Renda et al:[60]

— If private enforcement is effectively designed, the probability of detection of an illegal conduct increases, the accuracy of fact-finding increases and deterrence also increases. This, in turn, would increase workload for national courts, increase trial costs for private parties, increase the competitiveness of markets overall, and reduce the potential for strategic abuse of antitrust laws.

— If private enforcement is relatively more efficient than public enforcement, this leads private antitrust damages actions to gradually outnumber public enforcement cases. However, if private enforcement is not effectively designed, this can lead to an undue multiplication of private actions and an over-deterrence effect on firms.

— If private enforcement fosters strategic abuse of antitrust laws, this can lead to increased Type I errors (false convictions), and thus to inadequate investment, unmeritorious (strategic) suits and unmeritorious settlements.[61]

As a result, the potential impact of private enforcement on social welfare is not easy to determine, and can be said to depend on several factors, including:

— *The probability that an illegal action is deterred*: such probability should increase alongside with enhanced private enforcement, as the detection rates for anti-competitive conduct increase in jurisdictions that allow for private rights of action. However, the incentive to sue for private parties heavily depends on procedural rules introduced.

— *The probability that an illegal action is undertaken, but is then overturned by the court:* such probability should increase with both private and public enforcement, as private parties often hold superior information on the occurrence of anti-competitive behaviour, due to knowledge of the market and proximity to the damage. They can therefore sue for damages in their own interest, at the same time defending the public interest in maximising competition and its beneficial effects on the market. The likelihood of Type II errors (false acquittals) may encourage firms to undertake illegal actions, even if they know that they will be sued before a court or prosecuted by a NCA. For this reason, we consider the probability of conviction (after legal action has been

[60] Renda et al (n 7).

[61] Wils (n 3).

taken) as a separate variable from the probability of detection (the mere fact of being prosecuted for anti-competitive behaviour).

— *The probability that a legal action is deterred*: this also potentially increases when private enforcement is coupled with measures aimed at encouraging access to justice by competitors, direct and indirect purchasers, as well as consumers. The threat of nuisance suits and excessive litigation can act as a burden for firms, which will try to incorporate the risk of future settlements already in their prices. In this respect, strategic abuse of antitrust laws and over-deterrent damage multiples could, under certain circumstance, jeopardise the inherent goal of private enforcement.

— *The probability that a legal action is overturned*: this is the case of Type I errors (false convictions). If this probability turns out to be significant, then the overall welfare-enhancing potential of the competition rules may be threatened. Especially in some cases of allegedly anti-competitive conduct (for example predatory pricing, bundling), inaccurate antitrust scrutiny can harm society as much as absence of scrutiny. The same can be said when plaintiffs can exert an influence on judges in the discovery process, thus 'capturing' an imperfectly informed court: this at once harms incentives to undertake perfectly lawful actions, and undermines the foundations of competition law by creating uncertainty over the standards that will be applied to specific types of conduct.[62]

— *The expected trial costs*: depending on the extent to which private damages actions outnumber public cases, and on the relative costs of the two means of enforcing antitrust rules, measures aimed at facilitating private damages actions could result in increased costs due to lengthy proceedings, legal expenses and excessive transaction costs due to litigation. With a contingency fee system, widespread collective actions and aggressive rules on access to evidence, legal fees have reached very high stakes in jurisdictions such as the US.

In terms of social welfare, as the probability that illegal actions are deterred increases, social welfare also increases through the elimination of the deadweight loss resulting from non-competitive markets; likewise, if illegal actions undertaken are then overturned by a court, social welfare does not necessarily increase, but a welfare transfer occurs through damage compensation, net of the costs of trial.[63] On the other hand, cases of Type I

[62] For such reason, the standard to be applied to predatory pricing is normally conceived to minimise Type I errors, as evidence of low prices—normally beneficial for end consumers—should not lead to a prima facie case for infringement of the antitrust rules. See eg, *Brooke Group Ltd v Brown & Williamson Tobacco Corp* 509 US 209, 226 (1993).

[63] Normally damage awards do not take into account the deadweight loss resulting from anti-competitive conduct. For such reason, even with damage compensation aimed at *restitutio in integrum*—ie not taking into account damage multiples—no real recoupment of the deadweight loss caused by anti-competitive action will be achieved.

errors (false convictions) arising from strategic abuse of antitrust laws can have a negative impact on social welfare, by challenging otherwise welfare-enhancing conducts. Likewise, Type II errors (false acquittals) can legitimate anti-competitive conduct which produces a negative effect on society as a whole.

Renda et al estimate the potential for private antitrust enforcement to contribute to social welfare in the European Union.[64] The main results are the following:

— Under reasonable assumptions (for example, a detection rate of cartels of 20 per cent), if double damages with no prejudgment interest (to be considered as broadly comparable to single damages plus prejudgment interest) are available, the yearly damage recovery could reach €17.3 billion; whereas, if treble damages without prejudgment interest (or double damages with prejudgment interest) were awarded, the yearly damage recovery could reach €25.7 billion. This would amount to 0.23 per cent of EU GDP (Gross Domestic Product). If double damages plus prejudgment interest were introduced only for cartel cases, economic actors suffering antitrust injury may recover up to €20.9 billion Euros yearly. This would amount to 0.19 per cent of EU GDP.[65]

— The impact on deterrence is significant at the margin, although firms would still not be fully deterred from forming cartels and engaging in other anti-competitive conduct. Prospective infringers may face an expected liability of up to €29.4 billion yearly (including the opponents' legal fees).

— If private antitrust damages actions do not become more effective in the years to come, foregone benefits for victims of antitrust infringement would range between €5.7 billion and €23.3 billion.

— Expected costs are significant, but never offset the corrective justice impact of enhanced private antitrust enforcement. Lawyers' fees and court fees, which are by far the largest portion of expected costs, would amount to approximately 15 per cent to 20 per cent of damage recovery (this result was reached using US data as a benchmark, as no EU data were available).

— Overall, more effective enforcement of antitrust laws in Europe (with public and private enforcement) could bring about yearly social benefits as high as one per cent of GDP, or €113 billion in 2006. The contribution of private enforcement to this impact is expected to be substantial.

[64] Renda et al (n 7).

[65] Note, in this respect, that according to existing studies (eg RH Lande, 'Are Antitrust "Treble" Damages Really Single Damages?' (1993) 54 *Ohio State Law Journal* 115; MC Lovell, 'Are Treble Damages Double Damages?' (1982) 34 *Journal of Economics and Business* 263) treble damages without prejudgment interest would fall between single and double damage awards with prejudgment interest.

III. FROM THE GREEN PAPER TO THE NEW DIRECTIVE: WHAT GOT LOST ON THE WAY

A. A Decade of Preparatory Work

Achieving a more effective private antitrust enforcement in Europe was a very ambitious endeavour. It took, so far, a decade of proposals, external studies, guidance documents and a number of concessions on the side of the European Commission. As already mentioned, the first step was an external study (the so-called 'Ashurst study')[66] and a subsequent Green Paper, adopted in 2005.[67] The purpose of the Green Paper and of the companion Commission Staff Working Paper was to identify the main obstacles to a more efficient system of damages claims and to set out different options for further reflection, as well as possible ways to improve damage recovery both in follow-on actions (for example, when the civil action is brought after a competition authority has found an infringement) and in stand-alone actions (that is, actions which do not follow from a prior finding of an infringement by a competition authority). In order to achieve both deterrence and corrective justice, the Green Paper identified a number of alternative options. The Green Paper later led to the adoption of a White Paper on antitrust damages actions in 2008.[68]

The White Paper concluded, also on the basis of the 'Impact Study',[69] that:

— *Corrective justice is the main focus of the Commission's approach*—which rules out any possibility of imposing punitive damages. The Commission proposal instead focused on single damages, including compensation of the actual loss due to for example an anti-competitive price increase or the loss of profit as a result of any reduction in sales. In addition, compensation of the real value of the loss suffered implies a right to interest.[70]

[66] Waelbroeck, Slater and Even-Shoshan (n 6).

[67] European Commission, 'Green Paper—Damages actions for breach of the EC antitrust rules', COM(2005) 672 final.

[68] European Commission, 'White paper on damages actions for breach of the EC antitrust rules', COM(2008) 165 final. See Commission Legislative and Work Programme, Roadmap 2007COMP/001. Comments received during the consultation phase are available online at: ec.europa.eu/comm/competition/antitrust/others/actions_for_damages/gp_contributions.html.

[69] Renda et al (n 7).

[70] For the difficulties in assessing the actual value of damages see European Commission, 'Practical Guide on Quantifying Harm in Actions for damages based on breaches of Article 101 or 102 of the Treaty on the Functioning of the European Union', SWD(2013) 205 final, and the external study by Oxera and a team of lawyers led by Dr Assimakis Komninos, 'Quantifying antitrust damages: towards non-binding guidance for courts', available at: ec.europa.eu/competition/antitrust/actionsdamages/quantification_study.pdf.

— *Group litigation was the key instrument for the promotion of more effective private antitrust damages actions.* Notably, the Commission recommended allowing representative actions led by recognised consumer groups and actions in which victims can choose to participate, as opposed to class actions. That said, the Commission's proposal ventured into so-called 'opt-out' collective actions in addition to more traditional 'opt-in' schemes.
— *In terms of access to evidence, the Commission proposed some measures to facilitate disclosure*, but nothing close to the US discovery, which in the Commission's opinion would lead to procedural abuses, where defendants settle merely to avoid the heavy costs that excessively wide-ranging discovery would entail.
— To avoid the time and cost of re-litigation, *the Commission recommended that final infringement decisions of Member States' competition authorities be considered sufficient proof of an infringement in subsequent actions for damages.* This proposal was indeed very controversial, since some Member States considered it to be excessively constraining the independence of their judges.

Since then, a period of stalemate followed, in which other EU institutions have handled this hot dossier with (probably excessive) care. One of the key issues was the delicacy of proposing a set of remedies that would apply only to antitrust cases. A less ambitious proposal to introduce collective redress at the pan-European level had been under consideration at the European Commission's DG SANCO since 2008, when a dedicated Green Paper was published.[71] In 2011, the Commission carried out a public consultation, in which around 300 institutions and experts as well as 10,000 citizens expressed their views on the European framework for collective redress. The public consultation demonstrated a divergence of views among stakeholders and a need for balanced solutions. Finally, in June 2013 the Commission adopted a Recommendation, which invited all Member States to introduce national collective redress systems and proposed a number of common European principles, including securing the consumers' right to 'injunctive relief' and 'compensatory relief', and ensuring that collective redress procedures are fair, equitable, timely and not prohibitively expensive.[72]

[71] See ec.europa.eu/consumers/solving_consumer_disputes/judicial_redress/index_en.htm.

[72] Commission Recommendation of 11 June 2013 on common principles for injunctive and compensatory collective redress mechanisms in the Member States concerning violations of rights granted under Union Law [2013] OJ L201/60.

Most importantly, the Commission took some steps backwards compared to the original proposal made in the context of the DG COMP proposals, by recommending that:

- *Collective redress systems must be based on the 'opt-in' principle*: any exception to this principle should be duly justified by reasons of sound administration of justice;
- *Member States should not permit contingency fees risking creating an incentive for abuses.*
- *The entities which are representing claimants have to be of non-profit character*, to ensure that they are guided by the interests of those affected in situations of mass damages.
- *Punitive damages should in principle be prohibited* by Member States.

At the same time, the European Commission was putting forward a proposed Directive on private antitrust damages actions, which sought to introduce new rules for antitrust lawsuits.[73] The proposed Directive maintained the idea that the decisions of national competition authorities finding an infringement would automatically constitute proof before national courts of all Member States that the infringement occurred. In addition the proposed Directive sought to clarify some rules on limitation periods to ensure that victims can effectively claim damages, and the rules on passing-on, to ensure that those who suffered the harm in the end are the ones receiving compensation. The proposal finally became legislation in November 2014, confirming the scope and text of the 2013 Commission document.

B. The Directive on Antitrust Damages Actions: Much Ado About Nothing?

The text of the new Directive is very far from the balance originally struck by the White Paper in 2008. The most important rules are dedicated to access to evidence, the effect of decisions by national competition authorities in other Member States, and limitation periods.

i. Access to Evidence

The Directive contains a rather conservative set of rules on access to evidence, more prone to the protection of confidentiality than to the exchange of information between parties involved. The original emphasis on the need to relax the very strict standards applicable in many EU Member States

[73] Dir 2014/104/EU of 26 November 2014 on certain rules governing actions for damages under national law for infringements of the competition law provisions of the Member States and of the European Union [2014] OJ L349/1.

for what concerns disclosure of evidence is replaced by a very cautious approach, mostly aimed at preventing 'fishing expeditions' and protecting confidential information and business secrets. That said, the Directive is a step forward in that it allows victims to ask for disclosure of 'categories of evidence' (Article 5(2)), which need to be identified by reference to their common features such as the nature, object or content of the documents. Disclosure orders can also be directed to third parties that are not involved in the damages action. However, judges are given the final say in the disclosure system, since they have to assess the relevance and proportionality of a disclosure request. Proportionality depends on three main aspects (Article 5(3)):

a) The extent to which the claim or defence is supported by available facts and evidence justifying the request to disclose evidence;
b) The scope and cost of disclosure, especially for any third parties concerned, including preventing non-specific searches for information which is unlikely to be of relevance for the parties in the procedure;
c) Whether the evidence the disclosure of which is sought contains confidential information, especially concerning any third parties, and what arrangements are in place for protecting such confidential information.

In other words, there is no US-inspired discovery system, but a slight modification to the system applied in most EU Member States. In addition, the Directive contains a set of rules dedicated to the disclosure of evidence included in the files of a national competition authority. When assessing the proportionality of a disclosure order, national courts shall also consider whether the request is sufficiently specific, whether the party requesting disclosure is doing so in relation to an action for damages before a national court, and the need to safeguard the effectiveness of the public enforcement of competition law.

The need to preserve the incentives for undertakings to apply for leniency or to engage in settlement procedures spurred a number of additional restrictions: national courts cannot at any time order a party or a third party to disclose either leniency statements or settlement submissions (Article 6(6)); and documents prepared specifically for the purpose of the public enforcement proceedings, documents drawn up by the competition authority during the course of its proceedings, or settlement submission that have been withdrawn, may only be required to be disclosed after the competition authority has closed its proceedings.

The compromise struck by the EU institutions is certainly reasonable, but unlikely to significantly modify the incentive of victims of antitrust infringements to sue. The cost of access to justice would be only slightly reduced since the victim can now invoke the disclosure of categories of documents. Also, the relative difficulty in interpreting the links between different types of documents might generate legal uncertainty during trial. Only time will tell if this rather timid change will not be eaten up by the path dependency of judges, who might continue to apply their national rules as if nothing has changed.

ii. Effect of Decisions by National Competition Authorities

Article 9 provides that a final decision adopted by a national competition authority of a Member State will be binding only on the courts of that same Member State. Final decisions taken by the competition authorities or courts of another Member State must qualify as at least prima facie evidence that an infringement of competition law has occurred, but will not be binding. This arrangement avoids the problem of the lack of trust between Member States and also reduces the likelihood of forum shopping. At the same time, it limits the impact of the original proposal, introducing changes that will be confined mostly within each Member State.

The provision introduced by the new Directive appears rather weak, since it does not constrain the possibility for courts to discard the outcome of a previous case concluded in another Member State. At a minimum, what will be needed is some peer pressure within the European Competition Network, aimed at keeping momentum for the recognition of decisions by national competition authorities as important, difficult-to-rebut evidence for courts in other Member States.

iii. Other Provisions: Settlements, Limitation Periods, Treatment of Leniency Applicants, and the Passing-on Rule

The Damages Directive contains other interesting provisions:

— On limitation periods, Article 10 provides useful clarifications by prescribing that Member States must take as reference the time at which the infringement has ceased, and the claimant knows (or could reasonably be expected to know) of its claim. Limitation periods should be for a minimum of five years and must be suspended if a competition authority is investigating the infringement to which the claim relates. Any such suspension should end at the earliest one year after the infringement decision, or after the proceedings are otherwise terminated.[74] This provision brings more legal certainty for potential victims.

— On the issue of leniency applicants, the Directive introduces two provisions: (i) Based on Article 11(5), the liability of successful leniency applicants will be limited to harm caused to the applicant's direct or indirect customers or suppliers, unless the victim is unable to obtain full

[74] An infringement decision is final when it cannot be reviewed by an appeal court.

compensation from the other cartelists[75]; and (ii) under Article 11(2), small and medium-sized enterprises with a market share below five per cent will only be liable to their own direct and indirect purchasers, if having them jointly and severally liable would irretrievably jeopardise their economic viability.[76]

— The Directive also seeks to clarify the rules on the passing-on defence and offense (Articles 12–15). These provisions imply that the 'passing-on' defence should be allowed, but the burden of proof should weigh on the defendant. Indirect purchasers will be able to claim damage compensation upon proving that the overcharge was passed on to them: the burden of proof will be somewhat lighter if the indirect purchaser shows that the defendant committed an infringement of competition law, that the infringement resulted in an overcharge for the direct purchaser, and that the indirect purchaser purchased the goods or services that were the object of the infringement or that were derived from or contained in such goods or services. The rebuttable presumption of passing-on gives indirect purchasers affected by the infringement a credible chance of getting compensation. Under the current system in most EU countries, indirect purchasers claiming damages have to prove that the overcharge harm suffered was passed on down the supply chain until it reached them. This is burdensome and makes it even more difficult for victims to exercise their rights.

— Under the Damages Directive, undertakings which have infringed competition law through joint behaviour are to be held jointly and severally liable for the entire harm caused by the infringement. This means that a victim can bring a claim against just one or against several of the infringing entities until he or she has been fully compensated. For infringers, this means that even if they are not sued by a claimant there is still the possibility that another co-infringer may seek to recover a contribution for its share in the infringement. The position is different for immunity recipients, to which the Directive offers immunity from fines if they are the first to blow the whistle to the Commission.[77]

— The Directive introduces a rebuttable presumption that cartel infringements cause harm (Article 17(2)), and national courts determine the extent of the overcharge harm and the amounts passed on.

[75] The immunity applicant will remain liable as a last resort debtor if the victims are unable to obtain full compensation from the other infringers.

[76] This exception will not apply if the SME was the ringleader or coerced other undertakings to participate in the infringement, or if the SME has previously been found to have infringed competition law.

[77] In the event that an immunity recipient is sued for damages with respect to its activity in the cartel, its liability is limited to the harm it caused to its own direct and indirect purchasers and providers, unless full compensation cannot be obtained from the other entities involved in the infringements.

The presumption that cartels cause harm is supported by economic evidence that more than 90 per cent of cartel infringements result in price increases. On the quantification of harm, the Directive maintains a position already expressed in the White Paper, which entails that national courts are left with some degree of flexibility in quantifying the harm suffered by the victim, where it is practically impossible or excessively difficult to quantify harm on the basis of the evidence. The Directive adds that national competition authorities should be ready to assist national courts with this task upon request.[78] Where a national court is called upon to determine the quantum of harm it must ensure that the compensation awarded does not exceed the overcharge harm at each level of the supply chain. This is undoubtedly likely to pose significant practical challenges for the courts. The Commission intends to publish guidance for national courts to assist in the quantification of harm.

— Finally, based on recitals and Articles 18 and 19 the Directive explicitly seeks to promote the use of consensual dispute resolution (CDR). The Directive provides that national limitation periods should be suspended when parties are engaged in CDR. Equally, national courts will be granted discretion to suspend proceedings for up to two years where the parties are engaged in CDR. To ensure that claimants are not overcompensated, national courts must take account of any consensual settlements relating to a particular infringement when making an award of damages.

IV. CONCLUDING REMARKS

The rules contained in the new Directive have the potential to promote more vibrant private antitrust enforcement in those EU Member States in which no significant development has been observed in the past few years. However, the original Commission proposal has been significantly watered down: as a matter of fact, the most effective features of private antitrust enforcement in the US (contingency fees, opt-out class actions, one-way fee-shifting, discovery rules) are absent in the final text of the proposal. What's more, the Directive might hamper the attempts of some Member States to introduce some of these features: in particular, reference can be made to the opt-out collective actions system recently introduced in the UK for competition law claims only; to the gradual opening of, inter alia, the German and

[78] See Renda et al (n 7), discussing the possible role of NCAs as amici curiae.

Italian legal systems to the use of contingency fee arrangements, etc. Finally, the provisions on limitation are likely to generate a degree of uncertainty.[79]

The uncertainty that surrounds the potential impact of the newly proposed rules on social welfare is confirmed by an analysis of the original impact assessment (IA) that backed the Commission's 2013 proposal. There, the more ambitious set of options contained in the White Paper (option 2 in the IA) was discarded on rather shaky grounds, by claiming that the milder option 3 'provides for a more balanced system' since

> [i]t contains an overall improvement of the possibility to obtain access to evidence, while offering a stronger protection of effective public enforcement, by protecting more documents from the file of the competition authorities from disclosure in actions for damages.[80]

Also, the latter option was found to have lower litigation costs: this is understandable, since it is likely to lead to less private antitrust damages actions, but this is not by itself good news for the overall goals of the EU initiative.

Furthermore, the Directive is designed to promote the use of follow-on litigation, rather than to encourage meritorious stand-alone private antitrust damages actions. This is regrettable, since the latter are the only way in which private antitrust damages actions can contribute to both the probability that an infringing conduct is detected, and to the liability exposure of the infringing party. Absent an increase in stand-alone actions, private enforcement becomes less effective and might end up placing a very high burden on the few that get caught. This might lead to undesirable reactions among judges, who might decide to under-enforce certain rules if they know that conviction would lead to the likely bankruptcy of a company.[81]

In summary, given the limited scope of the Directive, it is unlikely that the new rules will achieve the estimated welfare impacts.[82] To the contrary, absent more far-reaching proposals on opt-out collective actions and contingency fees, and clearer rules on access to evidence and limitation periods, it seems unlikely that the EU will manage to strike a satisfactory balance between corrective justice and deterrence. The existing rules seem to impose

[79] Such uncertainty has occurred in the UK where similar rules have been enacted. See J Cary, L Kilaniotis, A McGregor and S Smith, 'United Kingdom: Private Antitrust Litigation' (2015) *European Antitrust Review* s 71. See also P Akman, 'Period of Limitations in Follow-On Competition Cases: The Elephant in the Room?', University of East Anglia CCP Working paper 8/2013.

[80] See European Commission, 'Impact Assessment Report: Damages Actions for Breach of the EU Antitrust Rules', SWD(2013) 203 final, para 168.

[81] Authoritative commentators such as Calkins (1986) and Kovacic (2004) have mentioned such 'equilibrating tendencies' as a possible key to interpret some developments in US antitrust enforcement over the past few decades. See S Calkins, 'Summary Judgment, Motions to Dismiss, and Other Examples of Equilibrating Tendencies in the Antitrust System' (1986) 74 *Georgia Law Journal* 1065; and WE Kovacic, 'Private Participation in the Enforcement of Public Competition Laws' (2004) 2 *Current Competition Law* 167, 173–74.

[82] Renda et al (n 7).

significant constraints on the nascent market for damages claims, and provide limited additional incentives for follow-on cases, unless Member States decide to attach almost binding force to NCA decisions in other EU countries.

What remains undoubted, though, is the symbolic value of the new Directive. EU institutions have recognised the importance of the enforcement of EU rules, and have tried to introduce some corrections to a system that was unfit to comply with the principle of effectiveness of EU rules. Whether these initial steps will lead to subsequent, more ambitious steps at either the EU or at the national level, remains to be seen. The need to ensure sufficient deterrence might soon lead the EU debate to focus on new forms of collective litigation and other, equally important pillars of antitrust enforcement, such as criminal sanctions.

Part VI

Globalising Justice: Transnational Enforcement Mechanisms

14

The Challenges of Transnational Contractual Enforcement: The Relative Merits of Arbitration and State Courts Litigation

SANDRINE CLAVEL

I. INTRODUCTION

HISTORICALLY, THE EXPANSION of international commerce has come together with the development of specific and private modes of enforcement such as international commercial arbitration.[1] Arbitration has been one of the drivers of the growing autonomy of commercial parties in terms of governance and regulation. But the success of arbitration is not the only sign of the emancipation of international business operators from state authority. Contractual relationships have gained density, including multiple parties and multiple contracts—which will be referred to as *contractual networks*. Powerful transnational private regulation instruments have emerged, aside from public regulation, building on transnational commercial contracts, such as standard contracts, usages, international standards, codes of conducts etc.[2] Although usually pictured in terms of competition, the relationship between public regulation and transnational private regulation is more complex. Over the last years, scholars have acknowledged the idea that transnational private regulation is more a complement to public regulation than a substitute, and that it needs strong public regulation to work efficiently.[3] The issue of enforcement is exemplary.

[1] G Born, *International Commercial Arbitration* 2nd edn (Alphen aan den Rijn, Kluwer, 2014) 23, 62.

[2] F Cafaggi, 'The Regulatory Functions of Transnational Commercial Contracts. New Architectures' available at: ssrn.com/abstract=2136632 and dx.doi.org/10.2139/ssrn.2136632; F Cafaggi, 'New Foundations of Transnational Private Regulation' (2010) *European University Institute Working Papers* 53, PR Series-04.

[3] Cafaggi, 'New Foundations' (n 2). See also on the collaboration of public and private 'communities' giving rise to contemporary international commercial arbitration: Born (n 1) 62, 63.

Along with the development of transnational private regulation, specific monitoring and enforcement mechanisms have emerged, such as certification processes, contractual penalties or exclusion mechanisms. However, at one point, it is necessary to rely on judicial-type or compulsory enforcement systems, in order to ensure the respect of transnational private contracts, and the efficiency of transnational private regulation.

According to this view, the relevance of enforcement through national State court systems may only be questioned. The constraints of the conflicts of laws—strongly present in State court litigation—will often undermine the efficiency of regulatory provisions included in transnational contractual networks. The main impediments are: the obligation to subject contracts to State law;[4] the full authority of mandatory provisions of the contract law; the application of internationally mandatory provisions (*lois de police*) of the forum; the intervention of the forum's international public order principles. Let us consider for instance a buyer obliging his foreign supplier to enter a certification contract, in addition to and as a condition for the conclusion of a sale contract in order to ensure the compatibility of the products with environmental or labour standards. There is absolutely no guarantee that the contractual 'scheme' will be enforced as such by the courts of the supplier's State. In case of breach of the contractual standards by the supplier, it could happen that the sellers' courts having jurisdiction over the case find these standards incompatible with internationally mandatory provisions of the local law; or find the certification contract to have been imposed on the supplier through an abuse of economic dependence sanctioned by the contract law.

These constraints may not be a fatality. It is imaginable to reshape conflicts of legal rules in order to make them compatible with the specificities of transnational contractual networks.[5] However, focusing on conflicts of laws applying in State courts' litigation is insufficient, given the extensive role played by international arbitration in the enforcement of transnational commercial contracts. In most legal systems, arbitrators' rulings are not constrained by conflicts of laws. The limits imposed by the prohibition of *contrat sans loi*, or by the impact of states' internationally mandatory provisions, are absent or reduced when it comes to international arbitration. Does it mean that international arbitration is a better or at least a more efficient enforcement tool for transnational contractual networks?

The question deserves more in-depth consideration. Arbitration is traditionally praised as the judicial enforcement mechanism best fitting the

[4] Usually referred to as the prohibition of *contrat sans loi*, still applying in many legal systems, in particular in European ones.

[5] F Cafaggi and S Clavel, 'Interfirm Networks across Europe: A Private International Law Perspective' in F Cafaggi (ed), *Contractual Networks, Inter-Firm Cooperation and Economic Growth* (Cheltenham, Edward Elgar, 2011) 201.

expectations of the international business community. However, arbitration has faced new challenges over the last decades. It has notably gone through important changes coming with the development of investment arbitration, changes which international commercial arbitration has not been immune to. The regulatory functions of transnational commercial contracts could just appear to bring more challenges. This is why it is interesting to confront the two 'judicial types' of enforcement —state courts and arbitration—with transnational contractual networks, in order to assess their relative merits. This analysis shall be conducted by considering three issues, selected as particularly relevant with respect to complex transnational contractual schemes: Concentration of proceedings (II); interpretation of contracts (III); and efficiency of proceedings (IV).

II. CONCENTRATION OF PROCEEDINGS

In complex contractual schemes, multiple parties and multiple contracts are usually involved. Efficient transnational contractual enforcement might impose that proceedings, instead of being limited to two parties with regard to one contract, be extended beyond the original litigants, to linked parties or linked contracts. The ability of the enforcement system to capture the contractual relationship as a whole is a condition of its capacity to give an accurate effect to this relationship. The issue at stake is the jurisdiction of the courts. Is it possible for State courts or arbitral tribunals to have jurisdiction over the whole contractual network? The answer to this question varies according to how parties have designed their provisions on jurisdiction. The situation is different depending on whether there is no jurisdiction clause (A), an arbitration clause (B) or a choice of forum provision (C), or even conflicting provisions on jurisdiction (D) in the contracts.

A. Absence of any Jurisdiction Clause

In complex transnational contractual proceedings, involving multiple parties and multiple contracts, it is not excessively difficult for state courts to assume jurisdiction over the whole case when the parties have not included any provision on jurisdiction. As a preliminary, it should be noticed that, contrary to what happens in arbitration, the adjudication power of state courts is not questionable. It pre-exists litigation. Courts are vested by the state with the power to adjudicate matters in dispute. If proceedings are to be extended beyond their initial scope, then the issue will be a simple matter of *international jurisdiction*.

When a national judge has international jurisdiction over a given contract, two possibilities exist in order to extend the proceedings beyond this contract, to different parties and/or different contracts. First, it is commonly admitted that several defendants can be sued in one single forum, as long as the claims are sufficiently connected. The rule of the 'co-respondents forum' is set, for instance, in Article 6(1) of the Brussels I Regulation:

> A person domiciled in a Member State may also be sued: 1. where he is one of a number of defendants, in the courts of the place where any one of them is domiciled, provided the claims are so closely connected that it is expedient to hear and determine them together to avoid the risk of irreconcilable judgments resulting from separate proceedings.[6]

If contracts AB and AC are linked and A sues B in the courts where B is domiciled, the rule will then allow A to sue C in the same forum. Second, some legal systems have specific jurisdiction rules according to which where a court has jurisdiction over a case, it may assume international jurisdiction over any related cases. For instance, if A and B have concluded two different contracts, and if A sues B in the courts having jurisdiction over contract number one, A will also be able to present a claim based on contract number two to the same courts, even if these courts do not have natural jurisdiction over this claim, as long as A can prove the connection between the two claims. This jurisdiction rule based on related actions is not as widely spread as the rule of the co-respondents forum. It does not appear, for instance, in the Brussels I Regulation. But it has been accepted in various national systems under different forms: *Compétence fondée sur la connexité* in French law,[7] or *forum conveniens* in some common law countries.[8] Both rules are useful for judges to globally apprehend complex transnational contractual litigation.

Arbitration proceedings are in a less favourable situation. If any arbitration clause is absent, arbitrators simply lack adjudication power. It is necessary to have at least one arbitration clause in one contract. The question is then to define the scope of such a clause when there is a contractual network.

B. Inclusion of an Arbitration Clause

In contractual networks, two different situations may arise, depending on whether parties have included several arbitration clauses in their different

[6] Council Reg (EC) no 44/2001 of 22 December 2000 on jurisdiction and the recognition and enforcement of judgments in civil and commercial matters. See also Brussels I bis: Reg (EU) no 1215/2012 of the European Parliament and of the Council of 12 December 2013 on jurisdiction and the recognition and enforcement of judgments in civil and commercial matters (recast).

[7] P Mayer and V Heuzé, *Droit international privé* 11th edn (Paris, Montchrestien, 2014) 295.

[8] B Schneider, 'Le *forum conveniens* et le *forum non conveniens*' (1975) 27 *Revue internationale de droit comparé* 601–42.

contracts (i), or only one arbitration clause in one contract and none in the others (ii).

i. Multiple Clauses for Multiple Contracts

When each contract of a contractual network includes an arbitration clause, the consent of parties to arbitration is not questionable. The issue is rather to decide if the procedures arising out of the different contracts can be dealt with by one single arbitration tribunal.

The case of arbitration with multiple parties or over multiple contracts is not ignored.[9] It has been recently acknowledged by arbitral institutions. It is now expressly considered in the 2012 International Chamber of Commerce (ICC) Arbitration Rules, or to a lesser extent in the 2010 United Nations Commission on International Trade Law (UNCITRAL) Rules.[10] Article 9 of the ICC Rules is particularly interesting:

> claims arising out of or in connection with more than one contract may be made in a single arbitration, irrespective of whether such claims are made under one or more than one arbitration agreement under the Rules.

Article 10, dealing with the consolidation of arbitrations, is also useful:

> The Court may, at the request of a party, consolidate two or more arbitrations pending under the Rules into a single arbitration, where: ... c) where the claims in the arbitrations are made under more than one arbitration agreement, the arbitration are between the same parties, the disputes in the arbitrations arise in connection with the same legal relationship, and the Court finds the arbitration agreements to be compatible.

The multiplicity of contracts and of arbitration agreements is therefore not an obstacle to the organisation of a single arbitration, more compatible with an efficient settlement of the case in the context of a transnational contractual network, than multiple arbitrations or litigations.

ii. Single Clause for Multiple Contracts

The situation is more problematic when, within a transnational contractual network, all interdependent or linked contracts do not include an arbitration clause. In the absence of any consent of some of the parties to arbitration, the option of arbitration is normally closed. The result is that some issues should be dealt with by an arbitral tribunal with regards to some parties of the network (and some contracts), while others should be treated by one or

[9] See generally: B Hanotiau, *Complex Arbitrations: Multiparty, Multicontract, Multi-issue and Class Actions* (Alphen aan den Rijn, Kluwer, 2006).

[10] Art 10 (1) of the Uncitral rules deals with the constitution of the tribunal in case of multiple parties.

several national courts with regards to other parties (and other contracts). This fragmentation is not always compatible with the good governance of the transnational contractual network. The issue, then, is whether the scope of the arbitration clause may be extended beyond the contract where it is stipulated. Because of the privity of arbitration agreements, such extension seems rather difficult.

However, there is a notable trend in contemporary arbitration, favouring the 'extension' of arbitration agreements to non signatory parties.[11] There are two main reasons for admitting the extension of an arbitration agreement beyond the contract where it is included and the parties to such contract. The first one is based on the well-known 'group of companies doctrine'. A review of arbitral awards and a comparison of legal systems reveal that it is possible to 'pierce the corporate veil', in order to extend an arbitration clause accepted by a company to another company of the same group, whenever the principle of independence between companies has been the occasion of a fraud or abuse.[12] Eventually, arbitrators will also accept the extension based on the presumed consent inferred from active participation of non signatory parties in the negotiation, the performance or even the ending of the contract including the arbitration clause.[13]

The second reason for admitting the extension of the scope of the clause, which is more relevant when dealing with contractual networks, is founded on the 'group of contracts' doctrine. The idea is to bring 'into one arbitral proceeding all the parties that have participated in a single economic transaction through various agreements',[14] although all of them have not expressed their consent to arbitration. French law—known as particularly arbitration friendly—provides a good illustration of how it may work. When there is a chain of contracts organising, primarily or incidentally, the transmission of the property of goods, French law recognises that the nature of the relationship between the original seller, and the final buyer, is contractual, even if there is no direct contractual link between them because of the presence of an intermediary seller. Consequently, French case law admits that the arbitration agreement included in the original sale contract (between the first seller and the intermediary one) is 'transmitted' along the chain, except if the subsequent contractors can prove their reasonable

[11] B Hanotiau, 'Non-signatories in International Arbitration: Lessons from Thirty Years of Case Law' in AJ Van den Berg (ed), *International Arbitration 2006: Back to the Basics?* (Alphen aan den Rijn, Kluwer, 2007) 341; Hanotiau (n 9) 7–48.

[12] Hanotiau (n 11); N Blackaby, C Partasides, A Redfern and M Hunter, *Redfern and Hunter on International Arbitration* 5th edn (Oxford, Oxford University Press, 2009) 99, para 2.40.

[13] See, for an analysis of the practice in arbitration: C Seraglini and J Ortscheidt, *Droit de l'arbitrage interne et international* (Paris, Montchretien, 2013) no 713.

[14] Hanotiau (n 11) 342.

ignorance of the arbitration agreement.[15] All parties along the chain are bound by the arbitration agreement. When the chain of contracts does not involve the transmission of a good's property along the chain (for instance in the case of subcontracting), the situation is a bit more complex. The principle should be that, in the absence of any transmission of property, the arbitration agreement does not bind subcontractors. However, French case law has decided that a sub-contractor can be bound by an arbitration clause included in the main contract, when the sub-contractor has been directly involved in the performance of the main contract and has been informed of the content of this contract hence of the existence of the arbitration clause.[16] The rule has been generally formulated by the French Supreme Court (*Cour de cassation*) with the result that in any group of contracts, an arbitration clause can be extended to all parties being directly involved in the performance of the contract including the clause.[17]

As we can see, there are means in order to bring to arbitration parties involved in the performance of a single economic operation, even when interdependent contracts do not all include an arbitration clause. In this view, arbitration can be seen as more favourable than national state court litigation, at least when there is a choice-of-forum clause.

C. Inclusion of a Choice of Forum Provision

The privity of contracts implies that choice of forum provisions do not bind parties who have not 'agreed' on the clause. This rule is strictly imposed, for instance in Europe by Article 23 of the Brussels I Regulation. As a result, a non signatory party cannot be sued in courts having jurisdiction according to a choice of forum clause, on the basis of the rule of the co-respondents' forum set in Article 6(1) of the Regulation. In this case, however, the reason is less the privity of the contract, than the wording of Article 6(1) which gives general jurisdiction to the court where one of several respondents is 'domiciled'. A different solution applies when, according to Article 6(3), the

[15] French Cour de cassation, 1ère Civ, 6 February 2001, *Peavy Company*, and the commentary: F Jault, 'Transmission d'une clause compromissoire dans une chaîne de contrats et pouvoir du juge auquel la clause est opposée' (2001) *Revue Critique de droit international privé* 522; French Cour de cassation, 1ère Civ, 27 March 2007 (2007) *Journal du droit international (Clunet)* 969, and the commentary by C Legros; French Cour de cassation, 1ère Civ, 17 November 2010, *legifrance* no 09-12442.

[16] French Cour de cassation, 1ère Civ, 26 October 2011, *legifrance* no 10-17708; French Cour de cassation, Com 25 November 2008, *legifrance* no 07-21888.

[17] French Cour de cassation, 1ère Civ, 27 March 2007, and the commentaries: Ch Seraglini (2007) *JCP Edition Générale* I, 168, no 11; S Bollée, 'Transmission de la clause d'arbitrage dans une chaîne hétérogène de contrats' (2007) *Dalloz* 2077; C Legros (2007) *Journal du droit international (Clunet)* 968; J El Adhab (2007) *Revue de l'Arbitrage* 785; F Jault-Seseke, 'Transmission de la clause d'arbitrage dans une chaîne hétérogène de contrats' (2007) *Revue Critique de droit international privé* 798.

respondent presents 'a counter-claim arising from the same contract or facts on which the original claim was based'. In this provision, there is no condition that the tribunal dealing with the original claim be the one where the original respondent is domiciled. Hence third parties may be introduced in proceedings before a court which jurisdiction is based on a choice of forum provision.

Apart from the case where a counter-claim is presented, the privity of contracts makes it difficult to extend the scope of a choice of forum provision. One remarkable exception is in maritime transport, where a choice of forum provision has been included in a bill of lading. The European Court of Justice (ECJ) recognises that, given that the bill of lading represents the goods and is transmitted from the original seller to the final recipient of the goods, the choice of forum provision is also transmitted along the chain and binds all successive holders of the bill of lading, if the law ruling the transport contract says so.[18] But the ECJ has strictly limited the scope of this solution to maritime transports. In 2010, the French *Cour de cassation* made a reference to the ECJ for a preliminary ruling, asking whether a choice of forum provision included in a sale contract could be imposed on subcontractors, that is, parties involved in subsequent contracts involving the good originally sold. The detail of the ECJ's answer in its decision *Refcomp*[19] is worth mentioning. Firstly, the ECJ reminds us that the link between operators which are not parties to the same contract is of a non-contractual nature;[20] consequently, the choice-of-forum provision included in a sub-sale contract cannot, normally, be relied on against the final buyer or contractor. Secondly, the ECJ proposes an interesting nuance: the provision may nevertheless apply if 'it is established that the third party has actually consented to that clause under the conditions laid down in' Article 23 of the Brussels I Regulation. This is interesting because it is possible to discuss the concept of 'actual consent'. It does not seem necessary for the third party to actually have signed the clause or the contract including the clause. For instance, one could discuss the possibility that the existence of a contractual network creates a situation where parties have established practices between themselves, in order to presume the effective consent.

However, even if the ECJ has not totally closed the door to the extension of the scope of choice of forum provisions in contractual networks, the risk of fragmented litigation is high. With this in view, the extension of the scope of arbitration clauses, to parties involved in the performance of a single economic operation, appears to be easier, at least if there is no conflict between provisions dealing with jurisdiction.

[18] Case 71/83 *Tilly Russ* [1984] ECR 2417; C 159/97 *Trasporti Castelleti* [1997] ECR I-1597; C 387/98 *Coreck Maritime* [2000] ECR I-9337.

[19] C-543/10 *Refcomp SpA v Axa Corporate Solutions Assurance SA*, 7 February 2013, nyr; and the commentary: S Clavel (2013) *Journal du droit international* 1201.

[20] C-29/91 *Jacob Handte* [1992] ECR I-3967.

D. Conflicting Provisions on Jurisdiction

In complex contractual schemes, it is not rare to have to deal with conflicting clauses on jurisdiction. Parties may have included an arbitration agreement in one contract, and a choice of forum provision in another. Or they may have agreed on arbitration at one moment of their relationship, and concluded a choice of forum clause at another. Conflicting provisions on jurisdiction are a major impediment to the concentration of proceedings.

Eventually, concentration is still possible if it is clear that the common intent of the parties was to *replace* a clause by another:[21] the court/arbitral tribunal designated in second place will have jurisdiction over the whole contractual relationship. But often, the interpretation of the will of the parties leads to assigning different scopes to different clauses. For instance, when an arbitration clause is included in a framework contract, while sales contracts concluded within this framework include choice of forum provisions, disputes related to sales contracts will be considered as falling under the jurisdiction of national courts, while disputes related to the framework contract (as claims based on the ending of the commercial relation) will fall under the jurisdiction of the arbitral tribunal.[22] In that case, there is no efficient means to ensure the concentration of proceedings. However, in legal systems recognising the positive effect of the competence–competence principle, concentration will usually occur at the earliest stage of litigation, because of the priority offered to arbitrators to decide on the respective scopes of the clauses.[23]

The comparison of the national court system and arbitration does not lead to a clear conclusion as to which one is more efficient for the purpose of ensuring the concentration of proceedings. However, it seems easier to extend the scope of arbitration agreements, than the scope of choice of forum provisions.

[21] See French Cour de cassation, 1ère Civ 11 July 2006, *legifrance* no 03-19838; *Bulletin civil I* no 366, (2006) *Dalloz* 2273; and the commentaries: F Jault-Seseke, 'Du contrôle de l'inapplicabilité manifeste de la convention d'arbitrage' (2007) *Revue critique de droit international privé* 128; E Loquin, 'Le contrôle de l'inapplicabilité manifeste de la convention d'arbitrage' (2006) *Revue trimestrielle de droit commercial* 764.

[22] French Cour de cassation: 1ère Civ 4 July 2006, *legifrance* no 05-11591, *Bulletin civil I* no 337, (2006) *Dalloz* 2127; and the commentary: Loquin, ibid; 1ère Civ, 12 February 2014, *legifrance* no 13-18059.

[23] In the French legal system, one of the consequences attached to the competence–competence principle is that if there is any doubt on the intent of the parties as to the applicability of conflicting clauses, then arbitrators should decide on the issue (Cour de cassation, 1ère Civ, 14 January 2015, *legifrance* no 13-23806; 1ère Civ, 25 June 2014, *legifrance* no 13-23669; and the commentary: S Clavel, 'Règlement des conflits de clauses de procédure: compétence judiciaire ou compétence arbitrale?' (2015) *Revue Critique de droit international privé* 413. If arbitrators decide that they have jurisdiction on the whole contractual networks, state courts control will intervene only once the arbitral award has been rendered (Cour de cassation 1ère Civ, 29 Jan 2014, *legifrance* no 12-26597).

III. INTERPRETATION OF THE CONTRACTS

In transnational contractual networks, the issue of the interpretation of the contract(s) is a crucial one. Different approaches may be favoured: objective or subjective, literal, teleological, analogical or systematic. Depending on the approach, parties can more or less expect that due consideration will be given to the choices they have expressly or implicitly made. The interpretation method also affects the ability of enforcement authorities to embrace the contractual framework (groups of contracts/interdependent contracts), as well as the economic and political context which might be important for the understanding of the regulatory part of the contract. Interpretation issues are all the more important that they are not only related to the meaning of the contract, but also directly linked to the taking of evidence, because they have a strong influence on the admissibility of extrinsic evidence (is it possible to contradict the terms of the written contract, for instance by using pre-contractual documents, or can parties incorporate provisions by reference?).[24]

In state court's proceedings, *interpretation of the contract* is normally a matter depending on the *law of the contract*. By choosing the appropriate law to rule their contract, parties should normally be able to rely on the fact that the interpretation rules of such law will prevail. However, the law of the *forum* cannot be neglected. Questions of procedure and evidence are mainly governed by the *lex fori*.[25] As a consequence, the *lex fori* will necessarily influence the understanding of the contract.[26] The interference of *lex fori* may be considered a problem, because it creates uncertainty: even if the parties have carefully chosen the law ruling their contract, important issues may depend on the application of the law of the forum, which is usually not predictable at the moment the contract is concluded. However, parties may secure their relationship by including, aside from the choice of law clause, a relevant choice of forum provision.

In international arbitration proceedings, the principles ruling the *interpretation of the contract* are not clearly defined.[27] If arbitrators were to be influenced by the general principles of private international law,[28] they

[24] J Rosengren, 'Contract Interpretation in International Arbitration' (2013) 30 *Journal of International Arbitration* 1, 6.

[25] *Lex fori* is not the law normally ruling evidence in the conflict of laws on contracts, where the *lex contractus* plays a major role. However, *lex fori* still has a strong influence.

[26] For instance, Art 18 (2) of Reg Rome I states that although the modes of proof of the contract law are normally admissible, this is only the case as long as 'such mode of proof can be administered by the forum'. This implies that the *lex fori* sets the limits of the *lex contractus* applicability.

[27] But see for recent analysis: J Resengren (n 24); LO Baptista, 'The Practice of Interpretation in Arbitration' in *Liber Amicorum S Lazareff* (Paris, Pedone, 2011) 55.

[28] H Muir Watt, 'Les principes généraux en droit international privé français' (1997) *Journal du droit international* 417.

ought to rely on the rules of interpretation defined by the law of the contract. Even if this was the case, arbitration would offer more latitude to the parties than most national state courts would. In many national court systems, the law of the contract is necessarily the law of a state, whereas the same legal systems accept that, in arbitration proceedings, parties decide to have their contract ruled by private rules (*contrat sans loi*). However, it seems that arbitrators do not rely on the law of the contract when it comes to interpretation.

Recent research, based on 246 arbitration awards from different origins, acknowledges that arbitral praxis endorses an eclectic interpretative approach.[29] This approach is primarily pragmatic, 'based on experience, on knowledge and on previous practice of interpreters'.[30] It means that it is the personality of the arbitrator which mainly drives the interpretation process. The result is that it may be difficult for parties to anticipate. Apart from the pragmatic approach, the research emphasises the use of: 1) interpretation according to the purpose, object and context of the provision/contract; 2) teleological interpretation; 3) literal interpretation; 4) interpretation influenced by *lex mercatoria*, trade usages and general principles (including Unidroit). It reveals that several of these methods are usually combined in the same award in order to justify the interpretation proposed. Such a 'cumulative' approach is frequent in arbitration awards (it is also applied, for instance, to decide which law should rule the contract). The combined application of different methods of interpretation may lower the risk of uncertainty, and increase the chances for arbitrators to be sensitive to the peculiarities of contractual networks. This conclusion is reinforced if one considers the discretion that is usually recognised of arbitrators in the taking of evidence,[31] making it possible for them to go beyond the strict wording of the contract, in order to consider extrinsic contractual and non-contractual elements for the purpose of interpretation.

For the interpretation of network contracts, both state courts and arbitration proceedings can be regarded as satisfactory modes of enforcement, but with different comparative advantages. State courts offer good certainty if combined with a choice-of-forum provision; however, the interpretation and evidence process may be seen as too rigid. Arbitration is less certain, but would provide better adaptability, given the discretion largely recognised in arbitrators both in interpretation and in the taking of evidence.

[29] Baptista (n 27).

[30] ibid, 61.

[31] See Art 25 (6) of the Uncitral Rules; Art 9 (1) of the IBA Rules on the taking of evidence; Art 25 of the ICC Rules.

IV. EFFICIENCY OF PROCEEDINGS

Efficiency of the proceedings is naturally a major concern. Will the decision effectively ensure compliance with the commitments entered into by contractual parties? This is, firstly, a matter of geographical scope of the decision or to put it differently, of the ability of the judgment or award to move freely from one legal system to another (A). It also depends, secondly, on the nature of the available remedies and consequently on the content of the decision (B). It has to do, finally, with the constraints imposed on jurisdictional authorities, and more precisely on the possible interference of internationally mandatory provisions (C).

A. Recognition and Execution of Judgments and Awards

The efficiency of transnational enforcement implies that the decision be capable of recognition and enforcement in several countries. The issue is too well known to be developed here.[32] Yet, it is remarkable that, thanks to the very broad accession to the New York Convention on the recognition and enforcement of foreign awards, it is nowadays much easier to enforce arbitral awards, than it is to enforce the decision of foreign courts.

B. Nature of Available Remedies

The nature of available remedies is a major issue. In the context of contractual networks—in particular when it comes to the regulatory part of the contract(s)—it will often be more important for parties to restore compliance, than to compensate non-compliance. Hence the focus should be on specific performance and injunctive relief. With this view, state courts might prima facie seem better armed, considering the protests against the power of arbitrators to order specific performance.

Specific performance is widely available in legal systems. However, in international contracts, the ability for judges to order specific performance is subjected to a triple constraint. First, remedies must comply with the law of the contract which, according to conflict of laws principles, normally defines the consequences of a breach. Second, they have to be compatible with the power of the judge, as defined by the law of the forum.[33] Finally,

[32] See generally, for the enforcement of arbitration awards: Born (n 1) 3409. Compare for the enforcement of foreign judgments: RE Lutz, *A Lawyer's Handbook for Enforcing Foreign Judgments in the United States and Abroad* (Cambridge, Cambridge University Press, 2006).

[33] Art 15 (1) (c) of Reg Rome I offers a good illustration of this double constraint: 'The law applicable to the contract ... shall govern in particular: (c) within the limits of the powers conferred on the court by its procedural lax, the consequences of a total or partial beach of obligations, including the assessment of damages in so far as it is governed by rules of law'.

they eventually have to be consistent with the law of the country in which performance takes place.[34] The result is that specific performance will be ordered only when all three laws—of the contract, of the forum and of the place of performance—converge in admitting specific performance.

In arbitration, academics have sometimes questioned the power of arbitrators to order specific performance.[35] Arguments refer to 'systemic interests': The proper functioning of the New York Convention should prevent arbitrators from ordering specific performance, because the enforcement of such remedy would require an undesirable degree of courts' involvement.[36] Notwithstanding such arguments, the prevailing doctrine recognises arbitrators having the power to order specific performance.[37] And, although there are very few arbitration rules dealing with specific performance,[38] it is clearly used in arbitral practice.[39] In theory, the issue of the law applicable to the remedy should be discussed in arbitration, as it is in courts. In particular, arbitrators should decide if it is a matter of jurisdictional power (common law approach) ruled by the *lex arbitri*, or a matter of substance (civil law approach) ruled by the law of the contract. But in practice, the question of the law governing the remedies does not appear to be of great importance.[40] Arbitrators usually feel free to resort to specific performance, within the boundaries set by the parties' agreement.[41]

Finally, the comparative approach of courts' practice and arbitration practice reveals that when it comes to specific performance, arbitrators are not in such a disadvantaged position as it could appear prima facie. Eventually, the arbitrators' position could be undermined if parties were to resort

[34] See for instance Art 15 (2) of Reg Rome I: 'In relation to the manner of performance and the steps to be taken in the vent of defective performance, regard shall be had to the lax of the country in which performance takes place'.

[35] TE Elder, 'The Case Against Arbitral Awards of Specific Performance in Transnational Commercial Disputes' (1997) 13 *The Journal of the London Court of International Arbitration*, available at ssrn.com/abstract=1833733.

[36] ibid, 25.

[37] S Jarvin, 'Non-Pecuniary Remedies: The Practice of Declaratory Relief and Specific Performance in International Commercial Arbitration' in AW Rovine (ed), *Contemporary Issues in International Arbitration and Mediation: The Fordham Papers (2007)* (Leiden, Martinus Nijhoff, 2008) 167; ME Schneider, 'Non-Monetary Relief in International Arbitration: Principles and Arbitration Practice' in ME Schneider and J Knoll (eds), *Performance as a Remedy: Non Monetary Relief in International Arbitration* (New York, Juris Publishing, 2011) 3.

[38] With one remarkable exception, in favour of specific performance in arbitration: Rule 43 (a) of the American Association Arbitration Rules: 'The arbitrator may grant any remedy of relief that the arbitrator deems just and equitable and within the scope of the agreement of the parties, including, but not limited to, specific performance of a contract'.

[39] Dominant doctrine and praxis are in favour of such power: Schneider (n 37).

[40] ibid, 42.

[41] Surely, parties may impose upon arbitrators a prohibition to order specific performance, as well as they could expressly agree to confer upon the arbitral tribunal the power to order specific performance.

to courts in order to enforce awards ordering specific performance.[42] In that case, the mandatory provisions of the state where specific performance is to take place could be an impediment. More generally, the interference of the mandatory provisions of states is to be considered.

C. Interference of Internationally Mandatory Provisions

The ability of judges and arbitrators to efficiently enforce a contract depends on the acceptability of the content of the contract for states. It is the role of internationally mandatory provisions of the state (*lois de police*) and of the international public policy *(ordre public)* exception to define some boundaries that the parties should not cross. But the application of these rules can result in the impossibility of enforcing the contract according to the parties' forecast.[43] It is not the place to question the legitimacy of such rules and principles. But it is important to acknowledge that, in this respect, the constraints borne by arbitral tribunals are often lighter than the ones applying in State Courts.

When enforcing a contract, national courts are bound to respect at minimum all internationally mandatory rules of the *lex fori*, as well as mandatory rules of the law of the contract, at least if they do not contradict the former. Eventually, they will also apply, or to a lesser extent take into consideration, the mandatory rules of the country where performance is to take place. The latter step is a condition for the enforceability of the judgment.

Arbitral tribunals are not subjected to any *lex fori*. In the application of the law of the contract, they have important freedom. Even if the issue is a much discussed one, it is commonly considered that states' internationally mandatory provisions and states' international public policy do not constrain arbitrators during arbitral proceedings.[44] Possibly, the obligation for arbitrators to conform to transnational public order is mentioned.[45] But the truth is that the scrutiny of arbitral awards by states is weak, and makes it very difficult for judges to detect potential infringements of transnational public policy.[46] As a result, arbitral awards are mainly subjected to the

[42] Although statistics acknowledge that compliance with arbitral awards is usually voluntary. See: 2008 International Arbitration Study—Corporate Attitudes and Practices: Recognition and Enforcement of Foreign Awards, Queen Mary, University of London, available at: www.arbitration.qmul.ac.uk/research/2008/index.html.

[43] F Cafaggi and S Clavel (n 5) 231–32.

[44] E Gaillard, 'Aspects philosophiques du droit de l'arbitrage international' in *Collected Courses of the Hague Academy of International Law* (Leiden, Brill, 2008) vol 329, no 107.

[45] ibid, no 115.

[46] See the study and conclusion by Born: 'public policy exception is in fact applied relatively infrequently to deny recognition to otherwise valid awards' (n 1) 3646.

mandatory provisions of the country where performance is to take place,[47] as a condition for the efficiency of the award.

V. CONCLUSION

On the basis of the three issues selected as relevant for the purpose of comparing the relative capacity of States' court litigation and arbitration to ensure the efficient enforcement of transnational contractual networks, the conclusion might not be as straightforward as expected. In the absence of any choice of forum provisions, state courts have powerful tools to concentrate in a single forum proceedings relating to a same complex contractual operation. However, arbitration agreements can, more easily than choice of forum clauses, be extended beyond the scope of the contract where they are included, in order to embrace the contractual relationship as a whole. For the interpretation of the contracts, state courts offer better certainty if combined with a choice-of-forum provision, while arbitration provides better adaptability, given the discretion largely recognised of arbitrators both in interpretation and in the taking of evidence. Finally, it is the issue of the efficiency of proceedings which seems, rather surprisingly given the lack of enforcement power of arbitrators, to give advantage to arbitration over state courts for the purpose of enforcing transnational contractual networks. Arbitration awards will often provide better satisfaction to the parties because state constraints will be reduced, without seriously challenging the possibility for parties to obtain an order for specific performance, or the probability to have the award actually enforced.

[47] More precisely, the award should be compatible with the internationally mandatory rules of the place of the seat of arbitration (where the award can be annulled) and of the place of execution (performance). However, some countries allow the execution of arbitration awards—as long as they are compatible with local internationally mandatory provisions—even if they have been annulled in the country of the seat of arbitration. See Born (n 1) 3621; Gaillard (n 44) no 127.

15

Competition Law Enforcement Beyond the Nation-State: A Model for Transnational Enforcement Mechanisms?

KATALIN CSERES

I. INTRODUCTION

IN 2004, REGULATION 1/2003 introduced a new enforcement system for Articles 101 and 102 TFEU (Treaty on the Functioning of the European Union). It has delegated enforcement powers to national competition authorities (NCAs), national courts, increased participation of private actors and introduced a fundamental role for networked governance. This *transnational governance* framework was considered as a major transformation of enforcement, however many of these changes grew out of long-established practices in EU competition law.

This broader transformation of enforcement in EU competition law merits closer examination for the following reasons. First, the transformation of EU competition law enforcement from a *supranational* EU policy to *transnational governance* became subject to similar problems of multi-level governance as other fields of EU law. Second, even though many feared the failure of this transformation, it seems to work smoothly and there are indications that the EU's enforcement model in competition law may serve as a model for economic governance in other policy areas. Third, this transformation has stimulated a remarkable Europeanisation process of competition rules and developed a commonly shared sense of competition policy and culture among the Member States. Fourth, the modes of governance in the enforcement of EU competition law form a mix of traditional governance tools such as hierarchical legislative instruments as well as new governance modes such as the use of soft law and networks.

The aim of this paper is to critically analyse the decentralised enforcement model established by Regulation 1/2003,[1] in particular the governance mechanisms within the European Competition Network (ECN). The paper aims to answer the question whether the decentralised enforcement of EU competition law has been effective, this is that national authorities share competences with the Commission and apply the Treaty rules in a uniform and consistent manner.[2] The effectiveness of decentralised enforcement will be assessed by analysing whether it can be characterised as a bottom-up, experimentalist governance model or rather a top-down hierarchical governance model. Additionally, the paper examines whether its effectiveness as a transnational governance model can be transferred to other fields of EU regulation. Can this enforcement model serve as a blueprint for emerging EU economic governance?

The paper is based on a case study of the new Member States in Central and Eastern Europe (CEECs). Analysing the EU's competition governance model through the involvement of the CEECs highlights the EU's internal governance model in the light of its external governance in the enlargement process and examines both vertical relationships between the national actors and the Commission as well as horizontal relations among the Member States.

II. THE TRANSFORMATION OF COMPETITION LAW ENFORCEMENT IN THE EU

The changes brought by Regulation 1/2003 were considered as a major transformation of enforcement, however many of these changes grew out of long-established practices in the enforcement of EU competition rules before 2004. EU competition law enforcement has developed from a 'first supranational policy in the European Union'[3] into a transnational governance[4] model by 2004. Regulation 1/2003 created an enforcement system of parallel competences and simultaneous application of EU and

[1] See also Commission Notice on cooperation within the Network of Competition Authorities [2004] OJ C 101/43.

[2] Reg 1/2003 of 16 December 2002 on the implementation of the rules on competition laid down in Arts 81 and 82 of the Treaty (Reg 1/2003) [2003] OJ L 1/1, Preamble point 8.

[3] L McGowan and S Wilks, 'The First Supranational Policy in the European Union: Competition Policy' (1995) 28 *European Journal of Political Research* 149.

[4] Governance can be understood as a shift from 'government' to 'governance', a diffusion and fragmentation of governmental arrangements with a decentring of the state; I Maher, 'Regulation and Modes of Governance in EC Competition Law: What's New in Enforcement?' (2007) 31 *Fordham International Law Journal* 1713, 1720; I Maher, 'Competition Law in the International Domain: Networks as a New Form of Governance' (2002) 29(1) *Journal of Law and Society* 116. In the EU context, governance has to be understood in the multi-level context of EU institutions, Member States and growing participation of private actors.

national competition law. In order to coordinate the enforcement of Articles 101 and 102 TFEU among the various enforcers, Regulation 1/2003 established a system of close cooperation between the European Commission and national authorities: the European Competition Network (ECN). The cooperation mechanisms within the ECN play a crucial role in the decentralised enforcement and in the Member States' compliance with EU law. They frame both the vertical mechanisms between the Commission and the Member States and created horizontal cooperation mechanisms among the Member States. These mechanisms accelerated a remarkable Europeanisation[5] process of competition rules.[6]

The transformation of EU competition law enforcement reflects diffusion and fragmentation of government.[7] Regulation 1/2003 introduced several hybrid modes of governance. The Regulation itself is a hierarchical tool of EU governance. European competition law is legislated through directly applicable Treaty provisions and regulations and thus directly enters national legal regimes. At the same time, the shift to a decentralised enforcement system introduced networked governance, a fundamental role for information sharing and increased participation of private actors (leniency, private actions) that reflect modes of new governance.[8] Soft law instruments such as Notices and Guidelines, on the other hand, had been part of the enforcement regime of EU competition law since the 1960s.[9]

A. The Enforcers

Before 2004, the Commission had a central role in the enforcement of EU competition law. Under the enforcement framework of Regulation 17/62 the Commission had a monopoly on the application of Article 101(3) TFEU

[5] Europeanisation is understood as 'the reorientation or reshaping of politics in the domestic arena in ways that reflect policies, practices or preferences advanced through the EU system of governance'. I Bache and A Jordan, 'Europeanization and Domestic Change' in I Bache and A Jordan (eds), *The Europeanization of British Politics* (Basingstoke, Palgrave Macmillan, 2006) 30.

[6] For example, when the candidate countries join the EU and its competition law regime, external incentives and conditionality end their function as governance modes and the mechanisms within the ECN become crucial.

[7] I Maher, 'Regulation and Modes of Governance' (n 4); Y Svetiev, 'Networked Competition Governance in the EU: Delegation, Decentralization or Experimentalist Architecture?' in C Sabel and J Zeitlin (eds), *Experimentalist Governance in the EU* (Oxford, Oxford University Press, 2010); K Yesilkagit and O Danielsen, 'National competition regulators between regulatory autonomy and political control: the case of networked competition governance in the European Union', Paper prepared for EGPA Conference, Toulouse 2010, study-group 'Temporalities, Public Administration and Public Policy', available at: soc.kuleuven.be/io/egpa/org/2010Toul/Papers/Yesilkagit_danielsen_EGPA%202010.pdf.

[8] I Maher, 'Functional and Normative Delegation to Non-Majoritarian Institutions: The Case of the European Competition Network' (2009) 7 *Comparative European Politics* 414.

[9] ibid.

and enjoyed a considerable margin of discretion in applying the conditions under Article 101(3).[10] This central role of the Commission in the enforcement of European competition law was an important exception to the decentralised enforcement of EU law. This meant on the one hand, that the relations between EU and national competition laws remained mostly unaddressed in contrast to the judicial supremacy doctrine in other substantive areas of EU law and on the other, that competition policy was immune from general problems of multi-level governance[11] such as the enforcement gap between substantive EU rules and Member States' procedures.

This changed in 2004, when Regulation 1/2003[12] (Article 3 (1))[13] imposed an obligation on the Member States' NCAs to apply Articles 101 and 102 TFEU parallel to their national competition rules when the effect on trade criterion is fulfilled and introduced a strict supremacy standard.[14] While the convergence rule of Article 3 acted as a radical intervention in the domestic legal systems of the Member States, it should be remembered that this convergence had been ongoing before Regulation 1/2003 came into force.[15]

[10] Council Reg No 17: First Reg implementing Arts 85 and 86 of the Treaty [1962] OJ 13/204. This had a number of reasons. First, many Member States lacked a proper competition law and enforcement regime until the 1980s or even late 1990s. Second, competition law in many Member States has not been regarded as an economic policy tool of primary importance. Third, the relationship between EU and national laws as well as the possible convergence or divergence between the different national regimes remained without significant legal or economic consequences.

[11] F Cengiz, 'Regulation 1/2003 Revisited' (2009) 42 *TILEC Discussion Paper* 26, 30.

[12] Reg 1/2003, 1.

[13] The new procedural framework abolished the notification system and Art 101 became directly applicable in its entirety, thus including Art 101(3). This required the Member States to enforce Arts 101 and 102 TFEU without the need for notification and a prior administrative decision on Art 101(3).

Art 3(1) defines the principle of simultaneous application of national law and competition law with the limitation posed in Art 3(2): Member States may not adopt and apply on their territory stricter national competition laws which prohibit agreements, decisions by associations of undertakings or concerted practices which may affect trade between Member States but which do not restrict competition within the meaning of Art 101(1), or which fulfill the conditions of Art 101(3) or which are covered by a Reg for the application of Art 101(3). In other words, stricter national competition laws are not as such objectionable, as long as they are not applied to agreements, concerted practices and decisions of associations of undertakings that fall within the jurisdictional scope of the EU competition rules, in breach of Art 3(2). The convergence rule contained in para 2, seeks to create a level playing field by providing for a single standard of assessment which allows undertakings to design EU-wide business strategies without having to check them against all the relevant national sets of competition rules. European Commission, 'Commission Staff Working Paper of 29 April 2009 accompanying the Report on the functioning of Regulation 1/2003', SEC(2009) 574 final, paras 141–42, 152. Supremacy of EU competition law over national competition law has been established by Case 14/68 *Walt Wlihelm v Bundeskartellamt* [1969] ECR 1, but only for cases where an exemption under Art 101(3) has been granted. See also more recently Case C-17/10 *Toshiba Corporation and Others v Úřad pro ochranu hospodářské soutěže*, judgment of 14 February 2012, nyr.

[14] This means that national provisions have to comply with the EU interpretations of Arts 101 and 102 TFEU when they are applied parallel to their national rules.

[15] RJ Van der Bergh and PD Camasesca, *European Competition Law and Economics: A Comparative Perspective* (Antwerp, Intersentia, 2001) 125, 126.

Many EU Member States abandoned their ineffective competition regulation based on the so-called administrative control model during the 1980s and 1990s and adopted a competition law system similar to the rules laid down in Articles 101 and 102 TFEU and the EU Merger Regulation.[16] Competition law and policy gained importance.[17] Waarden and Drahos found that this convergence was due to a subtle top-down pressure from the Commission and the European courts combined with the emergence of strong epistemic community of competition lawyer.[18]

B. The Procedures and Institutions

The decentralised enforcement system became subject to similar problems of multi-level governance as other substantive parts of EU law. Regulation 1/2003 contains some basic rules on the powers of the NCAs but leaves national procedures and institutional designs unaddressed. Article 5 lists their powers when they apply Articles 101 and 102 TFEU by, in fact, listing what type of decisions the NCAs can take in such cases. Article 5 is a very basic provision and does not formally regulate or harmonise the procedural rules to be followed by the NCAs or the ECN.[19] This means that the NCAs apply the same substantive rules, but in divergent procedural frameworks and may impose different sanctions. These procedural differences had been addressed to some extent in Articles 11 and 12 of Regulation 1/2003 through the cooperation of the NCAs within the ECN.[20] National competition laws differ on many aspects of the competition law procedures such as fines, liability of undertakings or setting priorities and these differences

[16] In the Member States, the basic conditions for free competition were introduced by the legal reforms between 1989 and 1991. From 1990 onwards, new national competition laws were enacted and thus the enforcement of competition law could begin. After 1990 accession to the EU became the most relevant external pressure to influence competition policies in Eastern Europe. See more details in KJ Cseres, 'The Impact of Regulation 1/2003 in the New Member States' (2010) 6 *Competition Law Review* 145.

[17] The new competition laws followed a prohibition system and enforcement was trusted to an administrative body with judicial-like decision-making. Enforcement became primarily administrative law based, with administrative law sanctions. These new competition regimes worked more effectively than their predecessors and indeed their main achievement was to gain social and political support for the enforcement of competition law. D Gerber, *Law and Competition in Twentieth Century Europe: Protecting Prometheus* (Oxford, Oxford University Press, 1998) 402–03.

[18] F van Waarden and M Drahos, 'Courts and (Epistemic) Communities in the Convergence of Competition Policies' (2002) 9 *Journal of European Public Policy* 913.

[19] European Commission (n 13) para 200.

[20] ECN's Working Group on cooperation issues and due process monitor this voluntary convergence among the Member States. Individual Reports provide an overview of the different systems and procedures for antitrust investigations within the ECN. See ec.europa.eu/competition/ecn/documents.html.

may have far-reaching consequences in decisions.[21] For example, custodial sanctions may be imposed on cartelists in the United Kingdom or Estonia while in most other Member States it is their firms that are subject to administrative fines.[22]

Under Article 35 of Regulation 1/2003, each Member State had a clear obligation to designate a competition authority responsible for the application of Articles 101 and 102 TFEU before 1 May 2004.[23] The chosen authorities could be administrative or judicial in nature. The only requirement was that they have to be designated in order to guarantee that the provisions of Regulation 1/2003 are effectively complied with.[24] Beyond Article 35 of Regulation 1/2003, neither further requirements nor additional formal rules have been formulated on the powers and procedures to be followed by the NCAs.[25]

Hence, Articles 5 and 35 of Regulation 1/2003 imposed very rudimental obligations on the Member States allowing for legal diversity in national procedures and institutional designs. This approach is in line with the general principle of subsidiarity, as enshrined in Article 5 TEU (Treaty on European Union), and respects the Member States' procedural autonomy. This freedom is, however, not unlimited. Article 4(3) TEU requires the Member States to take all appropriate measures to ensure fulfilment of the obligations arising out of the EU Treaty and facilitate the achievement of the Community's tasks.[26] The diversity of the national competition authorities'

[21] Further differences exist on criminal sanctions, liability in groups of undertakings, liability of associations of undertakings, succession of undertakings, prescription periods and the standard of proof, the power to impose structural remedies, as well as the ability of their NCAs to formally set enforcement priorities.

[22] See also K Ost, 'From Regulation 1 to Regulation 2: National Enforcement of EU Cartel Prohibition and the Need For Further Convergence' (2014) 5 *Journal of European Competition Law and Practice* 125.

[23] Art 35(1) of Reg 1/2003: 'The Member States shall designate the competition authority or authorities responsible for the application of Articles 81 and 82 of the Treaty in such a way that the provisions of this regulation are effectively complied with. The measures necessary to empower those authorities to apply those Articles shall be taken before 1 May 2004. The authorities designated may include courts'.

[24] Point 2 of the Notice on cooperation within the NCA provides that 'Under general principles of Community law, Member States are under an obligation to set up a sanctioning system providing for sanctions which are effective, proportionate and dissuasive for infringements of EC law'. See also Case C-176/03 *Commission of the European Communities v Council of the European Union* [2005] ECR I-7879, paras 46–55.

[25] Albeit their competences were very roughly set out in Arts 5 and 6 of Reg 1/2003. Although national procedural rules had to provide for the admission of the Commission as amicus curiae in national procedures, NCAs will have to be empowered to conduct examinations in accordance with Reg 1/2003, and Member States will have to report to the Commission. The Commission retains broad supervisory powers that allows it to intervene in proceedings before national authorities and which in fact enables it to act as 'primus inter pares'. See Art 11(6).

[26] Moreover, they should 'abstain from any measure which could jeopardize the attainment of the objectives of this Treaty'. On the basis of this loyalty principle the European Court of Justice has also developed the so-called useful effect doctrine in EU competition law. According to this doctrine the Member States may not introduce legislation or take decisions, which would

institutional design is largely determined by country-specific traditions.[27] For example, the CEECs gave broad market-regulatory tasks to their regulatory agencies, sometimes with overlapping competences. They have all created a single agency model with 'non-unitary' structure, where investigative and decision-making activities are separated functionally even though they are handled within one single administrative institution.[28]

One aspect of administrative capacity is gaining relevance in EU law: independence of national competition authorities.[29] EU law has traditionally focused on independence from market players,[30] and it is this very feature that Courts had established as a core element in regulated markets.[31] However, the relevance of political independence is a fundamental cornerstone of administrative authorities in the EU. While European legislation has become detailed with respect to the concept of independence, EU judiciary has not formulated any general principles on the independence of regulatory authorities.[32] Accordingly, EU law requires regulators to be

deprive the competition rules of their useful effect. This doctrine has no explicit legal basis. In the former EC Treaty this doctrine was founded on Art 3(1)(g) (now implemented in a Protocol No 27 on the internal market and competition) read in conjunction with Art 10 (now Art 4(3) TEU) and Arts 81 and 82 EC (now Arts 101 and 102 TFEU). Case C-267/86 *Van Eycke v ASPA* [1988] ECR 4769, para 16.

[27] Ost (n 22).

[28] Some of these authorities, including the Czech and Slovak ones, follow a 'unitary' structure and have integrated administrative hierarchies. In other words, they do not have different bodies carrying out different steps of the procedure, even though there may be different divisions (eg a competition department and a legal department) inside these authorities that deal with separate aspects of a given case. The Reports of the ECN's Working Group on cooperation issues and due process provide an overview of the different systems and procedures for antitrust investigations within the ECN. See European Competition Network, 'Decision-Making Powers: Report', 31 October 2012, 6–7, available at: ec.europa.eu/competition/ecn/decision_making_powers_report_en.pdf.

[29] European Commission, 'Commission Staff Working Document SWD (2014) 231—Enhancing Competition Enforcement by the Member States' Competition Authorities: Institutional and Procedural Issues', SWD(2014) 231/2, available at: ec.europa.eu/competition/antitrust/legislation/swd_2014_231_en.pdf.

[30] It was already in 1988, in Dir 88/301/EEC of 16 May 1988 on competition in the markets in telecommunications terminal equipment [1988] OJ L131/73, that the Commission introduced in Art 6 an obligation on the Member States to entrust the regulation of terminal equipment to a body independent from market parties active in the provision of telecoms services or equipment. This requirement of independence has also been implemented in the second liberalisation package in the energy and telecoms sector.

[31] See the judgments of the Court of Justice of the European Union Case C-202/88 *France v Commission* [1991] ECR I-1223, paras 51–52; Case C-18/88 *RTT v GB-Inno-BM* [1991] ECR I-5941, paras 25–26; Case C-82/07 *Comisión del Mercado de las Telecomunicaciones* [2008] ECR I-1265.

[32] The latest package of liberalisation Dirs of 2009 mentions a general principle of independence towards the legislative and executive organs. Art 35 of Dir 2009/72/EC of 13 July 2009 concerning common rules for the internal market in electricity and repealing Dir 2003/54/EC [2009] OJ L211/55, compels Member States to make the regulatory authority 'functionally independent from any other public or private entity' and give it the autonomy to decide 'independently of any public body'. Art 39 of Dir 2009/73/EC of 13 July 2009 concerning

independent from political institutions, yet without laying down the criteria of independence that regulatory authorities must meet.[33]

Regulation 1/2003 does not specify any kind of requirements on the formal independence of NCAs.[34] However, political independence from central government is not guaranteed in all countries, a fact that can be problematic as competition authorities have to use their expertise independently from political and market actors.[35] It is not surprising that the Commission is now urging for more independence for NCAs in order to enhance further the enforcement of EU competition law.[36]

In sum, Regulation 1/2003 posed a challenge to the uniform application of EU law. When NCAs apply Articles 101 and 102 TFEU, they make use of their national procedural rules and impose remedies and sanctions that are available in their respective legal systems. Consequently, the enforcement of EU competition rules has come to rely on the effective administrative enforcement of EU competition rules through national administrative procedures.

III. EVALUATION OF THE MULTILEVEL GOVERNANCE SYSTEM

The public enforcement of EU competition law takes place in a multiple layered system composed of EU and national law and supervised by

common rules for the internal market in natural gas and repealing Dir 2003/55/EC [2009] OJ L211/94, formulates the same obligation. Dir 2009/140/EC of 25 November 2009 amending Dirs 2002/21/EC on a common regulatory framework for electronic communications networks and services, 2002/19/EC on access to, and interconnection of, electronic communications networks and associated facilities, and 2002/20/EC on the authorisation of electronic communications networks and services [2009] OJ L337/37 states that 'national regulatory authorities responsible for ex-ante market regulation or for the resolution of disputes between undertakings ... shall act independently and shall not seek or take instructions from any other body in relation to the exercise of these tasks assigned to them under national law implementing Community law'.

[33] CJ Hanretty, P Larouche and AP Reindl, 'Independence, Accountability and Perceived Quality of Regulators', CERRE Report, 6 March 2012, available at: www.cerre.eu/sites/cerre/files/120306_IndependenceAccountabilityPerceivedQualityofNRAs.pdf.

[34] *Syfait* is an important case in this context where the Court of Justice of the EU has gone beyond the analysis of the formal independence of the Greek competition authority. Not only did the Court analyse the NCA's functional independence in detail, it even concluded that the Commission may remove a case from the NCA if the latter is not sufficiently independent. Case C-53/03 *Syfait* [2005] ECR I-4609, paras 31–36.

[35] The most recent and comprehensive study on the issue of the formal independence of NCAs is likely in the work of Guidi who shows extensive variations in independence among the NCAs. However, Guidi's study raises the question of how does an NCA's de iure independence reflect its de facto independence. M Guidi, 'Does Independence Affect Regulatory Performance? The Case of National Competition Authorities in the European Union', EUI Working Paper RSCAS 2011/64; M Guidi, 'Delegation and Varieties of Capitalism: Explaining the Independence of National Competition Agencies in the European Union' (2014) 12 *Comparative European Politics* 343.

[36] European Commission (n 29).

the Commission and 28 national competition authorities. The aim of the decentralised enforcement system under Regulation 1/2003 was to delegate enforcement powers to national competition authorities and national courts,[37] in order to relieve the Commission of its increasing administrative burden and make enforcement more efficient. Accordingly, a system of parallel competences and simultaneous application of EU and national competition laws was created and mechanisms of close cooperation between the European Commission and the Member States to achieve uniform and consistent application of Articles 101 and 102 TFEU.

The enforcement of EU competition law by national actors is crucial in evaluating the effectiveness of the compound procedural mechanisms of Regulation 1/2003.[38] It has been questioned whether an enforcement system where NCAs with diverging capacities and resources apply different national procedural rules and impose a variety of sanctions and remedies, could jeopardise the effectiveness of EU law. It has also been argued that consistent policy enforcement requires a certain degree of harmonisation of procedures, resources, experiences and independence of the NCAs.[39]

The Court of Justice of the European Union (CJEU) judgments, such as *Tele 2 Polska*[40] and *VEBIC*,[41] signal that an in-depth discussion is needed

[37] Arts 5 and 6 of Regulation 1/2003.

[38] The effectiveness of EU law enforcement had been defined in literature by 'the degree to which both the formal transposition and the practical application of supranational measures at the national level correspond to the objectives specified in the European legislation'. The main factors of effective competition law enforcement lie in: Effective administrative organisation, clearly worded national law provisions and the extent to which European rules are successfully transplanted into the existing institutional and regulatory traditions of the Member States. O Treib, 'Implementing and Complying with EU Governance Outputs' (2006) 1 *Living Reviews in European Governance* 1, available at: www.livingreviews.org/lreg-2006-1. C Knill and A Lenschow, 'Coping with Europe: The Impact of British and German Administrations on the Implementation of EU Environmental Policy' (1998) 5 *Journal of European Public Policy* 595.

[39] Cengiz (n 11); C Gauer, 'Does the Effectiveness of the EU Network of Competition Authorities Require a Certain Degree of Harmonisation of National Procedures and Sanctions?' in CD Ehlermann and I Atanasiu (eds), *European Competition Law Annual 2000: The Modernisation of EC Antitrust Policy* (Oxford, Hart Publishing, 2001) 187–201; F Jenny, 'Does the Effectiveness of the EU Network of Competition Authorities Depend on a Certain Degree of Homogeneity within its Membership?' in Ehlermann and Atanasiu, ibid 208–10.

[40] See Case C-375/09 *Prezes Urzędu Ochrony Konkurencji i Konsumentów v Tele2 Polska sp z o.o, now Netia SA w Warszawie* [2011] ECR I-3055.

[41] See Case C-439/08 *Vlaamse federatie van verenigingen van Brood- en Banketbakkers, Ijsbereiders en Chocoladebewerkers (VEBIC) VZW* [2010] ECR I-12471. As Advocate General Kokott in *T-Mobile Netherlands and Others* argued: '[i]n those circumstances, it is of fundamental importance that the uniform application of competition rules in the [European Union] be maintained. Not only the fundamental objective of equal conditions of competition for undertakings on the single market but also the concern for uniform protection of consumer interests in the entire [European Union] would be undermined if in the enforcement of the competition rules of Articles [101 and 102 TFEU] significant disparities occurred between the [NCAs] and courts of the Member States. For that reason, the objective of a uniform application of Articles [101 and 102 TFEU] is a central theme which runs throughout Regulation No 1/2003'. Opinion of AG Kokott in Case C-8/08 *T-Mobile Netherlands* [2009] ECR I-4529, 85. See also Case C-8/08 *T-Mobile Netherlands* [2009] ECR I-4529, paras 85 and 86.

on the legal puzzles that arise when NCAs apply Articles 101 and 102 TFEU in accordance with domestic procedural rules. The procedural differences had been to some extent addressed in Articles 11 and 12 of Regulation 1/2003 with regard to the cooperation within the ECN. Moreover, the Member States have voluntarily converged their procedural rules to those of the Commission. While there is a certain degree of 'voluntary' harmonisation towards the Commission's procedural model, Member States resist to further harmonise procedural rules.[42]

IV. VOLUNTARY HARMONISATION

Regulation 1/2003 did not formally intervene with the procedures of national competition authorities over and above Article 5 of the Regulation and the rules applicable to cooperation mechanisms.[43] Member States voluntarily harmonised certain elements of the procedural rules,[44] towards Regulation 1/2003 and the accompanying soft law instruments such as the leniency notice.[45] This convergence so far took place through legal transplants,[46] by implementing similar procedural rules as those of the Commission. The underlying reason for these transplants could be that once these rules and enforcement methods work effectively and efficiently in the

[42] The Commission argued that procedural divergences merit further examination and reflection. In fact, it has set an initial step to further harmonise substantive rules on unilateral conduct and procedural rules. The Commission has stated that it considers soft harmonisation or the adoption of certain minimum standards through legislative rules. European Commission (n 13) para 207. See also European Competition Network, 'Investigative Powers: Report' and 'Decision Making Powers: Report' of 31 October 2012, available at: ec.europa.eu/competition/ecn/documents.html.

[43] The Commission stated that in important respects, the Reg reconciled the requirements of substantive coherence with the existing procedural diversity amongst NCAs. European Commission (n 13) para 200.

[44] In 2012 the ECN's Report on decision-making powers reflected a high level of convergence among the NCAs and was intended to serve as a basis for further harmonisation on the NCAs' procedures for competition law enforcement. European Competition Network (n 28) 5. In 2013, this convergence of national competition law procedures was summarised in the ECN's Recommendations on key investigative and decision-making powers. See in particular the ECN Recommendation on the power to set priorities, ibid 3; European Commission (n 29) para 180.

[45] European Competition Network, 'Results of the Questionnaire on the Reform of Member States' National Competition Laws After EC Regulation No 1/2003', 22 May 2013, available at: ec.europa.eu/competition/ecn/convergence_table_en.pdf.

[46] Convergence between different legal rules towards an efficient model may take place as a result of a legal transplant or as an outcome of a competitive process between different legal formants, U Mattei, L Antoniolli and A Rossato, 'Comparative Law and Economics' in B Bouckaert and G de Geest (eds), *Encyclopedia of Law and Economics* (Cheltenham, Edward Elgar Publishing, 2000) 508–11. In the first case, legal transplants are implemented because they proved to be efficient in other legal systems. In the second case, convergence towards efficiency is the result of the interaction between different legal formants. So, while legal transplants are governed by hierarchy the second scenario is governed by competition among legal formants.

hands of the Commission, they will prove successful in the hands of the NCAs as well.

However, the effectiveness of the transplanted rules was not always successful in the different institutional frameworks of the Member States. An example is in the CEECs, where agencies often had to divide resources between several legislative competences and, crucially, depended on institutional capacity.[47] NCAs did not enforce the transplanted rules due to constraints in administrative capacity and the enforcement tools have not always delivered the expected results.[48] Moreover, the CEECs faced important questions on the (parallel) enforcement of national and EU law.[49] Some of these countries even voiced the need for more guidance from the Commission on the decentralised application of Articles 101 and 102 TFEU.[50] It has been argued that such guidance is most needed with regard to the national courts.[51]

It is beyond the scope of this chapter to provide a comprehensive analysis of judicial review, still it should be noted that NCAs express certain scepticism with regard to the expertise of national judges to assess competition law issues.[52] Certain NCAs even consider judicial review to be an important

[47] This has been confirmed by the most recent example of Croatia; M Kapural, 'New Kid on the Block: Croatia's Path to Convergence with EU Competition Rules' (2014) 5 *Journal of Competition Law and Practice* 218.

[48] This is, for example, the case with regard to the power to investigate private premises. There are no actual experiences of the use of this investigative tool in the Czech Republic, Estonia, Hungary, Romania, Slovenia and the Slovak Republic and in Bulgaria it does not exist at all. European Commission (n 13) para 202; European Commission (n 29).

[49] See Case C-17/10 *Toshiba* (n 13) and Case C-68/12 *Protimonopolný úrad Slovenskej republiky*, judgment of 7 February 2013, nyr.

[50] See Slovakian NCA, Z Šabová, 'Coherent Application of the EU Competition Law in Slovakia', Antimonopoly Office of the Slovak Republic, Visegrad 4 Competition Conference, Budapest 20 March 2014, available at: www.gvh.hu/en//data/cms1026431/2_panel_3_Z_Sabova_presentation.pdf.

[51] National courts apply European competition law when they review administrative decisions of NCAs, whose decisions are subject to judicial review by the national courts. Moreover, the national courts have the competence to enforce competition law in private law claims, especially in damages claims based on national tort law. Pursuant to Art 15 (3) of Reg 1/2003, the European Commission submitted a written observation to the Slovakian Supreme Court. In its amicus intervention, the Commission expressed its opinion on the parallel application of EU and national competition rules and the possibility to impose fines for abuse. The case concerned the application of the concept of economic continuity and the effectiveness of fines in relation thereto. The Commission's statement was consistent with the argumentation of the Slovakian NCA's appeal to the Supreme Court. In its judgment of 31 January 2012, the Slovak Supreme Court held that the approach of the appeal court to the issue of fines and their functions was not compatible with the need to ensure effective enforcement of EU competition rules. Available at: ec.europa.eu/competition/ecn/brief/03_2013/sk_dot.pdf and ec.europa.eu/competition/court/antitrust_amicus_curiae.html.

[52] 'About ten Member States have not sent any judgment yet to the Commission. The absence of feedback on judicial activity in those Member States and the overall small number of judgments received suggest that there are lapses in the cooperation mechanism that need to be corrected'. European Commission, Commission Staff Working Document SWD (2014) 230—Ten Years of Antitrust Enforcement under Regulation 1/2003, SWD(2014) 230/2, 9 July 2014, available at: ec.europa.eu/competition/antitrust/legislation/swd_2014_230_en.pdf, paras 7, 248 and 244–52.

impediment to the effective decentralised enforcement. They argue that judges are unfamiliar with the principles of competition law analysis and find it difficult to come to grips with competition law. The competition agency may find itself losing an unacceptable number of its cases in court. Moreover, judicial process may take too long and thus frustrates effective law enforcement.[53] While it can be argued that the cooperation mechanisms within the ECN and with the Commission represent a certain degree of administrative accountability control, national judicial review is indispensable with its complementary function of judicial accountability. Accordingly, the reluctance of national courts to review the decisions of the NCAs with more rigour is decisive in an effective enforcement framework.

These facts clearly challenge public views on the success of the decentralised enforcement system,[54] and support those commentators who argue that in fact a (re)-centralisation has taken place.[55] On the same basis some NCAs also argued for, in fact, more central steering from the Commission. In the next section, the governance mechanisms of the ECN and the close cooperation between the NCAs and the Commission will be analysed, as they are crucial indicators of the effectiveness of the governance framework of Regulation 1/2003.

[53] OECD, Global Forum on Competition, 'Questionnaire on the Challenges Facing Young Competition Authorities, Contribution from Latvia', DAF/COMP/GF/WD(2009)2, 5; OECD, Global Forum on Competition, Questionnaire on the Challenges Facing Young Competition Authorities, Contribution from Slovak Republic', DAF/COMP/GF/WD(2009)62, 5–6; OECD, Global Forum on Competition, Questionnaire on the Challenges Facing Young Competition Authorities, Contribution from Czech Republic, DAF/COMP/GF/WD(2009)6, 10–11; Experience showed that those countries where specialised courts existed faced fewer problems than where general courts dealt with competition cases. For more details, see Cseres (n 15).

[54] A Italianer, 'The ECN, convergence and enforcement of EU competition law: achievements and challenges', 3 October 2014, Vilnius, Lithuania European Competition Day of the Lithuanian Presidency, available at ec.europa.eu/competition/speeches/text/sp2013_08_en.pdf; WPJ Wils, 'Ten Years of Regulation 1/2003—A Retrospective' (2013) *Journal of European Competition Law and Practice*, published online 9 July 2013. B Lasserre, 'The Future of the European Competition Network', St Gallen International Competition Law Forum ICF, 16 May 2014, available at: ssrn.com/abstract=2567620; 'Focus, implementation, inclusiveness—The impact of the ICN', Interview of the President of the Bundeskartellamt and the Chairman of the ICN, Andreas Mundt, to Concurrences, *Competition Law Journal*, 15 November 2013, available at: www.bundeskartellamt.de/SharedDocs/Interviews/EN/Concurrence-ImpactICN_neu.html; H Kassim and K Wright, 'The European Competition Network: a European Regulatory Network with a Difference', Paper presented at ECPR Standing Group on Regulatory Governance, Third Biennial Conference, Dublin, 17–19 June 2010, available at: regulation.upf.edu/dublin-10-papers/2E3.pdf.

[55] G Monti, 'Independence, Interdependence and Legitimacy: the EU Commission, National Competition Authorities, and the European Competition Network' EUI Working Paper Law 2014/01, available at: cadmus.eui.eu/bitstream/handle/1814/29218/LAW_2014_01.pdf?sequence=1, 16; S Wilks, 'Agency Escape: Decentralization or Dominance of the European Commission in the Modernization of Competition Policy?' (2005) 18 *Governance* 431.

V. THE ECN

The ECN was created in 2004 in order to ensure uniform and consistent enforcement of Articles 101 and 102 TFEU. It lays down cooperation mechanisms for NCAs when they apply Articles 101 and 102 TFEU. The ECN was originally set up to provide regular contacts and consultations on enforcement policy between the Commission and the NCAs.[56] In the meantime, the network has moved beyond its original goals and it functions today as a forum to discuss enforcement strategies as well as for mutual learning and information sharing. The ECN makes Member States comply with EU law while peer accountability provides ways of conduct monitoring by the Commission as well as among the Member States.[57]

The two main pillars of the ECN are case allocation and information exchange. Information sharing within the ECN is based on formal obligations (Articles 11(3) and (4) of Regulation 1/2003): Member States share information about their investigations and about decisions to be taken. They may also share confidential information although respecting the safeguards associated with fundamental rights (Articles 11 and 12(1)).[58] These formal cooperation mechanisms also make it possible to exchange informal advice, experiences with regard to market analysis or regulatory processes, enforcement strategies and, ultimately, other 'softer' information. Furthermore, regular meetings and interactions prompt members to create personal contacts and to acquire institutional and cultural information about each other and the Commission. This socialisation process is an important aspect of the governance mechanisms within the ECN. It creates a commonly shared vision between ECN members of what competition rules are, what the goals are of competition law enforcement, and how it should be enforced. Members of the network share these common objectives and develop a shared identity.[59] These formal and informal mechanisms of information exchange are core features of the ECN's governance model.

The work of the ECN is organised at four different levels: the yearly meetings of the Directors General of the European Competition Authorities, the Plenary meetings, the horizontal working groups and the sector-specific

[56] Point 1 of the Notice on cooperation within the Network of Competition Authorities.

[57] For example, for the new Member States once accession to the EU's competition law regime is completed, external incentives and conditionality end their function as governance modes and so the mechanisms within the ECN become crucial.

[58] They may conduct inspections of premises or other fact-finding activities on behalf of another NCA investigating a case (Art 22 (1) of Reg 1/2003).

[59] I Maher, 'Regulation and Modes of Governance' (n 4) 1732; I Maher and O Stefan, 'Competition Law in Europe: The Challenge of a Network Constitution' in OD Prosser and T Rawlings (eds), *The Regulatory State: Constitutional Implications* (Oxford, Oxford University Press, 2010) 188.

subgroups.[60] The ECN is a highly juridified network with detailed cooperation mechanisms defined in Regulation 1/2003 and in the Notice on cooperation within the Network of Competition Authorities. The ECN is characterised by formalism to safeguard consistent law application, and by a quasi-hierarchical structure where the Commission has a central position.[61]

While the ECN has been formally set up with a vertical division of enforcement powers between the Commission and the NCAs, it has proved far more horizontal in practice.[62] It was primarily designed as a policy-enforcement network, and yet it functions as a policy-making network through informal discussions and mutual policy learning among the NCAs. For example, it is clear that the ECN is a platform where visible harmonisation efforts are made, such as the ECN Model Leniency Programme,[63] the review process of Article 102 TFEU and sector specific regulations.[64] While the functions of enforcement and policy-making and formal and informal information exchange are mutually supportive, it is this spill-over effect into informal soft law-making where the most criticism with regard to its transparency and accountability has arisen.[65]

VI. A MODEL OF EXPERIMENTALIST GOVERNANCE?

Research on the ECN has focused so far on the role of the Commission vis-à-vis the Member States rather than on the Member States as local actors.[66]

[60] The Director General's meeting is the forum for discussing major policy issues such as the review of the Commission's policy on Art 102, the ECN leniency model programme, increases in food and energy prices and the financial crisis. The ECN Plenary discusses horizontal issues of common interest policy such as the ability of national competition authorities to disapply state measures in their application of the EU competition rules. Under the ECN Plenary forum several working groups operate that deal with horizontal issues of legal, economic or procedural nature situated at the interface between EU law and the different national laws. The ECN's Working group on Cooperation issues and Due process follows up on the state of convergence of enforcement procedures in the different Member States. The Sectoral Subgroups deal with issues from specific sectors such as energy, food, banking and payments. The working groups are created by the NCAs as their needs dictate and they are composed of expert officials from the NCAs and the Commission and they share views and best practices.

[61] Compared to other European regulatory Networks, the ECN did not emerge as an initiative of the Member States, unlike other European regulatory networks but was centrally designed and established by the Commission. D Coen and M Thatcher, 'Network Governance and Multi-level Delegation: European Networks of Regulatory Agencies' (2008) 28 *Journal of Public Policy* 49.

[62] Maher and Stefan (n 59) 181.

[63] European Competition Network, 'ECN Model Leniency Programme', 2006, available at: ec.europa.eu/competition/ecn/model_leniency_en.pdf, and the 2012 revision, available at: ec.europa.eu/competition/ecn/mlp_revised_2012_en.pdf.

[64] European Commission (n 13) paras 248–49.

[65] DMB Gerard, 'The ECN—Network Antitrust Enforcement in the European Union' in D Geradin and I Lianos, *Research Handbook on EU Competition Law* (Cheltenham, Edward Elgar, 2013) 181; Maher and Stefan (n 59) 191; Cengiz (n 11).

[66] Kassim and Wright (n 54); Y Svetiev (n 6); Gerard (n 65); Cengiz (n 11).

The perspective of this paper is to analyse also the lower levels of the governance model by analysing the ECN's horizontal dimension among the Member States.

In the legislative framework of the ECN the Commission's role has been laid down as *primus inter pares* who guards uniform application of EU rules.[67] While it has been argued that the ECN functions as a successful 'joint enterprise' between the Member States and the Commission,[68] in practice the Commission still plays a key role. It may not make use of its legislative prerogatives on the basis of Article 11(6) of Regulation 1/2003 to relieve a national competition authority of its competence for reasons of coherent application,[69] but it does have an influential role. The Commission sets the agenda of the plenary meetings and even though the NCAs are invited to approve it and to add items to it,[70] the NCAs stated that agenda setting is a powerful tool and even though discussions are not dominated by the Commission, its officials take part in working groups and subgroups do take a very active role.[71]

The ECN has often been characterised as an experimentalist governance model[72] as it employs new governance modes such as consultations, negotiations and soft law instruments. It has been argued that there is a certain 'can-do-ness'[73] in the work of the ECN and that it has been functioning without any major conflicts or serious political or judicial challenges since its conception.[74] This alleged success rests on peer esteem, trust, confidentiality and credibility among the ECN members and is strengthened by a strong epistemic community of lawyers, officials and academics.[75]

[67] Reg 1/2003 granted the Commission new and extended some of its existing enforcement powers. Art 9 of Reg 1/2003 grants the Commission the power of accepting commitments from the parties under investigation in Arts 101 and 102 procedures and making these commitments binding. Reg 1/2003 also extended its search powers during sector inquiries. It has given it the prerogative to bring Arts 101 and 102 investigations of NCAs to an end by opening its own proceedings against the same violation. Art 11(6) Reg 1/2003; see also Opinion of AG Mazák in Case C-375/09 *Prezes* (n 40) para 47.

[68] European Commission (n 13); European Commission (n 52) paras 229–44; Kassim and Wright (n 54); Y Svetiev (n 6).

[69] European Commission (n 13) para 28.

[70] Kassim and Wright (n 54).

[71] Interviews with NCAs in CEECS.

[72] Svetiev concluded that the ECN leaves substantial scope for the emergence of experimentalist governance mechanisms. His analysis focuses on the ECN's Model Leniency Programme and conducts a textual analysis of the programme where he identifies the presence of experimentalist governance; Svetiev (n 6).

[73] Maher (n 8) 427; European Commission, 'Annual Report on Competition Policy: 2005', 14, 69, available at ec.europa.eu/competition/publications/annual_report/2005/en.pdf.

[74] Wilks (n 55); Cengiz (n 11).

[75] Van Waarden and Drahos (n 18) 928–29; Maher (n 8) 425.

However, there is also criticism arguing that there are important characteristics of hierarchical governance present in the ECN.[76] First, the formal governance framework of the decentralised enforcement system did preserve features of the Commission's central role.[77] Hierarchical governance is present in the form of directly applicable legislative instruments as the Treaty provisions and regulations, which directly enter national legal regimes. Accordingly, there is a strong top-down pressure from the Commission to the Member States to align national competition rules to the provisions of the EU.[78] The traditional forms of governance are further strengthened by a large body of case law, traditional application of economic analysis and the active involvement of the epistemic community of competition lawyers.[79]

VII. THE CEECs IN THE ECN

This section will answer the question whether the CEECs are mere passive users of the ECN or if they actively contribute to its work, for example, in setting the agenda and influencing decision-making. This analysis is based on legislative documents such as the Annual Reports of the NCAs in CEECs between 2005 and 2013 if available. This analysis was complemented by an open questionnaire sent to all 10 new Member States (except Croatia). Where possible, the questionnaire was discussed with the NCAs in CEECs in semi-structured interviews.[80]

Analysing the EU's competition governance model through the participation of the CEECs puts the EU's internal governance model in the light of its external governance in the enlargement policy. The accession process has been characterised by top-down rule transfer and the hierarchical governance mode of strong conditionality.[81] The routine of hierarchical

[76] I Maher, 'Regulation and Modes of Governance' (n 4) 1715, 1724; Wilks (n 55); G Monti, 'Independence, interdependence and legitimacy: the EU Commission, National Competition Authorities, and the European Competition Network' Working Paper EUI LAW; 2014/01, available at: http://cadmus.eui.eu/bitstream/handle/1814/29218/LAW_2014_01.pdf?sequence=1.

[77] Wilks (n 55) 431.

[78] This feature was a core characteristic of the accession process of new Member States in 2004, 2007 and 2013 where the candidate countries had to align their competition law regime to that of the EU due to EU conditionality.

[79] BF Van Waarden and M Drahos, 'Courts and (Epistemic) Communities in the Convergence of Competition Policies' (2002) 9 *Journal of European Public Policy* 6, 931–32; Maher (n 8) 424–25.

[80] Interviews were conducted so far with Slovenia, Slovakia, Hungary, Latvia, Lithuania, and Bulgaria.

[81] Schimmelfennig defines conditionality as a direct mechanism of Europeanisation. The EU disseminates its legal rules and governance by setting them as conditions that external actors have to meet in order to obtain candidate/ accession status or other rewards and avoid sanctions. '[C]onditionality is a bargaining strategy of reinforcement by reward, under which

governance created during the accession period has continued after accession and the CEECs continued to implement similar procedural rules and soft law instruments as those in EU competition law.[82] But the imperfections of conditionality,[83] that is, problems of implementation and monitoring, also continued after accession and explains the EU's focus on enforcement and institution-building,[84] and this is why the ECN has become a crucial learning and cooperation platform for the CEECs with regard to the legal and practical problems of competition law enforcement.

The CEECs consider the ECN a useful forum where they learn and share legal and practical problems.[85] They consider the ECN especially helpful for the exchange of ideas on enforcement strategies and it has been key to the introduction of new enforcement methods in new Member States, which are slowly growing into full-fledged members of the network and may even become its innovative drivers. For example, Hungary has clearly managed to do so. Many of its new concepts on enforcement, such as the interplay between damages claims and leniency, compliance programmes for SMEs, statutory presumption of damage in damages claims, or setting fining guidelines for unfair commercial practices, received increased attention through the ECN.

the EU provides external incentives for a target government to comply with its conditions'; F Schimmelfennig and U Sedelmeier, 'Governance by Conditionality: EU Rule Transfer to the Candidate Countries of Central and Eastern Europe' (2004) *Journal of European Public Policy* 670; F Schimmelfennig, 'EU External Governance and Europeanization Beyond the EU' in D Levi-Faur (ed), *The Oxford Handbook of Governance* (Oxford, Oxford University Press, 2012). It was only with regard to the CEECs that pre-accession conditionality became a regular feature of EU enlargement policy for all candidates; U Sedelmeier, 'Europeanisation in New Member and Candidate States' (2006) 1 *Living Reviews in European Governance* 1, available at www.livingreviews.org/lreg-2006-3.

[82] Reg 1/2003 formed part of the legal requirements imposed on candidate countries for their EU accession. Legal obligations associated with accession exercised considerable political and economic pressure on the candidate countries and exerted the most significant influence on the way competition laws developed in the CEECs.

[83] G Pridham, 'The EU's Political Conditionality and Post-Accession Tendencies: Comparisons from Slovakia and Latvia' (2008) 46 *Journal of Common Market Studies* 365.

[84] As a result, the obligations placed on candidate countries not only included the transposition of the competition acquis and the effective enforcement of competition and state aid rules, but also strengthening of the administrative capacity of the candidates through well-functioning competition authorities. See eg Arts 62 of the Hungary EA [1993] OJ L347/1; see European Commission, 'White Paper on Preparation of the Associated Countries of Central and Eastern Europe for Integration into the Internal Market of the Union', COM (95) 163 final, chapter 2, 8–16. These rules had to address the powers of the authority charged with the application of competition and state aid rules as well as the rights of the undertakings concerned. The authority had to be endowed with sufficient powers to carry out its tasks efficiently. ibid, 52–53, 55–56, 59.

[85] This statement is made on the basis of content of the annual reports of the CEECs' NCAs between 2005–2012 or 2013 when available, and on the basis of a questionnaire which has been sent out to the NCAs in the 10 CEECs, not yet including Croatia.

The CEECs have stated that they greatly profit from the 'side-effects' of formal cooperation mechanisms, which make the exchange of informal advice, experiences with regard to market analysis or regulatory processes, enforcement strategies and, ultimately, other 'softer' information possible. For example, in the framework of a sector inquiry, Hungary requested the ECN members to share their experience with the Hungarian NCA (Gazdasági Versenyhivatal (GVH)) with regard to the investigated sector.[86] The Czech Republic and Latvia also mentioned that informal information helped them in their investigations and others emphasised that they found support in the ECN documents for their competition advocacy work.

The CEECs consider their participation in the network as equal and relatively active members. They all emphasise though that their participation fundamentally depends on and is determined by their limited resources. While they all participate in the ECN's working groups and state that any agency can propose agenda issues and influence decision-making, none of them chairs any of these groups nor have they initiated any of the policy discussions. This indicates a passive rather than active role for the CEECs in the ECN. They have also indicated that there are some NCAs that play a more influential role in the network—that is, there are also NCAs with 'bigger voices' and ones that can formulate proposals better so that these proposals indeed make their way to the ECN agenda.

As to the Commission's role, even though they confirm that the Commission acts as an equal partner within the ECN, some of them admit that the Commission plays a key role through agenda setting and steering debates. This is clearly the case in the so-called 'voluntary' harmonisation process, which steers national procedural rules towards the Commission's procedural model.[87] Most CEECs seem to accept or even support this central role of the Commission, however they emphasised that the national procedural autonomy continues to be a hard principle and that the stability of the national administrative system is eventually what matters. Still, as mentioned above, there are CEECs that argued for even more guidance from the Commission on the decentralised enforcement of EU competition law.

[86] GVH, 'Országgyűlési Beszámoló (Annual Report)', 2008, 188, available at: www.gvh.hu//data/cms996954/9460AD08913A3368.pdf.

[87] In 2012 the ECN's Report on decision-making powers reflected a high level of convergence among the NCAs and was intended to serve as a basis for further harmonisation on the NCAs' procedures for competition law enforcement. European Competition Network (n 28) 5. In 2013, this convergence of national competition law procedures was summarised in the ECN's Recommendations on key investigative and decision-making powers. See in particular the ECN Recommendation on the power to set priorities (ibid, 3). The 'voluntary' convergence takes place within the ECN's Working Group on cooperation issues and due process, which monitors convergence among the Member States and provide an overview of the different systems and procedures for competition law investigations within the ECN. ECN's Working Group on cooperation issues and due process. Documents available at: ec.europa.eu/competition/ecn/documents.html.

The case of the ECN Model Leniency Programme,[88] which has often been praised as a success story of the ECN's cooperation mechanism and as a proof of experimental governance shows a different picture in the CEECs. The transplanted leniency model rules were not effective in the different institutional frameworks of the CEECs. The first adopted programmes proved to be unproductive due to insufficient transparency or uncertainty about eligibility. Many programmes had been therefore recently revised, and they now slowly begin to operate with a few cases in each country.[89] These facts thus contradict the basic premises of experimentalist governance, such as recursive learning and revision from the implementation of general goals in various local contexts. These findings confirm the presence of top-down processes rather than bottom-up processes and thus hierarchical governance mechanisms.

VIII. CONCLUSIONS

The goal of the decentralised enforcement system was to make EU competition law enforcement more effective by delegating enforcement powers to national competition authorities and national courts. The system of parallel competences was created to share the workload of enforcing EU competition law between the European Commission and the Member States and the system of close cooperation to achieve uniform and consistent application of Articles 101 and 102 TFEU.

This chapter has analysed the effectiveness of the decentralised enforcement system in the light of these goals. This analysis comes to three conclusions. First, the functioning of the decentralised enforcement is subject to the multi-level governance system where national actors apply EU law under diverging national procedural rules. This challenges uniform and consistent application of EU law and creates uncertainty for national actors how (not) to apply the Treaty provisions. The Commission reacted by encouraging harmonisation of national procedures, but these legal transplants often

[88] European Competition Network (n 63).

[89] The Czech NCA has applied its leniency programme for the first time in 2004 with regard to a cartel agreement in the energy drinks market. Poland had its first leniency case in a 2006 cartel agreement but had largely revised its 2004 leniency programme in 2009 due to several shortcomings of the previous model. In the Czech Republic, Hungary and Slovakia a marker system exists as well. However, in the Czech Republic the decision to grant a 'marker' lies fully at the discretion of the NCA. See M Zahradnik and H Madárová, 'Slovakia' in *International Comparative Legal Guide to: Cartels & Leniency 2009* (London, Global Legal Group, 2009) 214; A Braun and D Bicková, 'Czech Republic', in *International Comparative Legal Guide to: Cartels & Leniency 2009*, ibid 54; G Bacher and J Budai, 'Hungary' in *International Comparative Legal Guide to: Cartels & Leniency 2009*, ibid 102. In Hungary, leniency was applied for in a few cartel cases yet only one of them has already been closed by the NCA in 2007 (Vj-81/2006).

proved ineffective in the different procedural and institutional frameworks of the Member States. Some Member States argued that their national enforcers, especially the courts, need more guidance from the Commission on the (parallel) enforcement of national and EU law. These facts contradict the positive views on the decentralised enforcement system and in fact point to certain forms of (re)-centralisation taking place.

Second, the ECN, which has been characterised as a success of decentralisation and as experimentalist governance, also shows mixed results. While it provides a peer-accountability forum, which steers compliance and Europeanisation among the Member States, these positive features of the ECN are visible and intentionally highlighted by the Commission and the NCAs. There are relevant mechanisms in the ECN which remain invisible to the outside world leaving fundamental problems of legitimacy and accountability unanswered. The analysis of the CEECs' participation in the ECN shows that the Commission plays a central role and the CEECs are passive actors, who contribute to the work of the ECN, but who do not play an influential role in its decision-making processes. This conclusion challenges previous research which claimed that the ECN is a model of experimentalist governance and it works according to a bottom-up approach, where revision from the implementation of general goals in various local contexts would be possible. On the contrary, this paper finds that the ECN mechanisms are tilting towards hierarchical governance modes.

Third, what makes this decentralised enforcement model unique is the mixture of various elements that emerged gradually within the broader political, economic and social context of EU competition law. The basis of the present governance model is a constitutionally anchored field of EU law which is by now also deeply rooted in the economic constitutions of its Member States. The goals of competition law and enforcement are commonly shared objectives of the EU, its Member States as well as the epistemic community of competition lawyers.

Still, the EU's competition governance model is not something that has been created in 2004 by Regulation 1/2003 and it might not be effectively transplanted to other fields of economic regulation. Its elements developed throughout 50 years into the present model, which might not be readily present in other areas of EU economic law. The EU law in energy, financial and telecommunications markets emerged roughly in the last two decades and mainly operate through Directives. Moreover, while the European Regulatory networks in energy, gas telecommunications or the financial markets are in many respects similar organisations with similar competences and tasks, the ECN does have a different set up.[90] It is a strongly 'top-down'

[90] M Maggetti and F Gilardi, 'Network Governance and the Domestic Adoption of Soft Rules' (2014) 21 *Journal of European Public Policy* 1293, 1304.

driven organisation, which has been created by and is operating in the shadow of the EU Commission with its main goal of 'top-down' harmonisation. If informal network governance is the EU's way forward to enhance harmonisation and convergence of national laws and law enforcement, then the competition law model might be an important stage in the learning process. On the one hand, it might indicate that the EU trend towards 'agencification'[91] may not be the key to achieve an effective transnational governance model, on the other hand it also warns that 'bottom-up' processes have to be stimulated and strengthened in networks in order to nurture innovative policies and disseminate best practices among Member States. Even though supranational competences were traditionally strong in competition law, without providing space for national laboratories to shape the transnational regulatory space, the nation states will constrain transnational entities and remain the locus of rule-making and rule enforcement.

[91] D Levi-Faur, 'Regulatory Networks and Regulatory Agencification: Towards a Single European Regulatory Space' (2011) 18 *Journal of European Public Policy* 810, 812.

Part VII

Governing Justice: Public Accountability of Enforcement

16

The Role of Procedural Law in the Governance of Enforcement in Europe

BURKHARD HESS

I. THE PRESENT SITUATION OF CIVIL PROCEDURES IN EUROPE

IN THE EUROPEAN Union, there are at least 29 different systems of adjudication in which courts are differently composed, equipped and motivated. The procedures applied vary, and different languages are spoken. There are considerable variations with regard to the efficiency of the national systems, the length of proceedings and the effectiveness of the enforcement of judgments.[1] Some systems are still extremely formalistic, while others are based on the idea of managerial judging and procedural economy. In some of the EU Member States, the judicial landscapes have remained unchanged since the early nineteenth century, while other systems have been streamlined and modernised on the basis of sophisticated information technologies. There are considerable differences with regard to the costs of litigation and access to justice:[2] In some Member States, only wealthy parties and businesses can afford civil litigation.[3] Other Member States provide for far reaching legal aid schemes. In some EU Member States, a settlement culture has spread out in recent years, whereas settlements are still the exception in others. The modernity and the efficiency of the national systems do not depend on the accession of the respective State to the European Union: There are some new Member States with modern

[1] *cf* European Commission, 'The 2015 EU Justice Scoreboard', COM (2015) 116 final, available at ec.europa.eu/justice/effective-justice/files/justice_scoreboard_2015_en.pdf.

[2] C Hodges, S Vogenauer and M Tulibacka (eds), *The Costs and Funding of Civil Litigation: A Comparative Perspective* (Oxford, Hart Publishing, 2010) 11ff.

[3] The most prominent example in this respect is—unfortunately—England and Wales. See J Peysner, 'England and Wales' in Hodges, Vogenauer and Tulibacka (n 2) 289ff.

judicial systems,[4] whereas some of the founding Member States are notorious for slow and inefficient court systems.[5] One might consider this broad diversity as a 'richesse culturelle' entailing regulatory competition among and improvements of the national systems.[6]

II. THE ROLE AND FUNCTION OF EUROPEAN LAW

The perspective of European Union law is different. According to the case law of the CJEU (Court of Justice of the European Union), when applying EU legislation national courts act as 'Union courts' and must provide effective judicial protection to everyone, citizens and enterprises, whose rights guaranteed by EU law were (allegedly) violated.[7] However, as the CJEU respects the procedural autonomy of EU Member States when domestic courts implement EU law, national procedures are subject only to a restricted control by the principles of effectiveness and equivalence.[8] Nevertheless, the diversity of the adjudicative systems of EU Member States seems to be a bad starting point for the efficient (and equal) enforcement of EU law throughout the whole European Union.

From the perspective of European law, providing for efficient judicial systems is a major task of EU Member States. Regarded from a regulatory level, the EU Commission has the mandate to supervise the enforcement of EU law by the Member States and to initiate legislative steps in order to overcome shortcomings of the national systems. Therefore, the concepts of procedural autonomy and of a decentralised enforcement of EU law in the domestic systems of the Member States are per se not an impediment to additional law-making of the European Union.[9]

In 2013, the EU Commission started a new programme to supervise the efficiency of the national adjudicative systems. In this context, the EU Commission referred to the right to an effective remedy enshrined in the Charter of Fundamental Rights of the European Union (Article 47).[10] This fundamental right enjoins all EU Member States to provide for efficient

[4] Especially the Baltic States.

[5] In this respect, the Italian system is often blamed for its inefficiency.

[6] B Hess, Inaugural Lecture of the Max Planck Institute Luxembourg on May 8, 2013.

[7] Case C-295/04 *Manfredi v Lloyd Adriatico Assicurazioni SpA* [2006] ECR I-6619, para 62, 77ff; Case C-453/99 *Courage and Crehan* [2001] ECR I-6297, para 19; Case C-536/11 *Bundeswettbewerbsbehörde v Donau Chemie*, judgment of 6 June 2013, nyr, para 20ff.

[8] B Hess, *Europäisches Zivilprozessrecht* (Heidelberg, CF Müller, 2010) s 11, paras 41ff; S Prechal and K Cath, 'The European Acquis of Civil Procedure: Constitutional Aspects' (2014) 19 *Uniform Law Review* 179, 182ff.

[9] Hess (n 8) s 11 I paras 10ff.

[10] European Commission, 'The 2014 EU Justice Scoreboard', COM(2014) 155 final, 2, available at ec.europa.eu/justice/effective-justice/files/justice_scoreboard_2014_en.pdf.

justice systems. Consequently, the Commissioners for Justice clearly understand their mandate in a comprehensive way aimed at supervising the performance of the national judicial systems.[11] As the 'justice for growth' programme[12] demonstrates, procedural shortcomings within the EU Member States may entail legislative action of the European Union.

III. EU COMPETENCES IN PROCEDURAL LAW

However, the legislative empowerment of the European Union in procedural law is not unlimited. According to the principle of limited competences, the Commission must base legislative initiatives on the specific competences granted in the EU treaties. In procedural law, legislative initiatives may be based on two different competences: Articles 67 and 81 TFEU (Treaty on the Functioning of the European Union), on the one hand; Article 114 TFEU, on the other hand.[13]

The most pertinent competence is found in Article 81 TFEU, which has been constantly used for the coordination of the national systems in cross-border cases:[14] At present, the national judicial systems are coordinated by European instruments on jurisdiction, pendency and the recognition of judgments.[15] Cross-border service of documents[16] and the cross-border taking of evidence have been improved, judicial networks and judicial training programmes facilitate the practical handling of international civil litigation in the Area of Freedom, Security and Justice. Specific procedures for uncontested claims,[17] payment orders[18] and small claims[19] have

[11] EU-Commissioner for Justice Viviane Reding, 'Strengthening Mutual Trust: Towards a True European Area of Civil Justice', Speech at the MPI Luxembourg, 25 March 2014, available at www.mpi.lu/fileadmin/mpi/medien/news/2014/4/Speech_VP_Reding.pdf.

[12] European Commission, 'EU Justice Agenda for 2020: Strengthening Trust, Mobility and Growth within the European Union', COM (2014) 144 final, ec.europa.eu/justice/effective-justice/files/com_2014_144_en.pdf.

[13] Hess (n 8) s 2, paras 2ff.

[14] G Wagner, 'Harmonization of Civil Procedures: Policy Perspectives' in XE Kramer and CH van Rhee (ed), *Civil Litigation in a Globalizing World* (The Hague, TMC Asser Press, 2012) 97ff.

[15] Reg (EU) No 1215/2012 of 12 December 2012 on jurisdiction and the recognition and enforcement of judgments in civil and commercial matters [2012] OJ L351/1.

[16] Reg (EC) No 1348/2000 of 29 May 2000 on the service in the Member States of judicial and extrajudicial documents in civil or commercial matters [2000] OJ L160/37.

[17] Reg (EC) No 805/2004 of 21 April 2004 creating a European Enforcement Order for uncontested claims [2004] OJ L143/15.

[18] Reg (EC) No 1896/2006 of 12 December 2006 creating a European order for payment procedure (European Payment Order Reg) [2006] OJ L399/1.

[19] Reg (EC) No 861/2007 of 11 July 2007 establishing a European Small Claims Procedure (Small Claims Reg) [2007] OJ L199/1.

been adopted—however, without generating any considerable practical impact.[20] The (mere) coordination of the national procedural systems under Articles 67 and 81 TFEU does not, however, directly affect the autonomous procedural systems of the EU Member States. Recently, the focus of EU legislation in this area has shifted to combine private international and procedural law, especially with regard to maintenance,[21] successions[22] and other family matters.[23] A more comprehensive regime can be found in the European Regulation on the Attachment of Bank Accounts which, upon its entry into force on 18 January 2017, will provide for a direct cross-border seizure of bank accounts.[24] This instrument provides for a set of uniform norms on the seizure of bank accounts and will directly influence the enforcement laws of the EU Member States.[25] Yet, the specific competences of the Union in the area of judicial cooperation do not seem to be well suited for implementing a comprehensive framework of law enforcement as they only address cross-border situations. However, an instrument on the coordination of cross-border collective redress may be easily based on Articles 67(4) and 81 TFEU.[26]

On the other hand, there is a second set of EU competences permitting a sectorial and even a horizontal harmonisation of the national procedures. These provisions are found in Article 114 TFEU and in the more specific heads of competences at Article 103 TFEU (with regard to cartel damage claims) and Article 153 TFEU on Consumer Protection. Especially Article 114 TFEU has been used by the EU Commission to establish an equal

[20] This result is explained by the following figures. Under the European Payment Order Regulation, the local court of Berlin-Wedding (being the centralised court for all German proceedings) received 3286 applications in 2014. The total number of orders for payment in Germany amounted to 5,763,385 in 2013. Under the Small Claims Regulation, 500 proceedings were conducted by German courts in 2012—compared to 1.16 million civil proceedings in all Germany.

[21] Reg (EC) No 4/2009 of 18 December 2008 on jurisdiction, applicable law, recognition and enforcement of decisions and cooperation in matters relating to maintenance obligations [2009] OJ L 7/1.

[22] Reg (EU) No 650/2012 of 4 July 2012 on jurisdiction, applicable law, recognition and enforcement of decisions and acceptance and enforcement of authentic instruments in matters of succession and on the creation of a European Certificate of Succession [2012] OJ L201/107; B Hess and S Spancken, 'The Effective Operation of the EU Maintenance Regulation in the Member States' in P Beaumont, B Hess, L Walker and S Spancken (eds), *The Recovery of Maintenance in the EU and Worldwide* (Oxford, Hart Publishing, 2014) 385ff.

[23] At present, legislative initiatives under Art 81 TFEU mainly focus on jurisdiction and the law applicable to matrimonial property.

[24] Reg (EU) No 655/2014 of 15 May 2014 establishing a European Account Preservation Order procedure to facilitate cross-border debt recovery in civil and commercial matters [2014] OJ L189/59.

[25] B Hess and K Raffelsieper, 'Die europäische Kontenpfändungsverordnung' (2015) 35 *Praxis des Internationalen Privat- und Verfahrensrechts* 81ff.

[26] At present, most collective cases (with few prominent examples) concern domestic disputes. One of the largest cross-border lawsuits (of more than 25,000 claims) is pending at the Vienna District Court. See below n 71.

level playing field for the implementation of EU law by domestic courts of the EU Member States. The most prominent example is the Enforcement Directive 2004/48,[27] which provides for uniform rules on the protection of Intellectual Property (IP) rights, especially with regard to provisional relief and the preservation of evidence.[28] A similar, sectorial approach with regard to disclosure of evidence (and aimed at protecting leniency programmes) is found in the EU Directive on actions for the damages for the infringement of competition law of 26 November 2014.[29] One additional example is provided with the proposal of the EU Commission for a Directive on the protection and disclosure of business secrets of 28 November 2013.[30]

The practical advantage of a sectorial regulatory approach consists in the fact that it permits the European legislator, on the one hand, to experiment with new procedural devices in a limited area of law before implementing them generally. On the other hand, the sectorial European procedural instruments may be used by Member States as a model for reforming more generally their national systems.[31]

The law-making power of Article 114 TFEU is not limited to specific sectors, but permits general legislation in procedural law. One example is the Directive on Consumer Alternative Dispute Resolution (ADR) of 21 May 2013,[32] which establishes a framework for alternative consumer dispute resolution. This legal instrument introduces general binding procedural principles and sets up a comprehensive infrastructure for the resolution of consumer disputes based on EU law.[33]

The Recommendation on Collective Redress of 11 June 2013 equally provides for a horizontal instrument—although the proposed instrument does not clearly indicate its legal basis within the TFEU. In this area of procedural law, a horizontal approach based on Articles 114 and 153 TFEU

[27] Dir 2004/48/EC of 29 April 2004 on the enforcement of intellectual property rights [2004] OJ L157/45.

[28] Hess (n 8) s 11 II, paras 18ff; C Heinze, *Einstweiliger Rechtsschutz im Europäischen Immaterialgüterrecht* (Tübingen, Mohr Siebeck, 2008) 64ff.

[29] Dir 2014/104/EU of 26 November 2014 on certain rules governing actions for damages under national law for the infringements of the competition law provisions of the Member States and the European Union [2014] OJ L349/1. This instrument is based on Arts 103 and 114 TFEU.

[30] Proposal for a Dir of the European Parliament and the Council on the protection of undisclosed know-how and business information (trade secrets) against their unlawful acquisition, use and disclosure, COM (2013) 813 final.

[31] A pertinent example in this respect is the implementation of the Dir 2008/52/EC of 21 May 2008 on certain aspects of mediation in civil and commercial matters [2008] OJ L136/3. This instrument only addresses cross-border settings, but was implemented in several Member States with regard to domestic mediation (eg France and Germany).

[32] Dir 2013/11/EU of 21 May 2013 on alternative dispute resolution for consumer disputes and amending Reg (EC) No 2006/2004 and Dir 2009/22/EC [2013] OJ 2013 L165/63.

[33] B Hess and N Pelzer, 'Rechtsstaatlichkeit und Transparenz verbessern' in K Gelinsky (ed), *Schlichten statt Richten*? (Sankt Augustin, Konrad-Adenauer-Stiftung, 2015) 35ff; B Hess, 'Prozessuale Mindeststandards in der Verbrauchermediation' (2015) 70 *Juristen Zeitung* 548ff.

seems to be appropriate: Collective redress procedures require several considerable adjustments of the national procedures, especially with regard to legal standing, representation, the binding force of judgments (especially on third parties) and funding.[34]

IV. ACCESS TO JUSTICE AND ENFORCEMENT OF RIGHTS: TWO SIDES OF THE SAME COIN?

While civil justice, in its traditional perception, aims at the protection of the rights of private litigants—the constitutional concept of access to justice is also based on the perspective of protecting the individual's subjective rights.[35] In contrast, the concept of enforcing mandatory law (especially in EU competition law, in the areas of electronic communications,[36] intellectual property, public procurement,[37] or consumer protection) does not focus on the protection of individual rights but, rather, on safeguarding the underlying public interests. However, as long as public interests (for example the protection of the consumer) correspond to subjective individual rights, the two concepts correlate. At the same time, the examples mentioned above demonstrate that public interests often transgress the mere enforcement of individual interests. The traditional civil procedure (at least in the continental procedural systems) may appear inappropriate for the implementation of general public interests. Accordingly, the 'enforcement concept' aims at strengthening the procedural position of the plaintiff with regard to access to information, provisional relief, collective litigation, costs of the proceedings and the financing of litigation.[38]

Conversely, the concept of the private public attorney may entail an imbalance, as demonstrated by the Enforcement Directive 2004/48/EC:[39] Assimilating one party to the 'attorney' of a general interest may incline the legislator to confer unilaterally considerable procedural powers to one party in order to strengthen the enforcement of a given public interest. Yet, civil litigation is based on a general understanding that the parties must

[34] These issues are partially addressed in the Commission Recommendation of 11 June 2013 on common principles for injunctive and compensatory collective redress mechanisms in the Member States concerning violations of rights granted under Union Law [2013] OJ L201/60. See part V below.

[35] O Jauernig and B Hess, *Zivilprozessrecht* (München, CH Beck, 2011) s 1, paras 6ff.

[36] Framework Dir 2002/21/EC of 7 March 2002 on electronic communications networks and services [2002] OJ L108/33.

[37] Dir 2007/66/EC of the European Parliament and of the Council of 11 December 2007 amending Council Dirs 89/665/EEC and 92/13/EEC with regard to improving the effectiveness of review procedures concerning the award of public contracts [2007] OJ L335/31.

[38] B Hess, '"Private Law Enforcement" und Kollektivklagen' (2011) 66 *Juristen Zeitung* 66ff. These issues have been addressed in the Commission's Recommendation on Collective Redress (n 34).

[39] See n 27.

be treated equally in the course of the proceedings. In this respect, public enforcement still has a legitimate function for the enforcement of public interests.

Recently, with the adoption of Directive 2014/104/EU,[40] the EU Legislator significantly strengthened the public enforcement in cartel damages law, even to the detriment of private claimants, by giving preference to public enforcement, at least with regard to follow-on lawsuits for damage claims.[41] Accordingly, the Directive limits the access of private litigants to documents which are considered to be crucial for leniency programmes and settlements proceedings.[42] Furthermore, it protects the leniency recipients in the context of joint liability by providing for a kind of immunity.[43] At the same time, the Commission refrained from proposing any binding proposal on the introduction of collective redress mechanisms in the sector of cartel damages by giving preference to a horizontal framework of collective redress mechanisms in all areas of EU law.[44] Directive 2014/104/EU clearly provides for a far-reaching protection of public authorities engaged in the public enforcement of cartel law.[45] It remains to be seen whether this legislative initiative is the first step of a new regulatory approach aimed at strengthening public, instead of private, enforcement.

V. THE EU COMMISSION'S PROPOSALS ON COLLECTIVE REDRESS OF 11 JUNE 2013

Compared to the initial proposals of the EU Commission,[46] the Communication and the Recommendation on Collective Redress of Summer 2013 do not appear as an ambitious legislative initiative. With regard to the legislative instrument, the Commission opted for a non-binding Recommendation (Article 292 TFEU) and refrained from proposing any

[40] See n 29.

[41] Similarly, para 33 of the Recommendation on Collective Redress (n 34) states that 'collective redress actions should, as a general rule, only start after any proceeding of the public authority'.

[42] Arts 5–8 of Dir 2014/104/EU (n 29). See M Bakowitz, *Informationsherrschaft im Kartellrecht* (Heidelberg, Dissertation, 2015) 199ff.

[43] Art 11(4) of Dir 2014/104/EU (n 29).

[44] The introduction of collective redress had been a major objective of the Green Paper—'Damages actions for the infringement of EU-cartel law', COM (2005)672 final.

[45] As a result, this protection will also limit the current case-law of the ECJ. See Bakowitz (n 42) 204 et seq.

[46] Green Paper (n 44). See T Eilmannsberger, 'The Green Paper on Damages Actions for Breach of the EC Antitrust Rules and Beyond: Reflections on the Utility and Feasibility of Stimulating Private Enforcement through Legislative Action' (2007) 44 *Common Market Law Review* 431; C Hodges, 'Competition Enforcement, Regulation and Civil Justice: What is the Case?' (2006) 43 *Common Market Law Review* 1381; J Basedow (ed), *Private Enforcement of EC Competition Law* (The Hague, Kluwer, 2007).

mandatory mechanism.[47] The Recommendation provides for a set of common principles for injunctive and compensatory collective redress mechanisms. These principles contain legislative guidelines for the Member States on the enactment of collective redress procedures in their respective procedural systems. With regard to the content of the proposed instruments, the Recommendation is based on an understanding of collective redress which shall mainly avoid the implementation of a litigation culture similar to the American class action.[48] Accordingly, the recommendation strongly advertises the introduction of opt-in instruments,[49] limits the standing to representative actions brought by non-profit entities (and prohibits the standing of self-appointed law firms),[50] provides for a loser-pays principle (regarding the costs of the proceedings), and sets clear limits to the funding of litigation by third parties. Finally, the Recommendation proscribes punitive damages.[51]

All in all, the EU Commission adopted a restrictive approach to collective redress which will not legally bind the Member States (Article 292 TFEU).[52] Contrary to its title, the Recommendation does not provide for general principles of collective redress, and rather contains a kind of legislative toolbox aimed at assisting the Member States in implementing national procedures.[53] Against this backdrop, one may wonder whether the EU Commission finally abandoned its initial preference of promoting private enforcement and refrained from proposing a mandatory instrument implementing collective redress mechanism.[54] Obviously, the resistance of the Member States, the EU Parliament[55] and the diversity of the national systems[56] prevented a top down approach to collective redress.[57]

[47] Recommendation on Collective Redress (n 34). See also C Hodges, 'Collective Redress: A Breakthrough or a Damp Sqibb' (2014) 37 *Journal of Consumer Policy* 67, 79ff.

[48] HL Buxbaum, 'Class Actions, Conflict and the Global Economy' in A Bruns, C Kern, J Münch, A Piekenbrock, A Stadler and D Tsikrikas (eds), *Festschrift für Rolf Stürner zum 70. Geburtstag*, vol 2 (Tübingen, Mohr Siebeck, 2013) 1443.

[49] Recommendation on Collective Redress (n 34) paras 21–24.

[50] ibid, paras 4–7; contingency fees shall be prohibited (ibid, paras 29 and 30).

[51] ibid, para 31.

[52] In this respect, neither minimum procedural standards of collective actions, nor a maximum harmonisation have been proposed. The Recommendation and the Communication of the Commission appear as a kind of 'position paper' in an on-going political discussion.

[53] Same opinion: GE Kodek, 'Class Actions: Some Reflections from a European Perspective' in E Lein, D Fairgrieve, MO Crespo and V Smith (eds), *Collective Redress in Europe: Why and How* (London, BIICL, 2015) 117.

[54] The proposal equally demonstrates strong influence of lobbying business groups in Brussels and Strasbourg.

[55] European Parliament Resolution of 2 February 2012 'Towards a Coherent European Approach to Collective Redress' 2011/2089/INI.

[56] For a brief overview of class action rules in the EU Member States see Hodges (n 47) 79ff.

[57] A Stadler, 'Grenzüberschreitender kollektiver Rechtsschutz in Europa' (2009) 64 *Juristen Zeitung* 121, 122ff.

VI. POSSIBLE WAYS FORWARD: SELECTING THE APPROPRIATE LEGISLATIVE STRATEGY

Nevertheless, it would be premature to conclude that the legislative process has come to an end. It seems to me that, quite to the contrary, the EU Commission carefully reframed its political strategy to collective redress, but without giving up its principal ambition. The legislative activities were to be contextualised against the backdrop that the term of the Barroso II Commission was approaching its end, scheduled for Autumn 2014, and that elections of a new EU Parliament were to take place in mid-2014. Therefore, as of Autumn of 2013 onwards, the Commission lacked sufficient time for the initiation of comprehensive legislative initiatives which were expected to trigger controversial political reactions. Consequently, the Barroso Commission opted for the implementation of a limited instrument on cartel damages and for a comprehensive, non-binding recommendation on collective redress that did not need any adoption by the EU Parliament and the Council.

However, the preference of the EU Commission for a non-binding instrument does not preclude the implementation of binding instruments at a later stage. This approach corresponds to a long-term legislative strategy which was recently successfully implemented in the field of consumer ADR. In this area of law, the EU Commission initiated two recommendations on minimum procedural and fairness standards for consumer dispute resolution in the 1990s, which were finally accepted by the stakeholders in the EU Member States.[58] In 2011, the EU Commission made the second and decisive step by proposing a Directive for a comprehensive framework on consumer ADR.[59] This Directive, which was recently adopted by the EU Parliament and Council, endorses the principles of the former recommendations and implements a binding framework for consumer ADR to be set up by the EU Member States. The same strategy has been adopted in the area of insolvency law: here, a comprehensive reform of the Insolvency Regulation[60] on the coordination of insolvency proceedings in cross-border settings was adopted in the tripartite negotiations in Spring 2015.[61] In March 2014, the EU Commission published a Recommendation on business failure and restructuring providing for legislative action in substantive insolvency and corporation law.[62]

[58] Hess (n 8) s 10 VI.

[59] See n 32.

[60] Reg (EU) 2015/848 of 20 May 2015 on insolvency proceedings (recast) [2015] OJ L141/19.

[61] Document 16636/5/14, Justiz iv 319 of March 17, 2015.

[62] Commission Recommendation of 12 March 2014 on a new approach to business failure and insolvency [2014] OJ L74/65. An assessment of the impacts of the Recommendation in the Member States shall take place in September 2015.

If one looks at the final part of the Recommendation on Collective Redress, there appear some parallels to the Consumer ADR Directive: In the final part of the Recommendation, EU Member States are urged to adopt corresponding domestic remedies and to report their legislative activities to the EU Commission within two years. According to paragraph 41 of the Draft Recommendation, the EU Commission will assess the implementation of the instrument and propose further legislative action, if necessary. This context demonstrates that the Commission might still envisage additional legislative action.[63] Its objective is to lower the costs of assessing the risks of investing in another EU Member State, to increase recovery rates for creditors and to remove difficulties in cross-border restructuring.[64]

Furthermore, it must be noted that the Recommendation has already triggered legislative activities in the Member States. In 2015, the United Kingdom adopted a far reaching reform of the Financial Ombudsman Schemes providing for opt-out collective redress (in domestic situations). Germany is equally considering the implementation of a general collective redress remedy after earlier unsuccessful drafts from academia[65]—a legislative proposal is expected for the end of 2015.[66] In the current political debates on collective redress, references are often made to the principles of the Recommendation.

Finally, a fundamental question endures: will the principles and legislative guidelines of the Recommendation be the cornerstones of a future EU instrument on collective redress? Although it might be premature to give a definitive answer, the new legislative approach seems to be too defendant-oriented and, therefore, too reluctant in promoting effective collective redress. It may turn out that Member States will implement more effective instruments incompatible with the 'principles' of the Recommendation.[67] In addition, the coordination of cross-border relief has not been sufficiently addressed by the Recommendation[68]—in this area, further legislative action

[63] M Clough, 'Where to Next? The European Law Institute's Statement on Collective Redress and Competition Damage Claims' in Lein et al (n 53) 357 et seq.

[64] Recommendation on a new approach to business failure and insolvency (n 62) 5.

[65] H-W Micklitz and A Stadler, 'Gruppenklagen in den Mitgliedstaaten der Europäischen Gemeinschaft & den Vereinigten Staaten von Amerika' in T Gabriel and B Pirker-Hörmann (eds), *Massenverfahren: Reformbedarf für die ZPO?* (Wien, Verlag Österreich, 2005) 111–309.

[66] Entwurf der Fraktion der GRÜNEN eines Gesetzes über die Einführung von Gruppenverfahren, Bundestagsdrucksache 18/1464 as of 21 May 2014 [Legislative proposal initiated by the Green Party aiming at introducing group proceedings in the German Code of Civil Procedure].

[67] One example is the Dutch Act on Collective Settlements which serves as a model for similar redress procedures in other EU-Member States; I Tzankova and H van Lith, 'Class Actions and Class Settlements Going Global: The Netherlands' in D Fairgrieve and E Lein (eds), *Extraterritoriality and Collective Redress* (Oxford, Oxford University Press, 2012), paras 4.37ff.

[68] Paras 17 and 18 refer to the Brussels I Reg which is suited for two-party litigation and does only insufficiently address the coordination of cross-border collective actions, J Stefanelli, 'Parallel Litigation and Cross-Border Collective Actions under the Brussels I Framework: Lessons from Abroad' in Fairgrieve and Lein, ibid para 9.05.

is urgently needed.[69] The new regime of the Brussels I bis Regulation[70] does not enhance the present situation as it replaces the recognition (exequatur) proceedings in the Member State of enforcement by a form which is not suited for collective redress proceedings. Practical difficulties in the new regime will arise soon, at least in the context of collective redress mechanisms.[71] Therefore, the Recommendation does not seem to be the last step in European law-making—neither with regard to its binding effects, nor with regard to its substantive content.

[69] B Hess, 'Collective Litigation under the Brussels I Regulation' (2010) 30 *Praxis des Internationalen Privat- und Verfahrensrechts* 116, 120; A Stadler, 'Foreword' in Lein et al (n 53) IX, XIX.

[70] B Hess, 'Urteilsfreizügigkeit unter der Brüssel Ia-VO: Effektuiert oder ausgebremst?' in von J Adolphsen, J Goebel, U Hass, B Hess, S Kolmann and M Würdinger (eds), *Festschrift für Peter Gottwald* (München, CH Beck, 2014) 273ff.

[71] The current deficiencies are demonstrated by the lawsuit of an Austrian Internet activist against Facebook Ireland currently pending at the District Court Vienna. In this lawsuit, the plaintiff allegedly represents more than 25,000 persons whose personality rights were (allegedly) infringed by the defendant. Accordingly, 25,000 claims for damages (of €500 each) were assigned to the plaintiff. The claimant based the jurisdiction of the Austrian Court on Arts 15 and 16 of the Brussels I Reg as Facebook usually establishes contractual relations with its users. Yet, this head of jurisdiction only applies to his personal claim, but not to the claims of other consumers assigned to him. Recently, the Court dismissed the action on the ground that the plaintiff did not qualify a consumer.

17

The Legitimacy and Public Accountability of Global Litigation: The Particular Case of Transnational Arbitration

DIEGO P FERNÁNDEZ ARROYO

I. INTRODUCTION

THE TOPIC I have been asked to address is 'the legitimacy and public accountability of global dispute resolution with reference to lessons from supranational and international law as well as with reference to arbitration in particular areas of law (for example commercial contracts)'. I have also been invited to answer the question: 'Is there a need to legitimise global litigation beyond the consent of the parties and private and contractual autonomy?'

Based on this proposal, and having due regard to the content of the other esteemed contributors' work, I thought it wise to focus on the legitimacy and public accountability of transnational arbitration, the field that currently attracts many of the most significant cross-border commercial disputes containing European elements. While arbitration is mentioned several times in this volume, readers should note that other authors do not treat it in of itself. Nevertheless, transnational arbitration is particularly relevant when dealing with enforcement. Therefore, it is the very context of this colloquium that has compelled me to focus my contribution upon this particular angle.

The leading role of arbitration in the settlement of transnational commercial disputes (in its most *lato sensu* meaning) may be viewed (and criticised) from different perspectives. However, the factual evidence of the importance of arbitration is now beyond doubt: it is now clear that a shift from judicial to arbitral adjudication has taken place over the last two decades for a vast range of private, public and mixed disputes.[1] This shift represents a part

[1] For Pierre Tercier, this shift is a determinant moment in the history of law and commercial relations. See P Tercier, 'La légitimité de l'arbitrage' (2011) *Revue de l'arbitrage* 653, 654.

of the trend towards privatisation of enforcement, which has developed in parallel with the privatisation of the law-making process.[2]

Furthermore, I thought that it might be interesting to treat this subject here, within the context of the European Union (EU), as we are nearing a point where EU law and arbitration can no longer exist apart.[3] In the case of commercial arbitration a first view might be that the EU and arbitration are still worlds apart.[4] However, factual evidence demonstrates that arbitration has succeeded in Member States. Capital cities of some of these States (such as Paris, London or Stockholm) are among the most attractive venues for arbitral proceedings worldwide, while other Member States whose traditional procedural rules were far less favourable to arbitration (for example Spain, Italy or Portugal) have modernised their laws. These developments are, of course, not random but rather reflect increasingly more pro-arbitration policies.

The rise of the importance of investment arbitration within this geographical context is even more visible. In fact, almost the entirety of the debate surrounding the Transatlantic Trade and Investment Partnership (TTIP) agreement is focused upon the possible inclusion of investor–State dispute settlement in this agreement, even if there are many other aspects of this negotiation process that remain far more significant. Moreover, the newly consecrated EU competence in this field has provoked some unexpected situations, both *ad extra* and *ad intra*. For example, notwithstanding its observer status, the EU played a leading role in the elaboration of the 2013 United Nations Commission on International Trade Law (UNCITRAL) Rules on Transparency, and the (2014) United Nations (UN) Mauritius Convention on Transparency in Treaty-based Investor-State Arbitration.[5] As an

[2] See DP Fernández Arroyo, 'La multifacética privatización de la codificación internacional del derecho comercial' in J Basedow, DP Fernández Arroyo and JA Moreno Rodríguez (eds), *¿Cómo se codifica hoy el derecho comercial internacional?* (Asunción, La Ley/Thomson Reuters, 2010) 51; see also PB Stephan, 'Privatizing International Law' (2011) 97 *Virginia Law Review* 1573.

[3] In this vein, see GA Bermann, 'Navigating EU Law and the Law of International Arbitration' (2012) 28 *Arbitration International* 397. See also, GA Bermann, E Gaillard, C Kessedjian, H Muir Watt and DP Fernández Arroyo, 'L'arbitrage international et le droit de l'Union européenne: un dialogue constructif ou une collision inévitable' (2013) *Cahiers de droit de l'entreprise* 9.

[4] This impression may come, for instance, from the decision of the EU legislator to keep arbitration out of the scope of the Brussels 1 Reg Recast (Reg (EU) no 1215/2012 on jurisdiction and the recognition and enforcement of foreign judgments in civil and commercial matters), after a long discussion. However, it is apparent that the fact that the recast still excludes arbitration from its scope of application, besides some modifications introduced in the new text, should reinforce the protection of arbitration. See LH Wilhelmsen, 'The Recast Brussels I Regulation and Arbitration—Revisited or Revised?' (2014) 30 *Arbitration International* 169.

[5] See the texts of the Rules at www.uncitral.org/pdf/english/texts/arbitration/rules-on-transparency/Rules-on-Transparency-E.pdf, and the text of the Mauritius Convention at www.uncitral.org/pdf/english/texts/arbitration/transparency-convention/Transparency-Convention-e.pdf.

additional demonstration, the European Commission has been particularly active in monitoring the functioning of arbitral tribunals in cases involving EU Member States.[6]

Therefore, and even if the position that arbitration has become the default mechanism for dispute settlement seems difficult to reconcile with the apparent indifference of the EU,[7] it seems clear that a new period of mutual discovery between the arbitration and the EU, and not an easy one, is afoot. As a result, there are at least two good reasons to focus this contribution on arbitration.

Needless to say that the scope of all statements I am going to make depend on the specific matter under arbitration. So even though I am using the word 'arbitration' throughout this contribution, I am evidently not saying that commercial arbitration has the same features as arbitration in the context of sports, consumption, or investor–State disputes.[8] I will be dealing specially with commercial arbitration, a field where legitimacy has not been traditionally treated in depth. While some of my analysis may be generalised to other types of arbitration, this should not be assumed.

II. THE JUSTIFICATION OF LEGITIMACY

Legitimacy of transnational arbitration has often been taken as a *fait accompli*. And one does not discuss what is obvious. Whenever scholars have attempted to establish a proof of this legitimacy, emphasis has been placed upon:

- Party autonomy as a source of arbitrator power; and/or
- the effectiveness of arbitration agreements and arbitral awards (understood as a quasi-automaticity of enforcement).

Those assumptions, however, fail to provide either a solid argument for the legitimacy of arbitration as an institution or a sufficient explanation of its success. Indeed, arbitration has become the most common method of

[6] After the tribunal in *Micula v Romania* ICSID Case No ARB/05/20 rendered its award, the EU Commission prohibited Romania from complying with the award because of its alleged incompatibility with EU Law on State aid.

[7] Actually, rather than indifference, the EU's attitude appears to have been one of deliberate non-intervention in order to allow the growth and expansion of arbitration. The positive effect of arbitration on the dynamism of international trade has surely been taken into consideration.

[8] No legal subject has drawn more attention and generated more debate during the last months within the EU context than the proposed inclusion of investment arbitration rules in the draft US-EU Transatlantic Trade and Investment Partnership. Even though such rules would only be one small part—and certainly not the most significant—part of this broad treaty, most of the public discussions and criticism have focused on investment arbitration. This reaction of political, economic and legal circles (including, for the latter, some influential scholars) shows the current dimension of the topic. See, for example, www.kent.ac.uk/law/isds_treaty_consultation.html.

dispute resolution in a wide array of matters affecting global trade and the world economy. Even matters closely related to the public interest, formerly subject to the exclusive jurisdiction of national courts, are now submitted to resolution via arbitration. Arbitration has acquired, in this way, a fundamental importance. Consequently, enforcement in matters of arbitration requires a governance-based approach in addition to the classical party-oriented approach.[9] The fact that any single arbitration concerns primarily the parties involved should not prevent us from considering the broader picture. Taken as a whole, all such arbitrations constitute the lion's share of the settlement of transnational disputes, and from this perspective their impact on global governance is tremendous.

Whatever flavour of arbitration we consider, the success of arbitration is a matter of fact,[10] having regard both to the number and the type of disputes submitted to this form of adjudication. Unsurprisingly, certain scholars have argued that the systematic introduction of arbitral clauses into international contracts[11] (which can be taken as an *in principle-private-enforcement preference*) is to be seen as the expression of commercial usage, which would be another source of legitimacy.[12]

Summing up, there would be at least three sources of legitimacy: party autonomy, effectiveness and introduction of arbitration clauses in international contracts. Together with party autonomy, the systematic introduction of arbitration clauses into contracts could show, at best, a perception of legitimacy by the users, but they could hardly explain the existence of *lato sensu* legitimacy (in fact some authors have talked about 'internal' or 'relative' legitimacy by contrast with 'external' or 'absolute' legitimacy).[13] Effectiveness, on the other hand, may be the consequence of either the

[9] Mutatis mutandis both perspectives may also be used concerning judgment enforcement. See, for instance, CA Whytock, 'Domestic Courts and Global Governance' (2009) 84 *Tulane Law Review* 67.

[10] Even in fields traditionally less inclined to arbitration, such as banking law or insurance law, interest in arbitration is growing. See the report of the Working Group of the Comité français de l'arbitrage on Arbitration in banking and financial disputes (2014) *Cahiers de l'arbitrage* 419.

[11] The fact is not new. According to CR Drahozal, 'New Experiences of International Arbitration in the United States' (2006) 54 *American Journal of Comparative Law* 246–49, almost 10 years ago 90% of international contracts in the United States included an arbitration clause. In a survey conducted in 2013 for the Queen Mary School of International Arbitration the numbers were not as impressive, although one of the main conclusions is that 'overall, businesses continue to show a preference for using arbitration over litigation for transnational disputes, although concerns remain about the costs of arbitration'. See www.pwc.com/gx/en/arbitration-dispute-resolution/assets/pwc-international-arbitration-study.pdf.

[12] In this sense, reference has been made to the 'répétition du recours à l'arbitrage (il s'agit en partie d'une légitimité factuelle)' ['repetition of recourse to arbitration (it is about a factual legitimacy)']. J-B Racine, 'Éléments d'une sociologie de L'arbitrage: Actes de la Journée d'étude du Groupe Sociologie de l'arbitrage du Comité français de l'arbitrage' (2012) *Revue de l'arbitrage* 709, 714.

[13] Tercier (n 1) 655.

application of norms in force (that is norms imbued with legality but not necessarily with legitimacy) or the imposition of powerful actors (that is actors lacking specific interests in legitimacy).

From another perspective, it seems clear that if focus is to be placed on party autonomy and on repeated conduct, the discussion should almost be about contract legitimacy. But this is a dated and perhaps even circular discussion.[14] Nonetheless, there is an important aspect of these sources that relates to legitimacy: in transnational legal transactions, parties normally incorporate arbitration clauses, typically because no national judge appears 'appropriate' to adjudicate a dispute involving foreigners.[15] Effectiveness, even though it has a direct, essential impact on the parties themselves (and, by consequence, it might be seen as a contractual issue), goes beyond such relationships. It implies the recognition of private parties' power to settle their disputes without the intervention of State courts.[16]

However, there are at least two limitations to accepting effectiveness as a strong argument justifying legitimacy of arbitration:

— On the one hand, there are numerous examples (the mafia being perhaps the most egregious), of systems or structures that are fully effective without a drop of legitimacy;
— on the other hand, legitimacy based on effectiveness would be to a large extent external in nature (that is legitimacy given by public powers which have been ensuring the enforcement of arbitral award for decades).

Taking into consideration the limitations of all these three arguments in establishing the internal legitimacy of arbitration, other avenues should be explored. In particular, I will review the need (and the feasibility) for arbitration to reach legitimacy and public accountability. In order to do this, I will analyse three basic and intertwined elements: first, increasing transparency; second, the developing notion of 'precedent' in arbitral case law; and, finally, the monitoring of actors (in particular arbitrators) in the arbitral process.

[14] E Gaillard, 'Aspects philosophiques du droit de l'arbitrage international' (2008) 329 *Recueil des Cours* 49, nn 9 and 42.

[15] According to some views, national judges would lack legitimacy to adjudicate these disputes. See G Cuniberti, 'La légitimité de l'arbitre' in *Droit et technique. Etudes offertes à Xavier Linant de Bellefonds* (Paris, Litec, 2007) 131, 140–41. This author adds that arbitrator's legitimacy based on party autonomy may be complemented by legitimacy based on procedure—impartiality, equitable treatment of the parties, reasoning of the award.

[16] '[L]'arbitrage n'est pas seulement obligatoire; par la sanction de l'État, il devient même contraignant et exécutoire' ['Arbitration is not only binding; because of the State intervention it becomes mandatory and enforceable']; P Tercier, 'L'arbitrage et les entreprises' (2009) 52 *Arch phil droit* 223, 226.

III. TRANSPARENCY

At the dawn of the century, a significant discussion concerning the need for transparency sprung up in investment arbitration circles. It remains one of the main points of debate in a broader discussion about the legitimacy of investor–State dispute settlement.[17] Underpinning this debate were a series of controversial cases in which States' powers to regulate in the public interest were challenged.[18] At the time of these cases, a schism of sorts took place, as it was implicitly assumed that transparency would be acceptable for investment arbitration (because of State participation and public interest concerns arising from this participation), but that outside this relatively small sub-set, transparency should not be admitted into arbitration. This was a big mistake. And even worse: it implied a serious misunderstanding of the reality. One did not notice the beginning of an evolution that started at that very time in case law, legislation, and ultimately also in doctrine.

Of course, in some fields where the public interest is at stake (for example arbitrations involving State parties, and particularly investment arbitration) or high profile cases (for example sports arbitration) the tendency towards transparency has progressively prevailed. In fact, transparency is now the default rule in investment arbitration, despite a certain political reluctance. The adoption by the United Nations of a set of comprehensive procedural rules and a multilateral convention aimed at enlarging the scope of such rules[19] cannot but confirm the general state of affairs.[20] Indeed the

[17] The number of contributions on this matter is huge and is only likely to increase. See M Waibel, A Kaushal, C Balchin and L K-H Chung (eds), *The Backlash Against Investment Arbitration: Perceptions and Reality* (Alphen aan den Rijn, Kluwer Law International, 2010); S Besson, 'La légitimité de l'arbitrage international d'investissement' *Jusletter*, 25th July 2005, www.weblaw.ch/jusletter. More recently, see CA Rogers, 'The Politics of International Investment Arbitrators' (2014) 12 *Santa Clara Journal of International Law* 223; H Muir Watt, 'The Contested Legitimacy of Investment Arbitration and the Human Rights Ordeal: the Missing Link' in W Mattli and T Dietz (eds), *International Arbitration and Global Governance: Contending Theories and Evidence* (Oxford, Oxford University Press, 2014) 214. Evidently, the significance of transparency goes far beyond investment arbitration. See A Peters, 'Towards Transparency as a Global Norm' in A Bianchi and A Peters (eds), *Transparency in International Law* (Cambridge, Cambridge University Press, 2013) 534.

[18] Several of the most famous cases involved Latin-American States, such as *Compañía del Desarrollo de Santa Elena SA v Republic of Costa Rica* ICSID Case no ARB/96/1, *Metalclad Corporation v Estados Unidos Mexicanos* ICSID Case no ARB(AF)/97/01, and *Aguas del Tunari SA v The Republic of Bolivia* ICSID Case no ARB/03/2. We could include also the long saga of Argentinian cases based on some measures this state adopted to overcome the deepest crisis in its history. See J Alvarez, 'The Public International Law Regime Governing International Investment' (2009) 193 *Recueil des Cours* 344, 368–433, 442–69.

[19] See n 5 and accompanying text.

[20] Certainly, according to its Article 1, the UNCITRAL Rules on Transparency are not applicable to all investment-arbitration proceedings. However, both the content of discussions in the UNCITRAL Working Group on Arbitration during the elaboration of the Rules and the decision to adopt a multilateral instrument (the UN Mauritius Convention) to expand the scope of the Rules are strong indications of the assumption that transparency will not be exclusively limited to UNCITRAL arbitration proceedings. Furthermore, transparency is already a feature in some regional free trade areas such as NAFTA or CAFTA, a timid reality within the ICSID system, as well as a basic investment policy for some countries.

UNCITRAL (United Nations Commission on International Trade Law) Rules on Transparency provide for a framework—subject to some exceptions—in which almost all information concerning arbitration proceedings brought under an investor–State treaty is made available to the public by means of a registry administered by UNCITRAL.[21] Furthermore, the Rules on Transparency ensure open hearings and easy access of amici curiae to the arbitral proceedings. As regards sports arbitration, it is clear that the notion of transparency has shifted the rule of confidentiality in Article R59 of Court of Arbitration for Sport (CAS) Rules.

Although transparency has visibly infiltrated these specific areas of arbitration, this tendency has had a broader effect: within the field of commercial arbitration, judicial decisions from different jurisdictions and significant law reforms demonstrate that criticism of confidentiality is more than a fashion. The very notion that confidentiality is a fundamental principle of arbitration is now weaker than ever.[22] In fact, it is clear that traditionally arbitration-friendly States no longer regard it as an essential facet,[23] particularly in international arbitration.

From a technical point of view, transparency can be seen as the negation of confidentiality. Nevertheless, in a more picturesque way, it can be coupled with visibility and accessibility. Essentially, I am talking about accessibility to proceedings and decisions, but also about the visibility of arbitrator selection processes and, by extension, of arbitrators' qualities. Whenever one talks about confidentiality within the context of commercial arbitration, the first observation is that confidentiality is a technicality to be dealt with at the moment of a contract's conclusion.[24] In other words, the traditional view that confidentiality is an essential element of arbitration is waning—even if it is still considerably significant in commercial arbitration.[25] Nowadays, if

[21] See www.uncitral.org/transparency-registry/registry/index.jspx#economicSector.

[22] See Report on *Confidentiality in International Commercial Arbitration*, adopted in 2010 by the Committee on International Commercial Arbitration of the International Law Association (www.ila-hq.org/en/committees/index.cfm/cid/19). One of the findings of the ILA Resolution no 1/2010 on the same subject, states: 'Many users of international commercial arbitration assume when choosing arbitration that arbitration is inherently confidential. This assumption is not warranted because many national laws and arbitral rules do not currently provide for confidentiality and those that do vary in their approach and scope (including the persons affected, the duration and the remedies)'.

[23] A paradigmatic example is the elimination of the confidentiality rule for international arbitration in the French arbitration decree enacted in 2011. See E Gaillard and P de Lapasse, 'Le nouveau droit français de l'arbitrage interne et international' (2011) *Recueil Dalloz* 84. Other attractive venues where arbitration is not deemed to be necessarily confidential are Switzerland, Sweden, the United States and Australia.

[24] See E Silva Romero, 'De la confidencialidad del arbitraje internacional y materias aledañas' in E Gaillard and DP Fernández Arroyo (eds), *Cuestiones claves del arbitraje internacional* (Bogota, UR/CEDEP, 2013) 165, 175–77.

[25] See Queen Mary School of International Arbitration, *2010 International Arbitration Survey: Choices in International Arbitration*, s 6, available at www.whitecase.com/files/upload/fileRepository/2010International_Arbitration_Survey_Choices_in_International_Arbitration.pdf.

parties want to keep their arbitration proceedings outside of the public eye, they need to make a careful analysis of their potential or actual disputes and to draft appropriated clauses about it.[26] And even so, they must be aware that the 'confidentiality' agreed upon will not be absolute confidentiality, namely because of the existence of superior values concerning public interest.[27]

In this contribution, I argue that transparency may strengthen legitimacy alongside increasing public accountability—irrespective of the type of arbitration concerned. This powerful source of legitimacy can operate via the creation of a framework for 'virtuous' control of arbitration. I am not talking here about State control, which can be operated individually for any particular case by means of annulment and exequatur procedures (in fact, these procedures exist to sanction failures of arbitrability, due process, equality of the parties and violation of public policy), but rather about another form of control: 'Private general control' of users, advocates, arbitrators themselves, institutions, and, in certain hypotheses, of civil society. This control should include the selection of arbitrators,[28] conflicts of interests (independency, impartiality, availability), and the scrutiny of awards.[29]

Public access to awards should allow, in addition to the development of arbitration law, more efficient arbitrator selection. To be sure, such access may only be achieved through complete and traceable publication of awards. Publishing summaries or excerpts (even on a random basis) may help, but I argue that only the publication of all awards in full through a centralised mechanism would suffice.[30] This is a long-standing proposal of many distinguished arbitrators,[31] and its adoption is becoming more and more urgent. While the names of parties could be occluded where appropriate,

Nevertheless, in a large survey conducted by the American Arbitration Association in 2003, privacy appears in a very low position among the reasons to decide the mechanism of dispute settlement. www.adr.org/aaa/ShowPDF?doc=ADRSTG_004327.

[26] See the recommendations in the ILA Resolution no 1/2010 (n 22).

[27] Comparative case law is rife with significant decisions in this sense. See Australian High Court, 7 April 1995, *Esso Australian Resources v Plowman*; Sweden Supreme Court, 27 October 2000, *Bulgarian Foreign Trade Bank v Al Trade Finance*; and more recently Argentinian National Commercial Court of Appeal, Chamber B, 3 April 2014, *Accor Argentina v NSB DS*.

[28] B Oppetit, 'Le droit international privé, droit savant' (1992) 234 *Recueil des Cours* 331, 400–01, underlines the legitimacy provided by some arbitrator's personal and intellectual authority (called by him 'la légitimité du pouvoir du savoir' ['the legitimacy of the learning power']).

[29] See, in this vein, Tercier (n 1) 667.

[30] See J Karton, 'A Conflict of Interests—Seeking a Way Forward on Publication of International Arbitral Awards' (2012) 28 *Arbitration International* 447.

[31] For example, JDM Lew, 'The Case for the Publication of Arbitral Awards' in JC Schultsz and AJ van den Berg (eds), *Liber Amicorum Pieter Sanders* (Deventer, Kluwer, 1982) 223; A Mourre, 'Precedent and Confidentiality in International Commercial Arbitration: The Case for the Publication of Arbitral Awards' in E Gaillard and Y Banifatemi (eds), *Precedent in International Arbitration* (Huntington, Juris, 2008) 39.

the identification of arbitrators, on the other hand, should be systematically revealed.[32]

In arbitration proceedings under the aegis of an institution, this type of openness would be easy to achieve. In fact, several institutions have already taken significant steps to improve accessibility to their awards.[33] Equally, leading associations of arbitrators (although not themselves institutions to settle disputes) have declared fundamental commitment to other aspects of transparency.[34] In ad hoc proceedings, arbitrators should directly support transparency with parties' help. The arbitration community should develop soft rules and mechanisms to facilitate suitable transparency practices. Obviously, neither hard rules nor soft rules on transparency suffice to solve all legitimacy problems, but I do not think any author seriously claims that transparency is the magic cure for this issue. At best, transparency is one of the tools that may contribute towards a higher standard of legitimacy.

All this being said, transparency also has its detractors, and this is no surprise. Similar situations occur in respect of all other human activities in which a measure of transparency is implemented: the road to transparency is always sinuous, and rife with issues of special interest groups (as secrecy has its advantages, and therefore its beneficiaries). Therefore, additional time, cost and some procedural inconveniences have been singled out to lessen the advantages of pro-transparency developments—this is especially true in the particular field of investment arbitration.[35]

Without denying the negative effects that might arise in particular occasions, I have no qualms in qualifying such inconveniences as either exaggerated or easily manageable. The UNCITRAL Rules on Transparency demonstrate that it is possible to cope with conflictual situations by simply providing some discretionary authority to the arbitral tribunal. In any event, the possible emergence of negative effects in some particular cases is a small price to pay in order to achieve this unavoidable requirement of global governance. As regards commercial arbitration, critical opinions seem to be based upon putative users' wishes: even if such wishes do actually exist, they would not be affected by systematic publication of anonymised awards.

[32] See J Fernández Armesto, 'The Time Has Come: A Plea for Abandoning Secrecy in Arbitration' (2012–2013) *Les Cahiers de l'arbitrage* 583, 585.

[33] See, for instance, the interesting efforts made within the framework of the Milan Arbitration Chamber to optimise the publication of awards. See A Malatesta and R Sali (eds), *Arbitrato e riservatezza. Linee guida per la pubblicazione in forma anonima dei lodi arbitrali* (Padova, CEDAM, 2011).

[34] On the home page of the International Arbitration Institute (the 'IAI') (www.iaiparis.com/pages_p_html.asp) it is stated that 'one of the most important objectives of the IAI is to promote transparency in the international arbitration community. In the past, access to academic literature and other more practical information was not complemented by access to the international arbitration community itself'.

[35] See Silva Romero (n 24) 183–87. Some States' reluctant attitude during the negotiation of UNCITRAL instruments on transparency confirms this critical perception.

IV. PRECEDENT

The use of precedent is becoming a common feature for all flavours of international courts and tribunals[36]—and arbitral tribunals are no exception. Whenever arbitrators are able to overcome the obstacles embodied by the lack of access to other arbitral awards, basing their decision upon previous awards comes almost naturally. In fact, this behaviour is clearly perceptible within the framework of investment[37] and sport arbitration,[38] fields in which transparency is the rule. However, secrecy is not the only barrier to the creation of a system of arbitral case law. There is another obstacle of a conceptual nature: arbitration is traditionally conceived as a dispute settlement mechanism that embodies justice dispensed by tribunals specially appointed in order to settle a particular dispute, outside the reach of a hierarchically-organised jurisdiction and regardless of all other arbitral tribunals. Standing from this ground, it may be difficult to argue that there is a doctrine of precedent in arbitration. Moreover, and if adopting a dogmatic point of view, this may serve to bolster claims that the notion of precedent cannot possibly exist in arbitration.[39]

Certainly, random or spontaneous use of reasoning from prior awards can hardly be seen to constitute a real doctrine of precedent, not least in the sense of a stare decisis-type obligation upon arbitrators. But this is not the type of precedent necessary for arbitration. The thrust of my argument is that a more systematic attitude founded on persuasiveness, rather than on hierarchy and imposition, is necessary. By systematic I mean that arbitrators should be required to search for available prior decisions on the matter and that this search be neither random nor formalistic, nor used only to justify the decisions they have already made. By persuasiveness,

[36] Even constitutional courts when facing most sensitive (domestic) issues pay attention to other jurisdictions' decisions. The greater the significance of the issue at stake, the broader seems to be the reference to foreign prior decisions. See S Cassese, 'Legal Comparison by the Courts', paper for the Opening Plenary Session of the 18th Congress of the International Academy of Comparative Law (Washington DC, July 2010). www.irpa.eu/wp-content/uploads/2011/05/The_judge_as_a_comparatist.pdf.

[37] See JP Commission, 'Precedent in Investment Treaty Arbitration: A Citation Analysis of a Developing Jurisprudence' (2007) 24 *Journal of International Arbitration* 129, 149–53; L Reed, 'The *De Facto* Precedent Regime in Investment Arbitration: A Case for Proactive Case Management' (2010) 25 *ICSID Review* 95–103.

[38] See G Kaufmann-Kohler, 'Arbitral Precedent: Dream, Necessity or Excuse? The 2006 Freshfields Lecture' (2007) 23 *Arbitration International* 357, 365–66; E Loquin, 'L'utilisation par les arbitres du TAS des principes généraux du droit et le développement d'une *Lex sportiva*' in A Rigozzi and M Bernasconi (eds), *The Proceeding before the Court of Arbitration for Sport* (Bern, Weblaw, 2007) 85.

[39] For an in-depth treatment of the role of precedent in transnational arbitration and further citations, see DP Fernández Arroyo, 'Private Adjudication Without Precedent?' in H Muir Watt and DP Fernández Arroyo (eds), *Private International Law and Global Governance* (Oxford, Oxford University Press, 2014) 119. Actually, most of the statements in this section are directly taken from this source.

I mean the authority of prior decisions based on their substantive qualities (for instance, whether their authors are highly regarded, and, for instance, if there has been repetitive adoption of this solution by different tribunals).[40]

The fundamental reason to claim for the development of a precedent doctrine in transnational arbitration is that arbitration is now the prevailing method of adjudication for a large array of private and public–private disputes. Accordingly, it is apparent that the traditional view of individual arbitration proceedings constituting isolated portions of reality, and concerning only the parties and the arbitrators involved is no longer admissible. Since many among the most important transnational disputes (both by quantum and by quality) are settled by means of arbitration, the very functioning of this mechanism and the outcome of disputes submitted to it become relevant for all. States, international organisations, civil society and economic actors in general, are all interested in the manner and reasons that arbitral decisions are taken.

The particular reasons underlying this interest may differ depending on the stakeholders considered. However, for all of them, the interest is far from being a mere product of curiosity. On the contrary, it is a matter of necessity. Their view is that they need to be aware of the foundations of arbitral awards, and they expect appropriate procedures and a predictable way in which decisions are adopted. From this perspective, the question of precedent is closely related to the search for consistency. In fact, a minimum of consistency is inherent to any framework of dispute resolution. Arbitration cannot be an exception to this rule, even less if we understand it as a true legal order.[41] Indeed, a legal order that seriously intends to be considered as such may not allow the decisions it issues to appear as resulting from the caprices of its decision-makers. In principle, arbitral tribunals are not formally compelled to follow precedent.[42] However, no legal ground prevents them from doing so.[43]

If I use the expression 'a minimum of consistency', it is because there are obvious barriers to achieving consistency. Even in investment arbitration, where the use of precedent is as clear as it is widespread, it may not be said that full consistency has been achieved. Thus, neither the mass publicity of awards in general nor the implementation of an autonomous annulment

[40] See G Born, *International Commercial Arbitration* 2nd edn (Alphen aan den Rijn, Kluwer, 2014) 3826–27.

[41] At least, this is the claim of some renowned authors, the most famous being Gaillard (n 14) 40–67.

[42] The inclusion in the 2006 version of the UNCITRAL Model Law of an Art 2A, which makes reference to the 'need to promote uniformity' in the interpretation of this law, could be considered as a mandate in this direction. However, the provision is directed at national courts rather than arbitral tribunals. In fact, its very purpose is to prevent automatic recourse to domestic procedural law.

[43] See G Kaufmann-Kohler, 'Is Consistency a Myth?' in Gaillard and Banifatemi (n 31) 137.

mechanism within the specific framework of ICSID (International Centre for Settlement of Investment Disputes) have allowed investment arbitration case law to avoid serious disparities in decisions on some legal issues. Nevertheless, it cannot be seriously contested either that some kind of interpretative consensus has been reached on various issues. At the same time, other avenues to consistency have been proposed and even implemented in particular investment arbitration settings.[44]

Notwithstanding the obstacles for a consistent case law in investment arbitration, no doubts exist that all efforts toward this goal are justified by the essential public interest at stake. Under this assumption, one might conclude that the need for consistency is less pressing concerning commercial arbitration. However, the extensive use of arbitration and the absence of actual competition with State courts are as important justifications for having consistency as public interest concerns. Even more importantly, the fact that a significant portion of commercial disputes are solved by means of arbitration amounts to a major governance concern. Broadly put, the wider the scope (and therefore, the autonomy) of arbitration, the greater the demand for consistency on the part of arbitrators.[45] And that is the crucial point: of all the arguments in favour of arbitrators taking precedent into account and contributing to the creation and consolidation of arbitral case law, the need for consistency is paramount.

Needless to say, consistency will never be absolute. The same is true of any legal order—even in orders where the doctrine of precedent does in fact prevail. Contradictions are inherent to human relations, and law, as the regulator of certain aspects of these relations, is not (and may not be) insulated from such contradictions. The consistency to which I refer is an attitude rather than a final outcome: its essential goal is to prevent arbitration awards from being grossly at odds with a generally accepted solution or trend, unless there is a clear and sufficient reason why such a solution or trend should be put aside, whether in general or within the particular context of a specific case.

As a result, the argument for consistency bears a close relationship with the laudable intention to enhance arbitration law, since explaining why a previous authoritative decision should be excluded necessarily leads to the unravelling of a plethora of other arguments. Of course, arriving at different conclusions is allowed, and previous decisions may not automatically determine future cases. Obviously, the repetition of a 'bad' solution is likely to harm rather than to improve arbitration.[46] All of these assertions are far

[44] See Fernández Arroyo (n 39) 132–34.

[45] See WMC Weidemaier, 'Towards a Theory of Precedent in Arbitration' (2010) 51 *William & Mary Law Review* 1895.

[46] See the warning in T Schultz, 'Against Consistency in Investment Arbitration' papers.ssrn.com/sol3/papers.cfm?abstract_id=2318358.

too obvious to deserve to be answered. When well understood, the doctrine of (de facto, persuasive) precedent should not forestall the development of arbitration law, rather it should ensure it. Whenever a precedent has been created by means of the repetition of a given solution, and the consensus around it, the existence of such precedent does nothing but exert a greater level of pressure on the interpreter or enforcer. The step from the mere quotation to the identification of a precedent requires a considerable but unavoidable effort from arbitrators. In such cases, in which a particular issue has gained no consensus, careful analysis of case law can help to favour sensible over weak reasoning.[47] In doing so arbitrators are putting the right bricks in the building, as it were, of legitimacy.

V. ACCOUNTABILITY

Even though the notion of accountability is itself far from clear, it has always been linked with governance. These concepts are regularly used in relation to State powers, and particularly in relation to the manner in which these powers are exercised.[48] Within such a context, accountability circumscribes the responsibility or liability of governments (as bodies) and public servants (as individuals).[49] Lately, the notion of accountability has also been applied to transnational corporations and it has promptly become a major topic of debate in the social sciences. One may wonder, what impact accountability has (or should have) on the organs of the 'arbitral legal order'?[50] Or, in other words, whether arbitrators and institutions should be potentially liable based on their pivotal role in private enforcement?[51]

To begin with, the answer is a resounding yes. An adjudicatory mechanism that is preponderant in several areas of transnational law, and quasi-exclusively used in other fields cannot function properly without a framework requiring accountability. Private adjudicators must be at least as accountable as their public-sector colleagues. This assumption is not

[47] See J Paulsson, 'International Arbitration and the Generation of Legal Norms: Treaty Arbitration and International Law' in AJ van den Berg (ed), *International Arbitration 2006: Back to the Basics?* (Alphen aan den Rijn, Kluwer, 2007) 889.

[48] The World Bank, together with other international agencies, has been insisting upon this issue for more than two decades.

[49] See M Kamto, *Droit international de la gouvernance* (Paris, Pedone, 2013) 34–35, 53–56.

[50] In the sense used by Gaillard (n 14) no 62.

[51] H Muir Watt, 'Concurrence ou confluence? Droit international privé et droits fondamentaux dans la gouvernance globale' in J Foyer (ed), *Le droit entre tradition et modernité. Mélanges à la mémoire de Patrick Courbe* (Paris, Dalloz, 2012) 459, 464–65, refers to arbitrators together with multinationals, rating agencies, standards authors and other private entities, claiming for 'la nécessité de les canaliser et de les discipliner, au nom d'une justice de l'ordre international' ['the necessity of canalize them and discipline them in behalf of a justice of the international order'].

only based on possible cases of corruption (which, thankfully, are rare in arbitration), it deals also with the possible violations of professional requirements (comparatively more common in practice).[52] This is not a proposal in the abstract: numerous legal orders—from New Zealand to Peru through Singapore and several European States—have now enacted rules governing the civil and criminal responsibility of arbitrators.[53]

The remaining questions are, however, what type of accountability is needed within the field of private enforcement and, subsidiarily, how should it operate? In the remaining portions of this short contribution, I will offer some thoughts on these points. According to a well-known distinction, accountability is composed of a vertical dimension and a horizontal dimension. Yet, the concrete meaning of each of them differs.[54] In our context, I prefer to speak about exogenous and endogenous accountability. The former would refer to the means through which public authorities control and punish arbitrators' violations of legal requirements, while the latter would be primarily put in motion by the organs of the arbitral legal order themselves and also exercised by arbitration users.

One might think that a way to adequately 'punish' arbitrators would be to set-aside or refuse enforcement of the arbitral awards they issue. This would represent a type of quality control of the work products generated by arbitrators, and is possible because every national legal order has the power (within the scope of its jurisdiction and in the terms fixed by the rules in force) to control the legal regularity of all aspects of arbitration—from agreements to proceedings, to awards. All legal orders have and use this power. Needless to say, within the field of commercial arbitration, such control is always domestic in nature.[55] In other words, it is not necessarily

[52] See Y Derains, 'Le professionnalisme des arbitres' (juillet-août 2012) *Cahiers de droit de l'entreprise* 21.

[53] An example may be found in the 2008 Peruvian Arbitration Decree no 1071 (the most advanced arbitration national legal order in Latin America). Concretely, its Art 32 (Responsibility of arbitrators) allows the management of this situation by indicating that '[A]cceptance binds arbitrators and, where applicable, the arbitral institution, to comply with their duties, making them liable, if they fail to do so, for any loss or damage due to wilful misconduct or gross negligence'. With more detail, Art 813-ter (Responsibility of arbitrators) of the Italian Code of Civil Procedure (resulting from the reform introduced by the Legislative Decree of 2 February 2006, no 40), states that '[T]he arbitrator shall be liable for damages caused to the parties if he or she: (1) has fraudulently or with gross negligence omitted or delayed acts that he or she was bound to carry out and has been removed for this reason, or has renounced the office without a justified reason; (2) has fraudulently or with gross negligence omitted or prevented the rendering of the award within the time limit fixed according to Articles 820 or 826'. Furthermore, this article provides that the Act on Responsibility of Judges (Act of 13 April 1988, no 117) applies by analogy to arbitrators under particular circumstances. Although not specified in the text, Art 813-ter would apply to international arbitration seated in Italy.

[54] Available at siteresources.worldbank.org/PUBLICSECTORANDGOVERNANCE/Resources/AccountabilityGovernance.pdf.

[55] Concerning investment arbitration under the ICSID Convention, there is an autonomous control mechanism established in its Art 52 (see C Schreuer, *The ICSID Convention: A Commentary* (Cambridge, Cambridge University Press, 2009) 890–1091). According to Art 53 of

effective outside its own jurisdictional scope. Indeed, the effects of (national) control decisions on other legal orders as well as on arbitral tribunals are often limited.[56] In any event, beyond all considerations one might make about this external control of arbitration products (and without prejudice to the severe censure that annulment or refusal of enforcement represents), this is not the kind of exogenous accountability I refer to.

The notion of accountability retained in this chapter is rather related to arbitrators' behaviour. By consequence, the 'punishment' I am speaking of would impact the arbitrators themselves, rather than their work products. Accordingly, my argument hinges less of an 'objective' view of accountability than a 'subjective' one. Of course, arbitrator behaviour may also provoke the annulment of the award and/or the refusal of its enforcement,[57] but this kind of censure tends to punish users more than it does adjudicators.[58]

What must be stressed is that subjective accountability has two dimensions. According to the first, the arbitrator's responsibility is based on its role as an adjudicator. The arbitrator is, in this sense, to be considered as a (private) judge. Accordingly, the duties of independence and impartiality are mutatis mutandis comparable to those required of judicial judges. The second dimension of an arbitrator's subjective accountability deals with their condition as a contracting party in the arbitration, committed to follow the terms according to which they have been designated by the parties—together, the co-contracting party. In this second sense, if the arbitrator does not fulfil its duties under the contract, an action may be brought against it.[59]

Under this proposed understanding of the notion of accountability, it seems clear that risks are to be found in practical applications. The temptation for a losing party, naturally unhappy with the outcome of arbitration

the Convention, annulment decisions issued by ad hoc committees 'shall be binding on the parties and shall be not subject to any appeal or to any other remedy except those provided for in this Convention'.

[56] As examples of these limitations one can mention the enforcement in some jurisdictions of foreign arbitral awards that have been set aside by the national courts at the seat of arbitration and the rather weak success of so-called anti-arbitration injunctions. See, respectively, AJ van den Berg, 'Should the Setting Aside of the Arbitral Award be Abolished?' (2014) *ICSID Review* 1–26, and E Gaillard, 'Reflections on the Use of Anti-Suit Injunctions in International Arbitration' in LA Mistelis and JDM Lew (eds), *Pervasive Problems in International Arbitration* (Alphen aan den Rijn, Kluwer, 2006) 201–15.

[57] Contrary to what it might be imagined, such control is becoming stronger in arbitration-friendly countries. As proof, it is sufficient to look at recent French case law to find an increasing number of annulments of awards because of a violation of the duty of disclosure (as a parameter to measure the lack of arbitrator's independence). See T Clay, 'Panorama. Arbitrage et modes alternatifs de règlement des litiges, décembre 2012—novembre 2013' (2013) 44 *Recueil Dalloz* 2936, 2941–44. The *Cour d'appel* of Paris has confirmed its rigorous standard in matter of duty of disclosure in a judgment of 14 October 2014, *AGI v Colombus*.

[58] To be sure, users often deserve this punishment.

[59] On all these questions, it is necessary to read T Clay, 'De la responsabilité de l'arbitre' in E Silva Romero, *El contrato de arbitraje* (Bogotá, Legis, 2005) 543, and more extensively T Clay, *El árbitro* (Pontificia Universidad Javeriana, 2012).

proceedings, to attempt to hold members of the tribunal liable for supposed misconduct may be strong. I am not simply speculating upon this point, as situations like these occur relatively frequently. As it happens, and likely as a result of the proliferation of such claims, the rules of most institutions now include provisions on arbitrator immunity.[60] Case in point, the instrument most frequently used in ad hoc arbitration, the 2010 UNCITRAL Arbitration Rules, provide in their Article 16 for the waiver of 'any claim against the arbitrators, the appointing authority and any person appointed by the arbitral tribunal based on any act or omission in connection with the arbitration'. Of course, limits to such waivers are to be found in the applicable law (insofar as it establishes such a limit) and in the arbitrator's intentional wrongdoing.[61]

Unsurprisingly, the arbitration community seems overwhelmingly favourable to the principle of arbitrator immunity.[62] Nevertheless, rules providing for arbitrators' liability will likely promote additional care and caution among arbitrators, notwithstanding the seriousness of the risks they imbue. The development of this type of vertical accountability might enhance the legitimacy of arbitration. By sure, lawmakers will have to take into account the risks of facilitating abuses by means of these liability clauses. The risks of poor drafting, or of contradictions with existing legislation, are clear.[63] It seems natural that the goal of such provisions, although praiseworthy, should not open a route to abusive challenges before judicial courts, nor excessively jeopardise the necessary efficiency of arbitration proceedings. Accordingly, and as a matter of principle arbitrators should not be responsible for the substantive content of their decisions—except in cases of intentional wrongdoing or when they provoke a denial of justice.[64]

[60] On arbitrators' risks and the way to minimise these risks, see J Gal, *Die Haftung des Schiedrichters in der internationalen Handelsschiedsgerichtsbarkeit* (Tübingen, Mohr Siebeck, 2009). Amongst other elements to shield arbitrators (the main purpose of the book), the author proposes the generalisation of professional liability insurance (365ff). Actually in some legal orders insurance is mandatory both for arbitrators and institutions. See, in this vein, the addition incorporated by Act 11/2011 into Art 21.1 of the Spanish Arbitration Act (Act 60/2003).

[61] The introduction of the latter was decided after a long discussion within the UNCITRAL Working Group on Arbitration. By contrast, 2012 ICC Rules as well as other recent arbitration rules include the former but not the latter.

[62] 'Overwhelmingly' does not mean 'unanimously'. See the criticism expressed by P Lalive, 'Sur l'irresponsabilité arbitrale' in *Études de procédure et d'arbitrage en l'honneur de J-F Poudret* (Lausanne, Faculté de Droit de l'Université de Lausanne, 1999) 419–35.

[63] This would be the case of the arbitral tribunal's liability by damages caused to a party in adopting interim measures introduced by the Mexican legislator in the reform of Mexican Arbitration Law (2011). See F González de Cossio, 'La modificación al derecho arbitral mexicano. Un comentario', www.juridicas.unam.mx/publica/librev/rev/jurid/cont/41/pr/pr13.pdf.

[64] This was the solution adopted by the French Supreme Court in *Azran*, 15 January 2014. See comments of E Loquin in *La Semaine Juridique Édition Générale* 8 (24 fév 2014) doctr 255, and L Aynès in *Cahiers de l'arbitrage* (2014) 299. See also R Dupeyre, 'Les arbitres et centres d'arbitrage face à leurs responsabilités: le droit français à son point d'équilibre' (2014) 32 *ASA Bulletin* 265–85.

In order to avoid excesses from unsatisfied parties, an option could be to require the annulment of an award before requesting liability of an arbitrator. In more general terms, the objective accountability should be treated as a condition precedent for the implementation of subjective accountability.[65] Such a filter would thus operate as a balance between (desirable) full accountability, on the one hand, and the need to avoid baseless, abusive and costly challenges, on the other hand. Nevertheless, there may exist cases in which no award exists,[66] as well as cases in which annulment is impossible due to particular reasons (for example due to procedural requirements), while the inappropriate behaviour of an arbitrator has caused prejudice to a party. Consequently, implementation of admissibility filters would need to provide for clear and comprehensive exceptions in order to avoid a de facto immunity.

In furtherance of this solution, the problem with domestic punishments is that they are not very effective concerning transnational arbitration. They may affect local arbitrators but their extraterritorial effects are uncertain. I say 'may affect' because of the existence of a number of features that demonstrate increasing autonomy of arbitration from domestic legal orders.[67] Under this understanding, even local arbitrators adjudicating forum-seated arbitrations often feel free to disregard the 'orders' issued by domestic courts. But arbitrators cannot take such situations as a 'carte blanche': arbitrators or arbitral institutions should not need remonstrations from national legal orders in order to act responsibly. In fact, the arbitral epistemic community has already taken several steps towards implementing accountability via different means. For instance, increasing attention is being paid to the availability of arbitrators, and a lower threshold has been required to successfully challenge sitting arbitrators—particularly in cases involving State parties. Whether by happenstance or otherwise, the arbitration community is in search of broader social acceptance of this dispute resolution method—one of the characteristic elements of legitimacy.

All respected arbitration institutions around the world have now included some type of endogenous accountability provision, both in their rules and in their practice. All this increases their control over arbitrators' independence,

[65] An example in this direction is found in the above mentioned Art 813-ter of the Italian Code of Civil Procedure: 'In case the award has been rendered, the action for liability may be filed only after the recourse against the award has been upheld by a final judgment and for the reasons for which the recourse was upheld'.

[66] The same Art mentioned in the previous note contemplates also this hypothesis.

[67] The trend towards the so-called denationalisation or delocalisation of arbitration—with its progress and regress—is all but new. See, for instance, P Mayer, 'The Trends Towards Delocalisation in the Last 100 Years' in M Hunter, H Marriot and VV Veeder (eds), *The Internationalisation of International Arbitration* (London, Graham & Trotman/Martinus Nijhoff, 1995) 37. The persistence of that trend allowed the development of a theory about the emergence of an (autonomous) arbitral legal order. See Gaillard (n 14).

impartiality and availability.[68] It is worth underlining that when parties submit to institutional arbitration, they become bound by the rules and practices of the institution they choose—a measure of the significance of such legal frameworks. Besides this type of 'private hard law', a softer counterpart is taking a progressively more important role.[69] This is the case of instruments created by the International Bar Association, generally taken into consideration in the course of transnational arbitration.[70] Surely, endogenous accountability works better within a context of exogenous incentives.[71] However, the arbitration community is interested in increasing efforts aimed at strengthening this internal control as a matter of survival.[72]

Last but certainly not least, endogenous accountability needs to be complemented by arbitration users who suffer directly from the consequences of arbitrators' misconduct. It can be argued that 'bad' arbitrators suffer 'reputational' sanctions: arbitration users will not appoint an arbitrator with a record of misconduct. However, this type of potential downstream sanction will remain ineffective, so long as arbitrators' activity remains inaccessible for those not directly concerned by the proceedings. In order to make reputational sanctions effective, systematic publication of awards including arbitrators' names is required. In other words, endogenous accountability also depends on transparency.

VI. EPILOGUE

Public justice, as well as all legal manifestations, is required to accomplish high standards of transparency, consistency and accountability. Within such a context, any contention that arbitration must conserve its traditional attributes of secrecy, of disregard for precedent, and of total immunity

[68] These types of instrument have existed for a number of years now, although their significance has greatly increased as their application has become widespread. Sometimes such tools are called 'codes of ethics'. As an example, amongst many others, one can mention the well known Code of Ethics for Arbitrators in Commercial Disputes, issued by the American Arbitration Association and available at www.adr.org/aaa/ShowProperty?nodeId=%2FUCM%2FADRSTG_003867&revision=latestreleased. I cannot refrain myself from quoting U Draetta, *Behind the Scenes in International Arbitration* (Huntington, Juris, 2011) 4: '[those arbitrator's attitudes] amount, rather, to conduct I would tend to define much more simply, not as unethical but as unprofessional if not downright stupid, because of its often counterproductive effects for those guilty of it'.

[69] See G Kaufmann-Kohler, 'La codificación y la normatividad del *soft law* en el arbitraje internacional' in Basedow, Fernández Arroyo and Moreno Rodríguez (n 2) 107.

[70] This is particularly the case of the 2004 IBA Guidelines on Conflict of Interests in International Arbitration, reformulated as of 2014, and available at www.ibanet.org/Publications/publications_IBA_guides_and_free_materials.aspx.

[71] See BA Warwas, *The Three Pillars of Institutional Arbitral Liability: The Weaknesses of Present Regulations and Proposals for Further Reform* (PhD thesis, EUI, 2014).

[72] See J Paulsson, *The Idea of Arbitration* (Oxford, Oxford University Press, 2013) 147 ff, 290–91.

of arbitrators, is hardly justifiable. Only by parting ways with these three traditions will arbitration be able to aspire to any measure of genuine legitimacy.

The final issue regarding legitimacy of transnational arbitration would be the question of whether different options to settle disputes should exist. Yet, this question is similar to the debate concerning the reasons for having different types of legal rules (hard and soft; public and private; national, international, supranational and transnational) or about the reason for having different types of legal persons (essentially, private, public and mixed). The answers are quite similar: complexity and pluralism are the normal expressions of a transnational society—complex and plural by nature. Private enforcement is an evident feature which coexists with different types of public enforcement, and whose legitimacy should be reinforced given its increasing significance and massive use.

Part VIII

Conclusions

18

Conclusions: Enforcement in Europe as a Market of Justice

ANDREA WECHSLER AND BOŠKO TRIPKOVIĆ

I. INTRODUCTION

ENFORCEMENT IS A matter of justice.[1] A scheme of rights and obligations—no matter how well designed—is futile unless it achieves compliance, provides redress and sanctions non-compliance. This nexus with justice has for a long time attached the understanding of enforcement to the nation state. As the authority of the nation state is premised on its capacity to secure justice, enforcement has traditionally been perceived as the exclusive domain of its coercive power. This notion was never completely accurate—there were always non-state actors that enforced the rules along with the state—but it did emphasise an important intuition: the state was the actor that was able to make good on its promise of justice.

While the demand for justice persists, the context in which it is delivered has changed dramatically. In Europe, enforcement includes a myriad of practices that escape this traditional conception.[2] These practices not only exist and operate within, outside, above and beyond the state, but they also challenge the distinction between state and non-state enforcement.[3] The state now competes with a number of institutions and processes to retain its role in enforcement. While the state before had to *justify* its power to enforce, today it has to *advertise* it;[4] whereas the state before had to *explain*

[1] This claim does not assume any particular conception of justice; rather, it points to a common justice-related expectation from the system of law enforcement. Such an expectation can exist regardless of the disagreement about justice: people can disagree about the kind of justice law enforcement system ought to deliver but still agree that its purpose is to deliver justice.

[2] See more in Robert Wai's contribution to this volume.

[3] See Christopher Hodges and Naomi Creutzfeldt's contribution to this volume.

[4] See for example the brochure 'Law—Made in Germany', available at www.lawmadeingermany.de/Law-Made_in_Germany.pdf. It promotes the 'global, effective, affordable' system of dispute resolution in Germany and advertises German legal systems in the following way: '"Made in Germany" is not just a quality seal reserved for German cars or machinery, it is equally applicable to German law'.

the authority of enforcement, now it begins to *export* it.[5] This need not mean that the state is no longer at the centre of legal enforcement: to neglect the state's essential role would certainly be mistaken. But to ignore the fundamental transformation of enforcement would be equally detrimental. European states today find themselves in a complex system of enforcement mechanisms, and this system governs the realisation of justice. The aim of this chapter is to account for this change.

A satisfying account would have to include at least two elements. On the one hand, it would need to map the main tendencies that epitomise the transformation of enforcement in Europe. Any explanation that would neglect this empirical change would be deficient for it would miss important aspects of the phenomenon. On the other hand, it would need to offer a new conceptualisation of the architecture of enforcement. Given that enforcement cannot be properly understood outside of the context of justice, such conceptualisation should not only capture important features of enforcement, but also illuminate the ways in which it can better fulfil its purpose. The aim should be an empirically adequate account that is at the same time normatively suggestive: one that succeeds in organising our thoughts about the existing mechanisms of enforcement from the perspective of justice.

This chapter thus proceeds in two steps. First, it identifies general processes that challenge the traditional conception of enforcement. The argument here is that there are at least three important developments in this respect: new modes of *regulation* lead to *fragmentation* and then *collectivisation* of enforcement. Second, the chapter argues that as a consequence of these developments the *enforcement in Europe becomes a regulated market for dispute resolution*: competition between diverse enforcement mechanisms becomes the guiding norm, and the provision of justice becomes a service. This points to some problems in the design of enforcement in Europe that need to be adequately addressed. The chapter argues that the realisation of justice becomes a fundamentally different task in the new environment, and then suggests several ways in which enforcement in Europe could become more responsive to these novel circumstances.

[5] For example, Dutch Collective Settlement of Mass Damages Act (WCAM 2005) has become an export product. See T Arons and WH van Boom, 'Beyond Tulips and Cheese: Exporting Mass Securities Claim Settlements from the Netherlands' (2010) 21 *European Business Law Review* 857. The Nordic conception of enforcement that includes the institution of ombudsman has been exported to the European Union and many other countries worldwide. The European Ombudsman, *The European Ombudsman: Origins, Establishment, Evolution* (Luxembourg, Office for Official Publications of the European Communities, 2005) 3.

II. REGULATION, FRAGMENTATION AND COLLECTIVISATION OF ENFORCEMENT

An investigation into the transformation of enforcement in Europe reveals three interrelated tendencies. First, there is a shift in regulation from nation state to supranational and transnational levels. Second, this leads to fragmentation of enforcement, both vertically (between different levels of governance) and horizontally (on sectorial basis or along the public/private distinction). Third, policies that are countering fragmentation result in collectivisation of enforcement on both the supply and demand side of justice.[6] Let us address each of these tendencies in more detail.

A. Regulation

The governance of enforcement in Europe has changed. Transformations concern both the understanding of the goals of enforcement and the way they are attained. While compensatory and deterrent elements of enforcement have traditionally been kept distinct, they are now combined in an effort to achieve a balance between compensation, deterrence and vindication.[7] This not only implies a new regulatory function in addition to the traditional enforcement rationales, but also denotes a departure from command-and-control conception of enforcement.[8] As a consequence, judicial enforcement has been steadily replaced with stronger administrative and private elements: traditional regulation is substituted with cooperative mechanisms for dispute resolution that strike a different balance between the role of government and private actors in enforcement, and thus introduce—to some degree—private regulatory litigation.

These developments emanate from the interplay between *deregulation* and *non-regulation* at the national level, *re-regulation* at the European level, and *self-regulation* at the transnational level: deregulation and non-regulation at the national level have stimulated the involvement of private actors in the enforcement system; growing competences and re-regulation at the European level have empowered private litigants to bring regulatory litigation, and have also shifted enforcement from traditional judicial

[6] Note also the concept of diagonal fragmentation in C Joerges, 'The Idea of Three-Dimensional Conflicts of Law as Constitutional Form of Transnational Governance' (2010) RECON Online Working Paper 2010/05, available at www.europeanrights.eu/public/commenti/jeorges_testo.pdf.

[7] G Wagner, 'Prävention und Verhaltenssteuerung durch Privatrecht—Anmaßung oder legitime Aufgabe?' (2006) 206 *Archiv für civilistische Praxis* 352. G Brüggemeier, *Prinzipien des Haftungsrechts: Eine systematische Darstellung auf rechtsvergleichender Grundlage* (Baden-Baden, Nomos, 1999) 3–6.

[8] *cf* O Lobel, 'New Governance as Regulatory Governance' in D Levi-Four (ed), *The Oxford Handbook of Governance* (Oxford, Oxford University Press, 2012).

avenues towards public administrative enforcement; and globalisation and technological developments have facilitated the emergence of self-regulation at the transnational level that is beyond the reach of traditional national instruments and conflict of law mechanisms.

i. Deregulation and Non-Regulation at the National Level

One of the major driving forces behind the emergence of a new regulatory style is the liberalisation and deregulation of large parts of the market in the 1990s in a number of European Member States.[9] Privatisation was coupled with a corresponding transfer of responsibility for law enforcement from public to private actors, and with an increased importance of private enforcement mechanisms.[10] But the imminent threat of the growing volume of private enforcement has led to the strengthening of the deterrent function of enforcement.[11] The European Union has stepped into the regulatory void and started policy initiatives for addressing many of these emerging issues, such as the possible need to compensate consumers in antitrust cases. This has brought about a rather particular mode of regulation, whereby the increased empowerment of private actors is combined with public enforcement.[12]

Another tendency is non-regulation of enforcement on national level. A number of enforcement regimes in European Member States have suffered from reform gridlocks and extensive reliance on conflict of laws. In many cases, the reforms of the civil justice systems have come ex post facto, have not been deep enough, or have not been undertaken at all. For instance, this has been evident in relation to securities lawsuits in Germany. It was only when the Landgericht Frankfurt was faced with 17,000 private plaintiffs against Deutsche Telekom in a securities liabilities case that the collective action proceedings were reformed, and even then only under very limited circumstances.[13] A consequence of this was the adoption of Capital Markets Model Case Act (KapMuG) that allowed model proceedings that would streamline similar capital market related actions.[14] Even though its validity

[9] M Reimann, 'Präventiv-administrative Regulierung oder Private Law Enforcement?' in *Jahrbuch Bitburger Gespräche 2008/I* (München, CH Beck, 2009) 105.

[10] R Podszun, 'Vertragsrettung durch Zivilgerichte?' in P Kreutz, N Renftle, E Faber, D Arndt, N Huber, H-M Schellhase and M Steuer (eds), *Realitäten des Zivilrechts—Grenzen des Zivilrechts* (Stuttgart, Gesellschaft Junger Zivilrechtswissenschaftler, 2012).

[11] Reimann (n 9).

[12] R Daniel Kelemen calls this regulatory style 'Eurolegalism'. For a concise overview, see his contribution to this volume.

[13] See A Halfmeier, 'The KapMuG story: Failure of the Deutsche Telekom Collective Action', available at sustainableprivatelaw.files.wordpress.com/2013/02/halfmeier_handout_rucc88schlikon_20131.pdf.

[14] Kapitalanleger-Musterverfahrensgesetz 2005.

has been extended from 2012 until 2020,[15] the law was inadequate in many respects, and some of these inadequacies are feeding into the discussion about collective redress mechanisms at the EU level.[16]

ii. Reregulation at the European Level

Filling the void that was left by national deregulation and non-regulation—but also as a result of functional pressures, political incentives and activist judges—the EU has ventured into reregulation of enforcement at the European level. European regulatory intervention has taken a variety of forms ranging from judicial and administrative enforcement,[17] over Alternative Dispute Resolution (ADR) regimes and mediation,[18] to cross-border litigation concerning small claims.[19]

The regulatory style of the EU is marked by two tendencies. First, in contrast to some former approaches that negated the behavioural effect of private law enforcement, the EU has recognised deterrence as an objective of private law, in addition to the traditional compensatory goals. Rhetoric about 'policing the market through judicial and administrative enforcement'[20] and the European Union as '*Ordnungspolizei*' for the internal market corroborate this finding.[21] The European Commission has consequently attained extensive law enforcement powers in some domains, such as competition law.

Second—and in tension with this—the EU had to rely on national administration and courts for law enforcement.[22] This has led to the emergence of regulatory litigation: Judicialised mode of economic governance[23] in which

[15] See www.disputeresolutiongermany.com/2012/07/class-actions-in-germany-kapmug-extended-until-2020-modest-change-of-scope/.

[16] See Commission Recommendation of 11 June 2013 on common principles for injunctive and compensatory collective redress mechanisms in the Member States concerning violations of rights granted under Union Law [2013] OJ L201/60.

[17] eg Reg (EC) No 2006/2004 of 27 October 2004 on cooperation between national authorities responsible for the enforcement of consumer protection laws (the Reg on consumer protection cooperation) [2004] OJ L364/1.

[18] European Commission, 'Proposal for a Directive on Consumer Rights', COM(2008) 614 final.

[19] Reg No 861/2007 of 11 July 2007 establishing a European Small Claims Procedures [1973] OJ L199/40.

[20] F Cafaggi, 'The Great Transformation. Administrative and Judicial Enforcement in Consumer Protection: A Remedial Perspective' (2009) 21 *Loyola Consumer Law Review* 496.

[21] See G Oettinger, 'Wir sind die Ordnungspolizei', available at www.focus.de/finanzen/news/guenther-oettinger-kaempft-um-seinen-ruf-eu-kommissar-ich-bin-auch-ein-teil-des-volkes_aid_1017840.html.

[22] For example, this is demonstrated by the decentralisation of competition law enforcement. See C Baudenbacher, 'Decentralization of EC Competition Law Enforcement and Arbitration' (2002) 8 *Columbia Journal of European Law* 1.

[23] eg RD Kelemen, *Eurolegalism: The Transformation of Law and Regulation in the European Union* (Cambridge MA, Harvard University Press, 2011) 16.

social changes are brought about by litigation rather than regulation or legislation. The Court of Justice has played a central role in facilitating regulatory litigation.[24] This was, for instance, evident in the *Mohamed Aziz* case that symbolises the trust that societal actors put into the Court of Justice, and where enforcement mechanisms were used to remedy social deficiencies of national and EU legal orders.[25]

Nevertheless, the EU re-regulatory efforts have not succeeded on all accounts. For instance, the application of the Directive on Injunctions for the Protection of Consumers' Interests[26] is still very limited in transborder litigation.[27] The use of ADR procedures is also rather infrequent.[28] Finally, only two per cent of European citizens have been involved in civil justice procedures in other Member States.[29] But despite this mix of successes and failures of the European approach to law enforcement, the tendency towards regulatory enforcement as a new mode of governance is evident.

iii. Self-Regulation at the Transnational Level

Another driving force behind the emergence of a new regulatory landscape in Europe has been the rise of self-regulatory enforcement techniques at transnational level. The range of affected legal regimes is broad: it includes many areas of trade law, food safety law, financial services, professional standards, environmental and employment standards as well as advertising and data protection, to mention only a few.[30] In these areas enforcement transpires through contractual regulatory tools as developed by global supply chains.[31] Such self-regulatory mechanisms range from guidelines,

[24] See Marcus Norrgård's contribution to this volume.

[25] Case 415/11 *Mohamed Aziz v Caixa d'Estalvis de Catalunya, Tarragona i Manresa (Catalunyacaixa)*, judgment of 14 March 2013, nyr. For the analysis along these lines see H-W Micklitz, 'Unfair Contract Terms—Public Interest Litigation before European Courts—Case C-415/11 Mohamed Aziz' in E Terryn, G Straetmans and V Colaert (eds), *Landmark Cases of EU Consumer Law: In Honour of Jules Stuyck* (Antwerp, Intersentia, 2013) 615–34.

[26] Dir 98/27/EC of 19 May 1998 on injunctions for the protection of consumers' interests [1998] OJ L166/51.

[27] See Report from the Commission concerning the application of Dir 98/27/EC of the European Parliament and of the Council on injunctions for the protection of consumers' interest, COM(2008) 756 final.

[28] See European Commission, 'Special Eurobarometer 195: European Citizens and Access to Justice' (2004), and European Commission, 'Special Eurobarometer 292: Civil Justice in the European Union' (2007), available at ec.europa.eu/public_opinion/archives/ebs/ebs_292_en.pdf.

[29] European Commission, 'Special Eurobarometer 195', ibid and European Commission, 'Special Eurobarometer 292', ibid.

[30] See extensively F Cafaggi (ed), *Enforcement of Transnational Regulation: Ensuring Compliance in a Global World* (Cheltenham, Edward Elgar, 2012).

[31] F Cafaggi, 'The Transformation of Transnational Private Regulation: Enforcement Gaps and Governance Design 1' in Cafaggi (n 30).

codes of conduct, regulatory contracts, agreements and standard setting instruments, and are mostly stimulated by governmental and market failures, as well as technological pressures.[32]

The logic of enforcement in this domain is different from the traditional state-sponsored idea of enforcement. Instead on justice, such mechanisms primarily focus on achieving compliance. Because private regulations are voluntary instruments, compliance is understood as a precondition for participation in a particular association or regulatory space.[33] As opposed to traditional ex post enforcement devices, self-regulatory enforcement mechanisms at transnational level rely extensively on ex ante incentives for compliance or on a combination of ex post and ex ante enforcement techniques. Compliance is thus not only motivated by the threat of judicial proceeding, as it is assumed in the ordinary private law, but also—and perhaps in particular—by reputational implications.[34]

B. Fragmentation

The new modes of regulation lead to fragmentation of enforcement. The emergence of a complex system of interacting players, authorities and structures in the European political economy results in the multi-level system of governance of enforcement in European economic law.[35] Multiple regulatory regimes leave gaps between enforcement mechanisms and bring about usual concerns about fragmentation:[36] the lack of legal uncertainty and the loss of integrity.[37] It is helpful to distinguish between two dimensions of fragmentation: vertical and horizontal.

[32] See F Cafaggi, 'The Regulatory Functions of Transnational Commercial Contracts: New Architectures' (2013) 36 *Fordham International Law Journal* 1557.

[33] F Cafaggi, 'The Transformation of Transnational Private Regulation: Enforcement Gaps and Governance Design 5' in Cafaggi (n 30).

[34] For example, compliance is secured through 'outcasting' mechanisms whereby the disobedient members are denied the benefit of social cooperation and membership. See OA Hathaway and SJ Shapiro, 'Outcasting: Enforcement in Domestic and International Law' (2011) 121 *Yale Law Journal* 252.

[35] On enforcement of foreign judgments as a multilevel system of governance see Christopher A Whytock's contribution to this volume. On the concept of multilevel governance see S Piattoni, 'Multi-level Governance: A Historical and Conceptual Analysis' (2009) 31 *European Integration* 163.

[36] F Cafaggi, 'The Transformation of Transnational Private Regulation: Enforcement Gaps and Governance Design 6' in Cafaggi (n 30).

[37] M Koskenniemi and P Leino, 'Fragmentation of International Law? Postmodern Anxieties' (2002) 15 *Leiden Journal of International Law* 553; P Weil, 'Towards Relative Normativity in International Law?' (1983) 77 *American Journal of International Law* 413. See also G Hafner, 'Risks Ensuing from the Fragmentation of International Law' in International Law Commission, *Report of the Working Group on Long-term Programme of Work* (ILC (LII)/WG/LT/L.1/Add 1, 25 July 2000) 26.

i. Vertical Fragmentation

Vertical fragmentation occurs between the enforcement regimes of individual Member States and the European Union.[38] The emergence of vertical fragmentation results primarily from the expansion of European Union competences in the field of enforcement. For instance, the Lisbon Treaty (TFEU) has extended the legal framework for criminal legislation and judicial control.[39] Article 83(2) TFEU now allows for the adoption of common minimum rules on the definition of criminal offences and sanctions if they are essential for the effectiveness of EU policies.[40] The legal basis for European enforcement measures in private law—such as the Directive on ADR and the Regulation on Online Dispute Resolution (ODR)[41]—is the harmonisation of rules for the establishment and functioning of the internal market (Article 114 TFEU). Another example is intellectual property (IP) law, where the Article 118 TFEU establishes a shared competence between the EU and the Member States and allows for the 'creation of European intellectual property rights ... and for the setting up of centralized Union-wide authorisation, coordination and supervision arrangement'. While not exhaustive, these examples demonstrate a growing number and sophistication of legal bases for the regulation of enforcement on European level. A consequence of the expansion of EU competences in the field of enforcement is the creation of a wide variety of enforcement mechanisms, procedures and remedies in European economic law that either conflict, complement or compete with national enforcement mechanisms. In any area of European economic law—ranging from consumer protection, employment

[38] 'Vertical' here denotes a sense that there is a hierarchical dimension to these relations. The ECJ articulated its understanding of 'vertical' relations in C-26/62 *NV Algemene Transporten Expeditie Onderneming van Gend en Loos v Nederlandse Administratis der Belastingen* [1963] ECR 1, and asserted the supremacy of EU law in Case 6/64 *Falminio Costa v ENEL* [1964] ECR 585. These doctrines have been confirmed in 17th Declaration Concerning Primacy annexed to the Final Act of the Intergovernmental Conference which adopted the Treaty of Lisbon: 'The Conference recalls that, in accordance with well settled case law of the Court of Justice of the European Union, the Treaties and the law adopted by the Union on the basis of the Treaties have primacy over the law of Member States, under the conditions laid down by the said case law'. For a detailed account of the operation of enforcement in a vertically fragmented legal system from the political science perspective, see Marlene Wind's contribution to this volume.

[39] Treaty of Lisbon Amending the Treaty on European Union and the Treaty Establishing the European Community [2007] OJ C306/1.

[40] Not surprisingly, the adoption of Art 83(2) TFEU was followed by a communication from the Commission on the development of EU criminal policy under the Lisbon Treaty. Communication from the Commission, 'Towards an EU Criminal Policy: Ensuring the effective implementation of EU policies through criminal law', COM/2011/0573 final.

[41] Dir 2013/11/EU of 21 May 2013 on alternative dispute resolution for consumer disputes and amending Reg (EC) No 2006/2004 and Dir 2009/22/EC (Dir on consumer ADR) [2013] OJ L165/63; Reg No 524/2013 of 21 May 2013 on online dispute resolution for consumer disputes and amending Reg (EC) No 2006/2004 and Dir 2009/22/EC (Reg on consumer ODR) [2013] OJ L165/1.

discrimination, environmental policy, securities regulation to competition policy—there exists a certain degree of fragmentation.

Vertical fragmentation sometimes takes the form of strengthening of European administrative enforcement regimes at the expense of national judicial enforcement systems.[42] In competition law, for instance, the European Commission has taken the role of an investigator, prosecutor and decision-maker, with European courts providing only some degree of external control.[43] At times, fragmentation takes the form of decentralisation of law enforcement. For example, there has been a move towards decentralisation of competition law enforcement in Europe through Council Regulation 1/2003.[44] In the field of consumer law, the European Union has encouraged its Member States to establish appropriate public regulatory authorities and agencies at national level, thereby leading to a new balance between administrative and judicial enforcement.[45] And despite the attempted harmonisation in the field—for example, through the Regulation on Consumer Protection Cooperation which establishes an EU-wide network of national enforcement authorities with enforcement and investigation powers—the lack of de facto cooperation and the ongoing consultations about its effectiveness testify to the continued fragmentation.

Intellectual property law is another example of a vertically fragmented enforcement regime. The Enforcement Directive 2004/47/EC[46] requires all Member States to provide effective, dissuasive and proportionate measures, remedies and procedures against IP infringements; however, it does not regulate the way in which such remedies are to be provided.[47] Further fragmentation can be observed in trade mark law where the Regulation on the Community Trade Mark established the Community trade mark courts.[48] But in fact, the Member States have designated certain national

[42] H-W Micklitz, 'Administrative Enforcement of European Private Law' in R Brownsword, H-W Micklitz, L Niglia and S Weatherill (eds), *The Foundations of European Private Law* (Oxford, Hart Publishing, 2011) 563–92.

[43] H Schweitzer, 'The European Competition Law Enforcement System and the Evolution of Judicial Review' in C-D Ehlermann and M Marquis (eds), *European Competition Law Annual 2009: The Evaluation of Evidence and its Judicial Review in Competition Cases* (Oxford, Hart Publishing, 2011).

[44] Council Reg (EC) No 1/2003 of 16 December 2002 on the implementation of the rules on competition laid down in Arts 81 and 82 of the Treaty [2003] OJ L1/1.

[45] See F Cafaggi and H-W Micklitz, 'Administrative and Judicial Collective Enforcement of Consumer Law in the US and the European Community' (2007) EUI Working Papers Law 2007/22.

[46] Dir 2004/48/EC of 29 April 2004 on the enforcement of intellectual property rights [2004] OJ L195/16.

[47] Because of this, the directive is currently under review with the objective of assessing the effectiveness and functionality of the civil enforcement system put in place by the Member States. See 'Civil enforcement of intellectual property rights: public consultation on the efficiency of proceedings and accessibility of measures', available at ec.europa.eu/internal_market/consultations/2012/intellectual-property-rights_en.htm.

[48] Council Reg (EC) No 207/2009 of 26 February 2009 on the Community trade mark [2009] OJ L78/1.

courts and tribunals of first and second instance as their Community trade mark courts, while keeping the traditional enforcement avenues for national trade marks. A similar system has been established for the enforcement of community design rights under the Community Design Regulation.[49] While the reform to overcome the enforcement fragmentation in patent law has featured high on the EU agenda[50]—for example, through the Agreement on a Unified Patent Court creating the so-called Unified Patent Court (UPC) with the exclusive jurisdiction for litigation related to European patents and European patents with unitary effect[51]—few areas of European economic law have seen so many failed initiatives to strengthen and harmonise enforcement mechanisms. For example, not only has the Proposed Directive on Enforcement of Intellectual Property Rights failed,[52] but the Anti-Counterfeiting Trade Agreement (ACTA)[53] has also been rejected by the European Parliament.

Finally, the creation of rights at European level has substantially reshaped national law enforcement regimes.[54] *Bosman*, *Laval*, *Courage* and *Janecek* are only some examples of cases in which existing remedies under national law had to be refashioned, or in which new remedies had to be introduced into national legal regimes.[55] Likewise, the *Marshall II* case[56] demanded from Member States' legal systems to lift statutory damage caps and to ensure that damage awards provide full compensation for damages. These developments have contributed to an even stronger competition between European and national enforcement regimes.

[49] Council Reg (EC) No 6/2002 of 12 December 2001 on Community designs [2002] OJ L3/1.

[50] See A Wechsler, 'Europäische Patentorganisation' in A Hatje and P-C Müller-Graff (eds), *Enzyklopädie des Europarechts, Europäisches Organisations- und Verfassungsrecht*, vol 1 (Tübingen, Mohr Siebeck, forthcoming).

[51] Reg (EU) No 1257/2012 of 17 December 2012 implementing enhanced cooperation in the area of the creation of unitary patent protection [2012] OJ L361/1; Council Reg (EU) No 1260/2012 of 17 December 2012 implementing enhanced cooperation in the area of the creation of unitary patent protection with regard to the applicable translation arrangements [2012] OJ L361/89. The text of the draft agreement on a Unified Patent Court is available at register.consilium.europa.eu/pdf/en/12/st16/st16351-co03.en12.pdf.

[52] See A Wechsler, 'Strafrechtliche Rechtsdurchsetzung: Dysfunktionalitäten oder Funktionswandel?' in RM Hilty and T Jäger (eds), *Fehlstellungen im Europäischen Immaterialgüterrecht* (Springer, forthcoming) (copy on file with author).

[53] For more information see trade.ec.europa.eu/doclib/docs/2012/january/tradoc_149003.pdf.

[54] N Reich, 'Horizontal Liability in EC Law: Hybridization of Remedies for Compensation in Case of Breaches of EC Rights' (2007) 44 *Common Market Law Review* 705.

[55] Case C-415/93 *Bosman* [1995] ECR I-4921, Case 341/05 *Laval un Partneri Ptd v Svenska Byggnadsarbetareförbundet et al* [2007] ECR I-5751, Case C-453/99 *Courage and Crehan* [2001] ECR I-6297, Case C-237/07 *Dieter Janecek v Freistaat Bayern* [2008] ECR I-6221.

[56] Case 271/91 *Marshall v Southampton Health Authority (No 2)* [1993] ECR I-4367. See also Case C-36/02 *Omega Spielhallen* [2004] ECR I-9609.

ii. Horizontal Fragmentation

Horizontal fragmentation refers to the fact that several actors—whether public, private, national or transnational—either issue and enforce highly specialised and targeted policies in the same area, or apply different types of enforcement.[57] The first kind of horizontal fragmentation divides enforcement along the sectorial lines. There are manifold examples of such fragmentation in European economic law. For instance, the enforcement in consumer protection has not only been separated from the overarching private law regime but has also been internally fragmented. Let us mention but a few areas that have distinct treatment under European consumer law: unfair commercial practices, financial services, air travel, energy, product guarantees, consumer credit, package holidays and doorstep selling.[58] Likewise, the enforcement of intellectual property law has been both detached from the general private law regime of enforcement and internally separated into distinct systems. Discrete enforcement regimes have been created for trade mark law and design rights, and are currently being established for patents.[59]

The second kind of horizontal fragmentation occurs along the public–private divide. It denotes a situation in which mechanisms of public and private enforcement are implemented simultaneously or combined in hybrid public–private regimes of enforcement.[60] There are many examples of such fragmentation in European economic law. Most noticeably, there has been a rise in private enforcement services and self-regulatory mechanisms in recent years. The European Union has promoted private enforcement services in

[57] See: N Luhman, 'Die Weltgesellschaft' (1971) 57 *Archiv für Rechts- und Sozialphilosophie* 21; A Fischer-Lescano and G Teubner, 'Regime-Collision: The Vain Search for Legal Unity in the Fragmentation of Global Law' (2004) 25 *Michigan Journal of International Law* 1004.

[58] eg the Commission Dir 2011/90/EU of 14 November 2011 amending Part II of Annex I to Dir 2008/48/EC of the European Parliament and of the Council providing additional assumptions for the calculation of the annual percentage rate of charge [2011] OJ L296/35; Council Dir 85/577/EEC of 20 December 1985 to protect the consumer in respect of contracts negotiated away from business premises [1985] OJ L372/31; Dir 90/314/EEC of 13 June 1990 on package travel, package holidays and package tours [1990] OJ L158/59; Dir 1999/44/EC of 25 May 1999 on certain aspects of the sale of consumer goods and associated guarantees [1999] OJ L171/12.

[59] Narrowly tailored enforcement systems have sometimes been established to cope with challenges posed by digital technology and globalisation. See for example the Uniform Domain-Name Dispute-Resolution Policy (UDRP), available at www.icann.org/en/help/dndr/udrp. See also: J de Werra, 'Can Alternative Dispute Resolution Mechanisms Become the Default Method for Solving International Intellectual Property Disputes?' (2012) 43 *California Western International Law Journal* 39; and A Wechsler, 'WIPO's Policy Priorities in a World of Global Legal Pluralism—Alternative Dispute Resolution for Generic Top-level Domains (gTLD) and the Protection of Audiovisual Performances' in C Hermann, C Krajewski, JP Terhechte (eds), *European Yearbook of International Economic Law 2014* (Heidelberg, Springer, 2013).

[60] For the discussion of hybrid enforcement mechanisms see Christopher Hodges and Naomi Creutzfeldt's contribution to this volume.

the form of mediation, ADR and ODR.[61] Arbitration has also been a very popular, cost- and time-efficient mechanism of resolving disputes,[62] not only in cross-border contractual conflicts but also in public–private disputes, such as investment arbitration.[63] The growth of case volumes of institutions such as the London Court of International Arbitration (LCIA), the ICC International Court of Arbitration and—increasingly—Asian courts such as the Singapore International Arbitration Centre (SIAC), testifies to the growth of private justice in a global economy.[64] Private enforcement avenues have even appeared in the realm of proprietary rights, such as intellectual property rights. For example, the World Intellectual Property Organization (WIPO) Arbitration and Mediation Centre has provided dispute resolution services in a wide variety of conflicts since its foundation in 1994.[65] Self-regulatory enforcement mechanisms also develop in the realm of standard setting. While standard-setting organisations (SSOs) such as the International Standards Organization (ISO) have no power to enforce the implementation of its standards, a high degree of compliance can nevertheless be understood as a quasi self-enforcing mechanism.[66] And finally, whereas European competition law enforcement has primarily relied on administrative governmental enforcement, there has been a surge of interest in recent years in the expansion of private actions for damages.[67]

The problem with horizontal fragmentation is not the public or private nature of enforcement mechanisms as such, but one of complementarity between them. As with complementary goods, complementary dispute resolution services exhibit a negative cross elasticity of demand. Changes in the provision of one good affect the demand for the other. For instance, rising costs in judicial litigation affect the demand for arbitration and alternative dispute resolution. Moreover, transnational arbitration is not a self-sufficient enforcement mechanism. Rather, it operates in the shadow of judicial litigation that lends it authority by recognising arbitral awards.[68]

[61] See eg Dir 2008/52/EC of 21 May 2008 on certain aspects of mediation in civil and commercial matters [2008] OJ L136/3.

[62] KC Nobles, 'Emerging Issues and Trends in International Arbitration' (2012) 43 *California Western International Law Journal* 77.

[63] SD Franck, 'Development and Outcomes of Investment Treaty Arbitration' (2009) 50 *Harvard International Law Journal* 435.

[64] W Mattli, 'Private Justice in a Global Economy: From Litigation to Arbitration, International Organization' (2001) 55 *International Organization* 919.

[65] Available at www.wipo.int/amc/en/.

[66] *cf* J Freeman, 'The Private Role in Public Governance' (2002) 75 *New York University Law Review* 543, 644.

[67] J Stuyck, 'Class Actions in Europe? To Opt-In or to Opt-Out, that is the Question' (2009) 20 *European Business Law Review* 483.

[68] CA Whytock, 'Litigation, Arbitration, and the Transnational Shadow of the Law' (2008) 18 *Duke Journal of Comparative and International Law* 449. See also Robert Wai's contribution to this volume.

Horizontal fragmentation, thus, exposes the increasing interdependence of various mechanisms and underlines the need to pay due regard to all elements of the enforcement system. In particular—as we shall argue in the final part—it demands the reform and modernisation of the judicial system that seems neglected in comparison with the excitement over the advantages of alternative dispute resolution.

C. Collectivisation

Collectivisation is a tendency that emerges as a consequence of attempts to counter fragmentation.[69] It is driven by a general policy shift in European economic law from producerism (that is from an emphasis on the rights and interests of the supply side of the market) to consumerism (that is towards an emphasis on the rights and interest of the demand side of the market).[70] Collectivisation encompasses two distinct trends: coordination of enforcement services and the aggregation of claims. Let us discuss each of them in more detail.

i. Coordination

The rationale of coordination is the need for complementary and consistent decisions for the realisation of mutual interests. Globalisation has made this need evident, as the territorial limitations of traditional national governance regimes require novel forms of collaboration. There is a growing dialogue between national and supranational judges, and there is a growing interchange in almost any aspect of the law enforcement regime.[71] Coordination thus involves a range of activities: from informal consultation and collaboration, over connection of different activities, to formal cooperation. It also takes a range of different forms of coordination with regard to actors (for example judges), institutions (for example consumer authorities), policy-making (for example in the case of the unitary patent regime), procedures and substantive law.

Let us use some examples. Substantial and binding coordination has taken place in the area of conflict of laws with the adoption of the Brussels Convention on Jurisdiction and the Enforcement of Judgments in Civil and

[69] K Tuori, 'Towards a Theory of Transnational Law' (2010, draft, copy on file with the authors) 18.

[70] *cf* JQ Whitman, 'Consumerism versus Producerism: A Study in Comparative Law' (2007) 117 *Yale Law Journal* 340.

[71] S Cassese, 'The Constellation of Global and National Courts: Jurisdictional Redundancy and Interchange' in A Seibert-Fohr and M Villiger (eds), *Judgments of The European Court of Human Rights: Effects and Implementation* (Baden-Baden, Nomos, 2014).

Commercial Matters,[72] first replaced by the Regulation on Jurisdiction and the Recognition and Enforcement of Judgments in Civil and Commercial Matters, and now substituted with the Brussels I Recast in 2013.[73] Another form of cooperation takes place in the European Competition Network (ECN) which is based on the Commission Notice on Cooperation within the Network of Competition Authorities,[74] and on the Joint Statement of the Council and the Commission on the Functioning of the Network of Competition Authorities.[75] The network constitutes a discussion forum and method of cooperation of European competition authorities in cases where Articles 101 and 102 TFEU are applicable.[76]

In consumer law, Regulation on Consumer Protection Cooperation has set up an EU-wide network of national enforcement authorities with similar investigation and enforcement powers.[77] The system allows national authorities to ask other members of the network for assistance in investigations of consumer law violations. Moreover, also in consumer law, the European Consumer Centres Network (ECC-NET) assists consumers in the settlement of cross-border disputes by guiding them towards ADR mechanisms. The sheer number of 50,000–60,000 annual complaints demonstrates the success of this coordination mechanism.[78] For consumers of financial services, the so-called Financial Services Complaints Network (FIN-NET), established in 2001, coordinates 50 out-of-court schemes in the EU and beyond.[79] One year later, the Internal Market Problem Solving Network (SOLVIT) was created to support the handling of cross-border complaints that involve misapplication of EU law by public authorities within the EU Member States.[80] Another formal mode of cooperation has recently been initiated with a view of establishing a unitary patent system in Europe. In 2011, the Council authorised enhanced cooperation among EU Member States under Articles 326–334 TFEU for the creation of unitary patent and unitary patent court.[81]

[72] Brussels Convention on Jurisdiction and the Enforcement of Judgments in Civil and Commercial Matters [1972] OJ L 299/32.

[73] Reg (EU) No 1215/2012 of 12 December 2012 on jurisdiction and the recognition and enforcement of judgments in civil and commercial matters [2012] OJ L 351/1. See also Tuori (n 69).

[74] Commission Notice on Cooperation within the Network of Competition Authorities [2004] OJ C101/43.

[75] Available at ec.europa.eu/competition/ecn/joint_statement_en.pdf.

[76] For a detailed discussion see Kati Cseres' contribution to this volume.

[77] Reg (EC) No 2006/2004 of 27 October 2004 on cooperation between national authorities responsible for the enforcement of consumer protection laws (the Regulation on consumer protection cooperation) [2004] OJ L364/1.

[78] See Christopher Hodges and Naomi Creutzfeldt contribution to this volume.

[79] See ec.europa.eu/internal_market/fin-net/.

[80] See ec.europa.eu/solvit/site/index_en.htm.

[81] See European Commission, 'Towards a Unitary Patent Protection in Europe', 8 March 2011, available at www.consilium.europa.eu/ueDocs/cms_Data/docs/pressData/en/intm/119665.pdf.

Judicial cooperation has also become more formalised and is now governed by Articles 67–81 TFEU. The network of courts that cooperate with the Court of Justice of the European Union has expanded to 27 Member States. Some initiatives have even gone as far as promoting the emergence of international civil procedure law.[82] Apart from these judicial structures, there are multiple contractual networks that use new cooperative enforcement techniques both within and beyond public institutions.[83] These examples from a variety of European economic law regimes show that coordination has become an essential characteristic of European law enforcement.

ii. Aggregation

Aggregation denotes the summation of individual claims and dispute resolution interests into one or more collective claims. This tendency is typically justified on efficiency and distributional grounds, and primarily concerns the plaintiffs, that is the demand side of justice. The growth of legislation on aggregate litigation and collective redress in Europe does not necessarily demonstrate a failure of existing enforcement mechanisms, but rather reflects an awareness of the need to improve the access to justice.

Ever since the 1990s, collective redress has been on the rise in Europe. In European Member States, the instruments and mechanisms for collective consumer protection have been extensively included into either national consumer protection laws or the respective civil procedure laws.[84] It is possible to distinguish three waves of activities pertaining to collective redress. In the first wave—between 1990 and 2000—there was a growth in representative action that involved consumer associations.[85] During the second wave—from 2000 until 2008—there was a selective introduction of general class actions for damages in several Member States.[86] The third wave—which started in 2005 and thus partly overlapped with the second—is characterised by European policy initiatives in cross-border harmonisation. Following up on the *Courage* and *Manfredi* judgments,[87] considerable attention

[82] See the ALI/UNIDROIT Principles of Transnational Civil Procedure, available at www.unidroit.org/english/principles/civilprocedure/main.htm.

[83] Cafaggi (n 20).

[84] For an overview of, for instance, collective consumer protection laws see Christopher Hodges, *The Reform of Class and Representative Actions in European Legal Systems: A New Framework for Collective Redress in Europe* (Oxford, Hart Publishing, 2008) 10–12.

[85] For example, in the UK, the role of the Office of Fair Trading (OFT) has become more important in enforcing consumer law, and in 1999 the Group Litigation Order (GLO) was enacted for better claim management. R Mulheron, *The Class Action in Common Legal Systems: A Comparative Perspective* (Oxford, Hart Publishing, 2004).

[86] For instance, Nordic countries have enacted new legislation on group action. Hodges (n 84).

[87] Case C-453/99 *Courage and Crehan* [2001] ECR I-6297, Joined Cases C-295/04 C-298/04 *Manfredi* [2006] ECR I-6619.

has been devoted to the question of damages actions in antitrust law as well as to the question of collective redress for consumers.[88] A number of documents have been issued in this area, and there has been an intense academic discussion about the development of a coherent framework for collective redress in Europe.[89]

Even this cursory overview of the initiatives for collective redress shows that they have been growing substantially in recent years. This is not to say that these initiatives have always been successful and that they have not been severely criticised. The European Commission has been particularly careful to avoid the pitfalls of the United States regime for mass claim resolution and class actions. For instance, the Joint Information Note not only stresses the need to avoid the risk of abusive litigation of the US class action system,[90] but also goes beyond this by explicitly stating that the EU firmly 'opposes introducing "class actions" along the US model into the EU legal order'.[91] However—even though some initiatives have not been outright successful and others are still under discussion—the general trend remains: aggregation of claims on the demand side of the enforcement regime is on the rise.

III. ENFORCEMENT BETWEEN COMPETITION AND AUTHORITY

As the enforcement in Europe undergoes profound transformations—with changes in regulation that lead to fragmentation and collectivisation—it is also becoming clear that the default understanding of enforcement as the exclusive domain of nation state's authority is no longer adequate. But there is also a further question of whether enforcement becomes so detached from the nation state that it transforms into something fundamentally different? It could seem, in other words, that the change is not only in degree but also

[88] For an overview of the documents adopted (studies, green and white papers, and proposals) see ec.europa.eu/competition/antitrust/actionsdamages/index.html.

[89] See for example: European Parliament Resolution, 'Towards a Coherent European Approach to Collective Redress', 2011/2089(INI); Communication from the Commission 'Towards a European Horizontal Framework for Collective Redress', COM/2013/0401 final; Commission Recommendation of 11 June 2013 on common principles for injunctive and compensatory collective redress mechanisms in the Member States concerning violations of rights granted under Union Law [2013] OJ L201/60; Dir 2014/104/EU of 26 November 2014 on certain rules governing actions for damages under national law for infringements of the competition law provisions of the Member States and of the European Union [2014] OJ L349/1. For a detailed analysis, see Josef Drexl's contribution to this volume.

[90] 'Towards a Coherent European Approach to Collective Redress: Next Steps', SEC(2010) 1192, 6.

[91] ibid. On the pitfalls of class action system of enforcement in the US see Christopher Hodges' contribution to this volume.

in kind: whereas enforcement has always included a network of competing and complementary actors, institutions and processes, it might appear as if the enforcement in Europe has irreversibly turned into a heterarchically structured non-state affair.

Notwithstanding the depth of the change in the system of enforcement, this conclusion would be premature. The empirical picture outlined above reveals a complex structure of enforcement where both state and non-state actors play important roles. This calls for a more nuanced conceptualisation that would be able to capture the intricate dynamics between diverse enforcement practices. Enforcement in Europe is now best understood as a regulated market for justice: while competition between different enforcement mechanisms is its guiding norm, it operates with the state authority in the background. Here we aim to add more detail to this conceptualisation, and to draw attention to some of the setbacks of such architecture of enforcement. If enforcement in Europe is to achieve its primary purpose and facilitate justice, there is a need for a holistic approach that would take into account a number of important issues that may be overlooked in a purely market-driven system.

A. Enforcement as a Regulated Market of Justice

While the ultimate enforcement authority remains vested in public institutions, the European enforcement regime becomes a regulated market for dispute resolution. The state is not the only provider of justice anymore. Its dominant position has been challenged by the amount and relevance of private enforcement mechanisms that operate in the shadow of the law. However, while the state with its judicial apparatus stands in different relations to these new actors and process—and sometimes even competes with them—it also provides the authority that grounds the complex structure of enforcement.

There are two main features of this new system of enforcement. First, the connection between justice and state authority becomes indirect, and is mediated through *competition* between different actors and practices, which in turn becomes the guiding norm of enforcement. The state remains responsible for delivering justice, but achieves this through a set of market-driven mechanisms. Second—and related to this—*justice* becomes understood as a service to be provided to consumers in the market of enforcement, rather than as merely a virtue of public institutions. To put it roughly: Justice remains the motivating ideal of the enforcement system as a whole but is attained through competition, and this leads to compromises, gaps and frictions, whereby the realisation of justice—especially from the perspective of affected individuals—may become suboptimal. Let us explain.

i. Competition as a Guiding Norm

What does the analogy between enforcement and regulated market imply? In this model, enforcement regime is as a medium for providing justice, over which the court system exerts the ultimate level of control. This entails recognition of the crucial role of courts and of the continued hierarchy in the domain of enforcement, but with an important proviso: private elements in enforcement constitute a semi-autonomous domain which makes this hierarchy both less visible and eventually less important. Moreover, not all areas of enforcement entail the same level of hierarchical involvement of the state. To extend the analogy further, it is possible to think of different enforcement constellations in terms of different market structures. For instance, in criminal law there is a monopolistic market structure with a single enforcement service provider: the judiciary. The elements of this type of arrangement can also exist in other areas of legal regulation. They are visible in the tendency of public authorities to police certain types of behaviour by strengthening the punitive elements in economic law, for example in IP and competition law.[92] But the enforcement system in private law, by contrast, could be characterised as oligopoly in which there is competition among several enforcement institutions, including the competition between private and public enforcement mechanisms such as arbitrations and courts.

Today, only a portion of private law disputes requires action from national courts. Most disputes are resolved through mechanism of self-control within the company, ADR/ODR mechanisms or arbitration. Depending on the importance of infringement and especially its collective dimension, the dispute may involve the intervention by administrative agencies. Courts, in turn, interfere only in the most important infringements with strong socio-political importance.[93] As Micklitz explains—and this is the crucial point—'courts and agencies turn into managers of major conflicts'.[94] This is very far from the traditional picture of the state as the main actor responsible for law enforcement. Although courts provide the foundation of the system and get involved in most important cases, they neither exercise full control over enforcement nor determine all the details of the system. Instead, the market itself becomes an important architect of the edifice of enforcement.

This, of course, does not mean that competition in private law enforcement is the invention of our age. Such competition has taken a wide variety of forms throughout history. In the mid-to-late medieval period, there was a remarkable mixture of different laws governing enforcement, sometimes

[92] WPJ Wils, 'Is Criminalization of EU Competition Law the Answer?' (2005) 28 *World Competition* 117.

[93] See more in H-W Micklitz, 'The Transformation of Enforcement in EU Private Law: Preliminary Considerations', forthcoming in *European Private Law Review*, 24–25 (copy on file with the authors).

[94] ibid, 25.

conflicting, and sometimes complementary: local customs, general Germanic customary law, feudal law, the law or merchant or *lex mercatoria*, commercial law and customs followed by merchants, canon law of the Roman Catholic Church, and the revived Roman law. Various types of forums were in charge of enforcing these different regimes, such as manorial, municipal, merchant, guild, church and royal courts. Competition in the provision of legal services is, thus, a familiar feature of the European legal system.[95] However—while contemporary competition between modern public and private, national and transnational, sectorial and general enforcement techniques is at the bottom a very similar phenomenon—the extent of diffusion and fragmentation of enforcement mechanisms generates a more fundamental change in which competition provides the primary framework of incentives for legal enforcement. And with competition as the guiding norm, it is easy to expect that effects of such enforcement apparatus may not be completely satisfactory.

The expected functioning of the new Unitary Patent Court regime is a case in point.[96] The suggested regime would allow for extensive forum shopping which would most probably result in the plaintiffs choosing the court in which they are most likely to succeed. This rational commercial behaviour, in turn, would increase the popularity of divisions that are most likely to grant injunctions (either preliminary or final) or award high damages. It would also result in plaintiffs choosing a division which bifurcates, so that the validity is not considered at the infringement trial. Patent courts would either have to offer what their customers—mainly patentees—expect, or they would cease to exist. The effect of putting divisions of the court in direct competition with each other without any safeguards will probably be the growth of pro-patentee judgments. This could lead to further consequences: plaintiffs would move into pro-patentee regions, and defendants would move out of such regions. For example, the decision of Microsoft to relocate its distribution centre from Germany to the Netherlands to reduce exposure to the German bifurcated patent system demonstrates this possible impact.[97]

In this way, the institutions of enforcement—whether public or private, national or transnational—come to be in competition with each other and are consequently guided by market concerns.[98] This demands a cautious approach to the design of enforcement, and a careful balance between competition and regulation. There is a danger of idealising free markets and

[95] BZ Tamanaha, 'Understanding Legal Pluralism: Past to Present, Local to Global' (2008) 30 *Sydney Law Review* 375.

[96] For a detailed discussion see Marcus Norrgård's contribution to this volume.

[97] See Microsoft moves inventory to avoid German patent woes at mybroadband.co.za/news/general/46972-microsoft-moves-inventory-to-avoid-german-patent-woes.html.

[98] See also R Whish, *Competition Law* 6th edn (Oxford, Oxford University Press, 2009) 3–15.

competition in the field of enforcement: they can lead to both unjust and anti-competitive/inefficient outcomes which require a more robust state intervention. Much will also depend on the specificities of the area of regulation. For example, enforcement based on self-regulation works well where the organisations have relatively simple structures, competition is rigorous, the goods and services are well defined, and where relevant information is public.[99] By contrast, statutory regulation and state enforcement are more warranted in industries with more complex transactions and hierarchical structures. Informal enforcement mechanisms function well in well-defined environments—such as the diamond and cotton industries[100]—but probably cannot be applied across the board. Thus, whereas there is much enthusiasm about enforcement based on market principles, it should not be forgotten that public institutions must retain responsibility for the governance of enforcement as a justice-related matter. This brings us to our next point.

ii. Justice as Service

In the new architecture of enforcement in Europe, justice increasingly becomes understood as a service. To be more precise: This does not imply a change in the dominant understanding of justice, but rather a change in the dominant understanding of how justice is and ought to be delivered. There is a growing expectation for transparent, efficient, effective and affordable dispute resolution.[101] Even though enforcement in Europe still relies on public authorities quite strongly—and is thus still far from the US profit-driven approach—the change in the expectations from the justice enforcement system has a potential to affect the kind of justice it delivers.[102]

As we have argued, the dynamics between state deregulation and EU re-regulation creates a void that is filled by transnational self-regulation and enforcement mechanisms that replace the traditional judicial dispute resolution. These mechanisms are managed and funded by private entities, prioritise compliance and efficiency, and are motivated by competition concerns. Their prevalence and influence are not based on their ability to enforce rights

[99] C Doyle, 'Self Regulation and Statutory Regulation' (1997) 8 *Business Strategy Review* 35.

[100] L Bernstein, 'Opting out of the Legal System: Extralegal Contractual Relations in the Diamond Industry' (1992) 21 *Journal of Legal Studies* 115; L Bernstein, 'Private Commercial Law in the Cotton Industry: Creating Cooperation through Rules, Norms and Institutions' (2001) 99 *Michigan Law Review* 1724.

[101] These expectations are expressed in law: intellectual property law, for instance, requires enforcement to be 'effective, expeditious, deterrent' (Agreement on Trade-Related Aspects of Intellectual Property Rights ('TRIPS Agreement') 1869 UNTS 299; 33 ILM 1197 (1994)). As a consequence, there is also a dramatic increase in the size of the legal services industry in Europe. See RD Kelemen, *Eurolegalism: The Transformation of Law and Regulation in the European Union* (Cambridge MA, Harvard University Press, 2011) 79–88.

[102] On the US class action system, see Christopher Hodges' contribution to this volume.

that characterised state-based enforcement. It is then very likely that such enforcement mechanisms will sometimes provide inadequate safeguards for individual rights. This is for example visible in the domain of consumer protection, where alternative dispute mechanisms almost exclusively aim at consensual settlements and not at binding decisions.[103] While there are many reasons to prefer consensual settlements to authoritative decisions, this eventually changes the nature of enforcement: it brings about a system of enforcement which relies on reputational costs for businesses rather than on a robust right-based protection of consumers' interests.

The question is: what is the consequence in terms of justice? To stay with the same example, it is not hard to see why the system based on reputational incentives for businesses might generate satisfaction of all parties: ideally, it should make the interest of businesses to retain their position in the market work to satisfy the interest of consumers, who would themselves otherwise have to go through a costly and time-consuming judicial process. However, this often also means that enforcement does not guarantee the rights of the consumers to the fullest. The result can be seen as beneficial, but only against the baseline of an inefficient state-based enforcement system. For consider: if the ideal solution from the perspective of justice is a complete compensation of the consumer, the suboptimal realisation of this goal in most settlements that result from non-state enforcement procedures must somehow be justified.[104] Any such justification, however, can only hold insofar as there is no viable alternative; the conclusion that this is an all-things-considered optimal way to reach a certain level of consumer satisfaction must take the inability of state courts to deal with such problems for granted. A similar situation occurs as a consequence of collectivisation of enforcement procedures, which—inevitable as it may be—often fails to take the perspective of individuals into account seriously enough, because claims are dealt with selectively and do not lead to complete redress. There are thus important trade-offs between different objectives of enforcement which come as a consequence of the transformation: the context of enforcement has changed and so has the realisation of its underlying values.

It is important to emphasise that this conclusion does not hinge on any particular understanding of justice. Rather, it points out the fundamental change in the expectation from the law enforcement system in this regard. The understanding of justice becomes more service-like: justice is delivered because of market pressures but it is then also constrained by these pressures. The ordinary understanding was that legal enforcement should provide redress and protect individual rights, and not that it should accomplish

[103] See Horst Eidenmüller and Martin Fries' contribution to this volume.

[104] See ibid for an extensive discussion of this issue. We assume here that the full protection of consumer rights is a commonly shared justice-related expectation from the system of enforcement.

this to the extent that reputational costs of businesses allow it. There is of course much appeal to the idea that interests of businesses and consumers can work together to the satisfaction of both sides. But the question is one of degree of involvement of market-driven mechanisms in enforcement, and of the role of public authorities in such a system. If the courts had the capacity to deal with these challenges effectively, this would also change the system of incentives in the sense that both consumers would expect full compensation and businesses would operate on the assumption that full compensation is a possibility. In other words, the more the system escapes the shadow of the law, the more it transforms the traditional model in which justice concerns—expressed in the vocabulary of individual rights—were at least supposed to reign supreme.

B. A Holistic Approach to Enforcement in Europe

The notion of enforcement as a regulated market implies that public authorities play a much more limited role in enforcement than they used to. The danger in this system is to underestimate the need for public intervention to prevent abuses and secure justice. This danger is amplified in a fragmented system of enforcement where many different actors and practices interact, and where responsibility for delivering justice becomes much less tangible. There are several issues we would like to underline in this regard. First, enforcement effectively determines the scope of individual rights and cannot be simply subjugated to market forces. Second, new circumstances demand new roles and capacities of public institutions in order to address these justice-related concerns. Third, non-state mechanisms of enforcement should fulfil the expectations about legitimacy and accountability that are commensurate with their power. Fourth, enforcement procedures should allow for more inclusive access to justice and better achievement of the goals of enforcement.

i. Enforcement and Rights

The transformation of enforcement and the ensuing diffusion of responsibility for the protection of rights require a fresh look at the effects of enforcement. Enforcement is not only essential for achieving compensation, deterrence and vindication: it also defines the boundaries of rights and duties. Enforcement mechanisms fill the gaps in underdetermined legislation and private arrangements, such as contracts.[105] While this is a general feature of enforcement, it gains much more prominence in a fragmented and market-driven system. Such a system of enforcement can escape traditional

[105] On this issue, in the context of IP rights, see Reto M Hilty's contribution to this volume.

regulation in two different senses. On the one hand, enforcement fills the regulatory void left by deregulation on the state level, for example through regulatory litigation. On the other hand, enforcement fills the regulatory void that arises from the multi-level governance of economic affairs where traditional enforcement mechanisms are replaced by transnational enforcement regimes.[106]

The question is whether private and transnational enforcement techniques can give adequate shape to individual rights. There is reason to doubt that private actors have the legitimacy, authority and effectiveness to fill these regulatory voids. In fact, it is the behaviour of private actors—whether corporate or individual—that often constitutes the greatest challenge for enforcement regimes. Recent cases in the realm of human rights violation—such as *Kiobel*[107] and *AFPS and OLP v Alstom and Veolia*[108]—have demonstrated that a rights-based resolution of conflicts reaches far beyond the protection of consumer rights. It leads to corporate recognition of constitutional principles and fundamental rights. Economic liberalisation and globalisation of trade have diminished the role of the state in enforcement regimes, and the economic crisis has further shaken the foundations of the European legal order to such an extent that even the trust in the regulatory power of the European Commission is disappearing; however, it is important to recall that European enforcement system is not only about coherency, efficiency, fair trial and effective remedies, but also about fairness and the prevention of human right violations. As the enforcement is undergoing fundamental transformations, it is important not to neglect its impact on overarching social values and fundamental rights.

ii. The Role of Public Institutions

In the new system of enforcement, two important functions of public institutions should not be neglected. First, public institutions need to provide and supervise the enforcement environment. Even if alternative dispute resolution mechanisms are readily resorted to, they are not self-sufficient enforcement regimes but depend on judicial support.[109] Independent private orderings bring about the danger of market failures—as exemplified by the failure of regulatory regimes for financial products—and public authorities have an important role to play in preventing such developments.[110] This may include, for example, a more prominent role of private actors in the

[106] See Robert Wai's contribution to this volume.

[107] *Kiobel v Royal Dutch Petroleum Co* 133 SCt 1659 (2013).

[108] *AFPS and OLP v Alstom and Veolia*, Court of Appeal of Versailles, decision of 22 March 2013.

[109] CA Whytock, 'Domestic Courts and Global Governance' (2009) 84 *Tulane Law Review* 67.

[110] R Wai, 'The Interlegality of Transnational Private Law' (2008) 72 *Law and Contemporary Problems* 107.

realm of regulatory litigation that would reintegrate private enforcement initiatives into the framework of judicial and administrative enforcement, instead of letting them flourish beyond the state in the transnational realm. Despite the globalisation of trade, the state has remained the central institution of economic governance, and it is still the actor that has a capacity to exercise decisive influence over enforcement.[111] State institutions are premised upon principles of accessibility, accountability and legitimacy, and are thus a resource that should not be discarded without an appropriate alternative that would be able to replace it.[112]

Second, courts and administrative agencies need to be properly equipped and trained to deal with new challenges—for example mass disputes—in a competent manner, and to exercise effective control over regulation brought by private litigants and enforcement mechanisms.[113] This demands a system of enforcement that would combine the advantages of public institutions with the efficiency of private enforcement. Successful enforcement mechanisms typically rely on the complementary of administrative and judicial procedures, and are also supplemented by private enforcement techniques. Public and private techniques often have to be combined to achieve multiple goals of enforcement.[114] For example, public enforcement by administrative agencies in competition cases often has deterrent function, while private damages claims are directed at compensation. As a result of these different goals, there is a need for both public and private enforcement.[115] This is even more visible in times of severe budget constraints, when agencies are very likely to lack the resources necessary to research, inspect and pursue all entities that violate regulations.[116] Furthermore, judicial and administrative enforcement need to be better integrated: they should not only be

[111] Many global initiatives for the establishment of multilateral governance structures have failed and led to a surge of bilateralism in, for instance, IP law—demonstrating the continued role of the state. See Tuori (n 69).

[112] There is an important historical lesson in this regard. Opportunistic usage of highly fragmented enforcement mechanisms has eventually destroyed the 'justice monopoly' of courts and has consequently contributed to the fall of the judicial system in the late Roman Empire. The direct cause of this was lack of modernisation of judicial structures. See S Schmidt-Hofer, 'Ostentatious Legislation: Law and Dynastic Change, AD 364–365' in J Wienand (ed), *Contested Monarchy: Integrating the Roman Empire in the Fourth Century AD* (Oxford, Oxford University Press, 2015) and S Schmidt-Hofer, 'Staatswerdung von unten: Justiznutzung und Strukturgenese im Gerichtswesen der römischen Kaiserzeit (1-6 Jhdt n Chr)' in P Eich, S Schmidt-Hofer and C Wieland (eds), *Der wiederkehrende Leviathan: Staatlichkeit und Staatswerdung in Spätantike und Früher Neuzeit* (Heidelberg, Universitätsverlag Winter, 2011).

[113] See more on this issue in Ianika Tzankova's contribution, and on comparative advantages of courts and arbitrations in Sandrine Clavel's contribution to this volume.

[114] On relationship between different enforcement goals in competition law see Andrea Renda's contribution to this volume.

[115] Compare also DR Hensler, 'Sins of Omission, Sins of Commission: Why Modern Societies Need Public and Private Enforcement' (2013, draft, copy on file with the authors).

[116] *cf* Freeman (n 66).

complementary but also cooperative. In particular, the interface between administrative and judicial enforcement proceedings demands a careful design.[117]

iii. Legitimacy of Enforcement

The main advantage of private enforcement techniques is their efficacy. They are supposed to deliver outcomes faster and at a lower cost. The problem is that this often comes with a price: the loss of legitimacy. Inefficacy of judicial enforcement is directly related to the fact that it is based on an open and fair procedure which bestows legitimacy on its outcomes. While there are obvious benefits to the new enforcement mechanisms, it is important to notice that there is a need to enhance their legitimacy credentials. As private enforcement mechanisms gain more power, they must also take responsibility for the way in which such power is exercised. This is all the more true when the regulatory effects of enforcement on matters of public interest are taken into account.

Apart from the need for a more robust control of private enforcement by public institutions, private enforcement mechanisms must themselves incorporate some of the principles that would enhance their legitimacy in a more direct way.[118] The traditional conception of legitimacy of private enforcement was based on party autonomy: it was considered enough if parties to a dispute have agreed to resolve it in a certain way. However, not only may the parties not actually be fully autonomous and able to exercise a real choice in this regard, but the others may also be affected by the regulatory impact of private dispute settlement mechanisms without a chance to influence the process in any way. This becomes even more problematic in the context where the state effectively provides the backing for private enforcement mechanisms that do not respect the minimal standards of legitimacy.[119] There is thus a need to recognise the wide-ranging regulatory effects of private dispute resolution mechanisms, and accordingly demand from them to develop open and fair procedures that would lead to more public responsibility.[120]

[117] See Joseph Drexl's contribution to this volume. See also for Case C-360/09 *Pfleiderer AG v Bundeskartellamt* [2011] ECR I-5161 where the interaction between judicial and administrative side of enforcement was particularly visible.

[118] See generally in G de Búrca, 'Developing Democracy Beyond the State' (2008) 46 *Columbia Journal of Transnational Law* 221.

[119] On the role of public authorities in creating the structure in which private power is exercised see Robert Wai's contribution to this volume.

[120] These issues are discussed at length in Diego P Fernández Arroyo's contribution to this volume.

iv. Enforcement Procedures

Finally, there are two important procedural features that demand careful attention in the new constellation of enforcement. First—and related to the previous point—procedures should guarantee equal access to justice and due process principles in order to be legitimate. Collectivisation of enforcement brings about growing concerns about the access to justice. Procedural rules of standing substantially determine not only claim aggregation but also the ability of individuals to pursue their claims. For example, the choice between opt-in and opt-out mechanisms have a tremendous impact upon the exclusive or inclusive nature of law enforcement.[121] While a too inclusive procedure may lead to undesirable results, there is clearly a need to design an enforcement procedure that would be accessible to all affected individuals.

Second, enforcement mechanisms should provide for remedies that would maximise the purposes of enforcement. There is a need for a more comprehensive design of enforcement procedures—including prospective, retrospective and vindicatory techniques—that would be able to take into account different enforcement goals.[122] There are many examples of procedures that do not live up to the expectations in the new environment and fail to deliver expected results. In competition law, for instance, compensation has been difficult to achieve: the true economic victims of most antitrust violations are downstream consumers who are too numerous and remote from the violation to locate and compensate. Furthermore, deterrence has often been ineffective as the time between the violation and legal judgment is so prolonged that responsible corporate managers may already leave their corporation before it can internalise the cost of the violation.[123]

An integrated approach would address possible social losses through ex ante deterrence mechanisms and private losses through effective ex post compensatory schemes. This integrated approach would also clearly establish the relationship between different remedial options. Past violations or infringements should then be addressed by retrospective remedies: through

[121] There is also a need to balance effective collective enforcement against the danger of creating a profit-driven litigation culture. See Commission Recommendation of 11 June 2013 on common principles for injunctive and compensatory collective redress mechanisms in the Member States concerning violations of rights granted under Union Law [2013] OJ L201/60, and Burkhard Hess' contribution to this volume.

[122] In this context, it is important to notice the growing importance and increased regulatory functions of procedural remedies in European law. See Marcus Norrgård's contribution to this volume. For example, Dir 2004/48/EC of 29 April 2004 on the enforcement of intellectual property rights [2004] OJ L195/16 contains several procedures in relation to, for instance, preservation of evidence and right of information that should be reclassified as procedural remedies.

[123] DA Crane, 'Optimizing Private Antitrust Enforcement' (2010) 63 *Vanderbilt Law Review* 675.

compensatory harm- or loss-based damages, restitutive gain-based damages, restorative injunctions or orders to compensate third parties or to forfeit profits. Future violations or infringements should be addressed by prospective remedies: through preventive injunctions, punitive damages, declaratory relief, orders and fines. Finally, as the effectiveness of collective redress mechanisms often fails as a result of the impossibility to fairly compensate the victims, vindicatory damages—for example rights-based remedies such as expression of acknowledgement, nominal damages, *cy-près*, coupon settlements, apology and declaratory judgments—should play a more prominent role. One of the greatest challenges for enforcement in Europe will be to integrate these various measures and goals into a coherent system.

IV. CONCLUSION

This concluding chapter has attempted to outline the main features and some of the deficiencies of the system of enforcement in Europe. It has argued that new models of regulation have led to increased fragmentation and collectivisation of enforcement, and that this, in turn, has transformed the system of enforcement into a regulated market for delivering justice guided by the competition between different enforcement mechanisms. It has also argued for a more comprehensive approach to enforcement that would enable public institutions to perform their role in the new environment, demand from private enforcement mechanisms higher standards of legitimacy, combine different procedural mechanisms and remedies to achieve the goals of enforcement, and—above all—be sensitive to the fact that enforcement determines the scope of individual rights and decisively affects the realisation of justice. More importantly, this chapter has tried to map the transformed landscape of European enforcement and locate the central themes that have been explored, discussed and theorised in this volume at greater length, in more detail, and—crucially—from many different perspectives.

Index

www.ingramcontent.com/pod-product-compliance
Ingram Content Group UK Ltd.
Pitfield, Milton Keynes, MK11 3LW, UK
UKHW021341091225
9465UKWH00037B/1395